LATIN AMERICA
ITS PROBLEMS AND
ITS PROMISE

The Western Hemisphere
Reprinted, with permission, from Margaret Daley Hayes, *Latin America and the U.S. National Interest: A Basis for U.S. Foreign Policy* (Boulder, Colo.: Westview Press, 1984).

Third Edition

LATIN AMERICA
ITS PROBLEMS AND
ITS PROMISE

A Multidisciplinary Introduction

edited by
Jan Knippers Black
MONTEREY INSTITUTE
OF INTERNATIONAL STUDIES

WestviewPress
A Member of the Perseus Books Group

Photo Credits: The photographs in Chapter 8 were taken by Mary Grizzard. The collages introducing each part were prepared from photographs taken by Jan Knippers Black.

Copyright © 1998 by Westview Press, A Member of the Perseus Books Group

Published in 1998 in the United States of America by Westview Press, 5500 Central Avenue, Boulder, Colorado 80301-2877, and in the United Kingdom by Westview Press, 12 Hid's Copse Road, Cumnor Hill, Oxford OX2 9JJ

Library of Congress Cataloging-in-Publication Data
Latin America, its problems and its promise : a multidisciplinary
  introduction / edited by Jan Knippers Black. — 3rd ed.
    p.   cm.
  Includes bibliographical references and index.
  ISBN 0-8133-2757-1 (pbk.)
  1. Latin America.   I. Black, Jan Knippers, 1940–   .
F1406.7.L38   1998
980—dc21   97-40415
                                                                                                   CIP

Printed and bound in the United States of America

The paper used in this publication meets the requirements of the American National Standard for Permanence of Paper for Printed Library Materials Z39.48-1984.

10   9   8   7   6   5   4

To my parents
Judge Ottis J. Knippers
and
Opal Moody Knippers
of Lawrenceburg, Tennessee,

and to our
much loved and esteemed colleagues

E. Bradford Burns,
who died as this third edition revision
got under way, and

Eldon "Bud" Kenworthy,
who died shortly after it was published

CONTENTS

MAPS, TABLES, FIGURES, AND ILLUSTRATIONS

Maps

Tables

Figures

Illustrations

1

INTRODUCTION:
THE EVOLUTION OF
LATIN AMERICAN STUDIES

JAN KNIPPERS BLACK

Latin America, occupying through no fault of its own the same Western Hemisphere as the United States, has often been the testing ground for U.S. foreign policy initiatives. Like a long-suffering and not necessarily willing spouse, Latin America has been occasionally courted with false promises but more often taken for granted when the United States was feeling confident and battered when the United States was suffering from insecurity or delusions of invincibility.

For Latin America, as for the United States, the twilight of the twentieth century represents both the best and the worst of times—a new age of democracy but perhaps also a new kind of democracy: one that allows for election to office but not to power; one in which the vestment of office is all too often a straitjacket.

With respect to foreign policy challenges and opportunities, the administration of U.S. president Bill Clinton had the good fortune of taking the reins at a time—the first since the early 1960s—when most of the Latin American countries were under elected, constitutional, and more or less democratic governments. These democracies, however, are for the most part limited and very fragile. Although the middle classes have regained participation and relief from intimidation, the more numerous poor lack effective representation and remain vulnerable to abuse. Moreover, a debt crisis compounded by deep economic recession left newly elected leaders at the mercy of foreign creditors and thus with precious little latitude for national economic decisionmaking.

The same pressures and perceptions of the times that are brought to bear on U.S. and Latin American policymakers set the agenda and the parameters that govern academic discourse. Thus to the student who must launch his or her exploration of Latin America through the eyes and ears, the assumptions and perspectives, and the theoretical and ideological filters of others, it would be useful to know something of the intellectual paths that have been traveled by the specialists in the field. Those paths have circled, dead-ended, and U-turned, merged and diverged; they are now, as always, subject to turns in new directions. The attempt to understand social relations, especially in an area so diverse and complex as Latin America, can never be a simple matter of learning "the facts." There will always be many facts in dispute; answers depend on the nature of available data, on the interests of the sources consulted, and on how questions are asked. Confronted, as one must be in a multiauthored text, with differing points of view and, thus, differing interpretations of the same historical and social data, the student may find it worthwhile to begin the study of Latin America with a study of Latin Americanists.

It is to be expected that interests and interpretations of social phenomena will vary from one discipline to another. The geographer may find, for example, that soil quality, climate, and topography determine settlement patterns and socioeconomic relations, which in turn configure political systems. The anthropologist may find explanation for social harmony or social conflict in ethnic and cultural patterns. The economist may find that political trends derive from economic ones, while the political scientist may see power relationships as overriding. In the study of Latin America, however, there has always been a unifying theme.

From the perspectives of U.S.- and European-based scholars, as well as from those of Latin America's own creative and scholarly writers, the study of Latin America has been approached as the study of a problem, or set of problems. The problems might be capsulized as underdevelopment and political instability or, more simply, as poverty or inequality and the failure of democratic systems to take hold. The search for the roots, causes, and progenitors of these problems has generally led in one of three directions: to the Iberians—the conquistadores and the institutions, attitudes, and cultural traits they brought with them to the New World; to the Latin Americans themselves—the alleged greed of the elites, absence of entrepreneurship in the middle classes, or passivity of the masses; or to the United States and the international capitalist system it promotes and defends.

Long before U.S. scholars began to direct their attention to Latin America's problems, the area's own intellectuals were absorbed by the question of where to place the blame. Domingo Faustino Sarmiento and other nineteenth-century intellectual and political leaders of cosmopolitan Buenos Aires blamed the cycles of anarchy and tyranny their newly independent country was suffering on Hispanic influences.[1] Sarmiento in later life directed his scorn toward Latin America's own "melting pot." Influenced by social Darwinism, he diagnosed "the decadent state" of Argentine society as deriving from its racial components of Spanish, mestizo, Indian, and Negro.

Turning the tables at the turn of the twentieth century, José Enrique Rodó, Uruguay's foremost literary figure, urged the youth of his country—in his masterpiece, *Ariel*—to shun the materialism of the United States and to cling to the spiritual and intellectual values of their Spanish heritage. A strong current of Latin American social thought, reflected in art and music as well as literature, that gained momentum a few decades into the twentieth century has touted the strengths of native American cultures and blamed both Hispanic and North American influences for the prevailing instability and social injustice. Likewise, in the Caribbean, the Black Power movements of the sixties and seventies called Europe and Anglo-America to task for the region's underdevelopment.

Latin American studies as an interdisciplinary field in the United States and, by extension, the coming of age of analysis of Latin American social and political systems are clearly the illegitimate offspring of Fidel Castro. Prior to the Cuban Revolution, historians, anthropologists, and literary scholars had generally pursued their studies of Latin American subjects in disciplinary isolation. Political analysis had been largely limited to formal legal studies, highlighting the fact that Latin American regimes rarely lived up to the standards, borrowed from France and the United States, embodied in their constitutions. Such studies generally drew their explanatory theses from the distinctive historical and cultural traditions of the United States of North America and the disunited states of Latin America and, in so doing, contributed to the mystification of the political process in both areas.[2] The Iberian heritage of feudalism, authoritarianism, and Catholicism was seen as the major obstacle to democratic and socioeconomic reforms.

The surge of interest in Latin America on the part of U.S. politicians and academics (encouraged by newly available government-funded fellowships and contracts) that accompanied the Cuban Revolution followed closely upon the expansion of attention to the Third World generally by the previously parochial disciplines of economics and political science. Thus, development and modernization theory, formulated to address change processes in other parts of the Third World, came to dominate the study of Latin America as well. Studies falling under these rubrics generally posited that either the economic and political systems of Latin America would increasingly approximate those of the United States and Western Europe or the area would be engulfed in violent revolution.

The invalidation of many of the assumptions of development and modernization theorists by the onrush of events—particularly by the fall of democratic regimes and their replacement by military dictatorships—resulted in a theoretical backlash as well as in long overdue attention to the work of Latin American theorists. The backlash was expressed in a reassertion of the tenacity of tradition, of the fundamentally conservative character of Latin American society. This perspective has been endowed with greater theoretical and conceptual sophistication in studies using the corporatist model. Corporatism stresses the hierarchical organization of modern institutions and the persistence of control from the top.

There existed a large body of literature by Latin Americans, dating back to "the black legend" of Spanish rule, to support the historical and cultural explanations for the failure of democracy. But the trends that had dominated the social sciences in the major Latin American countries were variations on the Marxist themes of class conflict and imperialism. One such body of thought, known as dependency theory, came to rival development and modernization theory for predominance among U.S.

and European specialists in Latin American studies. Dependency theory held that Latin American underdevelopment should be understood as a by-product of the international capitalist system.

With the end of the Cold War, that system struck back with a force that suppressed all previously contending paradigms. Some Latin American theorists continued to urge attention to national and local markets, to social and economic democracy, and to a new kind of nationalism; but a triumphalist neoliberalism that stressed open markets, privatization, and elections-as-democracy and gave no quarter to social concerns came to dominate elite institutions throughout the hemisphere.

These theoretical trends and approaches have permeated all aspects of Latin American studies, because—to a far greater extent than in Europe or the United States—philosophy, literature, the arts, and other pursuits of the intelligentsia in Latin America tend to reflect national or regional concerns. It could hardly be otherwise; the cataclysmic episodes of insurgency and repression, revolution and counterrevolution, leave no one untouched.

BLAMING THE IBERIANS: CORPORATISM AND CULTURE

The historical-cultural approach to the study of Latin America and its problems draws attention to the persistence in contemporary Latin America of attitudes, institutions, and social relations that are said to have been characteristic of the Iberian peninsula in medieval times.[3] According to this view, the Spanish conquistadores, crown officials, and Roman Catholic missionaries transplanted in the New World a social system firmly based on elitism, authoritarianism, and militarism.

The Portuguese legacy differed from that of Spain in its greater tolerance of racial and cultural diversity, but, like the Spanish, the Portuguese inculcated in their New World offspring a rigid sense of social, political, and cultural hierarchy. The patriarchal view, deriving from Iberian monarchism, held that culture and personality were functions of education and that the uneducated man was incapable of participating in the dominant political culture. (That women, educated or otherwise, were to be seen but not heard was taken for granted.) The uneducated man was expected to accept his status in society as a function of a divinely ordered hierarchy. However, as the uneducated were not expected to be responsible for their own welfare, the dominant class was obligated to contribute to the amelioration of their suffering. Public morality was an integral part of the political culture, and the Catholic Church, also hierarchical in structure, absolutist in doctrine, and authoritarian in practice, shared with the institutions of government the responsibility for the maintenance of the political and moral order.

During the early colonial period, a great debate raged among intellectuals and governmental and spiritual leaders in Spain and its colonies as to whether native Americans were fully human. It was finally concluded that the Church's Christianizing mission implied recognition of the fundamental human attributes of the Indians. But in much of the empire, the slaughter or enslavement of the Indians proceeded nevertheless, and it is clear that many contemporary Latin Americans continue to see the Indians as belonging to a lesser order of humanity.

Corporatism

The corporatist model, drawn primarily from medieval Catholic thought and observed, to some degree, in Spain under Franco and Portugal under Salazar, was found to "fit" mid-century Latin American politics to a greater degree than some of the models derived from development and modernization theory. The model, elaborated in works by Wiarda, Schmitter, Malloy, Erickson, and others, has called attention to the tendency to vertical, as opposed to horizontal, organization among politically active groups in Latin America.[4] Such groups, in corporatist systems, are controlled and manipulated by authoritarian governments so that communications and power flow from the top down rather than from the bottom up.

Few Latin Americanists would dispute the observation that vestiges of medieval Iberia are still to be found in Latin America. Nor is the existence of corporatist tendencies a subject of great controversy. The point at which many Latin Americanists depart from the findings of some scholars pursuing historical-cultural or corporatist approaches is the supposition that contemporary manifestations of elitism and authoritarianism are due primarily to colonization by Spain and Portugal.

Critics note, for example, that some countries recently under fiercely authoritarian, military rule (Chile and Uruguay, for example) had enjoyed constitutional and more or less democratic rule throughout most of the twentieth century. Furthermore, the Southern Cone (Argentina, Uruguay, and Chile) was among the areas least influenced by colonial Spain. In Argentina, descendants of Italian immigrants, who arrived in great waves around the turn of the twentieth century, now outnumber the descendants of Spanish settlers. Surely some common denominators of vintage more recent than the colonial period are needed to explain the resurgence of authoritarianism in Latin America in the late twentieth century. Moreover, the qualitative difference between traditional corporatism and the modern bureaucratic-technocratic variety has often been understated. By the end of the 1980s, the popularity of the corporatist paradigm appeared to be waning, and some of its former proponents, including Howard Wiarda, had turned to an emphasis on cultural causation.

Cultural Causation

The late 1980s saw a revival of interest in the explanatory power of culture as an independent variable. Samuel Huntington, noting that contemporary concepts of modernization and of Westernization are beginning to diverge, suggests that development and modernization may be distinctively Western goals. He alleges that aspirations to wealth, equity, democracy, stability, and autonomy emerge from Western, particularly Nordic, experience, and that other cultures may prefer simplicity, austerity, hierarchy, authoritarianism, discipline, and militarism.[5] This view represents a considerable retreat for a theorist who once believed Western-style modernization to be irresistible.

BLAMING THE LATIN AMERICANS:
DEVELOPMENT AND MODERNIZATION THEORY

Whereas analyses of contemporary Latin America based on the traditional, or historical-cultural, approach tended to have a static quality, development and modernization theory introduced a new dynamism into the field. The new approach highlighted the facts that for better or worse, social change was indeed under way and that to a great extent, that change was in response or in reaction to the spread of the ideas and technologies of the more industrialized world, primarily the United States and Western Europe, to the Third World.

The body of thought that came to be known as development and/or modernization theory—terms often used interchangeably—was pioneered primarily by U.S. scholars in the late 1950s and the first half of the 1960s. In economics, development theory presumed that with the infusion of capital and the acquisition of business skills, and with the advantage of not having to reinvent the wheel, the nations that had yet to experience their industrial revolutions would pass at an accelerated pace along paths already broken by Western Europe and the United States. Walt W. Rostow further assumed that economic development, at least beyond a stage he called "take-off," was irreversible.[6]

From the perspective of anthropologists and sociologists, "modernization" generally meant the ingestion of the supposedly Western attitudinal traits of rationalism, instrumentalism, achievement orientation, and the like. This approach stressed the felicitous consequences of the spread of modern communications media, of education in science and the liberal arts, and of technology transfer. And it implied that Third World societies could (and should) become developed through the accelerated absorption of individuals into the middle class or the modern industrial sector.

Political scientists borrowed liberally from the other social sciences, often without seeming to notice that in their extreme formulations these theories amounted to a virtual denial of the stuff of their own discipline: power relationships. Political scientists did, however, add their own set of indices of development and/or modernization to those compiled by scholars of other disciplines. Gabriel Almond, for example, stressed structural differentiation (the elaboration of economic and political roles), whereas Samuel Huntington stressed the strengthening of political institutions.[7] Other scholars focused on participation, egalitarianism, and governmental capability. Some assumed that such attributes were mutually reinforcing. Huntington, however, seeing expanding participation in the absence of institutionalization as destabilizing, stressed the importance of stability. Martin C. Needler, perceiving the same contradiction, placed higher priority on participation but noted that in the absence of steady economic growth it would have a destabilizing effect on systems of limited democracy, threatening the imposition of authoritarianism.[8]

These trends in the social sciences coincided with the Cuban Revolution and thus with the Alliance for Progress and the emergence of interdisciplinary programs in Latin American studies. Development came to be one of the major goals of the Alliance for Progress; the other was security—the prevention of "another Cuba." These goals were deemed to be interdependent; it was rarely imagined that they might be contradictory. The few critical voices, such as that of Albert O. Hirschman, who argued that popular pressure, sometimes assuming violent form, was essential to the achievement of reform, were generally ignored.[9] The prevailing view, that "unrest" was an impediment to progress and had to be contained by strengthened security forces, won out in academic as well as in governmental circles until a wave of military takeovers forced a reevaluation.

Critics of development and modernization theory have pointed out that its adherents often emitted an optimism bordering on euphoria. Huntington had said that "modernization is not only inevitable, it is also desirable."[10] Such positivistic assumptions, that what was good was inevitable and vice versa, had predictable consequences for analysis. Researchers were inclined either to see what they wanted to see or to label whatever they saw as progress. Economists, for example, measured development by using aggregate data on the growth of gross national product or per capita income, data that were blind to the skewed distribution of income. While U.S. economists lavished praise on Brazil's "economic miracle," Brazil's own dictator, General Emilio Garrastazú Médici, commented in 1970 that "the economy is doing fine, but the people aren't."[11]

Critics have also argued that many of the supposed attributes of modernism are not even characteristic of the industrialized countries, much less of what they project to or promote in the Third World. Nor do the undeniable influences of the so-called developed countries necessarily contribute to the kind of development desired by leaders and peoples of the so-called underdeveloped ones. Technology transfer, for example, has generally meant a transition from labor-intensive to capital-intensive industry in areas where labor markets are glutted and capital is scarce.

A tendency common to much of the work based on development and modernization theory was a peculiar sort of ethnocentricity based on an idealized and class-delimited national or North Atlantic self-image. The terminology employed in such work, for example, was often charged with unacknowledged value judgments. All cultures other than our own, from a sophisticated ancient civilization such as China's to a preliterate society of nomads, were lumped together under the single epithet "traditional." Such terms as "secularism" and "rationalism" carried the thinly veiled implication that they referred to the thought processes of clear-headed folks like us. If Latin Americans and other peoples of the Third World had failed to achieve development or modernization, it was assumed to be because they lacked our industriousness and had failed to see their own problems as clearly as we saw them. In effect, the blame for poverty and powerlessness was placed squarely on the poor and powerless.

There were those, of course, who used some of the concepts and models of the developmentalists but rejected such ethnocentric assumptions. Scholars of the period were not necessarily in accord as to which of the indices of development and modernization were most relevant and useful. Nevertheless, distinctions between value-free and value-laden concepts were rarely well drawn. The behavioralist tendency in the social sciences, which was also coming into its own in the 1960s, sharpened the inclination of social scientists, attempting to be "scientific," to hold acknowledged bias in disdain. Thus, those scholars who argued that economic growth and stability were the most important indices of development and those who challenged that redistribution of wealth and the expansion of political participation were more important tended to maintain the pretense that they were arguing over facts rather than over values.

As military regimes swept the hemisphere in the 1960s and 1970s, replacing democratic ones, the development approach was discredited and superseded by newer theoretical trends, particularly dependency. Some of the theorists once attracted to the development paradigm became persuaded by the arguments of dependency theory. Others came to stress the interdependence of First and Third Worlds or to look for cultural causation in differing levels of development. Many of the attitudes and assumptions associated with development theory have been revived in the 1990s through the currency of neoliberalism, but the latter also embodies striking differences.

BLAMING THE UNITED STATES: DEPENDENCY AND RELATED THEORIES

In his earlier ideological incarnation as one of the originators of dependency theory, Brazilian social scientist Fernando Henrique Cardoso responded to the question, "What is dependency?" by saying, "It's what you call imperialism if you don't want to lose your Ford Foundation grant." (Elected president of Brazil in 1994, Cardoso now calls dependency theory his Frankenstein.) More precisely, as Susanne Bodenheimer Jonas has noted, dependency refers to the perspective from "below," whereas the Marxist theory of imperialism provides the perspective from "above."[12] As the Marxist theory of imperialism seeks to explain why and how the dominant classes of the dominant capitalist powers expand their spheres of exploitation and political control, dependency theory examines what this relationship of unequal bargaining and multilayered exploitation means to the dominated classes in the dominated countries.

Like most of the other trends and perspectives that have been designated theory, dependency by no means refers to an integrated set of if-then propositions. Rather, it is a focus of inquiry and a body of thought built upon common assumptions. Unlike the behavioral approach that has held sway over most aspects of social science in the United States since the mid-1960s, dependency is unabashedly normative. Its impulse derives largely from the attempts of the United Nations Economic Commission for Latin America (ECLA), under the leadership of Argentine economist Raúl Prebisch, to understand and counteract such problems as the deterioration in the terms of trade for producers of primary (nonindustrial) products. A renewed awareness of economic exploitation and dependency followed upon disillusionment with industrialization through import substitution, Latin American economic integration, and other solutions proposed by ECLA. Thus, a number of Latin American political scientists and sociologists, including Brazilians Cardoso and Teotonio dos Santos and Chilean Osvaldo Sunkel, renewed their efforts to explain patterns of social class structure and predict the structural changes that are inherent in the process of capitalist development in a dependent state. This new focus derived in part from a recognition that the form of this exploitative relationship was constantly subject to change and that the consequences of the industrialization of the periphery—that is, the Third World—through the medium of multinational corporations had not been adequately addressed by previously prevalent theories.

Among the assumptions that underpin dependency theory are the following. First, the distribution of power and status in national and international arenas is ultimately determined by economic relationships. Second, the causes of underdevelopment are not to be found in national systems alone but must be sought in the pattern of economic relations between hegemonic, or dominant, powers and their client states. The perpetuation of the pattern of inequality within client states is managed by a clientele class, which might be seen as the modern functional equivalent of a formal colonial apparatus. Third, both within and among states, the unfettered forces of the marketplace tend to exacerbate rather than to mitigate existing inequalities. That is, the dominant foreign power benefits at the expense of its client states, and the clientele class benefits at the expense of other classes.

Dependency theorists further held that development would not take place through the "trickle-down" of wealth nor through the gradual diffusion of modern attitudes and modern technology; that the upward mobility of individuals expressed by their gradual absorption into the modern sector is no solution to the problem of the impoverishment of the masses; and that stability is no virtue in a system of pronounced inequality. In fact, most dependency theorists, or, in Spanish, *dependentistas,* believed that only by breaking out of the international capitalist system and establishing socialist regimes will Latin American nations gain control over their own decisionmaking and expand the options available to them.[13]

Whereas modernization and development theorists see foreign investment and foreign aid as critical to development in the Third World, *dependentistas* see such investment and aid as means of extracting capital from client states. *Dependentistas* would probably agree with the observation of U.S. congressman Dante Fascell (D-Florida) that aid is a means whereby the poor of the rich countries contribute to the rich of the poor countries. They might also add that aid is yet another means whereby the poor of the rich countries contribute to the rich of the *rich* countries.

Andre Gunder Frank, comparing the experiences of the Latin American states during World War I and the depression of the 1930s with their experiences during periods when the links were stronger between those states and the industrialized West, concluded in 1970 that satellites, or client states, experience their greatest industrial development when their ties to the more developed states are weakest.[14]

Other scholars, noting, for example, the industrial expansion of Brazil in the late 1960s and early 1970s, maintain that rapid industrial growth may take place under conditions of dependency. There is general agreement, however, that to the extent that economic growth takes place under conditions of dependency, it is a distorted pattern of growth that exacerbates existing inequalities among both classes and regions within client states.

Like development theory, dependency theory has been limited by an excessive reliance on aggregate data and a "black box" approach—which treats nations like black boxes, shedding no light on internal dynamics or relationships. Such an approach deals with the outcome of unequal relations between nations but fails to elaborate the political mechanisms whereby dependent relationships are perpetuated.

Furthermore, in assigning primacy to economic relationships, *dependentistas* tend to give short shrift to other factors, such as the pursuit of institutional, or bureaucratic, interests, which may have an important bearing upon relations between dominant powers and client states and upon relations among political actors within client states. And in focusing upon international capitalism as the cause of inequities within and among states, the approach contributes little to an understanding of the similarities in relationships, for example, between the United States and Latin American countries and, until the late 1980s, between the Soviet Union and its East European client states.

Penetration Theory and Bureaucratic Authoritarianism

Other approaches that share many of the assumptions of dependency theory but that serve to elaborate or refine our understanding of politics in dependent states include penetration theory and the model of bureaucratic authoritarianism. Penetration theory seeks to identify the means whereby a dominant foreign power influences policy in a client state not only directly, through diplomatic pressures, but also indirectly, through the manipulation of political competition within the client state.[15] Bureaucratic authoritarianism, according to Argentine political scientist Guillermo O'Donnell, who coined the phrase, is the likely outcome of social and economic modernization in the context of delayed, or dependent, development. Such impersonal, institutional dictatorship is not a vestige of the feudalistic rule imposed by Spain or Portugal but rather a response to a perceived threat to the capitalist system. According to O'Donnell, the levels of coercion and of economic orthodoxy that are imposed depend upon the level of perceived threat.[16]

The Center-Periphery Model

The relationships hypothesized or described by dependency theorists have been incorporated by Norwegian scholar Johan Galtung into a model of elegant simplicity.[17] According to the center-periphery model, elites of the center, or metropolis, draw bounty from the periphery of their own state system (through taxes, for example), which they devote to the nurture and support of co-opted elites of client or "peripheral" states. In turn, elites of those client states, dependent upon elites of the center for assistance in exploiting and suppressing their own peripheral, or nonelite, populations, have no choice but to allow center elites to participate in, or share in the product of, the exploitation of the peripheral peoples of the peripheral states.

World Systems Theory

World systems theory, pioneered by Immanuel Wallerstein, also views the world economy as segmented into core and periphery areas.[18] Rather than focusing on the interactions of governments, however, this approach calls attention to the transnational interactions of nonstate actors, particularly multinational corporations and banks. The international economy is said to be driven by the initiatives of economic elites, particularly of the developed capitalist states, whose governments normally do their bidding. The control centers of the world economy then are financial rather than political capitals. The farther one lives from such a center, the less the "trickle down" of its wealth will be experienced.

Wallerstein, who sees the ideas of *dependentistas* as falling within the world system perspective, takes issue with more traditional Marxists and liberals alike for what he calls a rigidly developmentalist approach. That is, both schools assume that each nation-state must pass through the same set of stages, or modes of extracting surplus, in the same order. As he sees it, the nation-state system, which came into being in part as a convenience to economic elites of an earlier era, has ceased to be the essential institutional base of the global economy. The contemporary struggle, then, is not between rich and poor states, but rather between rich and poor classes in a global society.

SEEKING COMMON GROUND

None of the approaches, models, and theories discussed above wholly excludes the others. The differences among them are largely differences of perspective, emphasis, and value judgment. Adherents of development and modernization theory, like those of the historical-cultural approach, tend to focus on the attitudes of individuals and the behavior of institutions, though the former are more attuned to the indices of change whereas the latter more often stress continuity. Both pay tribute to the achievements of the modern West and deplore the antidemocratic influences of the Iberian tradition, but development and modernization theorists, more readily than historical-cultural analysts, see approximation to the Western model as a plausible solution.

Drawing explicitly on Marxist concepts, dependency theory looks to material interests and class conflict as well as to international patterns of trade, aid, and political control for explanations of political process at the national level. Thus, even when scholars of differing schools can agree as to what happened, they are likely to disagree as to why it happened. Whereas development and modernization theorists, for example, have generally viewed the public and private vehicles of U.S. influence as forces for democratic and social reform, dependency theorists have viewed them as antidemocratic and anti-egalitarian forces.

In the late 1980s, a number of scholars sought to resolve the debate between development and dependency theorists by seeking common ground or to supersede the debate by asking a different set of questions. One consequence has been a new emphasis on "interdependence." Another has been a wide-angle focus, reaching across disciplines and deep into the history of industrialization to explore, in particular, relationships between the state and the private sector, domestic and foreign. That approach has been labeled the new international political economy.

Interdependence

Whereas scholars dealing with relations between developed states and the Third World tended to focus in the 1960s on the benefits of such relations for the Third World and, in the 1970s, on the detriment of such relations to the Third World, many scholars in the 1980s began to focus instead on complementary needs and common problems. Some noted, for example, an increasing vulnerability on the part of the industrialized states to economic problems in the Third World. The high interest rates of the early 1980s in the First World, particularly the United States, were devastating to Latin American economies. The consequent debt crisis in Latin America has threatened the solvency of U.S. banks and closed markets for U.S. manufactured goods.

International Political Economy

The international political economy (IPE) agenda recaptures the scope of nineteenth-century social concerns for the purpose of addressing contemporary policy issues. Thus, the assumptions and findings of IPE theorists tend to cut across, and perhaps defuse, the development-dependency debates. In addressing Third World issues, IPE theorists, like dependency theorists, seek explanation for means and levels of development in class conflict rather than in assumptions about attitudes. Like modernization and development theorists, however, they generally find a positive relationship between development and democracy. They accept, to a point, the *dependentista* assertion that Third World countries have been disadvantaged by their participation in the global economy, but hold that positive results have on occasion been achieved where Third World governments had the capacity to negotiate the conditions of their participation.

International political economy shares with the world system school the conviction that development follows no preordained sequence of stages. IPE, however, faults the world system approach for underestimation of the role of the state in determining economic outcomes. Rejecting both the liberal preference for an unfettered market and the Marxist choice of state dominance of economic decision making, international political economy theorists contend that both state and market have important roles to play and that on occasion they are mutually reinforcing. Effective operation of the market may in fact be dependent upon the vigilance of a strong state, prepared to intervene where necessary.

Like dependency theorists, adherents of the IPE approach concern themselves with the contradiction between the geographic character of state power and the transnational character of economic power, but IPE theorists argue that the penetration of foreign capital does not necessarily shrink the economic role of the state. Studies of petrochemical and iron industries in Brazil by Peter Evans, of the oil industry in Venezuela by Franklin Tugwell, and of the copper industry in Chile by Theodore Moran have shown that foreign-owned extractive sectors may stimulate state entrepreneurial activity; that in itself, however, does not necessarily advance living standards or other indices of development.[19]

THE POST–COLD WAR PARADIGMATIC SHIFT

Though the Cold War ended with a whimper rather than a bang, the postwar period has had much in common with the aftermath of other wars—shifting boundaries and trade patterns, new categories of the displaced and the deprived. The winner in this case, however, was not a country or set of countries but an economic system. That system is not just capitalism; it is a socially premodern version of capitalism bulwarked by postmodern technology.

Spencerian capitalism, emerging triumphant, has demanded unconditional surrender not just of socialism in its extreme forms but also of many experiments in state planning and regulation, state-run enterprise and protected domestic industry, and welfare provisions—in Latin America, and particularly the most developed Latin American states, survivals of several decades of political development and economic nationalism. Such globalization of economic power and planning has meant also a level of hegemony in the realm of ideas unprecedented perhaps since the era of scholasticism. That is not to say that there is no dissidence or heresy. So long as there have been spokesmen of the haves proclaiming that trends and policies in their interest were in the interest also of the have-nots, there have been defenders of the have-nots having the nerve to say "not so." But one thing the have-nots have not in times like these is a forum.

The kind of economic devastation that followed the final cataclysms of the Cold War in the region of its epicenter got a long head start in Latin America. The debt crisis of the early 1980s left Latin American leaders at the mercy of creditors and currency speculators. The state itself, as a representative of a sovereign people, was so weakened that any line of policy, or even rhetoric, that smacked of economic nationalism threatened to set off a stampede of fleeing capital.

The surrender of economic policymaking seemed not to be a matter of choice, but domestic constituencies nonetheless demanded explanation and justification, which was scripted in neoliberal terms. Dependency theorists might claim that this turn of events had validated their analysis of the problem; but in a globalized economy—that is, without an alternative market or credit source—they were left without politically feasible solutions.

Liberalism and Neoliberalism

Like persons and places and religions, theories that acquire celebrity status—and thus usefulness to the powerful—become caricatures of themselves or their original versions; and liberalism was no exception. As elaborated in 1776 by Adam Smith, it was a progressive proposition, designed to redistribute wealth and opportunity from opulent courts and colonizers monopolizing trade under a system known as mercantilism to a new class of merchants and entrepreneurs whose interests and power would be limited by competition. Smith, however, recognized the danger of the evolution of monopolies and advocated strict governmental regulation to prevent such a development.

As liberalism came to be championed by an expansive Great Britain in the nineteenth century and the United States in the twentieth century, its qualifiers faded and its progressive features were transformed. The surviving core of the theory held that states had a common interest in the free flow of goods, services, and capital across national borders. Smith's laissez-faire principle was reinforced by David Ricardo's theory of comparative advantage. That theory posited that states should take advantage of their raw materials, low labor costs, technologies, or other strengths in order to specialize in those goods they could produce most efficiently, while trading for goods in which other states had the advantage. In colonial and neocolonial systems, the advantage accrued, of course, to mother countries, not colonies.

Development and modernization theory was a legitimate offspring of liberalism, and like its sire it served to explain and legitimate the seemingly limitless opportunities and responsibilities of an imperial power at its peak. Like liberalism also it sought to promote social and political change in adversary or client states, within limits dictated by economic interest.

Though its power center does not reside in a state, neoliberalism shares those circumstances and attributes of its forebears; but whereas development theory sought to strengthen state institutions, neoliberalism as expressed in policy tends to eviscerate them. Governments in general are seen as wasteful and corrupt, their deficits inflationary, their budgets a drain on resources that might otherwise be directed to attracting credit and investment. And privatization of government enterprises or services that might bring in a profit has commonly been a condition for the extension of credit. These and other measures that have come to be known collectively as "structural adjustment" are in the context of neoliberalism both policy prescriptions and factors in explanation and prediction of economic growth and stability or its absence. It is also assumed that an economy restructured along the lines prescribed is a prerequisite for a smoothly functioning electoral democracy. It has been conveniently forgotten that in general the "opening" of Latin American economies co-incided with the demise of democratic systems in the 1970s rather than with their return.

Critics and Heretics: What's Left of the Left

With the end of the Cold War, the right had lost its cover story, but the left had lost something harder to come by; it had lost its dream.

Criticism of neoliberalism as theory and as policy has exhibited little in the way of romanticism or radicalism. It is not in spite of the enormity of Latin America's problems and the pressures that private interests are able to bring to bear against the public interest but *because* of them that political strategies and policy alternatives from the left in the 1990s have been measured and modest.

The *dependentista* school has not vanished, though some might argue—since Cardoso was elected president of Brazil as a born-again neoliberal—that it has gone under deep cover. Osvaldo Sunkel, in his influential book *Development from Within*,[20] argues that while a strategy of export promotion may be unavoidable, a healthy economy, resistant to the effects of global market volatility, demands priority attention to the development of the domestic market. Andre Gunder Frank, who has joined world systems scholars in the study of long cycles of history, found Latin America in the early 1990s to be increasingly marginalized from world trading systems. More important, he sees commerce centering once again in the twenty-first century in the Orient, and particularly China.

Mexican scholar and political columnist Jorge Castañeda, in *Utopia Unarmed*,[21] observes that the entire political spectrum has shifted sharply to the right in the 1990s. In that context, he finds the left alive and well and living in the center—or what used to be the center. He does not interpret such repositioning, however, as surrender or battle fatigue; rather, he sees it as the outcome of learning through painful experience to see politics as the art of the possible. Castañeda calls for a revival of nationalism, but reformulated so as to promote transnational coalition building and to accommodate regional economic integration.

Alternative Perspectives and Concerns

The 1990s have seen the amassing of a great body of scholarly and popular literature inspired by needs and interests that run counter to those advanced by neoliberalism. This intellectual flourishing, however, particularly on the part of environmentalists, feminists, and advocates of grassroots community development, has yet to generate a great debate, mainly because economists, who now enjoy unchallenged disciplinary primacy in the business of theoretical legitimation, have generally ignored it.

Between these concerns and neoliberalism as now advanced there is little common ground. From the perspective of environmentalism, the global village is being stripped of resources by a feeding frenzy set off by deregulation and the new openness of markets and fueled by hard-currency debt-service requirements. Globe-hopping investors deplete, despoil, and depart, leaving communities and ecosystems devastated.

Likewise scholars engaging in gender analysis, along with chroniclers and supporters of the international women's movement, have noted that the front-line victims of the economic restructuring now sweeping the global village are women. Shrinkage of the public sector has cost women their best professional jobs at the same time that loss of family services, pensions, and benefits has expanded their responsibilities. While women are being squeezed out of the better-paying formal economy, they are being drawn in ever greater numbers into exploitative informal-sector work.

As governments, bound first to distant creditors, default on their obligations to their own citizens, the newly displaced and deprived are discovering what the long-suffering have always known—that the last bastion of security is the community, a community organized and aware of the need for general commitment and mutual support. Theorists of grassroots development note that such awareness and commitment runs counter to the dog-eat-dog or all-eat-dog options suggested by neoliberal individualism. Moreover, globalization—the alienation or distancing of decision-making about priorities and livelihoods—presents a dire threat to the ideal of individual and collective self-sufficiency, or "empowerment," that is the philosophical foundation of community development.

The momentum of these theoretical schools and activist movements continues to build, and separately or together they will bring ever greater pressure to bear on policymakers, ultimately laying the groundwork for a vibrant new debate on the fundamentals of democracy and development.[22]

NOTES

1. Sarmiento's best-known work is *Facundo* (in English translation, *Civilization and Barbarism: The Life of Juan Facundo Quiroga* [New York: Collier Books, 1961]).

2. This author submits that one of the reasons that Latin American politics has been so poorly understood by North Americans is that North American politics is also poorly understood by them.

3. Among the Latin Americanists whose works have tended to be in this vein are Fredrick Pike, John Mander, Charles Wagley, Claudio Veliz, Ronald Newton, William S. Stokes, and William Lyle Schurz.

4. Works highlighting corporatism or employing corporatist models include Howard J. Wiarda, *Corporatism and Development: The Portuguese Experience* (Amherst: University of Massachusetts Press, 1977); Howard J. Wiarda, ed., *Politics and Social Change in Latin America: The Distinct Tradition* (Amherst: University of Massachusetts Press, 1974); Philippe C. Schmitter, *Interest Conflict and Political Change in Brazil* (Stanford, Calif.: Stanford University Press, 1971); James M. Malloy, ed., *Authoritarianism and Corporatism in Latin America* (Pittsburgh: University of Pittsburgh Press, 1977); and Kenneth Paul Erickson, *The Brazilian Corporative State: Working Class Politics* (Berkeley: University of California Press, 1977).

5. Samuel Huntington and Myron Weiner, eds., *Understanding Political Development* (Boston: Little, Brown, 1987), pp. 21–28.

6. Walt W. Rostow, *The Stages of Economic Growth* (London: Cambridge University Press, 1960).

7. Martin C. Needler, *Political Development in Latin America: Instability, Violence, and Evolutionary Change* (New York: Random House, 1968). Other applications of development theory to the study of Latin America have included Charles W. Anderson, *Politics and Economic Change in Latin America* (Princeton: Van Nostrand, 1967), and Edward J. Williams and Freeman Wright, *Latin American Politics: A Developmental Approach* (Palo Alto, Calif.: Mayfield, 1975).

8. Gabriel Almond and G. Bingham Powell, *Comparative Politics: A Developmental Approach* (Boston: Little, Brown, 1966); and Samuel Huntington, *Political Order in Changing Societies* (New Haven, Conn.: Yale University Press, 1968).

9. Albert O. Hirschman, *Journeys Toward Progress: Studies of Economic Policymaking in Latin America* (New York: Twentieth Century Fund, 1963).

10. Samuel Huntington, "The Change to Change," *Comparative Politics* 3 (April 1971), p. 290.

11. Cited in Dan Griffin, "The Boom in Brazil: An Awful Lot of Everything," *Washington Post*, May 27, 1973.

12. Susanne Bodenheimer Jonas, "Dependency and Imperialism: The Roots of Latin American Development," *Politics and Society* 1:3 (May 1977), pp. 327–357.

13. Richard Fagen, "Studying Latin American Politics: Some Implications of a Dependency Approach," *Latin American Research Review* 12:2 (1977), pp. 3–26.

14. Andre Gunder Frank, *Development and Underdevelopment in Latin America* (New York: Monthly Review Press, 1968).

15. For an elaboration and application of penetration theory, see Jan Knippers Black, *United States Penetration of Brazil* (Philadelphia: University of Pennsylvania Press, 1977).

16. Guillermo O'Donnell, *Modernization and Bureaucratic-Authoritarianism: Studies in South American Politics*, Politics of Modernization Series, no. 9 (Berkeley: Institute of International Studies, University of California, 1973).

17. Johan Galtung, "A Structural Theory of Imperialism," *Journal of Peace Research* 8:2 (1972), pp. 81–117.

18. Immanuel Wallerstein, *The Modern World-System: Capitalist Agriculture and the Origins of the European World-Economy in the Sixteenth Century* (New York: Academic Press, 1974).

19. See Peter Evans, *Dependent Development: The Alliance of Multinational, State, and Local Capital in Brazil* (Princeton: Princeton University Press, 1979); Franklin Tugwell, *The Politics of Oil in Venezuela* (Stanford, Calif.: Stanford University Press, 1975); and Theodore H. Moran, *Multinational Corporations and the Politics of Dependence: Copper in Chile* (Princeton: Princeton University Press, 1975).

20. Osvaldo Sunkel, ed., *Development from Within: Toward a Neostructuralist Approach for Latin America* (Boulder, Colo.: Lynne Rienner, 1993).

21. Jorge B. Castañeda, *Utopia Unarmed: The Latin American Left After the Cold War* (New York: Knopf, 1993).

22. Some scholarly aspects of the current discourse are covered well in Mitchell A. Seligson and John T. Passé-Smith, *Development: The Political Economy of Inequality* (Boulder, Colo.: Lynne Rienner, 1993).

PART ONE
THE LAND AND THE PEOPLE

2

PHYSICAL LANDSCAPE AND SETTLEMENT PATTERNS

ALFONSO GONZALEZ

Latin America is among the largest world culture regions with an area of 20.5 million sq km (7.9 million sq mi), more than double the size of the United States. It has the greatest latitudinal range of any world region, extending from 32° north latitude to 56° south latitude. The airline distance from northwestern Mexico to northern South America is nearly 5,000 km (+3,000 mi),* and from there to Cape Horn, following the general curvature of the continent, is an additional 7,500 km (+4,600 mi). As a consequence, the region has a highly diversified ecology. Although it is primarily tropical, it encompasses some midlatitude environments, and there is great variation in the physiography, climate, vegetation, soil types, and minerals that are encountered in the region.

OUTSTANDING PHYSICAL CHARACTERISTICS

There are some outstanding physical characteristics in Latin America that combine to render a uniqueness to the region. The Andes, for example, comprise the highest continuous mountain barrier on earth with a lineal extent of +7,000 km (4,400 mi). The chain includes the highest summits outside of central Asia with at least three dozen peaks higher than Mt. McKinley (6,194 m [20,320 ft]), the highest summit in North America. Virtually every maximum or near-maximum elevation for most of the world's features (except summits) occurs in the Andes—the highest settlement, capital city, railroad, highway, mining activities, commercial airport, volcanoes, navigable lake, snowline, etc. Furthermore, the steepest coastal gradient anywhere occurs in Colombia.

The Amazon is physically the world's greatest river. Although second to the Nile in length, it has by far the greatest discharge volume, drainage basin, and length of navigable waterways of any river on earth. The highest and most voluminous water-

* + before a number means "more than"; – means "less than."

falls are located in South America. Two or three of the world's highest falls occur in the Guiana Highlands, and five of the seven greatest waterfalls in the world in volume of flow are in the Brazilian Highlands. Although the waterpower potential of Latin America is somewhat less than that of Asia, one-fifth of the world's potential hydroelectric power is found in Latin America.

Latin America is a unique faunal region, the Neotropical Zoogeographical Realm, which covers all of Latin America except northern and central highland Mexico and the Bahamas. Although the diversity of mammalian animal life is somewhat greater in the African region, no world region has so many unique mammalian families. Furthermore, Latin America also has the most diverse bird life and a highly varied and complex collection of lower animal forms.

Latin America has the highest proportion of any world region (nearly one-half) of its area in forests, and the regions of Amazonia and the Guiana Highlands represent the largest continuous tropical rain-forest area on earth. Latin America also contains the greatest absolute area in forest, almost one-quarter of the world total, and the highest per capita forested area of any world region. Unfortunately, perhaps only one-third of this forested area is both economically productive and accessible, so that Latin America, in reality, is a net importer of forest-based products. Currently, the reduction of the forests is occurring at an unprecedented rate: +300,000 sq km (+100,000 sq mi) of forested area were cleared for other uses in the past decade. This reduction is essentially all in South America. This is approximately one-fifth of the world's total loss of forests.

There are a number of extremes that distinguish the climate of Latin America. Some of the coastal lowlands and island stations approach the world record of only approximately 13°C (23°F) between the highest and lowest temperatures ever recorded. Probably the driest region on earth is the Peruvian-Atacama Desert, especially in northern Chile. Nevertheless, southern Chile is one of the rainiest places on earth, receiving measurable precipitation for as many as 325 days a year. The wettest place in the Western Hemisphere is located in the western Colombian Andes, which receive more than 8.5 m (335 inches) of rainfall annually.

Latin America is periodically beset by major natural disasters that are destructive of both lives and property. In this regard, the area is second only to the Orient in major natural disasters. Earthquakes occur with great frequency along the western highland margin of the region. Two of the greatest quakes outside the Orient occurred in 1868 and in 1970 in highland Peru, each causing the loss of 50,000 to 70,000 lives. Recently, devastating quakes occurred in 1972 at Managua, Nicaragua, in 1975 in central Guatemala, and in 1985 in Mexico City. There are fifty or more active volcanoes in the region (approximately one-quarter of the world total). The eruptions of Mt. Pelee (Martinique) in 1902, which resulted in the deaths of at least 30,000 people, and Nevado del Ruiz (Colombia) in 1985, with more than 22,000 killed, rank among the greatest volcanic eruptions of modern times. Hurricanes occur regularly within the Caribbean Basin and with less frequency on the Pacific coast of Mexico, often causing thousands of deaths. Perhaps the greatest avalanche ever recorded occurred in the Andean region of Peru.

OUTSTANDING POPULATION
AND SETTLEMENT CHARACTERISTICS

The population and settlement pattern of Latin America is also distinctive. The population in mid-1995 was approximately 486 million (see Table 2.1). More than 8 percent of the world's population now resides in Latin America compared to less than 2 percent during the colonial period. It is the only world region that has consistently increased in population faster than the world average since the mid-eighteenth century. Latin America became the fastest growing region in the early post–World War I period and continued to be so for half a century until it was equaled or surpassed by the Middle East and sub-Saharan Africa during the 1970s or even earlier.

Latin America's rate of population growth has been gradually decreasing since the early 1960s although very recently the decline has been more significant. Nevertheless, the region's population continues to increase by nearly 9 million annually. During the early post–World War II period, the average rate of growth was 2.7 to 2.9 percent per year. It is currently expanding at less than 2 percent annually. The greatest rates of growth occur in northern Central America and in Andean South America. Traditionally, the slowest growth has occurred in Argentina and Uruguay, although more recently these countries have been joined by Chile and most of the Antilles. The potential for further population growth remains in those few countries in which the death rate remains relatively high, notably in Haiti and Bolivia. Family planning programs in the region became generally significant only in the late 1960s.

The age structure of the population is characteristic of underdeveloped regions generally—a high proportion of the younger ages (now only 35 percent or more younger than 15) and a low proportion of older people (now 5 percent 65 years or older). Dependency ratios (proportions of the very young and very old in relation to the productive ages, 15–64) are generally high in the region, placing an additional burden on the economy. Partially related to this situation is the fact that only approximately one-third of the population is economically active (compared with two-fifths in developed regions). With reduced mortality, increasingly large numbers will be entering the labor force, currently about 3 million annually, which will result in heavy demands on employment opportunities as well as on educational and health facilities and housing.

In Latin America, infant mortality rates are the lowest of any underdeveloped region, and life expectancy is the longest. A subregion of the Orient, East Asia, however, now has rates that are an improvement over the Latin American average. Mortality aside, there is still a significant gap between the levels of living in Latin America and in the more developed regions.

The population density of Latin America averages approximately 23 inhabitants per sq km (+59 per sq mi), which is only slightly more than half the world average and is comparable to a number of other world regions. Most of the countries of Latin America are, therefore, below the world average in density; exceptions include the Antilles, El Salvador, Guatemala, Costa Rica, and more recently, Honduras, Mexico, and Ecuador. Partly as a consequence of relatively low crop yields, population pres-

Table 2.1
Latin America: Population Characteristics

	Area (thousand km²)	Population (million) 1996	Density per km² 1995	Percent Annual Population Increase 1990–95	Birth Rate^a	Death Rate^b	Infant Mortality Rate^c	Composition of Population by Age		Percent Population	
								-15	65+	Urban	Agricultural
Mexico	1,958	94.8	46.5	1.8	27	5	34	36	4	71	28
Guatemala	109	9.9	97.5	2.9	36	7	51	45	3	39	49
Salvador	21	5.9	274.1	2.2	32	6	41	40	4	45	35
Honduras	112	5.6	49.0	3.3	34	6	50	45	3	47	55
Nicaragua	130	4.6	33.0	2.3	33	6	49	44	3	63	35
Costa Rica	51	3.6	65.4	2.2	26	4	13	34	5	44	22
Panama	76	2.7	34.8	1.9	22	4	18	33	5	55	22
Belize	23	0.2	9.4	2.8	38	5	34	44	4	48	—
Cuba	111	11.0	99.8	0.8	14	7	9.4	22	9	74	18
Dominican Republic	49	8.1	161.5	1.9	29	6	52	37	4	61	32
Haiti	28	7.3	237.9	1.7	35	12	74	40	4	32	57
Puerto Rico	9	3.8	409.2	1.1	17	8	11.5	27	10	73	3
Jamaica	11	2.6	229.3	1.0	24	5	24	34	7	53	28
Trinidad/Tobago	5	1.3	246.7	0.6	18	7	12.2	31	6	65	7
Guyana	215	0.7	3.6	0.4	25	7	48	38	4	33	21
Surinam	163	0.4	2.6	1.3	23	6	28	35	5	49	15
Venezuela	912	22.3	24.0	2.3	26	5	23.5	38	4	84	9
Colombia	1,139	38.0	30.7	1.7	27	6	28	33	4	67	24
Ecuador	284	11.7	42.1	2.2	29	6	40	36	4	59	27

Peru	1,285	24.0	18.3	1.7	29	7	60	36	4	70	35
Bolivia	1,099	7.6	6.7	2.4	36	10	71	41	4	58	39
Paraguay	407	5.0	11.9	2.7	34	6	38	42	4	50	47
Chile	757	14.5	18.8	1.6	21	6	13.1	30	7	85	12
Argentina	2,780	34.7	12.4	1.2	20	8	22.9	31	9	87	9
Uruguay	177	3.2	18.1	0.6	18	10	20.1	26	12	90	13
Brazil	8,512	160.5	18.2	1.5	25	8	58	34	4	76	22
Latin America	20,533	486	23	1.8	26	7	43	35	5	71	24
Canada	9,971	30.0	3.0	1.2	13	7	6.2	21	12	77	3
United States	9,364	266.52	27.6	1.0	15	9	7.5	22	13	75	2
Underdeveloped Countries	84,933	4,594	54	1.9	27	9	68	35	5	35	54
WORLD TOTAL	135,641	5,771	42	1.6	24	9	62	32	6	43	43

[a] Number of births annually per 1,000 population.
[b] Number of deaths annually per 1,000 population.
[c] Number of deaths of infants (less than 1 year of age) annually per 1,000 population.

Sources: United Nations, *Demographic Yearbook 1994;* Population Reference Bureau, Inc., *1996 World Population Data Sheet; Britannica Book of the Year 1996;* Britannica World Data; Food and Agriculture Organization. *Production Yearbook 1994.*

sure on available cropland is greater in Latin America than in any developed world region, but such pressure is less than in any other underdeveloped area.

The pattern of population distribution in Latin America includes a concentration on the periphery, especially in South America and on the Pacific margins of Central America. Population is also concentrated in the highlands within the tropics, with one-half to three-quarters of the national populations in the upland areas. Major exceptions are the Antilles, Nicaragua, Panama, Belize, and the Guianas. Latin America has a larger population in the highlands than any other world region.

The region has a nucleated pattern of settlement, with semi-isolated population clusters and national population cores. Population clusters are detached, although this is diminishing with increased population and improved transportation. Generally 10 to 25 percent of the national area of a Latin American country contains one-half or more of the national population. As a result, in most countries there are large areas that are very sparsely settled—half of the area of Latin America contains only about 5 percent of the region's total population. The population pattern demonstrates that the effective area of settlement in most countries is still a small segment of the total national territory.

A rapid process of urbanization has characterized Latin America, especially since World War II. It is, by far, the most highly urbanized underdeveloped region. Its population was one-half urban by 1965 and is now more than two-thirds urban, the result of both natural increase (excess of births over deaths) and internal migration, with probably 3 to 4 million migrants moving into the urban centers annually in recent years. The causes of rapid urbanization include rural poverty (the "push" factors—expulsion from the countryside); the fast rate of natural increase in the rural areas; the scarcity of available arable land, especially in the traditional areas of settlement; the land tenure system (latifundia, the predominance of large estates, and *minifundia,* the prevalence of many very small landholdings); limited rural employment opportunities; and low wages; restricted social services provide an undesirable rural habitat over most of the region. Also, the attractions of the city (the "pull" factors)—the possibility of employment, higher wages, and improved social services—make the cities, especially the capitals, appealing to impoverished rural residents.

The largest city of each country (the capital except in Brazil, Ecuador, and Belize) tends to dominate the life of the country and is generally several times larger than the second largest city. This degree of primacy is more accentuated in Latin America than in any other world region. Some countries are highly urbanized, notably Venezuela and the Southern Cone countries of South America, while the most rural areas are Central America, Haiti, and the Guianas.

NATURAL REGIONS

Although there is a great variety of physical habitat in Latin America, it is possible to subdivide the area into thirteen natural regions (see Figure 2.1). These regions, although based fundamentally on physiographic characteristics, also possess some uni-

LATIN AMERICA:
NATURAL REGIONS

1 Gulf-Caribbean Coastal Lowlands
2 Antilles (West Indies)
3 Pacific Littoral:
     Coastal Plains & Valleys
4 Cordilleran Ranges,
     Intermontane Basins &Plateaus
5 Llanos
6 Guiana Highlands (& associated
     coastal lowlands)
7 Amazonia
8 Brazilian Highlands (& associated
     coastal lowlands)
9 Peruvian-Atacama Desert
10 Middle Chile
11 South Chile
12 Patagonia & Northwest Argentina
13 La Plata -Parana Basin

Kilometres
0 200 400 600 800

Compiled by Dr. Gonzalez and M.Styk. U of Calgary

Figure 2.1.   Latin America: Natural Regions

fying characteristics of climate, natural vegetation, and soils. Therefore, since these natural regions present differing sets of problems for human settlement and economic development, the human patterns are often in large measure a response to the prevalent locational and physical factors. Crude approximations of the areas, populations, and densities for the natural regions of Latin America are presented in Table 2.2.

Gulf-Caribbean Coastal Lowlands

The Gulf-Caribbean Coastal Lowlands are a continuation of the Atlantic-Gulf Coastal Lowlands of the United States, but south of the Rio Grande (Rio Bravo to the Mexicans) the coastal plain is narrower and interrupted. In the northernmost section, in the Mexican state of Tamaulipas, the climate is mostly subhumid (low-latitude steppe). This section is relatively sparsely settled, although the lower Rio Grande Valley has dense settlement because of agriculture and the newly developed gas fields. South of Tamaulipas, the coastal lowland is tropical in climate, vegetation, and soils.

The coastal plain becomes very restricted in portions of Veracruz and along sections of Central America; it becomes broadset in Yucatán and is fairly broad in Nicaragua and adjoining sections of Honduras and Costa Rica. Many portions of the coastal plain are characterized by poor drainage, resulting in swamps and marshes. Precipitation occurs throughout the year, but it is concentrated in the warmer months and is often twice as great as on the Pacific littoral. Many parts of the coastal lowlands are subject to violent tropical storms, especially from August through November. These hurricanes sometimes cause losses of thousands of lives and very extensive property damage.

The soils generally are not highly productive under continuous tillage. These lowland areas have traditionally had only scattered areas of settlement, frequently associated with commercial plantation agriculture, especially bananas, and with fishing and logging. However, in recent decades, there has been an influx of migrants into the lowlands.

The Yucatán peninsula, a platform of coral rock with limestone beds, is characterized by shallow, dry rendzina soil, with many sinkholes (*cenotes*) and few surface streams. The eastern and southern sections of the Mexican portion of the peninsula, Belize, and the northern third of Guatemala (the Petén) comprise one of the most sparsely settled areas of the coastal lowlands. Nevertheless, in pre-Columbian times, this area was the cultural hearth of the Mayan civilization, with population densities significantly above current levels.

The older petroleum fields of Mexico were centered in northern Veracruz. Reduced production continues from fields near Tampico, Tuxpan, and Poza Rica, but the great petroleum and natural gas fields were opened in the 1970s in southern Veracruz, Tabasco, adjacent Campeche, and on the offshore banks. Agricultural expansion in this region predates the development of the petroleum and natural gas industries.

The Gulf-Caribbean Coastal Lowlands extend into neighboring Colombia and Venezuela in South America. There they mainly comprise the Atrato and Magdalena valleys of Colombia and the Maracaibo Basin of Venezuela, which contains Latin

Table 2.2
Natural Regions of Latin America

	Area (thousand km²)	Population (thousand) 1995	Percent Annual Growth 1988–95	Density (per km²)	Percent of Total Area	Percent of Total Population 1995
Gulf-Caribbean Coastal Lowlands	743	28,676	1.78	38.6	3.6	6.1
Pacific Littoral	494	21,995	2.05	44.5	2.4	4.7
Cordilleran Highlands	3,233	151,497	1.49	46.9	15.7	32.1
Antilles	234	35,330	1.49	150.7	1.1	7.5
Llanos (Orinoco)	641	4,637	3.50	7.2	3.1	1.0
Guiana Highlands	1,104	2,535	1.65	2.3	5.4	0.5
Amazonia	4,958	13,347	3.47	2.7	24.1	2.8
Brazilian Highlands	4,370	144,362	0.95	33.0	21.2	30.6
Peruvian-Atacama Desert	402	12,093	2.38	30.1	2.0	2.6
Middle Chile	255	12,918	1.54	50.7	1.2	2.7
South Chile	241	239	0.97	1.0	1.2	0.1
La Plata–Paraná Basin	2,357	36,532	1.01	15.5	11.5	7.7
Northwest Argentina–Patagonia	1,538	7,290	2.05	4.7	7.5	1.5
TOTAL	20,570	471,451	1.43	22.9	100.0	100.0

Note: Figures are estimates and totals may not coincide with above data or with other data for Latin America because of rounding.

America's largest lake. These areas have been attracting migration from the more traditional highland centers of settlement because of the production of bananas and other tropical crops in Colombia and the great petroleum production in the Maracaibo district of Venezuela.

Antilles (West Indies)

The Antilles comprise one of the world's most important archipelagoes. The total area of the islands is only about 238,000 sq km (92,000 sq mi), approximately the size of Oregon. Cuba alone embraces one-half of the area; most of the remainder consists of the other Greater Antilles: Hispaniola, Jamaica, and Puerto Rico. The islands enclose one of the world's largest seas, the Caribbean, on the north and east.

The Greater Antilles are a complex folded and block-faulted mountain system that is mostly submerged. They consist of two ridges, separated by a deep trough. The Lesser Antilles, extending from east of Puerto Rico to the Netherlands Antilles off the coast of South America, consist of a great number of much smaller islands with an arcuate shape, convex toward the Atlantic Ocean, and structurally connected with the highlands of Venezuela. The northern section, the Leeward Islands, extend from the Virgin Islands to north of Guadeloupe, or possibly as far south as Martinique. The southern islands are the Windwards. The total area of the Lesser Antilles is less than 13,000 sq km (5,019 sq mi), about the size of Connecticut. The Antilles region, like the northern mainland of Central America and most of Mexico, is regularly exposed to hurricanes. The climate throughout the Antilles gives rise to either tropical rain-forest or tropical savanna.

The Antilles, except for the Bahamas and the Turks and Caicos, are far more densely settled than any other area of Latin America. Their populations are predominantly of African descent. The geographic location, combined with an equable climate and productive soils, gave rise to the earliest plantation economies of the New World. These were based primarily on sugar, although later bananas, coffee, and other crops were added.

The plantation agricultural economy has declined recently, especially on the smaller islands. Other economic activities, including tourism, subsistence agriculture, and commerce, have generally proved inadequate to support the dense populations. Mineral wealth in this region overall is minor but is of importance in eastern Cuba, Jamaica, and Trinidad. Relatively rapid population growth in the post–World War II period without compensating socioeconomic development caused a large exodus of emigrants to the United States, the United Kingdom, France, the Netherlands, and Canada.

Pacific Littoral: Coastal Plains and Valleys

The Pacific margins of Middle America and the northern section of South America represent a narrow zone of diverse physical landscapes. The peninsula of Baja

(Lower) California, in Mexico, represents the southern extension of the Pacific mountain system of North America and consists of a long series of blocks tilted toward the Pacific Ocean with a steep fault scarp on the Gulf of California side. This essentially desert, shrub-covered region has been, with parts of Yucatán, the most sparsely settled and isolated area of Mexico. However, in 1972 a paved highway was opened, and it runs the length of the peninsula, nearly 1,900 km (1,180 mi).

Across the Gulf of California lies the almost equally arid Sonoran Desert, the southward extension of the basin-and-range topography of the United States. Although the population is greater toward the more humid south, many of the river valleys of southern Sonora and northern Sinaloa are densely settled and intensively utilized due to the irrigation projects developed since the Revolution.

From approximately Mazatlán southward, the remainder of the coastal margin of Mexico, Central America, Colombia, and Ecuador is generally narrow; in places it disappears completely as the highlands reach the shore. The population along the Mexican section of this coastal zone is relatively sparse but increasing. The Pacific coastal margins of Central America tend to have greater population settlements than the Caribbean coasts, except in Honduras, but the coastal lowlands on both sides of the isthmus are undergoing a rapid increase in settlement. The great majority of the population of Panama is located in the Pacific lowlands, whereas that of Nicaragua is in the lake district lowlands close to the Pacific.

The extremely humid Pacific coastal margins of Colombia are sparsely settled and relatively isolated from the country's national settlement core. However, the growing commercial importance of the port of Buenaventura has stimulated population migration into this heavily forested area. The coastal margins and Guayas lowlands of Ecuador contain approximately half of that country's population and constitute a very rapidly expanding area of development. The cultivation of a number of tropical products, especially bananas, since World War II has encouraged settlement in this region where the ports and the largest city (Guayaquil) of the country are located.

Cordilleran Ranges: Intermontane Basins and Plateaus

The highland spine of the American Cordillera extends the length of Latin America near the Pacific margin of the region. Clearly, this is the most extensive of all the natural regions, with an airline distance of more than 12,000 km (7,458 mi); it is also one of the most populous, with about 150 million inhabitants. From Mexico to Bolivia, this highland zone contains from about half to more than three-quarters of the populations of every country except Belize, Nicaragua, and Panama.

The Cordillera is a young, complex mountain system with a considerable diversity of features, rock types, and geologic structures. Peaks attain elevations of nearly 7,000 m (22,966 ft). Aconcagua, rising 6,960 m (22,835 ft) on the Chilean-Argentine border just north of Santiago, is the highest summit in the world outside of central Asia. The passes are extremely high in the Andes, and throughout most of the Cordillera the high elevations, steep slopes, and extremely rugged terrain present very serious obstacles to transportation. Glacier and ice fields occur throughout much of the mountain system, even at the equator, and reach sea level in southern Chile. There are snowcapped peaks in the highland zones of Mexico and every country of South America within the Cordilleran system.

Within Latin America, the Cordillera attains its greatest width in northern Mexico (1,000 km [+600 mi]) and Bolivia (800 km [500 mi]). It becomes very narrow in portions of southern Central America and again in Chile. There are only four major topographic breaks in this formidable barrier: (1) the Isthmus of Tehuantepec in Mexico; (2) the Nicaraguan graben lowlands, which run from the San Juan River in the Caribbean coastal zone through the lake district northwest to the Gulf of Fonseca (part of this route was considered an alternate for a canal during the last century); (3) the Panamanian isthmus, where the canal is located; and (4) the Atrato–San Juan river valleys across northwestern Colombia.

The mountain system also contains numerous intermontane basins and plateaus, the largest being those of northern and central Mexico and the Altiplano of Peru and Bolivia. These plateaus are the major population zones of Mexico and Bolivia. The system contains some fifty active volcanoes—the greatest concentration in the world outside the Orient—concentrated in five zones: (1) the volcanic axis of Mexico, along the southern margin of the Mexican Plateau; (2) the Central American Pacific volcanic belt, extending from just inside the Mexican border to Costa Rica; (3) southern Colombia and Ecuador, including the Galápagos Islands; (4) central and southern Peru; and (5) Chile, where the two highest active volcanoes in the world are found. The only volcanic activity in Latin America outside the Cordilleran system occurs on three of the lesser Antilles. Throughout its length, except in northern Mexico, the Cordilleran region is one of the most earthquake-prone regions on earth. Very strong quakes occur regularly and cause considerable loss of life.

Most of the population in the western Cordilleran highlands of Latin America is found in the tropical zone or just on its margins where there is a considerable range of climate. Climates and vegetation vary in accordance with variations in altitude and temperature. The altitudinal boundaries of the climatic zones vary among localities because of latitude, windward/leeward location, exposure, precipitation, and humidity. In the highlands, although the seasonal range of temperature is comparable to that in the adjacent lowlands, the diurnal range is usually considerably greater, especially during the dry season. Table 2.3 gives a general overview of the major altitudinal zones in Latin America.

Throughout the Cordilleran highlands, the more productive basins have numerous urban communities and high rural densities. Increasing population pressure and the land-tenure system have stimulated a massive rural to urban migration, and, to a lesser degree, agricultural colonization of the more sparsely settled lowlands. The region has a great diversity of mineral wealth, but it is concentrated in northern and central Mexico and in Peru and Bolivia.

The higher zones have a very high proportion of Amerindians, especially in Guatemala and the central Andean counties. The *tierra caliente* zone, especially the Caribbean lowlands of Central America, the lowlands of Colombia, and to a lesser

Table 2.3
Altitudinal Zonation of Climates in Latin America

Lower Altitudinal Limit	Zone	Average Monthly Temperature	Major Agricultural Commodities
4,500 m (14,000 ft)	permanent snowfields (*nevados*)	<0°C (<32°F)	
3,000/3,500 m (10,000/ 11,500 ft)	alpine meadows (*tierra helada, páramos*)	6°–10°C (43°–54°F)	livestock grazing (especially sheep and goats, with llamas and alpacas in the central Andes) (above treeline and general crop cultivation)
2,000 m (6,000/ 6,500 ft)	temperate (*tierra fría*)	10°–17°C (54°–65°F)	midlatitude crops: wheat, barley, white potatoes, apples, and other deciduous fruits
600/1,000 m (2,000/ 3,000 ft)	subtropical (*tierra templada*)	17°–24°C (65°–75°F)	coffee, maize, cotton, rice, citrus, sugarcane
Sea level	tropical (*tierra caliente*)	24°–28°C (75°–83°F)	bananas, cacao, rubber, palms (coconut, oil), pineapples, mangoes (crops of subtropical zone also, except for coffee)

Note: Metric and English measure figures are rounded so conversion is not exact.

degree, the coastal zones of Venezuela and Ecuador, has the greatest concentration of blacks.

Orinoco Llanos

The Llanos ("plains") lie between the Venezuelan-Colombian Andes and the Guiana Highlands and are drained by the Orinoco River system. This basin, nearly evenly divided between Venezuela and Colombia, is the third largest in Latin America, accommodating the third greatest river discharge of the region. In size, the Llanos region approximates the state of Texas; it is one of the five very sparsely settled natural regions of Latin America.

Petroleum and iron ore have been exploited for some time in the eastern Llanos of Venezuela, but the most widespread activity, by far, is cattle ranching. In recent decades, there has been migration in both countries from the densely settled highlands to the forested margins and the open grassland districts of these lowlands. The settlers have reportedly encountered resistance from a few nomadic Amerindian tribes in the area.

Guiana Highlands

The Guiana Highlands, and the associated coastal lowlands, are perhaps two-thirds larger than the Llanos but contain even less population, making the Guiana region, Amazonia, and South Chile the most sparsely settled regions in Latin America. There is a narrow coastal lowland along the Guianas, which contains approximately nine-tenths of the population of those countries. There is also a narrow riverine lowland between the Guiana Highlands and the Orinoco River, which contains the greater part of the population and economic activity of the Guiana Highlands of Venezuela, nearly one-half the area of that country.

Much of the upland surface has been dissected by streams, and the world's highest waterfalls are located near the Venezuelan-Guyanan border. This highland massif and the Brazilian Highlands are composed of remnants of the oldest rocks on the continent—primarily a granitic base partially capped by a resistant sedimentary layer. Bauxite, iron ore, and manganese are the most important mineral deposits of the area, but gold and diamonds are also found there.

Amazonia

The Amazon Basin is the largest natural region of Latin America and one of the most homogeneous. Although nearly three-quarters of the basin lies within Brazil, portions of the region extend into Peru, Bolivia, Colombia, and Ecuador. Despite the basin's immense area, its population is extremely sparse: Only about 3 percent of the population of Latin America resides in this largest river basin on earth.

The Amazon River is, in volume, the greatest river on earth, although it is slightly shorter than the longest river, the Nile. The Amazon accounts for nearly one-fifth of the total world river discharge into the oceans. The outlet of the river is more than 300 km (186 mi) wide and contains an island the size of southern New England. It is the most navigable river system on earth. There is no bridge across the Amazon in its entire lowland traverse of the continent. Despite the river's immense silt discharge, the delta has undergone little development because of coastal subsidence and coastal currents. Few places on earth can match Amazonia with regard to the diversity of life-forms that are encountered.

The Amazon Basin can be generally divided into two major parts: the low-lying, level alluvial lowlands, or floodplain, and the upland plains. The floodplain is of varying width and comprises approximately one-tenth of the basin's area. This zone consists of a series of broad, disconnected swamps with natural levees. Much of the area is inundated at various times of the year. The most fertile soils, replenished by river silt, constitute the best agricultural land, and by far the greater part of the settlements lie within this zone. The upland plains are generally above the periodic river floodings and contain the highly leached and laterized soils typical of many tropical environments. The population in this zone is extremely sparse. Recently deforestation has accelerated to alarming proportions. Increasing areas are being devoted to crop cultivation and cattle ranching. Since the 1970s an extensive highway network is being constructed along with hydroelectric dam projects. Considerable mineral wealth has been discovered and is being exploited, especially iron, ferro-alloys, bauxite, gold, and petroleum. The destruction of the habitat is of serious concern for the aboriginal Amerinds; soil erosion, the loss of wildlife and plant species, and the alteration of regional and global climates are also sources of global concern.

Brazilian Highlands

The dissected Brazilian Plateau and its associated coastal lowlands make up the second largest natural region of Latin America and, with the Cordilleran Highlands, have the largest population of the entire region. Nearly one-third of Latin America's population is in this natural region, which accounts for half of Brazil's area and almost all of that country's population.

The diverse Brazilian Highlands consist of (a) a prominent seaward escarpment, the Serra do Mar of the southern section, which acted as a transportation handicap and barrier to early penetration of the interior; (b) the rolling, dissected plateau of the interior of this highland zone, which is inclined away from the ocean so that drainage is generally toward the interior before it eventually reaches the ocean; and (c) the old, eroded, and rounded mountain ranges that are found in different sections of the uplands. The east-central section of this Brazilian shield, notably in the state of Minas Gerais (General Mines), is highly mineralized with significant deposits of iron, ferro-alloys, diamonds, and gold.

The narrow and discontinuous coastal plain accounts for only 5 to 10 percent of the area of Brazil but at least a third of the population, including four of the half-dozen largest cities—Rio de Janeiro, Recife, Salvador, and Porto Alegre. The coastal lowlands have a tropical rain-forest, or monsoon, climate and broadleaf evergreen forests.

Tropical savanna occurs along much of the northeastern coast and the northern and central portions of the interior highlands. However, the interior northeastern section is a comparatively subhumid region. Its periodic droughts have had devastating effects on the nearly 30 percent of the national population residing in the poverty-stricken nine states of this section. This has been a zone of out-migration, primarily to the coastal plantation zone and the industrial and commercial centers in the south and southeast.

The southern highland section has a humid subtropical climate and, on the Parana Plateau, soil hospitable to coffee. Population growth is faster in São Paulo and the three southern states—which, combined, contain nearly two-fifths of the national population—than in the other eastern sections of the country. The interior plateau is also undergoing in-migration and rapid growth and development, although the region is still sparsely settled.

Peruvian-Atacama Desert

The Peruvian-Atacama Desert region consists of a narrow coastal zone that extends 3,000 to 3,500 km (+1,800 to +2,000 mi) from near the Ecuadoran-Peruvian border to Coquimbo, Chile. The coastal plain is extremely narrow or absent, and the coastline generally lacks enclosed, protected harbors. Isolated blocks and low coastal hills also characterize parts of the zone, and in places, there are low, but steep, escarpments behind the shore. There are few perennial streams, especially toward the south.

The combination of the Pacific anticyclone, the cool Humboldt current, and winds that parallel the coast makes this coastal zone perhaps the driest on earth. Arica, Chile, at the border with Peru, has the lowest average annual precipitation (0.5 mm [0.02 in]) of any weather station on earth. Another station, Iquique, less than 200 km (+100 mi) to the south, has experienced a period of fourteen years without measurable precipitation. However, the El Niño phenomenon occurs occasionally and brings heavy rains and floodings. Atmospheric and oceanic disturbances displace the cool Humboldt (or Peru) current farther offshore, permitting warmer water from the equatorial region to move southward off the coast of Ecuador and Peru. The loss of fisheries and marine birds can also be catastrophic.

The great mineral wealth in what is now Chile, first of nitrates and later of copper, opened sections of the arid north of that country to development. However, this one-third of the country contains less than one-tenth of the national population. Significant iron ore is exploited in southern Peru and the extreme south of the Atacama in Chile. In Peru, as in Chile, many stretches are barren both of vegetation and habitation, but fairly dense settlement occurs in the irrigated narrow coastal valleys, especially from Lima north.

Middle Chile

The relatively small Middle Chile region, lying between Coquimbo and Puerto Montt, comprises only one-third of the national area but contains slightly more than nine-tenths of the country's population, most of the agricultural land and industrial production, and much of the mineral wealth.

The northernmost section of this region is desert/steppe, a transition to the very arid region of the Atacama. Most of northern Middle Chile, however, has essentially a Mediterranean climate. In this sector, the summers remain dry; the mild winter is the season of precipitation. In some places, irrigation is necessary during the summer. This sector, which includes the capital, Santiago, contains more than 70 percent of Chile's population. The remainder of Middle Chile, south of Concepción, is less densely settled. Precipitation is greater in this area and occurs throughout the year. Southern Middle Chile is the most important forest-producing region of the country. The major mineral wealth is copper.

South Chile

South Chile, another small natural region, has a very sparse population. The coastal range is now partially submerged to form an archipelago, and much of the longitudinal valley is drowned. Andean glaciers reach sea level in this region, which is one of the four major fjorded coasts on earth. The region is rugged and isolated, cold, rainy, and dreary. There are no road or rail extensions south of Puerto Montt.

Only 2 percent of Chile's population resides in this third of the country. Most of those people are concentrated in the northern sector, on Chiloé Island—where forest quality and soils are relatively good—and in the Atlantic portion of Chile. There, in the rain shadow of the low Andean chain along the Strait of Magellan, the main economic activities are sheep raising, forestry, and the production of coal and petroleum.

Northwest Argentina and Patagonia

Patagonia and Northwest Argentina compose one of the larger of the natural regions of Latin America and lie entirely within Argentina. The Northwest is larger and more populous than Patagonia, yet the two subregions contain less than a quarter of the country's population in more than half the national territory. In addition to sparse settlement, aridity and uplands characterize this natural region.

Northwest Argentina is characterized by a series of pre-Cordilleran and Pampan ranges that attain their greatest breadth at 30°–35° south latitude and extend into the provinces of San Luis and western Córdoba. Most of the settlement and irrigated agriculture occur in the basin oases of the foothills.

The desert and steppe area of Patagonia is unique in that it is the only midlatitude arid climate in the Southern Hemisphere and the only major arid region on the east coast of a continent. The soils of Patagonia and part of Tierra del Fuego, like those of arid northern Mexico, are typical desert soils—productive when irrigated—and important agricultural output, especially of fruits, is obtained from the densely settled and intensively cultivated oases. There are some mining communities in Northwest Argentina. Petroleum is produced in both coastal Patagonia and in the

Andean foothills of the Northwest. Much of the region, however, is sparsely settled and devoted to livestock ranching.

La Plata–Paraná Basin

The La Plata–Paraná Basin, the third largest in the Western Hemisphere, after the Amazon and the Mississippi, encompasses the La Plata estuary, the master stream—the Paraná—and its tributaries, notably the Paraguay and Uruguay Rivers. The basin lies mostly within northeastern Argentina but also includes all of Uruguay and Paraguay and a portion of southeastern Bolivia. (A significant portion of Brazil is also drained by this river system, but most of that region of Brazil is included in the Brazilian Highlands natural region.) The La Plata–Paraná Basin is also one of the most populous of the natural regions and contains the Argentine nucleus of settlement.

This natural region has several subregions: the Gran Chaco (west of the Paraná and Paraguay Rivers from 29°–30° south latitude northward to Bolivia), eastern Paraguay (east of the Paraguay River), Mesopotamia (Argentina between the Paraná–Alto Paraná and Uruguay Rivers), the Pampas (grasslands radiating outward from Buenos Aires for +600 km [400 mi]), and Uruguay. The soils over much of the area are mollisols, deep and dark with organic matter and minerals, that develop near the humid-dry climatic boundary in the midlatitudes. These are the richest soils in Latin America and among the best in the world. The Pampa is the major food-surplus-producing region of Latin America. However, soil quality deteriorates toward the drier Northwest and Patagonia and, especially, northward into the humid tropics. The prevailing climate over most of the region is humid subtropical, comparable to the southeastern United States, with hot, rainy summers and mild winters.

SUMMARY AND CONCLUSION

The natural environments of Latin America are diverse and display varying degrees of settlement and development. The three largest regions—Amazonia, the Brazilian Highlands, and the Cordilleran system—comprise nearly two-thirds of the total area of Latin America. The Cordilleran highlands are very rugged, presenting enormous problems for cultivation and transport, but this has been the traditional area of settlement since pre-Columbian times for most of the countries that lie within the region. The Cordilleran and Brazilian highlands contain nearly two-thirds of Latin America's population. At the other extreme, five regions—Amazonia, Guiana Highlands, Northwest Argentina and Patagonia, Llanos, and South Chile—compose almost half of Latin America but contain about 5 percent of the population. Rates of population growth in these sparsely settled areas, however, are rapid, as pressures on land and resources in the traditional settlement areas stimulate internal migration. Despite this significant movement, the great migration within Latin America is into the major urban centers. This rural-urban migration is many times greater than the migration into sparsely settled regions.

SUGGESTED READINGS

Physical Geography

Clawson, David L. *Latin America and the Caribbean: Lands and Peoples.* William C. Brown, 1997. Chapters 2–4.

Handbook of Middle American Indians. Vol. 1, *Natural Environment and Early Cultures,* ed. Robert C. West. Austin: University of Texas Press, 1964. 570 pp. Eight of the chapters provide a good detailed study of the different aspects of the physical environment of Middle America. Probably the best overview of the physical geography of this part of Latin America.

Handbook of South American Indians. Vol. 6, *Physical Anthropology, Linguistics, and Cultural Geography of South American Indians.* U.S. Bureau of American Ethnology, ca. 1948/1949; reprinted New York: Cooper Square, 1963. 715 pp. The section by Carl O. Sauer, "Geography of South America" (pp. 319–344), pertains to the physical landscape of the continent and can serve as a companion piece (although not as detailed) to the *Handbook of Middle American Indians* to complete the coverage of all of Latin America.

Kendrew, Wilfrid George. *The Climates of the Continents.* 5th ed. Oxford: Clarendon Press, 1961. 608 pp. Part 6, "South America, Central America, Mexico, the West Indies" (pp. 464–527). Probably one of the best accounts, although perhaps too detailed, of meteorological and climatic conditions in Latin America.

Martinson, Tom L. "Physical Environments of Latin America," in Blouet, Brian W., and Blouet, Olwyn M. (eds.), *Latin America and the Caribbean: A Systematic and Regional Survey.* 3d ed. New York: John Wiley & Sons, 1997. Chapter 2.

Robinson, H. *Latin America.* 4th ed. London: MacDonald and Evans, 1977. Chapter 1.

Verdoorn, Frans, ed. *Plants and Plant Science in Latin America.* Waltham, Mass.: Ronald Press, 1945. 381 pp. Despite this work's age, it is still an informative source, not only for the phytogeography and agriculture of the region, but also for other aspects of the physical environment.

Population

Blouet, Brian W. "Population: Growth, Distribution, and Migration," in Blouet, Brian W., and Blouet, Olwyn M. (eds.), *Latin America and the Caribbean: A Systematic and Regional Survey.* 3d ed. New York: John Wiley & Sons, 1997. Chapter 5.

Gonzalez, Alfonso. "Latin America—Population and Settlement," in Boehm, Richard G., and Visser, Sent (eds.), *Latin America: Case Studies.* Dubuque, Iowa: Kendall Hunt Publishing Co., 1984. Chapter 6.

Merrick, Thos. W., et al. "Population Pressures in Latin America." *Population Bulletin* 41:3 (1986).

Sánchez-Albornoz, Nicolás. *Population of Latin America: A History.* Berkeley: University of California Press, 1974. 299 pp. A very good and thorough study of the growth and development of Latin America's population (chapters 1–4) but also contains chapters (6–8) that deal with recent trends and prospects.

Sargent, Charles S. "The Latin American City," in Blouet, Brian W., and Blouet, Olwyn M. (eds.), *Latin America and the Caribbean: A Systematic and Regional Survey.* 3d ed. New York: John Wiley & Sons, 1997. Chapter 6.

3

THE INDIAN POPULATIONS
OF LATIN AMERICA

KARL H. SCHWERIN

In order to understand the contemporary character and distribution of Indian populations in Latin America, it is necessary to know something about the nature of indigenous societies at the time of European discovery. The native inhabitants of the New World represented a great range of cultural development, from simple hunting and gathering bands to complex and literate civilizations. Within the area of present-day Latin America, the great majority of the peoples had reached levels of significant cultural achievement. Most societies were food producers, and in many respects, the region from central Mexico southward was far more advanced than the area lying to the north in what is today northern Mexico, the United States, and Canada. In fact, North America is the only major world region where the majority of the aboriginal peoples relied on gathering, hunting, and fishing for their subsistence. By contrast, South America was inhabited by predominantly agricultural societies.[1]

Nonetheless, a full range of cultural variability also existed in the Latin American region. Although specialists might want to differentiate a great number of categories, it is more instructive for our purposes to treat the early Indian societies as belonging to one of three major types. Marginal hunters and gatherers were restricted for the most part to Argentina, Uruguay, and parts of coastal Brazil. They were also predominant on the northern frontier of the Spanish Empire, the arid deserts of northern Mexico. Lowland extensive agriculturists were much more widespread, ranging from central Chile throughout most of interior Brazil to the whole of the Amazon Basin, including those portions now within the territorial borders of Bolivia, Peru, Ecuador, Colombia, Venezuela, and the Guianas. They also occupied the rest of Colombia and Venezuela and ranged northward through the whole of Central America and the Antilles. The third principal type was the highland intensive agriculturists, many of whom achieved state-level societies in the mountains and plateaus of Mexico, Guatemala, Ecuador, Peru, and Bolivia.

During the past generation, a vigorous debate has raged among historical demographers concerning the aboriginal population of the Americas at the time of European discovery. Estimates range from 13 million to more than 100 million. For the Latin American region, however, an estimate of 80 million seems likely. Sixty million of these people belonged to the civilized states of Middle America and the central Andes. Most of the remaining, numbering about 18 million, were lowland agriculturists in the interior of South America, the northern coastal region, the Caribbean, and Central America. Hunting and gathering peoples accounted for no more than 2 million persons, and the figure was probably closer to 1 million.

European conquest radically disturbed the aboriginal societies. Perhaps the most drastic effect was a rapid and massive population decline, characterized by modern investigators as a "demographic disaster." The principal cause of the disaster was the introduction of several new diseases that decimated the native populations through repeated epidemic outbreaks. The wars of conquest also took their toll, as did slavery and other abuses of Indian labor, and there were ecological repercussions because of interference with the seasonal rhythm of native agriculture (by removing native labor for Spanish needs at critical periods in the agricultural calendar) and the introduction of livestock (which competed with natives for land and invaded their planted fields).

Estimates of the rate of depopulation differ, but the best calculations suggest an average decline of 95 percent in 130 years, leaving only about 4 million Indians south of what is now the United States in 1650. It must be remembered, however, that an unknown portion of this decline is represented by the mestizo offspring of European or African fathers and Indian mothers, who were treated as a class or caste apart from their parents and who often sought to "pass" into the higher-status European category.

The Caribbean population, which was conquered first, was wiped out in less than fifty years. African slaves were introduced to replace the Caribbean Indians as a labor force. Most of the continental hunters and gatherers have also become extinct. The lowland agriculturists declined drastically, with many groups becoming extinct (some continue to disappear today); others, however, have survived and are today increasing in number. In the areas of highland civilization, there was also a drastic population decline, but the population reached its low of perhaps 3 million to 5 million around 1650. Thereafter it grew slowly until around the beginning of the nineteenth century. Since that time, the Indian population of Middle America and the central Andes has been growing at an increasingly rapid rate.

PRECONQUEST SOCIETIES

A moment's reflection about the areas occupied by these three major culture types helps one realize that these regions are still characterized by distinctive populations today. Elman Service has dubbed these areas Euro-America, Mestizo-America, and Indo-America, respectively.[2] Why are such differences of aboriginal culture type reflected in differences among the modern populations? Commonly, this is explained as resulting from differences in administrative policies of the European colonial powers. Not only did such policies differ among Spain, Portugal, and Great Britain, but there were differences in the way the policies were implemented in various parts of the colonial empires. Thus, it is frequently maintained that colonial policies were enforced more rigorously in the Antilles, Mexico, and Peru and that greater control was exerted over the colonists in those areas, both because these colonies were more valuable and because they contained greater numbers of colonists. In contrast, there was less interest in colonies like Venezuela and Buenos Aires, and consequently, crown control was much more lax in those areas.

There is, however, another way of looking at the question of contemporary differences. This approach begins by looking at the diversity of aboriginal cultures encountered by the white man and recognizing that the Europeans were forced to adjust differently in accordance with the basic differences in native cultures.[3]

The object of European conquest was to profit from these newly discovered areas. The preferred ways of doing so were to assess tribute from the native populations (by means of the *encomienda* and the *corregimiento*) or to exploit native labor in profit-making enterprises (through forced labor projects, or the *repartimiento*) such as construction, mining, ranching, and later, textiles.

In the highland areas of Mexico and Guatemala and in the central Andes, native societies had achieved a high level of cultural development, with complex state organization. The native peoples were integrally involved with complex economic, social, and political institutions and depended upon them to maintain their traditional way of life. It would not have been easy to survive on their own if they had been cut off from these state-level institutions. In addition, most of them had no easily accessible refuge areas to which they could flee from Spanish domination. Given the existence of well-defined state institutions, within which the native populations were accustomed to function, it was relatively easy for the European conquistadores to take these institutions over from the top and continue to control the population in much the same way as had the native elite. Such control was particularly effective because of the system of indirect administration that was worked out. Only minor modifications were made in most native institutions (except for religious ones), especially on the lower levels where native intermediaries continued to be employed in governing the mass of the population.[4]

Throughout the colonial period, there was a fair amount of racial mixture, and the native elites were gradually absorbed into the dominant Spanish ruling class. Among Indian commoners, local community and familial institutions retained strength in spite of racial mixture with the Spanish overlords and their African slaves. To this day, many Indian languages continue to be spoken throughout these areas, many rural communities have maintained their identification as Indian, and many aboriginal and/or ethnically distinct customs have been retained as central features of the local cultures. These are the areas Service characterizes as Indo-America.[5]

Lowland areas were occupied mostly by extensive agriculturists who were organized principally as independent localized tribes or villages.[6] Here there were no large organized communities or state-level institutions. It was much more difficult to control these small independent tribes, for conquest of one did not give the victor authority over its neighbor. The European strategy was to capture single families and individuals and force them to become household servants or to work as agricultural slaves. The intimacy that existed between masters and household slaves or small numbers of agricultural slaves led to a rapid mestization of the native groups. Mestizos tended to identify with the dominant European population and to be absorbed into its lower levels. Thus, there was a continuing need to acquire additional slaves from the native groups. The Paulistas of Brazil are the best-known example of this type of exploitation. Their periodic expeditions ranged far and wide throughout the interior to capture Indian slaves. This type of exploitative relationship between the European colonists and native societies led to a breakdown of the more accessible Indian communities and the flight of many more to remote refuge areas where they might avoid the depredations of slavers. In some of these isolated locations, the Indians have been able to survive to the present day, particularly in southern Chile, parts of Amazonia, the interior of Venezuela, parts of Central America, and the extremely rugged and isolated regions of northern Mexico. These are the areas that Service identifies as Mestizo-America.[7]

Where plantation agriculture developed, there was need for large numbers of laborers. Because of the social and physical separation between owners and field laborers, the latter, which existed in large numbers, were treated impersonally. Under the rigors of the plantation system, Indian slaves often fled to the interior, which they could easily do because they were familiar with the environment and knew how to survive there. Even when they were unable to return to their own community, other native communities and social systems were similar enough that they were usually able to plug into them with relatively little difficulty. The very serious problem, for plantation owners, of runaway Indian slaves led to the introduction of African slaves who were much easier to control. The Africans were in a wholly unfamiliar environment— an alien terrain filled with unknown plants and animals. They could not speak the native languages, and they did not know how to behave or participate in the aboriginal social systems. Consequently, African slaves were much more inhibited from fleeing the slave situation. These plantation areas developed principally in coastal Brazil, the Caribbean, and coastal Peru. In most of these areas, the African racial type remains predominant today, and I would therefore characterize them as Afro-America.

Where the European intruders found it impossible to control the native population, even as slaves over the short term, their only recourse was to exterminate the natives or to drive them from the areas of settlement. Hunters and gatherers lived a simple life, unburdened with abundant possessions or a complex technology. They were more or less nomadic and thus could readily flee areas of control. They could survive quite well away from European control. In some cases, they found it possible to survive on the margins of European settlement. And in some instances, they actually developed a new and highly successful adaptive strategy of attacking and living off the European settlements. Among such groups we may count the Tehuelche and Puelche of Argentina; the Pehuenche of Chile; the Argentine Araucanians; the Abipón, Mbayá, and other Guaicuruan tribes of the Gran Chaco in Paraguay; and the Charrúa of Uruguay. At the northern limits of the Spanish colonies, in northern Mexico and New Mexico, similar groups developed; Apache, Ute, and Comanche raiders preyed on Spanish settlements for several hundred years. The result in most of these cases of active raiding by native groups was chronic warfare between them and the Spanish colonists. The Spanish settlements grew gradually over time and eventually reached the point at which the Spanish were able to carry on intensive warfare against the native raiders, usually exterminating them completely. These areas, where the native populations have been wholly eliminated, are what Service calls Euro-America,[8] and they include Argentina, Uruguay, and Costa Rica.

One other point is worth emphasizing in this analysis of differential relations between the conquering Europeans and native societies. European culture was structurally complex, representing a state level of organization. In this sense, it was most like the cultures of the highland state-organized peoples, less like those of the lowland agriculturists, and most distinct from the cultures of the marginal hunters and gatherers. It is clear that there was a more or less direct correlation between the cultural complexity of a native society and its survival after European conquest. It thus appears that the more alike the conquerors and the conquered, the more simple and easy the adjustment to conquest; the less difficult and disruptive the adjustment, the more likely the survival of the conquered people and the preservation of at least the local basis of their native social organization and cultural forms.

CONTEMPORARY LATIN AMERICA

Euro-America and Afro-America

Table 3.1 gives the current distribution of the Amerindian population in Latin America according to the latest more or less complete data readily available, which are centered on 1990. It will be noted that in Euro-America and Afro-America, the indigenous population generally accounts for 1 percent or less of the total population. In Euro-America, it is about 1 percent, and in Afro-America it actually averages much less than that.

The principal exception is in the three Guianas, where population is sparse and total population numbers are low. There, because of the limited population and the concentration of intrusive groups along the coast, the indigenous groups that occupy the interior of those countries have not previously been faced with as much direct competition as in Brazil or the Antilles. This situation is now changing because, since independence, the Guianas have increasingly looked to development of the interior as integral to their goals of national economic development, although it is likely that as the nonrenewable resources are depleted, the perceived usefulness of the indigenous population will diminish at the same time. In the case of Guyana, development

Table 3.1
Amerindian Population of Latin America, 1990

	Total Population	Indian Population	Indian Percent of Total
Euro-America (approx. 1 percent)	38,187,000	379,470	1.0
Argentina, Uruguay, Costa Rica			
Afro-America	163,838,499	224,594	0.1
Coastal Brazil	122,218,922	61,485	0.05
Guianas	1,338,000	63,771	4.8
Northern Colombia	6,931,577	91,338	1.3
Antilles	33,350,000	8,000	–
Mestizo America (1–7 percent)	128,741,314	3,195,327	2.5
Northern Mexico	24,354,529	184,368	0.8
Central America (excl. Costa Rica)	16,648,000	1,189,746	7.1
Southern and eastern Colombia	25,911,248	328,668	1.3
Venezuela	19,738,000	308,762	1.6
Braz. Amazonia	24,598,537	167,329	0.6
Paraguay	4,314,000	84,892	2.0
Chile	13,177,000	931,562	7.1
Indo-America (>10 percent)	105,460,335	24,792,906	23.5
Central and southern Mexico	55,975,116	5,097,969	9.1
Belize	189,000	25,799	13.7
Guatemala	9,197,352	5,604,214	60.9
Ecuador	10,559,000	2,624,304	24.9
Peru	21,662,000	8,317,919	38.4
Boliva	7,877,867	3,122,701	39.6

Sources: National censuses data; World Bank 1991; Matos Mar 1993.

of the interior is also a means of asserting and consolidating rights to territory claimed as well by neighboring Venezuela.[9]

In Euro-America population growth has been slow, although the indigenous population has increased by nearly 26,000 in the past decade, growing more than one and a half times faster than the general population. In Afro-America the indigenous population has declined by about 12,000 in the same time period and now represents less than 0.1 percent of the total population. Significant changes in coastal Brazil (from 34,165 in 1980 to 61,485 in 1990) and northern Colombia (from 139,596 in 1980 to an estimated 91,338 in 1990) probably represent differences in the definition of an "Indian" as well as different methods of enumeration. There has been no major change in the Guianas. There is increasing evidence, however, of significant numbers with indigenous ancestry who are systematically excluded from census enumeration and denied as "real Indians." There may be a half million or more in the Antilles and Central America alone.[10]

Mestizo America

Most of the surviving indigenous populations of this region are tribal Indians. In general, they retain their aboriginal cultures and their identity as members of a tribal community. They are not integrated into national society but continue to function as members of distinct cultures within national boundaries of the modern state, thus leading some authorities to characterize them as "Fourth World" societies. But numerous native groups in this region are currently in the process of acculturating to the dominant national cultures, including significant numbers that are migrating to the cities.

There are slightly more than 3 million Indians out of a total population of more than 100 million. It is worth noting that the indigenous population of this region has doubled since the early 1980s while the population as a whole has grown by only 27 percent—the Indians have increased from 1.6 percent to 2.5 percent of the total. On a country-by-country basis, the Indians mostly represent more than 1 percent but less than 7 percent of the total population (see Table 3.1). Their numbers have declined in northern Mexico and Brazilian Amazonia, increased modestly in southern and eastern Colombia and Paraguay, and grown dramatically in Central America, Venezuela, and Chile.

In northern Mexico, the principal group is the Tarahumara—subsistence farmers widely scattered throughout their rugged mountain homeland. In Central America, interior Venezuela, and the vast Amazon Basin, the aboriginal populations were relatively sparse at the time of European contact. Disease, slavery, and European warfare against these highly divided groups led to their decimation and extinction in many localities. Nonetheless, a number of tribal groups persist in more isolated localities or on reserves protected by missionaries or national governments. Most of these populations are found in the lowland, tropical areas.

The economy of these lowland tribes is based on subsistence slash-and-burn farming of tropical crops. The most important staples are manioc, bananas, and yams, but these are supplemented by a variety of other crops. Some tribes, like the Karinya of Venezuela, cultivate nearly a hundred different crops. Fishing is also an important subsistence activity, providing the principal source of dietary protein. Hunting is generally less important, and even this activity is often oriented toward riverine and aquatic species (turtle, caiman, ducks, manatee, etc.). In some groups, which lack ready access to the rivers—such as the Jivaro and the Yanomamö—hunting assumes greater importance. By exploiting the diverse resources of agriculture, fishing, and hunting, most of these groups have maintained a nutritionally balanced diet. Their crafts are generally simple, although many tribes make excellent baskets and some like the Jivaro are known for their fine pottery.

Villages are politically independent, and tribal identity is recognized only as a consequence of sharing a common language, common customs, and a mutual ethnic consciousness. Settlements generally number fewer than 300 inhabitants, although they may occasionally range up to as many as 1,000 to 2,000. Traditional residence was in communal houses, with one or more located in each settlement. Sociopolitical organization is based on kinship ties. Marriage tends to be endogamous within the local group. The headman or chief has limited authority over the group; he usually enjoys few, if any, special privileges. His influence is based on personal prestige and does not extend beyond the local village. The division of labor is based strictly on age and sex. With the exception of the shaman, there is no full-time specialization.

Warfare is frequent and often bitter, but it is never pursued for purposes of conquering territory or exacting tribute. Usually it is justified in terms of revenge, or sometimes to gain prestige or to acquire trophies that are supernaturally powerful. Many anthropologists subscribe to an ecological explanation for warfare among these tribes—seeing it as a mechanism for acquiring and maintaining access to scarce resources, such as rivers, with their abundance of fish and game; good farmland, also mostly along the rivers; and, among the Yanomamö, women. Warfare may also serve to keep populations dispersed so as not to overexploit the limited resources of the tropical environment.

Except for marriage, which tends to be treated in a matter-of-fact way, life crisis rites are particularly emphasized among these peoples. Shamanism is also important and highly developed. The shaman works to cure illness, to affect the weather, and to ensure success in warfare. Often he organizes magical-religious festivals and dances as well. He is generally the guardian of tribal religious tradition. The shaman may also practice witchcraft and sorcery, though he rarely admits to doing so unless it is directed against tribal enemies. A wide variety of narcotics are used by the shamans, and sometimes by all adult men, in curing and other religious ceremonies. Although the concept of a high god may exist, it is relatively unimportant in religious belief and ritual. Instead, religion centers on culture heroes, who made the world as it is today, and on nature spirits who are closely associated with subsistence concerns, particularly fishing and hunting.

The Mapuche of southern Chile are somewhat distinct from the other groups being discussed here, since they have adopted European crops and farming techniques and participate, to a certain extent, in the national society. Crop surpluses are sold in the regional market, children receive formal schooling, and the Mapuche participate, at least marginally, in national political, legal, and judicial institutions. Under the Pinochet regime, however, they suffered severe discrimination and many communities lost their land.

All of the groups in Mestizo America are under increasing pressure from national societies because the isolated areas they have occupied up to now are being opened up by the construction of highways, spontaneous colonization by peasant farmers, national development programs, and projects for the exploitation of natural resources by numerous multinational corporations. In Central America, the native groups seem to be holding their own so far, although there are concerns for the future. In Nicaragua the revolutionary Sandinista government was startled to find the 120,000 Miskito Indians living in the Caribbean lowlands resisting efforts to absorb them into national society. After several years of tense relations, the Mosquitia region was formally recognized as an autonomous region within the Nicaraguan state.

In Venezuela the government has been attempting to protect Indian lands through legal action. This protection was called into question, however, when the Karinya were denied legal rights to the lands they have occupied for generations, rights confirmed by royal decree during the colonial period. Authorities in Colombia, Bolivia, and Paraguay have generally ignored the problems of the natives, but in Colombia indigenous peoples have suffered high levels of violence perpetrated by security forces, drug traffickers, leftist guerrillas, and paramilitary groups, as well as severe poverty. Efforts to legislate more rigorous paternalistic control over indigenous groups were defeated. Instead, indigenous groups contributed to the writing of a new constitution in the late 1980s that recognizes indigenous peoples as Colombian citizens with full rights. Indigenous representatives have also been elected to the Colombian congress.[11]

Brazil has vacillated between looking the other way while natives are pushed out or exterminated and attempting to resettle them on reserves. Brazil continues to have one of the worst human rights records with respect to its Indian population.[12] When faced with pressures from development interests, responsible officials have generally allowed these reserves to be fragmented or whittled down. For example, in spite of a vociferous international outcry, Brazil has made no concerted effort to keep thousands of prospectors, miners, and traders from intruding on Yanomamö territory. The democratic Constitution of 1988 includes a chapter on indigenous peoples that revises relations between them and the state, terminating five centuries of integrationist policy. On paper it increased enormously the rights of Indians, recognizing their right to land and the existence of collective (community) Indian rights. But Brazilian practice continues to be integrationist, while state and local governments ignore abuse of constitutionally guaranteed Indian rights.

Although most of these Indians have remained in distinct, small-scale tribal communities, increasing numbers have also followed the general demographic trend in Latin America of rural to urban migration. While it has often been recognized that there are significant numbers of Indians in Latin American cities, it has been nearly impossible to get any reliable estimate of their numbers. To judge from the available figures, at least 200,000 Indians are probably urban dwellers in Mestizo America.

These tribal peoples cannot be ignored as human beings. Certainly, they are equal in importance to any other identifiable group in the nations of Mestizo America. Many of their current difficulties arise from the fact that in terms of their gross numbers and the economic or political impact that they exercise within those nations, they represent a very small segment of the modern population.

Indo-America

By far the most significant indigenous populations, in terms both of numbers and of their place in national society, are the modern Indian types found in Indo-America, comprising most of Mexico, Guatemala, and the central Andean countries of Ecuador, Peru, and Bolivia. These Indians, most of whom live in the highland regions of those countries, must be included in any consideration of modern Latin America. Although their way of life differs from that of the non-Indians in the countries in which they live, they share many patterns and institutions, mainly of European origin, with the other citizens. Numerically, they are an important segment of the population, constituting more than 10 percent in almost all of these countries. In some countries, such as Guatemala, Peru, and Bolivia, they make up from 40 to 60 percent of the population, respectively (see Table 3.1).

Taking Indo-America as a whole, the indigenous population amounts to nearly 25 million, or 23.5 percent of the total population. This represents an increase of more than 7.5 million, or 44 percent, since about 1980. Compare this to the growth in the general population of about 22 million, or 27 percent. It is clear that the indigenous population is increasing more than one and a half times as fast as the general population.

During the colonial period, the Indians of these countries were taught Catholicism and often were concentrated into Spanish-type villages, where European forms of community organization were forced upon them. They borrowed freely from the European culture of the sixteenth and seventeenth centuries—a culture that in many respects contained as many "folk features" as their own. By at least the beginning of the eighteenth century, the fusion of the aboriginal and colonial Spanish patterns had formed a new culture among these peoples. This culture persists today, unchanged in its main outlines, and constitutes an important variant of *national* patterns in these highland countries. Because this culture is relatively unchanged from colonial times, it contrasts markedly with modern cultural patterns and is sometimes erroneously believed to represent a survival of aboriginal cultural practices.

Modern Indians in these countries generally speak an aboriginal language, although they frequently speak Spanish as well. Community cohesion tends to persist at a high level despite the encroaching power of the national states. The Indians of each community generally think of themselves as ethnic units, separate from other Indian groups and from non-Indian nationals of the country in which they reside. They are people of the village or town rather than Mexicans, Guatemalans, or Peruvians. Frequently, they wear a distinctive costume that identifies them as members of a particular pueblo.

Community structure is characteristically of the type known as the closed corporate peasant community. It is an organized communal structure with clearly defined social boundaries; in other words, it is very clear who does and who does not belong to the community. The community generally does not identify with the nation; its members find their personal and social satisfactions within the community by adhering to its traditional value system. The corporate peasant community is held together not by ties of kinship but by co-ownership of a landholding corporation. Members are not allowed to sell or rent land to outsiders, and this taboo severely limits the degree to which factors outside the community can affect the structure of private property or the development of class differences within the community. This is one of the most important ways of promoting and maintaining community integration.

Another common pattern, especially in the central Andes, is for the Indians to be clustered as peons on large hacienda estates. These Indians have no secure rights to property; instead, they provide labor to work the land belonging to a non-Indian owner. In exchange, they receive a plot of land on which to build a house and grow subsistence crops. Although a small wage may be paid, the plot of land serves in lieu of most wage income. The hacienda owner discourages community organization and tries to establish personal ties between himself and each laborer, thereby exercising greater control over his labor force. At the same time, by encouraging maintenance of the peons' native language and distinctive ethnic identity, with its own traditional customs, he ensures that the peonage community will remain isolated from the larger society.

These peasant communities depend on agriculture as their principal means of subsistence. Most of the land that the peasants receive for their own use is of marginal productivity. It is exploited by means of traditional technology, which involves continuous physical effort and much manual labor. Peasants rely on both the hoe and the plow drawn by draft animals, but there is little use of modern machinery. Their staple crops include the principal cereal grains (corn, wheat, barley), a variety of legumes (beans, broad beans, lentils, garbanzos, peas), chile peppers, and in the Andes, a variety of root crops, including potatoes. Most agriculture follows a short fallow cycle, with fields being rested for one year after several years of cropping. There is little use of fertilizers, although insecticides have become popular in recent years. In some areas irrigation is important.

Crafts are highly developed. The great variety of objects being manufactured includes textiles, pottery, baskets, wood carvings, jewelry, and toys, which often achieve a high degree of aesthetic creativity. The economy of the closed corporate community is closely linked to a peculiar sort of regional marketing system. Different villages specialize in different commodities, and these are brought together and exchanged in the market. For the same reason, the market brings together a much larger supply of articles than merchants in any one community could afford to keep continuously in their stores. Thus, there is much wider access to the products of each community. A shortage of money requires that sales and purchases in the market be small. The producer typically offers his or her goods for sale in order to obtain small amounts of cash, which can be used to purchase other needed goods. In recent years, increasing quantities of cheap manufactured goods have also been introduced into the regional market system and in some cases, they have provided stiff competition for locally produced handicrafts. Another source of cash income is seasonal migration to work on plantations and *fincas* that produce sugar, coffee, or other goods for export. Typically, this migration involves movement from highland peasant communities to lowland areas. In Mexico increasing numbers of indigenous peasants are traveling to the northern part of the country or even further, into the United States, as migrant workers employed by agribusiness enterprises.

The basic social unit of these communities is the nuclear family. Households average about six persons. Marriage may be consecrated through formal religious ceremonies, but there is also a high incidence of marriages that are the result of elopement or abduction. Marriage is usually with an unrelated person, but it is preferentially endogamous within the village. This preference serves as another mechanism for local community integration. Fertility is high among these people, and although the rate of infant mortality has also been high, the mortality rate has been declining over the past several decades, leading to a rapid growth of population. The institution of *compadrazgo,* which establishes a special relationship between the parents and godparents of a child, is another important mechanism for social integration and mutual support.

Settlement patterns vary considerably. In some areas, such as central Mexico, residence is concentrated in a compact village. In others, such as southern Mexico or highland Ecuador, the preference is to scatter residences throughout the community's territory. In the organization of the local community, traditional native officials are often maintained alongside representatives of the national bureaucracy. The community's system of power embraces the male members of the community and makes achievement of power a matter of community decision rather than one of individually achieved status. This system of power is tied into a religious system or a series of interlocking religious systems. The politico-religious system as a whole tends to define the boundaries of the community and acts as a symbol of collective unity. Prestige within the community is largely related to rising from office to office within this system. Conspicuous consumption, principally by putting on elaborate fiesta celebrations, is geared to this communally approved system of power and religion, and it serves to level differences of wealth within the community. The system thus avoids the development of class divisions that might undermine the corporate structure of the community. Various psychic mechanisms of control, such as institutionalized envy and the concept of "limited good," serve as additional conservative factors that help in maintaining the traditional values and way of life.[13]

The modern Indian is nominally Catholic, but his religious beliefs and practices have incorporated a considerable amount of aboriginal belief as well. In addition, Catholic saints are endowed with local characteristics and powers. Fiestas are held to honor the patron saint and other locally important saints, and *cargos,* or magical practices, are assumed to preserve and promote these saint cults. Maintenance of traditional fiestas and associated ceremonies and celebrations is an important part of the traditional culture, and it serves as one more way of preserving a distinctive local identity. Some communities maintain folk priests—cantors, for example—who have contributed to the survival of the folk beliefs and practices in the absence (sometimes for several generations) of Catholic priests. Since the 1970s, however, various evangelical Protestant sects have successfully recruited large numbers of indigenous adherents, particularly in Mexico and Guatemala. This often creates conflict between new converts and traditional segments of the community. *Evangélicos* typically abjure alcohol and dancing, refuse to participate in the traditional fiesta system, and tend to withdraw from customary practices of community reciprocity, thus creating factionalism and undermining community integration.

Illness and disease are explained as resulting from an imbalance in the hot and cold humors that occur in the body, in the foods consumed, and in other objects with which the individual comes into contact. Certain psychological disorders are also explained as a result of *susto* or *espanto* ("fright"), in which the individual is frightened by an encounter with a supernatural entity, sometimes resulting in loss of the soul. The curing of these disorders is usually in the hands of local *curanderos* ("folk doctors") who may attempt to restore the hot-cold imbalance, call upon aboriginal supernaturals or Christian saints, apply herbal remedies, etc. Ethnographic reports suggest that many of the empirical remedies of these *curanderos* are effective and that their treatments are largely successful. If the family members of the sick person can afford it, however, they may try to hedge the probabilities of a successful cure by also consulting a modern physician.

Adherence to the traditional culture validates membership in an existing society and acts as a passport to participation in the life of the community. The amount of wealth that can be gained by a typical peasant is enough to gain the prestige symbols of the Indian system, and thus, the individual is encouraged to maintain his identification with that system. The particular traits held by an Indian help him remain within the equilibrium of relationships that maintain the community. On the other hand, the non-Indian individual is attempting to gain wealth within the national system, where it is impossible to accumulate enough wealth through hard work to permit access to the prestige symbols of the upper sector. The non-Indian peasant is thus perpetually frustrated in his attempt to achieve meaningful goals.

These modern Indian populations are important elements of the national societies. Numerically, they represent a significant proportion of the total population. They participate, if only marginally, in the economic, political, and religious institutions of the nation, and they represent a large, inexpensive pool of labor that can be recruited whenever unskilled labor is required. There is a slow but constant interchange of ideas between the Indian subcultures on the one hand and the national culture on the other.

The 1990s have been marked by increasing Indian activism and political participation. The Zapatista uprising of January 1994 in Chiapas is perhaps the most widely reported. It was motivated by limited access to land, the threat of increased economic disadvantage with the implementation of the North American Free Trade Agreement (NAFTA), long-standing abuse of the indigenous population by the dominant mestizo inhabitants, and government inaction in addressing these problems. Negotiations to resolve these complaints have continued so long that one wonders how willing the Mexican government really is to deal with them.

In Guatemala the genocidal policies of the government in the 1970s and early 1980s were directed against suspected Mayan subversion. Over 400 villages were destroyed and their inhabitants massacred. By the late 1980s massive oppression had abated, with new protections for "Indigenous Communities" being written into the 1985 Constitution. Still, considerable tension exists between Maya and ladino in that country. The Maya community continues to be fragmented, but a new intellectual leadership is emerging, new forms of organization are being developed, and Mayan towns are defending themselves from government abuse. That the Maya themselves are taking an active role in defining their own identity may give hope for eventual development of a plurinational state in Guatemala.

Similar developments may be seen in growing Indian political participation in Bolivia, where the Aymara leader Víctor Hugo Cárdenas was elected vice-president in 1993. In Ecuador the indigenous movement has created a strong organizational base that is now an important actor in the national political arena. It has organized indigenous communities, established bilingual education, and resisted neoliberal economic policies. It has created a place in the political agenda where indigenous people are not merely subjects but active members of civil society. The cultural demands of the indigenous movement have allowed them to create a political force that came as a surprise to both the state and the left in Ecuador.

With modernization, education, improved communication, and other developments, Indian interaction with the national culture is increasing all the time. Continuing population growth and the resultant pressures on the land have led to a large-scale migration to the cities. Today, there are probably 5 million Indians or more living in the towns and cities of Indo-America. Once they arrive in the cities, there is rapid acculturation to urban life. But at the same time, they maintain their ties to and identification with the home community. Urban residents frequently return to visit their relatives or to attend major fiestas. There is also evidence that with increased incomes and greater sophistication, traditional customs and practices are being revived and even intensified in many of these communities.[14] Thus, in spite of modernizing influences, there are indications that for the immediate future, many of these contemporary Indian communities will retain their ethnically distinctive subcultures, while the activism cited above may produce newer forms of nationwide indigenous identity.

NOTES

1. Herbert Barry III, "Regional and Worldwide Variations in Culture," *Ethnology* 7:2 (1968), pp. 207–217, and George Peter Murdock, "Ethnographic Atlas," *Ethnology* 6:2 (1967).

2. Elman R. Service, "Indian-European Relations in Colonial Latin America," *American Anthropologist* 57 (1955), pp. 411–412.

3. Ibid., p. 411.

4. Ibid., p. 418.

5. Ibid., pp. 411–412.

6. Some lowland societies were organized as chiefdoms—small, weakly centralized societies that were transitional between independent villages and strongly centralized states; in fact, they generally integrated a number of dependent villages. Chiefdoms were typically unstable, and with European conquest removal of the ruler usually resulted in social disintegration. The constituent villages then reverted to the level of independent communities (Karl H. Schwerin, "The Anthropological Antecedents: Caciques, Cacicazgos, and Caciquismo," in *The Caciques:*

Oligarchical Politics and the System of Caciquismo in the Luso-Hispano World, ed. Robert Kern and Ronald Dolkart, pp. 5–17 [Albuquerque: University of New Mexico Press, 1973]).

7. Service, "Indian-European Relations," pp. 411–412, 418.

8. Ibid., pp. 411–412, 420.

9. William Heningsgaard and Jason Clay, "The Upper Mazaruni Dam," *Cultural Survival Newsletter* 4:3 (1980), p. 103.

10. *Cultural Survival Ouarterly* 13:3 (1989); for 1980 population figures, see table 3.1 in my chapter in Jan Knippers Black, *Latin America, Its Problems and Its Promise,* 2d ed. (Boulder: Westview, 1991).

11. Donna Lee Van Cott (ed.), *Indigenous Peoples and Democracy in Latin America* (New York: St. Martin's Press, 1994).

12. Amnesty International, *Brazil. "We Are the Land": Indigenous Peoples' Struggle for Human Rights* (New York: Amnesty International, 1992).

13. George M. Foster, *Tzintzuntzan: Mexican Peasants in a Changing World,* rev. ed. (New York: Elsevier, 1979), pp. 122–166.

14. See, for example, Hugo Nutini, *San Bernardino Contla: Marriage and Family Structure in a Tlaxcalan Municipio* (Pittsburgh: University of Pittsburgh Press, 1968), and Frank Cancian, *Economics and Prestige in a Maya Community: The Religious Cargo System in Zinacantan* (Stanford: Stanford University Press, 1965).

SUGGESTED READINGS

Allen, Catherine J. *The Hold Life Has. Coca and Cultural Identity in an Andean Community.* Washington, DC: Smithsonian Institution, 1988. Discusses the social and ceremonial life of a highland community, emphasizing the ritual importance of mountain peaks and the socially and ceremonially integrative functions of coca use.

Amnesty International. *Brazil. "We Are the Land." Indigenous Peoples' Struggle for Human Rights.* New York: Amnesty International, 1992. Details abuses of indigenous human rights in Brazil.

Barry, Herbert, III. "Regional and Worldwide Variations in Culture." *Ethnology* 7:2 (1968), pp. 207–217. A cross-cultural statistical analysis, based on the *Ethnographic Atlas* (see Murdock 1967), of the distribution worldwide, and by continents, of the major types of subsistence economy, family customs, and social structure.

Buechler, Hans C., and Judith-Maria Buechler. *The Bolivian Aymara.* Case Studies in Cultural Anthropology. New York: Holt, Rinehart and Winston, 1971. One of the few complete ethnographic descriptions of an Andean community and the best short study available.

Cancian, Frank. *Economics and Prestige in a Maya Community: The Religious Cargo System in Zinacantan.* Stanford: Stanford University Press, 1965. Offers a thorough analysis of a typical religious *cargo* system and shows how traditional practices have been modified and elaborated in response to population growth and increasing wealth differentiation within the community.

Chagnon, Napoleon A. *Yanomamö: The Fierce People.* Case Studies in Cultural Anthropology. New York: Holt, Rinehart and Winston, 1968. The classic study of an extremely warlike people who inhabit an isolated area in the northern Amazon Basin.

Cultural Survival. "Nicaragua." *Cultural Survival Newsletter* 4:4 (1980), pp. 8–9. Cultural Survival is an international organization of anthropologists and other concerned individuals who seek to document cases of injustice, exploitation, and ethnocide suffered by indigenous peoples and, where possible, to bring pressure to bear or to intervene to protect the interests of the native groups.

Davis, Shelton H. *Victims of the Miracle: Development and the Indians of Brazil.* Cambridge: Cambridge University Press, 1977. Attempts to document the disruptive impact on the native peoples of the tropical forest of programs to develop the Amazon in Brazil.

Denevan, William M., ed. *The Native Population of the Americas in 1492.* Madison: University of Wisconsin, 1976. A collection of papers that treats the historical demography of the Americas. Each paper considers some aspect of the basic disagreement about the relative size of the aboriginal population of the New World.

Faron, Louis C. *The Mapuche Indians of Chile.* Case Studies in Cultural Anthropology. New York: Holt, Rinehart and Winston, 1968. An excellent summary of contemporary culture among the peasant Araucanian farmers of southern Chile.

Foster, George M. *Tzintzuntzan: Mexican Peasants in a Changing World.* Rev. ed. New York: Elsevier, 1979. The best general account of peasant society and worldview in Latin America. Although most inhabitants of Tzintzuntzan are mestizo, they share many characteristics with the modern Indian, or the closed corporate peasant communities of Indo-America.

Gregor, Thomas. *Mehinaku: The Drama of Daily Life in a Brazilian Indian Village.* Chicago: University of Chicago Press, 1977. The peaceful Mehinaku, who live in the southern Amazon Basin, contrast strikingly with the warlike Yanomamö (see Chagnon 1968).

Heningsgaard, William, and Jason Clay. "The Upper Mazaruni Dam." *Cultural Survival Newsletter* 4:3 (1980), p. 103. A brief account of the economic and political factors behind the construction of the dam and why this project means the Akawaio are being deprived of their land.

Isbell, Billie Jean. *To Defend Ourselves. Ecology and Ritual in an Andean Village.* Austin: University of Texas, 1978. Good analysis of a typical Andean community that treats both traditional culture and the processes of accommodating to a changing nation.

Matos Mar, José. "Población y Grupos Étnicos de América." *América Indígena* 53(4), pp. 155–234 (1994). The most recent effort at a comprehensive calculation of the indigenous population of the Americas, including Canada, the United States, and Latin America.

Murdock, George Peter. "Ethnographic Atlas." *Ethnology* 6:2 (1967). The culmination of Murdock's lifelong interest in tabulating the occurrence of cultural traits on a worldwide basis.

Murphy, Yolanda, and Robert F. Murphy. *Women of the Forest.* New York: Columbia University Press, 1974. An excellent account of a typical Amazonian society with an emphasis on the role of women and the woman's point of view.

Nutini, Hugo. *San Bernardino Contla: Marriage and Family Structure in a Tlaxcalan Municipio.* Pittsburgh: University of Pittsburgh Press, 1968. A good account of a typical central Mexican community.

Schwerin, Karl H. *Oil and Steel: Processes of Karinya Culture Change in Response to Industrial Development.* Latin American Studies, 4. Los Angeles: UCLA, 1966. A comparison of social and cultural characteristics in two Venezuelan Indian communities with a theoretical analysis of the processes of culture change that have occurred there during the present century.

———. "The Anthropological Antecedents: Caciques, Cacicazgos, and Caciquismo." In *The Caciques: Oligarchical Politics and the System of Caciquismo in the Luso-Hispano World,* ed.

Robert Kern and Ronald Dolkart, pp. 5–17. Albuquerque: University of New Mexico Press, 1973. A summary statement on the general nature of chiefdoms, or *cacicazgos,* in pre-Columbian Latin America with discussion of their distribution and principal social and cultural characteristics.

Service, Elman R. "Indian-European Relations in Colonial Latin America." *American Anthropologist* 57 (1955), pp. 411–425. Presents the thesis that major differences in the character of modern Latin American states can be traced to European responses to differences in aboriginal cultural patterns, especially in relation to subsistence and sociopolitical complexity.

Stephen, Lynn. *Zapotec Women.* Austin: University of Texas Press, 1991. Explores how commercial weaving for export has altered the lives of Zapotec women in recent decades. Class, ethnicity, and gender determine women's roles and standing in the community. Yet, while the expansion of capitalism has produced class differentiation, it has also reinforced kin-based institutions supporting local ethnic identity.

Van Cott, Donna Lee, ed. *Indigenous Peoples and Democracy in Latin America.* New York: St. Martin's Press, 1994. Analyzes, within a broader theoretical framework, indigenous movements in eight Latin American countries: Bolivia, Colombia, Peru, and Ecuador; Mexico and Guatemala; Brazil and Paraguay.

Vogt, Evon Z. *The Zinacantecos of Mexico: A Modern Maya Way of Life.* Case Studies in Cultural Anthropology. New York: Holt, Rinehart and Winston, 1970. Since 1960, Vogt has directed the Harvard Chiapas Project in the *municipio* of Zinacantan in southern Mexico. This project has been dedicated to twenty years or more of continuous observation and study in the same community in order to gain a better understanding of the types of directional processes that are at work in social and cultural systems.

PART TWO
HISTORICAL SETTING

4

COLONIAL LATIN AMERICA

PETER BAKEWELL

The colonial period in Latin America lasted just over 300 years. That is an impossible amount of history to describe even broadly in a few pages. So this chapter does not try to give a summary of events in colonial times. Rather, its aim is to examine two broad themes: What, in a quite practical way, is meant by "colonialism" in Latin America in the 1500s, 1600s, and 1700s? and What features and influences of colonial times have carried over into, and helped to form, the Latin America of today?

CONQUEST AND SETTLEMENT

We begin with some basic dates and geographical data. The colonial period of Latin America began when Columbus sailed across the Atlantic from Spain in 1492 and claimed the lands he touched on for Spain. They were, on that first voyage of 1492–1493, the islands of Cuba and, as the Spaniards came to call it, Hispaniola (now divided between the Dominican Republic and Haiti). It is illogical to say that Columbus "discovered" the Americas, because, obviously, the true discoverers were the people who first entered and settled them. And people from Asia had done those things many tens of thousands of years before Columbus arrived, becoming in the course of time what are now referred to as "native Americans." From the point of view of Spain and Europe in general, however, Columbus did find the Americas, and more important, his "discovery" led to the establishment of a permanent link between the two sides of the Atlantic—something that the Norse expeditions to North America from Greenland, around A.D. 1000, had failed to do.

As soon as Columbus reported the existence of Cuba and Hispaniola to the Spanish crown, Spain claimed the right to settle and govern those islands and other lands that might be found in the same direction. The pope of the day, Alexander VI, who was a Spaniard, confirmed the claim. His confirmation was sought because, as the chief representative of God on earth, he was the highest authority in the world known to Christian rulers. In any case, no other European state, with the possible exception of Portugal, was strong enough to challenge Spain's claim to possess and govern the lands Columbus had found.

The Portuguese had themselves been exploring westward and southward in the Atlantic for many decades before 1492 and were understandably disturbed by Spain's claim to all land on the west side of the Atlantic. Conflict was averted, however, by an agreement (the Treaty of Tordesillas), drawn up in 1494, that divided the tasks of exploring and settling the world between the two countries. To the west of an imaginary north-south line in the Atlantic, Spain should explore and settle, and to the east of that line, Portugal should do so. Although it was not realized at the time, that agreement was to give to Portugal a large section of eastern South America since, as defined in the treaty, the line passed down through the mouth of the Amazon, leaving the coastline again at about 30° south latitude. Hence, the eastern "bulge" of South America, once it was discovered in 1500, became Portuguese territory, forming the basis of modern Brazil.

The colonial history of Spanish America, having begun in 1492 with Columbus, ended in the years 1810–1825. This was the period in which the various Spanish colonies in the Americas, with two small exceptions, fought for and gained their independence. The exceptions were Cuba and Puerto Rico, which did not become free of Spain, for various reasons, until 1898. Brazil broke from Portugal in 1822. So, in both the Spanish and Portuguese cases, the colonial period was long—almost twice as long, in fact, as the time that has elapsed between independence and the present.

Colonial Spanish America was much larger than Portuguese America. Even though the Portuguese did gradually push westward beyond the Tordesillas line, still Spanish America covered a greater area, extending ultimately from the southern tip of South America to well within the present limits of the United States. In the 1700s, Spain had settlements as far north as San Francisco in California, southern Arizona, most of New Mexico, and much of Texas—as well as in a substantial part of Florida. And all territory, with a few exceptions—by far the most notable being Brazil—between that northern frontier and the far tip of South America was Spanish. Spain also held the larger Caribbean islands and some of the smaller ones. The empire in the Americas—Las Indias (the Indies), as the Spanish called their possessions—was truly vast: some 9,000 mi (almost 14,500 km) from north to south.

COLONIAL GOVERNMENTS AND ECONOMIES

What is meant by saying that these great areas explored and settled by Spain and Portugal were colonies? First, certainly, is the fact that the two home countries governed them. One of the remarkable features of Latin American colonial history is that governments were set up and actually worked. The difficulties of accomplishing this task were forbidding. For one thing, distances were enormous, not only within the Americas, but also between the Americas and Europe. The whole colonial period was, of course, a time of sailing ships, which were slow and unreliable. (Ships improved technically with time, but not until the 1700s were they good enough to allow regular sailings around Cape Horn to the colonies on the west coast of South America. Before then, communication between Spain and the west coast was by Atlantic shipping to the Isthmus of Panama, barge and mule across the isthmus, and Pacific ships to the various west coast ports.) Travel in the colonies themselves was difficult in most cases because of mountains, deserts, forests, and extremes of temperature. One basic necessity of effective government—communication—was therefore difficult to achieve from the start. Nevertheless, governments were installed, and their authority was extended into remarkably remote areas. A brief explanation of how this task was accomplished is necessary.

The Spanish had the greater problems because of the size and the distance from Spain of their colonies. (Brazil was quite easily reached by sea from Portugal.) The Spanish home government saw, once the size of the Americas began to be appreciated, that it would have to delegate a great deal of responsibility to administrators in the colonies, because it would be simply impossible to make all the necessary decisions in Spain. So two very powerful positions were created—those of viceroys who would live in Mexico City and Lima. The holders of these offices were usually Spanish noblemen of much experience, who were to act in their areas in place of the king (which is precisely the meaning of the word "viceroy"). They had authority to make all but the largest of decisions, and each was ultimately responsible for everything that happened in the area under his command. The first viceroy appointed to Mexico City arrived there in 1535. As the area of Spanish exploration expanded, this viceroy came to have control of the whole of Mexico, the Spanish islands of the Caribbean, and all of Central America except Panama. This area of authority, or jurisdiction, was known as the viceroyalty of New Spain. The first viceroy in South America reached Lima in 1544. The territory of this official eventually came to include everything from Panama in the north to Tierra del Fuego in the south, excluding, of course, Portuguese America. The jurisdiction centered on Lima was known as the viceroyalty of Peru. In the 1700s, for closer control, two further viceroyalties were created in South America: New Granada (corresponding roughly to modern Colombia) in 1739, and River Plate (roughly speaking, modern Argentina) in 1776.

It was obviously impossible for individuals to run these vast viceroyalties unassisted. So the Spanish government at home quickly created, in the 1500s, a series of councils to assist the viceroys and to carry their authority far from the two viceregal capitals of that time. These councils were called *audiencias*. Besides having the task of advising the viceroys and in many matters making executive decisions themselves, these councils also functioned as regional courts of appeal. By 1570, there were ten *audiencias*, each with authority over a large sub-area. At a lower administrative level than the *audiencias* were local governors, some of them in charge of large frontier regions and others, of lesser rank, administering towns and villages.

There was much wrong with this system. By modern administrative standards, it was certainly clumsy and corrupt. Many officials, for example, paid more attention to preventing other officials from intruding on their powers than they did to implementing the king's law. And nearly all officials, in the general manner of the times in Europe, saw their positions as means of enriching themselves far beyond the rewards of their salaries, which were often low. Nonetheless, in view of the difficulties, it is a near miracle that the system worked at all. Also very surprising was the speed with which the system was constructed. Generally speaking, within a few years of the conquest of a given region, there were royal administrators in place to enforce laws, collect taxes, and send reports home. Although Spanish America was a vast and rough place, the king's men made their presence felt throughout most of it, and they commanded respect.

The Portuguese set up a rather similar system in Brazil, centered on Bahia (until the mid-1700s when Rio de Janeiro became the capital). They never, however, succeeded in achieving quite such a powerful grip on their colony as Spain did. There were various reasons for this difference. Two important ones were that Portugal, being a smaller and poorer country than Spain, simply did not have the resources of cash and men to create such a powerful administrative machine as Spain built in the Americas and that for many decades after locating Brazil, Portugal was far more attentive to its spice-yielding colonies in the Far East than it was to the apparently rather poorly endowed coast of Brazil.

The first outstanding feature of colonization, therefore, was government. The second was the extraction of wealth from the Americas—the Spanish themselves freely admitted that they had gone to and conquered the Americas for the sake of gold and God. One of the main tasks of the colonial governments was certainly to ensure that Spain and Portugal received as large an income as possible from the colonies. The main type of wealth that Spain received from its colonies was silver. We tend to think of Spanish gold, sunk perhaps in galleons off the coast of Florida, and the conquerors did seek, and find, large amounts of gold. But the more plentiful precious metal proved, in the long run, to be silver. One of the main reasons for Spain's very rapid exploration and settlement of the Americas (and hence, for the quick expansion of government) was that the conquerors ranged far and wide in search of mines. In a surprisingly large number of places, they found them, especially in the highlands of Mexico and what is now Bolivia. These mines were the greatest sources of silver in the world throughout the Latin American colonial period, and they made Spain the envy of its neighbors in Europe. Other profitable goods that Spain took from the Americas were red and blue dyes, chocolate beans, hides, sugar, and some spices.

The Portuguese also did well from their colony in Brazil. Before 1560 or so, the main export was a wood that yielded a red dye. From then until about 1700, a far more profitable export predominated: sugar, which the colonists produced on large plantations. For fifty years thereafter, gold and diamonds were the most spectacular products of the Brazilian economy, stimulating substantial population of the interior for the first time and an increase in immigration from Portugal. Finally, in the last half-century or so of colonial times, there was a recovery of the sugar trade and an increase in the cultivation of other crops, such as chocolate and rice.

The term "exploitation" is often applied to the extraction of wealth by Spain and Portugal from their American colonies. It is a term of criticism, signifying an unjust and greedy grasping by the colonizing powers of the natural riches of Latin America—a process that had the result, among others, of leaving the states of Latin America considerably poorer than they otherwise would have been after independence. But an unqualified charge of exploitation against the Spanish and Portuguese is too crude to be convincing. In some cases, the valuable export product was something that the colonizers had introduced into the Americas: sugar, for instance, in the case of Brazil, or hides from cattle introduced into Mexico by the Spanish. And even where the exported wealth was something already existing in the Americas, such as silver, that wealth was not merely lying on the ground waiting to be picked up and sent back to Europe. In all cases, and especially in that of mining, successful extraction of the product was the result of the application of new techniques, investment of capital, and use of freighting methods not known in the Americas before the Spanish and Portuguese arrived. The wealth of the Americas was great, but it did not come for nothing, even to the greatest of the conquerors or the most fortunate of settlers.

EXPLOITATION OF LABOR

That said, it cannot be denied that the term "exploitation" is a just description of the use made of the native Americans by Spaniards and Portuguese for labor. Within a very few years of the conquest, the idea became firmly rooted among settlers, and even among some theologians and government officials, that the native Americans were by nature inferior to Europeans. It seemed, therefore, quite natural to both sets of colonists and both governments that the natives, once conquered, should work for their conquerors. Some enlightened Spaniards and Portuguese opposed this reasoning, but their views were far outweighed by Iberian public opinion. So the American native peoples were forced in one way or another to work for the colonists. Sometimes they were enslaved. This was particularly common in both Spanish and Portuguese America between the conquest and the mid-1500s. Also in the 1500s, many natives were distributed among Spanish settlers in a system called *encomienda* ("entrustment"). According to this system, the people who had been "entrusted" were to work for the settler, or to supply a tribute in goods or cash, in return for being taught Christianity and the Spanish way of life in general. Settlers were also charged with protecting the people entrusted to them from any enemies who might appear. On paper, this *encomienda* arrangement had strengths. The natives were not legally slaves of the settler in question, but free people. In return for services rendered, they were at least to receive physical security and what was for the Spanish, at least, the highest spiritual gift imaginable: Christianity. In fact, however, few Spaniards fulfilled their part of the bargain, and the *encomienda* often became an oppressive means of making the native people work for the settlers.

Because of its damaging effects and because it tended to direct disproportionate amounts of native tribute and labor toward the conquerors and early settlers at the expense of later Spanish immigrants, the *encomienda* soon ceased to be the home government's preferred arrangement for the supply of native labor to the colonists.

Indeed, from the 1540s on, the home government actively opposed the *encomienda* and tried to take native people away from those settlers to whom they had been entrusted—much to the settlers' anger. Another system for obtaining native labor then became needed, and draft labor was introduced in many places from the 1550s on. Rather elaborate arrangements were made according to which a small proportion of the adult men from each Indian town would be assigned each year for a period of time—between a week and a month, generally—to a Spanish employer. The assignments were made by a Spanish official, and, at least in principle, workers were directed to tasks that were of public utility: agriculture, road and bridge building, and mining (because it was so central an economic activity).

When the system began, draft labor was probably less of a burden on the natives than *encomienda* had been. It also probably made more effective use of native labor than *encomienda* had, because the draft spread the available workers more evenly among Spanish employers. During the second half of the 1500s, however, the number of settlers wanting workers increased while the native population decreased, with the result that draft work also soon became a very great burden for the native people. Their solution to this problem was to offer themselves for hire to individual Spanish settlers, evading the draft as best they could. Since many employers were in great need of workers, the native volunteers could obtain much higher wages than they were paid under the draft system. Wage labor by volunteer workers naturally appeared first in situations in which the settlers were both very short of labor and able to pay high wages. Silver mining was one of these. By 1600, for example, three-quarters of all mining workers in Mexico were native people who had been drawn to that sort of labor by the high pay. After 1600, wage labor became increasingly common in many occupations in Spanish America. Broadly speaking, it gave the workers more freedom and better conditions than the previous labor arrangements had done. So it is generally true that the years of harshest exploitation of native workers by the Spanish were the 1500s.

Where, for one reason or another, there were not enough native people to do the Europeans' work, black slaves were imported from Africa. Exactly how many slaves were brought across the Atlantic in colonial times to Latin America is not known, but the number was certainly in excess of 3 million, with the main importing regions being Brazil and the Spanish Caribbean. Demand for black slaves was high in both of these regions because both produced sugar on plantations—a strenuous sort of labor that blacks proved more able to tolerate than native Americans. In the Spanish Caribbean, there was, in any case, little choice in the matter. Nearly all the native populations of the large islands were destroyed in the sixteenth century by maltreatment, enslavement, and above all, disease. In Brazil, the natives survived in larger numbers, but they proved too primitive to be easily adapted to plantation labor. The importation of blacks into Brazil was, furthermore, simplified and cheapened by the proximity of Brazil to the West African coast, which was the source of most slaves in colonial times, and by the fact that Portugal had several small colonies and bases on that coast in which slaves were traded.

The need for the labor of black slaves was greatly increased after the Spanish and Portuguese conquests in the Americas by the drastic decline in the native populations. There were several reasons for this decline. The battles of the conquest killed some natives. More serious, however, were the aftereffects of conquest: the seizure of good agricultural land by the Europeans; the disruption of families resulting from the imposition of labor burdens on the natives; and the fall of the birthrate of the native peoples as a result of poorer nutrition, dislocation of society, and above all, discouragement at finding themselves, their beliefs, and their gods so easily overcome.

Even more damaging to the native populations, however, were the diseases that the Europeans, quite unintentionally, brought with them. Many diseases common in Europe, Africa, and Asia were unknown in the Americas because of the geographical separation of the continents. Consequently, the American native peoples suffered very severely from diseases that today seem minor: the common cold and measles, for example. Other diseases that are still considered dangerous were also transmitted to the Americas by the conquest: plague and most damaging of all, smallpox. These sicknesses cut great swaths through the natives in conquered areas in the 1500s. In most regions settled by the Spanish, native populations had fallen, by the end of the 1500s, to one-tenth or less of what they had been just before the conquest. In Brazil, the drop may have been smaller. It is hard to tell because many native people there fled into the inland forests so it is not clear how many fled and how many died.

This terrible destruction of the native populations is one of the striking features of the social history of colonial Latin America, and its effects were equally striking. It made necessary a far larger importation of black slaves than would otherwise have taken place. It made the fate of the surviving Indians considerably harder since they were forced to do the work of those who had died (although some survivors at least received higher wages for their work if they chose to become wage laborers), and it reduced the difference in numbers between the native population and the white population, thus accelerating the rate of racial mixing between whites and natives. As a result, the present-day populations of Latin America are notably whiter and more European in culture than they would have been if the natives had survived in their original numbers.

ROMAN CATHOLIC EVANGELISM

In view of the work burden placed on the native Americans by the conquerors and the many very clear cases of harsh treatment, it might seem contradictory to say that Roman Catholic evangelism was one of the two main motives for the conquest and settlement of Latin America. But it was indeed so, especially for the Spanish. Spain was the most powerful Christian country in the world when Columbus crossed the Atlantic, and it continued to be strong for a century thereafter. The Spaniards were sure, for a variety of reasons, that it was not a matter of chance that their expedition, led by Columbus, had established the link between Europe and the Americas. They felt that Spain, as the leading Christian nation of the time, had been singled out by

God to conquer and settle the Americas and to carry the Christian faith (for them, of course, the only true faith) to the native peoples of that region. Some Spaniards held an even more extreme belief. These were the believers in certain biblical prophecies that stated that once the whole world had been converted to Christianity, Christ would return and rule in justice and peace for a thousand years (the millennium). Clearly, the Americas made up a very large piece of the world, and until Christians knew of it and converted its peoples, the millennium could not begin. God, therefore, in apparently entrusting the Christianization of the Americas to Spaniards, had given Spain a central part to play in the history of the world. Spain's work in spreading the true faith was to be a large and direct contribution to the second coming of Christ. Only a small minority of Spaniards, mainly some rather mystically inclined Franciscan friars, truly believed in this prophecy, but the fact that even a few priests could see Spain's mission in the Americas as having such cosmic importance is some indication of the religious zeal of the Spanish as a whole.

That zeal resulted in great efforts to convert American native peoples during the first fifty years or so after the conquest in various regions of the Americas. Many remarkably tough and intelligent missionaries—drawn mainly from the Franciscan, Dominican, and Augustinian orders—set to work in Spain's expanding colonies. Their efforts were especially vigorous in Mexico, as manifested by the many church buildings that have survived from the 1500s. Millions of native people were baptized. Most of them did not understand Christianity very well and ended up with a faith consisting of elements of their preconquest religion mixed with elements of Christianity. The friars, however, generally took the view that it was better to convert many people partially than a few thoroughly.

After the mid-1500s, Spain's missionary zeal wore off considerably for many reasons. One was an understandable fatigue among the missionaries after many years of effort and after the newness of the challenge had gone. Another reason was that by then, many native people in the central areas of Spanish settlement had been converted up to a point and could be entrusted to the more humdrum care of parish priests. There were always missionaries active in some parts of the colonies, however—mainly in remote frontier areas where there were new peoples to convert. Among the best-known and longest-lasting of these later missionary enterprises were those of the Franciscans in New Mexico and the Jesuits in Paraguay.

The Portuguese were, on the whole, rather less concerned than the Spanish with making natives into Christians. From the start, the Portuguese had less religious zeal than the Spaniards, and their possession of colonies in Africa and Asia, as well as in the Americas, meant that the effort they made was spread rather thin. Precisely because of this lack of effort by the state, however, the Jesuits found in Brazil, from about 1550 onward, an open field for mission activity. The Jesuits, indeed, dominated the religious history of colonial Brazil as no single order managed to do in Spanish America. The spread of Jesuit missionary villages into the interior became, in fact, one of the means by which Portuguese America advanced westward beyond the Tordesillas line in the 1600s and 1700s.

CONCLUSION

Those, then, are some of the main features of colonization by Spain and Portugal in the Americas: rapid exploration and settlement (particularly by the Spanish), rapid installation of government (again more noticeable in the case of the Spanish than the Portuguese), economic employment of the settled lands for the profit of individual colonists as well as the home governments, exploitation of native labor, importation of black slaves, and the spreading of Christianity. Some of the processes, of course, took place only in the 1500s, though their influence persisted long after that time. Others—the utilization of land and other resources and the exploitation of native and black workers—continued through colonial times. They continued, though, in changing forms, as illustrated, for example, by the progression from slavery and *encomienda* to draft labor and finally to wage labor.

Similarly, there were changes, as time passed, in the strength of colonial governments. The initial, rapid formation of an administrative apparatus in Spanish America in the 1500s was a strenuous business, and there was a natural tendency toward a relaxation in the system once it had been built. This tendency was increased by the growth of Spain's problems in Europe in the late 1500s, which distracted the home government's attention from the colonies. As a result of these and other influences, colonial governments were less effective and disciplined in the 1600s than in the previous century. In the 1700s, Spain attempted, with some success, to remedy this weakness. The creation of the two new viceroyalties already mentioned was part of this effort (New Granada in 1739 and River Plate in 1776). Many other administrative reforms were introduced. The results were that the force of Spanish government was felt by the colonists in areas where it had never been strongly present before and that Spain's income from taxes on the colonies increased several times over. These were gains that Spain enjoyed only briefly, however, for the increasing pressure of government and taxation that the colonies felt in the late 1700s was resented by many colonists. Such pressures helped turn their thoughts toward greater self-determination and, in the end, toward outright independence from Spain.

SUGGESTED READINGS

Chevalier, François. *Land and Society in Colonial Mexico.* Berkeley: University of California Press, 1963.

Gibson, Charles. *The Aztecs Under Spanish Rule: A History of the Indians of the Valley of Mexico.* Stanford: Stanford University Press, 1964.

Haring, Clarence H. *The Spanish Empire in America.* New York: Oxford University Press, 1947.

Hemming, John. *The Conquest of the Incas.* New York: Harcourt, Brace, Jovanovich, 1970.

Lockhart, James, and Enrique Otte, eds. *Letters and People of the Spanish Indies: The Sixteenth Century.* Cambridge: Cambridge University Press, 1976.

Lockhart, James, and Stuart B. Schwartz. *Early Latin America. A History of Colonial Spanish America and Brazil.* Cambridge: Cambridge University Press, 1983.

68   *Peter Bakewell*

Lynch, John. *Spain Under the Hapsburgs.* 2 vols. Oxford: Oxford University Press, 1964–1969.
_____. *The Spanish-American Revolutions, 1808–1826.* New York: Norton, 1973.
Maclachlan, Colin M., and Jaime E. Rodríguez. *The Forging of the Cosmic Race: A Reinterpretation of Colonial Mexico.* Berkeley: University of California Press, 1980.
Parry, John H. *The Spanish Seaborne Empire.* New York: Knopf, 1966.
Phelan, John L. *The Kingdom of Quito in the Seventeenth Century: Bureaucratic Politics in the Spanish Empire.* Madison: University of Wisconsin Press, 1967.
Schwartz, Stuart B. *Sovereignty and Society in Colonial Brazil: The High Court of Bahia and Its Judges, 1609–1745.* Berkeley: University of California Press, 1973.

5

THE CONTINUITY OF
THE NATIONAL PERIOD

E. BRADFORD BURNS

Interpreting the Latin American past from the period of independence to the present challenges the imagination of any historian. A wide range of peoples descended from Europeans, Africans, and Indians inhabits diverse lands. No one can doubt the great variety of human experiences, nor underestimate the individuality of the numerous regions. Yet, on another level, there exists a certain similarity of experiences that allows us to consider also broad and common themes pervading the past of all—or most—of Latin America. At any rate, for the purposes of a short introduction to the topic, I will have to dwell on broad themes to the exclusion of details.

One prominent theme emerges to provide a sobering interpretation of the past, to give meaning, to impart understanding of Latin America's national period. It emerges in the form of an enigma: Poor people inhabit rich lands. Most Latin Americans are poor, yet Latin America boasts an impressive array of natural resources. Most Latin Americans are malnourished, yet only a small fraction of the arable land has ever been cultivated.

Efforts to explain the enigma have been numerous but less than satisfactory. Many experts point to the population increase as the cause of persistent poverty. Latin America's population grew from approximately 15 million in 1820 to over 425 million in 1990. The increase sounds impressive, of course, but we must remember that these 425 million people are dispersed over almost 8 million sq mi (20,566,000 sq km). That area is over twice the size of Europe but contains only one-third of Europe's population. To put it in yet another perspective, Latin America occupies 19 percent of the world's land but contains only 7 percent of the world's population. It is, in short, underpopulated. Food experts estimate Latin America could feed many, many times its present population. At any rate, a century ago, when Latin America had but a fraction of its present population, it nevertheless suffered a proportionate amount of poverty. Population pressures, which exist in El Salvador and a few small Caribbean islands, do not offer a rational explanation for Latin America's persistent poverty.

Other specialists have blamed the region's geography. They term it "stingy." However, Latin America boasts of natural resources, including fertile lands, proportionate to any other comparable area in the world. There are rugged mountains, trackless swamps, and bone-dry deserts but no more so proportionately than in the United States and Canada. Furthermore, Latin America has supplied the world for five centuries with an impressive catalogue of mineral and agricultural products. The argument has been persuasively made more than once that the gold and silver flowing from Latin America financed much of Europe's industrial revolution. Further, Latin America has become a major supplier of food to the world's markets. In fact, Latin America probably has been dispossessed of more natural wealth over a longer period of time than any other part of the Third World. A harsh or stingy geography cannot be accepted as an explanation of the enigma.

Although now disguised by polite language and an impressive arsenal of euphemisms, the charge persists that Latin Americans, for one reason or another, lack the skill, intelligence, drive, ability, or will to enrich themselves. It is—it always has been—an insidious argument. The Latin Americans certainly have been capable of enriching others: Spain in the sixteenth century, Portugal in the eighteenth, England in the nineteenth, and—some might argue—the United States in the twentieth. Considering that their diets are minimal to inadequate, their education rudimentary, and their limited health facilities concentrated in the capital cities, the Latin Americans excel at work.

Other experts argue the lack of technology as a major contributor to the enigma. They counsel that only as the technology transfer accelerates will poverty diminish. This explanation puzzles because Latin America has been importing the most up-to-date technology from abroad for at least the past century. Perhaps it has been the wrong kind of technology, or perhaps it has been put to the wrong use, but a very persuasive case can be made that as "modernization" increased, both poverty and dependency in Latin America deepened. Recent transfers of technology seem to aggravate unemployment and to multiply the stockpiling of industrial goods a poor population is unable to buy. Technology contributes disproportionately to the export sector. It seems only to have helped foreigners exploit Latin America's resources. It has contributed minimally—if at all—to raising the standard of living of the average Latin American.

A more profound explanation of the persistent poverty in the midst of potential wealth is needed. History, I think, will provide a better explanation if we examine the institutional structures of Latin America from the time of independence to the present. We will find not only an astonishing similarity of institutions between otherwise diverse regions but an impressive uniformity of consequences resulting from those institutions as well as of reactions to them.

INSTITUTIONAL CONTINUITY
AND INCOMPLETE INDEPENDENCE

Iberian institutions, which is to say those institutions developed by Spain and Portugal, embodied a curious mixture of feudalism and capitalism at the time of the discovery and conquest of the New World. The Iberians transferred their institutions to the New World, imposing them on the Indians and on the black slaves imported from Africa. The presence of both feudalism and capitalism (highly modified forms to be sure) can be seen and contrasted in the hacienda and plantation, both key rural institutions. Both were immense estates. The hacienda was the more self-sufficient of the two, a world almost unto itself, governed by the family patriarch with minimal outside contacts. It produced almost secondarily for an international marketplace. It resembled the fief of the late Middle Ages. The plantation, in contrast, produced in quantity for the international market. It shipped its products away from the plantation; it catered to and became involved in rather complex commercial systems, a part of the expanding capitalist system. The sugar plantations of Brazil in the sixteenth and seventeenth centuries, of the Caribbean in the eighteenth century, and particularly of Cuba in the nineteenth century offer some excellent examples of the New World plantation producing profitably for foreign trade. Other examples would be cacao, coffee, bananas, and wheat. By the late nineteenth century, ranches—the equal in size and purpose to the plantations—supplied beef, mutton, hides, and wool. All these great capitalist enterprises linked Latin America ever more tightly with the interests and markets first of Western Europe and then of the United States.

Both Madrid and Lisbon devised mercantile policies to ensure their own benefits in the lucrative export trade of the New World. The mother countries reaped profits from agriculture but also from mining, particularly of gold and silver. Spain and Portugal considered the New World their "milch cow." Clearly, the colonies existed to benefit the two mother countries, but through them, much of Western Europe profited, especially England. The dynamic part of the Latin American economy— the part that grew and prospered—was both capitalistic and export oriented. The neofeudal heritage, however, imparted a peculiar pattern to local social, economic, and political life. The great landowners ruled like the lords of the manor, which, indeed, they were.

During the long colonial period, the psychology of the Latin Americans, particularly the elite, a majority of whom were Europeans born in the New World—called Creoles in Spanish-speaking regions, *mazombos* in Brazil—changed significantly. A feeling of inferiority before the Iberian-born gave way to a feeling of equality and then of superiority. At the same time, nativism, a devotion to one's locality, matured into feelings of nationalism, a group consciousness attributing supreme value to the land of one's birth and pledging unswerving dedication to it. Such changes of attitude also resulted from a fuller understanding on the part of the local elites that their own interests could be better served if they, not distant Iberian monarchs, made the fundamental economic and political decisions. Inspired by the example of the United States and encouraged by the changes wrought in Napoleonic Europe, they declared the independence of the new Latin American nations. The elites took command of those new nations, exercising the powers once reserved for the Iberian masters.

The independence of the new nations proved to be nominal. The ruling elites depended spiritually on their Iberian past, culturally on France, and economically on Great Britain. They tended to confuse their own well-being and desires with those of the nation at large, a fallacious identification since they represented considerably less than 5 percent of the total population. Nonetheless, that minority set the course upon which Latin America has continued to the present. Since the elites had bene-fited handsomely from the colonial institutions, they were loath to tamper with them. As one newspaper editor of the period put it: "Let us have no excesses. We want a constitution not a revolution." In sum, they sought to institutionalize the past, not to challenge or change it.

The elites first faced the questions of what type of government they would insti-tute and who would rule. These problems have never been satisfactorily resolved. Brazil and Chile were the most successful in establishing and maintaining order. It took Argentina and Mexico, for example, more than half a century to do so. With the notable exception of Brazil, the nations eventually chose a republican form of government that centralized almost all power in the presidency. A handful of men se-lected and supported the presidents, who, with some interesting exceptions, did not even pretend to represent the majority of the citizenry. A powerful emperor ruled Brazil for most of the nineteenth century.

Independence provided no panacea for Latin America's economic ills. A Chilean intellectual asked at the end of the colonial period, "Who would imagine that in the midst of the lavishness and splendor of nature the population would be so scanty and that most of it would be groaning under the oppressive yoke of poverty, misery, and the vices which are their inevitable consequences?" He blamed the unhappy eco-nomic condition of Chile on the unequal distribution of the land that favored a few large landowners but condemned most of the population to the role of overworked, underpaid, and landless peons. His diagnosis of Chile's economic ills applied equally to the rest of Latin America as it entered the national period.

The economy after 1825 remained as subordinate to the economic needs of Europe as it had throughout the long colonial period. In fact, it became increasingly integrated into the widening network of international capitalism, in which the Latin Americans were a junior partner, subordinate or dependent. The very institutions that the elite preserved from the Iberian past perpetuated dependency, a situation in which Latin America's economy was subordinate to the development or expansion of the mother countries. Such economic dependency presupposes a political subordi-nation, encourages cultural imitation, and perpetuates social iniquity.

During the first half of the nineteenth century, Europe and the United States en-tered an active period of population growth and accelerated industrialization and ur-banization. They demanded raw products: food for their urban centers and materi-als for their factories. In turn, they sought markets in which to sell their growing industrial surpluses. The newly independent Latin American nations, with their abundant natural resources but limited industries, were pressed into a working rela-tionship with the burgeoning capitalist centers: They exported the raw materials re-quired in Europe and the United States and imported the manufactured goods pour-ing from the factories. Latin America's exports depended upon and responded to the requirements of Europe and the United States. In catering to the caprices of an unpredictable market, the Latin Americans encouraged the growth of the reflexive economy, little different, except perhaps more hazardous, than the previous colonial economy. External factors, over which the Latin Americans had little or no influence, determined whether the economies prospered or vegetated. The economic cycles of boom and collapse repeatedly occurred in all regions of Latin America. Responding to the needs and requirements of Europe and the United States condemned most of the area to remain on the periphery of international capitalism.

The governing elites, always closely related to the great landowners and merchants, had selected by default policies that favored growth over development. Of all the elements of society, the governing elites profited most from growth, and the immediate advantage they reaped wed them to their policies. Furthermore, development would have required changing some basic institutions—those governing land and labor, for example—from which the elites drew immediate benefits. From their own point of view, then, the elites favored growth, simple numerical accumulation, over development, the maximum use of a nation's potential for the greatest benefit of the largest number of inhabitants. That particularly helps to explain why the new governments tampered very little with the well-established colonial institutions that had maintained rigidly the precedence of growth over development.

A remarkable continuity existed between the colonial period and the decades following independence. Economic changes were few. Agriculture and the large estate retained their prominence, and the new nations became as subservient to British economic policies as they once had been to those of Spain and Portugal. The wars of independence had shaken and weakened some of the foundation stones of society, but the edifice stood pretty much intact. A small, privileged elite ruled over the muted masses. Fewer than one in ten could read, and fewer than one in twenty earned enough to live in even modest comfort. Land remained the principal source of wealth, prestige, and power, and only a few owned the land.

THE MODERNIZATION OF INEQUALITY

The continuity, however, was not perfect. Two major political changes marked the early national period. The first and most obvious was the transmission of power from the Iberians to the Creole and *mazombo* elites. Political power no longer emanated from Europe; it had a local source. The second was the emergence of the military in Spanish America as an important political institution destined to play a decisive role in history. It did not emerge as a powerful institution in Brazil until the late nineteenth century. The military forces were the elite's only guarantee of order; initially, the officer class provided prestigious employment for the sons of the wealthy as well as one means of upward mobility for talented and ambitious plebeians. Early in the national period, the liberals challenged the status of the military, thus alienating them and driving them into the welcoming embrace of the conservatives. The elites, intent upon conserving the past—tantamount to preserving their privileges—found useful allies in the military and the Roman Catholic hierarchy, both powerful institutions in their own right. The remarkable early stability of both Chile and Brazil can be partially explained by the close identification and harmony among the Church, the conservatives, and the military.

By mid-nineteenth century, it was possible to see that some of the nations were achieving political stability and enjoying greater economic prosperity. Foreign threats had diminished. Stronger centralized governments exerted greater authority over larger areas. Nationalism became a better defined force as more and more Latin Americans expressed greater pride in their homelands, appreciated their uniqueness, and pursued their visions of progress.

In the second half of the century, Positivist ideology dominated in many governmental circles. The "scientific laws" of society codified by Positivism seemed to promise the Latin American elite and emerging middle class the progress they sought, primarily a material progress. Outward manifestations of progress—railroads and industrialization were prime examples—assumed great importance in Positivism, emphatically so among Latin Americans. With an emphasis on material growth and well-being, Positivism favored a capitalist mentality, quite different from the communal spirit pervasive among the indigenous peoples of Latin America. Indeed, private accumulation of wealth was viewed as a sign of progress as well as an instrument for progress. Because of the weakness of domestic, private institutions, the state had to assume the role of directing progress, which, in turn, required the maintenance of order and guarantee of stability. With its special emphasis on political order and material progress, Positivism reached the height of its influence between 1880 and 1900. It became almost an official doctrine of the regime of President Porfirio Díaz in Mexico (1876–1911). Some of his principal ministers were known as *científicos* as they offered "scientific" solutions to the problems confronting the nation.

As their warm embrace of the ideas associated with Positivism might indicate, the elite and middle class customarily adopted the latest ideas from abroad, even if they ill suited the local scene. They ordered the capital cities to be rebuilt to resemble Paris as much as possible. Not all of them understood that anything more than "cosmetic" modernization was impossible in nations whose basic institutions retained the neofeudalistic, neocapitalist orientation of the colonial past. Still they persisted.

The progress or modernization pursued by the Latin American governments required increasing sums of money to import the machinery, railroads, luxuries, and technology that would be used to try to transform their nations into replicas of the European nations the elites and middle class so much admired. To earn that money, the Latin Americans increased their exports, the foods or minerals they traditionally had sold abroad. The export sector of their economies received the most attention. In that sector, they increasingly concentrated investments, technology, and labor, leaving the domestic economy weak and increasingly inadequate. The number of those exports was limited. Usually each nation or region depended on the sale of one or two, possibly three, such exports: for Brazil, it was coffee; for Chile, nitrates and copper; for Bolivia, tin; for Argentina, beef and wheat; for Peru, guano. The highly prized railroads, built at staggering expense, opened new lands for exploitation but always were linked to the export sector, rushing the material products of the interior to the coastal ports where ships waited to transport them to Europe and the United States. Most of the modernization concentrated in the export sector. It contributed to some impressive growth but did little to develop Latin America. In fact, modernization contributed to deepening dependency.

Most significantly, the nineteenth century witnessed the growth in size, importance, and power of the latifundia, those huge estates that produced all too often for the export market. The latifundia grew at the expense of the Indian communities, peasants, and small landowners. Inefficiency characterized most of the large estates. The owners used only a fraction of their extensive lands. They kept large acreages under their domination in order to control labor, always in scarce supply. By denying access to land, they assured themselves of a ready supply of workers who otherwise would have been independent peasants.

The growth of large and inefficient estates raised serious social and economic questions. An editorial in the Buenos Aires newspaper *El Río de la Plata,* September 1, 1869, lamented: "The huge fortunes have the unhappy tendency to grow even larger, and their owners possess vast tracts of land that lie fallow and abandoned. Their greed for land does not equal their ability to use it intelligently and actively." Similar complaints were voiced everywhere. It became all too obvious that the expansion of cultivation for export was accompanied by a decline in food production for local consumption. The province of Rio de Janeiro, undergoing a coffee boom at mid-century, provided the perfect example. The landowners quickly converted their land to coffee plantations. Foods that had been grown in such abundance in 1850 that they were sold outside the province had to be imported a decade later. The price of basic foodstuffs—beans, corn, and flour—rose accordingly.

For the majority of the Latin Americans, progress resulted in an increased concentration of lands in the hands of ever-fewer owners; falling per capita food production, with corollary rising food imports; greater impoverishment; less to eat; more vulnerability to the whims of an impersonal market; uneven growth; increased unemployment and underemployment; social, economic, and political marginalization; and greater power in the hands of the privileged few. In fact, the more the majority of Latin Americans were forced to integrate into world commerce, the fewer the material benefits they reaped. But poverty through progress must be understood in more than the material terms of declining wages, purchasing power, or nutritional levels. A tragic spiritual and cultural impoverishment debased the majority, forced by circumstances to abandon previously more satisfactory ways of life and to accept alien ones that provided them little or no psychic benefits.

The impoverished majority both bore the burden of the inequitable institutional structures and paid for the modernization enjoyed by the privileged. The deprivation, repression, and deculturalization of the majority by the minority created tensions that frequently gave rise to violence in the nineteenth century. The poor protested their increasing misfortunes as modernization increased. For their part, the privileged were determined to modernize and to maintain the order required to do so. They freely used whatever force was necessary to accomplish both. Consequently, the imposition of progress stirred social disorder that took the form of Indian and peasant rebellions, slave uprisings, banditry, and millenarian movements. Those popular protests tended to be local and uncoordinated. Thus, despite the frequency of such protests, the elites using the military forces at their disposal imposed their will and brand of progress. The triumph of that progress set the course for the twentieth-century history of Latin America: It bequeathed a legacy of mass poverty and continued conflict.

Although the overwhelming majority of the Latin Americans lived in the countryside during the nineteenth century, the population began to shift toward the cities during the last quarter of the century. Argentina's urban population doubled between 1869 and 1914, so that in the latter year, the urban sector represented 53 percent of the population. Chile, too, witnessed an impressive urban surge. In 1875, approximately 27 percent of the population could be classified as urban dwellers, but a quarter of a century later, the figure reached 43 percent. During the three decades after 1890, the population of Rio de Janeiro—Brazil's primary city and port as well as capital—doubled while São Paulo increased eightfold in size. A few cities played increasingly important roles in each nation. The government and administrative apparatus, commerce, and industry were located in those cities. Increasingly, they served as hubs of complex transportation and communication networks. Further, they provided important recreational, cultural, and educational services. Urban growth resulted from the arrival of greater numbers of foreign immigrants, a constantly increasing population (Latin America had 61 million inhabitants in 1900), and the rising tide of rural migrants who arrived attracted by the promise of the city or propelled by the grinding poverty of the countryside.

Unfortunately, the cities did not contribute to national development. The urban facade of modernization deceived. Dependency shaped the cities just as it molded other aspects of life. The high concentration of land in few hands weakened the urban network throughout Latin America. The large estates, combined agrarian-industrial units, demonstrated little need for the intermediary services that support small trading, servicing, and processing towns. A national economy whose most dynamic sector was export oriented encouraged the rapid growth of maritime ports, a transportation system focusing on the ports, foreign investment in or connected to export products to the neglect of the rest of the economy, the spending of export wealth to beautify and service the capital city, and the concentration of landowners in the capital to be near the center of power. The capital and the ports (in the cases of Argentina and Uruguay, for example, the capitals are also the principal ports) served the dynamic export sector of the economy. They shared in the growth and prosperity while other cities and towns played secondary roles, stunted in both growth and development, just as overreliance on the export sector restricted national growth and development on yet another level. Dependency helps to explain why there were only one, two, or three major and "modern" cities in each Latin American nation and even further why that modernity remained more a facade than a reality.

THE NEW URBAN CLASSES AND
THE RISE OF NATIONALISM

As Latin America approached its independence centennial, two trends, one of external origin and the other internal, emerged with greater clarity. Together they would have a mighty impact on events in the twentieth century. The first was the emergence of the United States as a major world power preoccupied with its security in the Western Hemisphere and with a strong drive to invest in and trade with Latin America. The other was the emergence of a more clearly defined middle class within Latin America. The two trends intertwined, reinforcing and supporting each other. The growing middle class looked for its own sources of inspiration, its own example to emulate. The industrializing and progressing United States attracted the attention of that class. Members of the Latin American middle class visited New York before Paris; they learned English rather than French. Above all else, they admired the new technology associated with the United States. They saw in industrialization their key to advancement, and no country industrialized more rapidly and more thoroughly than the United States. They may have feared the expansion of their mentor and ridiculed its materialism, but nonetheless, they were drawn toward it, and the lifestyle of the Latin American middle sectors increasingly reflected that of the United States.

Commerce, business, and industry contributed heavily to the ranks of the middle class, and foreign immigrants continued to compose a disproportionately large percentage of its members. Certain characteristics of that class became increasingly evident. The majority lived in the cities and boasted an above-average education. Their income level placed them between the wealthy few and the impoverished many. Although the varied groups within that class never unified, on occasion a majority of them might agree on certain goals—such as improved or expanded education, increased industrialization, or more rapid modernization—and on certain methods—such as the formation of political parties or the exaltation of nationalism. They consented to the use of the government to foment change (a change that, following their perceptions, most closely resembled growth), and with minimal dissension, they welcomed the government's participation in—even direction of—the economy. Still, political preferences within their ranks varied from far right to far left.

As urbanization and industrialization grew, a larger, more cohesive, and more militant proletariat appeared. Slowly becoming aware of their common problems and goals, these workers unionized despite relentless government repression. By 1914, about half a dozen nations boasted well-organized unions, and at least some attempt had been made in the rest to institute them. The economic dislocation caused by World War I and the financial collapse of 1929 sparked labor unrest, militancy, and strikes. A working-class consciousness took shape as labor thought in terms of changing the national institutions to suit its own needs.

In their periods of formation and expansion, the unions could and did cooperate with other urban elements, specifically the middle class. Both groups sought change, however modest, and realized they had to challenge the traditional elites to foment it. The privileged oligarchy resented and opposed that alliance. Once the middle class achieved its more limited goals and began to participate in the national institutions, it broke that alliance to align itself with the elites.

The Brazilian middle class was the first to exercise power. It allied with the military to overthrow the monarchy in 1889 and for five years governed through an uneasy or uncertain cooperation with the generals. The coffee elite nudged both from the government in 1894, and the Brazilian middle class did not get its second taste of power until 1930. In Argentina, the middle class entered power through the election of President Hipólito Irigoyen in 1916, and shortly thereafter, in 1920, the Chileans elected a middle-class president, Arturo Alessandri. But it was in Uruguay that the Latin American middle class won its greatest victory in the early twentieth century. Uruguay changed dramatically under the government of the middle class, providing one of the best examples of peaceful change in Latin America. José Batlle, the outstanding political representative of the middle class, served twice as president (1903–1907 and 1911–1915), but his influence over the government lasted until his death in 1929. During those decades, he sought to expand education, encourage industrialization, restrict foreign control, enact a broad welfare program, and unify the republic. Succeeding brilliantly in each instance, he transformed Uruguay into a model bourgeois nation. In the long run, however, the middle class throughout Latin America proved to be cautious, if not conservative. Its members came to fear that too much reform might harm rather than benefit their interests. As they began to participate in the major institutions of their nations, they saw less reason to challenge or to reform them.

Forces favoring basic institutional change continued to grow, and mounting pressure on the static institutions ranks as one of the major historical trends of the twentieth century. Ambitious new groups—organized labor, nationalists, intellectuals, and students, for example—in an increasingly complex society opposed the rigid institutions that impeded their rise or stunted national development as they perceived it. They demanded a more fluid society, and they sought to alter the old one. They sought national development rather than simply the unsatisfactory growth of the past. They repudiated the dependency that they rightly identified as a restriction on development. At the same time, under skillful direction, nationalism emerged as a potent force favoring change and development.

The Fate of Revolutions

Five nations have attempted change by revolution in the twentieth century: Mexico, 1910–1940; Guatemala, 1944–1954; Bolivia, 1952–1964; Cuba, 1959 to the present; and Nicaragua, 1979 to 1990. Revolution is a very specific—and widely abused—term. It denotes the sudden, forceful, even violent overturn of a previously stable society and the substitution of new institutions for those discredited. Similarities characterize the five Latin American revolutions (although notable differences also distinguish one from the other). All five of the revolutions had in common a desire to modify or eradicate traditional institutions considered incompatible with the drive for meaningful modernization and greater social equity. All recognized the importance of land reform in the restructuring of society and set about to radically change the ownership patterns. All were manifestations of intense nationalism. All involved the participation of the masses. All accelerated efforts to educate the masses. All favored one or another form of socialism. All hoped to increase the economic viability and the independence of action of their nations. All favored greater industrialization. All removed from power—at least temporarily—representatives of the old oligarchy.

The fates of the five revolutions have varied. The Mexican Revolution seemed to be succeeding until it grew rigid and conservative after 1940. The Guatemalan Revolution was first halted and then reversed. The Bolivian Revolution accomplished much in its first years, grew increasingly timid after 1956, and expired with the military coup d'état in 1964. The Cuban and Nicaraguan Revolutions continue.

Since the Cuban and Nicaraguan experiments continue, any judgment of their success or failure would be premature. The Cuban experiment with change is the most radical to date. For the first time in the Western Hemisphere, a revolution has been put through in the name of socialism. Scarcely any of the prerevolutionary institutions remain, and much of the prerevolutionary privileged class is gone and without ready access to power. Cuba thus provides an example of socialist solutions to the old problems that have beset Latin America.

The United States reacted hostilely to four of the five revolutions. It took nearly three decades for Washington to reconcile itself to the new turn of events in Mexico. Washington has steadfastly opposed the Guatemalan, Cuban, and Nicaraguan Revolutions. In alliance with Guatemalan dissidents, the U.S. Central Intelligence Agency (CIA) succeeded in ending the Guatemalan experiment, and in cooperation with Cuban exiles, the CIA later tried to remove Fidel Castro and blunt the Cuban Revolution. Thus far, its efforts have failed. From 1979 to 1989, the CIA armed, financed, and trained Nicaraguan exiles who repeatedly invaded Nicaragua from Honduras. Only the Bolivian Revolution received support from the United States, and that aid went to the moderate wing that eventually came to dominate the revolutionary process. Such a record doubtless reflects a nervous metropolis fearful of any change in or challenge from its client states.

The Backlash Against Democratic Reform

Reform, the gradual change or modification of institutions, has had no greater success in changing old and iniquitous institutions than revolution. (Once again, I make the exception of the ongoing revolutions in Cuba and Nicaragua.) The two longest experiments with democratic reform, those in Uruguay and Chile, collapsed in dismal failure in 1973, to be replaced with brutal military dictatorships that held sway in Uruguay until 1984 and Chile until 1990.

Uruguay long had been judged the Latin American bastion of reform and democracy, a kind of middle-class paradise, thanks largely to the changes brought about by

José Batlle. Commendable as his reforms were, they did not adjust the mainsprings of the economy: land monopoly and overdependence on the export sector. When events after the mid-1950s shook and crumbled the foundations of the economy, the edifice of democracy came crashing down.

Between 1955 and 1970, Uruguay witnessed the worst inflation and the poorest economic performance in Latin America. The complex causation of this disaster had its roots in the countryside. The land provided Uruguay's wealth, but it was used inefficiently. Uruguayan prosperity depended on wool and beef exports, but Uruguayan producers made a poor international showing, their productivity barely half that of some of their major world competitors. As the population of the small nation increased in the twentieth century, agricultural production declined proportionately. The weakening agrarian sector undermined industrialization. Those who suffered most called for reforms: land reform, socialization of industry, and the expropriation of foreign-owned banks, businesses, and industries. As the economy continued to deteriorate, demands for change escalated and intensified, the level of violence rose, the frightened middle class swung more to favor order and the status quo than reform, the government proved its ineffectiveness, and the military intervened in 1973 at the insistence of the wealthy and middle class to overthrow the government. Uruguay, for half a century the model of democracy and reform in Latin America, was reduced to a shameless military dictatorship devoid of any freedom, reform, or hope. The military officers were unable to revive the economy because they were unwilling to challenge the institutions that perpetuate its inefficiency.

At the same time, events in another "model democracy," Chile, followed an all-too-familiar course. There, too, the middle class demonstrated an equal distaste for democracy and a fear of reform in late 1973. A combination of increased political participation of the lower classes, the declining economic position of the poor, and the inability of unimaginative governments to bring about reform had brought Salvador Allende to the presidency in the hotly contested elections of 1970. The aims of his Popular Unity government were to transform Chile from a capitalist and dependent society into a socialist and independent one and to do so gradually within the democratic and constitutional framework of the nation.

Once in office, President Allende nationalized the foreign-owned copper industry, the source of three-quarters of the value of all Chile's exports. He accelerated agrarian reform, distributing during his first year in office more land than his predecessor had in six. The government bought control of most of the banks, thus controlling the use of credit in order to favor development over mere growth. Allende paid considerable attention to improving the living conditions of the poor. Salaries rose, and real buying power increased. Unemployment dropped sharply. The government rechanneled distribution to favor the underprivileged. Those changes took place within a democratic framework; all liberties were respected.

The shifting balance of political and economic power frightened the middle class, unaccustomed to sharing the nation's political decisionmaking or its limited resources with the poor. Allying with the traditional elite, the middle class refused any cooperation with the Allende government. Hostile to the socialization process, the international banks and the U.S. government cut loans and aid to the Allende government to a trickle. A process of economic destabilization was planned and carried out by the still economically powerful middle and upper classes. The United States contributed to that destabilization. The resulting economic chaos generated a class conflict. The middle and upper classes called on the military to intervene. It did on September 11, 1973, imposing a barbaric military dictatorship.

Democracy, freedom, and reform in Latin America suffered a staggering blow in Chile. Events there, coupled with those in other key nations, indicated that the middle class has no commitment to either democracy or change. Indeed, the arguments for democracy in Latin America now seem hopelessly idealistic, as does the case for reform. They simply have no historical support.

The Bitter Fruit of Military Governments

Military governments have a poor record of economic and political performance. They are authoritarian, some exceedingly barbarous; they permit little or very limited popular participation. They sometimes facilitate economic growth for limited periods but never encourage development. Development would necessitate reform of basic institutions, most notably landowning and land use, anathema to the middle class and elites and—with the exception of Peru in the early 1970s—to their military allies as well.

Brazil offers a splendid recent example of military governments wed to growth but hostile to development. When the Brazilian middle class and elite summoned the soldiers from their barracks in 1964 to overthrow a democratic government that promised reforms, the soldiers repressed every form of freedom and liberty. Economically, they concentrated on controlling inflation and accelerating the growth rate. The phenomenal growth rate during the years 1969–1974, averaging 10 percent a year, attracted considerable envy throughout Latin America. That economic record emphasized a rising gross national product (GNP). Pursuit of an ever-higher GNP is never, however, a search for social objectives but rather, a blind chase of numbers that can be expanded to infinity without much social value resulting. Brazil, in fact, provides the perfect example of an upwardly spiraling GNP without much development or resultant social benefit. As a matter of fact, the gap between the rich and the poor widened during those years. Instead of solving any basic problems, the military government intensified them. Inflation surpassed the 100 percent rate in 1980, higher than it had ever been in 1964 or before. Foreign debt reached alarming proportions. By 1990 the government had run up an international debt of over $110 billion, for which the annual carrying charges consumed half of the country's export earnings. At least by the end of 1990, no sign had appeared that economic growth, which had declined to a 4 percent average after 1975, might promote development. Thus, in the short run, the military governments fostered growth, but in the long run, they not only were unable to sustain their earlier growth but they accelerated inflation and drove the economy to the brink of bankruptcy. The Brazilian military provided no solutions to old problems; they did not speak to the tragic enigma besetting their nation. The army assured order; it prolonged the status quo, but the officers merely postponed for the middle class and the elites the day of reckoning.

In the past decades, the aspirations of larger and larger numbers of the Latin American population for change and development have vastly outpaced actual change. Too few enjoyed the benefits of whatever growth took place, and too many of the age-old political, economic, and social structures and patterns remained to permit any real development. As the rate and extent of change and development have failed to meet expectations, frustrations have mounted. Further, the failure of change and development has created a widespread feeling of disillusion with democracy and capitalism and has contributed to mounting violence in contemporary Latin America, well exemplified by the present civil war in El Salvador. Violence, disillusionment, the failure of democracy, the propensity for economic growth at the expense of development, and continuing dependency are characteristics of contemporary Latin America.

ECONOMIC GROWTH WITHOUT DEVELOPMENT

From the vantage point of the present, we survey the Latin American past and contemplate its future. There is much to admire: the blending of races and cultures to create unique civilizations; the beauty of the lands; the talents of the peoples; intellectual achievements such as the brilliant twentieth-century literature of Jorge Amado, Carlos Fuentes, Gabriel García Márquez, and Jorge Luis Borges; the enviable ability to settle international disputes peacefully; magnificent examples of contemporary architecture such as Brasília; among other things. Yet, the grim reality of social, economic, and political inequity remains. Injustice seems to predominate. A series of challenging questions confront us in our effort to better understand Latin America. Why does dependency tend to deepen rather than recede? How can the quality of life for the majority be improved? What is the best role for the United States to play in Latin America, and how does a knowledge of the past help us prepare for it?

In considering these difficult questions, it is useful to recall a challenging historical judgment made by Will and Ariel Durant, authors of the widely acclaimed, multivolume historical survey, *The Story of Civilization*. They capped their survey with a slender volume based upon their observations of the past. Entitled *The Lessons of History*, it observed, "When the group or a civilization declines, it is through no mystic limitations of a corporate life, but through the failure of its political or intellectual leaders to meet the challenges of change." The ability—or lack of it—of Latin America's leadership to meet these tough challenges of change will determine the course of the future.

Change always occurs. Change has taken place in Latin America. Latin America in the 1990s differs considerably from Latin America in the 1890s. Perhaps most noticeable among the changes is the presence of a significant middle class exercising a dominant role in the social, economic, and political life of each nation. Many of the most vigorous political parties spring from that class. Some leaders from that class direct the potent force of nationalism, encourage industrialization and progress, and contribute to the vitality of the cities. Urban unionized laborers constitute a relatively new and important group as well. Some of them enjoy a reasonable wage and impressive social benefits. On occasion, they have exerted political influence. Transportation and communication networks now cover large parts of most of the nations, giving them a greater cohesion than ever before. Increasingly, Latin Americans use their own natural resources to promote national growth—Mexico's use of its own oil to propel local industrialization illustrates that trend. But to balance this assessment of change we must return to a familiar theme: Despite pockets of change, a veneer of progress, and apparent modernity, much of Latin America retains the flavor of a distant past. In short, the change and modernization that have occurred in the last century have had little positive effect, particularly on the quality of life of the majority.

A major reason for this constancy is that one characteristic still dominates—and enervates—Latin America: The economies grow but do not develop. The most dynamic part of each economy remains linked to exports. The economic policies and performance strengthen institutions nurturing dependency. It is those institutional structures, minimally altered by time, that create the ever-present enigma of widespread poverty amid potential wealth.

As Latin America moves through the decade of the 1990s, the problems created by the remarkable continuity of those institutions weigh heavily, perhaps more heavily than ever. They beg for a solution. No reason exists to believe that time alone will solve these problems. On the contrary, the passage of time has only compounded them. The level of frustration felt by the majority certainly seems higher than ever. It will require some imaginative restructuring of institutions to solve the problems and to relieve the frustration.

The human dimension of these problems staggers the mind. The terrifying reality is that most of the population is hungry, malnourished, and sick. In 1990, nearly three-quarters of a population of 425 million, which was increasing at a rate of nearly 2.5 percent a year, were physically undernourished in one form or another. The social problems assume yet other directions. The overall illiteracy rates still hover at about 40 percent. The workforces grow at a faster rate than the creation of new jobs. The annual per capita income remains low, about one-tenth that of the United States. However, in reality, even that income is highly unbalanced, with a few receiving most of it. In Mexico, for example, about 1 percent of the gainfully employed population receives 66 percent of the national income, while most of the workers receive an income insufficient to satisfy minimal needs. There, as elsewhere in Latin America, the actual purchasing power of the worker has been declining since the early 1960s. In sum, the quality of life for the majority remains abysmally low.

In analyzing the institutional causes for these many problems, one should look first at the utilization of the land. It continues to be used inefficiently, not by the small farmer and peasant, but by the owners of the large estates. Roughly 90 percent of the land belongs to 10 percent of the owners, a degree of concentration far greater than that in any other world region of comparable size. The agrarian sector of Latin America is less and less able to satisfy the needs of the population. Although it has been estimated that in the 1970s population increase and agricultural production kept pace with each other, the statistics deceive. Large amounts of agriculture went into export. A growing proportion of the cereal crop became cattle feed. In other words, the amount of grain available to feed people decreased. At the same time, one must remember that beef feeds the wealthy only, so that the majority benefited in no way from increased cattle feeding. The distressing reality is that Latin Americans do not feed themselves. Latin America expended 60 percent more for the importation of food in 1978 ($6.4 billion) than it had in 1971 ($4 billion). Under present conditions in Latin America, there is no justification for predicting a decline or even a stabilization of mounting food imports. The tragedy of hunger remains a dominant characteristic of Latin America at the end of the twentieth century. After a visit to El Salvador in 1977, Father Timothy S. Healy, president of Georgetown University, noted the arresting contradiction: "An agricultural people . . . starve to death on rich land while they farm it."

It is a measure of Latin America's underdevelopment—its traditional propensity to grow rather than to develop—that this vast region, which must spend its hard-earned international currencies to import food to feed the population, is in reality a net exporter of foods, the primary exports. Latin America continues to export grains, meats, sugar, bananas, coffee, cacao, and soybeans because the large landowners, foreign as well as domestic, earn handsome profits from such exports, more than they might earn selling food in the domestic market. It is a further measure of Latin America's underdevelopment that most of the arable land lies unused or underused: Only about 10 percent is in use.

Latin America is fully capable not only of feeding its own population well but of contributing significantly to world food supplies. One must recall, as a point of comparison, that the vast and relatively populous Incan Empire fed its inhabitants well and maintained large food surpluses to compensate for lean years and natural disasters. That same area has been unable to do so since the Spanish conquest. In this particular case, we are challenged to understand why Incan technology, efficiency, and productivity surpassed Western technology, efficiency, and productivity. The Incan Empire in the fifteenth century was more developed than Peru or Ecuador or Bolivia in the twentieth century.

One probable solution to the staggering agrarian problems of contemporary Latin America is to put the unused and underused lands into the hands of the unemployed and underemployed. The newly created peasant class could feed itself and provide surpluses for the local marketplaces. Furthermore, access to land might reduce the flow of migrants from the countryside into already overcrowded cities. The answer sounds easy; its implementation would be extremely difficult. The middle class, and particularly the elite, owning the land partly for speculative and investment purposes, partly for profit, and partly to control the labor supply, have no intention of divesting themselves of their lands for the benefit of the impoverished masses, for national development, or for any other reason. It would take all the force of a strong government to alter the landholding structure in Latin America and then to sustain the new peasants with the agrarian reforms they would need. But until that agrarian reform takes place, no amount of investment, certainly no amount of rhetoric, will fundamentally alter the unjust institutions inherited from the past.

THE BURDEN OF THE PAST

There was little evidence, in the twilight of the twentieth century, of an emergence of greater agricultural efficiency, and where the efficiency does manifest itself, it usually produces for export rather than for national consumption. Those oases of efficiency are capital intensive, supplanting people with machinery. Besides forcing hundreds of thousands of would-be peasants to trek to the cities, that machinery consumes gasoline, the price of which has skyrocketed in all but a few privileged regions. The high cost of oil imports already has burdened Latin America with an unprecedented debt that threatens some nations with bankruptcy. Thus, mechanized agriculture is a risky, and possibly even a negative, answer to rural deficiencies of production.

In a few regions of Latin America—Peru and Bolivia, for example—land reform has taken place in recent times. But a land reform that does not give people access to water, credit, and/or services is not the correct answer either. It becomes increasingly clear that land reform and agrarian reform are not synonymous. The former constitutes changes in ownership; the latter includes changes in production and service structures as well, a much deeper institutional change.

Current patterns of landownership and use exemplify perfectly the prevalence of the institutions of the past. Furthermore, they illustrate a basic theme that runs through Latin American history: The historical institutions contribute significantly to the creation and perpetuation of mass poverty. There seems little doubt that so long as those historical institutions predominate, poverty will remain a major characteristic of Latin America. To bring about development, basic institutional changes will be needed, although, it must be emphasized, basic institutional changes legislated but not enforced, in law but without spirit, will not produce development.

Solution to the prevalent poverty in the midst of potential plenty lies not in exotic formulas eagerly imported into or imposed upon Latin America by the left or the right or any political hue in between. Unfaltering loyalty to imported solutions for domestic problems has reaped few rewards for Latin Americans. That a solution might lie within Latin America itself, within the pragmatic communal approach of the majority, is a possibility governments shun. Yet, solutions to old problems might well be found in local values and experiences. Given access to land, seeds, tools, water, and credit, the rural masses conceivably could make Latin America flourish. They could feed themselves, supply the local marketplace, and minimize dependency. Such a solution entails the restructuring of power because it would remove land from the monopoly of the few and distribute it to the many, thereby diminishing the former's wealth, prestige, and power while enhancing the latter's position; the luxuries and privileges of the few might diminish as the basic welfare of the many improved.

Accompanying that fundamental shift in landownership and productivity, there must be a centrally administered national plan for development. Massive public works projects would alleviate urban unemployment and underemployment while providing needed housing, schools, and hospitals. Industry would be directed to meet the basic needs of the many, not the exotic tastes of the few. A rational manufacturing plan would produce trucks to transport food, not sports cars for the privileged; pasteurized milk for schoolchildren, not carbonated soft drinks; sturdy sandals for the barefooted, not expensive leather shoes for export. Such a government would have to respond to the desires of the majority; it would have to lean upon and be supported by the majority. Identification between the people and the government would have to be complete. Through that identification, the local culture would triumph. The challenge for change would have been met.

Well-defined institutions from the past, enshrined by the elites and middle classes and relying on the strength of the military and the support of foreign allies, still prevail. Brazil, Uruguay, Chile, Nicaragua, and El Salvador have given us proof in the last two decades that those who enjoy privileges and benefits from society will not freely give up their position. If history does in fact suggest "lessons" on which we can draw, then it teaches that change of any fundamental nature will not be achieved easily. Eventually, change will probably result from the dialectic of violence so long a characteristic of Latin America—the violence expressed by those who feel oppressed, who desire to share in the benefits of society, and who seek change and the violence imposed by those who enjoy power, who benefit from the status quo, and who desire to perpetuate their domination. As we have seen, it is much easier to maintain an existing system than to bring about authentic change. In the late 1980s, Latin America entered another phase of formal democracy. The new leaders offer no innovative ideas to spur development. They raise the haunting questions of whether democracy in its present form is capable of addressing the challenges of change.

The Latin American experience indicates that change will require that strong, determined, and well-led governments break with the past and pursue an innovative course. Until such governments appear, Latin American countries, with the exceptions of Cuba and Nicaragua, manifest all the signs of being underdeveloped: low per capita income, unequal distribution of wealth, economic dependency, high birth and death rates, endemic diseases, undernourishment, and illiteracy. The enigma remains: Poor people inhabit rich lands.

SUGGESTED READINGS

Burns, E. Bradford. *Latin America: A Concise, Interpretive History.* Englewood Cliffs, N.J.: Prentice-Hall, 1982. This text sweeps through history from pre-Columbian times to the present and emphasizes those forces that shaped and are reshaping Latin America.

Conde, Roberto Cortés. *The First Stages of Modernization in Spanish America*. New York: Harper and Row, 1974. The author concentrates on the growing export economies of Latin America in the last half of the nineteenth century and details the consequences of those exports and the accompanying modernization for Latin America.

Lindquist, Sven. *Land and Power in South America*. New York: Penguin Books, 1979. With an incisive understanding of South American problems, Lindquist grasps the fundamental significance of landownership patterns. The book first treats the need for agrarian reform and then proceeds to study the efforts to make such reforms.

Mariátegui, José Carlos. *Seven Interpretive Essays on Peruvian Reality*. Austin: University of Texas Press, 1971. In the mid-1920s, Mariátegui isolated and discussed the major issues in Peruvian society—and by extension, in most of Latin America. Most discussions in the last half century of Latin America's past have only expanded on the sharp insights of Mariátegui.

Mörner, Magnus. *Race Mixture in the History of Latin America*. Boston: Little, Brown and Company, 1967. Discusses the mixing of the races on a scale unprecedented in world history and the resultant emergence of new cultures, which constitute some of the most dramatic chapters in Latin American history.

Reed, Nelson. *The Caste War in Yucatán*. Stanford: Stanford University Press, 1964. Using the example of nineteenth-century Yucatán, Reed offers a splendidly thought-provoking study of the rejection of Europeanization and modernization in favor of a folk society.

Stein, Stanley J., and Barbara H. Stein. *The Colonial Heritage of Latin America: Essays on Economic Dependence in Perspective*. New York: Oxford University Press, 1970. This succinct and sophisticated book is the classic statement on the imposition and growth of Latin America's dependency.

Wolf, Eric R., and Edward C. Hansen. *The Human Condition in Latin America*. New York: Oxford University Press, 1972. These two anthropologists indicate how both the dominant and the popular institutions of Latin America have affected large groups of people.

PART THREE
CULTURAL EXPRESSION

6

PHILOSOPHY AND THE
INTELLECTUAL TRADITION

FRED GILLETTE STURM

From the early years of colonization to the contemporary period, philosophical speculation and analysis have played important roles in the development of Latin American culture. Indeed, it might be argued that whether one's concern is with literature and the arts, or with history and the social sciences, a full and adequate comprehension of the Latin American scene can be achieved only if the philosophical dimension is included in the study.

Until recently, the educational systems in Spanish America and Brazil have followed a classical tradition as far as the curriculum of secondary schools is concerned, philosophy being included as a compulsory subject during the last year or two of studies. In this way, all secondary school graduates have been exposed to the European philosophical tradition—its history, major movements, and principal problems—however cursory the survey may have been. In many instances, the textbooks used have included an appendix that introduces the reader to the philosophical history of the particular country itself, so that the student understands that philosophy is not confined to Europe but is practiced in the Americas as well.

On the university level, philosophy has been closely linked to the human and cultural sciences. Until recently, no sharp distinctions have been drawn between psychology and philosophical anthropology, sociology and social philosophy, political science and political philosophy, or jurisprudence and the philosophy of law. Earlier in the history of Latin American education, the same was true of the natural sciences. Physics had been an integral part of the philosophy curriculum in Spanish and Portuguese universities during the centuries of colonization, so that concern with physical, chemical, and biological phenomena was considered to be a branch of philosophical investigation termed "natural philosophy." Although this close relationship between philosophy and the sciences was not peculiar to university studies and research in Latin America and Iberia—the same was the case in the United States and the countries of northern and Western Europe well into the nineteenth century—the tradition tended to remain in effect longer, only recently falling victim to the fragmentation of learning and research into increasingly self-contained specializations.

If philosophy has had a close relationship with the sciences in Latin America, it has been even more closely linked to the literary arts: poetry, the novel, theater, and especially the essay form. Any study of Latin American intellectual or philosophical history must take into account the history of literature in order to understand the philosophical ideas that were being considered and debated at any given period. Today, philosophy continues to have a close link with literature and theatrical expression. Many philosophers use, to good advantage, the essay form for the transmission of their thought, and Sunday newspapers often feature such essays in their supplements of art and culture.

The close connection between philosophy and the arts and sciences can be noted in many cultures, but it is especially true in Latin American culture, a fact that is often overlooked by U.S. students of Latin America to the impoverishment of many of their analyses, whether in the area of the social sciences, literary criticism, or history.

INTELLECTUAL DEPENDENCY AND THE "NEW WORLD" CONCEPT

It has become fashionable to use the word "dependency" to describe the Latin American situation, whether one is referring to economics or to the world of culture in general. Political independence from Spain and Portugal did not bring with it either economic independence or intellectual independence. Instead, there was a clear transference of dependency. Economically, the relationship of dependency was shifted from the Iberian colonial powers to the industrial and commercial establishments of northwestern Europe, Britain, and "the colossus of the North" and has largely remained in that state to the present. Intellectually, a similar transference of dependency occurred earlier, during the latter half of the eighteenth century, as ideas from France and Britain, and to a lesser extent the United States, began to gain dominance in those circles that were calling for reform and eventually, independence. To a large degree, it is accurate to refer to Latin American culture as being one of dependency, an extension of the Western European and Anglo-American worlds. In this respect, Latin America does not differ from many other regions of the world that are equally dependent, culturally as well as economically.

The profound interrelationship between ideas and institutions, or philosophy and culture, can be studied more easily, perhaps, in the case of societies that are classified as being culturally and intellectually dependent. The dominant ideas come from outside the culture and are adapted to specific historical situations, making it easier for the analyst to identify the components and the relations involved. Although the originating process of ideation emerging directly out of a cultural problematic is lacking, the mutual interaction of idea and sociohistorical situation can be observed under circumstances in which the two are readily identifiable.

There is an important sense, however, in which Latin America differs from all other regions of cultural and intellectual dependency in the world. This difference has its center in the notion of "new world," a concept born in Europe in the early decades of the sixteenth century when attention was directed to the Western Hemisphere, which hitherto had been ignored, if not largely unknown. What "new world" signifies has varied from period to period, but it has been a persistent idea throughout the history of Latin America from the time of European discovery, conquest, and colonization. This concept of a "new reality" was especially evident at the time of Spanish American independence. Suddenly, new nations were born, seemingly ex nihilo, whose previous history was solely that of politico-juridical units within a larger colonial administrative entity. There was a consciousness not only of having constituted a new national identity but of having become a new social entity that needed to address the problems of forging institutions suited to its peculiar needs and of creating a cultural tradition expressive of its own concerns and values.

PHILOSOPHY: "PERMANENT ACTIVITY OF THE HUMAN SPIRIT"

Before proceeding, it is necessary to indicate what is to be included in a study of "philosophy," a controversial topic in professional philosophical circles. This chapter is concerned with more than just academic philosophy, however, and in it, the word shall be used in its broadest possible meaning.

In common linguistic usage, there are three ways in which the word is employed. First, we talk about a person's "philosophy of" something. It could be a general philosophy of life or a more specific philosophy of art. In this sense, "philosophy" translates into "attitude toward" or "way of understanding." This use can be generalized to make reference to an entire society's "philosophy of . . . ," so we can refer to "the ancient Egyptian philosophy of death" or "the Japanese philosophy of beauty." In this use of the term, philosophy refers to a basic comprehension and means of approaching a given dimension of experience or existence. Considered in its broadest dimension, philosophy in this sense is equivalent to what the Germans have called *Weltanschauung* and *Lebensanschauung*: a particular way of "looking at the world" and "looking at life," a worldview and a life view. More often than not, an individual's "philosophy of *x*" has never been thought through carefully, unless some situation has arisen that posed a serious challenge to it, and almost always the *Welt- und Lebensanschauung* of a society is inarticulate, a matter of taking for granted a certain set of attitudes and values and a system of acceptable behavior. Employed in this sense, it can be said that every human being and every society has a philosophy, even though the task of philosophizing is not "being done."

Second, we refer to the philosophy of a given social movement or institution. It is possible to discuss the philosophy of Marxism, or of a given Marxist political party, for example; the philosophy of a given society's educational system, or the philosophy of higher education held by the board of regents and administration of a particular university; or the philosophy of artistic creativity held by a group of artists who have banded together to achieve certain common goals in the creative use of a particular medium or set of media. The positions taken are almost always clearly articulated and published in party platforms, charters, manifestos, constitutions, legislation, and the like. Here philosophy of *x* is equivalent to ideology, in the broad sense of referring to a set of agreed-upon perspectives and goals that can serve as the basis for determining directions of common action.

Third, we use philosophy to refer to a specialized intellectual activity, often, but not necessarily, associated with institutions of higher learning. In this instance, people who have received training in effective techniques engage in critical analysis of the various dimensions of experience and existence, as well as in a continual reassessment of the techniques of critical analysis itself. The dimensions of critical philosophy are many and include such disciplines as the philosophy of science, the philosophy of art, ethics, and political philosophy as well as the technical fields of logic, epistemology, and ontology. Histories of philosophy usually confine themselves to activity corresponding to this third usage of the term "philosophy."

That there are three major ways in which "philosophy" is used does not mean that we are dealing with a case of simple ambiguity—the same word being employed to designate separate meanings because of some vague associations, often lost in linguistic history. The three ways of using the term are, in fact, interrelated. The task of the critical philosopher often involves undertaking the articulation of a position that has been taken for granted. On the other hand, critically articulated positions often filter down into common usage and become assumed worldviews after a generation or two. Marxism is a good example of the appropriation of a critically articulated philosophical system for the purpose of creating a political and social ideology. Indeed, it could be argued that critical analysis and ideological articulation have advanced in conscious interaction within the history of Marxism. An excellent example of the interrelationship of all three usages of the word is to be found in the philosophy of the Quechua-speaking Amerindians of the Andes. They share, of course, an unarticulated (except in the case of nonverbal religious ritual and artistic expression) *Weltanschauung,* the result of many generations dwelling in, and interacting meaningfully with, a common environment. Several attempts have been made during this century to articulate some of this outlook verbally and transform it into an ideology, one of the most notable being that of the sociopolitical movement associated with the charismatic Peruvian figure, Victor Raúl Haya de la Torre. More recently, a concerted effort has been undertaken in the University of Cuzco's department of philosophy to provide a complete articulation of the Quechuan worldview on the basis of linguistic and behavioral analysis for the purposes of critical analysis and restatement. Because the university serves the predominantly Quechua-speaking highlands of Peru, students who enroll in the philosophy program are required to take courses in the scientific study of the Quechuan language so they will be prepared to deal critically with Quechuan philosophy.

Keeping these three interrelated usages of the word in mind, we may define philosophy as being the effort to comprehend human existence and experience coupled with a continuing effort on the part of certain intellectuals to evaluate critically the articulation of such comprehension. This is undertaken, not only for the sake of a better understanding of the human situation, but in order to designate directions for action toward the achievement of desired goals, involving the discovery of values and the imposition of norms.

THE PROBLEM OF PERIODIZATION
IN LATIN AMERICAN PHILOSOPHY

A fundamental problem in the writing of any history is that of periodization, a determination of the meaningful temporal units that permit an adequate comprehension of the development of that which is being studied. Periodization is especially important when attempting an intellectual history of a given culture in which the development of ideas must be correlated with the wider history of the society in which those ideas were articulated. When more than one society is being considered, as in the case when dealing with Latin American intellectual history, the question becomes even more acute. Can the problem of periodization be resolved uniformly for all Latin American societies?

Efforts at writing overall histories of Latin American philosophy have been divided, in general, into six periods.

1. Colonial thought during the sixteenth and seventeenth centuries
2. The impact of the European Enlightenment on Latin American intellectual circles during the eighteenth century
3. The search during the first decades after independence from Spain and Portugal (and in the case of Haiti, from France) for adequate and appropriate philosophical bases to serve the task of constructing new national states and "peoples"
4. The dominance of Positivism throughout almost every aspect of social and cultural life during the final decades of the nineteenth century
5. The reaction against nineteenth-century Positivism in the early decades of the twentieth century, with the search for national cultural identity
6. The contemporary period

Although this periodization is very rough and needs much modification, it will serve as an introduction to the subject of the history of Latin American philosophy.

The first two centuries of colonial rule in Spanish America witnessed a remarkable richness in intellectual life. Universities that often rivaled those of Europe were founded throughout the viceroyalties and attracted outstanding European professors as teachers. Such universities later produced competent scholars who not only served their own institutions but found employment on European university faculties as well. Philosophical works published by scholars in Spanish America were read and discussed in European university circles, and there was a healthy interchange of ideas between American and European intellectuals. Only recently has serious work been undertaken to uncover and analyze this rich body of sixteenth- and seventeenth-century Spanish American philosophical literature. The very thorough bibliography of that literature prepared by Walter Redmond indicates the work that is yet to be done before we can appreciate it to the fullest extent.

The great bulk of this academic philosophy in Spanish American universities falls within the movement known as the Second Scholasticism; this movement involved the renaissance and reinterpretation of the great medieval philosophical traditions that occurred within Catholic university circles, especially in Spain and Portugal, as the intellectual phase of the Counter-Reformation as well as the effort to stem the tide of "new thought" that was sweeping across northwestern Europe. There were examples in the sixteenth century, however, of Latin American followers of such Renaissance figures as Erasmus and Thomas More and later, in the seventeenth century, of Latin American intellectuals who were influenced by the new ideas of such European philosophers as Descartes, Gassendi, and Malebranche.

What was most exciting, perhaps, about this first period in Latin American intellectual history was the appearance of a new set of problems that were debated not only in the Americas, where they originated, but in European circles as well. The central focus had to do with the indigenous populations of the New World. Were they fully human? If not, then they could not be said to enjoy the rights that humans enjoy under natural law, including the rights to hold property and to lay claim to sovereignty. They could be employed as beasts of burden. On the other hand, missionaries were sent along with the conquistadores and colonists to proclaim the gospel and save the souls of the indigenous populations, a mission that implied the fundamental human nature of the Amerindians. Two names loom large in the articulation and discussion of this issue: Bartolomé de las Casas in Spanish America and Manuel da Nóbrega in Brazil. The repercussions were strong and led, among other factors, to the development of the discipline of international law in European legal circles as well as to laying the groundwork for a new articulation of the notion of fundamental human rights during the Enlightenment.

During the second period, Latin American intellectual circles were increasingly influenced by contemporary developments in England and France, a phenomenon that occurred also in the mother countries of Spain and Portugal but to a much lesser degree. There was a proliferation of intellectual activity outside the universities. In Brazil, where all requests for establishment of a university had been denied, this was of special import. Academies flourished in the form of literary and debating societies in which new ideas were expounded and discussed through the reading of learned papers and poetry. The "new thought" from Europe, including developments in the natural sciences and French *enciclopedismo,* made its way into the Latin American mind largely by way of these academies. An important influence at this time was the new approach to economics being taken by Adam Smith, whose ideas became a rallying cry for the nascent Latin American bourgeoisie.

It was not merely the scientific and technically philosophical ideas from French Encyclopedism that were promulgated in the academies but the political concepts as well, which, along with an acquaintance with John Locke's social contract theory and certain revolutionary ideas from the Anglo-American colonies, helped to forge the ideologies that were adopted by the various groups that began to speak of independence.

Alongside the academies there emerged Masonic lodges, centers of the new rationalism of the Enlightenment and seedbeds for revolutionary discussion and activity.

With independence came the problem of defining the newly emerged national identities. It was not only necessary to articulate political and economic ideologies but to lay the foundations for a new cultural tradition as well. These were confusing decades in the history of most of the new republics, and the intellectual scene mirrored this turmoil. One movement does seem to predominate in the philosophical literature of the time, however, viz., the Eclecticism of Victor Cousin. Philosophically, Cousin had insisted on the harmonization of what at first sight were conflicting doctrines. This stress on pluralistic harmonization was welcomed by many Latin American intellectuals, although by no means all, in a time of emergent nationhood with all its attendant instability and strife. Eclecticism especially influenced the Brazilian mentality of the period, which had important political consequences, notably in the "moderative power" granted to the emperor and the eventual coalition formed between the Liberal and Conservative parties.

The concern for the inauguration of a new cultural tradition, growing out of the consciousness of having become suddenly a new entity—the awareness of being Argentinean, Chilean, Mexican, and so on, and thereby constituting a new "peoplehood" as well as "nationhood"—led to a great debate in several of the Spanish American republics concerning the desirability, and feasibility, of severing all linguistic and literary ties with Spain. Closely allied with this was Sarmiento's well-known plea for large-scale, non-Hispanic European immigration in order to create the new Argentine nation and culture.

Perhaps the most important figure in Latin American philosophical circles during this third period was Andrés Bello, the Venezuelan native who spent years in London in the service of Simón Bolívar and the cause of Spanish American independence. He later accepted the invitation of the Chilean government to provide important services in educational and juridical reform. Thoroughly versed in Lockeanism, Utilitarianism, and the Scottish school of "common sense philosophy," and with an impressive knowledge of Roman law as well as international law, Bello made a profound contribution toward the establishment of Chile as a nation state with a distinguished cultural tradition, not only through a life of practical administrative activity, but especially through his prolific literary production.

By the middle of the nineteenth century, it is clear that if any generalizations are to be made concerning Latin American developments, they must be made in a highly tentative fashion and accompanied with many qualifications as the situations in the individual countries were markedly diverse. Despite this diversity, there was a common thread, linked somewhat to an awareness of the highly successful northern European phenomenon known as the industrial revolution, along with a strong desire for stability in many of the societies. This common thread was the prevalence of the movement to which reference was made earlier, viz., Latin American Positivism. It was not a monolithic movement by any means, and it was marked by much internal controversy, but the component elements can be identified as Comtean Positivism, Spencerian Evolutionary Naturalism, and the Utilitarianism and inductive logic of John Stuart Mill.

There are three studies of this period, focusing upon developments in individual societies, that have become classics in their own right. The earliest, which includes a careful analysis of the preceding intellectual period as well, is by one of Argentina's own Positivists, José Ingenieros. Leopoldo Zea, in several works, has traced the introduction, ascendancy, and fall of the doctrines of Positivism within the fabric of Mexican history. João Cruz Costa has done much the same with reference to Positivism in Brazil. If and when a general analysis of Positivism in Latin American culture is undertaken, it will reveal a very deep imprint made by these rather heterogeneous ideas upon a wide spectrum of social life, including the political, economic, religious, educational, and literary sectors.

The reaction against Positivism was as vocal as Positivism's impact had been profound. In Mexico, it was first articulated through the Ateneo de La Juventud (Atheneum of Youth), which provided the intellectual base for the Mexican Revolution that toppled the old Porfirian establishment. Francisco Romero, who belonged to the second generation of anti-Positivists in Argentina, referred to such figures as José Vasconcelos and Antonio Caso in Mexico, Alejandro Korn in Argentina, Raimundo de Farias Brito in Brazil, Alejandro Deústua in Peru, and Carlos Vaz Ferreira in Uruguay as *Los Fundadores* (the Founders), intellectuals who were striving to create a new philosophical stance that would be authentically Latin American. Ironically, these philosophers were greatly influenced by similar work being done in European circles at the time in the sense of reacting to Positivism and Evolutionary Naturalism, the greatest influence coming from the French philosopher Henri Bergson. Strong emphasis was given in their writings to aesthetics, which had been downplayed during the reign of Positivism, and metaphysics, which had been virtually eliminated, along with a concern for the study of the spiritual dimension of human life.

Contemporary periods are always difficult to characterize because one lacks the necessary historical perspective to evaluate them adequately, but four features seem to stand out over the past half century. First, there has been a continuation of the work of *Los Fundadores* through a second, as well as a third, generation in several of the countries. This is evident especially in Mexico, where first Samuel Ramos and then Leopoldo Zea were seen as standing in the tradition of Vasconcelos and Caso. Ramos is remembered for his work in philosophical anthropology, through which he attempted to clarify the uniqueness of the Mexican personality. Zea is known for the impetus that he has given to the study of Mexican intellectual history as it relates to the development of national institutions.

Second, there has been the forging of what has become a dominant ideology for much of Latin America, a concern for liberation from a status of dependency of national political economies and for the liberation of the underprivileged classes within those economies. On the one hand, this ideology has been expressed through heterodox Marxist positions, perhaps most clearly in the writings of the Peruvian José Mariátegui. On the other hand, it has found its roots in Catholic tradition, where Liberation Theology has arisen to make its revolutionary impact felt far beyond the Latin American geographical area. This new theology has spawned in Latin America philosophies of liberation and pedagogies of liberation as well.

What may be designated as the golden age of Latin American philosophy of law falls within this mid-century, and it is exemplified by important works by Luís Racaséns-Siches and Eduardo García-Maynez from Mexico, Juan Llambías de Azevedo of Uruguay, Carlos Cossio of Argentina, and the Brazilian Miguel Reale.

Within academic philosophy, the present period has witnessed a new maturity that recalls the situation described in the discussion of the sixteenth and seventeenth centuries in Spanish American universities: Work being done by philosophers in the Americas has paralleled that being accomplished by European faculties. Important contributions have been made in the methodologies both of phenomenology and of analytic philosophy, as well as in the disciplines of philosophy of science, philosophy of mathematics, epistemology, ethics, and the history of philosophy. Mario Bunge, whose father was an important figure in Argentinean philosophy earlier in the century, can be considered representative of this new philosophical maturity, although he has left his native Argentina to teach in the United States and Canada. The University of Campinas (Brazil) is the site of an internationally recognized center for logic and the philosophy of science. At the National Autonomous University of Mexico (UNAM), the Institute for Philosophical Studies has become a center for work in analytic philosophy and publishes *Crítica,* an important journal of analytic work in philosophy.

Shortly after mid-century, the Pan American Union was instrumental in publishing a series of brief panoramic histories of philosophy in Latin American countries. Regular Latin American congresses of philosophy are held under the auspices of the Latin American Society of Philosophy.

To approach Latin American philosophy exclusively in terms of the Euro-American tradition, however, is to ignore two of the three cultural strains that have characterized the region from the time of European invasion and colonization, accompanied shortly thereafter by the introduction of a significant population from a number of different African societies. There is growing evidence that at least three historic civilizations had developed before the European/African invasion: the Meso-American, the Andean, and the Tupian-Guaraní.

Miguel León-Portilla has undertaken an analysis of the philosophical dimension of Meso-American civilization. A periodic frame can be indicated from the Olmec horizon through the Aztec. An almost parallel periodic frame designates the philosophic dimensions of Andean civilizations beginning with the Chavin horizon and continuing through the Inca. I have begun a study of the philosophical dimensions of Tupian-Guaraní civilization, although much remains to be done. It might be claimed that these traditions have either stagnated or atrophied, but for large segments of the population they still determine worldviews, attitudinal stances, value judgments, and behavioral patterns. With the appearance of Indianist movements and with "consciousness-raising" by leaders within these movements, we may look forward to a revitalization of these traditions and the intellectual development that occurs whenever there is new cultural self-awareness.

Afro-American communities are the result of gradual merging of disparate linguistic and cultural traditions from several sixteenth-, seventeenth-, and eighteenth-century African societies. Many of these syntheses have incorporated Amerindian elements; all have incorporated elements of Iberian and colonial Roman Catholicism. Afro-American religious movements remain vital and have become critically articulate. A growing literature is being produced by the intellectual leadership, and a level of articulation is emerging that has its own technical language, logical structure, and methodology.

There has been a tendency to consider Amerindian and Afro-American developments as peripheral, exotic, subcultural specimens of "pre-philosophy" existing outside the mainstream of Ibero-American intellectual life—fit subjects of study by sociologists, cultural anthropologists, and historians of religion but irrelevant to the concerns of intellectual historians and philosophers. It is important that we change this attitude. We should consider these to be *peer* cultures on a level with the Europeanized American culture rather than *sub*cultures peripheral to the mainstream, thereby admitting the truly pluralistic nature of "Latin American" thought and culture. The study of Latin American philosophy is concerned with the total spectrum of thought in this geographical area of the world.

A much more difficult problem will remain even if, and when, a successful periodization is worked out for the Indo-American and Afro-American dimensions of the cultures of Latin American nations; namely, the effort to correlate the histories of Indo-, Afro-, and Euro-America. A periodization might then be formulated that would serve as a framework for the writing of a history of Latin American philosophy faithfully reflecting and reporting the pluralistic nature of the subject matter. The question raised at the outset of this section must, then, be restated this way: Can the problem of periodization be resolved uniformly for Latin American societies that are culturally and intellectually pluridimensional?

REPRESENTATIVE PROBLEMS IN THE STUDY OF LATIN AMERICAN PHILOSOPHY AND INTELLECTUAL TRADITION

It is necessary to develop more adequate techniques for uncovering and studying Indo-American and Afro-American philosophical thought. Much of the source material is not written, of course. Required for the task of analyzing it are scholars who are trained both as philosophers and historians of ideas on the one hand and as anthropologists, linguists, or art historians on the other. A multidisciplinary effort will be necessary to work fruitfully in the areas of Indo-American and Afro-American intellectual history.

A perennially controversial question is: Can a genuinely Latin American philosophy be identified and distinguished from European philosophy in the Americas? A parallel problem is whether a genuinely Afro-American mentality can be identified and distinguished from the philosophies of traditional African societies.

The question of what is distinctively Latin American about intellectual activity in the Americas is related to a third set of problems: How have certain words, concepts, and themes, which have their origins in European thought, been modified through use in the context of Latin American realities? Three configurations of terms come to mind immediately:

1. The terms *libertad* (Port.: *liberdade*) and *liberación* (Port.: *libertação*) have been used throughout most of the intellectual history of Latin America with varying meanings in each of the periods. There has been a cumulative effect in this history of usage so that it might be argued that there has come to be a peculiarly Latin American range of connotative significance attached to them.

2. *Independencia, dependencia,* and *interdependencia* are used in more than a political and economic sense to encompass the cultural and intellectual as well. The relationship between Latin American populations and the powers that have exercised political and economic colonial domination is not the same as the relationship that characterizes other colonial and former colonial situations in the world. This difference gives a special nuance of meaning to the notion of cultural dependence and independence that deserves to be carefully delineated.

3. The associated terms of "sovereignty," "international law," and "human rights" have been important throughout Latin American history. We have already noted that the discipline of international law owes its origin to the controversy over Amerindian nature and rights and what should be the correct political and juridical relations between the European colonizing powers and the Amerindian societies they had to deal with. The question of human rights, with reference to certain segments of the population, has been a perennial issue in Latin American history, from the days of Bartolomé de las Casas and Manuel da Nóbrega to the present-day concern of liberationists and freedom fighters. An analysis of the contributions made by Latin American intellectuals who have been dealing with these issues to world understanding would help to reveal the creative edge of the Latin American intellectual tradition.

The analysis of Latin American philosophy and intellectual history is an important dimension of Latin American studies and constitutes a fascinating field for the student who has an interest in the life of the mind and the close interaction of ideas and social institutions. It is an area that has been relatively neglected in the past and therefore offers an especially challenging opportunity for fresh and innovative research and interpretation.

SUGGESTED READINGS

General Works

Davis, Harold Eugene. *Latin American Thought: Historical Introduction.* New York: Free Press, 1974. A brief, informative survey from pre-Columbian times to the present.
Encyclopedia of Philosophy. 8 vols. New York: Macmillan, 1967. In addition to a general article on Latin American philosophy, there are separate articles about several of the leading figures. A listing of periodicals is given in the article "Philosophical Journals."
Pan American Union. *Revista interamericana de bibliografía/Interamerican Review of Bibliography.* A quarterly publication of the Pan-American Union (OAS), which includes articles about Latin American intellectual history.

Amerindian Thought

León-Portilla, Miguel. *Aztec Thought and Culture.* Norman: University of Oklahoma Press, 1963. Reconstruction of Nahuatl thought during the period before the Spanish conquest of New Spain based on a careful analysis of the available codices.

_____. *Time and Reality in the Thought of the Maya.* Boston: Beacon Press, 1968. Reconstruction of Mayan thought prior to the Spanish conquest based on studies by leading investigators of available sources.

Sturm, Fred Gillette. "The Concepts of History and Destiny Implicit in the Apapokuva Guaraní Myth of Creation and Destruction of the Earth." In Mary H. Preuss, ed., *"In Love and War: Hummingbird Lore" and Other Selected Papers from LAILA/ALILA's 1988 Symposium.* Culver City, Calif.: Labyrinthos, 1989. Pp. 61–66.

_____. "Problems in Articulating the Traditional Tupi-Guaraní Welt-und-Lebensanschauung." In *Latin American Indian Literatures Journal* (Vol. 2, No. 1 [Spring, 1986] pp. 124–145.

_____. "A Comparative Analysis of the Mbya Guaraní and Apapokuva Guaraní Myths of Creation and Destruction of the World." In Mary H. Preuss, ed., *LAILA Speaks: Selected Papers from the VII Symposium on Latin American Indian Literatures.* Culver City, Calif.: Labyrinthos, 1990. Pp. 89–93.

_____. "Ontological Categories Implicit in the Mbya Guaraní Creation Myth." In Mary H. Preuss, ed., *Past, Present, and Future: Selected Papers on Latin American Indian Literatures.* Culver City, Calif.: Labyrinthos, 1991. Pp. 117–121.

Afro-American Thought

Bastide, Roger. *The African Religions of Brazil.* Baltimore: Johns Hopkins University Press, 1978. A thorough and sympathetic analysis of the Afro-Brazilian religious communities by a leading French sociologist who, as a convert, has a unique perspective.

Herskovits, Melville J. *The New World Negro: Selected Papers in Afroamerican Studies.* Bloomington: Indiana University Press, 1966. A variety of essays including studies of cult life in Brazil, the worldview of blacks in Paramaribo, Trinidad "Shouters," "Voodoo," and Afro-Catholic syncretism.

Philosophy During the Colonial Period

Redmond, Walter. *Bibliography of the Philosophy in the Iberian Colonies of America.* The Hague: Nijhoff, 1972. A listing of books and articles written and published by philosophers in Spanish America and Brazil during the centuries of colonial rule that reveals the breadth and richness of philosophical production during the period.

Eighteenth-Century Enlightenment

Whitaker, Arthur P., ed. *Latin America and the Enlightenment.* 2d ed. Ithaca: Cornell University Press, 1961. A collection of short essays about various aspects of Enlightenment thought throughout Latin America.

Intellectual Developments During the Nineteenth Century

Crawford, William Rex. *A Century of Latin-American Thought.* Rev. ed. Cambridge: Harvard University Press, 1963. A survey of social and political thought in Latin America during the nineteenth century with brief summaries of the positions of individual writers.

Davis, Harold Eugene, ed. *Latin American Social Thought: The History of Its Development Since Independence, with Selected Readings.* Washington, D.C.: University Press of Washington, 1961. An anthology of selections from the writings of leading social and political thinkers of Spanish America and Brazil during the nineteenth century.

Zea, Leopoldo. *The Latin American Mind.* Norman: University of Oklahoma Press, 1963. An analysis of Liberalism during the first half of the nineteenth century, and Positivism during the second half, throughout Spanish America.

Intellectual Developments During the Twentieth Century

Boff, Leonardo, and Boff, Clodovis. *Introducing Liberation Theology.* Maryknoll, N.Y.: Orbis Books, 1987. A good, brief introduction to the historical development and basic tenets of Liberation Theology by one of the best-known Brazilian leaders in the movement and his brother.

Chavarría, Jesus. *José Carlos Mariátegui and the Rise of Modern Peru, 1890–1930.* Albuquerque: University of New Mexico Press, 1979. A study of the intellectual development of one of Peru's best-known political ideologists.

Freire, Paulo. *Pedagogy of the Oppressed.* New York: Seabury Press, 1970. The "bible" of the Pedagogy of Liberation Movement in Brazil, Spanish America, and the Third World.

García, Jorge J. E., ed. *Latin American Philosophy in the Twentieth Century: Man, Values, and the Search for Philosophical Identity.* Buffalo: Prometheus Books, 1986. An anthology of leading Spanish-American and Brazilian philosophers that supplements the Sanchez-Reulet volume with some overlapping.

García, Jorge J. E., et al., eds. *Philosophical Analysis in Latin America.* Dordrecht: Reidel, 1984. A study of the impact of Anglo-American analytic philosophy in Spanish America and Brazil.

Gutiérrez, Gustavo. *A Theology of Liberation: History, Politics, and Salvation.* Maryknoll, N.Y.: Orbis Books, 1973. One of the germinal works of the Latin American Theology of Liberation Movement.

Handbook of Latin American Studies. Gainesville: University Presses of Florida, 1935– . An annual report of publications in which the section on philosophy provides a yearly overview of philosophical activities in Latin America.

Himelblau, Jack. *Alejandro O. Deustua: Philosophy in Defense of Man.* Gainesville: University Presses of Florida, 1979. Analyzes the thought of Peru's great philosopher of art.

Ireland, Gordon, trans. *Latin American Legal Philosophy.* Cambridge: Harvard University Press, 1948. English translations of works by Luís Recaséns-Siches, Eduardo García-Maynez, Juan Llambías de Azevedo, and Carlos Cossio.

Kunz, Josef L. *Latin-American Philosophy of Law in the Twentieth Century.* New York: New York University School of Law, 1950. A brief survey of the golden age of Latin American legal philosophy, placing it within the broader context of European philosophy of law and dealing with several minor figures as well as the major ones.

Sánchez-Reulet, Aníbal, ed. *Contemporary Latin-American Philosophy.* Albuquerque: University of New Mexico Press, 1954. An anthology of selections from writings of late nineteenth-century and early twentieth-century philosophers from various Spanish American countries and Brazil. Although a few Positivists are included, the majority of writings belong to *Los Fundadores*.

7

LATIN AMERICAN
LITERATURE

TAMARA HOLZAPFEL

More than a century before the Pilgrims reached the shores of North America, Spanish and Portuguese explorers were busy discovering, conquering, and colonizing the vast territory to the south. It was at this time of feverish activity that Latin American literature came into existence. The discovery of a strange new continent inhabited by hitherto unknown peoples with exotic customs had the greatest impact imaginable on the European mentality. The conquerors and colonizers took on the additional task of describing and interpreting this amazing discovery to the European world. They recorded living history in chronicles and heroic deeds in epic poems. These two genres begin the history of Latin American literature.

During the three-century colonial period, Latin American literature followed the literary models of the mother countries. The coming of independence in the first quarter of the nineteenth century brought forth a large number of separate nations, and literature in Latin America acquired national characteristics. To the original complexity of the two languages dividing Latin American literature into two distinct literatures, Spanish American and Luso-Brazilian, was now added the difficulty of distinguishing among the literatures of nineteen Spanish-speaking countries. If it is obvious that Luso-Brazilian literature is unique in Latin America, it is quite another matter to define the characteristics that separate Argentine from Nicaraguan or Colombian from Mexican literature.

Nevertheless, similar historical circumstances—from conquest, colonialism, and independence to the political turmoil of the present—provide a common denominator for scrutinizing Latin American literature. Another unifying characteristic of this literature is a persistent concern with social issues. In contrast to European literary tradition, always preoccupied with the discovery of new literary techniques, Latin American literature has had to deal with a myriad of extraliterary factors. From the beginning, it was the strangeness and the diversity of a new reality that asserted itself

over a mere concern with literary form. History and politics, geography and sociology, have always been an integral part of Latin American literary expression.

Although Latin American literature has been in existence for nearly half a millennium, it is only since the mid-1960s that it has broken through the barrier of silence
that has surrounded it. At this recent point in time, an unprecedented interest in the
literary productions of Latin America developed simultaneously in Europe and
North America. This became known as "the boom" of Latin American literature.
Critics everywhere agreed that Latin American literature had finally emerged from
obscurity and that Latin American writers could now stand comparison with the best
of Europe and North America.

Latin Americans are proud of such names on their literary roster as Pablo Neruda,
Jorge Luis Borges, João Guimaraes Rosa, Miguel Angel Asturias, Gabriel García
Márquez, and a score more. Their books, readily available in good translations in all
major languages, are read, discussed, and admired throughout the world. But with the
discovery of a "new" literature, it is easy to overlook the fact that Latin American literature did not develop out of nowhere. Let us now look at the highlights of the literary
tradition that helped forge a new and significant literature in the twentieth century.

THE COLONIAL PERIOD

The entire literary expression of the sixteenth century was devoted to the description
of the American experience. The conquerors, the colonizers, and the missionaries
were the authors. They found a vast land of untamed nature that they proceeded to
explore and subjugate. At the time of the conquest, novels of chivalry were at the
height of their popularity in Europe. These stimulated the imagination of the early
explorers, and they came to the Americas with their minds filled with legends of the
Fountain of Youth, the Seven Enchanted Cities, and the myth of El Dorado. In
many instances, even the style of the chronicles is taken from the novels of chivalry.
The Americas, from the beginning, became lands of "magical realism" to the
European imagination. Magical realism denotes the fusion of two planes, the real
and the fantastic, or marvelous. The term has been used extensively in the critical literature of the fictional writings of contemporary authors who have readily acknowledged the chronicles as a source of inspiration.

These historical accounts begin with the log book of Christopher Columbus
(1492) and include the famous dispatches, *Five Letters* (1519–1526), Hernán Cortés
sent from Mexico to Charles V of Spain as well as histories of every stage of colonization. The most vivid of these first-person narratives is *The True History of the
Conquest of New Spain* (1552) by Bernal Díaz del Castillo. Bernal Díaz was a simple
soldier who accompanied Cortés in the conquest of Mexico. He took part in 119
battles and skirmishes and at the conclusion of the conquest, was rewarded with an
encomienda in Guatemala where he spent the rest of his long life. Although he wrote
his book when he was eighty-four, he seems to have had phenomenal powers of recall, remembering the names and the colors of horses in the expedition. The book

stands out because of the author's individuality of character and his personalized point of view, both traits much appreciated in contemporary writing. Bernal Díaz relates in great detail and in a natural, colloquial language the events in which he took part. He does it with much bragging about himself and praise for the 400 soldiers who achieved the conquest rather than for their commander, Cortés.

The second generation of chroniclers was born in the Americas. Creoles, mestizos, and even Indians contributed a number of significant narratives during the second half of the sixteenth century. By far superior are the *Royal Commentaries* (1609–1617) by Inca Garcilaso de la Vega of Cuzco, Peru. Son of a conquistador (who was a cousin of the gifted Castilian poet of the same name) and an Incan princess, Garcilaso wrote a historicist account of the Incan Empire and its conquest, stressing the parallels between the civilizations of the New World and the Old. Much of the information he gleaned from oral tradition and the memories his relatives had of preconquest times. He was a gifted scholar who established his reputation as a humanist in Spain. But what attracts the modern reader is Garcilaso's imaginative bent. Legendary and fantastic episodes enliven the narrative. He and Bernal Díaz represent authentic Americanism in colonial letters, their works being typical of the contribution made by the chronicles.

Epic poetry was the other genre cultivated in the sixteenth century. Two works in particular stand out, one in Spanish, the other in Portuguese. The Spanish nobleman Alonso de Ercilla participated in the struggle to subdue the hardy and warlike Araucanians of Chile. He was so impressed by their bravery and their stoic composure that he dedicated his epic poem *La Araucana* (1569–1589) to them. Although he could not help but extol the prowess and valor of his countrymen, he was not blind to their greed and cruelty. Yet he admired unquestioningly the fortitude and patriotism of the Indian chieftains. Caupolicán, Lautaro, Colocolo, and Rengo have truly Homeric stature and their names have retained resonance to this day.

The first colonial poet in the Portuguese language was Bento Texeira Pinto who is remembered for his epic *Prosopopéa* (1601). Here, as in Ercilla's *Araucana,* American man and American nature play the principal roles. Both works may be considered truly American even if their authors were not born in the New World.

The seventeenth century in Latin America was dominated in life and in art by a Spanish import: the baroque style. Characterized by excessive ornamentation in the plastic arts and sumptuousness and artificiality in dress and manners, it appeared in literature as *culteranismo,* a complicated stylistic obscurity, and as *conceptismo,* which refers to the complexity of concepts and sharpness of wit. *Culteranismo,* especially, also known as *gongorismo* after the Spanish poet Luis de Góngora y Argote, caught on as a literary style in the cultural centers of Latin America: Mexico City; Lima, Peru; and Bahia, Brazil. Colonial society was rigidly stratified, and this stylistically sophisticated literature was produced exclusively by and for an aristocratic class. The baroque has been persistent in Latin American literature. It reappeared with a new face in the contemporary novel in which it creates tension and paradox in imagery and translates into a rich, hedonistic use of language.

The greatest literary figure of the baroque was Sor Juana Inés de la Cruz. She was Mexican by birth and a woman of rare beauty and intelligence. She learned to read at the age of three, when she stopped eating cheese because she had heard it made people stupid. She learned Latin in twenty lessons. Because of her beauty, she was invited to live at the court of the viceroy, the Marquis de Mancera. Much impressed with her intelligence, the marquis brought forty great scholars to the court to question her on their particular subjects. Sor Juana answered all questions to everyone's satisfaction and amazement. At the age of sixteen, she entered a convent to pursue her genuine and considerable intellectual interests. Her literary achievement earned her great fame in colonial society, and she became known throughout the Spanish-speaking world as "the tenth muse." But Sor Juana had also considerable talent for empirical observation, and had she lived in a more propitious environment, she might have become the world's first woman scientist.

Sor Juana's literary production is varied, representing all the different genres cultivated in colonial Latin America: lyric and metaphysical poetry, comedies and religious plays, satirical and theological writings. Her poetry is technically skillful and reveals a personality beset by intellectual problems. It shows that she was torn not only between religious obedience and her passion for learning but also between following the *autoridades* ("authorities") or turning to the new pragmatic methods.

Among her prose writings, *The Critique of a Sermon* (1690) provoked a sensation in the Church because she had daringly criticized a sermon by the celebrated Jesuit, Father Antonio Vieira. This resulted in an exchange of letters between the nun and the bishop of Puebla, who had published her critique. Her most famous piece of prose forms part of this correspondence. *Answer to Sor Philotea* (1691) is autobiographical and explains her lifelong pursuit of learning. She defends her intellectual inclination as a God-given gift, but modern readers consider this candid self-analysis an important forerunner of feminist expression.

One great literary figure of colonial times is usually classified as a Spanish author. He was the Mexican Juan Ruíz de Alarcón, gifted as a dramatist, who became, together with Lope de Vega, Tirso de Molina, and Calderón de la Barca, an original contributor to the creation of a national theater in Spain. Today, Alarcón's comedies—he wrote twenty-five of them—are considered more modern than those of his colleagues, for he gave more importance to construction, restraint, and psychology. His masterpiece, *The Liar* (1630), was rewritten by Pierre Corneille for the French theater and became the model for Molière's comedies of manners. That this talented Creole writer had to seek his fortune in Spain is an indication of cultural domination by the mother country over its colonies. By the seventeenth century, the excitement over the conquest had subsided, and the robust Americanism that had developed earlier in Spanish America had almost disappeared.

In Brazil, on the contrary, the heroic spirit of the conquest was prolonged into the eighteenth century by the *bandeirantes*, or explorers of the hinterland, the Brazilian *sertões*. They were adventurers of the first order who audaciously and brutally fought against Indians and nature in their search for lodes of precious metals and stones. In the second half of the seventeenth century, the inland mining center of Minas Gerais became the home of the *mineira* ("miner") school of Brazilian poetry. José Basilio de Gama was its greatest representative, and his masterpiece, *The Uruguay* (1769), of lasting literary merit, describes the war of Spain and Portugal against the Paraguayan Indians in 1756. Santa Rita Durão, a contemporary of da Gama, was another important poet inspired by native elements. His *Caramurú* (1781) is the epic of Brazil. It tells the story of the discovery of Bahia by Diogo Alvares Correa about the middle of the sixteenth century.

The eighteenth century was in every way a sterile period for Spain. The country was spent as a world power, and its two-centuries-long golden age had come to an abrupt end when the last great poet and dramatist of the age, Calderón de la Barca, died in 1681. The cultural decadence was still more pronounced in the colonies; it was only toward the end of the colonial period that a few writers, influenced by the French philosophes Voltaire, Rousseau, Diderot, and Montesquieu, took up the struggle for literary emancipation. But they did not form a cohesive group. Scattered all over the huge continent, they only shared in the hardships imposed by censorship and persecution.

THE MODERN PERIOD

Literary activity almost came to a halt during the years of the struggle for independence. Instead of imaginative literature, the first quarter of the nineteenth century produced war reports and descriptions of battles. But one work, published in 1816, made a unique contribution to Latin American letters. *The Itching Parrot,* a picaresque novel by the Mexican journalist José Joaquín Fernández de Lizardi, was the first novel to appear in the Americas. Lizardi had managed to become well acquainted with the ideas of the French philosophes, and when Father Hidalgo initiated the revolutionary movement in 1810, Lizardi became an eager supporter of the struggle for independence. He founded a journal, *The Mexican Thinker,* in 1812 and became famous as a propagandist and pamphleteer. His novel was the result of censorship rather than artistic vocation. Lizardi wrote *The Itching Parrot* to express opinions that were unpublishable in the journals of the time.

The novel satirizes Mexican middle-class life on the eve of independence. The hero Periquillo (Little Parrot) is an all-around rogue who goes through every imaginable adventure in late colonial Mexico City. The novel's faithful portrayal of social life and its racy and popular language made it the most readable work of the period.

Romanticism

During the turbulent and chaotic independence years, there was a pronounced antagonism toward everything Spanish and Portuguese, and the cultures of France, England, and Germany began to exert a strong influence on the new nations. Literary groups were founded with the express purpose of encouraging a national literature. These circles were often political as well as literary and were exceedingly important in the nineteenth-century history of Latin America.

The most pressingly discussed topic in these literary circles was Romanticism, a movement encompassing political, social, and philosophical concerns as well as changes in sensibility and literary form. Romanticism was identified above all with individual freedom and nationalism. In Cuba and Argentina, literature and politics were linked through the novel. In those two countries, the genre served as a vehicle to promote a national cause. In Uruguay, the historical novel was to provide a sense of national identity. A new genre, *tradiciones* ("traditions"), based on national themes, appeared in Peru. Its creator, Ricardo Palma, combined legendary material with historical anecdotes taken from every period of Peruvian history, from preconquest times to his own. The pure-blooded Aztec, Ignacio Altamirano, pursued in his writings and teachings the cause of a national literature in Mexico. By precept and example, he showed the younger generation of writers the value of using local customs, village types, and the dramatic events of their times as literary material. Brazil's concern with national themes is notable in novels dealing with the Indian and the hinterland.

The most significant body of Romantic literature in Latin America is associated with the Rosas reign of terror in Argentina. Juan Manuel Rosas, dictator of the eastern La Plata provinces, persecuted Argentine intellectuals as his natural enemies. The writers fought back through revolutionary societies and by recording his infamies in a variety of literary genres.

First among the writers was Esteban Echeverría, who introduced Romanticism into Argentina. He had espoused the new movement while in France, and he hoped to bring about a cultural revolution upon his return to his country in 1830. But the romantic conventions he learned in Europe conflicted with American reality. In an Argentina where Rosas had established a bloodthirsty tyranny with the aid of gaucho troops, it was difficult to idealize the common people and the noble savage. Thus, in Echeverría's important works, *The Slaughter House,* a long short story, and *The Captive,* a narrative poem, he depicts the conflict between the forces of primitive barbarism and the civilized, Europeanized individual. *The Slaughter House* is an allegory of the Rosas dictatorship: Under his rule, Argentina has been turned into a veritable slaughterhouse in which the civilized person is destroyed by the forces of barbarism.

Another important Argentine writer of this time was Domingo Faustino Sarmiento, who became one of Argentina's presidents after the fall of Rosas. His *Civilization and Barbarism: The Life of Juan Facundo Quiroga* (1845) has become a classic of Latin American literature. It is first of all a biography of a gaucho *caudillo* ("strongman") who duplicated Rosas's terror in the western provinces. He was eventually assassinated by the more powerful tyrant. The book is also a study of the influence of the physical environment in shaping the gaucho mentality. A seminomadic people, the gauchos roamed the vast Pampa, fiercely independent and antisocial. Sarmiento ultimately blames the rise of strongmen like Quiroga and Rosas on the gauchos who opposed civilized life because they could not understand it.

With this work, Sarmiento captured the lasting conflict in Latin American society, between civilization and barbarism, between the law and order imposed by the city versus the lawlessness of the frontier. He was the first writer to articulate this dichotomy, one that has remained a constant in Latin American literature.

But the most original contribution of Latin American Romanticism was the gauchesque genre that derived from the songs of the gaucho minstrels who roamed the pampas of southern Brazil, Uruguay, and Argentina. The masterpiece is a narrative poem, *Martín Fierro* (1872) by José Hernández, who opposed his citified countryman Sarmiento and actively conspired against him. In politics and in literature, Hernández took the side of the gaucho *caudillo* against the city.

The protagonist of his narrative poem is a gaucho persecuted by the authorities because he represents a different view of life. Martín Fierro does not believe in the right of private property and takes justice into his own hands. His moral enemies are judges, mayors, army officers, and the police—all of them corrupt. They have destroyed his way of life. They have taken him away from his loved ones and sent him to the frontier to fight the Indians. But despite his great suffering, he retains his sense of dignity and achieves heroic stature as a champion of liberty.

Hernández imitated the speech and the manner of thought of unlettered country people and was the first writer to break down the barrier that divided the cultural elite and the masses. The poem was a huge popular success, and in time, attained the status of a thoroughly American epic independent of European norms and influences.

Many of the nineteenth-century Romantic novels were written as a result of the support writers received from literary circles formed to promote the publication of literary works and to offer encouragement and criticism. The best Romantic novel of Latin America, *María* (1867) by Jorge Isaacs, was published with financial help from the Colombian literary group El Mosaico. Jorge Isaacs was the son of an English Jew who had settled on an estate called El Paraíso in the beautiful Cauca Valley. Unsuccessful business ventures and the civil war of El Cauca ruined the family financially. Between 1864 and the year of his death, 1873, Isaacs made every effort to win back his fortune in order to own again the home of his childhood. He never succeeded, but in his novel he charmingly re-creates his patriarchal country home. *María* is an elegiac love story of two young people who enjoy an enchanting moment of happiness under the protective care of their parents and faithful servants. But María is fatally ill and dies while Efraín is in London where he has gone to complete his studies. This sentimental story, with its combination of realistic detail and delicate romantic melancholy, has enjoyed continuing success and has been more widely read than any other Spanish American novel of the time.

Realism and Naturalism

During the latter part of the nineteenth century, Romanticism began giving way to Realism and Naturalism in fiction and in drama. In Chile, Alberto Blest Gana wrote *Martín Rivas* (1862), a novel that is a social document of the times. He was one of the first writers to describe social change in Latin America. The novel portrays a poor young man from the country and parasitic lower-class city people trying to improve their situation by marrying into upper- and middle-class families. The young provincial succeeds because of his admirable qualities. Clorinda Matto de Turner became the author of the first novel of social protest on behalf of Peruvian Indians. *Birds Without a Nest* (1889) strongly denounces the exploitation of the Indians by a village priest but does not offer a viable solution to their problem. The more sordid aspects of life in Buenos Aires were the subject of the novels of Eugenio Cambaceres. *Aimless* (1885) reflects the helplessness of people in a period of rapid social change. The protagonist of the novel, having lost his traditional faith, comes to the pessimistic conclusion that "knowing is suffering: knowing nothing, eating, sleeping and not thinking of the exact solution of the problem is the only happiness in living."

Throughout the nineteenth century, and everywhere in Latin America, native dramatists amused audiences with plays depicting local types and customs. But it was only in the Río de la Plata region that a realistic drama of originality based on rustic gaucho themes began to develop in the early 1880s. This theater, featuring gaucho heroes such as Juan Moreira and Santos Vega, grew from pantomime and crude melodrama and ranged from improvised representation without scripts to written drama of an original type. The earliest and best playwright of this period was Florencio Sánchez of Uruguay, who wrote his many plays on both rural and urban themes in Argentina. He brought to the stage typical problems of the Río de la Plata region: conflicts between original settlers and new immigrants, the individual and conventional social institutions, parents and children, city and countryside. His use of Argentine dialect and native characters accounts for his great success in Buenos Aires. *Downhill* (1905), his best play, dramatizes the decline and death of an old-fashioned Creole farmer. His downfall and suicide are brought about by social change and opposition to his ways, even by members of his family. Swindled of his land and surrounded by hostility, he loses all hope and self-respect and hangs himself. The play has been interpreted as the swan song of rural Argentina.

A mixture of Realism and Naturalism was used by many novelists and short-story writers at the turn of the century. On the whole, the quality of the writing is not impressive. An important exception, however, was the work of Brazil's Machado de Assis, author of *Dom Casmurro* (1900) and a number of other highly original works of fiction. A truly sophisticated novelist, Machado was profound in his treatment of character and was a forerunner, along with Henry James, in the use of an unreliable narrator as the central figure of a novel. Dom Casmurro (whose nickname means Sir Grumpy) is an aging widower who recounts his life story since the day he fell in love, at the age of fifteen, with the girl next door. He describes his long but successful campaign to avoid the priesthood and marry his true love, a captivating girl/woman named Capitu. Once married to her, he becomes jealously possessive and ultimately destroys their marriage and his love for their son. Thus, the novel becomes an old man's justification for having exiled his wife and son forever. Because the reader has only Dom Casmurro's version and because Machado made him exceedingly convincing by endowing him not only with intelligence but with Machado's own erudition and firsthand experience of jealous imaginings, Dom Casmurro's unreliability is not usually fully comprehended. Another reason why the reader tends to accept his account is that Machado diverts attention by creating a mystery that teases the reader's curiosity: Was Capitu innocent or guilty of adultery and can the reader figure out the truth? But the mystery is insoluble because the narrator's subtle and often undetected unreliability taints all the "evidence." Rarely has an unreliable narrator been so believable in presenting not just his side of the story but a view of life that seems convincing.

Modernism in Spanish American Poetry

In poetry, the move was not so much a departure from Romanticism as a rebellion against its excesses and an assimilation of new techniques from French Parnassianism and Symbolism. This gave rise to Spanish America's most important literary innovation. *Modernismo* (Modernism) revolutionized the Spanish language and the form of poetry. It derived its greatest impetus from the publication of *Azul* (1888) by the Nicaraguan poet Rubén Darío. It was Darío who gave the movement its name and definition. Although *modernista* poets were a disparate group of individual writers, Darío saw three essential strands that bound them together: (1) the rejection of any overt message, (2) emphasis on beauty as the highest goal, and (3) the need to free verse from traditional forms. Darío became the central personality of the whole movement because of his creative example and his extensive travels in Spanish-speaking countries. His presence helped link poets of different places and gave them a sense of solidarity. He participated in the founding of many literary magazines that spread the message of Modernism all over the continent. These magazines, or *revistas,* significantly influenced the literary climate throughout the Spanish-speaking world and did much to increase the importance of literature in Latin America.

Modernismo was guided in its literary innovation principally by models from France. Spain was too traditional, but France had undergone a literary revolution represented by Romanticism, Parnassianism, and Symbolism, three schools that offered the greatest variety imaginable of techniques and poetic resources. The *modernistas* learned from these models everything they could, but their poems were far from being mechanical imitations. Their search for new poetic methods and themes led them still further into foreign literatures: English, German, Italian, Scandinavian, and Russian. From all these multifarious elements, Spanish American poets created a poetry all their own, one that was entirely new in form, vocabulary, subject matter, and feeling.

Initially characterized as an art for art's sake movement, by a cosmopolitan outlook, and as a cult of the exotic, Modernism in its later years became increasingly concerned with American themes and thus was a forerunner of what was to follow: a period of literary rediscovery of the New World. The force of the Modernists' renovation of poetry also spread to prose and has extended in contemporary times to the writers of both Spanish America and Spain. *Modernismo* was Spanish America's first original contribution to world literature and was eminently representative of the cultural life of the times.

During the same period, poets in Brazil were classified as Romantics, Parnassians, and Symbolists, although at least one poet, Joaquín María Machado de Assis, transcends these categories. His poetry resembles that of Rubén Darío, and Machado, like the Nicaraguan poet, was a writer of refined temperament who modernized Brazilian poetry.

One of the last consequences of Modernism was the emergence of feminine literature. The movement had been decidedly masculine in character. Most of the women who participated were either too conservative or too timid in assimilating the essentially innovative and revolutionary manner. But one woman, Delmira Agustini of Uruguay, can truly be called a Modernist. She carried furthest the sensuality and eroticism expressed in the poetry of Rubén Darío. In her poems, she yearns for a higher kind of love, one that would more nearly satisfy both her carnal and her spiritual needs. Her poetry has been defined as the "first spectacle in the open of a woman's heart." Delmira had many followers, the most famous among them being the Chilean Gabriela Mistral, who became known everywhere as a great humanitarian and poet. Gabriela Mistral was the first Latin American writer to receive the Nobel Prize for literature (1945).

Brazilian Modernism and Spanish American Vanguard Poetry

Brazilian *modernismo* (not to be confused with the Spanish American movement of the same name) dates from 1922, when a new poetic era was ushered in, one that broke completely with the past. It proclaimed the destruction of the old and the idea that modernity was more important than beauty itself. The extremists among these modern poets founded *The Cannibalistic Review,* which proclaimed reversion to cannibalism and destruction of everything foreign in Brazilian literature. Yet this school also produced such outstanding contemporary poets as Jorge de Lima (Negro poetry), Mario de Andrade (futuristic poetry), and Carlos Drummond (revolutionary poetry).

A new, radical poetry also came into existence in Spanish America in the years following World War I. Early practitioners of this avant-garde poetry were the now internationally famous Jorge Luis Borges (Argentina), Pablo Neruda (Chile), and César Vallejo (Peru). Vanguard poets sought their inspiration in the new isms of the day, principal among them being Surrealism. But the best of these poets eventually found their own original expression. Brazilian and Spanish American poets of our day, like contemporary poets everywhere, seek their own inner voice to faithfully and aesthetically interpret their experience in the world.

Pablo Neruda, the most prolific and widely known of the major Latin American poets, won the Nobel Prize for literature in 1971. His most ambitious work, *Canto general* (1950), is a vast and diverse epic of the American continent, a poem of patriotism and propaganda. It has also been described as a poetic version of Latin

American history. Neruda begins his history in primeval times in order to trace the tellurian nature of man. Poems on the flora and fauna, on rivers and minerals, constitute the first section. Following is a meditation on the Inca ruin of Machu Picchu and sections on the conquerors, on the geographical panorama of the continent, on Chile with its workers and peasants. The poem concludes with an address to the United States, invoking the spirit of Lincoln and condemning imperialism, and a final Whitmanesque affirmation of his life and an expression of gratitude to the Communist party. *Canto general* was Neruda's attempt to reach the common man, to express his concern for social problems, and to proclaim his faith in communism.

Credited with being the poet who made the most revolutionary break with tradition and creating the most original style in Spanish America, César Vallejo came from a modest *cholo* (part Indian, part Spanish ancestry) family from a provincial Peruvian town. In 1920, at the age of twenty-eight, he was imprisoned for 112 days on charges that included attempted homicide. During this time, he wrote some of the finest poems in *Trilce* (1922), expressing his sense of having been orphaned in a cruel world. In 1923 he left for Europe, where he joined the Communist Party and lived in poverty until his death in 1938. Vallejo invented a totally new vocabulary that included colloquialisms, neologisms, and innovative metaphors to express the anguish he (and modern humanity) felt.

Another major literary figure who began writing in the early 1930s is the Mexican poet, essayist, and critic Octavio Paz. He was awarded the Nobel Prize in literature in 1990 in recognition of his "impassioned writing with wide horizons, characterized by sensuous intelligence and humanistic integrity." His most famous essay, *The Labyrinth of Solitude,* explores beliefs and myths that structure the Mexican character but expands to include the idea of human isolation in modern society. Paz believes that myth offers the individual a way to transcend subjectivity and that poetry, too, is a way to communion. One of his most ambitious poems, "Sunstone," is composed in the circular pattern of the Aztec calendar stone and has the same number of lines as there are days in that calendar year. The circular form of the poem has the effect of unifying the contradictory aspects of experience and the self. The poem is Paz's answer to the tragic situation in *The Labyrinth of Solitude.*

Regionalism

Perhaps the most notable development in the literary panorama of the twentieth century has taken place in fiction. Novelists moved in the right direction when they chose to take a closer look at American nature and man. At first, they concentrated on the semisavage areas of the continent, the vast hinterlands of mountains, plains, and jungles, thus bringing the regions largely overlooked since conquest times to the attention of the reading public. With this renewed interest in the regional peculiarity of Latin America, the novelists discovered a genuine American theme.

One result was the novel of the *selva* ("jungle"), which was cultivated in all countries with tropical forests, from Brazil to Bolivia. *The Vortex* (1924), by the Colombian José Eustasio Rivera, became a forerunner of many novels that recognized the importance of the natural environment. Rivera, as a member of the Venezuela-Colombia boundary commission, had traveled along the great jungle rivers, lived among the Indians there, and experienced the horrors of the jungle—in which he had become lost. He wrote his only novel at the journey's end. Against the background of the vast tropical forest, which comes alive in all its beauty and savagery, Rivera deals with a sociological theme: the plight of Colombian rubber gatherers in the upper Amazon region. The setting dominates. Nature represents primeval chaos, and the men who inhabit this green hell—be they the enslaved extractors of rubber or their more "civilized" exploiters—all degenerate to the extent that they lose their human feelings and social control. The jungle is a tentacular force, attacking the mind and the body, incubating fevers that bring on hallucinations and insanity. It drives men to kill each other or to commit suicide, and those who try to escape are devoured by the forest.

The novel par excellence of the llanos, or tropical plains, is *Doña Bárbara* (1929) by Rómulo Gallegos of Venezuela. Its focus is the exposition of the traditional theme of civilization versus barbarism. Doña Bárbara is an incarnation of the lawlessness and primitivism of the llanos. She is strong-willed and dominates a band of ruthless men whom she uses to enlarge her estate. Her opponent is Santos Luzardo, a city-educated lawyer, who has to resort to violent means to defeat her. Although the novel is as powerful as *The Vortex* in its natural setting and in the violent passions nature engenders in the characters, it provides us with a view that is less pessimistic. As the ending of the novel suggests, violence can be overcome by education. Santos Luzardo educates Doña Bárbara's daughter and marries her.

The greatest of the novels in this series is *Don Segundo Sombra* (1926) by Ricardo Güiraldes. The Argentine Pampa forms the background for the adventures of a boy on the threshold of manhood. He becomes a cattle driver and reaches maturity under the expert guidance of Don Segundo Sombra, a gaucho of mythical stature. Nature is portrayed here as a blind force, and without man, it is chaotic and malevolent. To mature as a man is to learn to control nature and to control one's own nature.

The treatment accorded nature in these novels was opposite to the European concept of nature as civilized by art and literature. For the first time, Europeans found something stimulating in Latin American literature. Many novels of this type were translated into the major European languages and were influential in bringing about a change in European attitudes toward non-European cultures.

At the same time, Latin American novelists also discovered a new protagonist, rural man, who appears not as an individual but as a mass protagonist: the Indian, the mestizo, the Negro, the miner, the fisherman, the peasant—in other words, the little, forgotten people of Latin America. The outstanding example of the novel of the mass protagonist is *The Underdogs* (1915). Written during the Mexican Revolution, the novel went unnoticed until after the Revolution had triumphed. Its author, Mariano Azuela, was a physician who had participated in the fighting. He chose his hero from the anonymous mass of Mexican illiterate peasants. Demetrio Macías and each member of the band he leads in the Revolution, including the women who follow the camp, represent some aspect of Mexican society, so that characters and history form an inseparable whole. Azuela's view of the Revolution is a pessimistic one. He presents the self-interested element in society as the winner, while the peasants, because they are ignorant, fail to bring about a change in their position as underdogs.

Through the 1930s and 1940s, Azuela's numerous followers in Mexico shared his concern for the plight of Indians and peasants whose condition had hardly improved after the Revolution. Elsewhere in Latin America the picture was similar. In the Andean countries, writers exposed the exploitation of Indians and mine workers. In Chile, fishermen, dockworkers, and the lumpen proletariat received sympathetic treatment in fiction. In Brazil, novelists showed the misery of the sugar plantation workers in the poverty-stricken northeast and the helplessness and wretchedness of slum dwellers, street urchins, and blacks.

Fantasy and Magical Realism; Experimental Theater

Although fiction writing during the first half of the twentieth century was dominated by an overwhelming interest in social and national problems that were best expressed in a realistic style, there were also some early adventures in innovation. These included the aesthetic novels and short stories of Modernism and the avant-garde period as well as experimentation with psychological, philosophical, and fantastic fiction. A masterful early innovator was the Argentine short-fiction writer Jorge Luis Borges, who has become an international cult figure. Borges began his literary activities in the 1920s as an avant-garde poet. In the 1930s, he wrote his first stories, called *ficciones* ("fictions"). He achieved literary maturity in the following decade when he published his best collections, *Ficciones* (1944) and *El Aleph* (1949).

Borges's stories have no message, no social or psychological concerns. They are rather in the nature of computer programs, patterned analogously on the way the human mind works. A common theme, for instance, is that of a man caught in a trap he has unwittingly created for himself. "Death and the Compass" (1942), one of Borges's most widely read stories, illustrates this situation. The detective Lönnrot, in his effort to solve three mysterious murders, quickly discovers a pattern that shows clearly the place and time of each crime. With the help of this pattern, it is possible for him to establish where and when a fourth murder will occur. He thinks he can now trap the murderer, but when he meets him, he finds himself face to face with an old enemy who tells him that he has invented the scheme to trap and kill Lönnrot.

This story gives us a nightmarish view of man's understanding of the universe, showing how the human intellect, bent on seeking meaningful patterns and solutions, is its own worst obstacle. Most of Borges's fictions present us with such a view of the universe and with man's consistent failure to decipher it or make sense out of it. Yet his universe is not entirely nihilistic, for man has the ability to dream and to use his imagination creatively. This Borges proves with his own puzzlelike creations, which absorb our attention and thoroughly entertain us.

In the 1940s, writers everywhere in Latin America began to experiment widely with new narrative techniques. They concerned themselves with authenticity and experimented with language and literary devices. The "new" novel, or the novel since the mid-1940s, like its predecessor, is largely the result of the writers' confrontation with national problems—including the struggle between man and hostile nature—but the technique is no longer realism. Fantasy and what has been called "magical realism" (an offshoot of European Surrealism) have become weapons against dictatorship and a variety of other social ills.

The first novelist to abandon conventional realism was Miguel Angel Asturias of Guatemala, winner of the 1967 Nobel Prize for literature. His novel *El Señor Presidente* (1946), although inspired by the Guatemalan dictatorship of Estrada Cabrera, takes place mostly in the subconscious of the characters living in the nightmare of dictatorship. They express their true feelings through dreams, memories, and imaginings rather than through straightforward language that the ever-present ear of a spy might intercept. Reality is further distorted through the grotesque and the way language is used. It is thus that the novel convinces us that dictatorship is a distortion of social function.

Asturias was alone in his creative enterprise to transform objective reality in 1922 when he started writing *El Señor Presidente*. But by the time of its publication in 1946, he had been joined by a substantial group of writers. Alejo Carpentier (Cuba), Juan Rulfo and Agustín Yáñez (Mexico), Eduardo Mallea and Ernesto Sábato (Argentina), and Carlos Onetti (Uruguay) all published novels in the 1940s that incorporated a large variety of new techniques and used fantasy or magical realism. From this moment on, we can speak of "the new novel" in Latin America.

Ever since Florencio Sánchez had signaled a more serious approach to the theater by probing into the social problems of the Río de la Plata region, more and more dramatists contributed to a growing repertoire of thesis plays that "dissected" a variety of conflicts and social ills. On the whole, however, they initially failed to achieve an interpretation of Latin American life in universal terms. The change came after World War I when experimental groups, either on their own or with support from the government, began to search for new approaches and techniques, discovering in the process such important European and North American innovators as Shaw, Pirandello, O'Neill—in the 1920s and 1930s—and Sartre, Camus, Miller, Brecht, and Beckett—in the 1940s and 1950s.

Rodolfo Usigli (1905–1979), dramatist and critic, was the leading figure of the Mexican theater during three decades. In the 1930s, 1940s, and 1950s, he wrote for and about the theater and virtually single-handedly created a generation of new dramatists, among them Emilio Carballido and Luisa Josefina Hernández. The 1950s and 1960s saw an unprecedented development of the theater craft everywhere in Latin America. Such well-known dramatists as René Marqués (Puerto Rico), Egon Wolff and Jorge Díaz (Chile), Virgilio Piñera and José Triana (Cuba), and Osvaldo Dragún and Griselda Gambaro (Argentina), among others, were instrumental in revitalizing the professional stage, producing plays of universal appeal and based on sound aesthetic principles. This experimental theater has increased its ranks in recent decades with new talent, including such major novelists-turned-playwrights as Carlos Fuentes and Mario Vargas Llosa. The theater continues to be a vital force in Latin American culture today.

The Boom in Latin American Fiction

There has been some confusion in the use of the terms "new novel" and "the boom." The latter is part of the new novel, but it refers to a different period. "The boom" began in the mid-1960s and refers to the international recognition of the quality of Latin American fiction. Many of the writers who began publishing novels and short stories in the 1940s are prominent figures of "the boom."

The first book of literary criticism that called attention to the maturing of Latin American fiction was published in 1966. *Los Nuestros* by Luis Harss—the English version, *Into the Mainstream* by Luis Harss and Barbara Dohmann (1967)—discusses the ten most important authors of the new fiction. This selection is representative of the variety and geographical distribution as well as indicative of the time it took for this fiction to develop. The ten authors are from seven Spanish-speaking countries and Brazil. The oldest members of the group were born at the turn of the century, 1899 and 1900, and the youngest was born in 1936, a generation later. Two are cosmopolitan writers, four are regionalists, and the remaining four fall somewhere in between the regional and the urban, categories that are not necessarily incompatible. What all these writers have in common is that they invented a literary form that could encompass the uniqueness of their experience. By combining linguistic virtuosity with fantasy and temporal and spatial superimposition, they created a verisimilitude that the earlier realistic novelists had failed to achieve.

The cosmopolitan writers are Jorge Luis Borges and Julio Cortázar, both Argentines. Argentina, as Borges himself has stated, can only follow European tradition since it has nothing comparable to the indigenous heritage of Mexico or Peru. Cortázar, who lived for many years in France, can be considered an expatriate writer, unlike Borges who lived and wrote in Buenos Aires. Cortázar's major work is *Hopscotch* (1963), its title referring to the idea of reading as play, to the structure of the novel, and to the protagonist's search for fulfillment. The game element is apparent from the start when readers find an "Instruction Chart" telling them that *Hopscotch* is many books but principally two. One is to be read in the traditional manner and consists of chapters 1–56; the other, to be read in a hopscotch manner, consists of all chapters in an order indicated in the "Instruction Chart" (73–1–2–166 and so on). The first 56 chapters tell the story of an uprooted Argentine student, Horacio Oliveira, who lives first in Paris and later in Buenos Aires. These two sections are titled "About That Side" and "About This Side," respectively. A third section, "About Other Sides" and subtitled "Expendable Chapters," serves primarily to bring about an awareness in readers of the act of creating. Readers wishing to read the entire book will most likely choose the hopscotch manner. In this reading, they will get only patterns and events instead of a plot. Readers may even lose sight of Horacio, whose search never ends, and they will certainly never know whether Horacio has gone completely mad or whether he will finally commit suicide. The book itself has no end because the next to last chapter sends readers to the last chapter, but the last chapter sends them back to the next to last chapter, a process that can go on forever.

Miguel Angel Asturias was the first Latin American writer to transcend regionalism in the novel, to go beyond the photographic and the picturesque in order to probe deeply into the experience of the region. João Guimarães Rosa, Juan Rulfo, and Gabriel García Márquez are the other authors included in Harss's book who have contributed to the new regionalism.

The Brazilian *sertão,* the vast desert hinterland of Minas Gerais, is the setting of Guimarães Rosa's *Grande sertão: veredas* (1956). The novel contains factual information, accurate in the smallest detail, as well as insight into the psychology of the inhabitants of the *sertão* derived from observation of life and from legends and songs. The narrator and protagonist is Riobaldo, whose nickname, Tatarana, means firefly but is a euphemism for sharpshooter. Now settled on his estate, Riobaldo tells of his early adventures as a *jagunco.* The *jaguncos* were a mixed lot of individuals—outlaws, mercenaries, homeless peasants, even idealists—who fought under different political chieftains and local warlords. They were mostly violent and destructive, but when led by a man with vision, they could be a civilizing force. Riobaldo embodies this duality. He has lived life both physically and spiritually, and his memoir is replete with experience and wisdom.

Juan Rulfo's *Pedro Páramo* (1955) imaginatively transposes the deep-rooted Mexican belief in the life of the dead. The reader soon discovers that in the story of a landowner turned into a powerful *cacique* ("boss"), all the characters are dead. The story is about the Mexican's inner solitude and inability to communicate, but it also explores several Mexican myths such as the two facets of the macho myth through the characters Pedro Páramo and his son Miguel.

In *One Hundred Years of Solitude* (1967), García Márquez tells the story of the rise and fall of a town in the tropical lowlands of Colombia and of a family. Macondo, founded by the Buendía family, has its beginning in primal innocence. But though isolated, it does not remain immune to outside influences. Gypsies, civil war, the railroad, and North Americans bring the world to Macondo. In the long run, however, no real progress is made. Macondo is destroyed by a deluge that lasts four years, and the family dies out, as prophesied, when a child is born with a pig's tail, the fruit of an incestuous union. The novel depends for most of its effects on magical realism and on comic exaggeration. It brings to mind the facts that Latin America was conquered by men who had read the novels of chivalry and believed in the myths of the Fountain of Youth and El Dorado, and that on the new continent, nature was the great adversary of man.

Alejo Carpentier, Juan Carlos Onetti, Carlos Fuentes, and Mario Vargas Llosa deal with the confrontation of civilization and primitive life in Latin America and life in

Latin American cities in contemporary times. Carpentier made an original contribution when his novels broached the theme of the coexistence of primeval jungle and European civilization in the tropical countries of Latin America. *The Lost Steps* (1955) has as its protagonist a sophisticated musician who, overwrought by civilized life, is given a chance to escape it. He is sent from New York on an expedition into the Venezuelan jungle in search of primitive musical instruments. He and a band of adventurers he meets on the way discover a Garden of Eden, a spot unspoiled by man's presence, on the upper reaches of the Orinoco River. Here is an opportunity for them to start anew, to found a life based on living in harmony with the environment. But the musician abandons the experiment. Despite his alienation from the modern world, he is not able to give it up. Carpentier traces the conflict between marvelous nature and overordered society, between spontaneity and intellect, and between creative activity and everyday routine—a conflict that ultimately remains unresolved.

Juan Carlos Onetti gives us a sordid vision of Uruguayan city life. In his masterpiece, *The Shipyard* (1961), a city of his own invention, Santa María, provides the setting. The protagonist is the old and worn-out Junta Larsen, who has spent his life dealing in dubious businesses. His attempt to resurrect the defunct shipyard of Santa María is his last effort to gain for himself a measure of security. To achieve his purpose, he courts the idiot daughter of the shipyard owner, and, upon becoming the manager of the shipyard, he studies old records and supposedly oversees the work of two clerks. They had stopped doing any meaningful work a long time before. They make their living by selling off old machinery and machinery parts. In the end, Larsen must face defeat, and he leaves the shipyard only to die within a week of pneumonia. The novel expresses, as few other Latin American works do, a complete sense of futility, decay, and bitterness.

Carlos Fuentes analyzes in his works different aspects of contemporary Mexico. His first novel, *Where the Air Is Clear* (1958), has Mexico City as its central locale. A character, Ixta Cienfuegos, symbolizes the dynamism and human suffering of the metropolis and incarnates the values and myths of Indian Mexico. There is no main protagonist in the novel. Many characters' lives are woven into the texture of its narrative, and most of them are significant as prototypes, not as individuals. The novel shows the confrontation of a cosmopolitan mind with a semiprimitive country that has a whole range of institutionalized myths hiding reality and stifling authentic life. The theme is that of the Revolution betrayed. Fuentes deals even more effectively with this theme in *The Death of Artemio Cruz* (1962). Artemio, who began life as an illegitimate outcast, was able to rise to the top of Mexican society because of the Revolution and a series of successful schemes. The novel is set in the last months of Artemio's life as he lies dying in a Mexico City hospital, and the story is told from three different points of view: in the first person, stream-of-consciousness of the dying man; in the second person, Artemio's alter ego, in the future tense; and in the third person, omniscient, in the past tense. This technique allows the reader to penetrate deeply into the human psyche. In the course of the novel Artemio emerges a fully rounded figure, revealed in all his strengths and weaknesses. In both of these novels, Fuentes projects the view that man is not the maker of history but rather that he is caught up in it, with little opportunity for movement or freedom of choice.

The youngest of the authors included in Harss's book is the Peruvian Mario Vargas Llosa, who won the prestigious Seix Barral Prize for his first novel, *Time and the Hero,* in 1962. The work is based on the author's personal experience of life in a Lima military school. Here boys are encouraged to develop the false value of machismo, all-pervasive in Peruvian society. A far more difficult novel is *The Green House* (1966). It is composed of several interlocking stories and is set in the town of Piura in the northwestern part of Peru and in the *selva* in the department of Amazonas. The lives of many characters—nuns, military men, adventurers, underdogs—intersect in a nonsequential order so that the reader cannot establish a clear pattern of development or the identity of the characters. The theme of this novel, however, is similar to that of *Time and the Hero:* Civilization corrupts. The central figure, Bonifacia—also known as "La Selvática," or "Jungle Woman"—is exploited by the Church, by the army, and by modern commercialism as symbolized by the brothel called the Green House. Vargas Llosa's novel *The War of the End of the World* (1981) is curiously not about Peru but about Brazil. The novel is based on a historical event, a popular insurrection that was both revolutionary and reactionary, which took place in northeastern Brazil at the end of the nineteenth century. Through the striking intermingling of Portuguese words with the Spanish of the narrative, the novel takes us beyond the limitations set by national borders and becomes a moral and political parable of the Latin American continent.

The ten writers included in *Into the Mainstream* by no means exhaust the list of authors who have enhanced the sophistication of contemporary Latin American literature. Since 1967 numerous and equally innovative writers have joined their ranks, among them many women of the stature of Clarice Lispector (Brazil), Elena Garro (Mexico), and Isabel Allende (Chile). The writers of the present continue the tradition of linguistic experimentation initiated by the modernist and avant-garde poets who sought, and eventually were able, to liberate Latin American writers from the bonds of Spanish rhetoric and to decolonize their imaginations. Contemporary writers carry on as well with the experimentation in prose introduced in the 1940s by Asturias, Borges, Carpentier, and others, who transcended the photographic realism of an earlier period by inventing literary forms to encompass their experiences of the extraordinary and often overwhelming reality of Latin America. Brazil and Spanish America may remain underdeveloped and exploited economically and politically, but they have achieved in this century a new cultural maturity in the resonant and profound voice of their literature.

SUGGESTED READINGS

Brushwood, John S. *The Spanish American Novel: A Twentieth-Century Survey.* Austin: University of Texas Press, 1975. Traces the development of the Spanish American novel during the twentieth century. Emphasis is on works, not authors. The novel is viewed as a cultural organism; therefore, consideration is given to the cultural milieu that created a work.

Castro-Klarén, Sara, Sylvia Molloy, and Beatriz Sarlo, eds. *Women's Writing in Latin America.* Boulder, Colo.: Westview Press, 1991.

Englekirk, John E., et al. *Outline History of Spanish American Literature.* New York: Appleton-Century-Crofts, 1965. Literature is divided into three major periods in the history of Latin America. Further sectioning is made along literary-cultural lines, each section being devoted to the three principal genres of poetry, prose, and drama. The introductory summaries to these sections are fairly detailed and complete, and the author entries are essentially bibliographical.

Foster, David William. *Currents in the Contemporary Argentine Novel.* Columbia: University of Missouri Press, 1975. A study of the contemporary Argentine novel focusing on the major work of four major novelists—Roberto Arlt, *The Seven Madmen;* Eduardo Mallea, *The Bay of Silence;* Ernesto Sábato, *On Heroes and Tombs;* and Julio Cortázar, *Hopscotch.* The introductory chapter surveys the contributions of the principal novelists of the nineteenth and early twentieth centuries. The final chapter deals with future trends.

Franco, Jean. *An Introduction to Spanish American Literature.* London: Cambridge University Press, 1969. A most readable history of Spanish American literature from the conquest to the mid-1960s. Emphasis is on general tendencies, but there are references to a national context. This work can be read as a gloss of the principal literary texts.

————. *The Modern Culture of Latin America: Society and the Artist.* Rev. ed. London: Penguin Books, 1970. Although this work deals with modern culture in general, a great deal of attention is given to literature. All modern periods are discussed in detail with a special view toward the problematic nature of Latin American artistic endeavor.

Gallagher, D. P. *Modern Latin American Literature.* London: Oxford University Press, 1973. The core of this book consists of seven monographic essays on major contemporary Spanish American writers—César Vallejo, Guillermo Cabrera Infante, Jorge Luis Borges, Gabriel García Márquez, Mario Vargas Llosa, Pablo Neruda, and Octavio Paz. The introduction surveys the literature of the nineteenth century. Two additional chapters give an overview of poetry between 1880 and 1925 and of regionalist fiction.

Guibert, Rita. *Seven Voices.* New York: Knopf, 1973. The author interviews a group of notable Latin American writers—Pablo Neruda, Jorge Luis Borges, Miguel Angel Asturias, Octavio Paz, Gabriel García Márquez, and Guillermo Cabrera Infante. The discussion ranges over a wide variety of topics of concern to Latin American writers, from Che Guevara to technology as well as literature.

Harss, Luis, and Barbara Dohmann. *Into the Mainstream.* New York: Harper and Row, 1967. Based on interviews with ten representative Latin American writers identified with "the boom." The question-answer format of the interview is replaced with a narrative description of the authors and a literary analysis of their works. The introductory chapter reviews the strengths and weaknesses of traditional Latin American fiction.

Schwartz, Kessel. *A New History of Spanish American Fiction.* 2 vols. Miami: University of Miami Press, 1972. The most detailed history of Spanish American fiction from colonial times to the late 1960s. Organized according to traditionally recognized literary movements, the book contains plot synopses, critical judgment, and analytical commentary.

Sommers, Joseph. *After the Storm: Landmarks of the Modern Mexican Novel.* Albuquerque: University of New Mexico Press, 1968. An operating premise of this study is that the Mexican novel reached a new level of maturity with the publication in 1947 of *The Edge of the Storm* by Agustín Yáñez. An introductory discussion of the Mexican novel of the Revolution is followed by four monographic chapters on the novel by Yáñez, Juan Rulfo's *Pedro Páramo,* and Carlos Fuentes's *Where the Air Is Clear* and *The Death of Artemio Cruz.* Several emerging younger writers are dealt with more summarily in the last chapter.

Spell, Jefferson Rea. *Contemporary Spanish American Fiction.* Chapel Hill: University of North Carolina Press, 1944. A collection of essays on authors who are considered to be the big names of the first forty years of this century. The book provides detailed plot summaries and critical evaluations.

Torres-Ríoseco, Arturo. *The Epic of Latin American Literature.* Berkeley: University of California Press, 1961. When originally published in 1943, this literary history was the most complete work to appear on the subject in English. Covering Latin American literature from the colonial period to 1940, most of the volume is devoted to Spanish American literature; only the final chapter deals with Brazilian letters. Written with enthusiasm and an emphasis on the exotic nature of Latin American literature, the work nonetheless provides a scholarly treatment of the significant authors and the main currents and movements.

8

NATIONALISM AND MODERN LATIN AMERICAN ART

MARY GRIZZARD

Today there is often a basic disagreement about what art is and what it should do. This point is very evident if one visits art galleries in any one of the major cities of the world. There are exhibits that represent every new twist and turn of modern art. Probably the most startling thing about twentieth-century art has been its tendency to swing back and forth from one extreme to another. We are no sooner comfortable with one style or movement than a new one erupts on the scene. Thus, in the United States, the pendulum has swung from turn-of-the-century neoclassicism to impressionism, the ashcan school, the synchromists and other modern movements of the 1910s and 1920s, the regionalist and American schools of painting, abstract expressionism, pop art, minimalism and conceptualism, photorealism, new-imagism, and now to whatever is new in the galleries of New York or the West Coast.

It is therefore with something of a sense of relief that one looks at twentieth-century Latin American art and finds some consistency of purpose and focus, although still a great diversity of styles. Although one certainly finds representatives of most of the modern-art isms, or movements, in the galleries of Latin America, there is an identifiably nationalistic current in Latin American art that reflects aspects of Latin American culture—its color, its folk traditions, its history, its heroes, even its social problems.

Art in twentieth-century Latin America tends to be an extension of society—it does not exist of and for itself. Latin American artists seem never to have lost sight of the simplest and most obvious fact of all: Art is the product of a person in society, and society, therefore, is intrinsic to art's identity and purpose. A painting without some echo of humanity is a thing. It is not art. The artist does not create more objects with which to litter this globe. He or she creates symbolic projections of human realities and human ideals—or, at the very least, clues to what people want, are, or dream about.

International modernism, and art that is totally abstract, subjective, and intuitive, are foreign to the Latin American experience. From pre-Columbian to Spanish colonial times, and through the nineteenth century to the present, Latin American art has manifested a variety of styles, but it has traditionally been a narrative, representational art. The most characteristic feature of modern Latin American art is its tendency to focus on social and political issues. This feature, which tends to criticize society's ills in an effort to reform them, is called "social realism." This term refers to content rather than style. It is quite different from Soviet socialist realism, a term coined by Maxim Gorky at the Soviet Writer's Congress in 1934. Soviet socialist realism does not embrace a variety of styles and tends to result in Zdanovism, a rigidly controlled program of positive, nationalistic images done in an idealized, dry, neoclassical style.

MEXICO

The modern muralist movement was largely responsible for the momentum given to modern Mexican social realism. The muralist movement was the product of artists who viewed art in its sociopolitical context. This was almost inevitable, for they first became active artists during the immediate aftermath of the 1910 Revolution, a time of national consolidation and class realignment.

Postrevolutionary Mexican social realism, also variously known as the Mexican school or the muralist movement, consisted primarily of gigantic murals and popular graphic art. It was the primary manifestation of Mexican nationalist painting from the 1920s through the 1960s. Although the participants in this movement did not completely eschew easel painting, commercial galleries, museums, and other cultural paraphernalia of the middle and upper classes, they did generally strive to direct their explicit, didactic art to the people. Each of the participants knew that art is potentially more than a thing of beauty, that it is also a very powerful means of communicating ideas in an effort to reshape society.

Not only had the Revolution in Mexico changed the economic and political status of a great many people, it had also unleashed a tide of nationalism in reaction to the European-influenced culture of the Porfirio Díaz era. Under government patronage, muralism became a key part of the plan to reeducate the masses according to the ideals of the Revolution.

Although mass communication had also been one of the primary objectives of Spanish colonial art, the 1910 Revolution thoroughly changed the context of art in Mexican society. In the colonial period, art had been patronized and preserved primarily by the Church. This patron had imposed the most severe standards of style and content, resulting in an art that served as an educational tool. Examples of extreme originality in style or content were rare, since a standard format was expected for the purpose of providing a consistent model for teaching. With independence and the later Reform period of the nineteenth century, the state urgently needed new types of artists who could communicate its ideological program. The Academy of San Carlos, the official school for artists in Mexico City, did not produce an identifiably Mexican art in the nineteenth century. However, one does find a vigorous style, very much reflecting the sociopolitical ambience in the popular art forms, specifically among the printmakers.

A very important root of the modern, Mexican social realist movement is the country's strong tradition in graphic art, which often appeared in the poorly funded opposition newspaper, *Gaceta callejera* ("pennyrag"). The best-known newspaper illustrator of the late nineteenth century was José Guadalupe Posada, who worked for the publisher Vanegas Arroyo in Mexico City. Posada's anti-Díaz cartoons, as well as those that chronicled the rise of such revolutionary protagonists as Madero, Zapata, and Villa, are especially well known today. In Posada's engravings for the newspapers, figures were often represented as *calaveras,* or dressed skeletons, acting out parts. A famous example from 1910 (Illus. 1) shows Francisco Madero as a *calavera,* recognizable by the mustache and beard as well as by the brandy bottle he carries, for the distillery business was the source of his family fortune. The use of penny newspapers and broadsides by Mexico's prominent graphic artists as a forum for communicating socially oriented issues to the people established an important precedent that was continued by artists of the postrevolutionary period.

According to the muralist David Alfaro Siqueiros, the modern Mexican school began during 1911–1913. At that time, when Siqueiros was an art student at the Academy of San Carlos in Mexico City, students revolted against the remaining "Porfirian faculty." In place of the traditional, academic training, which included drawing the casts of antique statues, the new director, Ramos Martínez, installed in 1913, started "open-air schools" that sent artists into the communities to depict the Mexican people and to reflect their artistic traditions.

When Alvaro Obregón was inaugurated as president of Mexico in November 1920, the country entered a new era of improving the general quality of education. Government patronage of mural art became part of the program to educate the masses. Only the title and general description of the painting were specified by the government patron; the artists all employed different styles and were free to design their own compositions. Most of the credit for the Obregón administration's encouragement of muralism belongs to the secretary of education, José Vasconcelos. It was because of this patronage that Diego Rivera returned from Europe in 1921 and later painted a series of murals depicting the triumph and struggle of the Revolution on the walls of the Department of Education.

Mexican nationalistic painting flourished with this new freedom, and in 1922, artists organized the Syndicate of Revolutionary Painters, Sculptors, and Engravers. The executive committee included Siqueiros as general secretary, Rivera as secretary of the interior, and Xavier Guerrero as treasurer. José Luis Orozco also belonged to the syndicate, although he was not an officer. The painters' syndicate, only one of several peasants' and workers' organizations formed in the 1920s, had two major objectives: to abandon easel painting and to recognize that subject matter is as important as style in painting.[1]

The climate of social and economic reform during the Lázaro Cárdenas presidency fostered some of the finest products by the Mexican muralists, such as Orozco's and Rivera's paintings (both of 1934) in the Palace of Fine Arts in Mexico City. Lithography, linoleum prints, and woodcuts were also employed to defend the agrarian reform and the nationalization of the oil fields in 1938 and to combat the international threat of fascism.

The graphic artists used flyers, posters, and pamphlets and illustrated them with caricatures, *calaveras,* and representation of historic events. Theirs was not a commercial art, but an art directed to the people, to the streets. They used direct symbols, but also drew from the sentimental and the picturesque, in order to lend familiarity and recognition to their social and political satire. As seen in José Chávez Morado's lithograph *Clergy and Press* (1939) (Illus. 2), artists were vigilant against any aspect of Mexican society that threatened the objectives of social reform fostered by the revolution. But Chávez Morado did not shrink from showing some of the weaknesses of Mexican society that the people inflicted on themselves. In one of his best-known prints, *Calaveras Against the People* (1950) (Illus. 3), he showed the Mexican people fleeing from *calaveras* that bear such labels as "Black Market" and "Bribes."

Murals had shown man's place among the priests and the gods of pre-Columbian society; they had also been used in the Spanish colonial period to teach the stories of the saints and the Spanish social and religious order to the New World. The postrevolutionary Mexican muralists used a medium familiar in history, but they depicted subjects that were in keeping with the sociopolitical focus that Mexico's graphic artists had already achieved.

The dominant members of the muralist movement were Siqueiros (1898–1975), Orozco (1883–1949), and Rivera (1886–1957), or *los tres grandes* ("the big three") as they were sometimes called. Although each emphasized different aspects, they agreed on the need to represent certain didactic themes. These included the exposition of the historic struggle to achieve liberty and independence and the teaching of the ideals of the 1910 Revolution. Among the legacies of the Revolution were the glorification of the indigenous heritage of Mexico and the celebration of the modern mestizo civilization, that which resulted from a blend of Indian and Spanish peoples. In addition, several members of the muralist movement, including the big three, espoused socialist, antimilitarist, and anti-imperial views. Within this broad spectrum of agreement, Siqueiros emphasized the struggle of the working class; Orozco, the Revolution and the formation of the nation; Rivera, the Revolution and the indigenous culture.

Each of *los tres grandes* painted in a distinctive style. For instance, Siqueiros's figures in the Polyforum Cultural in Mexico City (1961) show a strong illusion of movement (Illus. 4). The telescoped positions suggest the rapid movement of sequential frames in a film. Siqueiros's images are also shown from many points of view at once. These polyangular compositions are comparable to the achievements of cubist painters, such as Picasso, in the first decade of the twentieth century. Although Siqueiros's methods of achieving the illusion of space were not new, he did combine different surface textures and materials to achieve bold, startling effects. The combination of sculpture and painting on one surface resulted in a three-dimensionality that contributed greatly to the power of his representation. The Polyforum murals, encircling an entire large room, present a complex picture of the progress of humanity through history and evolving technology toward a hopeful future.

Orozco was an expressionist who conveyed emotion by using vivid colors, vigorous lines, active composition, and when necessary, distorted figures. The results were very exciting paintings, similar in many respects to the style of German expressionists such as Max Beckmann after World War I. Orozco tended to emphasize good versus evil as universals, as in the transcendent, positive figure of the *Man of Fire* (1938–1939), Hospice of Cabañas, Guadalajara (Illus. 5). This figure in flames ascends with humanity's aspirations toward the heavens. In other sections of the vast fresco cycle in the Hospice of Cabañas, it is apparent that humanity has had much to overcome. There are unidealized representations of the pre-Hispanic culture, including sacrifices to Huitzilopochtli. Cortés is shown as a terrifying hybrid man/horse, as he must have appeared to the Indians of Mexico. Later episodes of history that are depicted include phalanxes of fascist troops and dictators wielding whips.

Rivera drew from a wide variety of sources, including the murals of proto-Renaissance Italy, cubism (particularly Picasso), Mexican folk murals (especially those of the *pulquerías*),[2] and pre-Columbian artifacts. His technique was conservative, with bold outlines containing largely flat, even colors. Among his best-known frescoes are those in the National Palace in Mexico City (1945). As in the portion of the fresco shown in Illus. 6, which depicts a preconquest view of life in the Valley of Mexico, Rivera tended to idealize indigenous culture, depicting an idyllic, ancient utopia in which no class or intertribal strife occurred. The problem with celebrating such a mythical view of the past, however well intentioned its nationalistic aims, is that the modern, native people can no longer identify with such a remote, alien culture. Also, the portrayal of exotic Indian costumes and artifacts tends to become a picturesque cliché by its frequent repetition.

By the 1950s, expository nationalistic murals were an established postrevolutionary tradition, and Mexican architects designed buildings with the anticipated need for mural space in mind. In response to the growth of a middle-class market, however, easel painting and a newer group of nonpolitical and even formalist artists developed alongside the continuing muralist tradition. Although second- and even third-generation muralists have emerged since the days of Orozco and Rivera, the majority of Mexican artists today are independents who produce easel paintings. Their work may be sometimes theoretical in concept, but they react to the times in their own ways and have never divorced themselves from their environment.

Rufino Tamayo (1899–1991) is an example of a Mexicanist who rejects the muralistic tradition and who himself does not fit exactly into any modern art movement. The shape of the animal in his howling-dog series (Illus. 7) draws as much from the pre-Hispanic ceramic Colima dogs as it does from Picasso's fragmented forms in *Guernica*. Vivid colors, a dry meridional light, and the frequent depiction of masked figures, native musicians, dancers, fruit vendors, and tropical still lifes all indicate that Mexican culture dominates his memories. On the other hand, modernity constantly thrusts its emblems into this dream: wheels, clocks, workers' tools. From this collision between mythical time and measured time, an extraordinary poignancy arises, and the best of Tamayo's works have not become dated.

Surrealism has long had a strong role in Mexican art, beginning in the 1930s with artists such as Frida Kahlo and the photographer Manuel Alvarez Bravo. Quite often the Mexican Surrealists' work contained a bitter social commentary. As an example of this, there is a Manuel Alvarez Bravo photograph entitled *Striking Worker Murdered* (1934). It is a disturbing close-up of a dead worker's body, lying at an angle on the pavement, with blood streaming from his nose and mouth. As grisly as it is, it has not lost that special visual quality of art—and belongs in a line with Mantegna's *Dead Christ* (fifteenth-century Italian) and Manet's *Dead Toreador* (nineteenth-century French). Other important Mexican Surrealists include European immigrants to Mexico, such as Leonora Carrington and Remedios Varo. Surrealism in their work especially illustrated fantasy, dreams, and imagination, as celebrated by the French Surrealist theorist André Breton in his attack on the "reign of logic" in the first *Surrealist Manifesto*. In a Mexico full of myths, *brujos,* and legendary animal-human gods, Surrealism found a receptive home. At times, a retreat to these traditions may have provided some comfort, given the bewildering reality of social and political events enveloping Mexico through the Depression, World War II, and the postwar period of rapid but unequal economic growth.

While Kahlo, Alvarez Bravo, and others never saw themselves as Surrealists, likewise there are several artists still producing in this vein today who express the same denial. Alfredo Castañeda, for example, creates beautiful, meticulously painted, hallucinatory images of persons with extra or even oddly formed body parts, set on an empty terrain. These compositions coincide with his own dream-like poetry. One cannot help but be reminded of the singular reality that myth and illusory dreams appear to have as phenomena in Mexico's cultural tradition.

The major creations of José Luis Cuevas, Francisco Corzas, Rafael Coronel, and Emilio Ortiz—those fantastic and even macabre paintings, drawings, and prints, at times viciously sardonic and farcical, which they produced between 1960 and the present—have been troublesome to many spectators, critics, and art historians since their appearance. In Francisco Corzas's painting *My Mother's Visitors* (1963), there are violent contrasts of light and dark with great dislocations and exaggerations in the shape and expression of the faces (Illus. 8). The figures in this painting, as in others by Corzas, are often received as memories of disagreeable actual situations. They recall the lonely vendors of newspapers, *chicles* ("chewing gum"), and lottery tickets— the hungry, the sad, and the despairing faces of Mexico's poor.

These and other artists with similar objectives exhibited together for a short period of time during the 1960s, when their artistic movement was known as Los Interioristas. They echo many of the themes emphasizing loneliness and the sense of tragedy in the Mexican personality that are found in Octavio Paz's *The Labyrinth of Solitude,* popular in the 1950s. Above all, these artists were shaped by contemporary social and historical forces, especially the witnessing of major urbanization, concentrated in Mexico City, which, in turn, emphasizes the growing gap between the cultural and economic lives of rural and urban areas.

Perhaps it is therefore ironic that one of Mexico's urban abstract artists, Mathias Goeritz, is acclaimed for the strong Mexican quality of his works. He came from

Germany in 1949 and found his eclectic body of abstract work rejected by Rivera and Siqueiros. Goeritz created in Mexico of the 1950s and 1960s an architecture-sculpture of an imposing gigantism, which presaged the work of North American minimalists. The sculpture by which he is best known is a piece called *The Five Towers* (1957–1985), a group of sharply angled concrete slabs in Satellite City, Mexico City. These seem to celebrate the promise of progress in Mexico's modern city centers and in its industry. Yet, significantly, the heroic scale of the buildings poignantly dwarfs and dehumanizes any human being in the vicinity.

The modern independent Mexican artists are sensitive to popular feeling, social and intellectual issues, and the function of art in their society. They have reaffirmed the Mexican tradition of a socially oriented art—a thread that has continued from the nineteenth-century Reform period's graphic art through the politically didactic muralists of the postrevolutionary period to the present day.

PERU, BOLIVIA, ECUADOR

The art of Peru, Bolivia, and Ecuador has been greatly influenced by the indigenous heritage of the large Indian populations in those countries. Peru, the former center of the Incan Empire, retains a panorama of indigenous culture, including imposing ancient ruins, "native" agricultural methods, music, costumes, dances, festivals, etc. (though often mixed with European elements). After the disastrous defeat of Peru by Chile in the War of the Pacific (1879–1883), there began a long, often politically charged, search for the "reality" of Peru. Many historians, politicians, and artists found this Peruvian reality in indigenous life and customs. At first, during the early years of the twentieth century, there was a glorification of the picturesque aspects of the native culture, as found in Riva Aguero's *Paisajes peruanos* (Peruvian landscapes) (1912–1915). As the level of poverty and suffering of the modern heirs of the Incas became more apparent, more radical studies ensued, such as *Siete ensayos de interpretación de la realidad peruana* (Seven interpretive essays on Peruvian reality) by José Mariátegui. This study, published in 1928, combined Marxism with nativism, a stance that became increasingly influential. There have also been several strong, nationalistic movements in Peruvian painting since the 1920s. Especially during the 1930s and 1940s, Peruvian art shared many of the objectives of Mexican art, including nativism, nationalism, and a tendency toward Marxism.

José Sabogal (1888–1956), born in Cajabamba in northern Peru, was the founder and first leader of the *indigenista* ("indigenous," or "native") movement in Peruvian painting. Cajabamba is a region in which Indian traditions persist, but Sabogal was also influenced by the picturesque costumbrism of the Spanish artist Ignacio Zuloaga and the nationalism of the Mexican muralists. He became director of the National School of Fine Arts in Lima between 1933 and 1943, during which time his influence on Peruvian art greatly increased; he gained many followers, including Julia Codesido, Camilo Blas, and Enrique Camino Brent. The painters who were the closest followers of Sabogal have been called *indigenistas sabogalinos* to distinguish them from the independent nativists.

Among the most interesting independent nativists is Juan Manuel Ugarte Elésperu, who was at one time much influenced by the Mexican muralists, especially Rivera. Although there has never been much demand for mural painting in Peru and most modern Peruvian works are easel paintings, Ugarte Elésperu's early masterpiece was a large fresco in the Santo Tomás School in Lima. The fresco strives to represent in a detailed, ambitious composition the past, present, and future of Peru. Ugarte Elésperu taught at the National School of Fine Arts in Lima between 1946 and 1953 and was its director from 1956 to 1973.

There is also a form of indigenism in Peruvian painting called "abstract nativism," founded by the Limeñan artist Fernando de Szyszlo. He represented in abstract form the geometric designs found in pre-Columbian textiles, ceramics, and architectural sculpture. In 1963, Szyszlo exhibited at the Institute of Contemporary Art in Lima a series of paintings inspired by a Quechuan elegy on the death of the last ruling Inca, Atahualpa. Each of the paintings in the series was named after a line from the anonymous Quechuan poem, *Apu Inca Atawallpaman.* The "search for Peruvian reality" proclaimed by writers and artists in the early twentieth century continues even in the art influenced by international stylistic trends some sixty years later.

Bolivian art was also affected by the example of *indigenismo* in Peru. The leader of Bolivian indigenism was Cecilio Guzmán de Rojas, who returned from Spain in the early 1930s under the art deco influence of Romero de Torres. This influence accounts for Guzmán de Rojas's use of hard, curvilinear outlines on human forms set in geometric, stylized landscapes (Illus. 9). His subjects were usually Indians, mountains, Lake Titicaca, and the towns of the Altiplano. Between 1935 and his death in 1950, there was little else depicted in Bolivian painting.

By 1950, the tide of Bolivian nationalism had given rise to a group of followers of Guzmán de Rojas who were also influenced by the Mexican muralists. Miguel Alandia Pantoja headed this group of artists who were particularly interested in depicting the plight of miners and agricultural workers. In Sucre, a politically motivated group of artists formed an organization called ANTEO, led by Solón Romero. Inspired by the example of Diego Rivera, the group painted murals on the telephone building and at the San Francisco Xavier University.

The beginning of the 1950s also saw the disappearance of traditional liberal and conservative parties and the emergence of Marxist and other worker movements. The accompanying strong surge of nationalism resulted in agrarian reform and nationalization of the mines. Realizing that state promotion of the arts could further the cause of Bolivian nationalism, the government sponsored the first Salon Pedro Domingo Murillo in 1952 as a national forum for Bolivian artists.

As might be expected, Ecuadoran art also has many similarities with that of Peru, since both countries have large indigenous populations and have experienced a long, polemical search for national identity. Several Ecuadoran *indigenistas* especially well known, not only in Latin America but in Europe and North America as well, are Camilo Egas, Bolívar Mena, Diógenes Paredes, Eduardo Kingman, and Oswaldo Guayasamín.

Camilo Egas began as an academic painter, but early in his search for national expression he was influenced by the example of the Mexican muralists. He was for a time also influenced by surrealism, as is seen in his painting *Dream of Ecuador* (1939). The ground is barren, scattered with shabby huts, populated by emaciated peasants. Egas's paintings, which are often allegories of despair, are credited with popularizing the indigenist movement in Ecuadoran art.

Eduardo Kingman was long the leader of the indigenist movement in Ecuador, especially during the 1940s and 1950s. His first important recognition came in 1936 when he won the Mariano Aguilera Prize, the country's highest artistic award. He was later the founder and director of the Caspicara Art Gallery in Quito, director of the National Museum of Art, and director of the National Artistic Patrimony. He was influenced by the Ecuadoran *indigenista* novelists, such as Jorge Icaza, and by the example of nationalism and nativism in the work of the Mexican muralists. In Kingman's painting *Los Guandos* (1941), the tyranny of unjust labor practices is apparent, as the foreman cracks a whip over the backs of the Indians who are already bent double under the weight of an enormous cargo (Illus. 10).

Eduardo Kingman continued the *indigenista* theme through his later works, but adopted a very powerful form of expressionism that uses dark, angular lines and vivid colors to convey the force of its feeling. A recent work of his (1983) (Illus. 11) celebrates the victory of the Battle of Pichincha (May 24, 1822). It is a huge outdoor mural that covers the entire side of El Templo de la Patria, located on the side of Mount Pichincha, overlooking Quito. The mural may be seen from the city, and highlights Atahualpa, Eugenio Espejo, and the 1809–1810 Junta of Quito, which ultimately proclaimed independence. Spread magnificently below the above figures is a massive pair of indigenous, copper-colored hands, which break apart heavy chains.

Oswaldo Guayasamín, eight years younger than Eduardo Kingman, became well known in the United States during a State Department–sponsored tour during 1942–1943. He won the Mariano Aguilera Prize the same year and also traveled to Mexico where he met Orozco, with whom he worked for three months. After 1942, Guayasamín's style evolved into the synthesis of influences from Orozco and Picasso by which we recognize his work today. After a tour of several countries in South America in 1944–1945, he produced the series of paintings entitled *Path of Tears* (1952), which laments the difficult life of the underprivileged throughout the world. An extension of this series is represented in his set of paintings *Age of Anger,* which was exhibited in Mexico and several cities of Europe during the 1960s. Among his most recent works are two murals in government buildings in Quito. One is a large mural entitled *El mural Ecuador* (1980), sponsored by the Provincial Council of Pichincha. It is composed of several separate panels representing the stoic faces of Ecuador's national heroes, such as the Inca Atahualpa, and the eighteenth-century nationalist leader Eugenio Espejo. Other panels depict geometricized, anonymous faces and torsos wrenched into expressions of agony. Near the center are a jack-booted, military dictator (Illus. 12) and a bearded, helmeted Spanish *conquistador.* The subject is an amplification of an earlier theme by Guayasamín: the suffering of the indigenous Ecuadoran people throughout history. In a more recent mural (1988) in the Ecuadoran Congress of Quito, there is a similar montage of the social and political history of Ecuador.

COLOMBIA AND VENEZUELA

Although abstract art is not unimportant in Colombia—the work of Eduardo Ramírez Villamizar in painting and of Edgar Negret in sculpture would prove otherwise—the two most influential artists in Colombia today are neofigurative painters. The influence and fame of Alejandro Obregón and Fernando Botero have emphasized the importance of representational painting in Colombia.

Obregón, the older of the two artists, was born in Barcelona in 1920. He continues to live in the Colombian town where he grew up, the seaport of Barranquilla, and his paintings are rich in anecdotes from that environment. There are repeated images of Colombian flora and fauna, condors and cocks, bulls and iguanas. Some of his work has strong sociopolitical overtones, such as the *Mourning for a Dead Student* (1956). Despite the seriousness of the theme, the painting contains semiabstract representations of several of Obregón's favorite Colombian emblems: a bird, flowers, and tropical fruit.

Fernando Botero, born in Medellín, Colombia, produces paintings that have much in common with the work of Latin American writers of the magic realism movement. As the Argentine critic Enrique Anderson has said, "magic realism does not show magic as if it were real, but reality as if it were magic." Botero paints the parochial Colombian middle class, a class composed of businessmen, professionals, generals, and politicians. In this class, there are no extravagant luxuries or terrible tragedies, but time to enjoy family gatherings and long, relaxed dinners. It is a calm, peaceful world, which none of its inhabitants would think of disturbing. His paintings of activities in this placid world may be considered social criticism, but Botero's gaze never trivializes or demeans his subjects to the point of vulgarity. In Botero's painting *Junta militar* (1971), which is more real, the monumental personages or, wheeling above them, the tiny, astonishingly veristic flies? Which is the president's family, the two generals and the clergyman or the diminished figures of the wife and child? Who is playing the game, the father in military uniform or the child, also in uniform, who believes in the reality of his own game?

Although Latin American art is often mistakenly perceived as an undifferentiated whole, it is, in fact, a complex amalgam of different styles, approaches, and concerns. The art of Venezuela demonstrates a wide variety of styles and objectives, but a vital form of expression that has undergone a revival in recent years is realism. Venezuelan realism, however, is more lyrical than that of many other Latin American countries and often displays the spirit of fantasy.

The first internationally acclaimed Venezuelan realist of this century was Armando Reverón (d. 1954), an eccentric recluse who lived in the coastal town of Macuto. His studio was populated with large rag dolls, for which the artist made clothes, furniture, and musical instruments. His paintings often depicted the surrounding Venezuelan landscape, as well as these rag dolls, in a style influenced by the French impressionists.

The neofigurative movement in Venezuelan art continues to draw many followers. It is perhaps surprising that the currently best-known artist, who depicts contemporary Venezuelan racial types, local urban and rural scenes, as well as religious subjects, emigrated to Venezuela from Czechoslovakia in 1949. Guillermo Heiter combines expressionism and cubism to depict the faces and colors of the Caribbean. Although he has depicted people and communities of all social classes, his most acclaimed works are industrial urban scenes such as *Cranes,* a semiabstract composition of verticals and horizontals. Such paintings express the rapid commercial and urban development associated with Venezuela's petroleum industry.

HAITI AND CUBA

There was no national movement of painting in Haiti until the Center of Art opened in Port-au-Prince in 1944. Before the existence of this art center, there was no encouragement or recognition of artists, no systematic training, and no outlet for Haitian art. A North American painter, Dewitt Peters, filled this void by establishing the Center of Art in a large old building in the capital.

Since that time, Haiti's popular art movement has gained momentum and has become one of the richest national expressions in Latin America. It is much influenced by Haiti's rich folklore and the vital African element of voodoo. The strongly geometrized, blocky figures that populate the canvases of Haitian painting stem in part from the *vêver,* a voodoo geometric design traced on the ground. The *vêver* is essential to the voodoo ceremonial rites and is used to invoke particular divinities. Many of the subjects in Haitian painting are identical to those in the *vêver,* but one also sees its influence in the flat, symmetrical compositions and the linear, simplified outlines of the figures. All of these are characteristics of folk art in general, but certainly not to the degree of development that one finds in Haitian art.

Most prominent in Haiti's popular national art movement are the so-called primitive, or naif, painters, whose style is described above. Of these, the late Hector Hyppolite is probably the most famous, in part because he was also a voodoo *hougan* ("priest") whose art depicted supernatural aspects of his religion. Before his death in 1948, his paintings were praised in a UNESCO exhibit in Paris. Other primitive painters, such as Philomé Obin, are popular realists who draw their inspiration from their native rural backgrounds.

The accepted masterpiece of Haitian primitive art is the mural cycle at the Episcopal cathedral of St. Trinité in Port-au-Prince. Among the artists who contributed to these murals were Philomé Obin, Castera Bazille, and Wilson Bigaud. Bigaud (Illus. 13), who won recognition at the Center of Art, is a self-taught artist whose *Miracle at Cana* covers 528 sq ft (49 sq m) in the St. Trinité mural cycle. The cycle is especially noteworthy for the depth of spirituality that it conveys, a characteristic that is also the heart and soul of Haitian music and dancing.

In 1950, a group of painters broke away from the primitive-style national Haitian art movement associated with the Center of Art and founded the Plastic Arts Gallery (Foyer des Arts Plastiques). The chief encouragement and inspiration for the non-primitives came from Europe. It is significant that three of the leading semiabstract and abstract "international" artists—Luce Turner, Roland Dorcely, and Max Pinchinat—have lived in France for several years. Proof of the vitality of Haitian art is the fact that primitive, popular art continues to flourish amid the many modern art movements represented in the Plastic Arts Gallery.

The strains of patriotism and indigenous identity that began in the representation of folklore, social classes, and political caricature in such countries as Ecuador and Mexico found their continuation in the most pronounced nationalistic medium of Cuba, the poster. Previously, Cuban commercial posters, especially those advertising beverages, cosmetics, and the cinema, were imported from the United States and bore the imprimatur of the northern culture. Since the Revolution, Cuban artists and designers have produced posters for domestic use as well as for export to other Latin American countries. In Cuba, the poster industry is under the supervision of the revolutionary government, which seeks to diffuse its cultural viewpoint by using a medium that is readily accessible to all levels of society. A study of the Cuban poster is, in effect, a study of a contemporary living chronicle of the views of the Revolution. Although few of the posters are signed, the most unified, collective group has been done by members of the Cuban Institute of Art and Cinematographic Industry (Instituto Cubano de Arte e Industria Cinematográfica), who have produced many of the archetypal Cuban iconographic forms. In this institute are two of the most important producers of popular Cuban imagery, the graphic artist Alfredo Rostgaard and the painter Raul Martínez. The latter has developed a very successful and unusual style, based on colonial reminiscences as well as on modern imagery, which draws heavily on the influence of the Mexican muralists. Two main themes emerge in Cuban poster art: portraits of Cuban heroes such as José Martí, Fidel Castro, and Che Guevara and the images of unidentified people who represent the aspirations of the masses.

This chapter is but a brief introduction to the iconography and style of the art of Mexico and some of the countries of South America and the Caribbean. It is the strong appeal to nationalism, to indigenous identity, or to the potential for massive social reform that links the twentieth-century Latin American art movements.

Latinos in the United States

It might be said that Latin American cultural contributions are not confined to artists living and producing in their respective native countries, for there is now a phenomenon that might be described as a Latin American diaspora, which is changing the nature of North American society.

Substantial numbers of persons of Latin American origin are moving to the United States and forming communities in certain specific urban areas. The leading metropolitan areas of intended residence for Latinos include New York; Los Angeles–Long Beach; Chicago; Miami-Hialeah, Florida; Washington, D.C.–Maryland–Virginia; Orange County, California; and Boston-Lowell-Brockton, Massachusetts. Particular national groups favor certain areas; for instance, according to the Immigration and Naturalization Service, more than seven out of every ten Mexican immigrants live in either California, Texas, or Illinois, and over 84 percent of all Cubans admitted to the United States in 1995 intended to reside in Florida, where already 24 percent of the state's residents were registered as having been born in Cuba. (All figures are official Immigration and Naturalization Service statistics for 1995.)

Similarly, there are large communities of immigrants from El Salvador who have settled in Queens, New York, and in the Maryland–northern Virginia area, as well as in Washington, D.C. As it has been for the past several decades, in 1995, Mexico was the leading source country for both legal and illegal immigrants to the United States. In the same year, 12.5 percent of the total of legal immigrants to the United States were from Mexico. Of the estimated 3 million illegal Mexican immigrants, only about 300,000 are recorded as staying in the United States each year, which means that traditional migratory patterns are continuing, with persons crossing and re-crossing the border several times. From these figures we may conclude that there are large Latino communities in the United States, thus amplifying our connection with Latin America, especially with Mexico.

The cultural contributions these immigrant communities bring is obvious to any-one who has read recently published literature and periodicals, attended street festivals, eaten in restaurants, conversed with persons in the communities, and attended concerts and art exhibitions. In a recent exhibit entitled *Ceremony of Spirit: Nature and Memory in Contemporary Latino Art (1993–96)*, which began in the Mexican Museum in San Francisco and traveled throughout the United States for several years, works included those by sixteen artists from origins such as Brazil, Chile, Cuba, Mexico, Panama, Puerto Rico, and the southwestern United States. All artists were living and working in the United States. The works centered on spirituality and the struggle to maintain cul-tural identity in the United States. According to the show's curator, Amalia Mesa Bains, "Spirituality becomes an ultimate act of resistance against cultural domination" (*Ceremony of Spirit* [San Francisco: Mexican Museum, 1993], p. 9).

The pieces in the exhibit collectively assert that art may form a kind of "social imagination" by which a gap in one's knowledge of the past may be filled. When per-sons of Latino, Chicano, and Caribbean origins are living in the United States, in a society different from that of their ancestors, the broken thread of continuity with their ancestral past may be regained through a kind of spirituality centered in certain cultural symbols, represented in art. The idea is that one's *antepasados,* or ancestors, lived with an awareness of certain symbols and even a sense of spirit that must be taught to today's descendants in order to maintain continuity.

Several of the depictions in the exhibit relate to religious imagery and to genealogy. Through tracing genealogy, there are a series of ancestral mother figures, but as cul-tural symbols there are those which have bridged the Mexican/Chicano worlds: the Madre de México, Tonantzín (Nahuatl for "mother"), and the Virgin of Guadalupe. As the writer Zamudio-Taylor says, "Tonantzín/Guadalupe has functioned historically as an emblem of struggle and identity. From the rebellions against taxation in Colonial Mexico, independence from Spain, social change in the Mexican Revolution to the struggles from economic and social justice of the U.S. Southwest, Tonantzín/ Guadalupe has been approached for sustenance and solace" (Victor Zamudio-Taylor, *Ante América* [Bogotá: Biblioteca Luis Ángel Arango], p. 145).

One of the paintings in the *Ceremony of Spirit* exhibition is by a Chicano from Laredo, Texas, named César A. Martínez. It is a wooden triptych, a three-leafed wooden *retablo,* or altarpiece, depicting a modern conflation of images: human handprints, the pre-Columbian mother goddess Tonantzín, and an empty outline of the Virgin of Guadalupe. The latter is an image revered since the colonial period in Mexico, recognizable by the crescent moon below; the rays of light surrounding the figure; her blue, starry cloak; and the outline of her crowned head. The human hand-prints are aligned in such a way that the viewer's face would have to be directly con-fronting the empty space where the Virgin of Guadalupe should be. The interpreta-tion of this may be that the connection with such images is not static but continuous, with the present-day spectator forming part of that continuum. It is im-plied that both the viewer's face and handprints form a part of the image. Identity of the present and the past are thus linked.

Such is the reach of Latin American cultural identity and political expression through art that now its presence must be recognized in North America as well.

NOTES

1. For a statement of their objectives in the manifesto, see Bernard Meyers, *Mexican Painting in Our Time* (Oxford University Press, New York, 1956), p. 25.
2. Rural beer halls.

SUGGESTED READINGS

Arguin, Florence. *Diego Rivera: The Shaping of an Artist.* 1971. A general biography and artis-tic history of Rivera.

Art in Latin America. The Modern Era, 1820–1980. Exhibition catalogue by Dawn Ades. The Hayward Gallery, London. 18 May to 6 August 1989. The South Bank Center.

Atl, Dr. *Como Nace y Crece un Volcan.* 1950. A profile of the early days of the muralists and Mexican revolutionary politics by Gerardo Murillo (Dr. Atl), one of the ideologues of the group.

Charlot, Jean. *Mexican Art and the Academy of San Carlos, 1785–1915.* 1962. The role of the primary school for Mexican artists during the crucial pre- and postrevolutionary years.

———. *Mexican Mural Renaissance.* Primarily a history of the early period of the muralists in the 1920s.

Fondo de Cultura Económica. *La pintura mural de la revolución mexicana.* 1967. Especially valuable for the plates.

Helm, Mackinley. *Man of Fire: J. C. Orozco.* 1971. A general biography and artistic history of Orozco.

Mérida, Carlos. *Modern Mexican Artists.* 1968. Contains short biographical sketches of twenty-five Mexican artists.

Murillo, Gerardo. *See* Atl, Dr.

Reed, Alma. *The Mexican Muralists.* 1960. A general survey of the muralists and their politi-cal objectives.

Rodríguez, Antonio. *A History of Mexican Mural Painting.* 1969. A general survey of the mu-ralists; good plates.

Schmeckebier, Laurence. *Modern Mexican Art.* 1971. A brief general survey.

Siqueiros, José David Alfaro. *Alfaro Siqueiros.* 1968. Autobiography of Siqueiros; especially in-teresting for the views of artists on politics.

Illustration 1 (*left*). *Madero as a Calavera* (1910), José Guadalupe Posada.

Illustration 2 (*above*). *Clergy and Press* (1939), José Chávez Morado.

Illustration 3 (*below*). *Calaveras Against the People* (1950), José Chávez Morado.

Illustration 4 (*above*).
Mural in the Polyforum
Cultural (1961), David
Alfaro Siqueiros.

Illustration 5 (*right*). *Man
of Fire* (Hospice of
Cabañas) (1938–1939),
José Luis Orozco.

Illustration 6 (*above left*). *Tenochtitlán* (National Palace) (1945), Diego Rivera.

Illustration 7 (*above right*). *Howling Dog* (1942), Rufino Tamayo.

Illustration 8 (*below left*). *My Mother's Visitors* (1963), Francisco Corzas.

Illustration 9 (*below right*). *Mujeres Indias en Llojera* (1946), Cecilio Guzmán de Rojas.

Illustration 10 (*above*). *Los Guandos* (1941), Eduardo Kingman.

Illustration 11 (*left*). Mural on El Templo de la Patria, Quito, Ecuador (detail) (1983), Eduardo Kingman.

Illustration 12 (*right*). Military dictator (detail) in *El Mural Ecuador* (1980), Oswaldo Guayasamín.

Illustration 13 (*below*). *Papa Zaca* (1949), Wilson Bigaud.

PART FOUR
ECONOMIC AND
SOCIAL STRUCTURES

9

THE LATIN AMERICAN ECONOMIES RESTRUCTURE, AGAIN

WILLIAM P. GLADE

Recent years have brought a lively interest in Latin American economic restructuring, both on the part of the policy community in the countries involved and by scholars, development experts, and journalists who in their respective ways are concerned with studying and reporting on what is happening. If this literature does not yet amount to an equivalent of the Harvard 5-foot shelf of books that decorated so many American homes earlier in this century, it may soon exceed that number of linear feet—even if it never acquires the cachet of the older volumes as a documentation of household literacy.

It almost defies good judgment to try to compress into one short essay the complexity and variety that currently characterize the Latin American economies, which range from the semigiant dimensions of an economically dynamic Brazil, the eighth largest GDP in the world, to tiny and deeply impoverished Haiti, which ranks among the poorest nations of the world and is of negligible importance to anyone but Haitians. Just about every combination of size and income level and, correspondingly, structure of national production can be found in between—along with an exceedingly complicated medley of geographical and climatic conditions. Nevertheless, with the exception of Haiti, Honduras, and Nicaragua, the countries of the region have at least made it out of the poorest category in the World Bank's four-category classification scheme and are more or less firmly ensconced in the lower middle income and upper middle income categories.[1]

Performance, recently as well as historically, has been no less varied, though all the countries have since the 1970s been outdistanced in this respect by Asian "tigers," both old and new. It might seem foolhardy to inject an historical dimension into what is unavoidably an already overly baroque narrative of development and back-

Table 9.1
Economic Dimensions of Selected Latin American Countries, 1994

	GDP ($ million)	Population (millions)	GNP Per Capita ($)
Brazil	555,000	159	2,970
Mexico	377,000	89	4,180
Argentina	282,000	34	8,110
Chile	52,000	14	3,520
Uruguay	16,000	3	4,660
Colombia	67,000	36	1,670
Peru	50,000	23	2,110
Venezuela	58,000	21	2,760
Ecuador	17,000	11	1,280
Guatemala	13,000	10	1,200
Costa Rica	8,000	3	2,400
Haiti	1,623	7	230
Honduras	3,333	6	600
Nicaragua	1,833	4	340

Source: World Bank, World Development Report 1996.

wardness, but since what one sees today is very much an accumulation of institutional overlays from consecutive episodes of systemic reorganization, a quick romp through the centuries may be the most effective way to reach our central objective: that of understanding the problems that today vex the countries of the region, along with the exceptional opportunities that have led young investment bankers, perhaps rashly, to "enthuse" about its emerging—and reemerging—markets. Let us hope that Böhm Bawerk's faith that roundaboutness increases productivity applies to this short digression.[2]

THE PARADE OF RESTRUCTURINGS

The current episode—which the Inter-American Development Bank has rightly labeled a silent revolution in economic policy—is only the latest of five restructurings that have been visited on the region since the arrival of Columbus and his crew. Something remains of each of these in the contemporary economic landscape, and from the second restructuring onward, those advocating new policies have thoughtfully left us a diagnostic interpretation of what went before. Taken together, these recognizably edited versions of economic history are immensely helpful in piecing together a record of how the region got to where it is today.

The first "structural adjustment" began when the Spanish replaced sundry indigenous economic systems with one that was more in accord with imperial aspirations and European norms.[3] What emerged was a bureaucratically administered and intricately regulated system that brought under royal direction an ensemble of new local and regional economies, dispersed over a far vaster and more challenging territory than any European monarchy had yet tried to govern. It was in effect an integrated trading territory larger than any that has been cobbled together in more recent times in Latin America.

Agriculturally based, the economy was in time organized by a growing latifundism that defied stated royal objectives and was hastened in its expansion by demographic and other factors: for example, a steep decline in the native population from exposure to European diseases, the regrouping of indigenous peoples for ease of governance and a limited acculturation (which process vacated customary occupancies), a fundamental incompatibility between pre-Columbian land claims and those based on European custom, the need to devote much acreage to the production of food crops for the Spanish towns and cities and to pasturage for the draft animals on which the colonial transport system rested, and the ever present attempts of settlers to lay hold of the huge expanse of land claimed by the crown and often poorly defended by the royal bureaucracy. Private estates of considerable size eventually became the basic unit in agriculture, displacing some of the community-held lands the crown had reassigned to the indigenous population, and over the centuries church institutions also became owners of extensive landholdings, often the best managed in the colonies. Inasmuch as land was the fundamental productive resource in an agrarian economy and the source of livelihood for the overwhelming majority of the labor force, the evolution of this pattern of land tenure in effect established an inequality system the vestiges of which have persisted to the present.[4]

Trade, among the urban centers of Spain's overseas kingdoms and between them and Spain itself, was a major activity, closely supervised by the crown to ensure the collection of the taxes that formed the bulk of the structure of public finance, and there grew up a considerable number of artisan manufactures, based on both indigenous and Spanish craft technologies. These, too, were regulated by royal and municipal ordinances and, in the case of the nonindigenous craftsmen, by guild regulations—except where larger workshops, known as *obrajes,* developed. Capital for settlement and other purposes was supplied by the public sector, merchant financiers, and, above all, ecclesiastical institutions. The technological stagnation that was perpetuated in agriculture, mining, and manufacture by this imperially sheltered system of production had its institutional counterpart in the astonishingly stunted development of the financial sector, where nothing remotely resembling the contemporary European developments could be found—leaving the region singularly ill equipped to venture onto the territory of capitalist economic organization when Spain's empire came to an end.

The ambitious imperial enterprise was punctuated by the establishment and growth of important mining centers that supplied treasure for the Spanish crown and its never-ending dynastic wars in Europe, nourished an administrative machinery that grew in size and complexity as the centuries passed, and salted huge amounts of bullion amongst the European suppliers who furnished the New World its luxury imports. Even more important in many respects was the heavy and continuing investment of the New World economy's resources in the construction of urban centers and their linkage by costly transport networks, so that Spanish government, society, and culture—all of which could be considered analytically as produced public goods—could take root and prosper in the American setting.

A quadruple legacy, therefore, was bequeathed to Latin America from the colonial period. Local political organization was arrested by Spanish bureaucratic centralism, so that the insurgents who threw off Spanish rule had no real experience in self-government to draw on as they set about devising their new republics. Technological backwardness was pervasive, shielded as Spanish America had been from the exchanges of goods, services, and technologies that propelled the European economies toward modernity. Organizational or social capital remained little changed from the sixteenth and seventeenth centuries—at a time when the commercial revolution was reshaping the institutional architecture of Europe (and North America). And perhaps most nefarious of all, a foundational system of inequality came into being that was to continue to the present, so that a pronounced inequality in the distribution of wealth and income (and access to the opportunity structure) has been a dominant characteristic of Latin America ever since.

The second restructuring, which was launched in the eighteenth century by the Bourbons, sought a modest liberalization of trade, a revivification of the American production system, and greater efficiency in the administration of the imperial enterprise—objectives not too distant from those that are motivating today's structural adjustment programs. What is mainly interesting for our purposes, however, is that this second restructuring occasioned a considerable amount of analytical reflection on the conditions then prevailing in Spain's overseas kingdoms, both to diagnose ills and prescribe remedies. Indeed, from the economic writings of the Spanish mercantilists, who were surprisingly sophisticated in their understanding of economic processes, and the commissioned reports of special reconnaissance missions, of which the tour by Alexander von Humboldt may be the best known, we catch more than a passing glimpse of what needed to be done, and why, to remedy the accumulated weaknesses of the colonial economy.[5] Though the second restructuring program was only very partially implemented, it seems to have had a generally positive impact, as revealed by the quickening tempo of economic life as the eighteenth century drew to a close. The institutional architecture laid down by the first restructuring, however, remained very much in place.

A sidelight to this period, of more than passing interest, was the divergent growth path taken by Brazil, which virtually from the outset was conceived by the Portuguese as a commercial venture, supplementing the trading opportunities their earlier voyages along and around the African coast to Asia had opened up. There being no traded goods ready for the picking, however, commercial viability required the transfer to northeastern Brazil of the sugar plantation technology the Portuguese had developed on islands in the eastern Atlantic. When the native labor supply proved insufficient (the indigenous population was quite sparse compared with

Mexico, Guatemala, and the Andean highlands), manpower, in the form of slaves from Africa, had to be imported to run the enterprise. The high initial fixed costs this entailed ensured that earning a return on the sunk investment in labor supply would motivate plantation owners to extract an exportable surplus for sale to European markets.

Apart from northeastern Brazil, where the colonial capital was located, the rest of the colony served mainly to supply the plantation economy with a simple range of commodities, until the eighteenth century brought a mining boom in east central Brazil and pulled population southward, giving an additional impetus to growth in regions previously quite marginal, making Rio a more important port, and shifting the labor regime away from slave labor. The mining boom served also to reinforce the export orientation of the Brazilian economy and to consolidate its trading ties with the commercial network the Portuguese had constructed in Europe, including, not least, with Portugal's ally Great Britain.

The third restructuring, a much more ambitious enterprise than the second, arrived after the half-century hiatus of economic dislocation that beset the region with the arrival of independence, from which Brazil and Chile were the principal exceptions. The economic wreckage of the aftermath of independence—the wiping out of most artisan manufactures by cheap factory-made imports from Europe, the wholesale neglect of public investment in infrastructure, repeated defaults on external debt (both public and private), the chronic plundering of enfeebled fiscal systems by political adventurers, the removal of royal and clerical safeguards against exploitation of the indigenous population, the rape of the public domain, and the instability in the policy framework—all had composed a scenario very different from what the fighters for independence said they had in mind when they chased out Spanish bureaucrats. Public finances were a shambles, high risk levels undermined the investment environment, and a region now hitching its fortunes to the increasingly vibrant international economy did so bereft of even the rudimentary banking institutions needed to mobilize and allocate resources in the increasingly monetized capitalist system that was spreading out of Europe. In a sense, the third restructuring, launched when the political picture finally settled down a bit, was a bold remediation for this half century of failure.

To the disarray that prevailed in Spanish America up to the third restructuring, Brazil was again a contrast, providing a favorable climate for the germination of the new economic system that in time spread over the whole of Latin America, albeit unevenly. Owing to circumstances in Europe, the Portuguese court moved to Brazil to escape Napoleon and, when it finally returned to Lisbon, left behind an emperor to take charge of an independent Brazil that was governed from Rio, the city to which the court had fled under British protection. Thanks to the close commercial and political ties the new country inherited from its metropole with the center of the industrial revolution and to the effortless way it attained independence, Brazil was spared the turmoil that proved so costly elsewhere on the continent. And with the climate for economic modernization undisturbed by political change, the way was laid for a third dramatic export boom.[6] This time the product was coffee and the lo-cation was in the south of the country, so that the rapid spread of coffee cultivation on Brazilian-owned plantations around São Paulo triggered an explosion of eco-nomic expansion in this previously frontier region, based on a free labor force, the attraction of substantial capital and immigration from Europe, and the stimulation of capitalistic development throughout the south of the country.

From around 1870 to 1930, the third restructuring, which centered on the devel-opment of export economies, came to Spanish America and paid off handsomely for those not trapped by the inequality systems that had developed after 1492. As in Brazil for the whole of the nineteenth century, two engines of growth—the produc-tion and sale to world markets of a growing variety of primary commodities and the influx of foreign capital that made the export production system possible—propelled Latin America into the modern economic arena and transformed the economic dy-namics of the region. Even more than the second restructuring, this project antici-pated some of the main features of the so-called Washington consensus,[7] the chief difference being that there was no stable of deficit-generating public enterprises to privatize. Trade liberalization and the creation of a climate favorable to investment, both domestic and foreign, proved to be the foundations of the new economic order.

The third restructuring was an institution-building period par excellence as most of the organizational accoutrements of modern capitalism appeared around the con-tinent, carried to all the principal urban centers, and in some cases beyond, by the vectors of modern transport and communications systems. Commercial banks, ship-ping companies, firms specialized in new legal and accounting transactions, engi-neering firms, portworks, new railway, street railway, and telecommunications com-panies, smelters, capitalistically organized mining companies, insurance companies, plantations using narrow-gauge railways and steam-engine-powered refineries, and a slew of other enterprises provided the social or organizational capital on the basis of which Latin America belatedly joined the modern economy of the West and began to generate, or attract, the human capital needed to keep the ensemble in operation. Harbingers of a new age of factory production also sprang up here and there, fol-lowing the needs of export-fed markets and new structures of production. Most of the new manufacturing was, naturally enough, of consumer goods, but foundries, smelters, and machine shops were indicative of the possibilities for industrial deep-ening, and around the turn of the century the first integrated iron- and steelworks appeared in Monterrey, Mexico.

Over much of the region, these new developments occurred in scattered enclaves, for growth was markedly uneven. Interregional disparities came to be immensely greater than they had been in earlier times, setting the stage for the notorious un-evenness of development that characterizes most of Latin America today. Much of the area and population was thus left behind by the modernizing forces of interna-tional capitalism and its domestic offshoots, including substantial numbers of peo-ple trapped in subsistence cultivation.[8] Shorn of their communal holdings and pro-letarianized by the unrestricted expansion of large landholdings, the indigenous peoples in particular seemed destined for cultural obliteration in the liberal project that most governments pursued.[9] In the south of Brazil and the Rio de la Plata, however, the new economic influences spread untrammeled by colonial residues or sizable indigenous populations, with a transformative power that brought into being a region that today constitutes the economic heartland of South America (and the Mercosur, the Southern Common Market). Argentina even managed to reach the end of this era as one of the world's most prosperous economies, so that "rich as an Argentine" gained currency in Europe to describe vast wealth.[10]

As in the second restructuring, there was an abundance of new writing, this time mostly in the vein of the classical/neoclassical school of political economy and positivism, to reinterpret the past for its diagnostic value and prescribe ingredients for the policy armamentarium the governments of the day were putting together to ensure continued growth—and even progress, a term still very much in vogue in that pre-postmodern intellectual ambiance. It would be stretching a point to call this an age of unbridled laissez-faire, but it most certainly was one filled to overflowing with capitalist sentiments and language.

But beyond the Rio Plata and broad swatches of Chile and central and southern Brazil, the spottiness of the transformation made for glaring inequalities and a plethora of organizational and cultural disparities—contradictions of such severity as to delight the heart of a Marxist. In Mexico these were particularly acute, so that only a decade into the century, the ancien régime, as the nouveau régime soon came to be perceived, was cast aside and a kind of anticipatory glimpse of the next restructuring hove into view: one that would use a kind of economic nationalism to accelerate the process of industrialization. In Mexico, almost uniquely until the Bolivian revolution of the 1950s, agrarian reform was at first the dominant policy priority, but when the fourth restructuring set in, during the late 1930s and 1940s, it was manufacturing that was to call the tune.

ISI: THE FOURTH RESTRUCTURING

During the closing decades of the nineteenth century, the first modern factories appeared here and there in Latin America: in Argentina, Chile, Brazil, and Mexico especially but with scattered outposts of the industrial revolution popping up elsewhere as well. Population growth, modest urbanization, the enrichment of the area's human resources by immigration (which brought entrepreneurs as well as skilled labor), and a rise in incomes, together with the knitting together of a greater area by railways and telecommunication lines, gradually expanded domestic markets and with them the number of local manufacturing establishments. As the twentieth century unfolded, these market-based trends produced a further widening of the industrial base—spurred on, briefly, by the interruption of European imports during World War I. In interpreting the record of growth in more recent decades, we need to remember that several of these factors—an accentuated population growth, more rapid urbanization, the filling in of national infrastructure, and the upward trend in per capita incomes—have continued to operate in ways supportive of manufacturing development, both broadening and deepening the industrial structure independently of the effects of policy.

When the Great Depression hit and export earnings collapsed, the depreciation of Latin American currencies favored the further expansion of domestic industry to replace the unavailable imports, while by this time tariffs originally designed for revenue had gradually been raised to levels according a measure of protection for competing local products. And while depression thus knocked out one of the props of the age of export-led expansion, the other engine of the region's third-restructuring growth, foreign investment, was likewise rendered hors de combat by the massive disorganization of capital markets in the centers of capitalism.[11] Import supplies and capital imports continued to be disrupted when World War II began, and while domestic manufacturing was spreading to meet the gap between domestic aggregate demand and imports, governments increasingly questioned the wisdom of continuing to rely on the external sector as the mainstay of economic growth. The conditioning of such circumstances lasted into the postwar era while traditional sources of import supplies continued to be choked back by reconstruction priorities, which effort also absorbed most of the capital Europe could generate and the United States could export.

It only remained for the new UN Economic Commission for Latin America (ECLA), based in Santiago, Chile, to fashion out of these circumstances a rationale for systematic promotion, under state leadership, of accelerated industrial development.[12] Thereafter, until the debt crisis struck in 1982, the policies that had evolved by ad hoc adaptation to circumstances in the 1930s and 1940s were reshaped into a well-articulated development program that justified a wide variety of interventionary measures and in time spawned the movement toward regional integration as an expedient to keep industrialization's momentum unabated. Protective tariffs, fiscal incentives, exchange-rate controls, parastatal financial and industrial enterprises, and a host of other policy instruments were deployed to push industrial development forward and, from the early 1960s, to promote such schemes as the Central American Common Market, the larger Latin American Free Trade Area, and the smaller Caribbean Free Trade Area—to which were added, a bit later, the Andean Pact and the Caribbean Common Market. None of these regional associations lived up to the initial expectations, but in most there was a significant growth of intraregional trade—and, most likely, equally significant trade diversion effects.

Amid these changes there were also notable shifts in inter-American economic relations. The 1930s had brought the reciprocal trade agreements to build preferential commercial ties between the United States and Latin America, and the inauguration of the Export-Import Bank introduced government financing into the web of economic relationships. Technical assistance and additional intergovernmental financing for capital projects began during World War II, when the United States had need of increased Latin American production capacity. A trickle of economic aid of these types, especially technical assistance, continued through the 1950s, during which decade the World Bank became a significant external source of development financing and the Organization of American States a modest supplier of economic counsel and technical assistance through such entities as the Pan American Health Organization.[13] While the regional integration movement was reaching its heyday, the Inter-American Development Bank was instituted at the end of the 1950s as a multilateral regional supplier of development finance (and technical counsel), and soon thereafter the Alliance for Progress, sometimes misleadingly equated with the Marshall Plan, was introduced to mobilize public resources on a large scale for a concerted regional development push.[14] By the 1970s, however, these initiatives were playing out.

Baptized "import-substituting industrialization (ISI)," the strategy came to be administered carelessly, distorted from the pristine ECLA vision by the tug of rent-seeking interest groups and by populist policies that have been characterized as macroeconomic populism.[15] Bedecked also with some of the trappings of the modern welfare state, to placate the crucial urban constituencies, the public sector came to exemplify a concept of the state as the great piñata. Inflation was rampant, balance-of-payments crises were frequent, agricultural and traditional export sectors were undermined, and in time the policy environment turned increasingly hostile to foreign direct investment.[16] To cap the mounting list of problems, Latin America's export market share was generally eroded in favor of other Third World exporters, and fiscal profligacy and excessive bureaucratization combined with the discouragement of foreign investment and the need to cover growing trade imbalances to produce an increasing reliance on commercial loans from money-center banks—while domestic savings rates were depressed by adverse policies and capital flight was even unintentionally stimulated. Meanwhile, it transpired that the industrialization that had been designed to replace imports had in fact made Latin America more dependent on imports than ever before.

The jig was up when the oil shocks of the 1970s worked their effects, and (on top of all the external-sector adjustments) the industrialized countries more or less simultaneously undertook to put an end to accelerating inflation, causing export prices and earnings to drop precipitously. The repercussions in Latin America produced the debt crisis, which struck all the countries save Colombia in the early 1980s and effectively ended the half century of accelerated industrialization and the policy framework that had sustained and nurtured it.[17] As the Inter-American Development Bank has noted, the longer-term effect of the crisis was to usher in a major shift in economic policy that gradually spread over the continent.[18]

THE FIFTH RESTRUCTURING AND WHAT IT REVEALS

Chile, Mexico, Argentina, and latterly Peru have been at the forefront of the new policy agenda, which has promoted macroeconomic stabilization, the ending of financial repression (the freeing of interest rates to find market-determined levels), and the removal of most exchange-rate controls so that the prices in the foreign exchange market would be anchored in supply-demand relationships. The deregulation of other prices and the withdrawal of subsidies have also furthered the marketization of economic decisionmaking, whereas trade liberalization has been relied on to widen the scope of contestable markets and intensify competitive pressures, bringing about greater productive and allocative efficiency while aligning domestic price structures with those prevailing in the world market. In greater or lesser measure, deregulation has also been used to create a more favorable climate for capital formation, both domestic and foreign.

Privatization, once the most controversial of the new policies, has been employed for a variety of objectives: to strengthen the fiscal system by removing deficit-generating enterprises from the public portfolio and using the sales proceeds to reduce national debt; to link local production facilities more securely into the globalized production, financing, and marketing networks; to tap the more ample supplies of capital available in the private sector; and to pave the way for continuing technological upgrading. Secondary objectives have included the reduction of labor redundancy and making national capital markets more robust, both by spreading the ownership of shares and by enriching the options available to investors for portfolio diversification.

The recent peso crisis and its repercussions aside, the benefits of structural adjustment have been swifter to materialize than one might have expected, given all that has been said about the distortions and other shortcomings of the previous policy era—during which so many of the canons of orthodox economic theory were violated. No doubt it was indeed the flagrant character of these "violations" that led many to interpret the debt crisis as a well-deserved day of reckoning, in which policy sins of omission and policy sins of commission alike would finally be paid for. Yet, just as the three preceding restructuring episodes were the occasions for retrospective diagnoses of the economic orders that led into the restructurings, so also the present turnabout affords a useful vantage point from which to reflect on what legacy the twentieth century has left for the Latin American economies. A summing up of sorts, in other words, is plainly in order—not only for an accurate reading of the policies of the neoliberal model that critics have called the great restoration of capitalism but also to interpret the costs and benefits of the two eras that have brought Latin America to this point.

It is clear that the foundations of growth were established in the 1870–1930 era, which, while it lasted, did so much to bring substantial parts of Latin America, finally, into the modern age, with a much-needed filling in of institutional deficits left over from the colonial age and repair of the damage inflicted in the first decades of independence. Amid the new organizational infrastructure through which Latin America was increasingly engaged with the world market, incipient industrialization appeared as the harbinger of the more sweeping changes that redrew the economic map of the region after 1930.

Notwithstanding the obvious costs of the ISI policies that followed in the wake of the Great Depression and World War II, considerable strength was nevertheless added to the Latin American resource base, expanding the array of production options and creating the basis for considerably more production versatility than the region exhibited in, say, 1929. Not only was the structure of production totally transformed, and along with it the distribution of the labor force, but compared with the state of the region's economy at the close of the era of export-led growth, the Latin America of 1997 was richer by far in its human resources and in the organizational or social capital on which everything in the last analysis rests. The feverish pace of institution building that has characterized Latin America since the 1930s has been deeply flawed and often haphazard. Protectionism run riot most certainly contributed to both misallocations of resources among sectors and industries and suboptimal efficiency at the microlevel, just as it made rent-seeking pervasive and spread the opportunities for a socially corrosive corruption. Both no doubt contributed to the lopsided distribution of income for which Latin America has become notorious.

Yet, real factor productivity has nonetheless chalked up impressive advances in most of the region, and there has been an enormous amount of learning by doing, in both public and private sectors. For all the problems and setbacks, per capita income for an awesomely larger population has reached levels far above those that prevailed before market-induced industrialization was joined by policy-induced industrialization.

In country after country, the comparative advantages based on natural endowments have thus been supplanted by comparative advantages derived from organizational growth and the accumulation of human capital. For example, Brazil, noted as late as the mid-1960s for its overwhelming export dependence on coffee, became, thanks to policy adaptations that began in the latter part of that decade, a country whose exports have consisted primarily of manufactures, including a range of sophisticated exports (to highly competitive markets) that extends from *telenovelas* and oil field services to aircraft and automobiles. Colombia, another coffee country, has learned to export coal, petroleum, flowers, and a considerable variety of other products, just as Chile has moved away from a lopsided dependence on copper into a varied basket of higher-value products and Mexican industrial products are eating into the commanding lead acquired in the 1970s by petroleum exports.[19]

The Chilean case is particularly instructive. Given the disruptive policy shifts introduced by the Allende regime of the early 1970s and the Pinochet regime that followed, one might have expected the Chilean industrial sector to vanish in the face of rapid trade liberalization and a deliberately overvalued currency, policies adopted as the cornerstones of restructuring—especially when the banking system, which was ruined under Allende, collapsed a second time in the midst of the restructuring. Nevertheless, the manufacturing sector managed to survive and grow stronger, in organizational capacity and efficiency if not in scale, and the economy as a whole eventually turned in a stellar performance year after year.

In short, behind the debt and peso crises and all the Sturm und Drang of the restructuring controversies, the evidence is unmistakable that the three consecutive policy regimes that began around 1870 have enabled the current restructuring to be carried out with considerable success. The new climate has also made the Mercosur, North American Free Trade Agreement (NAFTA), and the general economic opening effective catalysts for economic revival and renewal. In this, the reborn regional integration movement offers a notable contrast to the various experiments that characterized the 1960s: the Central American Common Market (CACM), the Latin American Free Trade Agreement (LAFTA), the Caribbean Free Trade Agreement (CARIFTA), and the Andean Pact, all of which petered out after their initial momentum—victims of economic nationalism, contradictory policies, feckless bureaucrats, and faulty design. Today, the Mercosur (which groups Brazil, Argentina, Uruguay, and Paraguay) has emerged as the largest and most successful example of regional economic cooperation in the Third World, and the NAFTA, for all its stresses and strains, represents a boldly unique attempt to meld economies more disparate than any of those brought together in the European Union.[20]

There are, to be sure, a number of troubling accounts payable still remaining on the national ledger sheets: what has come to be called the social deficit. Environmental conditions have deteriorated over much of the continent, and the cities have patently exceeded the carrying capacity of their infrastructure, with consequent decay in the living conditions of all who dwell therein, even the rich, whose walled compounds nevertheless admit increasingly polluted air and who must from time to time sally forth to confront growing congestion and social disorder.[21]

Huge numbers of people and much of the rural sector have been left on the sidelines in the sweeping renovation effort, and the disparities among regions and income classes are greater than ever before.[22] Compared with the high-performance Asian economies, the most unequal Asian income distributions are more equitable than the least unequal of the Latin American cases. And the people Columbus encountered on his voyages live still in a state of economic and cultural anorexia, as powerless politically as they are deprived of assets and purchasing power in the economic arena.[23]

Much remains to be done, in other words, to make the current national projects credible as a path for general progress.[24] But it is hard to escape the conclusion that for all its ills, Latin America has more resources today than it has ever had before to enlist in the needed cleanup and social rectification efforts, which cannot be postponed much beyond the close of this millennium, and more social capability and institutional capacity as well. Considering that these assets, too, are products of development, albeit nonmeasured public-goods components that are not conventionally reckoned in the national accounts, and considering as well that these contribute importantly to the future capacity to produce, one could reasonably conclude that the recorded growth figures for much of this century, high as they have been, have actually understated the rate of change—though a full and balanced accounting would have to tally the accumulated social costs as a major offset to this record of achievement. Perhaps only the outcomes in the next century will enable us to judge with some assurance of accuracy the net asset or liability position.

NOTES

1. The World Bank groups the economies into four categories. Low-income countries are found mostly in Africa and Asia and include the majority of the world's population. Most of

Latin America has climbed into the lower-middle-income or upper-middle-income category, alongside Turkey, the central and Eastern European countries and those spun off from the former Soviet Union, as well as the high-performance Asian economies. None has made it into the most prosperous group of countries, although Hong Kong and Singapore have reached those levels.

2. This literature on Latin American economic history is now enormous. Readers with an interest in examining it can conveniently begin with the relevant volumes in Leslie Bethell, ed., *The Cambridge History of Latin America* (New York: Cambridge University Press, 1984), or William Glade, *The Latin American Economies: A Study of Their Institutional Evolution* (New York: American Book Company, 1969). See also B. R. Mitchell, *International Historical Statistics: The Americas and Autralasia 1750–1988* (Detroit, Mich.: Gale Research Co., 1983).

3. The large city-state empires run by the Aztecs (in Mexico) and Incas (in Peru, Ecuador, and Bolivia) at the time of the conquest were agriculturally based and boasted extensive trade routes within them, partly to collect tribute and sacrificial victims from subjugated peoples. The Maya were by then in an advanced state of decline, and apart from a few other indigenous peoples, such as the Chibcha in Colombia, most of the other Amerindian groupings were still in the hunting and fishing stage of technological development—with scattered regions of sedentary agriculture. It should be noted that most long-distance traffic moved by human bearers over footpaths, there being no wheeled carts or draft animals (other than the llamas used as pack animals). Thus, two immense adjustments had to occur with European colonization: the shift of much cropland to pasturage to fuel the new transport technology based on pack and draft animals and a massive dedication of resources to road and bridge construction, an undertaking made immensely costly by the nature of the topography and distances involved.

4. It should be stressed that the latifundiary foundations of the New World order were not part of the original aims of the Spanish crown, which in principle was also committed to protection of the native population. A voluminous corpus of decrees, partly administered by royal officials and partly overseen by a parallel ecclesiastical bureaucracy, was designed to safeguard the social blueprint on which the empire was theoretically constructed. But the chronic hunger of the royal treasury had to be fed by all kinds of expedients, ranging from the sale of lower-level offices to payments by which land claims, even illegal ones, could be regularized, and problems of communication and bureaucratic oversight reduced the efficiency (and integrity) of administration. Thus, the collision between metropolitan ideals and New World realities left a deposit of institutions that shaped social relations in ways that were unintended but were foundational for what came afterward.

5. Had these economists had a better address, say, in England or France, they would undoubtedly have been credited with great contributions to the embryonic science of economics. But in Spain they worked beyond the intellectual pale defined by the upcoming liberal modernization movements of the Enlightenment and hence never figured much in any citation index of the day.

6. Neither the ending of the empire in exchange for republican government nor the abolition of slavery, both of which events came at the dawning of the Belle Epoque (1890–1914), occasioned serious conflict in Brazil.

7. The term is widely used today to refer to the standard policy package recommended by the IMF and the World Bank for countries in need of economic resuscitation: macroeconomic stabilization programs, trade liberalization, deregulation of prices (including interest rates) and general business activity (including foreign investment), market-based exchange-rate policies, and privatization, inter alia.

8. For a convenient introduction into the huge literature on agrarian development, see Robert G. Keith, *Haciendas and Plantations in Latin American History* (New York: Holmes and Meier, 1977).

9. The spread of latifundism, to dimensions unimagined even by the end of the colonial age, was fostered by factors both political and technological. In the political realm, the ownership of government was held by the class most interested in expanding its landholdings, and liberal ideology provided a cloak for the self-aggrandizement of this group. In the technological realm, the spread of railways and telecommunications conferred value on parts of the public domain that had formerly held no interest for anyone save the native population that lived there.

10. In this region, where a relatively gentle topography and temperate climate facilitated agriculture and ranching, the cheap construction of roads and railways, supplemented by South America's most important inland waterway, spurred development and heightened the productivity of the immense amount of human capital that arrived through mass immigration from Europe.

11. The period is well covered in Rosemary Thorp, ed., *Latin America in the 1930's: The Role of the Periphery in World Crisis* (New York: St. Martin's Press, 1984).

12. The ECLA became in effect a graduate school for training a new generation of Latin American economists, the principal source of doctrinal inspiration for national industrial policies, a major purveyor of technical assistance for project and program planning, and the generator of a systematic strategy of development that was widely borrowed in other less developed parts of the world.

13. The International Labour Organisation, the Food and Agriculture Organization, and an assortment of other UN-related entities also came onto the Latin American stage in this era.

14. Smaller but important inter-American contributions were made by the Peace Corps and the Inter-American Development Foundation. Private U.S. foundations such as Kellogg, Rockefeller, and Ford were also enlisted on behalf of Latin American development, especially in institution building. The private foundations, however, had in some instances begun their Latin American programs before the 1960s, and by the end of that decade they were drawing back in favor of new programs in the United States. Significant advances in building Latin American intellectual capital resulted from their efforts as well as from the investments of others such as the Tinker Foundation, the Latin American Scholarship Program of American Universities, the U.S. Agency for International Development, a variety of church-related undertakings, and the Fulbright program.

15. Extremely effective analysis of the destabilizing patterns of policy that developed is contained in Rudiger Dornbusch and Sebastian Edwards, *The Macroeconomics of Populism in Latin America* (Chicago: University of Chicago Press, 1991).

16. An ever increasing overburden of regulation was applied to foreign direct investment, and restrictive regulation was also applied to technology transfers. A culmination of sorts was reached in the Andean Pact countries in the form of provisions to accelerate foreign disinvestment.

17. A different set of events had brought the Chilean economy to collapse in 1973, with the result that the fifth restructuring began there as a pioneering experiment in the mid-1970s, a decade before similar policies were introduced elsewhere in the region. For the Chilean case, see Dominique Hachette and Rolf Luders-Schwarzenberg, *Privatization in Chile: An Economic Appraisal* (San Francisco: ICS Press, 1993), and Barry Bosworth, Rudiger Dornbusch, and Raul Laban, eds., *The Chilean Economy: Policy Lessons and Challenges* (Washington, D.C.: Brookings

Institution, 1994). For the debt crisis, see S. Griffith-Jones and Osvaldo Sunkel, *Debt and Development Crises in Latin America: The End of an Illusion* (New York: Oxford University Press, 1986), and Robert Devlin, *Debt and Crisis in Latin America: The Supply Side of the Story* (Princeton N.J.: Princeton University Press, 1994).

18. Sebastian Edwards, *Crisis and Reform in Latin America: From Despair to Hope* (New York: Oxford University Press, 1995), provides an excellent review of the reform measures and their impacts.

19. Montague Lord, "Manufacturing Exports," in Inter-American Development Bank, *Economic and Social Progress in Latin America, 1992* (Washington, D.C.: Inter American Development Bank, 1992).

20. Greece and Portugal, the poorest members, were much, much smaller than Mexico and also relatively closer to European levels in per capita income—and therefore more readily "digestible." The closer counterpart to the NAFTA combination would have been the admission of Turkey into the European Community, a challenge the Europeans prudently declined.

21. Gordon J. MacDonald, Daniel L. Nielson, and Marc A. Stern, eds., *Latin American Environmental Policy in International Perspective* (Boulder, Co.: Westview Press, 1997); Michael Painter and William H. Durham, eds., *The Social Causes of Environmental Destruction in Latin America* (Ann Arbor: University of Michigan Press, 1995).

22. Samuel A. Morley, *Poverty and Inequality in Latin America* (Baltimore: Johns Hopkins University Press, 1995), William Thiesenhusen, *Broken Promises: Agrarian Reform and the Latin American Campesino* (Boulder, Co.: Westview Press, 1995).

23. George Psacharaopoulos and Harry A. Patrinos, eds., *Indigenous People and Poverty in Latin America* (Washington, D.C.: The World Bank, 1994), and Donna Lee Van Cott, ed., *Indigenous Peoples and Democracy in Latin America* (New York: St. Martin's Press, 1994).

24. Dagmar Raczynski, ed., *Strategies to Combat Poverty in Latin America* (Washington, D.C.: Inter-American Development Bank, 1996).

SUGGESTED READINGS

Agosin, Manuel R., ed. *Foreign Direct Investment in Latin America*. Washington, D.C.: Inter-American Development Bank, 1995. With its focus on the revival of capital inflows into a restructured region, this book is well paired with another book from the same publisher, Jose Antonio Ocampo and Roberto Steiner, eds., *Foreign Capital in Latin America* (1994). Both are strongly technical in their analysis.

Baer, Werner. *The Brazilian Economy: Growth and Development*. New York: Praeger, 1995. It is not hard to understand why this masterful analysis of Latin America's largest economy has gone through so many editions of which this is the latest.

Bethell, Leslie, ed. *The Cambridge History of Latin America*. New York: Cambridge University Press, 1984. This landmark work has chapters on economic aspects scattered among its multiple volumes.

Bresser Pereira, Luiz Carlos. *Economic Crisis and State Reform in Brazil: Toward a New Interpretation of Latin America*. Boulder, Co.: L. Rienner, 1996. A noted specialist who grew to professional maturity under ISI speaks his piece on what has come to pass with the structural adjustment reforms, though Brazil has lagged notably on making many of these.

Glade, William. *The Latin American Economies: A Study of Their Institutional Evolution*. New York: American Book Company, 1969.

Gordon, Wendell. *The Political Economy of Latin America*. New York: Columbia University Press, 1966. The last edition of one of the best of the several textbooks written in the 1960s and 1970s on Latin American development.

Hachette, Dominique, and Rolf Luders-Schwarzenberg. *Privatization in Chile: An Economic Appraisal*. San Francisco: ICS Publishers, 1993. A magisterial analysis of this controversial policy in Latin America's trailblazing country.

Huber, Evelyn, and Frank Safford, eds. *Agrarian Structure and Political Power: Landlord and Peasant in the Making of Latin America*. Pittsburgh: University of Pittsburgh Press, 1995.

Inter-American Development Bank. *Economic and Social Progress in Latin America*. An annual report containing current economic information on the different countries, a useful set of time series data, and an extended analytical treatment of some particular aspects of Latin American development, such as fiscal decentralization, social security reform, manufacturing exports, and suchlike. Earlier volumes have titles that vary slightly from the latest volumes.

Maddison, Angus, et al., *The Political Economy of Poverty, Equity, and Growth: Brazil and Mexico*. New York: Oxford University Press, 1992. One of a series of paired country studies by World Bank specialists, this one provides an intimate look at the two most important Latin American economies that for all their historical differences have gone through many of the same development policy hoops in recent years.

Ozorio de Almeida, Anna Luiza, and João S. Campari, *Sustainable Settlement in the Brazilian Amazon*. New York: Oxford University Press, 1995. A well-reasoned and well-documented analytical foray into one of the most controversial facets of Latin American development, for the problem explored is far wider than just Brazil. See also Charles H. Wood and Marianne Schmink, *Contested Frontiers in Amazonia* (New York: Columbia University Press, 1992), for an authoritative treatment of the demographic forces in environmental degradation.

Prebisch, Raúl. *Change and Development: Latin America's Great Task*. New York: Praeger, 1971. A rethinking of the Latin American predicament on the eve of the great borrowing spree and the oil shocks, by the man who, more than any other, shaped Latin American economic policy in the postwar period. The classical statement of the prevailing diagnosis of Latin American conditions and the policy that flowed from it is found in UN, ECLA, *The Economic Development of Latin America and Its Principal Problems* (Santiago: United Nations Economic Commission for Latin America, 1950). Ibid., *Development Problems of Latin America* (Austin: University of Texas Press, 1970), is a handy compilation of documents from the UN Economic Commission for Latin America that define the guiding vision of ISI policies.

Story, Dale. *Industry, the State, and Public Policy in Mexico*. Austin: University of Texas Press, 1986. See also, for Mexico, Roderic Ai Camp, *Entrepreneurs and Politics in Twentieth Century Mexico* (New York: Oxford University Press, 1989). For an equivalent glimpse of the policy process in Brazil, see Ben Ross Schneider, *Politics Within the State: Elite Bureaucrats and Industrial Policy in Authoritarian Brazil* (Pittsburgh: University of Pittsburgh Press, 1991). These three books, and their equivalents for several other countries, afford an insight into the dynamics that generated the economic outcomes analyzed by Maddison and associates. Although the neoliberal model has somewhat altered the institutional arrangements that these three studies examined, we would be rash to assume that the old order has altogether vanished in policy determination. In Latin America, as in the United States, policymakers listen selectively.

Thiesenhusen, William C. *Broken Promises: Agrarian Reform and the Latin American Campesino*. Boulder, Colo.: Westview Press, 1995. An important retrospective assessment by one who has followed the vagaries of agricultural policy for many years.

Tokman, Victor. *Beyond Regulation: The Informal Economy in Latin America*. Boulder, Colo.: Lynne Rienner, 1992. Although the informal sector, so baptized, was first spotted in Africa by ILO researchers, its Latin American twin has inspired a huge volume of studies, of which this is a good example. Hernando de Soto, *The Other Path: The Invisible Revolution in the Third World* (New York: Harper and Row, 1989), did much, in its earlier Spanish-language version, to stimulate scholarship on the Latin American phenomenon, though housing studies in squatter settlements during the early 1960s were perhaps the first to note the rise of the informal sector or the underground economy.

Urrutia, Miguel, ed. *Long-term Trends in Latin American Economic Development*. Washington, D.C.: Inter-American Development Bank, 1991. Especially chapters 1 and 2.

Weeks, John. *The Economies of Central America*. New York: Holmes and Meier, 1985. Though written before this troubled region began to settle down, the survey is nonetheless useful for understanding what democratic governments will have to deal with today.

10

SOCIAL STRUCTURE AND CHANGE IN LATIN AMERICA

HENRY VELTMEYER AND JAMES PETRAS

For close to three decades, from the 1950s to the end of the 1970s, Latin America experienced historically unprecedented high rates of economic growth—more than 5 percent in the aggregate and 2.5 percent on a per capita basis. This growth, together with associated developments, was based on a model characterized by (1) a high rate of government or state intervention in the economy, including regulation of private activity and restrictions on foreign investment; (2) an "inward orientation"—producing for the domestic rather than the world market; (3) import substitution—protecting and encouraging the growth of domestic industry; and (4) populism—the incorporation of the working and middle classes into the development process and politics.

In the 1970s, this process of development was arrested and reversed by the policies of governments acting in the interest of the economically dominant propertied class, which was deeply concerned about the mounting claims made by a restive working class against their property. In the 1980s, under conditions of a regionwide debt crisis and a redemocratization process, a solution was found to both the growing and unsettling power of the working class and the widespread economic imbalances. The Structural Adjustment Program (SAP), as it was called, was a series of economic stabilization measures and "structural" reforms designed by the economists of the World Bank and the International Monetary Fund, two international organizations set up to promote free-market capitalist development on a global scale.

Introduced by Chile's military regime but eventually adopted by or imposed on virtually every other government in the region, SAPs provide a standard recipe for curing a country's ills: (1) stabilization of the currency (adoption of a "realistic" exchange rate, i.e., devaluation); (2) liberalization of trade and capital flows, eliminating or reducing trade barriers and favorable treatment of domestic capital; (3) reorientation of production toward the world market and opening up the economy to foreign competition; (4) deregulation of private activity; (5) privatization of state enterprises and all means of social production; (6) downsizing the state, reducing the scale and scope of its market intervention, eliminating subsidies and control of prices; and (7) fiscal austerity—a policy of fiscal discipline and balanced budgets. After a decade and more of such policies, Latin America today is a very different place from what it was in the 1970s and what it was becoming. In the process, a revolution—or rather a counterrevolution—has been wrought in the social structure of Latin American society.

It is of critical importance to understand the nature of this social structure. For one thing, the capacity for people to change the structure and thereby to improve the conditions of their social existence to some extent depends on this understanding. For another, it is not possible to understand the development of Latin American society in its various dimensions (economic, social, political) without a solid grasp of the social structure that underlies this development.

THE SOCIAL STRUCTURE OF LATIN AMERICA

There are three basic levels of social analysis in Latin America as elsewhere. One is in terms of the distribution or composition of a population's social characteristics. At this level, we can identify a number of ascribed or socially constructed features such as gender, age, race and ethnicity, and achieved characteristics such as level of education. A second form of analysis operates at a different (structural) level, identifying sets of positions occupied by groups of people and the social and economic conditions associated with these positions. Arguably, this is the most critical level of social analysis, requiring a combination of theoretical abstraction and empirical analysis. A third type of social analysis is based on the subjective and political conditions of people's behavior and experience, identifying the forms of their social consciousness and action. In practice, the problem is how and where to combine these three forms of social analysis—to make the appropriate or necessary connections.

At the structural level, a number of critical factors and defining characteristics can be identified. One is spatial distribution and location. In terms of this factor, Table 10.1 distinguishes between two groups of Latin America's population, one located in the region's urban centers and the other in the countryside, in the smaller communities and farms of rural society. Table 10.1 also points toward a fundamental change in the urban-rural distribution of the population as well as in the gender composition of the labor force since 1970.

Table 10.1 not only identifies significant country-by-country variations in the urban-rural distribution of the population but highlights major changes in the structure of this distribution over the past two and a half decades. In most cases, the shift of the population toward the urban centers has involved a change of at least ten percentage points in just two decades. Table 10.1 also identifies a general trend toward the feminization of the labor force. This trend has accelerated since the early 1970s,

Table 10.1
The Population of Latin America and the Caribbean: Some Basic Distributions, 1994

	Population (thousands)		Percent Urban			Labor,[a] Percent Female		
	No.	*%*	*1970*	*1993*	*Ch[b]*	*1970*	*1993*	*Ch[b]*
Argentina	33,875	7.5	78	87	(09)	25	28	(3)
Bolivia	7,238	1.6	41	59	(18)	21	26	(5)
Brazil	159,000	35.1	56	71	(15)	22	28	(6)
Colombia	34,545	7.6	57	72	(15)	21	22	(1)
Chile	14,026	3.1	75	84	(09)	22	29	(7)
Ecuador	11,226	2.1	45	57	(12)	16	19	(3)
Mexico	88,431	17.2	59	74	(15)	18	27	(9)
Peru	23,381	5.1	57	71	(14)	20	24	(4)
Paraguay	4,767	1.1	37	51	(14)	21	21	(0)
Uruguay	3,167	0.7	82	90	(08)	26	32	(6)
Venezuela	21,051	3.7	72	92	(20)	21	28	(7)
Belize	21	.05						
Costa Rica	3,347	0.7						
Cuba	10,682							
Dominican Republic	7,769	1.7	40	63	(23)	11	16	(5)
El Salvador	5,641	1.2	39	45	(06)	20	25	(5)
Guatemala	10,322	1.9	36	41	(05)	13	17	(4)
Honduras	5,497	1.2						
Nicaragua	4,275	0.9						
Panama	2,583	0.6						
Caribbean-ES[c]	6,108	6.7						

[a]The official labor force, i.e., those registered as employed or seeking employment (employed/unemployed). In the Latin American context, this excludes large categories of workers, in particular women, who do not offer their labor sale or whose labor is otherwise not accounted for.

[b]Percentage point change.

[c]Includes English-speaking islands of the Caribbean (Trinidad and Tobago, Bahamas, Barbados, Dominica, Grenada, Jamaica, St. Lucia, St. Kitts, St. Vincent), Surinam, and Guyana.

Sources: General Secretariat, OAS, *Statistical Bulletin of the OAS* (Washington, D.C.: OAS, 1994); World Bank, *World Development Report 1995* (Oxford: Oxford University Press, 1995).

even though the vast majority of women enter the informal sector of the labor force, where their numbers are notoriously undercounted.

Even with the most limited demographic analysis, it is possible to identify clear patterns to these variations that correspond to differences in the social structure. To some degree this is reflected in other elements of the social structure, such as the distribution of economic activities (Table 10.2) and the associated structure of income

Table 10.2

The Structure of Economic Activity, Selected Countries, Ranked (out of 132) in Reverse Order of Per Capita Income, 1994

		GDP	*Percent*	*Percent Share of Total Production*			
		(million $)	*Share*	*Agriculture*	*Industry*[a]	*Manufacturing*	*Services*[b]
49	Bolivia	6,760	0.6	16.4	25.7	13.8	48.4
63	Ecuador	14,718	1.2	12.6	39.8	19.0	47.7
67	Colombia	53,367	4.5	14.9	32.2	19.2	50.3
69	Peru	44,074	3.7	6.9	41.2	28.1	51.4
70	Paraguay	6,911	0.6	26.7	22.2	16.2	47.7
87	Venezuela	61,527	5.2	4.7	48.3	20.5	44.5
89	**Brazil**	**412,747**	**34.9**	**10.5**	**33.1**	**25.2**	**53.7**
94	Chile	40.248	3.4	9.1	40.7	19.9	38.8
96	**Mexico**	**268,892**	**22.7**	**7.6**	**29.0**	**22.3**	**61.9**
98	Uruguay	11,516	1.0	10.7	25.2	20.7	61.9
103	**Argentina**	**266,005**	**17.4**	**6.5**	**41.5**	**26.1**	**56.8**

Note: Selected countries make up 84.9 percent of the region's population and 95.2 percent of the region's GDP. The biggest three economies (89, 96, 103) make up 59.8 percent of the population and 75 percent of the GDP.

[a]Composed of mining, manufacturing, and construction.

[b]Composed of commerce, transport/communications, finance, government, others.

Source: General Secretariat, OAS, *Statistical Bulletin of the OAS* (Washington, D.C.: OAS, 1994), tables A-5, A-6, B.

distribution (Table 10.3). A cursory examination of these patterns indicates that the corresponding structures are interconnected and form a system.

Within the economic and social system in place throughout Latin America and elsewhere, income is a critically important determinant of an individual's—and each household's—"life chances." Most people require money or income for meeting their basic needs, and the major source of this income is work, either for wages or a salary (employment) or on one's own account (self-employment) or commodity production (the direct production of goods and services for sale). In every Latin American society, with the exception of Cuba, there exists a class of individuals who receive income in the form of rent or profit derived from their ownership of property or some means of social production. Most people, however, have to work for a living. That is, they are part of the working class, dependent on the sale of their labor power. Table 10.4 provides a graphic if theoretical representation of the class structure of Latin American society and of the position of workers and producers within this structure.

THE NEW SOCIAL ORDER IN LATIN AMERICA

In order to gauge the social and political forces that are generated in support of or in resistance to the neoliberal (market-oriented) economic reforms implemented in the

Table 10.3

Distribution of National Income, by Top/Bottom Quintiles (1–2) and Top Decile (3), for Selected Countries, Listed in Rank Reverse Order by Per Capita Income Levels, 1993

| | GNP Per Capita | | Income Distribution[a] | | | | Percent Rural Pop. |
| | | | (1) | (2) | (3) | | |
	% U.S.	Int'l $	L 20%	H 20%	H 10%	2/1	in Poverty
Bolivia	9.8	2,420	5.6	48.2	31.7	9.6	97
Colombia	22.2	5,490	3.6	55.8	39.5	15.5	45
Peru	13.0	3,220	4.9	51.4	35.4	10.5	75
Brazil	**21.7**	**5,370**	**2.1**	**67.5**	**51.3**	**32.1**	**73**
Chile	34.0	8,400	3.3	60.4	45.8	18.3	56
Mexico	**27.5**	**6,810**	**4.1**	**55.9**	**39.5**	**13.6**	**51**
Argentina	**33.3**	**8,250**	**4.4**	**50.3**	**–**	**11.4**	**20**
Hong Kong	87.1	21,560	5.4	47.0	31.3	8.7	
Korea	38.9	9,630	7.4	42.3	27.6	5.7	
Southeast Asia	–	–	6.3	45.8	–	7.3	
Japan	84.3	20,850	8.7	37.5	22.4	4.3	
United States	100.0	24,740	4.7	41.9	25.0	8.9	

[a]Various years 1988–1991. Figures break income earners into quintiles: (1) the lowest 20 percent; (2) the top 10 percent; and (3) the top decile.

Source: World Bank, *World Development Report 1989, 1990, 1991, 1995* (Oxford: Oxford University Press, 1989, 1990, 1991, 1995).

Table 10.4

The Latin American Class Structure in the 1990s (% distribution of the EAP)

	Urban	Rural
Capitalist class	4	2
Middle class		
Professional/bureaucratic	6	2
Small business operator	10	4
Independent producers		12
Working classes		
Formal sector/proletariat (waged)	20	25
Informal sector/semi-proletariat	60	20
Peasant producers		35

Note: These rough estimates of the class distribution are based on official data on the economically active population (EAP), which includes those who are employed, self-employed, and those seeking employment in the labor force.

Source: Calculations made on the basis of estimates and projections from data by Alejandro Portes, "Latin American Class Structures: Their Composition and Change During the Last Decades," Occasional Paper 3, School of International Studies, Johns Hopkins University, table 4.

1980s, it is important to examine the underlying structure of class relations. Changes in this structure over the past two decades of reforms have had a significant impact on the politics of economic reform—on the forces that have been mobilized in support of or opposition to the SAPs. The reforms have also produced changes in class relations and associated conditions, mobilizing social forces for change.

The major element of this structure is the relation of capital to labor, which encompasses both those who own and control the means of production and those who have been dispossessed of all means of production except for the capacity to labor, which they have to exchange for a wage. In addition to these two basic classes, there exist several classes of individuals who occupy a position somewhere in between or located entirely outside the structure of the wage-labor relation. The most important of these is composed of individuals who own some means of production, physical and tangible or mental and intangible, but who are not in a position to purchase the labor power of the direct producers. These individuals are generally viewed as part of the traditional "middle class," sharing this position with intellectuals, professionals, and low-level managers of capitalist or public enterprises.

The Capitalist Class

Members of the capitalist class are easy enough to identify by the size of their capital (big, medium, small) and by functional criteria (industrial, commercial, financial, rentier), as well as by the perquisites of their position, such as wealth and power. Estimates as to the size of the capitalist class range from a low of 2 percent in countries like Bolivia and Ecuador to 5 or 6 percent for Argentina, Brazil, Chile, and Mexico, with a weighted regional average of 4 percent.

The core of this class is composed of individuals connected to the "big economic groups," a complex of banking, industrial, and agro-export conglomerates. In each country a core of such conglomerates can be identified, in addition to larger groupings (the new bourgeoisie) formed specifically as the result of the free-market reforms implemented since the 1980s. It is possible in each country to identify various fractions and groupings within the dominant capitalist class on the basis of the source of their capital. For example, in Mexico and to various lesser degrees in other countries, there is a large and politically significant bureaucratic class formed on the basis of privileged access to state resources and its regulatory and other powers. This part of the Mexican bourgeoisie is internally divided into different factions and connected through ties of common interest to other fractions of the capitalist class such as the industrialists, financiers, and bankers. In addition to these capitalists, there are groups of individuals who serve as CEOs of the transnational corporations that operate in each country or are connected to institutions such as the IMF. They form a powerful faction of the capitalist class as a whole, with resources and connections that constitute a significant factor in the internal and political dynamics of the class struggle.

Policies instituted in the 1980s created the basis of several other elements of the dominant capitalist class. Of particular significance here is the large-scale privatization of state enterprises undertaken by many regimes. In the case of Mexico, the privatization of hundreds of state enterprises under the administration of Carlos Salinas from 1989 to 1994 spawned a number of enormous private fortunes, which are reflected in the identification by *Forbes* in 1993 of twenty-four billionaires in Mexico, more than the number identified for all of Latin America just two years earlier. These billionaires, together with their not quite so wealthy associates (the thousands of mere millionaires created in the economic reform process), form the core of the region's new bourgeoisie, a propertied and entrepreneurial class well connected to the local political establishments as well as to international capital.

The Middle Class

Important sources of the middle class are the holding of land for the purpose of direct agricultural production and the operation of small businesses. Although these two components of the middle class vary significantly by country and have been subject to forces that have tended to decimate them, they remain numerically—and politically—important in most countries. The expansion of corporate capital has had a negative impact on the conditions of existence and survival of both the independent smallholders of land and urban-centered businesses (the "class media," as they see themselves). The specific impact of the government's economic policies on their enterprises and activities is more difficult to gauge. What *is* clear is that in every country a large number of small businesses and landholdings—over 50 percent in many cases—involve very marginal economic operations, microenterprises, the owners of which are barely able to survive in what is called "the informal sector." In this connection it is possible to distinguish between the formal petite bourgeoisie (the traditional middle class) and an informal petite bourgeoisie, which, it has been estimated, compose 10 percent or so of the region's economically active population (EAP).

Another element of the middle class is often self-identified as "professionals." These individuals provide a broad range of intellectual services, from the semiprofessional services of teachers, technicians, social workers, bureaucrats, and managers of office work to the professional and high-level management and business services provided by the legion of well-paid functionaries (of capital as well as government). A number of sociologists view these high-level functionaries and managers of capitalist and state enterprise as a distinct (professional-technical/bureaucratic) class that, it is estimated, constitutes an estimated 6–8 percent of the EAP in most countries. This is probably a fair estimate if restricted to the upper stratum of paid functionaries and distinguished from the two other major elements of the middle class—small proprietors (independent producers and business operators) and lower-level paid functionaries (salaried employees in public and private enterprises, semiprofessionals, and intellectuals).

The size of this social category in different societies is difficult to measure, largely because of the ambiguity of their position in the class structure. As salaried employees, they can also be regarded as part of the working class—as its white-collar element concerned with some form of mental or nonphysical labor. In any case, whether viewed as a stratum of the middle class or of the working class, these individuals probably make up 10 to 20 percent of the EAP. In Table 10.4 they are subsumed under the formal working class, with no attempt to differentiate among different categories of stratification or possible political divisions—manual and mental, waged and salaried, urban and rural, private and public sector, male and female, organized and unorganized.

Whether or not any of these categories relate to political differences is a matter of empirical analysis. A cursory look at the political responses to SAPs suggests that there is a strong element of resistance and opposition from groups tied to the education system, state enterprises, and the bureaucracy. Individuals and groups in this public sector have been seriously affected by policies of privatization and the cutback of the state apparatus. To a considerable but varying degree in different countries, neoliberal policies have produced a bifurcation of this class, with some elements doing well and accommodated to the neoliberal agenda and other elements doing poorly and disposed toward resistance. In a number of contexts like Argentina and Mexico, this class constitutes an important if not critical factor in the dynamics of social change.

The Working Classes

The working class comprises the vast majority of the population, but it takes diverse forms and in many countries it has been substantially restructured as a result of policy-induced and political conditions associated with SAPs. A sharp distinction has traditionally been made between wage laborers and those who work for themselves or without pay (housewives and unpaid family members). In the context of developments since the 1980s, the latter has assumed a growing proportion of the working class in all countries.

The Formal Sector.   Together with the big and the petite bourgeoisie, these workers make up the so-called modern sector of the economy, which accounts for an estimated 30 percent of the regional EAP. Estimates as to the size of this class fluctuate widely but essentially define three categories of countries: the Southern Cone (Argentina, Chile, Uruguay), where the formal proletariat represents a clear majority of the EAP; an intermediate grouping of countries (Brazil, Costa Rica, Panama, Peru) in which this class amounts to at least one-fourth of the EAP; and the rest of Latin America, where it represents on average barely 10 percent of the population.

In the 1960s and 1970s, these workers formed the social base of organized labor, of the union movement that in each country led the struggle against capital for better wages and conditions of work. And in the 1970s, in the context of a regionwide (indeed worldwide) counteroffensive by capital, this class was also the chief target of state repression, of the "dirty war" against subversives waged by the "national security" military regimes that took state power all over the region. In the 1980s context of a regionwide debt crisis, the institution of market-friendly reforms, and a redemocratization process, the formal proletariat also bore the brunt of efforts to restructure the economy and the society. In this process, the industrial proletariat, the backbone of the labor movement, was severely retrenched and in some cases decimated. From 1988 to 1992, these industries lost 1.3 million workers. As a result of these developments, by the early 1990s the formal proletariat was reduced to but a shadow of its former self—decimated numerically, weakened organizationally, and everywhere on the defensive, with a weak leadership accommodated to tripartite *concertaciones,* unable to mount any effective campaign or to mobilize political forces against capital.

The Informal Sector.   The largest component of the working class, representing in some countries up to one-half of the labor force and as much as 70 percent of workers, the informal proletariat is characterized by a diverse mix of production relations: irregular and nonstandard forms of wage labor for operators of small and unstable enterprises; part-time or casual labor without the benefit and protection of a legal contract; wage labor for subcontractors; self-employment (namely, the operation of unregulated microenterprises producing or selling goods and services from the home, in makeshift workplaces, and in the streets); domestic services to middle-class and bourgeois households; and an array of illegal activities ranging from petty thievery, burglary, and smuggling to the manufacture, distribution, and sale of drugs. By all accounts the size of this class, combined with the small-firm sector, has been on the rise—from 1980 to 1992 increasing its share of the EAP from one-third to over 55 percent (accounting for four out of every five new jobs generated over these years).

The Peasantry and the Rural Proletariat

As a region Latin America is highly urbanized, overly so in relation to the capacity of industry to absorb the large numbers of individuals dispossessed of productive land or otherwise led to migrate to the rapidly growing towns and cities. In the postwar period, a large part of the rural population was pushed into the towns and cities, converted into an urban proletariat. This process also led to the formation of a huge sector of informal enterprises and activities.

At the same time, in the countryside, an even more complex structure of economic activities and relations of production evolved. This sector incorporated various classes of producers and workers, including both middle-class and capitalist operators of farms and businesses; a rural proletariat composed of wageworkers in these sectors; a large class of smallholders, composed of individuals and households involved in farming or work under diverse relations of subsistence, independent commodity production, sharecropping, and other forms of tenancy (including—as in the case of indigenous communities in Bolivia, Ecuador, and Mexico—various forms of communal tenure); the semiproletariat, who make up the majority of direct producers in each country; and large numbers of landless workers, in the case of Brazil totaling up to 4.2 million families.

Although the EAP includes large numbers of children under working age, elders, retirees, the disabled, and other dependents, it also includes an equally large number of individuals, mostly women, whose contribution to either or both domestic and social production is not accounted for and whose labor is not remunerated at all. The majority of rural households have at least one member in this position, accounting for a significant number—perhaps 25 percent of the entire rural population.

The penetration of capitalism into the countryside has resulted in variations of this class structure. In addition, it has generated various processes of change within this structure: the transformation of the hacienda system of tenant farming into capitalist farming and agribusiness—what the Inter-American Development Bank defines as "the entrepreneurial sector of commercial enterprises"; the growth of temporary, casual, and seasonal forms of wage labor; the feminization of rural wage labor; and the urbanization of this labor.

THE SOCIAL IMPACTS OF ECONOMIC REFORMS

The announcement by the Mexican government in the summer of 1982 that it was unable to pay the interest on its accumulated external debt sent shock waves throughout the community of international finance. Under widespread structural conditions of extraordinarily high interest rates and plummeting export commodity prices, Mexico would not be alone, threatening the entire fabric of global capital. However, the international financial institutions, under the guardianship of the IMF, rallied in defense of the system.

Their solution, imposed on or adopted by country after country in the region, was a program of market-oriented economic reforms or structural adjustments. The major stated goal of this program was growth and macroeconomic equilibrium (restoration of growth in the total output of goods and services under conditions of balanced budgets, the control of price inflation). There are, however, major unstated goals of these sweeping reforms, including making sure of the capacity of countries in the region to service their external debts. But the major means of internal adjustment has been a restructuring of labor, particularly with reference to its share of national income. Table 10.5 shows for most countries in the region a significant reduction in the share of wages in both national incomes and in value added to production. With these declines in the share of labor come corresponding increases in the share of capital in national incomes and added value, both of them critical measures of the rate of labor exploitation.

Tables 10.6–10.8 provide other glimpses into the heavy social cost of this achievement: a deepening and extension of poverty, the conditions of which (unemploy-

Table 10.5
Share of Wages in (a) Value Added (Manufacturing) and (b) National Income, Selected Countries

	a		b	
	1970	1991–92	1970	1985–90
Argentina	28	19	40.9	24.9
Bolivia	37	8	36.8	26.9
Brazil	22	–	34.8	36.3
Chile	19	18	42.7	37.8
Mexico	–	21	37.5	27.3
Venezuela	31	19	40.3	31.1
Canada	53	48		
Japan	32	35		
Netherlands	52	60		
United States	47	35		
China	–	14.5		

Sources: (a) World Bank, *World Development Report 1995;* table 7; (b) ECLAC, *Statistical Annual,* various years.

Table 10.6
The Growth of Poverty in Latin America

	1980	1986	1989[a]	1992[b]
Millions of people				
Poor	136	170	183	266
Indigent	64	81	–	–
As a % of population				
Poor	41	43	44	62
Indigent	19	21	21	–

[a]Projection made by ECLAC on the basis of figures for mid-1980s.
[b]Based on estimate made during the second regional conference on poverty (Quito, 1990).
Sources: ECLAC, UNDP; cited in Latin American Special Reports (SR-92-5), October 1992.

ment, informalization of work, economic insecurity, falling wages, low income, homelessness, malnutrition, disease, illiteracy) have been borne mainly by the working class. A large part of this class has been impoverished in the process of structural adjustment, as has a part of the middle class, constituting in some countries a significant element of the "newly poor." Table 10.8 makes clear that there are significant gender as well as class dimensions to poverty and other conditions of structural adjustment. In terms of the basic indicators of social development, Cuba, as the one

Table 10.7
Social Impact Indicators, 1980–1990, Selected Countries (1980 = 100)

	Consumption Per Capita		Average Wages		Minimum Wages		Social Expenditures	
	1985	1990	1985	1990	1985	1990	1985	1990
Argentina	78.1	71.1	107.2	76.2	113.1	40.2	71.8	82.3
Brazil	89.1	93.8	116.1	102.9	88.9	53.4	–	–
Chile	83.7	98.2	93.5	104.8	76.4	87.5	87.8	90.7
Mexico	95.6	93.1	75.9	77.9	71.1	45.5	103.1	59.5
Venezuela	88.4	80.9	75.7	41.5	96.8	59.3	92.9	95.9

Source: Patricio Meller, "Latin American Adjustment and Economic Reforms: Issues and Recent Experiences," paper presented at the Conference "Economic Reforms in Market and Socialist Economies," Madrid, July 6–8, 1992.

Table 10.8
Social Dimensions of Latin American Development, Selected Countries, Ranked in Reverse Order by Per Capita Income

	Rural Pop. Percent Poor 1988/90	Percent Illiteracy 1990		Life Expectancy			Infant[a] Mortality	
		M	F	1965	1988	1993	1970	1993
Bolivia	97	29	23	46	53	60	153	73
Ecuador	65	16	14	58	66	69	100	49
Peru	75	21	15	54	62	66	116	63
Venezuela	58	17	8	65	70	72	53	23
Brazil	73	20	19	59	65	67	85	57
Chile	56	7	7	62	72	74	77	16
Cuba	35	6	5	–	74	76	–	9
Mexico	51	15	13	62	69	71	72	35
Argentina	20	7	7	67	71	72	52	24

[a]Rate per 1,000 live births.
Source: Idriss Jazairy, Mohiuddin Alamgir, and Theresa Panuccio, *The State of Rural World Poverty* (London: IFAD, 1992), table 8; World Bank, *World Development Report 1995* (Oxford: Oxford University Press, 1995).

country that has pursued a socialist rather than a capitalist path, stands out as a striking anomaly, with levels of education, health, and welfare comparable to the most industrially developed countries in the world.

By the 1980s, after three and a half decades of sustained economic and social change, the material conditions of social existence for the majority of the population had substantially improved. In the 1980s, however, under conditions of a widespread debt crisis and structural adjustment, these gains were wiped out. With a fall of up to 60 percent in the value of wages or purchasing power, the situation of most people—the working classes of the population—seriously deteriorated.

Despite a minimal and fragile "recovery" after close to a decade of sweeping economic reforms, in many countries the average level of income and standard of living in the early 1990s was lower than that achieved as early as 1970. Under the economic and social conditions of structural adjustment that included growing unemployment, informalization, a drastic decline in the value of wages, and cutback of government services, the 1980s saw a substantial worsening in the distribution of wealth and income, already among the most inequitable in the world (see Table 10.3). Within this distribution, the gap between the incomes of the poorest 40 percent of households and the richest 10 percent widened, in some cases dramatically. In 1993 the top decile received over 40 percent of total income in countries with the most highly concentrated income distribution, and in every case at least 30 percent. Also, the sharp decline in real wages and employment opportunities in most countries had a particularly strong impact on those at the bottom of the income pyramid and class structure. The overall result was a significant increase in income inequalities for most countries in the region.

These inequalities have produced striking differences in social situations for different groups and classes of the population. At one extreme they have spawned a small number of billionaires, whose combined wealth exceeds that of half of the population and whose conditions of social existence are almost unimaginable and certainly obscene. At the other extreme, the grossly unequal distribution of wealth and income is reflected in a widening and deepening poverty. As Table 10.5 shows, the number of those living in poverty has substantially increased over the course of the 1980s. By the end of the decade, according to some estimates, up to 46 percent of all households were poor, unable to meet their basic needs. Most of these households are located in the urban centers, although the incidence of poverty is higher in the rural areas, home to the landless, masses of marginal small landholders and producers, and most indigenous peoples who form 10 percent or so of the total population (50 percent in some countries). Typically, this element of the population suffers the most blatant forms of exploitation and oppression and the resulting conditions of abject poverty.

THE DYNAMICS OF CLASS STRUGGLE: POLITICAL RESPONSES TO SAPS

Over the years, there has been a recurring debate as to the social base and political dynamics of social movements for change in the region. However, the policies and conditions of structural adjustment have recast some of the issues involved, especially as relates to the popular sector of civil society. But two important questions remain. One is whether the objective and subjective conditions of struggle, resistance, and protest are structural and class based or based on localized struggles for and the politics of "identity," defined by gender, ethnicity, and other culturally specific struggles. A second contested area has to do with the specific structural source of the conditions that have given rise to social movements and the politics of resistance and social protest.

Apart from the problem of determining how relations of exploitation and marginalization fit in the social structure of Latin American societies, the political conditions of these relations—the social and political forces that have been generated and are subject to mobilization—are not clear. Forms of popular resistance and political protest and the conditions that produced them need further study. Some preliminary results of such a study are briefly summarized below.

Work on One's Own Account

The dramatic growth of the informal sector reflects decisions made by members of income-poor households (often recent rural emigrants) in the failed search for income-generating employment. These "decisions" are generally shaped by conditions over which their agents have absolutely no control and that provide few if any options. In other words, to the degree that there is agency involved in these decisions and actions, it represents a survival strategy, a defensive response to the economic and social conditions of poverty—the deprivation of basic needs. As such, it represents a form of self-exploitation by household members who are generally constrained to provide labor power, or the products of their self-organized labor, at a level of remuneration well below its value. As for the women in these households, their rate of exploitation tends to be considerably higher than that for men, given their general responsibility for household and reproductive labor, which, when added to their social production, often leads to working days of twelve to sixteen hours, or seventy-eighty-work-hour weeks.

However, as a household "strategy," self-exploitative informal economic activities, even with all members participating, generally have not enabled the household to meet its basic needs for food, nutrition, shelter, clothing, education, and human development. As a result, in the context of deepening economic crisis and adjustment, the female heads of some of these income-poor urban households in the 1980s came together to pool their limited resources and cooperate in the provision for these needs. Such interhousehold forms of cooperation and association can be found in most shantytowns in cities such as Lima, Mexico City, São Paulo, Rio de Janeiro, Santiago, and Guayaquil.

The Popular Economy: Community-Based Cooperation

In Lima in 1979, a number of *comedores populares* (popular canteens/dining halls) were set up and cooperatively run by a group of around fifty women from income-poor shantytown households. By 1982 there were an estimated 1,500 such organizations, in addition to 6,500 or so "glass-of-milk" committees that brought together and serviced over 100,000 households. In Santiago similar forms of popular economic organization (PEO), the *ollas comunes* (communal stew-pots) and community soup kitchens, were formed on the basis of various associations of women in *las poblaciones,* the shantytowns that surrounded the city. Such associations existed in Chile in the early 1970s, but under conditions created by the sweeping free-market reforms of the Pinochet regime and the worst economic crisis in the region, they pro-liferated. In 1982, when the country was in the throes of another economic crisis, there were thirty-four *ollas comunes* in Santiago; by 1988, fifteen years into the Pinochet regime, there were 232 of them. By the 1980s, entire networks of such PEOs, based on associations of women, were formed throughout the shantytowns. In addition to the *ollas comunes,* they included self-help groups, production work-shops (small units with three to fifteen people producing and selling goods and ser-vices such as bread, clothing, laundry, carpentry, etc.), organizations for the unem-ployed, housing committees, committees for the homeless, and organizations related to housing problems such as water and electricity.

Similar women's organizations of the urban poor were formed in Brazil, Mexico, and other countries in the region subject to the·same conditions of crisis and adjust-ment or austerity measures. By taking charge in this manner, the women of poor working-class households have come to feel collectively stronger and more self-reliant. In a number of cases, the PEOs have also provided a grassroots base for mo-bilizing resistance to the austerity and repressive policies of the military regime. In this context, these PEOs represent the transition made by a number of associations of the urban poor from community action to collective protest.

From Community Development to Street Protest

It is difficult to distinguish between forms of community-based cooperative actions and collective forms of resistance and to see where the former end and the latter begin. But in the context of spreading reforms, worsening socioeconomic conditions, and military rule, the urban poor took to the streets and moved from collective com-munity action to collective forms of protest, including rioting and demonstrations. There is no question about the effectiveness and political impact of these collective acts of protest. In the outburst of political protest from 1983 to 1986, the urban poor were center stage, and the women in the popular classes were among the first to protest the regressive and repressive free-market policies. Unionized workers, in contrast, were slow to respond and took their cue from the urban poor. And the in-tellectuals and politicos associated with the traditional parties were even slower to react and were manifestly ineffective in attempts to direct the self-mobilized forces of the urban poor, who in specific situations were joined in their struggles by unionized workers, students, teachers, public employees, shopkeepers, and other elements of an impoverished middle class.

The most widely documented form of overt resistance and protest against neolib-eral policies of stabilization and structural adjustment is the riot: the spontaneous outbreak of street protests against publicly announced increases in the price of food, gasoline, kerosene, or means of transportation. In the contemporary context of debt and adjustment, the first recorded street riots occurred in Peru in 1976. In subse-quent years there were sporadic outbreaks in various countries and a veritable wave of riots in 1982–1983 in Argentina, Bolivia, Brazil, Chile, Ecuador, and Panama. The forty-nine recorded riots in these years (fifty-two if we add the riots of 1984 in the Dominican Republic) represented more than one-third of all recorded riots worldwide. A second wave of rioting hit the region in 1985–1986, followed by a series of riots in Venezuela that left over 300 dead.

The immediate trigger of these riots is beyond dispute: They were invariably in response to policy measures and conditions attributed by the rioters themselves to the IMF, the symbolic if not immediate target of protest. In this connection, rioters tend to be manifestly unsympathetic to the efforts of various Latin American governments "to get prices right" by cutting or eliminating subsidies and price controls or other such austerity measures.

Riots are but one of a number of politically overt forms of resistance and acts of street protest against austerity measures. They have often been combined with other tactics such as mass demonstrations, marches on public buildings, encampments, land occupations, roadblocks, hunger strikes, boycotts, work stoppages, nonattendance at work or school, labor strikes (the traditional and well-tried tactic of organized labor), as well as civic strikes.

These acts of resistance and protest are significant in that they bring together diverse groups and classes in the popular sector and lead to concerted action. An example of such concerted action took place in Ecuador in 1994, when an association of urban women, the Federation of Trade Unions, and the National Association of Indigenous Peoples took to the streets in a carefully orchestrated and scheduled series of marches, mass demonstrations, and strikes. Similar associations were formed in other countries in response to the same conditions. For example, after the devaluation of the peso in December 1994, more than 1,200 demonstrations and 550 marches—a daily average of five acts of protest—were organized in Mexico City in the space of a year. On one day alone (March 10, 1995), there were over 100 separate acts of protest. This wave of street protests was followed by the formation of a huge coalition of diverse social movements and organizations of farmers, peasants, independent business operators, workers, and nongovernmental organizations (NGOs) that came together to reject the government's economic model, which has generated only misery and unemployment.

Protest and Resistance in the Workplace

In the context of widespread economic restructuring, the Latin American working class no longer is what it once was. A traditional stratum of full-time workers remains in place, strategically situated in various expanding industries, well organized to defend and advance their collective interests, able to negotiate collective contracts with managers of capitalist enterprises and to engage in effective workplace strike action. However, in the 1990s, such workers were in the minority. Where found they tended to be very much on the defensive, with a weakened capacity for collective action in an inhospitable if not hostile environment and an accommodating and compromised leadership, disposed to engage in tripartite pacts with business and government.

Under these conditions, the politics of resistance by workers in the formal sector of capitalist firms, public institutions, and remaining state enterprises tends to take different forms than before. Class struggle still involves strikes and electoral activity, but resistance to and protest against government policies of structural adjustment are now more likely to take the form of street demonstrations, mass rallies, and marches on government buildings.

It is clear that many workers remain opposed to the neoliberal agenda, as evident in the mass actions of workers all across the region in March and April 1995. In Bolivia, mass actions included the declaration of a general strike, orchestrated by the powerful Bolivian Center of Labor (COB). Despite the "understanding" reached between the COB and the government on April 29, leading to among other things the ending of the fifty-day teachers' strike that had forced the government to arrest hundreds of union leaders and to declare a state of siege, organizations of affiliated workers affirmed their commitment "to continue the struggle against neoliberal policies." A similar commitment was expressed by over 150,000 workers in Mexico City on May Day in a massive rally against privatization, the announced 50 percent increase in the value-added tax (VAT), and other elements of the government's neoliberal policy.

Protest and Resistance in the Countryside

The penetration of capitalism into the countryside has been associated with a number of developments, including the transformation of the hacienda system of tenant labor into a wage-labor-based system of agro-export production; a crisis in peasant agriculture based on communal forms of land tenure; the expulsion of many proletarianized producers from the land, leading to a massive outmigration from the countryside to the urban centers; and a marked increase in temporary and seasonal forms of wage labor in the agricultural sector, with a significant gender dimension.

The combination of these developments has had a decided impact on the political capacity of workers and producers in the countryside and on the form of their organized resistance. For one thing, noted changes in employment practices toward more casual, precarious, and feminized forms of "flexible" labor have tended to increase the control of capital and the bargaining power of employers vis-à-vis labor. For another, the casualization of rural labor has contributed to the fracturing of a long-standing and at times militant peasant movement. Although seasonal and casual laborers can be highly militant, they are notoriously difficult to organize in part because of their mixed composition and shifting residence. As for the mass of landless workers that has been generated, the pressures to migrate and the possibilities of doing so have also undercut their capacity to organize and fight in the countryside.

At the same time, throughout the countryside conditions of capital accumulation and policies of structural adjustment have spawned numerous associations of producers and workers, organized with the objective of resistance and political protest. The central issue for these organizations has been to agree on a form of struggle appropriate to their conditions and for which resources and cross-class support can be generated. The internal debates on this issue have been long and were relatively inconsequential until the January 1994 outbreak of armed insurrection in Chiapas. Among the highland peoples in the area, such uprisings have not been unusual, this one having been in the works since the early 1980s. But in Chiapas on January 1, 1994, a number of distinct but interrelated processes led to the formation of the Zapatista Army of National Liberation.

The demands of the Zapatistas relate to conditions generated by economic and political structures that are deeply embedded in the history of the state's indigenous peoples, but a subsequent declaration by subcomandante Marcos, the official spokesperson for the Clandestine Revolutionary Indigenous Committee, points to the right of rebellion against the inhumane and unjust policies of neoliberalism. In this declaration, the Zapatistas threatened to march on Mexico to press their demands, a similar approach to that taken by indigenous peoples in both Bolivia and Ecuador. In Bolivia the blockade of highways and mass marches on La Paz in 1993 and again in 1995 came in response to the call by the federation of organized urban workers for support of their struggle. However, in Mexico, as in Ecuador, there was no such call. It was the action of indigenous peoples that provoked the response of urban workers, leading to widespread mobilization and the creation of a social movement in solidarity with the Zapatista struggle in Chiapas and with similar struggles waged by indigenous peoples and peasant producers elsewhere.

CONCLUSIONS

The political dynamics of economic restructuring in Latin America are complex. Popular resistance and opposition to it takes multiple forms. It is clear, though, that these dynamics derive from conditions of class relations (exploitation, marginality, etc.) and not from the localized politics of gender and ethnic "identity," as some would argue. In the context of the restructuring experienced by most countries in Latin America, the widespread and multiform politics of protest and social movements of opposition and resistance relate to and arise out of the economic costs of structural adjustment, which have been catastrophic for the majority of the working population. The dynamics of this political opposition, of responses to conditions of structural adjustment, need to be better documented and further analyzed.

SUGGESTED READINGS

Alvarez, Sonia E. *The Making of Social Movements in Latin America: Identity, Strategy and Democracy.* Boulder, Colo.: Westview Press, 1992.

Chinchilla, Norma Stoltz. "Women's Movements in the Americas: Feminism's Second Wave," *Report on the Americas* 27 (1993):17–23.

Eckstein, Susan, ed. *Power and Popular Protest.* Boulder, Colo.: Westview Press, 1989.

Escobar, Arturo, and Sonia Alvarez, eds. *The Making of Social Movements in Latin America.* Boulder, Colo.: Westview Press, 1992.

Halebsky, Sandor, and Richard Harris, eds. *Capital, Power, and Inequality in Latin America.* Boulder, Colo.: Westview Press, 1995.

Leiva, Fernando, and James Petras, with Henry Veltmeyer. *Democracy and Poverty in Chile.* Boulder, Colo.: Westview Press, 1994.

Petras, James, and Morris Morley. *US Hegemony Under Siege: Class, Politics and Development in Latin America.* London: Verso, 1990.

Veltmeyer, Henry, and James Petras. *Neoliberalism and Class Conflict in Latin America.* New York: St. Martin's Press, 1996.

11

NATURE IN LATIN AMERICA: IMAGES AND ISSUES

ELDON KENWORTHY

"If you consent, neither you nor any other human being shall ever see us again: I will go to the vast wilds of South America." With those words the monster created by Victor Frankenstein implored his maker to provide him with a mate and let them flee to a place where they would pose no danger to civilization. In Mary Shelley's novel, the scientist Frankenstein first considers the plan, then rejects it. "You propose to fly from the habitations of man, to dwell in those wilds where the beasts of the field will be your only companions. How long can you, who long for the love and sympathy of man, persevere in this exile?"[1]

Who knows how many human beings lived in South America when Shelley's novel was first published in 1818, since thousands of aboriginal communities remained unknown to census takers. Only recently have archaeologists determined that the Amazon Basin—that stereotypical jungle primeval—hosted large human settlements. My guess is that 20 million humans inhabited South America in the year Shelley described it as "those wilds" far from "the habitations of man." Official records for 1850 point to 15 million in "tropical South America" alone,[2] comparable to the numbers then living in England or Spain or the United States.

The "savages" may reason there, thought the philosopher Thomas Hobbes two centuries earlier, since they have language. But as hunting and collecting are inferior to agriculture, so must aboriginal peoples lack the intellectual equivalents of fences and barns: the books and schools necessary for philosophy. Unable to "sow" knowledge, how could such savages discriminate reason's fruits from those generated by the "weeds" of "conjecture"?[3] It is a telling metaphor that lives on in the two meanings of "cultivated" and "culture": one associated with farming, the other with learning.

In much of the world, progress continues to be visualized as something wrested from nature, then defended against it—as land is cleared before a crop is planted, then defended from pests that enter from beyond the fence. Midway into the twentieth century, the U.S. historian Samuel Flagg Bemis wrote off the "lowland tropics" of Latin America as inhospitable to "civilization" due to a climate and geography that make taming nature difficult.[4] Where moisture and heat combine, nature eats away at the linearity of progress, as Gabriel García Márquez suggested in his novel *A Hundred Years of Solitude*. Roots buckle concrete, insects invade music, time slows, and fences fail.

No less intrigued than Hobbes with "the Caribs of Venezuela," Jean-Jacques Rousseau fostered a different reading of nature. Some of our finest qualities as humans, including the capacity to empathize with other species, arise from our prerational selves, wrote Rousseau. "Let us not conclude with Hobbes that because [primitive] man has no idea of goodness, he is naturally evil." As with advocates of "sustainable development" today, Rousseau sought to balance nature's and civilization's strengths. Halt Western civilization at the point where acquisitive drives and status preoccupations have not overcome natural wisdom and links to place: That is what Rousseau advocated in 1754.[5]

Although they quarreled, what Rousseau sought Voltaire visualized five years later. Voltaire refurbished the myth of a city of gold that lay somewhere in deepest Latin America, probably Amazonia. Only he turned the early explorers' quest for riches on its head by describing "Eldorado" as a place where gold is considered mud, where rubies lie undisturbed in the streets, where inhabitants are hospitable, and where the arts and sciences thrive in a society free of law courts, churches, and jails.[6]

No, this is not a chapter mislaid from a different book. This introduction merely reflects the truth that nature does not speak for itself. How we see nature in Latin America, and those whose lives are most deeply imbedded within it, continues to be shaped by northern projections. I use "northern" as shorthand for those Western European, North American, and East Asian centers that dominate the image-making, trade, technologies, and financial decisions that daily reshape this planet into a more interdependent and artificial place. Until recently, the North that impacted Latin America consisted of the United States and Europe. Today, Japanese preferences—such as for building with wood while keeping Japan forested—are among the many ways that Asia impacts nature in Latin America.

Latin America long has provided sites for the northern imagination to project its fantasies, be they dark or bright, surreal or strategic. That imagination has peopled Latin America with noble savages and cannibals, women warriors (Amazons) and señoritas in distress, chocolate and cocaine, a "new world" of liberty and the last redoubt of "old world" corporatism. Today at a store near you the rain forests still yield up the elixir of youth (remember Hernando de Soto?) in the form of politically correct cosmetics. Next door perhaps you can purchase a CD with Kayapó warriors backing a rock star who performs only on guitars made of certifiably environmentally friendly wood.

I received this solicitation from Randy Hayes, director of Rainforest Action Network (RAN)—dated only "Wednesday, past midnight"—in October 1996. In it Hayes recalls how in the Amazon, "I met with indigenous activists—people on intimate terms with the incredible variety of soaring trees, the rainbow-hued birds, the chattering monkeys and swift jaguars, the wild orchids. They dared to oppose the industrial machine to save their centuries-old way of life." On RAN's letterhead appears one of those swift jaguars (or some other wild cat) just as on the World Wildlife Fund's is the panda. Strange how the insects, reptiles, and fungi that proliferate in these forests are upstaged by creatures least likely to be seen there, not just today but historically. Strange, too, how little is said of the use indigenous cultures such as the Kayapó make of modern technology or of their willingness to have their own forests logged on occasion.

In his 1983 novel *The Mosquito Coast*,[7] Paul Theroux updated Joseph Conrad's *Heart of Darkness* in a Central American setting. Both books show confident northerners, motivated by the best of intentions, doing harm. A partner on an ecotour of Amazonia recalls waiting for Randy Hayes to meet up with the group: "It's a vast, chaotic place, the Amazon. What we need is somebody to put it in order, to name it, tame it, render up its teachings. We need a shaman, and ours [Hayes] is missing in action." As Kurtz was missing upriver, leaving his colonial company uncertain what to do? Midway into the trip Hayes was "out of sorts" because "the enemy is hard to define out here in the bush."[8] Was Bemis right?

No, Hayes is no Kurtz and RAN no colonial outpost. Yet neither hesitates to speak for the rain forest and its inhabitants or to play upon northerners' sense of the exotic. In the ongoing struggle over the meanings humans give nature—which influences the uses we make of nature—enchantment and empathy certainly are preferable to commodification (viewing nature as raw material). An ingredient missing in both, however, is humility. Rather than a place or species we get to save, nature is a design in which we live no matter where we are or what we do—a design in which the local is nested in the regional which is nested in the global like a series of Russian dolls.

So far I have noted several recurring ways of constructing nature in Latin America: as something other and apart (Shelley), as something in need of our improvement (Hobbes and countless capitalists), and as our second chance, our connection to goodness, wholeness, or righteousness (Rousseau and Hayes). Since projections are not made out of whole cloth, there are elements of truth in each. There also are large amounts of narcissism and denial, as later pages attempt to show.

HORIZONTAL SLICE: INVENTORYING WHAT'S THERE

One perspective on nature, then, is nature as cultural construct. Opposing that is the scientific perspective, especially science in its descriptive mode. As an introduction to nature in Latin America and the Caribbean (LAC), this chapter would be remiss if it did not provide a reasonably objective description of what is out there. I give the most attention to a third perspective, however, that of human-nature interactions. Since these interactions reach from village to planet, this "cut" manifests a vertical dimension in contrast to the more horizontal overview of descriptive science, to which we now turn.

Scientists sponsored by the World Wildlife Fund (WWF) and the World Bank recently collaborated on an inventory of Latin America's ecosystems.[9] To learn from their mapping, we must understand their terminology. Thinking that readers may

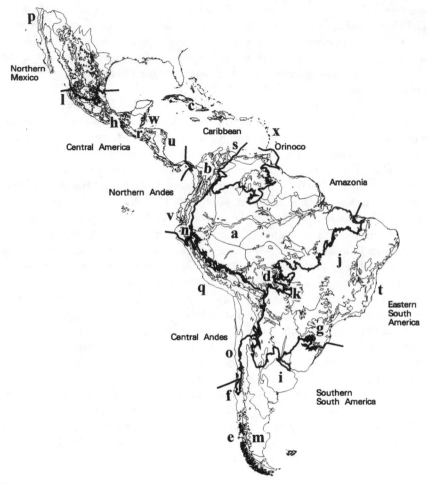

Figure 11.1. Ecoregions and Bioregions
Bold lines mark the boundaries of the nine bioregions, while thin lines delineate ecoregions. Lowercase letters indicate the approximate location of the ecoregions listed in column 3 of Table 11.1.

Adapted from Eric Dinerstein et al., *A Conservation Assessment of the Terrestrial Ecoregions of Latin America and the Caribbean* (Washington, D.C.: World Bank, 1995), map 1, p. 131. Reproduced with the permission of the World Bank and the World Wildlife Fund. Basemap data from the Digital Chart of the World.

find that task easier with a stable point of reference, this chapter periodically returns to one country for illustrations. Probably no nation better exemplifies the "problems and promise" of Latin America on this topic, nature, than Costa Rica.

Costa Rica (right below "u" on the map) is part of the Central American bioregion that extends from southern Mexico to the Isthmus of Panama. Each of the nine bioregions of LAC is composed of many smaller ecoregions. Within the Central American bioregion, for example, are thirty-two forest ecoregions, eleven grassland ecoregions, and so on. Although smaller than West Virginia, Costa Rica exhibits five distinct forest ecoregions, one paramo ecoregion, and several mangrove and coral reef ecoregions.

Ecoregions vary in size and often spill across national boundaries. All of Mexico could fit inside one in Brazil: the Cerrado (j). A glance at the map tells us that ecoregions tend to be smaller in areas riven by mountains or abutting oceans (both true of Costa Rica) while larger on inland plains (the Cerrado being an example). Two rules of thumb are: (1) The more ecoregions in a given area, the greater the variety of species inhabiting that area; (2) the larger the land area of an ecoregion, the better it can absorb human-induced change.

With its many small and varied ecoregions, Costa Rica supports a higher number of species than its landmass would suggest. Were maps drawn to reflect species diversity (one dimension of "biodiversity"), Costa Rica would be larger than the United States. I will illustrate this with birds since, unlike insects, most bird species have been identified and most birds need land for habitat. Costa Rica hosts 855 different bird species, or 9 percent of the world's total. The percentage of the world's land surface occupied by Costa Rica, however, is only one-third of 1 percent! With 12 percent of the world's land area, the United States and Canada host roughly the same number of bird species as Costa Rica. Why, from the perspective of genetic richness, is the region between the tropics of Cancer and Capricorn more valuable than temperate zones? As Bemis recognized, but deprecated, life proliferates in water and warmth. For Costa Rica, this effect is accentuated by the conditions described in the first rule of thumb.

The second rule of thumb tells us why conserving species presents a special challenge to the Costa Ricas of the world. There individual ecoregions are small, thus easily damaged. A movement is under way to create "biological corridors" larger than existing nature reserves, both within and between Central American countries. This is critical for the survival of larger mammals (e.g., panthers or tapirs) and species that fly.[10]

A forest ecoregion obviously consists of more than trees, a grassland ecoregion of more than grasses. An ecoregion is an "assemblage of natural communities" in interaction.[11] It is the high degree of interaction within an ecoregion that distinguishes it from neighboring ecoregions, even though species of one interact with those of another. Whether an ecoregion is spatially of a piece, as most are, or discontinuous, as mangroves, reefs, and dunes usually are, each is tangible. You can go there and observe it. The Costa Rican paramo, for instance, is found above timberline in the cloudy Cordillera de Talamanca accessed by the Interamerican Highway. Take the

Table 11.1
Three Levels of Ecological Classification

Six Major Ecosystem Types, Composed of	⇒	Thirteen Major Habitat Types, Found in	⇒	200+ Ecoregions, of Which Two Are Listed for Each Habitat Type: First an Extensive Site, Then a Highly Threatened Site
1. tropical broadleaf forests (42.8% of LAC landmass)		1.1 Moist (38.0% of LAC)		a. Amazon Basin (Brazil) b. Cauca Valley mountains (Colombia)
		1.2 Dry (4.8%)		c. Cuba's interior d. Lowland eastern Bolivia
2. Conifer/temperate broadleaf forests (5.1%)		2.1 Temperate (1.5%)		e. Valdivian forests (Chile) f. Chile's winter rain forests
		2.2 Tropical and subtropical conifers (3.6%)		g. Arucaria forests (Brazil) h. Sierra Madre del Sur (Mexico)
3. Grasslands/savannas/ shrublands (40.6%)		3.1 Dry, lowland (32.7%)		i. The Pampas (Argentina) j. The Cerrado (Brazil)
		3.2 Flooded (1.3%)		k. The Pantanal (Brazil) l. Jalisco palm savannas (Mexico)
		3.3 Montane (6.6%)		m. Patagonian steppe (Argentina) n. Andean paramo (Ecuador)
4. Xeric (arid) formations (11.5%)		4.1 Mediterranean scrub (0.8%)		o. Chilean matorral (central coast) p. Baja California coast chaparral (Mexico)
		4.2 Deserts and xeric shrub (10.5%)		q. Peru's coastal Sechura desert r. Motagna thornscrub (Guatemala)
		4.3 Restingas (dunes) (0.2%)		s. Paraguaná restingas (Venezuela) t. Brazil's Atlantic coast
5. Mangroves (0.2%)		5.1 Mangroves (0.2%)		u. Nicaragua's Atlantic coast v. Manabí (Ecuador)
6. Coral reef[a]		6.1 Continental shelf		w. Belize's barrier reef
		6.2 Oceanic		x. Lesser Antilles' fringing reefs

[a]Since this source omits marine ecoregions, I have added the sixth ecosystem type. Lacking reliable information on which coral reefs are most threatened, for the two types of reef systems only one example of each is provided. Oceanic islands might also be considered a major ecosystem type because of their high endemism (e.g., the Galápagos archipelago).

(continues)

Table 11.1
(*continued*)

Note: Several ecoregions span more than one nation. The list of one host country in column 3 is intended to facilitate location on the map, nothing more. For each habitat type, both of the examples given in column 3 may be threatened and both may be extensive. The selection process ensures *at least* one of each. With the exception of ecosystem 3, all of the second examples of each habitat type have been classified by the source as either "critical" or "endangered" *and* as being significant either globally or bioregionally. "Significance" refers to rarity, whereas "critical" and "endangered" refer to the probability that the site will lose its key species within ten years unless heroic conservation efforts are undertaken. No examples of ecosystem type 3 are as threatened as the first two types, but they have been classified "vulnerable" and are of global importance. Although no "threatened" ranking is provided for ecosystem type 6, coral reefs throughout the hemisphere suffer from agricultural runoff, industrial and marine pollution, overfishing, and global warming.

Source: Adapted from Eric Dinerstein et al., *A Conservation Assessment of the Terrestrial Ecoregions of Latin America and the Caribbean* (Washington, D.C.: World Bank, 1995).

bus from San José to San Isidro, and you will see "a chaparral like formation of tall, gnarled shrubs in sheltered situations, a small, stiff, broomlike bamboo in open sites, and a cycadlike tree fern in the numerous swampy spots."[12]

Such specificity is not the case with the "types" listed in the left-hand columns of the table. "Types" clump scattered ecoregions that have key characteristics in common. For example, Costa Rica's paramo resembles the Patagonian steppe of Argentina enough that both are included in a single category (3.3 in the table). Types help us summarize the bewildering diversity in nature and guide conservation practice. The WWF–World Bank inventory was undertaken to set priorities for conservation in a world where saving it all no longer is possible.

Two goals currently are sought in conserving nature. How compatible they are depends on how each is defined and applied. Popular with policymakers is "sustainable development," which basically means not destroying the natural resource base in the process of using it for economic ends.[13] Popular with scientists and environmentalists is "biodiversity," which seeks to arrest the human contribution to the extinction of other life-forms.[14] Both are responses to the destructive outcome of northern forms of economic development. The earth is believed to hold in excess of 10 million species—and perhaps as many as 50 million; no one really knows—of which fewer than 2 million have been classified. Human activity is causing extinctions on a scale comparable to such global catastrophes as the asteroid strike that ended the age of reptiles 66 million years ago. It took 10 million years of evolution to replenish the biodiversity lost in that event.[15]

To the U.S. Agency for International Development (USAID), which champions both goals, biodiversity serves sustainable development and vice versa.[16] The many new technologies that are biologically derived support this linkage, as does an increasing awareness of agriculture's dependence on the genetic resources of the wild.

To those who see biodiversity more as a matter of intergenerational or interspecies justice, however, or who simply value nature independent of human uses, USAID's emphasis on the good that humans derive from biodiversity seems misplaced. These critics suspect that "sustainable development" is merely "economic development" in politically correct clothing. To really save biodiversity, they argue, a clean break is needed from the perpetual growth assumptions imbedded in capitalism.[17]

At a practical level, a third group would argue that nothing in nature is likely to survive unless humans, especially those living in the ecosystem in question, perceive some benefit from its survival. While not all benefits need be economic, this third view pulls us back to "sustainable development."[18] As a goal, "sustainability" is hard to fault in that it directs us to discover complementarities between environment and economy, between a good life for all humans and the survival of all species. But it remains a goal, not yet an accomplishment on any scale that matters.

While humanity works at inventing "sustainable development," the World Bank–WWF study pinpoints the ecosystems that most need saving now, using such criteria as their uniqueness and their not having passed a point of no return. Preserving the full range of species naturally found in each bioregion is one of the study's priorities, which in practice means prioritizing the sole mangrove in one bioregion over a comparable mangrove in another that has three other mangrove systems. The reality, of course, is that each mangrove plays an important role in the functioning of all ecoregions within its vicinity. Nature knows no spare parts.

At the LAC level, the highest priorities assigned by the World Bank–WWF study include tropical *dry* broadleaf forests, such as those near the Pacific coasts of Ecuador and Peru. Top priorities also include tropical and subtropical coniferous forests, such as the pine-oak forests of Mexico's Sierra Madre range. While many tropical moist broadleaf forests—what usually is meant by "rain forest"—also are rated highly, these tend not to be in the Amazon but scattered along the Pacific slopes of the Andes in Colombia and Ecuador, in the Venezuelan Andes and Peruvian Yungas, and on the Atlantic coast in northeastern Brazil.

Why this reversal of the common perception that to "save nature" we must first save the rain forests, especially those of the Amazon? Although the vast fires used a decade ago to clear the Amazon for ranching and settlement have abated, the answer is not that conservation has succeeded there. As Southeast Asia is stripped of its hardwood, the pressure to log the Amazon increases.[19] Rather, the answer lies in the immensity of these forests, which makes them harder to compromise than the smaller forests listed above (our second rule of thumb). Only 3 percent of tropical dry broadleaf forests of Latin America are rated "relatively stable" or "relatively intact," whereas 27 percent of the tropical moist broadleaf forests remain so.[20] Another source claims that despite an annual rate of deforestation that reached 5,750 sq mi in 1994, 88 percent of the Amazonian forests remain intact.[21]

Another surprise is that of top priority for conservation are dune formations in Brazil and Mediterranean scrub in Mexico and Chile, hardly the poster children of environmental organizations. A parallel study agrees on prioritizing the Sonoran

Desert of northern Mexico.[22] In all, the northern Andean and Central American bioregions have more "critical" and "endangered" ecoregions than other bioregions.

Whether one agrees with its recommendations or not, the overview provided by the World Bank–WWF study alerts us to the variety of ecologies found in LAC: 178 distinct terrestrial ecoregions plus twenty-two mangrove units. Adding aquatic formations—which this study does not—would push the total into the two hundreds. Species that repel most nonindigenous humans, such as fungi, insects, plankton, and spiders, play indispensable roles in the health of these ecoregions. At the bioregional level, the same could be said of mangroves, wetlands, and scrublands. Many coastal resorts clear mangroves believing that northern tourists seek sandy beaches with swaying palms.

This brief excursion into Latin America's natural diversity reminds us that the size of a nation's landmass, population, or economy has little to do with its biological importance. LAC's diversity, with all of its hidden synergies, means that whoever arrives searching for some Disneyesque Eden their culture has lost or for wilderness in need of improvement probably will make bad choices. They may assume that economic activity has no place in "fragile" ecoregions or, to the contrary, that only a stiff infusion of northern techniques will permit "development" to occur. Just remember that virtually all LAC ecoregions have sustained human populations for millennia. What is problematic has not been the human presence but northern technologies and priorities.

On the steep and dry slopes of Andean Peru, long before Europeans arrived, humans developed bench terraces to hold topsoil and guide runoff. In the dry arroyos of the Sonoran Desert, Mexican farmers over generations developed the technique of using rocks and brush to trap the volcanic sediments washed down by the water that flows in torrents only a few days each year. Where the problem is too much standing water, peoples throughout LAC have devised *chinampas*, or raised beds, dredging by hand "green manure" from canal bottoms to build these beds. As with water, so with fire. On the phosphorous-deficient soils of the Amazonian forests, indigenous cultures practiced slash and burn with success for them and for the rest of the ecosystem.

Although sometimes archaeology is needed to retrieve these practices, in most instances all it takes is an observant eye not clouded over by northern assumptions. A blending of tradition and modernity that would have pleased Rousseau is evident in the new boundary-crossing fields of ethnobotany and agroecology. Contrary to what Hobbes wrote, cultivation can mimic nature, not displace it, and good science can be teased out of local knowledge.

SLICING IT VERTICALLY: HUMAN-NATURE INTERACTIONS

Such an overview does not lend itself to exploring the human-nature interactions typical of LAC today, since these require close attention to particular situations. When we explore any one case, however, we uncover a chain of reciprocal influences that links watershed to region to planet, giving this exercise verticality. What follows is as good an example of this process as any, although each beginning point tells a different tale.

On July 27, 1996, hurricane Cesar tore through Costa Rica. In a country of 3 million, forty were killed in the landslides, flooding, and rescue efforts that followed. Over 100 communities were isolated as roads washed out and bridges buckled. Over 3,000 homes, schools, and clinics were destroyed. A total of 5,000 acres of crops were lost, affecting not only the key exports, coffee and bananas, but the staples, rice and beans. The Interamerican Highway linking Costa Rica north and south was out of commission for weeks, halting regional trade. When it was over, the damage attributed to the hurricane totaled $177 million. For reasons soon evident, add the damage caused by all unusual weather that year: $227 million, or 3 percent of Costa Rica's national product.[23]

At first cut, hurricanes seem a normal manifestation of a bioregional pattern. All of Central America experiences storms that arise in the Caribbean, are carried by the prevailing winds west, hit the backbone of the mountain Cordillera, and dump their rain. This is as much a feature of this bioregion as the warm temperatures, which, by persisting year around, promote coral reefs offshore and prolific vegetation on land, particularly on the Caribbean side. The absence of a killing frost helps account for the traditional use of fire for weed control and the modern temptation to overuse pesticides.

The perpetually wet, warm, and level east side, ideal for growing bananas, is less hospitable to cattle and humans than the drier, sparser forests of the Pacific slopes. Cattle-raising is the one option poised to invade Central America whenever the international price of beef beckons. Cattle is the crop that walks (a boon for small landholders), and clearing forest for pasture has permitted landowners of all sizes to demonstrate the "improvements" that still play a role in establishing and defending title to land.[24] Even when not in cattle, agricultural expansion is more likely to occur west of the Cordillera. Only a few crops and fewer human beings can tolerate the diseases that proliferate in the saturated lowlands to the east.

But to many Costa Ricans, the impact of hurricane Cesar seemed unusual, even extreme. Costa Rican television and newspapers asked, "¿Por qué tanto daño?" (Why so much damage?). The answers local scientists gave were that soils cleared of forest absorb more water, become heavier, and are less impeded by friction, leading to more and larger landslides; that deforestation leaves rivers running faster and carrying more debris, a combination that rips out bridges and culverts, collapsing highways. What a San José daily termed a "tragic education" bore the formula: "Deforested terrain plus excessive precipitation" equals "landslides, highway destruction, bridge undermining and flooding."[25]

Excessive precipitation comes with the turf—with the bioregion, that is—but deforestation? Is Costa Rica not known for its progressive environmental policies, especially for preserving forest? According to international sources, Costa Rica ranks sixteenth in the world in protecting its territory, with 12 percent of it reserved.

Costa Rican authorities claim up to 28 percent,[26] the discrepancy arising from differing degrees of protection on different types of reserves. For so small a country, Costa Rica protects a larger share of its territory than most. So this is a puzzle worth exploring.

Nature set-asides and deforestation may not be as incompatible as they first seem; they may even drive each other to the point where the only forests remaining are inside reserves. Understanding how deforestation prompts the creation of reserves comes easier than the other way around. During the 1980s, Costa Rica's forests disappeared at an average annual rate of 150,000 acres a year, one of the highest rates of deforestation in the world. Given the burgeoning tourism industry, along with a policy of creating forest reserves—the first was announced in 1964—the government responded with a series of laws that cut the rate of deforestation to only 1,000 acres a year by 1994. Of course this slowing owes something to the exhaustion of big, old timber in accessible areas, since the easier-to-reach trees are taken first. By 1990 only one-third of Costa Rica remained forested, down from two-thirds just a half century before. That third was closing in on the government's claim that 28 percent was "protected."

So when a *New York Times* reporter wrote in 1997 that Costa Rica "has some of the largest untouched primary forests in the world," he reflected less the reality than the publicity generated by many organizations, in and outside the government, at home and abroad, seeking to save this natural treasure.[27] Following the passage of new environmental and forestry laws in 1995–1996, the government could claim that reforestation finally had overtaken deforestation. But trees do not a forest make, especially not a forest rich in biodiversity.

Flipping the preservation and deforestation relationship around—asking how preservation could abet deforestation—we find ourselves back in the cultural constructions with which this chapter opened. Nature set-asides may perpetuate an attitude of business as usual on less-protected lands. One of the dangers of ecotourism, for which Costa Rica is rightly known, is that it abets such compartmentalization by associating nature with time-outs and spaces-away from the "real world." "We live in a world filled with material goods," states a recent government brochure intended to attract foreign tourists: "We are protected from the elements in our safe cocoon of concrete, glass and steel but, somehow, something is missing. Only when we escape this artificial environment do we recognize how strong is our human need for contact with the natural world."[28] True, but also typical of a northern tendency to separate economic activities from nature, to think that we are "saving nature" when at best we may be saving specific places or specific species (usually the more exotic ones). In any other discourse, this would be labeled tokenism and considered more part of the problem than of the solution.

Half the Costa Rican population lives in the greater San José metropolitan area, where the average concentration of lung-damaging particulates in the air is 42 percent higher than what is considered safe for humans and where carbon monoxide levels register at twice the acceptable level.[29] High rates of certain cancers along with growing resistance to certain antibiotics testify to the indiscriminate use of chemicals in agriculture, which the government monitors in name only. Are we surprised, then, when forests outside high-profile reserves show stress?

The lesson delivered by natural disasters, such as hurricanes, is that nature is of a piece, farm and forest, "protected" and "nonprotected" alike. So we would do well to return to our case study. Cesar's effects were most felt in Pérez Zeledón, a canton created in 1931 in a region thinly populated before 1920. Before the Interamerican Highway made travel easier between the *meseta central* (the highland where a majority of Costa Ricans live) and the valley where Pérez Zeledón is located, travel was possible only by ox cart across mountain passes graced with such names as Cerro de la Muerte. Built soon after World War II with U.S. assistance, this new highway simplified that passage, opening the region beyond to small farmers looking for land in a small country where, by then, most of the good land had been taken.

Contributing to the scarcity of land along the Pacific watershed was the 62 percent expansion in cattle pasture during the 1960s, "much of it [in] extremely rugged country of steep slopes that would have been much better left in forest, if only for watershed protection."[30] Since cattle-raising uses a lot of land per laborer, this expansion pushed campesinos out of cultivated areas in search of land elsewhere. Cattle-raising increased not because Costa Ricans were consuming more meat—they were not—but in response to increased demand from the fast food and pet food markets of the United States. Encouraged by U.S. development agencies, the Costa Rican government made low-interest loans to cattle ranchers.

"As new roads were pushed into the Valle del General," where Pérez Zeledón lies, and into other "colonization fronts," "these areas became increasingly devoted to pasture."[31] In a country that was 95 percent forests when the nineteenth century dawned and in which the optimal use of half the territory remains forest, when hurricane Cesar hit only 20 percent of the land remained in old-growth forests and no more than 35 percent in forests of any kind.[32]

This story is repeated elsewhere in LAC. I have used Costa Rica's experience with roads, cattle, migratory peasants, and environmental destruction not because it provides an accurate picture of that country today but because it shows the completion of a cycle that other countries are still entering. Elsewhere bioregional climate and geology conspire with social inequities to nudge rural populations into situations where their search for livelihood threatens their lives—and those of other species. New roads continue to play the role seen in this example. Western Amazonia, for example, will be drastically changed if Japanese efforts to link that region to the Pacific by road succeed, as will be Panama's wild Darien province, where a similar scheme remains under consideration.

Cattle mania has been replaced by new exports to northern markets, coupled to new agendas within northern development agencies, but the pattern seen above is being repeated as commercial shrimp farming damages vulnerable mangroves (Honduras, Ecuador) and as winter produce for northern markets is being grown with pesticides friendly to northern consumers, pesticides that harm LAC field workers and their families (Mexico, Chile). The countries cited do not exhaust the list but merely provide well-documented examples.

Nor is Costa Rica the only government not to have made it worthwhile for campesinos to conserve rather than clear forest. The reasons vary but among them are governments' desire to promote exports to meet the demands of neoliberal structural adjustments, urban-based policymakers' lack of familiarity with campesino and indigenous cultures coupled with their suspicion of popular organizations outside the national parties, and finally the tendency of national governments to shift policy so often that no policy gains credibility among those asked to implement it. Compliance is a hurdle in many rural areas where the central authority shares power with armed landlords, indigenous communities, multinational corporations, or all three.

So the deforestation that exacerbated the impact of Cesar and that finally is being slowed in Costa Rica continues to run its course elsewhere, degrading habitat and drying up water sources. In Venezuela, where an area the size of Costa Rica was deforested during the single decade of the 1980s, at a rate double that in Brazil, the damage has yet to run its course. Of enormous value as watershed and habitat, Venezuela's forests give up 3,000 acres a day with unsurprising "increases in both the intensity and severity of droughts and floods."[33]

Participating in Venezuela's deforestation once more are campesinos in search of land. The opening wedge, however, is logging done by companies that treat forests as if they were mines. Since the lumber from 1 cubic yard of mahogany can fetch $1,000, loggers push new roads into primal forests to raze single trees. Using those roads, the land-seeking poor enter and complete the destruction. And after Venezuela? Surinam and Belize are current targets for logging by Southeast Asian firms that have exhausted hardwoods at home.

So we see how local cases bring us to Japan's hunger for tropical hardwoods or the United States' hunger for a 99-cent hamburger. Can we rachet one notch higher on this vertical scale? After Cesar struck, Costa Ricans commented on the unusual bad luck of four major weather disasters within a year and a half. Most did not know of a growing scientific consensus linking global warming not just to a slow rise in temperatures around the earth but to "more intense tropical storms."[34] Since 1983 Costa Rica has experienced sixteen major floods as a result of such storms.[35] Are these "acts of God" or of Homo sapiens?

Billions of tons of carbon dioxide and other "greenhouse gases" are introduced into the earth's atmosphere each year, primarily by industrialized nations. These gases trap the sun's heat near the earth's surface in what is known as the "greenhouse effect." Although originally scientists focused on the gradual "warming" that results, in recent years the term "global environmental change" is being substituted in recognition of the erratic and extreme changes the greenhouse effect produces.

When the earth is warmed, more surface moisture evaporates; a warmer atmosphere holds that additional moisture until natural forces send it back to earth. This pattern produces not just greater precipitation in some places at some times but greater drought elsewhere. In short, weather becomes more extreme. Eventually a warmer planet may experience the huge swings in climate that have occurred before, albeit in geologic time (e.g., the Eemian interglacial era) and from natural causes. "According to this line of thinking, a present-day warming caused by carbon dioxide emissions could ultimately force the [earth's] climate system to flip to a new, unstable state."[36]

Even if global climate change came gradually, different components of nature would respond differently. The warming that wipes out coral reefs and paramo may produce bumper crops of rice, unraveling the uneasy alliance between those who prioritize "development" and those who prioritize "biodiversity." The "shifts in competitive advantage among plant species" so induced "could produce far-reaching changes in the wild and even reduce the number of species."[37]

The post–Cold War consensus among elites in the Americas may fracture into temperate-tropical polarities. While agriculture in the northern Mexico, Central America, and eastern South America bioregions (consult Figure 11.1) will confront desertlike conditions, agriculture in the upper United States and Canada will enjoy bumper crops. Preventing global warming with timely actions today needs the *reverse* of the current cost structure, with its higher costs in the North for remediation (transportation, energy) than in the South, where relatively few benefit from the deforestation that would have to be curbed.[38] That imbalance between perceived winners and losers explains why "the North will not act and the South cannot," as one climate change scholar put it.[39] Five years after the 1992 Earth Summit in Rio de Janeiro, the world could boast an impressive new set of international institutions to promote sustainable development, biodiversity, and a reduction in greenhouse emissions—but few real gains on the greenhouse front.

What goes around eventually must come around. A hotter and stormier Central America and Caribbean will threaten the southern United States with malaria and other tropical diseases, including some new ones. North America may create a bird-friendly environment yet still slide into Rachel Carson's "silent spring" because of habitat loss in Central and South America, some of that directly attributable to climate change, some to deforestation and pesticide use.[40] Hawks and osprey, warblers, flycatchers, orioles, and tanagers are just a few of the species that migrate between these regions. Even now, according to one expert, "all migratory birds from the neotropics . . . have declined by about 30 percent."[41]

Nor will hurricanes stay south of the tropic of Cancer. They do not now, of course, but they are likely to increase in severity and number—as will snowpack and flooding further north. The environmental organization Greenpeace has interested some insurance companies in exploring the connection between recent hurricane damage within the United States, company payouts (hence profits), and northern governments' collective failure to reduce greenhouse emissions.

A CODA FOR THE CITIES

Tracing hurricane Cesar up and down the vertical scale makes the point that most needs making, which is that ultimately everything is connected to everything else (one of Barry Commoner's three rules of thumb). Had we started, however, with a storm's impact on the *favelas* (slums) perched above Rio de Janeiro, cattle and defor-estation would not have been featured, although we still would have noted the role of property titles, incomes, and migration. Since a majority of Latin Americans live in cities, two of which are among the four largest in the world (São Paulo and Mexico), and since cities impact vast areas around them with their thirst for water and power, they deserve at least passing mention.

The attempt of the urban poor to stay within a few bus rides of jobs means that shacks are often built on wetlands, estuaries, and steep hillsides—the only land left open and cheap in an urban environment—in a pattern that parallels the campesinos' clearing of mountain slopes and ravines: right instinct, wrong place. These same urban poor, however, supply the labor needed for recycling, sanitation, and greenbelts where those functions are organized into paying jobs. Their housing could be upgraded with the provision of clear titles and donated materials. Such so-lutions are visible in the poor neighborhood of Coelhos in Recife. Sustained solu-tions can produce cities as livable as Curitiba, another Brazilian city.

What seems distinctive about the environmental problems of cities is the increased role of the middle and upper classes. Having to keep their children home from school and indoors during episodes of high ground-level ozone has brought air quality issues home to those most likely to demand solutions as well as those whose collaboration is most needed to effect solutions. For the private automobile is a major contributor to the respiratory disorders that the middle and upper classes fear. One tank of gas in the average automobile emits 300 pounds of carbon dioxide. The diesel that most trucks and buses burn generates the inhalable particulates laced with sulfates that render even mass transport an environmental nightmare. Stir in nitrogen oxides, add sunlight and temperature inversions, and you have the smog that renders even a medium-sized LAC city less healthy than Tokyo or New York. On some days you are better off smoking a pack of cigarettes in Fargo than breathing Mexico City's air.

It is not that LAC policymakers are unaware of these problems or unwilling to find solutions. Rather, the development model followed for decades—industrialize first, deal with the consequences afterward—has closed off most of the inexpensive options for remediation, those that deal with street layout, for instance, or with fac-tory location.

Upper class or lower, citizen organizations focused on urban issues probably out-number all other environmental groups in LAC. With the possible exception of those along the U.S.-Mexico border, northerners are less aware of and less involved in these urban organizations for reasons that the opening section of this chapter il-luminates. Saving the jaguar or protecting an indigenous culture feels better to many of us than dealing with people like ourselves around issues we confront at home, such as urban sprawl and the private automobile.[42]

SOLUTIONS?

The same globalization that makes difficult place-sensitive solutions offers new col-laborations that hold promise. I close with an almost random sample of these simply to make the point that whether these particular innovations pan out or not, they evidence the dynamism of our topic. What you have seen here is but a snapshot of a moving target.

In 1990 the Costa Rican National Institute for Biodiversity signed a contract with the U.S. pharmaceutical company Merck to search for naturally occurring compounds that might yield new manufactured drugs. Such "bioprospecting"—also under way in Amazonia—promises an income stream for old-growth forests left in their natural state and for those who know them best, be they shamans or scientists. Later in that decade, Costa Rica began selling carbon bonds to European governments through a "joint implementation" approach to greenhouse gases. Here is how it works: Norway taxes its offshore oil fields for the carbon dioxide they contribute to the atmosphere, then transfers that money to Costa Rica to maintain forests that sequester (lock up) carbon dioxide. Behind this experiment is the as yet unsolved task of affixing prices to the multiple benefits of nature instead of to just its raw material component.

As has happened in the past, private corporations have not waited for government ministries and universities to solve problems but have plunged ahead on their own, reinventing trade and technology as they go. Many corporations are adopting new management systems (International Organization for Standardization 14000 is one) intended to yield certifiable compliance with environmental standards. Some LAC governments use such certification as a condition of entry of foreign corporations or as a guide to their own purchases, while some LAC industries use certification as a way to gain entry into northern markets or as a means to respond to their own governments' demands for better environmental practices.

Just as conservation for biodiversity has broadened its focus from species to habitats and from small habitats to ecoregions so large that public-private collaboration now is required (recall the "corridors" mentioned earlier in this chapter), so a green agenda that at Rio seemed tightly focused on the environment now is being mainstreamed into economic practice, with what results we do not yet know.

NOTES

1. Mary Shelley, *Frankenstein*, ed. Johanna M. Smith (Boston: St. Martin's Press, 1992), 125–126.

2. Nicolás Sánchez-Albornoz, *The Population of Latin America* (Berkeley: University of California Press, 1974), 169.

3. Thomas Hobbes, *Leviathan*, ed. Richard Tuck (New York: Cambridge University Press, 1991), chap. 46, 459.

4. For a discussion of Bemis's writings, see Mark T. Berger, *Under Northern Eyes* (Bloomington: Indiana University Press, 1995), 58–63.

5. Just as individuals may wish that their lives would halt at the point where youthful vigor and mature reflection are in balance, so you—Rousseau challenges his readers—"will seek the age at which you would desire your Species had stopped" evolving culturally. *Discourse on the*

Origins of Inequality, vol. 3 of *The Collected Writings of Rousseau*, eds. Roger Masters and Christopher Kelley (Hanover, N.H.: University Press of New England), 20, 35.

6. François Marie Arouet de Voltaire, *Candide, Zadig and Selected Stories*, trans. Donald Frame (New York: Penguin Books, 1961), "Candide," chaps. 17–18.

7. Paul Theroux, *The Mosquito Coast* (New York: Avon, 1983).

8. Bob Buchanan, "Looking for Rainforest Heroes," *Utne Reader*, March/April 1993, 78, 81. Maybe irony is intended; in writing that tries so hard to be entertaining it is hard to know.

9. Eric Dinerstein, David M. Olson, Douglas J. Graham, Steven A. Primm, Marnie P. Bookbinder, and George Leder, *A Conservation Assessment of the Terrestrial Ecoregions of Latin America and the Caribbean* (Washington, D.C.: World Bank, 1995).

10. In 1996 the environmental ministers of the governments of Mexico, Panama, and the five Central American countries signed an agreement to create a "Corredor Biológico Mesoamericano." Within Costa Rica, a new National System of Conservation Areas (SINAC) envisions several large corridors uniting public, indigenous, and private lands in common conservation regimes.

11. "An ecoregion represents a geographically distinct assemblage of natural communities that share a large majority of their species, ecological dynamics, and similar environmental conditions, and whose ecological interactions are critical for their long-term persistence." Dinerstein et al., *A Conservation Assessment*, 14.

12. F. Gary Stiles and Alexander Skutch, *A Guide to the Birds of Costa Rica* (Ithaca: Cornell University Press, 1989), 11.

13. The most widely quoted definition of "sustainable development" comes from the 1987 report of the World Commission on Environment and Development (Brundtland Commission), *Our Common Future* (New York: Oxford University Press, 1987): "development that meets the needs of the present without compromising the ability of future generations to meet their own needs." This definition begs a number of questions, as Sim Van Der Ryn and Stuart Cowan point out, such as whether all needs are equally legitimate (*Ecological Design*, Washington, D.C.: Island Press, 1996, 5). The conventional focus evaluates inputs, not the goods produced. In this view, development should proceed without denying future generations a resource base comparable to that enjoyed at present. Resources may include genetic resources, a human-use approach to other species that "deep ecologists," for one, reject. A *renewable* resource probably is being "sustainably" used if "yields" (or other desired economic functions) do not fall over time, given historic inputs. Imagine soil, for example, that produces as good a crop ten years from now as ten years ago without an escalating use of artificial inputs that mask the soil's declining productivity. *Nonrenewable* resources are "sustainably" used if comparable replacements (such as solar or hydropower for oil) are phased in as the original resource is used up.

14. "Biodiversity," an abbreviation for "biological diversity," is "an umbrella term for the degree of nature's variety, including both the number and frequency of ecosystems, species, or genes in a given assemblage. It is usually considered at three different levels: genetic diversity, species diversity, and ecosystem diversity." Jeffrey McNeely et al., *Conserving the World's Biological Diversity* (Washington, D.C.: World Resources Institute, 1990), 17.

15. Edward O. Wilson, "Is Humanity Suicidal?" *New York Times Magazine*, May 30, 1993.

16. J. Brian Atwood, head of USAID, "Administrator Atwood National Wildlife Federation Speech," in [usaid_press_release@info.usaid.gov], May 15, 1996.

17. A particularly far-ranging critique of "sustainable development" is Arturo Escobar's in *Encountering Development* (Princeton: Princeton University Press, 1995), chap. 5.

18. For a persuasive example of this view, see William Ascher, *Communities and Sustainable Forestry in Developing Countries* (San Francisco: Institute for Contemporary Studies, 1995), chap. 2.

19. The species most sought after is mahogany, for which the United States is a major buyer. An average logger will damage thirty trees of other species to extract one mahogany tree. In July 1996, the Brazilian government stepped in, expanding the Amazonian forest reserves and suspending new mahogany contracts for two years while it studied the situation.

20. Dinerstein et al., *A Conservation Assessment*, xvii.

21. Official Brazilian figures for 1994 as given in Brazilian government press release forwarded by the EnviroNews Service [newsdesk@envirolink.org], "E-Link: Brazil Suspends All Logging Contracts," in [environews@envirolink.org], July 26, 1996.

22. USAID-sponsored Biodiversity Support Program is reviewed on page 46 of Dinerstein et al., *A Conservation Assessment*. Grasslands also emerged as a top priority in both studies.

23. Information from the San José daily *La Nación*, July 29 through August 7, 1996, and from the weeklies *Tico Times* and *Semanario Universidad*, both August 16, 1996; and from Costa Rican television during this period. Also, the "year in review" issue of the *Tico Times*, December 27, 1996.

24. "Cleaning" the land (*limpiar* in Spanish) is one more episode in the West's fondness for cultivation (recall Hobbes). For an analog closer to home, visit the "lawn care" section of any garden supply store.

25. "La naturaleza pasa la factura" (Nature passes the bill), *La Nación*, August 2, 1996. Critics of neoliberal policies long have claimed that the costs of economic gains were being "endorsed over" to nature. *La Nación*'s headline implies that nature passes that bill back to society.

26. World Bank, *World Development Report 1992* (Washington, D.C.: World Bank, 1992), table 33. Allen Hammond, ed., *The 1994 Information Please Environmental Almanac* (Boston: Houghton Mifflin, 1993), 361. *Costa Rica: Datos e Indicadores Básicos*, 3d ed. (San José, Costa Rica: Market Data, 1993), 12.

27. Warren Hoge, "Where Wildlife Meets Wild Surf," *New York Times*, February 16, 1997, section 5.

28. "Costa Rica: Tan Your Soul," a 1996 brochure published by the Costa Rica Tourist Board (ICT), 1.

29. "Ticos Got the Word: S. J. Air Is Bad," *Tico Times*, December 27, 1996.

30. J. J. Parsons, "Beef Cattle (Ganado)," in *Costa Rican Natural History*, ed. Daniel H. Janzen (Chicago: University of Chicago Press, 1983), 77.

31. Ibid.

32. Estimates vary according to what degree of deforestation is the cutoff point and what is considered a forest (old growth/new, mixed stand/monoculture). One estimate for 1983 shows only 17 percent of natural, mixed stands remaining. Using the more generic "forest, pasture, cropland" categories, forests covered 32 percent of Costa Rica in 1990, down from 58 in 1970. Nicholas Brown, "Deforestation in Costa Rica," photocopy, March 1994; Proyecto Estado de la Nación, *Estado de la nación en desarrollo humano sostenible,* 1st *informe* (San José, Costa Rica: Lara Segura, 1996), 46–47. The second *informe*, or annual report, of *Estado de la nación*, chap. 4, updates the situation to 1995, showing a shift from harvesting trees in forests to growing and harvesting them on agricultural lands.

33. Julio Cesar Centeno [jcenteno@ciens.ula.ve], "Deforestation Out of Control in Venezuela," in ELAN [elan@csf.colorado.edu], January 17, 1996.

34. "Experts Confirm Human Role in Global Warming," *New York Times*, September 10, 1995.

35. Proyecto Estado de la Nación, *Estado de la nación*, vol. 1, 50.

36. "Data Give Tangled Picture of World Climate Between Glaciers," *New York Times*, November 1, 1994.

37. "Rise in Carbon Dioxide May Alter Plant Life," *New York Times*, September 18, 1990.

38. Deforestation in LAC contributes to the greenhouse effect, although not on the scale of the fossil fuel emissions of northern countries and China. Carbon dioxide emissions per person are 8 metric tons in Brazil versus 20 in the United States. Virtually all U.S. emissions come from the energy, transportation, and construction sectors, whereas in Brazil 80 percent stems from a deforestation that, many would argue, is driven by and benefits foreign interests. Centeno, "Deforestation Out of Control."

39. Daniel Bromley, remarks at the Third Scientific Symposium on Human Dimensions of Global Environmental Change Programme (Geneva, 1996), *Proceedings*, v. 1, *Report* 8, 31.

40. One season of controlling grasshoppers in Argentina by pesticides led to a 5 percent kill-off of Swainson's hawks in Oregon. Since for years this bird's population has been declining throughout its northern range, a single "accident" does not tell the whole story. "Pesticides Kill Migrating Hawks," *Walla Walla Union Bulletin*, May 13, 1996.

41. Roberto Roca, chief zoologist of the Nature Conservancy's Latin American division, speaking at the congress of neotropical ornithology, in an Associated Press article distributed over the internet by [C-ap@clarinet.com (AP)] as "Bird Decline Worries Meeting," in ELAN [elan@csf.colorado.edu], August 7, 1995.

42. Margaret Keck, "Parks, People and Power," *NACLA Report on the Americas* 28, 5 (March/April 1995): 36.

SUGGESTED READINGS

A selection of recent books plus a film that tap various aspects of this topic. Some treat "southern" or Third World nations in addition to LAC.

Ascher, William. *Communities and Sustainable Forestry in Developing Countries.* San Francisco: Institute for Contemporary Studies, 1995. Good on the unintended effects of governmental and NGO action at the grassroots.

Day, Bill, and Terry Schwartz. *Saviors of the Forest.* Film/video released in 1992 by Camera Guys, Los Angeles. Comic documentary on outsiders' efforts to save the rain forest.

Dinerstein, Eric, David M. Olson, Douglas J. Graham, Steven A. Primm, Marnie P. Bookbinder, and George Leder. *A Conservation Assessment of the Terrestrial Ecoregions of Latin America and the Caribbean.* Washington, D.C.: World Bank and World Wildlife Fund, 1995. Scientific basis for conservation priorities in LAC.

Escobar, Arturo. *Encountering Development: The Making and Unmaking of the Third World.* Princeton: Princeton University Press, 1995. A Colombian criticizes various conceptions of development, including "sustainable development."

Ghai, Dharam, and Jessica Vivian, eds. *Grassroots Environmental Action: People's Participation in Sustainable Development.* New York: Routledge, 1995. Case studies of local people managing their natural resources.

Goulding, Michael, with Nigel Smith and Dennis Mahar. *Floods of Fortune: Ecology and Economy Along the Amazon.* New York: Columbia University Press, 1996. Recent contribution to analyzing this complex, large region.

Hajek, Ernst, ed. *Pobreza y medio ambiente en América Latina.* Buenos Aires: Centro Interdisciplinario de Estudios sobre el Desarrollo Latinoamericano in association with Grancharoff J. A., 1995. The relationship between poverty and environment in seven LAC countries.

Hammond, Allen, ed. *The 1994 Information Please Environmental Almanac.* Boston: Houghton Mifflin, 1993. World Resources Institute data summarized. Short entries for each country of the world sketching its environmental issues. Data need updating.

Holmberg, Johan, ed. *Making Development Sustainable: Redefining Institutions, Policy and Economics.* Washington, D.C.: Island Press, 1992. Implications of sustainable development for cities, energy, and industry, topics slighted in this chapter.

Kane, Joe. *Savages.* New York: Knopf, 1995. One of several firsthand accounts of cultural and economic clashes in the Amazon to feature indigenous peoples up against foreign influences. Also see books in this genre by Marc Plotkin and Alex Shoumatoff. All make for exciting reading.

MacDonald, Gordon, Daniel Nielson, and Marc Stern. *Latin American Environmental Policy in International Perspective.* Boulder, Colo.: Westview Press, 1997. Essays on domestic and international factors that shape environmental policies within several Latin American nations.

Pearce, David W., and Jeremy Warford. *World Without End: Economics, Environment, and Sustainable Development.* Washington, D.C.: World Bank in association with Oxford University Press, 1993. A large text covering the economics and politics of sustainable development at both the national and international levels.

Van Der Ryn, Sim, and Stuart Cowan. *Ecological Design.* Washington, D.C.: Island Press, 1996. Not a book about LAC at all but a short and highly readable introduction to the choices embedded in "sustainability" wherever people practice it.

Vandermeer, John, and Ivette Perfecto. *Breakfast of Biodiversity: The Truth About Rain Forest Destruction.* Oakland, Calif.: Institute for Food and Development Policy (Food First), 1995. How agriculture impacts biodiversity in Central America, principally Costa Rica.

Wright, Angus. *The Death of Ramón González: The Modern Agricultural Dilemma.* Austin: University of Texas Press, 1990. How the evolution of agricultural technologies and markets has impacted peoples and environments in Mexico. Good historical perspective.

Sampling of Internet Web Sites Germane to This Chapter

Biodiversity and Ecosystems Network: http://straylight.tamu.edu/bene/bene.htm
Earth Council: http://terra.ecouncil.ac.cr/ecweb.htm
EnviroLink Network: http://envirolink.org/
Environment in Latin America Network (ELAN): http://csf.colorado.edu/elan/index.html
Latin American Data Base of the University of New Mexico: http://ladb.unm.edu/
Rainforest Action Network: http://www.igc.apc.org/ran
United Nations Environmental Program: http://www.unep.ch/
World Bank: http://www.worldbank.org//
World Conservation Monitoring Centre: http://www.wcmc.org.uk/
World Wildlife Fund: http://www.panda.org/

PART FIVE
POLITICAL PROCESSES AND TRENDS

12

PARTICIPATION AND POLITICAL PROCESS: THE COLLAPSIBLE PYRAMID

JAN KNIPPERS BLACK

All political systems are systems of limited participation. Even the societies we might call primitive—societies in which essential tasks and rewards are shared more or less equally among families—generally limit participation on the basis of sex and age; that is, women and minors are excluded. Such systems of exclusion may enjoy "legitimacy," or acceptance, even by the excluded, but they are ultimately based on physical prowess. Exclusion in more-complex societies, like the modern nation state, typically follows the lines of class, often reinforced by racial or ethnic divisions. Exclusion may also be based on political ideology.

In the United States, for example, the franchise was generally limited to property-holding white males until the 1830s, when the populist movement headed by Andrew Jackson led to the elimination of property-holding requirements. The franchise was extended to women in 1920 only after years of struggle on the part of the suffragettes. Suffrage for blacks in the South did not become effective until the issue was forced by the civil rights movement, led by Dr. Martin Luther King, in the early 1960s. It was only after university students were mobilized in opposition to the Vietnam War that the voting age was lowered from twenty-one to eighteen. In parts of the country, poor blacks or Hispanics are still turned away from the polls by one device or another.

Furthermore, as suffrage has been extended, the vote, which is only one of many forms of political participation, has become devalued as a consequence of the preponderant role of money in the U.S. electoral system. As campaigns have become outrageously costly media events, the candidate or elected official has become far more attentive to the wishes of major campaign contributors than to those of an amorphous electorate. The low level of voter turnout in the United States suggests, among other things, that a great many eligible voters see campaign promises as hollow and electoral choices as meaningless.

Likewise in Latin America, participation takes many forms, and effective participation is by no means automatic. For all but the wealthiest it must be earned or won, often through protracted struggle and great sacrifice.

INEQUALITY AND THE BID FOR PARTICIPATION

Most complex, highly stratified social and political systems can be traced to armed conquest, and the national systems of Latin America as we know them today are no exception. The subjugation upon which contemporary social inequality in Latin America is based included not only the conquest and enslavement by Spaniards, Portuguese, and other Europeans of native American populations, but also the kidnapping, by European merchants of flesh, of Africans and their subsequent enslavement in the New World.

The preponderance of brute force thus led to wealth, as the conquistadores acquired land and slaves or serfs and passed them on to their legitimate offspring. Over time, this system of exploitation acquired a measure of legitimacy, as it was moderated and condoned by the religious system imposed by the conquerors. In Latin America as elsewhere, the violent roots of such systems of inequality have been progressively obscured from subsequent generations of the conquered populations, and the myth has been established that differential reward and punishment and limitations of access to wealth and power rest somehow on divine purpose or merit. Those who would challenge that interpretation of the social reality are branded subversive and dealt with accordingly.

Through miscegenation, immigration, and an increase in the categories of tasks to be performed, classes of intermediate social and economic rank—that is, between the masters and the "slaves"—have come into being. It is quite possible, as social and political systems become more complex, for individuals, through accepting the social myth and incorporating the values of the conquering class, to rise above the status of their birth. The masters, however, do not voluntarily relinquish a share of their authority to a lower stratum on the social pyramid. Such a sharing of power across class lines comes about only when organization and the potential for the use of force on the part of a lower social stratum are such that the masters conclude that they must share their wealth and power or risk losing it all.

The great political theorists, at least since Aristotle, have noted that power systems and the distribution of wealth and opportunity are interdependent. Thus, the concepts of social class and class struggle introduced by Karl Marx are crucial to an understanding of the political process in its broadest implications. These concepts are, however, abstractions. Social classes do not compete as such. Individual competitors for political power act through or on behalf of groups, which, in turn, represent more or less limited sectors of society. Such groups may represent one or more social classes, or a sector within a single class. They may act on behalf of one class at one time and on behalf of another at a later date. They may act on behalf of very narrowly construed organizational or institutional interests, which only indirectly impinge upon the class struggle. They may represent interests fundamentally alien to their own societies. Or they may represent a combination of national and foreign, class and institutional interests.

Political parties constitute only one of many categories of group actors in politics. The alignment of groups that participate or seek to participate in political competition in a particular national system depends to a large extent on the level of differentiation, or complexity, of the socioeconomic system. In any system based on marked inequality, those in power will maintain armed bodies (vigilante squads, police, and/or military units) to keep the have-nots from going after what the haves have and to ensure that the labor force fulfills the role to which it has been assigned.

A ruling class cannot perpetually maintain its position through the use or threat of brute force alone, however. Thus, it will seek to fortify itself by propagating a religion or ideology that sanctions the existing order. The groups or institutions that provide force (e.g., the military) and legitimacy (e.g., the Church), since they are essential to the maintenance of the power position of the ruling class, will soon acquire a measure of power in their own right. In fact, at any level of development ruling elites must stabilize their own power positions by balancing the enforcers, or wielders of force, against the bestowers of legitimacy.

In an international system characterized by colonialism or hegemony (dominance by a foreign power), the ruling class of a colony or client state may be highly dependent on a foreign power. In most of Latin America, the conquering class remained Spanish or Portuguese, protected and legitimized by Spanish or Portuguese troops and clergymen for some 300 years.

Typically, in Latin America, participants in the political system at the time independence was achieved were the *hacendados,* or members of the landowning class; the military; and the Roman Catholic Church. The hegemony that had been exercised by Spain and Portugal during the colonial period was soon assumed by the United States in Mexico, Central America, and the Caribbean and by Great Britain (with lesser participation by other European powers) in South America. The United States gave strong competition to the British and other European powers in South America during the first half of the twentieth century and, by the end of World War II, had consolidated its position of dominance over the whole of Latin America.

The pace and order of the admission of new groups and classes to political participation have varied from country to country, having proceeded most rapidly in the Southern Cone countries and most slowly in the Andean and Central American highlands. In general, a commercial sector, associated with export-import operations, was admitted during the last half of the nineteenth century, and industrial elites and middle classes began participating in the first decades of the twentieth century. By the 1920s and 1930s, labor was organizing and making its bid, but in few countries was it admitted to participation before the 1940s and 1950s. The admission of peasants, by nonrevolutionary means, was scarcely even at issue until the 1960s, and it

was not until 1979 in Ecuador and 1980 in Peru that new constitutions gave illiterates—that is, the Indian peasants—the vote for the first time in those countries.
Peasant participation has been rare and tenuous, and the peasants' gains, like those
of organized labor, were reversed in several countries in the 1960s and 1970s through
counterrevolution. In politics, there is no "final analysis"; as far as we know, participation and its perquisites may be won and lost and won again ad infinitum.

POLITICAL ACTORS AND ARENAS

The means of seeking entry into, or control of, a political system depends upon the
strengths of the particular group, or political actor, and the openness of the system.
In general, however, elections and other processes associated with the democratic system become available to groups previously excluded only *after* they have become organized and have demonstrated, through illegal or extralegal means, their ability to
disrupt the system and to threaten seriously the interests of the power elite.
Furthermore, as Charles Anderson has noted, election results are by no means considered sacred by all participants; elections are but one of the many means of gar-
nering and demonstrating power.[1]

Anderson has pointed out that there are certain resources, or "power capabilities,"
without which governments would find it difficult or even impossible to function.
These resources include, for example, a cooperative labor force, agricultural or industrial production, control over the use of armed force, moral sanction, popular
support, and the support of a dominant foreign power. In order to secure participation in or control over the political process, political groups, or "power contenders,"
must demonstrate control of a power capability.

In most contemporary Latin American countries, these power contenders would
include landowners, industrial and commercial elites, religious leaders, military
factions, labor unions, political parties, students and intellectual leaders, foreign corporations, and agencies of foreign governments. In distinguishing between power
contenders and power capabilities, Anderson notes that within the military establishment, the business community, the labor movement, or even the Catholic
Church, there are generally various factions seeking to speak for the institution or the
community. (One might add that even agencies of the U.S. government have been
seen marching to different drummers. Civilian politicians in several countries have
found, to their dismay, that the support of the U.S. ambassador did not assure the
support of the Pentagon and the CIA as well.) In order to be "taken into account"
by those groups that are already participants in the system, a new power contender
must flex its muscles. A military faction might demonstrate control of a power capability without firing a shot by establishing a credible claim to the loyalty of a few
important garrisons. A labor federation might demonstrate such control by calling a
successful general strike; a peasant group, by seizing a significant amount of land; a
student group, by amassing a large turnout for a march; a political party, by receiving a sizable vote. Traditional participants, feeling threatened, might in turn demon-

strate their own capabilities; disinvestment and capital flight are among the many ways economic elites may respond to threat.

When a new power contender demonstrates its capabilities, the power elite must decide whether the greater risk lies in admitting the new group to participation in the system or in attempting to suppress it. The new group may be admitted if the risk of suppression appears to be as great as the risk of recognition, and if groups that are already participating believe that the new group will be willing to abide by the rules of the game—that is, to respect the perquisites of the other players. Thus, what Anderson calls the normal rule of Latin American political change, and what we shall call the defining principle of the evolutionary process, is that new power contenders may be added to the system but old ones may not be eliminated.

Political conflict, as Martin C. Needler notes, takes place simultaneously in various "arenas," differing in accessibility to social groups, in methods or "weapons" of competition, and in visibility to the public.[2] In the least-developed political systems, the dominant arena is the private one, where family pressures, personal contacts, bribery, blackmail, and graft determine the outcome of political conflict. In the most highly developed polities, decisions are reached through popular election, parliamentary debate, and judicial review. Between the development levels of court intrigue and constitutional mediation of conflict is a level in which conflict takes place in the streets—in which demonstrations, strikes, and riots determine the outcome of the conflict.

Merging the models of Needler and Anderson, we might say that the "street arena" holds sway while the political elite is unwilling to admit new participants to the system but unable to repress them fully. It might be added that the street arena is employed not only by nonelites on the way up but by elites who fear that they are on the way down. When elites in a more highly developed constitutional system begin to feel that their interests are threatened by electoral and other constitutional processes, they will use the street arena—the provocation of highly visible "instability"—along with other arenas in preparing the way for counterrevolution.

SOCIAL CHANGE AND POLITICAL PROCESS

What factors, then, determine when and how participation will be won or lost by various groups and classes of Latin American societies? Many of the factors that contribute to pressure for social change fall into the category Karl Deutsch has labeled "social mobilization"—that is, urbanization, education, and mass communication and the consequent "revolution of rising expectations."[3] The transistor radio has been called the greatest force for change in the twentieth century.

The circulation of new ideas or ideologies imported from other societies (Liberalism at the turn of the nineteenth century, Marxism at the turn of the twentieth) or revived from earlier eras of preconquest or national experience (Mexican and Andean *indigenismo* or "nativism," Nicaraguan *sandinismo*) may give momentum and a sense of direction to otherwise sporadic or unfocused social unrest.

Likewise, hope may be aroused and organization promoted by the appearance of agents of change. These agents may be foreigners with new ideas and ambitions, such as labor leaders who immigrated from Europe at the turn of the century or representatives of foreign or international development agencies who have descended on Latin America since the 1960s. Or they may be Latin Americans associated with new institutions or with old institutions that are assuming new roles. Students, for example, became agents of change after national universities came into being in the early twentieth century, and Catholic clergymen and nuns, inspired by Liberation Theology, became powerful agents of change in the 1970s and 1980s. Pressure for change may also be generated by natural or man-made disasters, such as earthquakes or wars, by an abrupt downturn in the economy, or by a particularly greedy or brutal move on the part of the ruling classes—a paranoid overreaction, for example, to some minor incident of protest or insubordination.

The factors that contribute to pressure for social change do not, however, in themselves predetermine what the nature of that change will be. The nature of the change that comes in response to social mobilization is a product of the interaction of the forces of change and the forces of resistance. If the political elite is willing and able to share power, incorporating new groups into the polity, change will follow the evolutionary pattern. If the elite is unwilling to share, determined instead to repress would-be participants, change may take the form of revolution, of counterrevolution, or of a holding operation (indecisive cycles of insurrection and repression) we shall call "boundary maintenance." The outcome will depend largely upon the relative strength, unity, and determination of the opposing forces.

Thus, the major political processes that may flow from social change or pressure for additional social change will be labeled, for the purposes of a model that we shall call "the collapsible pyramid," as evolution, revolution, and counterrevolution (Figure 12.1). Political evolution implies the incorporation of new political actors, representing previously unrepresented social strata, without the displacement of previous participants in the system. Revolution is defined as the displacement or disestablishment of groups representing one or more strata from the upper reaches of the social pyramid. Our definition of counterrevolution is implied in that of revolution. It is the displacement, or elimination from effective participation, of groups representing strata from the base of the social pyramid.

Evolution

The experiences of Latin American countries suggest that limitations on a client state's links to the dominant foreign power and racial or ethnic homogeneity are among the factors that make it more likely that change will follow the evolutionary pattern. Each of these two factors has independent explanatory power, but in Latin America, the two are also related historically.

Limitations on colonial or neocolonial control may be a consequence of, among other things, physical distance, competition among prospective hegemonic powers, or the relative absence of strategic or material assets. The political significance of such

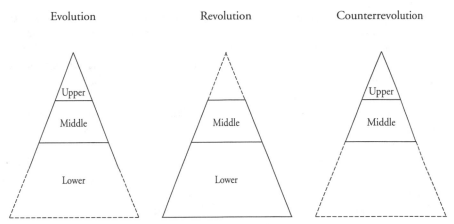

Figure 12.1.   Political Participation by Social Strata: The Collapsible Pyramid
Model

limitations is that, unable to rely on the backing of the dominant foreign power, the political elite may find it necessary to come to terms with new groups seeking participation. The first Latin American states in which the middle class, and to a lesser extent the working class, gained access to political power were those of the Southern Cone—Argentina, Uruguay, and, somewhat later, Chile. This area, which offered neither the gold and silver nor the exploitable Indian civilizations of the Andean and Middle American highlands, was of little interest to the Spanish crown. The Rio de la Plata Basin was among the last areas of the New World to be settled by Europeans and among the first to declare and win independence.

Relative to the rigid hierarchical systems of Mexico, Peru, and other early centers of royal domination, the social systems of the Southern Cone were loosely stratified, and their political systems were fluid. The nomadic Indians of the pampas were gradually exterminated, while those across the Andes in Chile—fewer than 100,000 in the late nineteenth century—were confined on reservations. Most of the African captives who were delivered to the Rio de la Plata Basin were subsequently transshipped north to zones where plantations were dominant. Argentina and Uruguay, predominantly mestizo at the time of independence, became overwhelmingly European as a consequence of large-scale immigration in the late nineteenth century. Chile's predominantly mestizo population was also relatively homogeneous. Thus, the social distance to be bridged in those countries in the incorporation of new groups into the polity was not nearly so great as in the countries of predominant Indian population, presided over by a tiny Hispanic elite.

From the late colonial period until the end of World War II, the Southern Cone countries were subjects of competition among hegemonic powers. Great Britain had competed very successfully with Spain for dominance in matters of trade even before the struggle for independence was undertaken. Britain then remained the dominant, though not unchallenged, foreign power in the area until World War II. The rise of the middle classes and the beginnings of labor organization occurred long before the United States acquired dominance over the area.

Other areas that have experienced evolutionary change have displayed some of the same characteristics. Venezuela and Costa Rica, for example, had sparse native American populations and were of little interest to the Spanish. Both have relatively homogeneous populations. Both were among the last areas to be settled by Europeans, and Venezuela, along with Argentina, was one of the first settlement areas to develop important trade ties with Britain and to rise in revolt against Spain. Representative government has been the rule rather than the exception in Costa Rica since the 1880s. In abolishing its army in 1948, Costa Rica eliminated a major threat to participation.[4]

The bid of the middle classes for participation has generally come about in conjunction with urbanization and the expansion of national institutions and government services. Spearheaded by merchants, bureaucrats, or students and intellectuals, middle-class movements have often led to the organization of new parties advocating social reform and appealing to incipient labor organizations. Victory at the ballot box, however, has generally been the confirmation, rather than the means, of middle-class ascent. The strength of the movement or party has had to be demonstrated first in the street arena, and its initial assumption of power has often been assisted by "young Turks" within the military.

As middle-class parties have generally needed the support of organized labor, and to a lesser extent of peasants, in order to confront the traditional political elite, the assumption of power by such parties has meant at least limited participation for the working classes as well—participation expressed, for example, in the right of collective bargaining as well as in the vote. Working-class groups may also be admitted prematurely to the political system, before their capabilities for disruption are fully developed, through the initiatives of one sector of the political elite that is seeking to enhance its position over another or by power holders seeking to maintain some degree of control over the development of labor's capabilities. Brazilian *caudillo* Getúlio Vargas cultivated labor as a counterpoise to the economic elite, but he kept it under the firm control of the labor ministry. In Colombia, the preemptive admission of organized labor and its incorporation into the pyramidal structures of the traditional parties delayed labor organization along horizontal lines of class interest.

The redistribution of power implied in the evolutionary process should be reflected in the long term in a redistribution of goods and services toward the newly participant groups. But this does not necessarily imply a redistribution toward all disadvantaged classes. For example, the economic position of a participating organized labor force may be enhanced while that of unorganized peasants or of unemployed and underemployed urban workers deteriorates. In the case of Venezuela, the middle-class parties gained admittance to the system by incorporating the strength of organized labor into their own. Nevertheless, while organized labor has reaped the benefits of political participation, there is a large and growing class of unorganized poor in Venezuela for whom the resultant inflation has only made things worse.

Effective working-class participation and thoroughgoing redistribution have been known to come about, even in Latin America, through the evolutionary process. In the early twentieth century, Uruguay, without suffering the devastation of social revolution, came to enjoy one of the most fully democratic systems and most highly developed welfare states in the world. In 1973, however, Uruguay's social and political advantages were erased by a brutal counterrevolution that brought the military to power until 1984.

While economies were expanding (in Uruguay, for example, from early to mid-twentieth century), the demands of newly participant social strata, such as urban labor, could be met without undue threat to the perquisites of traditional elites and middle classes; a concession to one pressure group was not necessarily at the expense of another. Moreover, the illusion of economic expansion could be maintained for a while by artificial means such as inflation or foreign borrowing. But when economies began to decline, the upper and middle classes came to fear that the gains of labor could only be at their expense. Moreover, in highly dependent economies, like those of Latin America, foreign businesses that feel threatened may appeal to their home governments and to public and private lending institutions to initiate measures, such as credit freezes and trade embargoes, that damage all economic interests in the client state.

Thus, the economic elites, both foreign and domestic, with substantial middle-class support, backed by the dominant foreign power and fronted for by the armed forces, move to silence lower-class demands and to regain control of the processes whereby wealth and power are allocated. Such was the fate of Brazil and the Southern Cone.

Costa Rica and Venezuela, the countries that most successfully maintained their evolutionary systems through the 1970s, were blessed with relatively healthy economies. But Costa Rica's economy, disabled by a drop in coffee prices, took a nosedive in the early 1980s. That country's democratic system was made more vulnerable by the efforts of the Reagan administration to transform its nonprofessional civil guard into a professional military establishment, and its social welfare system has been stripped in the 1990s to meet the conditions of creditors.

Petrodollars have freed the Venezuelan government to meet the most urgent demands of lower and middle classes without seriously taxing the rich. But petroleum wealth has not been converted into agricultural development and industrial diversification fast enough to alleviate the effects of oil-induced inflation and to bridge the gap between rich and poor. Rather, its social welfare system has been stripped in the 1990s to meet the conditions of creditors the oil bonanza has served, for the most part, to bloat the bureaucracy. The global oil glut of the 1980s, coupled with the foreign debt and the austerity measures imposed by creditors, has brought social tensions closer to the surface. Those tensions erupted in early 1989 in a popular rampage that left more than 300 dead and demonstrated the fragility of Venezuela's democracy.

Revolution

The displacement of a social stratum through revolution does not necessarily mean the physical elimination of individuals or the blocking of their participation, as individuals, in the political system. Rather, it means the removal of the resources (material or institutional) that have enabled them to exercise power as a class.

The revolutionary process is likely to involve violence both in the initial phase of insurgency and repression and in the secondary phase of struggle among insurgent groups. If the redistributional phase is delayed, renewed violence is likely to accompany that phase as well. But politics is the process whereby power relationships are established, so violence—or the threat of it—is implicit in all political processes. The violence accompanying revolution is not necessarily greater than that which accompanies other political processes.

The Cuban Revolution claimed several thousand lives, but considerably fewer than the Chilean counterrevolution, which claimed some 10,000 to 30,000. About 50,000 people were killed in the course of the Nicaraguan Revolution, and another 30,000 or so were killed in postrevolutionary struggles against the U.S.-sponsored "Contras," or counterrevolutionary forces, but an even greater number of Guatemalans have been killed, mainly by vigilantes and official security forces, in the "boundary-maintenance" effort—the effort, essentially, to keep the Indians "in their place"—that characterized Guatemalan politics from 1954 at least until 1997. The Colombian *violencia,* suggestive of the pattern whereby elites maintain their position while nonelites fight only among themselves, claimed more than 200,000 lives over more than a decade (mainly 1948–1958) of sporadic, nonpurposeful fighting. Revolution is only one—and perhaps the least likely—of many possible outcomes of violent confrontation.

The term "revolution" has been used very loosely, especially since the success of the Cuban Revolution in 1959 spread hope or fear, depending on one's point of view, throughout the Americas. It has been used as a synonym for violence, for social change, or for regime change; it has even been appropriated by rightist military rulers, like those who seized the Brazilian government in 1964, in vain attempts to legitimize their own counterrevolutions. In fact, however, successful revolutions are most rare.

In the Western Hemisphere, the only society to dismantle an entire ruling class (the French planters) in the process of ousting the colonial power was that of Haiti. Haiti was not only the first Latin American country to gain independence (1804) and to undergo a successful revolution, but the first state in the modern world to be born of a slave revolt.

The other Latin American countries that have experienced successful revolutions are Mexico (1911), Bolivia (1952), Cuba (1959), and Nicaragua (1979). Insurrectionary forces showed great strength in El Salvador in the 1980s and remarkable tenacity, at least, in Guatemala, but counterrevolutionary forces, backed by the United States, also remained strong, as conflict surged and ebbed and surged again without resolution (see Chapter 19).

Facilitating Factors.   Reams have been written on the causes of revolution in Latin America. Most of the causal factors cited fall into the category we have labeled "social mobilization." Such factors may rightly be viewed as causing pressure for political change, but they do not in themselves cause violent revolution. A necessary, though not sufficient, cause of violent revolution is the violent arrest of the nonviolent pursuit of change—that is, the blocking of the evolutionary process.

Factors that have facilitated or contributed to the perpetual blockage of the evolutionary process, and thus to the maintenance of a very low level of political participation, have included great social distance between elites and masses and proximity to the hegemonic power. The importance of the social distance factor lies in part in paranoia. The small elites of European origin who preside over a different racial group with an alien culture tend to feel exceedingly vulnerable and to fear that the slightest break in the traditional system of authority will unleash the contained wrath of centuries. Rather than welcoming the development of an incipient middle class that might serve a brokerage role and accepting the marginal political changes that might allow "things to go on as they are," the elites systematically eradicate would-be political brokers and strive to maintain a vacuum in the political center. This pattern has been particularly clear in recent decades in El Salvador and Guatemala.

The significance of close ties between dominant and client states has several facets. The most obvious is that, bulwarked by the might of the colonial or hegemonic power, colonial or client-state oligarchies are under little pressure to offer incremental concessions to middle or lower classes. But, as previously noted, there is also a historical connection between the factors of social distance and external control. European civilization in the New World was built quite literally on the ruins of Indian ones, and figuratively on the backs of Indians and transplanted Africans; so it is not coincidental that the areas of earliest and deepest penetration by the colonial powers are also the areas of least racial homogeneity and greatest social distance. Those are also the areas in which landed aristocracies, with the long-term backing of colonial military, religious, and bureaucratic authority, became most firmly entrenched.

Furthermore, even after routing the Spanish, the supposedly free states of Middle America and the Caribbean had little respite from foreign domination. After seizing half of Mexico's territory, the United States, devastated by its own Civil War, had to suffer competition from the French in Mexico and from the British in Central America in the latter half of the nineteenth century—but by the turn of the twentieth century, U.S. control over that area was virtually complete. In the Dominican Republic, Hispanic elites, frightened by Haiti's successful slave revolt and a subsequent period of Haitian occupation of their end of the island, scrambled to exchange national sovereignty for security under the flag of some stronger country. They succeeded in persuading the Spanish to return for a brief sojourn. Cuba, after the Spanish American War, merely exchanged one foreign master for another.

Thus, there was rarely a time when middle-class pretenders, sporting reformist ideas, could pose a credible threat to ruling aristocracies. As major U.S. corporations became an integral part of the power elite of those countries, the U.S. government made it clear that it would intervene militarily, if necessary, to protect the economic order from the greed and depredations of hungry natives. In fact, the United States did intervene extensively in the area and established constabularies in several countries that, in time, replaced the original landholding oligarchy at the pinnacle of power.

Finally, the greater the economic and political dominance or penetration of a foreign power, the fewer will be the nationals with a major stake in the old order. By the mid-twentieth century, the extent of U.S. economic holdings in much of Middle America and the Caribbean, and the fact that ruling constabularies answered to the United States rather than to any sector of local society, meant that relatively few families had extensive economic interests to protect and fewer still had a stake in the political order. Furthermore, the crudeness of U.S. power plays enhanced the importance of nationalism as a unifying theme. All of these factors facilitated the construction of a multiclass alliance in opposition to the ruling groups, particularly in Cuba and Nicaragua and to varying extents in Mexico, Guatemala, and the Dominican Republic. In the last two countries, reformist, potentially revolutionary, movements were crushed in 1954 and 1965, respectively, by U.S. military intervention.

Another social phenomenon that has correlated with insurgency and, in some cases, with successful revolution in Latin America has been the physical uprooting of subject populations. In the case of the Chaco War between Bolivia and Paraguay (1932–1935), peasants on both sides of the border, mobilized for the war, were not prepared to be demobilized when the fighting was over. In Paraguay, they contributed to the rise of a new party, which seized power in 1936. In Bolivia, they organized other Indian peasants, who ultimately seized the land and disestablished the Hispanic landholding aristocracy.

Throughout Middle America in the late nineteenth and early twentieth centuries, Indians were driven from their traditional communally held lands by Hispanic planters or U.S. corporations intent upon cashing in on the expanding market for export crops, particularly coffee. Many of the peasant uprisings of the period, including that led by Zapata in Mexico, represented efforts to take back land that had been seized.

In Central America, the cycle of planter encroachment, peasant uprising, and government reprisal that gave rise, for example, to El Salvador's notorious *matanza* of 1932—the massacre of some 30,000 Indian peasants—has continued up to the present. The creeping uprootedness of Salvadorans was exacerbated suddenly in 1969 when the Soccer War, fought against Honduras, resulted in the displacement of some 300,000 Salvadoran peasants who had settled on uncrowded land across the Honduran border. These peasants were thrust back upon a rural society in which a majority of the peasants were already landless migrants in desperate competition for seasonal labor at meager wages. In northern Guatemala, the pace of seizure of Indian land by non-Indians was accelerated in the 1970s as a consequence of the discovery of oil in the region.

The Phases of Revolution.   The phases of a successful revolution that runs its full course—that is, without falling prey to counterrevolution—might be described as (1) power transfer, (2) redistribution, (3) institutionalization, and (4) reconcentration.

Power Transfer.   The political, or power transfer, phase is a twofold one, comprising the toppling of the offending regime and the consolidation of the new power structure. The first step of a revolution, the displacement of the old regime, calls for the launching of insurrectionary movements on different social levels, either independently or in coalition. Intra-elite political conflict is not, in itself, revolutionary. On the other hand, uprisings of workers or peasants stand little chance of success unless there are important pockets of alienation in the middle class as well or unless the ruling class is sharply divided.

The dethroning, however, is only the beginning of the reallocation of political power. The affluent and the indigent, who might agree on the kind of government they do not want, cannot be expected to agree on the kind they want in its place. The struggle then continues within the coalition itself. As has often been noted, revolutions consume many of their authors.

In Mexico, after the demise of the dictatorship of Porfirio Díaz in 1911, armed struggle continued intermittently for another ten years; yet another decade was to pass before power was consolidated in a predominantly middle-class party representing predominantly middle-class interests. In Bolivia, the middle-class party, the National Revolutionary Movement (MNR), which took power in 1952, chose to embrace the rampaging Indian peasants rather than attempt to suppress them. Nevertheless, the brevity of the tenure of the Bolivian Revolution may be attributed in part to the facts that the competing interests of the three elements of the revolutionary triad—the MNR, the miners, and the peasants—were never reconciled and that no element of the triad was able to gain control over the others.

In the Cuban case, the consolidation of power in the hands of Castro and his rebel army, who favored, in particular, the rural poor, was facilitated by the mass exodus of middle- and upper-class Cubans to the United States. In Nicaragua, the multiclass coalition that strained to project unity when Somoza fled with the national treasury in 1979 began to unravel within the year. Anti-Somoza businessmen, overwhelmed in their bid for power by the workers and peasants mobilized in support of the Sandinistas, turned to subversion in league with exiled National Guardsmen and the U.S. government.

Class Demolition and Redistribution.   The fate of the various upper-level social strata, and the organizations and institutions representing them in political competition, in the aftermath of revolution has varied greatly from country to country. In general, however, a successful revolution requires the displacement of the colonial or hegemonic power that has backed the ruling elite and underwritten the old order. Such displacement does not imply that the external power is stripped of influence over the client state; rather, it means that that power is deprived of some of its prerevolutionary points of access or of its means of participating directly and overtly in domestic power struggles and policymaking. (It is not uncommon, for example, in Latin American countries that have not undergone revolution, for U.S. officials to exercise a veto over presidential candidacies or cabinet appointments.)

In the case of Haiti, the colonial power and the landowning aristocracy were one and the same. French officials and planters were expelled (or killed) in the course of the fighting, along with the military and religious institutions that protected and legitimized the rejected social order. Fifty years were to pass before Catholic priests again appeared on the scene.

In the Mexican case, the Revolution disestablished the landowning aristocracy and the Church, which, until the reforms of the late 1860s, had itself been a major landowner. The Revolution also displaced that sector of the business elite whose wealth and power were based on export-import operations and other external ties and weakened the role of the United States in the manipulation of domestic power relationships. The national industrial sector was not a casualty of the Revolution, but rather a product of it; that sector was nurtured by the strengthened postrevolutionary state while the state itself began to fill the vacuum left by the displacement of foreign business interests from infrastructure (e.g., transportation and utilities) and the primary production sector.

Bolivia's landowning aristocracy was displaced in 1952 along with the private interests controlling the country's major industry, the tin mines. The Church, which had never been strong in Bolivia, was relatively unaffected, but the military officer corps was purged of the protectors of the prerevolutionary order. Although the United States had previously sought to suppress the MNR, that country had little visibility in Bolivia and thus was not a major target of the revolutionary process. Consequently, the new MNR government accepted U.S. economic and military assistance under conditions that contributed to the disintegration of the revolutionary coalition, the nurturing of a new military elite, and, ultimately, to counterrevolution. Hernán Siles Suazo, president from 1956 to 1960, commenting later on the strings attached to U.S. assistance, said that the United States had given him just enough rope to hang himself.

Prerevolutionary Cuba was so thoroughly penetrated by U.S. businesses that its patriarchal landholding elite and its nationally oriented industrialist class were relatively small and weak. Thus, the most important displacements of the revolution were those of the hegemonic power (the United States) and the military establishment that served it and of the businesses based in or linked to the United States. Ultimately, however, almost all owners of income-producing property were deprived, as the economy was thoroughly socialized.

The initial targets of the Nicaraguan Revolution were the Somocistas—that is, the dictator, his relatives and cronies, and the National Guard that propped up the Somoza dynasty on the local level—and the United States, which had been the ultimate benefactor and protector of the dynasty. The removal of the Somocistas provided the first fruits of victory for the purpose of redistribution. The economic squeeze imposed by the United States and the counterrevolutionary stance adopted by much of the remaining commercial elite led to some additional nationalizations. Nevertheless, some 60 percent of the economy remained in private hands.

The role of the Catholic Church in the Nicaraguan Revolution represents a first. Whereas in revolutions past the stance of the Church had ranged from moderate opposition to outright hostility to insurrectionary groups and revolutionary goals, the

Nicaraguan Church was among the most potent and committed elements of the revolutionary coalition. In the aftermath of the Revolution, however, while most parish-level priests and nuns continued to support the Sandinista leadership, the bishops withdrew their support or made it highly conditional.

Just as there has been considerable variation in the extent of displacement and deprivation suffered by the upper classes in the aftermath of revolution, there has been great variation in the extent of redistribution of wealth and power and in the actual benefits reaped by lower social strata. The revolutionary process may be a protracted one. In the case of the Mexican Revolution, the constitution that set forth the principles of the new social order did not appear until six years after the overthrow of Porfirio Díaz in 1911, and the participation of workers and peasants was not reflected in significant redistribution until the 1920s, under the presidency of Alvaro Obregón. It was not until the administration of Lázaro Cárdenas (1934–1940) that the most far-reaching redistribution was undertaken. During that period, some 20 million hectares (49 million acres) of land were distributed to peasant communities (*ejidos*), workers' rights were expanded and wages raised, and the very important petroleum industry was nationalized.

The extent of redistribution, and thus the success of a revolution, depends, in large part, on how much wealth there is to redistribute. Cuba, at the time of its Revolution, was a relatively prosperous country as measured in GDP or per capita income. Redistribution took the form, primarily, of the extension of services, and within a few years, Cuba's public health and educational systems were among the most comprehensive in the hemisphere. In Bolivia and Nicaragua, by contrast, there was relatively little wealth to redistribute. Haiti, where prerevolutionary wealth evaporated with the abolition of slavery, presents the starkest proof that successful revolution does not necessarily mean living happily ever after.

Institutionalization.   The process of institutionalizing a revolution includes the creation of an entirely new set of political support groups as well as new constitutions, laws, and behavior patterns. The process is complete when a mechanism for regulating succession to power is functioning more or less smoothly. The most important umbrella organization for the new support groups is usually a political party. The Mexican revolutionary party took shape in 1929. It was reorganized in the 1930s and again in the 1940s, when it was renamed the Institutional Revolutionary Party (PRI). Presidential elections take place every six years, and the revolutionary party has never acknowledged defeat, though the 1988 margin was the closest ever.

The institutionalizing vehicle of the Bolivian Revolution was to have been the MNR. The MNR's first president, Victor Paz Estenssoro, attributed the survival of the Revolution in its early years to the creation of armed peasant militias.[5] But the party did not succeed in fully incorporating or co-opting the miners or in institutionalizing succession by prohibiting reelection; thus, the uninstitutionalized Revolution succumbed, within twelve years, to counterrevolution.

In the Cuban case, the dominant vehicles of institutionalization on the national level have been the Communist Party and the Revolutionary Armed Forces.

However, the levers of power in both organizations have remained in the hands of Castro and his rebels of the Sierra Maestra campaign. The national political super-structure is built upon an extensive base of popular organizations. Although the mechanisms for succession at the pinnacle of power remain untested, local representation has been regulated by direct election since 1975 and members of the national legislative assembly have been chosen by direct election since 1992.

In Nicaragua, the Sandinista National Liberation Front (FSLN), which began in 1959 as a tiny insurrectionary group composed largely of university students, was already in a clearly dominant position at the time of the triumph of the revolution. Groups mobilized for fighting Somoza and his National Guard were quickly expanded and converted into vehicles for reconstruction and political support. Prerevolutionary political parties continued to operate after the Revolution, but without numerical significance.

In the first elections of the postrevolutionary period, in November 1984, the Sandinistas won 67 percent of the vote. Under pressure from the United States, a coalition of prerevolutionary parties and factions withdrew from the race; but several other small parties participated and claimed seats in the National Assembly. Elections were held again in February 1990. This time, after a decade of suffering economic strangulation and proxy war mounted by the United States, the Sandinistas succumbed to defeat. The National Opposition Union (UNO), a U.S.-funded coalition of fourteen organizations, won about 55 percent of the vote. Elements of the same coalition prevailed again in 1996, though the Sandinistas, as before, remained the largest party in the National Assembly, with about 40 percent of the seats.

Reconcentration.   Thomas Jefferson once quipped that every country needs a revolution every twenty years. There is no "happily ever after" in politics. Revolutions, like other secular readjustments of power relationships, are impermanent. Wealth and power tend to reconcentrate.

Reconcentration is akin to evolution in reverse. It refers to a gradual weakening of the power and income positions of political participants from the lower echelons of the social pyramid. If a revolution is not subsequently undermined by counterrevolution, a period of reconcentration may be expected to follow the institutionalization of the revolution.

Revolutionary leaders may themselves become a "new class"—an economic as well as a power elite, as happened in Mexico. Or the new class may derive from the bureaucrats who inherit power when the revolutionary generation passes from the scene. In the Cuban case, although Castro and his rebel cohorts have conspicuously avoided the material trappings of elite status, rank differentiation, with accompanying privileges, has already crept into what was once a "people's" army.

Nevertheless, countries that have undergone successful revolutions tend to be far more stable than those in which progressive movements have been thwarted. And countries in which revolutions have been aborted, or reversed by counterrevolution, are the least stable of all. The redistribution that generally takes place within the first few years following the consolidation of a revolution gives most citizens a stake in the new government. That loyalty is likely to last at least for a couple of decades, until the passing of the revolutionary generation, and may, in fact, last long after the redistributional phase has given way to the reconcentration of wealth and power in a new class. On the other hand, where reform has been thwarted or revolution aborted, a vicious cycle of insurgency and repression generally sets in, a cycle that likewise may last for several decades.

Counterrevolution

Counterrevolution has been defined, for the purposes of this model, as the displacement of one or more strata of political participants from the base of the social pyramid. It may take place in response to an incomplete revolution or to rational or irrational fear of revolution. But it may reflect simply the recognition by economic elites that the logical long-term consequence of a political process that allows for the effective participation of nonelites will be redistribution of wealth as well as of power. In fact, since counterrevolution requires a military and paramilitary establishment at the service of an elite and/or of foreign interests, it is more likely to take place in countries in which political development has been evolutionary than in countries that have undergone successful revolution. It is precisely because the power bases of the economic elites and the connections of those elites with the military and the dominant foreign power have remained intact that a minority is able to override the apparent will of the majority—as imperfectly expressed, for example, in elections—and reverse the tide of redistribution. (The crushing of a political order through direct foreign occupation is not encompassed in this concept of counterrevolution.)

Although dictatorship has been the rule rather than the exception in the history of most Latin American countries, counterrevolution, as such, is largely a phenomenon of the latter half of the twentieth century; in earlier eras, there were rarely "participant" lower classes to be displaced. Among the first clear cases of counterrevolution was the overthrow of Guatemala's President Jacobo Arbenz in 1954, followed by the withdrawal of rights recently won by labor and the recovery by non-Indian *hacendados* of land that had been distributed to Indian peasants. Both Brazil and Bolivia underwent counterrevolution beginning in 1964, as did Chile and Uruguay in 1973. Argentina has experienced counterrevolutionary episodes periodically since 1930, the most dramatic having been those accompanying the military coups of 1966 and 1976.

Facilitating Factors.   Deterioration of an economy, expressed particularly by runaway inflation, is among the most obvious factors that contribute to counterrevolution. In the face of a shrinking economic pie, middle-class elements, generally dependent and insecure, begin to see the demands of the working classes as a threat to their own precarious positions. Thus, a major portion of the middle class, anxious perhaps because of popular agitation and/or elite-inspired scare propaganda, aligns itself with the upper classes in a bid to reverse the trend toward redistribution.

Since the proponents of counterrevolution are a minority element of the population (were they not in a minority, their interests would not be threatened by democratic processes), counterrevolution can only be successful if that minority can rely upon military and paramilitary forces that are alienated from the majority of the population. Furthermore, as the military role is central, the ultimate provocation leading to the overthrow of a reformist president and his replacement by a military government—typically, the first overt step of a counterrevolution—is often a threat to the military itself: rank-and-file insubordination, a military budget cut, or a threat of suspension of foreign military aid.

Even so, national economic elites and military establishments are not likely to undertake counterrevolution unless they can rely upon the help, or, at the very least, the benign neutrality, of the dominant foreign power. With the possible exception of some of Argentina's counterrevolutionary episodes, all successful counterrevolutions in Latin America since the middle of the twentieth century have had the direct or indirect support of the United States. In some cases, economic deterioration, military alienation, middle-class fear, and other facilitating factors have been intentionally exacerbated by the actions of U.S. government agencies. The complicity of the United States was particularly apparent in the Guatemalan, Brazilian, and Chilean cases.

The Phases of Counterrevolution.   The initial phases of counterrevolution are related to those of revolution in that the struggle between proponents and opponents of counterrevolution is immediately followed by struggle among the counterrevolutionary conspirators themselves. Counterrevolution, like revolution, calls for a multiclass alliance—in this case, of upper and middle classes. It also requires a coalition of military and civilian elements. Even within the military, there are various factions with differing perspectives and objectives. In the Chilean case, the counterrevolution began with a bloody purge of the military itself.

The initial agreement among military conspirators to topple the incumbent president and to assume power in the name of the armed forces by no means assures agreement on longer-term objectives. Thus, simultaneously with the process of demobilizing the nonelites—the disarming of opponents in the street and constitutional arenas—the conspirators engage in fierce competition among themselves in the private arena. In general, power is first consolidated in the hands of the military faction favored by the dominant foreign power, though rivalry within the military is perpetual and the balance of power among factions may shift over time. Meanwhile, civilian parties and political leaders who expected to profit from the demise of their civilian opponents soon find themselves stripped of their power bases and vulnerable to the whims of the new military authorities.

Political Demobilization.   The most immediate and dramatic manifestations of counterrevolution are political. The street arena is the first to be closed down. Labor, peasants, and student leaders, for example, are killed or arrested, and their organizations are dissolved or "intervened" (taken over) by the new government. The constitutional arena is the next victim. Congress is dissolved or its less malleable members are purged. Courts and local governments are purged of uncooperative individuals. Some or all political parties are dissolved, and government ministries, university faculties, and communications media that might be obstructive or critical are purged and brought under government control. The political process moves back into the private arena, which is now centered in the military establishment but continues to embrace economic elites and representatives of the dominant foreign power.

The extent of violence involved and of government control required is dependent, of course, upon the country's level of political development: The greater the proportion of the population that had come to participate in the political system, the greater the violence required, at least initially, to demobilize it. In the cases of Argentina, Uruguay, Chile, and to a lesser extent, of Brazil and Bolivia, counterrevolution called for overt executions; disappearances (usually unacknowledged executions); the establishment of concentration camps; and systematic, highly modern, and sophisticated techniques of torture. In the case of less-developed Guatemala, counterrevolution was manifested in a reversion, so to speak, to the campaign of conquest and the Indian wars.

Although the Catholic Church, like most middle-class or nonclass national institutions, is subject to marked factionalism in the face of either revolution or counterrevolution, the severity of the violation of human rights in the course of modern counterrevolution has made the Church the primary bastion against the excesses of counterrevolutionary regimes. As the only national institution that cannot be crushed outright by military authorities, the Church becomes the refuge of last resort for the dissident and the devastated.

Once power has been consolidated in a dominant military faction and effective opposition to counterrevolution has been crushed, authorities are free to move ahead with the transformation of the economy.

Economic Transformation.   Counterrevolutions do not merely freeze socioeconomic relationships or maintain the status quo. The expulsion of lower social strata, e.g., workers and peasants, from the political arena results in redistribution of wealth from the bottom up. This may be accomplished through a combination of tax, tariff, budget, wage, and land tenure policies. Land reform measures may be revoked, or squatters may be expelled. Graduated personal and corporate income taxes may be diminished or abandoned in favor of regressive taxes. Social services may be cut, and wages may be frozen in the face of inflation.

The central role of the military and paramilitary forces dictates that their budgets will be expanded. The involvement of the hegemonic power and/or the requirement of external aid and investment dictate acceleration of the denationalization of resources and the adoption of policies that favor foreign enterprises over national ones. Thus, the national industrialist class, which supported counterrevolution as a means of containing the demands of labor, finds itself crippled by tariff and credit policies and foreign competition. And the middle class, having lost free expression and political participation, suffers also the shrinkage of its economic mainstay—government employment.

Institutionalization.   Institutionalization does not come easily to counterrevolutionary regimes, partly because of the difficulty of achieving legitimacy. Establishing procedures to routinize policymaking and the succession to power in a manner that does not threaten the power position of the ruling faction or of the counterrevolutionary elite also proves difficult.

Counterrevolutionary regimes have often sought the support, or at least the acceptance, of certain sectors or institutions by labeling themselves "revolutionary" or "Christian." Such regimes in Bolivia were able to court, or at least to neutralize, most peasant groups for the better part of the decade by waving the revolutionary banner while crushing the miners and other elements of organized labor. The revolutionary label adopted by Brazil's military rulers in 1964, however, did not appear to impress anyone.

Regimes claiming to be bastions of "Western Christian values confronting atheistic communism" often succeeded initially in attracting support from some element of the Church hierarchy. But as the oppressed tend to cast their lot with any institution that dares to speak for them, the weight of the Church's influence has shifted to those members of the hierarchy who have defied the government. In defending the poor and other victims of government oppression, the Church itself becomes liable to government reprisal. Once clergymen and nuns have been added to the ranks of those subjected to imprisonment, torture, and execution, it becomes more difficult for any element of the Church hierarchy to continue to serve as apologist for the regime. Thus, appeals to the pious soon lose their credibility, and counterrevolutionary regimes fall back upon the slogans of "national security" and "free enterprise" that appeal to their own limited constituencies.

Counterrevolutionary regimes, like other ruling elites, have sometimes attempted to co-opt or to establish political movements or parties on the supposition that such movements or parties could be controlled from the top and grassroots initiatives could be blocked. But they have generally found that organizational initiatives carry unwarranted risks and may prove counterproductive.

Military governments are not necessarily counterrevolutionary, but counterrevolutionary governments are necessarily military, generally with considerable paramilitary support (police, vigilantes, "death squads," etc.) as well, because the abrupt reconcentration of wealth and power can be carried out only by armed force. Such regimes have begun their tenure as institutional ones, or what we shall call "militocracies." Power is seized and exercised in the name of the armed forces, as such, rather than by a *caudillo,* and the military establishment as a whole becomes the first-line political base of the government. The nominal president may be civilian, as was the case in Uruguay from 1973 to 1981, and a congress may be allowed to convene, as was usually the case in Brazil between 1964 and 1985, but such officials hold their posts for the convenience and at the sufferance of the military. Elections and plebiscites, held with varying degrees of regularity and under varying degrees and techniques of control, are the rule rather than the exception.

The failure of such regimes to achieve legitimacy may be compensated for by the maintenance of a high level of repression and coercion, but the failure to routinize succession to power means continual instability and vulnerability. The process whereby the most powerful position, be it the presidency or the highest military or army post, changes hands among individuals and factions is generally one or another form of palace coup, although it may be bloodless and may be sanctified by "elections."

In the Brazilian case, probably the most successful institutionalization of a counterrevolutionary regime, the succession process generally involved an "election" or polling process carried out among the highest-ranking officers—e.g., four-star generals. The victor of that process was then "nominated" by the official party and duly elected by an electoral college including members of the national congress and representatives of state legislative assemblies. Military elections—formal or informal polling among upper-echelon officers—are not simulations of democratic process; rather, they are simulated battles, as votes are weighted in accordance with command of firepower.

Decompression. Decompression (in Portuguese, *distensão*) is one of the terms used by Brazilians in reference to the process that got under way in their country about 1978. The term will be used here in the same sense, but to refer to the process in other countries as well—a process of attenuation of the power and control of the military and other counterrevolutionary forces, resulting in a lessening of repression and an increase in political participation, particularly by the middle class.

The factors that tend to weaken the grip of a counterrevolutionary elite are not unlike those that undermine other elites and other systems. They include division within the ruling group or between that group and its constituencies, economic stress, and external pressure. Commonly, all of these factors come into play simultaneously and reinforce each other.

The headiness of power and the spoils of office, not to mention the occasionally genuine conflicts of ideologies, are just as conducive to competition within a military caste as within a ruling civilian elite. If power becomes highly concentrated in the hands of an individual or a clique, other factions that have ceased to profit adequately from military rule may garner support from civilian groups in order to unseat the offending individual or clique. The price of civilian support will be a commitment to some degree of political opening.

Economic stress is likely to exacerbate divisions within the military as well as to alienate some elements of its constituency. The support of the dominant foreign power may be weakened or even withdrawn as a consequence of the regime's economic mismanagement. Also the level of repression may reach such proportions as to embarrass the hegemonic power. Such was the case in the mid-1970s when human rights policies adopted by the U.S. Congress and highlighted briefly by the Carter administration served to weaken, at least temporarily, some of Latin America's counterrevolutionary regimes.

In the Brazilian case, all of these factors were apparent in the 1970s. But Brazil's decompression gained additional impetus as the facade of democracy—the apparatus of parties, elections, and representative bodies that had served the regime well in the process of institutionalization—blossomed into a reality beyond the facile control of the still-dominant military. In Bolivia, neither revolution nor counterrevolution has gained any semblance of institutionalization; instability has reigned supreme. When the military abandoned power in 1982 to the government of Hernán Siles Suazo—elected, but suppressed, in 1980—it was primarily because the economy had collapsed under the weight of military corruption. Economic collapse was also a major factor in the disintegration of the Argentine regime that occurred in early 1983, but the disintegration had been accelerated by humiliating defeat in the Falklands/Malvinas War of 1982.

FROM ARISTOCRACY TO MILITOCRACY

In general, the constitutional and legal systems of Latin American countries were borrowed from France and the United States and, at least until the twentieth century, served merely to legitimize political arrangements that had been reached in private—in the smoke-filled rooms of men's clubs and other gathering places of the wealthy. In such arenas, competition among landholding families, and later between landholders and representatives of new wealth based on international commerce and industry, could be regulated. Such competition was not necessarily peaceful; it often led to clashes among armed hirelings of families or sectors of the economic elite. But electoral and parliamentary systems were little more than a ritualistic adjunct to a process based on wealth, force, and interpersonal intrigue.

It was only with the successful bid for participation by the middle classes that electoral and parliamentary systems came to have a serious function. In general, however, Latin America's middle classes have not constituted an intermediate level of property holders. Nor have they represented other independent sources of wealth. Rather, they have been a salaried class, derived from and dependent upon the expansion of commerce and government. Their bid for effective participation, beginning in the late nineteenth century in Argentina and continuing into the late twentieth century in Central America and the Andean highlands, could not (and cannot) rest upon their own numbers and resources alone. They found it necessary to incorporate the numbers and the potential disruptiveness of lower social strata, particularly the incipient labor movement, into their power bases. Middle-class bids for political power have generally been spearheaded by university students and intellectuals and carried to fruition by political parties, but they have rarely been successful unless they were believed to have the backing of organized labor. Thus, the effectiveness of the ballot box has been preceded by an effective demonstration of power on the streets and in the factories.

Where, for reasons of social distance based on racial and ethnic difference, the original postconquest aristocracy has concluded that it *dare* not expand political participation, and/or, for reasons of powerful external support, the economic elite has concluded that it *need* not expand political participation, the upshot has been either revolution or "boundary maintenance" depending on the relative strengths of contending forces.

Where aristocracies have felt constrained to give in to middle-class demands for effective political participation, democratic processes have acquired substance—for a time and to a point. But middle-class leaders have generally proved unable or unwilling to extend fully effective participation, through the electoral system, to urban workers and peasants, particularly when economic decline has sharpened competition between middle and lower classes.

Uruguay's felicitous early experience with the evolutionary process does not seem likely to be repeated in Latin America in the near future. Although a middle class may rise to the full exercise of political power through the evolutionary process, recent developments in Latin America suggest that, at least for the time being, there is a high threshold of participation that manual workers and peasants will not be allowed to cross.

Once middle-class parties and labor organizations have been incorporated into the system, political conflict may come to be centered in the constitutional arena. But, at least in Latin America and perhaps in most dependent states, limited participatory democracy contains the seeds of its own destruction. The greater the level of effective participation and the longer the unbroken tenure of constitutional rule, the more policy will incline toward nationalism, nonalignment, and egalitarianism. Thus, the middle class, dependent upon salaries from the government or the property-holding upper class and insecure in its status, begins to align itself with the upper class. These classes, seeing their power slipping away and their economic interests threatened, abandon the constitutional arena. They enlist the military establishment and the United States in their defense against the perceived threat—until recently "the menace of communism." Thus, counterrevolution is most likely and most violent precisely in those systems that have achieved the highest levels of political development through the evolutionary process.

The destabilized constitutional system is then replaced by a militocracy—a system in which the military establishment as a whole serves as a ruling elite. Competition for power within this system assumes the form of simulated battles, as command of firepower confers political power. Civilian instigators and supporters of counterrevolution soon find that military rulers are not content to become their pawns. Although economic policy initially reflects the interests of the counterrevolutionary coalition, over time it increasingly reflects the institutional and personal interests of military officers themselves.

Counterrevolutionary systems, like evolutionary and revolutionary ones, and the political and economic gains and losses they represent, are impermanent. But the praetorianism, or militarism, that facilitates counterrevolution and is, in turn, strengthened by it appears more durable. The Argentine military has often withdrawn in the period since the overthrow of Perón in 1955, but never to a safe enough distance to allow labor a free rein. Even though the military establishments of Chile and Uruguay have withdrawn from the direct exercise of power, it is most unlikely that those countries will return by the end of the century to the free-wheeling democracies that flourished before the counterrevolutions of the 1970s. Even if elections are unfettered, it will remain clear that full powers are not vested in the electorate. The experiences of Latin American countries suggest that nothing short of revolution would be likely to bring those military establishments under civilian control. And, as Bolivia can attest, even revolution offers no long-term guarantees against militarism. At any rate, in countries having acquired a large middle class, revolution is no longer an option. And in the post–Cold War global village, where economic policymaking is centrally controlled by a creditor cartel, conquest of the state would no longer be much of a prize.

TRANSITIONS AND ILLUSIONS: DEMOCRACY ON A LEASH

The end of the Cold War, and with it the end of the dialogue as to optimal and feasible means of organizing a new order, coincided with the end of militocracy in Latin America and the spread of democracy—at least the input, or electoral, side of it—over much of the globe. This welcome development may have become possible, however, precisely because those whose interests would be most threatened by egalitarianism do not feel threatened by the U.S.-marketed election-as-spectacle approach to democracy, with its soaring costs and sinking value.

By the end of the 1980s—particularly after the elections in Paraguay and Chile in 1989—all of the South American countries had acquired a facade, at least, of civilian, constitutional rule. The "redemocratization" of Central America responded to a somewhat different set of pressures and dynamics, including greater sensitivity to the peculiarities of foreign policy decisionmaking in Washington. The Reagan administration, seeking to roll back the revolution in Nicaragua and to crush rebellion in El Salvador and Guatemala, had found that scheduling elections throughout the region would persuade a recalcitrant Democratic Congress to continue appropriating military assistance. It was only in the 1990s, when U.S. interests and priorities changed, that the process of pacific settlement, initiated by Latin American leaders and supported by the United Nations, bore fruit and elections acquired a meaningful role in the political process. Even then, however, elected leaders generally operated within parameters narrowly drawn by military and paramilitary bodies and domestic and foreign economic elites.

Redemocratization has been accompanied by increasing indebtedness and surrender of economic sovereignty, the discrediting of reformist leaders and programs, and a return to economic elitism buffered by parties and parliaments and the ritual of elections. Civilian leaders have sometimes appeared to be virtual prisoners in their own presidential palaces, and violence, particularly against the poor, continues unabated. A Brazilian social worker commented that the military dictatorship had "democratized" the violation of human rights. The subsequent redemocratization has meant that violations have once again been restricted to the poor, who have always been vulnerable.

In the late 1990s, as in the early 1960s, most Latin American governments are considered democratic because elections have taken place. Now, as then, there is less to such democracy than meets the eye. The obstacles and deceits are, however, of a different order. In the early 1960s, "democracy" was being discredited in Central America and the Caribbean by fraud, in the Southern Cone by vulnerability to military intervention. Now, in the 1990s, democracy is being discredited by irrelevance—by the absence of options and expectations. The democracy of the 1960s was unstable precisely because there was hope—hope that political democracy might lead in the direction of economic democracy. The democracy of the 1990s is more nearly stable because there is little such hope (and consequently little fear). More than ever, electoral politics is the moral equivalent of sport. Military force is no longer required to hold the line. The politically articulate are kept in check by the lack of options— and the lack of an alternate theoretical paradigm; and the desperate are distanced from the comfortable by gated communities and new categories of police.

Challenges of the New Order

The problems facing the continent's old and new democratic regimes in the 1990s are staggering, but they are not the same problems that most preoccupied national leaders during the last interlude of optimism a generation ago. That earlier generation of civilian leaders sought means of modernizing their economies at minimal cost to traditional and marginal sectors. As it happened, the cost has been scandalous, but modernization has indeed taken place. The overriding problems now are not those associated with traditionalism but rather those of the flotsam of modernization: Inflation and unemployment, population growth, migration and displaced persons, crumbling cities, crime, pollution, and dwindling resources.

Those Latin Americans who had dared to hope that the end of militocracy would bring economic development and social justice have been sadly disillusioned. In fact, the retreat of the generals has been only partial. And inequitable socioeconomic systems are reinforced by the demands of foreign creditors and international financial institutions. Civilian elites who can no longer blame the military for policies that serve to line their own pockets at the expense of the impoverished masses can now pass the buck to the seemingly omnipotent International Monetary Fund.

The resurgence of electoral politics since the 1980s has sometimes meant that both military and civilian elites had come to recognize the need for an institutional buffer zone between management and labor, or between haves and have-nots. That is, elites had become willing to share their power—or at least their stage—in exchange for sharing also the blame for inequitable policies. Even so, in many cases Latin America's return to democracy was instigated in large part by genuinely popular movements, parties, and leaders. Particularly in those cases, organization charts notwithstanding, the elected leaders have lacked the full powers normally associated with the office: most important, control over military and paramilitary forces, including the police, and over resource allocation.

The End of the Trend, or Simply a Mixed Scorecard?

Only a year or two into the democratic new world order, the redemocratization trend in Latin America began to be challenged. The overthrow in September 1991 of Haiti's civilian president, Father Jean-Bertrand Aristide, elected in 1990 by an impressive 68 percent majority, unleashed a savage assault on the Haitian people and prompted an exodus of refugees toward an unwelcoming United States. Less than a year later, in April 1992, Peru's elected president, Alberto Fujimori, in league with the country's military high command, staged a coup of his own, dissolving the congress and detaining many of its members, particularly leaders of the dominant party, APRA.

In Venezuela, characterized for more than three decades by high per capita income and stable civilian rule, the debt crisis of the late 1980s forced incoming president Carlos Andrés Pérez of the social democratic party, Acción Democrática, to adopt extreme austerity measures. The upshot was rioting and police countermeasures that resulted in some 300 deaths by official count, 1,000 or more by unofficial count. The instability and discontent that followed generated a climate propitious for military conspiracy, which expressed itself in two abortive coup attempts in 1992.

Much of Latin America may be settling once again for a system relatively open but heavily compromised, a midpoint on the political spectrum between positions long known as *dictablanda* and *democradura* (soft dictatorship and hard democracy). New forms of authoritarianism have not been widely recognized as such, however, because in most cases repression has been selective or subtle, and elections, complete with hoopla and foreign observers, continue to take place regularly. In that regard, the Peruvian case appears to be a harbinger. New elections several months after the coup restored credit and international respectability even though they were boycotted by the major parties.

The new round of elections in Latin America may also serve to legitimate older authoritarian systems, thus giving them a new lease on life. The Paraguayan elections of May 9, 1993, are a case in point. They aroused international interest in that they offered the prospect that after almost a half century of military dictatorship Paraguay might at last undergo a transition to democracy. Paraguay had indeed come a long way since the corrupt and brutal thirty-five-year rule of General Alfredo Stoessner was ended by a coup d'état in 1989. But in 1993 the ruling triad of military, bureaucracy, and official party (the Colorados) still had control of most of the money, all of the weapons, and all of the electoral machinery. Even so, a new generation mobilized to force a democratic opening, freedom of expression and of assembly gradually came to be generally respected, and the electoral process, flawed as it was, gave the opposition a leverage point from which to extract concessions. By 1996, the judiciary and the electoral tribunal had undergone major reform.

Meanwhile, in the 1990s, elections in Mexico were becoming more competitive in partisan terms, as the business-oriented National Action Party (PAN) and the left-leaning Revolutionary Democratic Party (PRD) wrested major provincial and municipal posts as well as congressional seats from the control of the PRI, seriously weakened by assassination, increasingly transparent corruption, and ever bolder narco-traffickers. Mexico's economy, now linked with those of the United States and Canada in the North American Free Trade Agreement (NAFTA), remained a crap game for the high rollers and a downward escalator for the majority, whose frustrations were being expressed in strikes and demonstrations as well as a rash of new guerrilla movements.

Renewed or continuing momentum toward redemocratization since the mid-1990s has taken the form of U.S. intervention in Haiti to restore civilian rule; the ratification of accords ending a struggle of more than thirty years between the Guatemalan government and the Guatemalan National Revolutionary Unity (URNG), a rebel coalition that has sought to represent the Mayan community; and serious attempts on the part of the Honduran government to prosecute military and intelligence agents accused of human rights abuse.

On the other hand, even Haiti, one of the world's poorest countries, is responding to creditors' demands for austerity measures; and the weapons used so freely by political adversaries in Central America in the 1980s have given rise in the 1990s to a rash of routine street muggings. Guerrilla activity, along with narco-trafficking, continues in Peru and Colombia, provoking extralegal and often brutal military and paramilitary responses.

The bad news in Ecuador in early 1997 was that the imposition of austerity measures generated a crisis that deposed a president and left the country at one time with three claimants to the office. The good news was that the crisis did not—at least in the short term—give rise to a direct military takeover.

For the most part, contemporary manifestations of authoritarianism take the form of police power, its relevance to politics shrouded as unrest degenerates into anomic street crime and economic problems giving rise to it become increasingly untreatable at the national level. Still, to say that democracy in the 1990s is failing to live up to its promise is not to say that parties and elections and parliaments are likely to be abandoned. In many countries, though progress in demilitarization has been halting and exasperatingly slow, military power has continued to ebb. Few other than would-be autocrats see promise, at this point, in autocracy. And only those having very short memories could fail to find hope in an increased measure of respect for human and civil rights.

NOTES

1. Charles W. Anderson, *Politics and Economic Change in Latin America* (Princeton, N.J.: Van Nostrand, 1967).

2. Martin C. Needler, *An Introduction to Latin American Politics: The Structure of Conflict* (Englewood Cliffs, N.J.: Prentice-Hall, 1977).

3. Karl Deutsch, "Social Mobilization and Political Development," *American Political Science Review* 55:4 (September 1961).

4. Some scholars have viewed the outcome of Costa Rica's civil strife of 1948 as revolutionary. Others have viewed it as counterrevolutionary. The outcome, in this author's view, was a mixed one, with gains and losses for elements of both upper and lower social strata, but one that did not fundamentally alter the evolutionary course of change.

5. Conversations with Paz Estenssoro, Albuquerque, spring 1978. Paz told of a visit during his presidency by a delegation of peasants from a village on the Altiplano. They had come to plead for a telephone for the village and for a bridge to connect the village with a road leading to La Paz. Paz Estenssoro responded that the demands on his administration were enormous and the treasury was bare. Thereupon, the spokesman of the delegation said: "Mr. President, I'm sure you remember that an angry mob hanged former president Villarroel from a lamppost. When the counterrevolutionaries come for you, you can call us on our telephone and we'll come running across our bridge and save you!" Paz said they got their telephone and their bridge.

SUGGESTED READINGS

From the perspective of development theory, Charles W. Anderson, *Politics and Economic Change in Latin America* (Princeton, N.J.: Van Nostrand, 1967), has provided a useful model of political actors—who they are, and how they go about seeking participation and power. Martin C. Needler, *Political Development in Latin America: Instability, Violence, and Evolutionary Change* (New York: Random House, 1968), foreshadowed more recent work on the relationships between economic and political development.

The paradigm that has had greatest currency for dealing with the counterrevolutionary trends of the 1970s was provided by Guillermo O'Donnell in *Modernization and Bureaucratic-Authoritarianism: Studies in South American Politics* (Berkeley: Institute of International Studies, University of California, 1973). Penny Lernoux, *Cry of the People* (New York: Doubleday, 1980), depicts the changing role of the Church in the face of revolution and counterrevolution. The roles of Latin America's modern military establishments are treated in Philippe C. Schmitter, ed., *Military Rule in Latin America: Function, Consequences, and Perspectives* (Beverly Hills, Calif.: Sage Publications, 1973). Military withdrawal and the trend to "redemocratization" during the 1980s are covered in James M. Malloy and Mitchell A. Seligson, eds., *Authoritarians and Democrats: Regime Transition in Latin America* (Pittsburgh: University of Pittsburgh Press, 1987); Larry Diamond, Juan J. Linz, and Seymour Martin Lipset, eds., *Democracy in Developing Countries*, vol. 4, *Latin America* (Boulder, Colo.: Lynne Rienner Publishers, 1989); and Robert A. Pastor, ed. (with a foreword by Jimmy Carter and Raul Alfonsin), *Democracy in the Americas: Stopping the Pendulum* (New York: Holmes and Meier, 1989).

Cole Blasier, *The Hovering Giant: U.S. Responses to Revolutionary Change in Latin America* (Pittsburgh: University of Pittsburgh Press, 1976), deals with the U.S. stance vis-à-vis revolution, and Jan Knippers Black, *United States Penetration of Brazil* (Philadelphia: University of Pennsylvania Press, 1977), outlines the U.S. role in destabilizing democratic governments and promoting counterrevolution. More general coverage of U.S. involvement in the politics of Latin American and other Third World countries is found in Noam Chomsky and Edward S.

Herman, *The Political Economy of Human Rights,* vol. 1, *The Washington Connection and Third World Fascism* (Boston: South End Press, 1979).

Among the many noteworthy books on mature and fledgling revolutionary regimes are Martin C. Needler, *Mexican Politics: The Containment of Conflict,* 3d ed. (New York: Praeger, 1995); Jorge Domínguez, *Cuba* (New Haven: Yale University Press, 1979); and Thomas W. Walker, *Nicaragua: The Land of Sandino* (Boulder, Colo.: Westview Press, 1981). Late-developing Andean countries receive good coverage in David Scott Palmer, *Peru: The Authoritarian Tradition* (New York: Praeger, 1981), and Osvaldo Hurtado, *Political Power in Ecuador,* trans. Nick Mills (Albuquerque: University of New Mexico Press, 1980).

Roots and branches of counterrevolutionary regimes are covered in Alfred Stepan, ed., *Authoritarian Brazil: Origins, Policies, and Future* (New Haven: Yale University Press, 1973); Arturo Valenzuela, *The Breakdown of Democracy in Chile* (Baltimore: Johns Hopkins University Press, 1978); and Peter G. Snow, *Political Forces in Argentina* (New York: Praeger, 1979).

Among the many outstanding books on tumultuous Central America are Stephen Schlesinger and Stephen Kinzer, *Bitter Fruit: The Untold Story of the American Coup in Guatemala* (New York: Doubleday, 1982); Cynthia Arnson, *El Salvador: A Revolution Confronts the United States* (Washington, D.C.: Institute for Policy Studies, 1982); Peter Calvert, ed., *The Central American Security System: North-South or East-West?* (Cambridge: Cambridge University Press, 1988); Peter Kornbluh and Malcolm Byrne, *The Iran-Contra Scandal: The Declassified History* (New York: New Press, 1993).

More recent assessments of the political potential of the military are found in Alfred Stepan, *Rethinking Military Politics: Brazil and the Southern Cone* (Princeton, N.J.: Princeton University Press, 1988), and Brian Loveman and Thomas M. Davies, Jr., eds., *The Politics of Antipolitics: The Military in Latin America,* 3d ed. (Wilmington, Del.: Scholarly Resources, 1996).

Post–Cold War works on the Caribbean and Central America include Anthony Payne and Paul Sutton, *Modern Caribbean Politics* (Baltimore: Johns Hopkins University Press, 1993), and Thomas W. Walker, ed., *Nicaragua Without Illusions: Regime Transition and Structural Adjustment in the 1990s* (Wilmington, Del.: Scholarly Resources, 1997).

13

THE POLITICS
OF INSECURITY

JORGE NEF

This chapter provides an overview of Latin American politics in the larger context of the Americas. The term "Latin America" is somewhat deceiving, since it encompasses many different national experiences. However, there is one common feature: Despite a seemingly chaotic pattern of politico-institutional development, the societies south of the Rio Grande are part of the New World. They are also an offshoot of Western civilization. My perspective is broadly historical and systemic, concentrating on the intersection between domestic and regional factors. The countries that compose the area are inserted in an extremely asymmetrical system with manifold linkages. In it, U.S. elites, by themselves or in alliance with external groups, enjoy relational control, or metapower.[1] That is, they have the ability to alter the outcomes of the interaction not only by force or the threat of force but by setting and changing the rules of the game. For all intents and purposes, the inter-American system is hegemonic and unipolar, with some structural similarity to pre-1989 Eastern Europe.[2]

Partly for the reasons outlined above, the unified study of Latin America is replete with facile generalizations, intellectual vogues, and fallacies.[3] A case in point is the use by mainstream analysts of the concept "democratic transition" to characterize contemporary politics.[4] This expression is often made synonymous with the change from military (or in any case authoritarian) to civilian rule—one of a number of dramatic transformations that allegedly indicate a worldwide victory of American ideals. This transition also involves a perceived decline of populism, the proliferation of "limited democracies," and the emergence of semicorporatist and governable "pacts of elites" geared to preventing overparticipation.[5] Its economic correlate is the replacement of economic nationalism and socialism by neoliberalism[6] and market-oriented reforms. Its international manifestations include the collapse of Eastern Europe at the end of the Cold War, the reversal of the Sandinista revolution in Nicaragua, the isolation of Cuba, and the demise of the Nonaligned

Movement. The sum total of these trends is construed as a vindication of modernization theory,[7] bringing about conservative triumphalism and a surge of business confidence.

Yet, even if popular revolt looks unlikely for the moment, the long and deep social antagonisms festering under the democratic veneer have not vanished. Rather, they have resurfaced in the familiar spiral of poverty and institutional, repressive, and insurgent violence. The weak civilian governments that replaced the militocracies of the past and those electorally generated regimes that survived the 1970s are paralyzed by ineffectiveness and low legitimacy. A careful look at the emerging literature and the mass of statistical and qualitative data renders a view far from optimistic.[8] The much-proclaimed business and official confidence, therefore, has little to do with social equity, political democracy, or even the state of real economic well-being, nor with actually existing security for its inhabitants. It rests instead on the ideological illusion that a felicitous correspondence between market politics and market economics has finally emerged, preventing turbulent social change from below.[9]

Two central propositions are advanced. The first is that the repressive military regimes of the 1970s and today's limited democracies manifest greater continuity than the proponents of transition theory and the popular media suggest. Despite the political turmoil of the past, persistent violence, and a normalization allegedly taking place, the underlying social, economic, and international forces that have enjoyed extraterritorial power and privilege still prevail. Contrary to myth, the Americas as a whole and with few and reversible exemptions have not undergone profound social revolutions. Their social and economic systems are mostly stable and conservative. The second proposition is that stability in the long run has hampered sustainable, equitable, and democratic development. In fact, the current style of modernization hinders real democracy and increases rather than decreases poverty and insecurity for most people in the hemisphere.

THE HISTORICAL ROOTS OF
THE LATIN AMERICAN STATE

Since the conquest, the region has been subordinated to one or another more highly developed part of the world. The patterns of production, trade, and finance have reflected an enduring satellite-metropole international division of labor. The insertion of Latin America in the international economy, with its boom-and-bust cycles, was firmly established by the latter part of the nineteenth century. This export economy was based on the overseas marketing of raw materials, the import of manufacture, and the superexploitation of labor. The "modernization" of these commodity-states has been largely antidevelopmental, as endogenous development has been overdetermined and distorted by external factors, has been undermined by flights of local capital, and has resulted in the marginalization and exclusion of most of the population. Nearly two centuries after formal independence, structural underdevelopment persists.

Under the above conditions, social backwardness has predictably endured. The ranch, the hacienda, the mining town, and the plantation created conditions favorable to the perpetuation of an outward-looking and parasitic commercial elite[10] and facilitated the emergence of a patrimonial system of labor relations based upon indenture, paternalism, and servitude. Class and racial barriers have been intertwined in a highly hierarchical, rigid, and exploitative social structure. The very existence of the privileged groups has been a function of their role as a link to an external power, having objectively benefited from social inequities and foreign domination. These structural circumstances have been incorporated into the Latin American states and the system of inter-American relations,[11] bringing about a vicious cycle: The key function of the regional and local political systems has been by and large the maintenance of a socioeconomic order based on inequality and underdevelopment.

Independence (1803–1823), though generally violent and convoluted, resulted more from European power politics and imperial delinking than from homegrown social movements. The disintegration of the Spanish and Portuguese empires did not alter the socioeconomic order. The process of national consolidation unfolded in the absence of a revolutionary bourgeoisie, a revolutionary ideology, and most important, a radical national-capitalist transformation. On the contrary, authoritarian institutions inherited from the Iberian peninsula, such as the Roman Catholic Church, a closed class system, the practices of local bosses (*caciquismo*), clientelism, and familism, became entrenched in the New World and continued to shape the national period. Despite the presence of violent cyclical crises, which contribute to the stereotype of almost perpetual revolution, Latin American societies have remained mostly unrevolutionary. Social revolutions have occurred in Haiti (1803), Mexico (1910–1917), Bolivia (1952), Cuba (1959), and Nicaragua (1979), but with the qualified exception of Cuba they have all run astray or been reverted. Likewise, contemporary counterrevolutionary modernizations "from the top" have also been rare.[12] If one discounts the foiled attempt in authoritarian Brazil (1964–1984), only Chile stands today as a problematic case of elite modernization.

In the decades following independence, the frequent civil wars between "conservatives" and "liberals," "unitarians and federalists," "presidentialists and parliamentarists" were more often expressions of struggles for booty and power over the spoils of a disintegrating postcolonial system than manifestations of clear class alliances or national projects. The prosperity brought about by increased demand for raw materials beginning in the 1880s facilitated intra-elite compromise and the cessation of civil strife. The military and to a lesser extent the bureaucracy were gradually professionalized, though not necessarily democratized, following European molds. Toward the end of the century, most countries had developed various forms of stable oligarchical rule: "gentlemen politics." By and large, and for as long as there was enough surplus to distribute among the elites, the dangers of regionalism, intra-elite conflict, and civil wars remained subdued. However, repression by the now professionalized and oligarchically controlled military and police forces was effectively directed against lower-class mobilization, the latter also a by-product of the modernization and internationalization of the economy. While the military establishment acted as an insurance policy against popular challenges to the status quo, intra-elite consensus was maintained by facilitating private accumulation of the export bonanza. In a few instances (Uruguay, Argentina, Chile, Costa Rica, Mexico), the process of economic modernization gave rise to a greater degree of social differentiation, above and beyond the "butler" strata of officers and patrimonial clienteles on the public payroll. Instead, a middle class of sorts, constituted by professionals, employees, schoolteachers, bureaucrats, small retailers, and the like, emerged as a "buffer" between the oligarchy and the mass of workers and peasants.

The postwar economic recession of the 1920s, culminating in the Great Depression of the 1930s, shattered the old status quo. With the collapse of markets, the tenuous system of elite accommodation that sustained the oligarchical republics crumbled. As intra-elite tensions increased, so did the challenges to the existing order coming from labor, the peasantry, and the dispossessed. In the aftermath of economic collapse, the "dictator of the 1930s" became a dominant feature practically everywhere.[13] Yet, depending upon the previous modality of socioeconomic development and institutional consolidation, the long-term effects of the crisis in each country were quite diverse. In the relatively more industrialized South American nations and in Mexico, where middle-class reformism had evolved in the previous decades and where republican practices had become institutionalized, import-substitution industrialization (ISI) with populism[14] became the dominant form. Under the leadership of a middle-class controlled state, an alliance with national entrepreneurs and unionized labor was constructed. Their program was one of reactivation, employment, and national development. In the lesser-developed societies in Central America and the Caribbean, where (with the exception of Costa Rica) a constitutional order had not emerged and a professional and bureaucratic middle class played no meaningful role, the populist alternative was impossible. The political pattern was essentially exclusionary for the nonelite sectors, and for the next thirty or forty years dictatorial rule continued unabated.

Both patterns of conflict management began to fall apart between the mid-1940s and early 1950s. Riots, revolts, and generalized political turmoil exploded in Colombia, Costa Rica, Guatemala, El Salvador, Argentina, Venezuela, Peru, Bolivia, Cuba, and Puerto Rico. U.S. administrations, mesmerized by the Cold War, the Truman Doctrine, and the newly established Rio Treaty for the collective defense of the Americas (1947), responded to these domestic events in their backyard as threats to U.S. national security. Latin American oligarchies, besieged by social unrest and unable to withstand popular mobilization and pressures for democratization, took advantage of the new international environment by playing on the anti-Communist fears of their allies in the United States. Entangling transnational alliances between U.S. and Latin American business, political, and military elites were built. The East-West conflict created the conditions for a new North-South confrontation. It also marked the return of an active U.S. interventionism reminiscent of the "big stick" and gunboat diplomacy that preceded the Good Neighbor Policy, inaugurated by the administration of President Franklin D. Roosevelt in 1934. Interventionism was justified by a new and compelling ideological motif: the struggle between the "free world" and "communism."

The CIA-orchestrated overthrow of the elected government of Guatemala in 1954 was paradigmatic of the new mood. The long-term effects of U.S. interventionism were destructive for the region's institutional and democratic development. Washington became in the eyes of many the principal force for the preservation of oppressive regimes and an unabashed supporter of military dictatorships. Yet, even this support proved insufficient to prevent the popular uprisings that precipitated a crisis of domination in Venezuela and Cuba. Neither the Pérez Jiménez nor the Batista dictatorships and their external supporters were able to exercise effective control by force. The Venezuelan dictator was overthrown in 1958 and Batista fled Cuba shortly thereafter. Cuba represented the first of a wave of national revolutionary movements backed by a wide array of popular forces. Its revolution was one of the most important developments in the region since the Mexican Revolution four decades earlier. It set in motion a fateful chain of events involving confrontational U.S. responses and a growing internationalization of domestic conflicts.

Attempts by the United States to destabilize and subsequently overthrow Fidel Castro and undo the revolution culminated in both the calamitous Bay of Pigs invasion and President Kennedy's Alliance for Progress, launched in 1961.[15] Washington's main purpose was to prevent "another Cuba" by encouraging social and economic reforms in the region. With it, U.S. policy moved away from the open support of dictators of previous years. Instead, economic and social development was perceived as the antidote to insurgency. It was to be accomplished by propping up middle-class, progressive reformist and anti-Communist governments. But the alliance was no Marshall Plan, and it was a case of too little too late. Import-substitution industrialization had already come to a dead end, populism had run its course, social tensions were mounting, and a profound fiscal crisis had set in. The inability of the reformist governments to deliver and quell social unrest rendered the alliance virtually useless.

Though calamitous for the region's long-run democratic development, the other side of the strategy met with more verifiable success. It involved the isolation of Cuba as well as a massive effort to give the collective defense of the Americas outlined in the Rio Treaty a new meaning: the introduction of counterinsurgency and civic action as the central preoccupation of the region's security forces.[16] A radical reorganization of the Latin American military ensued. The change in military doctrine from the defense of territorial security (external aggression) by conventional forces to fighting the "internal enemy" by special forces was a blow to the precarious sovereignty of the Latin American countries. It transformed the U.S. security establishment into the head of a vertically integrated regional counterrevolutionary system, giving the local military a new self-justifying and professional mission: fighting "subversion," however loosely defined. In a relatively brief period and with a modest expenditure, the United States, irrespective of its declared intentions, had turned the local military and police forces (the latter through USAID's public safety programs) into the dominant internal linkage groups,[17] operating the lower rungs of the hemispheric security regime. With the reformist and preventive side of the Alliance for Progress marred by internal and external inconsistencies, the counterinsurgency and containment elements took precedence over democratic considerations. This reorientation became manifest during the Johnson administration, with its encouragement and nurturing of the Brazilian counterrevolution of 1964.

In the more institutionalized democracies, the exhaustion of import substitution and populism led to a breakdown of consensus and civic confidence.[18] In the 1960s, wage and price spirals had become a muted and protracted form of civil strife in many countries. Political deadlock eroded both the legitimacy and the effectiveness of these regimes. Labor practices inherited from the populist years reproduced and accelerated the "push-up" effect of institutionalized social conflict. The rules of the pluralistic game decomposed in the midst of rapid mass mobilization. In these countries, the existing socioeconomic order, both domestic and international, was maintained by resorting to naked yet highly bureaucratized repression under a new political alliance. The latter involved a coalition between the externally linked business elites, which gave content to a neoliberal economic package, and the security establishments transnationalized by the ideological "professionalism" of the Cold War. The military, representing a unique U.S.-trained, -indoctrinated, and -financed fraction of the middle class, provided the force required to keep the population at bay.

AUTHORITARIAN CAPITALISM

The national security doctrine, defined by an internal enemy ("subversion") and an external "friend" (the United States) and by ideological frontiers, eroded the legitimacy of the local military institutions and decisively transnationalized the state. The explicit articulation of this U.S. strategic posture was the Nixon Doctrine, contained in the Rockefeller Report of 1969.[19] The document clearly showed a change in the U.S. normative ideal of political development, from democracy and participation to authoritarianism and order.[20] For the duration of the Nixon-Ford regime, and with a few notable exceptions,[21] the number of military dictatorships steadily climbed: ten in 1969, twelve in 1970, fourteen in 1972, and fifteen in 1973.[22]

The liberal-authoritarian projects that unfolded in the 1970s rejected the nationalist and protectionist overtones of import substitution and induced development policies. Instead, economic growth was seen as a function of a reinsertion of the countries' economies into the international division of labor as exporters of raw materials: a return to a widened export economy. With the exception of Brazil in the late 1960s and the 1970s, economic modernization, far from "deepening industrialization," meant increased reliance on the natural resource sector and heavy borrowing. The foreign debt, which in 1960 amounted to about one-third of the regional annual exports, had grown by 1970 to 1.7 times the total value of exports. Just before the oil crisis in 1973, it had climbed to 1.9 times that value. The strategy of accumulation also involved the creation of favorable conditions, through deregulation, denationalization, and the disarticulation of labor organizations, for domestic and transnational elites to increase their share of profits.

The era of national security[23] was not only extreme in its persistent abuses of human rights; the early neoliberal design of its economic strategies implied the tearing down of the welfare state and import-substitution industrialization policies developed since the 1930s. Authoritarian capitalism rejected the demand-side implications of the early Cold War liberalism of the Alliance for Progress and was more concerned with direct containment and the protection of the status quo than with development. Other than offering "economic miracles" financed by foreign investment, the orthodox policies imposed monetarism (later identified with the Chicago School) over the structuralist doctrine of the UN Economic Commission for Latin America (ECLA). These measures were far more effective as a shock therapy—by atomizing labor, freezing wages, letting prices float to world levels, and privatizing the economies—than in raising living standards. They were much more effective in the short run as weapons in a social war than as instruments of national development. On the contrary, the long-term socioeconomic consequences of these policies were by and large disastrous for the region. So were their social, environmental, and financial implications. In fact, far from generating stability and bringing prosperity, the combination of dictatorial rule with unrestricted free-market policies created a serious governability problem. The authoritarian capitalist formula also set the conditions for the subsequent debt crisis and recession of the 1980s.

The bureaucratic-authoritarian states[24] that emerged in South America, patterned on the example of post-1964 Brazil, were attempts at modernizations from the top, with strong U.S. inducement. The benefits of this new order accrued to a small alliance of domestic entrepreneurs and speculators supported by a technocratic-military middle class and their business, political, and military associates in the United States.[25] The crisis of legitimacy was managed by military force, through strengthening the alliance between themselves and the domestic socioeconomic elites and also by including external constituencies from the North (military, business, political, and diplomatic), while demobilizing and excluding the bulk of the population by force. Dictatorship had became a fundamental component of economic freedom.[26] The social cost for the majorities was enormous, since overall living conditions declined and the gap between haves and have-nots widened. Nor did these regimes succeed in unleashing real counterrevolutions. At best the national security regimes provided a repressive brake against social mobilization, economic nationalism, regional integration, and a perceived threat from the left. The effective operation of the neoliberal model required large amounts of external financing, which was facilitated in the 1970s and early 1980s by massive deposits of recycled petrodollars in Western private banks. Indebtedness, fueled by the illusion of prosperity, ensued. As both the governments and especially the private sector in the region increased their financial obligations, the failure of production and exports to keep pace with borrowing and, most important, with swelling interest rates, resulted in huge debt burdens.[27] In this, the hard-line military regimes in Brazil, Argentina, Chile, Uruguay, and Bolivia did not behave very differently from the more populist ones in Peru, Panama, or Ecuador or those in civilian-controlled oil-producing countries (Mexico and Venezuela) or in the island governments and microstates of the Caribbean, though the ideological framework was quite different. Irrespective of the intent of the policies, their effects were similar: unmanageable indebtedness in the region.

The crisis of the dictatorships in Brazil, Argentina, Uruguay, and Chile involved the erosion of the political alliances that had permitted the implementation of the repressive socioeconomic projects. Meanwhile the sui generis military regimes in Peru, Ecuador, and Panama quietly faded away. The main political limitation of the national security regimes was that government by force was ultimately untenable. The Nicaraguan uprising of 1979 and the long civil wars in El Salvador and Guatemala signaled another form of transition: popular, radical, and potentially democratic. To Washington, these endogenous developments posed a more serious threat to the maintenance of the hemispheric order than the erosion of the bureaucratic-authoritarian regimes in South America. The combined impact of economic crises, a growing inability to manage conflict among internal factions, and a new "post-Watergate" political coalition in Washington fearful of the long-run effects of authoritarian solutions created the conditions for military withdrawal. The transitional strategy was outlined in 1975 by the Linowitz Report.[28] This document was heavily influenced by the views of the Trilateral Commission[29] and was critical of the previous "Pentagonist" U.S. policy toward Latin America. It constituted the blueprint for President Carter's initiative on democratization.

Democratic transition for most of Latin America was largely the result of intra-elite negotiation superintended by the United States. The orderly retreat of the national security regimes preserved many authoritarian traits. In this, the reemerging democracies shared some of the political characteristics of older "managed democracies" such as those in Colombia, Venezuela, and Mexico, which did not experience direct military rule. Such closely watched transition to democracy had strict limits. Although authoritarian capitalism proved to be largely a developmental failure, the radical restructuring of the economies along radical free-market lines by means of political repression was profound enough to prevent a return to economic nationalism. Likewise, the restructuring and transnationalization of the security establishment made the pursuit of nationalist and nonaligned foreign policies impossible. In this sense, the political arrangements that emerged in Latin America as a result of redemocratization may possess the formal trappings of sovereignty and democracy yet have been neither truly democratic nor sovereign. They have produced precariously balanced civilian regimes, based on negotiations within the elites, with exclusionary political agendas and narrow internal support. In these the popular sectors are effectively maintained outside the political arena, while external actors, both economic and military, enjoy de facto veto power over the state.[30]

The central role of the state changed from at least symbolically promoting development and providing public services to that of manifestly servicing the foreign debt and implementing IMF-inspired structural adjustment policies. The ultimate effects of these policies have been the perpetuation of dependence and underdevelopment. The latter express themselves in chronic vulnerability to external economic and political influences, requiring ever increasing doses of external supports.[31] This vulnerability can be dramatically illustrated by the inability of the countries to extricate themselves from chronic indebtedness: the "debt trap."[32] Debt management became the number-one political concern in the regional agenda[33] in the early 1980s. The service, both principal and interest, grew from slightly over 40 percent of the total value of annual exports in 1979 to over 65 percent in 1983. The total indebtedness figure for 1988 was over $400 billion, with Brazil, Mexico, Argentina, Chile, Venezuela, and Peru incurring the highest sums. In 1990–1991, even though about one-half of the countries had reduced their liabilities, the overall debt had grown to $421 billion (a 5.2 percent increase). In fact, out of the seventeen most indebted countries in the world in 1992, twelve were in the Latin American region. On an average the annual interest rate payments fell from 33 percent of all exports in 1987 to 22 percent in 1991 as the "lost decade" came to an end. Between 1992 and 1996, the burden was reduced even further, but at a high social cost.

The end of the cycle of national security in the 1980s was a direct consequence of the insoluble contradictions between and within the nature of the reactionary coalitions in power and the centrality of external supports for authoritarian capitalism. Given limited resources, there was a long-run impossibility of reconciling the interests of the national security bureaucracies with those of domestic and foreign business. There was also the additional problem emerging from the extreme vulnerability of the countries to external factors (e.g., the unmanageable debt burden, deteriorating terms of trade) and constituencies (e.g., members of the U.S. administration, Congress, corporations). As power conflicts intensified in Washington in the post-Nixon era, the loss of crucial support from liberal political sectors and also U.S. business compounded the internal erosion of power suffered by the Latin American dictatorships. Democratic transition became the alternative to popular revolt. The conversion from dictatorship to limited democracy has to be seen in the context of the previous transition to national security, both in the bureaucratic-authoritarian context of the Southern Cone and in the less institutionalized setting of Central America. Growing participation and dependent development could coexist only under conditions of economic expansion and for as long as such participation did not threaten the perceived interests of the local and U.S. elites.

THE PREDICAMENT OF THE RECEIVER STATE

The mounting debt crisis set the parameters for the emergence throughout the Americas in the mid-1980s of a new political formula: a "receiver state,"[34] splicing together limited democracy and neoliberal economics.[35] It is a highly transnationalized and weak state, acting in partnership with foreign creditors and international financial institutions as manager, executor, and liquidator of national bankruptcy.[36]

The central function of this arrangement has been the administration of the debt combined with the implementation of structural adjustment policies (SAPs) geared to massive privatization and denationalization of the economy. This state reflects the nature of the transnationalized political alliances and the narrow spaces for political participation, where economic and fiscal policies have been effectively left out of the political debate. Yet these policies define the rules of the game and set the limits for social policies.

The various national incarnations of receivership exhibit important differences. These depend upon the transition processes as well as on the particular coloration of the civilian management to appear in the postauthoritarian period and in the early adjustment phase. At close scrutiny, regardless of the elected origin of the government in charge, the economic agenda has had striking resemblances to those imposed by authoritarian rule. The present arrangements are not a mere transitional phase from elite domination to genuine democracy: free and participatory politics, with effective popular control. Rather, the repressive state of the 1970s and the receiver state of the 1990s are two different manifestations of a similar cluster of elite interests.

The receiver state expresses the consensus of a largely transnationalized and conservative coalition, though at times managed by tamed center-left governments. Limited democracy with narrow mobility opportunities and exclusionary agendas provides a thin cushion to confront the deep structural problems once controlled by repression. The current modality of conflict management, though it has reduced the most blatant and ugliest human rights abuses, has left the region's most pressing and fundamental socioeconomic and political problems largely unresolved. The combination of the transnational integration of the domestic elites (economic, military, technocratic, and bureaucratic) with the demobilization and marginalization of the popular sectors is not a formula for stable governance. In the absence of tangible rewards to buy legitimacy, insurgent, repressive, institutionalized (as well as criminal) violence has become common.

Despite the phasing-out of the national security regimes, contemporary Latin America is not necessarily undergoing a change toward substantial democratization. Demilitarization and return to limited democracy are not synonymous with an alteration of the status quo. Nor is democracy nowadays any more "real" in those countries in the hemisphere where civilian governments have remained in control. On the contrary, the "new" discourse on democracy among the official intelligentsia in the United States, Canada, Latin America, and the Caribbean involves a juxtaposition of a substantially tamed democracy with neoliberal economics.[37] Although this "low-intensity democracy"[38] may appeal to the regional core—the consumption-intensive, high-income groups in the Americas—it is not majority rule. This elitist view,[39] espoused by the Trilateral Commission, considers that the basic cause for the crisis of democracy is democracy itself. This mode of conflict management entrenches under a legal facade a corporatist pact of elites representing basically the same economic, social, and political alliances that sustained the antidemocratic regimes: transnational business, the military, the local bourgeoisie, and upper segments of the middle classes.

The regressive socioeconomic policies implemented under authoritarian rule were enshrined both in the pacts of transition and in ad hoc constitutional mechanisms. The emerging democracies are constrained by other factors, too. One is the weakness of the governing centrist political alliances, since the transition arrangements effectively excluded most left-of-center and populist political forces from holding power. Another is the crucial, autonomous role played, as a parallel state, by the security forces to maintain the status quo and prevent investigation of human rights abuses. Then there are the odious and massive debt obligations incurred mostly under the previous repressive regimes. They severely limit the rendering of services to those in need, and fiscal "austerity" inevitably leads to confrontation politics and increasingly repressive governmental responses. The impact of the debt service on already exiguous fiscal resources is compounded by the strict conditionalities imposed by the international financial institutions (the IMF, the World Bank, and private banks). Structural adjustments resulting from such conditionalities have gravitated against demands for reform, equity, and social justice, already frozen by the old dictatorships.

By most statistical accounts and with very few exceptions (Haiti, Honduras, Bolivia), Latin America makes the upper layer of the Third World. Moreover, unlike the Middle East, Africa, and especially Asia, the balance and diversity of resources to population is most favorable. In this sense, Latin America and the Caribbean, other than by virtue of their proximity to the overdeveloped "North," appear to be out of the condition of critical poverty. Business confidence and the post-1990s recovery (3.3 percent average growth between 1992 and 1995), which has made investments profitable once again, have fueled a bullish wave of optimism among Western business and political elites. However, distributional inequity, rooted in powerlessness and exclusion, is more pronounced than in other regions of the world. Democratic development, with the sole exception of Costa Rica, is weak and unstable at best. Most of the Latin American population lives under very precarious and vulnerable circumstances. Even, when economic recovery is factored in, the overall income levels are below those of 1980.[40] As is the case throughout the globe, the slow economic improvement has failed to translate into social well-being. Nor are there signs of the aforementioned distributional inequities being arrested, let alone reversed. Perhaps the unintentionally ironic remark made by Brazil's dictator, General Emilio Garrastazú-Medici, in 1975 still holds true: "The economy is doing well; people aren't."

Between 1980 and 1990, those living below the poverty line in Latin America and the Caribbean *increased* from above 120 million to over 200 million and from 41 to 46 percent of the population.[41] A 1994 ECLAC study on accessibility to the basic food basket indicated a significant but persistent increase in poverty and destitution, as seen in Table 13.1. Central America has been the most seriously affected by the double impact of concentration of wealth and the spread of poverty. Nearly 80 per-

Table 13.1

Estimates of Percent of Population in Poverty and Indigence in Nineteen Countries in Latin America, 1980, 1986, and 1990

	Poverty			Indigence		
	1980	*1986*	*1990*	*1980*	*1986*	*1990*
Nationwide	41.0	43.0	46.0	19.0	21.0	22.0
Urban	30.0	36.0	39.0	11.0	14.0	13.0
Rural	60.0	60.0	61.0	33.0	36.0	37.0

Source: Oscar Altimir, "Income Distribution and Poverty Through Crisis and Adjustment," *CEPAL Review* 52 (April 1994), p. 12.

cent of its inhabitants were reportedly unable to access a basic food basket, and half of these were destitute.[42] According to the same report, between 1977 and 1994 Guatemala witnessed an acceleration in the concentration of wealth and resources,[43] with fewer than 2 percent of the landowners owning more than 65 percent of the total farmland. Between 1990 and 1993, after just two years of structural adjustment, the poverty rate in Honduras increased from 68 percent of the total population to 78 percent. In Nicaragua, as a result of the Contra war and the implementation of President Chamorro's austerity package, 71.3 percent of the economically active population were unemployed.[44] Illiteracy, which had been effectively reduced to 12 percent between 1979 and 1989, actually *increased* in 1993 in absolute and relative terms. The same was the case with infant mortality, from 50 per 1,000 in the 1980s to 71 per 1,000 in 1991 and 83 per 1,000 in 1993.[45]

Even the much-hailed economic "miracles" have not produced lasting development. The combination of entrenched elite interests, extreme free-market agendas, and structural adjustment policies have left a lasting legacy of poverty and despair. The areas of health, education, and community development have suffered continuously. Hardest hit have been those sectors lacking political influence: women, children, natives, peasants, the urban poor. Since the end of the boom of the 1970s, Brazil's only enduring feature has been the most unequal income distribution in the Western Hemisphere. Chile's "success story" does not fare any better under close scrutiny. Between 1970 and 1987, the proportion of people defined as poor increased by an average yearly rate of 7.2 percent. Meanwhile, real income per capita grew at an annual average rate of 0.3 percent. Despite a democratic government and a slowdown in the velocity of impoverishment, widespread privation has persisted since 1990. There is an extremely skewed distributional profile despite impressive GNP annual growth rates between 4.5 and 10 percent. Pauperization and expanding inequity are not limited to the cases mentioned above. They are present all over the region: throughout the Caribbean, in Argentina, Uruguay, Paraguay, Venezuela, Colombia, Peru, Bolivia, Ecuador, Panama, Costa Rica, the Dominican Republic, Haiti, and particularly Mexico.[46] The most affected are the rural and urban poor, but white-collar, middle-class sectors have also seen their economic opportunities and social safety nets dramatically eroded. In fact, in Latin America, as in Canada and the United States today, the middle classes are disintegrating in the growing gap between the extremities of wealth and poverty.[47]

Praetorianism has a lingering presence. Given the polarized and violent nature of political conflicts, militarization has been a long-standing feature of the Latin American state. With few exceptions, the military establishment has played a disproportionately large role in virtually all the countries, whether under civilian executives or not.[48] Even in the supposedly exceptional cases, a careful examination reveals that direct military rule or militarized repression have always been present. Although with the withering away of the Cold War the military is less conspicuously present in politics than in the recent past, a closer examination reveals a more complex picture. True, the ending of the civil conflicts in El Salvador and Nicaragua, declining insurgent threats in Colombia and Peru, as well as the effects of structural adjustment packages upon defense budgets, suggest a trend toward demilitarization.[49] Yet, overall budget reductions have not necessarily been matched by personnel reductions. Rather, a small increase in manpower has taken place. But this smallness is deceiving: Downturns in countries with large establishments, such as Argentina (–39.8 percent), Chile (–9.1 percent), Nicaragua (–76.6 percent), and Peru (–12.5 percent), reduce the impact of significant upturns in most other countries. Twelve out of twenty of the countries actually increased the size of their defense forces between 1985 and 1991. Colombia topped the list with 76.7 percent, followed by Venezuela (53.1 percent), Guatemala (40.7 percent), and Mexico (35.6 percent). The largest establishment, that of Brazil, with nearly 270,000 forces, grew 7 percent.[50]

Though in comparison with the United States, Western Europe, the former Soviet Union, and the Middle East, the size of the Latin American forces is relatively modest, the impact, influence, and transnationalization of the security establishment, especially of its officer corps, remain extensive. Not including some 760,000 paramilitary and an indeterminate number of reserves, Latin America has over 1.3 million individuals under arms and spends close to $9 billion in defense. In this, Latin America follows the U.S. lead. Despite the alleged "peace dividend" and a substantial decline in budgets and personnel, the United States still has over 1.9 million on its military payroll and spends over $227 billion on its war machinery—about 22.6 percent of its central government expenditures. The leverage of the U.S. military in that country's hemispheric policy and upon its Latin American clients remains considerable. Put bluntly, the Americas are overmilitarized; the security sector still is a voracious competitor for the scarce resources needed for development. It constitutes a persistent obstacle to the sovereignty of and cooperation among nations and continues to be the single most serious threat to political stability, integration, sustainable democracy, and human rights. With the end of the Cold War and with the insurgency threat reduced, the fundamental security issue in the Americas is not so much how to protect society from external and internal "enemies" but how to safeguard the population from its own security forces. Thus, we must reconsider civil-military relations in the emerging inter-American order, especially in light of new factors. One is the influence of the new right in U.S. politics. Another is the resurgence of border tensions, exemplified by the 1995 Ecuadoran-Peruvian war. And yet another is the growing militarization of conflicts, as in Chiapas and Colombia's and Peru's narco-wars.

Post-1990 political developments in Latin America, although they convey a more democratic picture, especially in contrast to a somber past record, exhibit at best mixed signs. On the positive side, most of the region is now ruled by governments generated through formally free, fair, and competitive elections. In some instances, some sort of consolidation has taken place, as a second and even a third generation of elected governments have been inaugurated. There have also been sporadic yet significant attempts to hold governments accountable to the electorate. Instances of torture, disappearances, and state terrorism, with notable exceptions, have become less frequent. However, there are also disturbing signs. One is the persistence and even revival of authoritarian and oligarchical traditions. Power remains highly concentrated. Other less tangible but basic values such as respect for human life, honest government, and the reduction of discrimination and official abuse are not widely adhered to. Corruption is widespread, deep, and fast growing. Limited democracies, based upon pacts of elites, are distinctively exclusionary. Electoral processes, despite their becoming a common sight throughout the Americas, are increasingly void of choice and even meaning: Voters can cast a ballot, but the choices and the policy options are roughly the same—something North Americans are beginning to see happening at home, too. The socioeconomic and institutional pillars of the former national security regimes (landowners, businesspeople, foreign investors, and authoritarian preserves within the military, the judiciary, and the technocracy) are also those of the new democratic orchestration. The large majority of the perpetrators of crimes against humanity are still at large and have gone unpunished. Thus, it is hardly surprising that public apathy and cynicism are at an all-time high, while governmental legitimacy is shrinking. Despite the unfolding of formally contested elections during 1993 and 1995 in six countries and apparently normal constitutional reforms in four, these processes failed to provide real alternatives. The above-mentioned alienation of the population from the political process has resulted in extremely high rates of electoral abstention.[51] In addition, many of these contests were tainted with serious irregularities.[52]

Beyond ceremonial transfers of offices by electoral means and the absence of direct military rule, democracy in Latin America has not been consolidated in the 1990s, and transition remains incomplete. Political elites throughout the continent have shown a remarkable continuity. The old practice of executive *continuismo,* the elimination of which was central to the region's past democratic agenda, has resurfaced. There is also a remarkable continuity of policy. Neoliberal recipes have become entrenched in the conditionalities attached to debt alleviation, regional trade agreements (such as NAFTA and MERCOSUR), and the so-called macroeconomic equilibrium policies that effectively remove fiscal, monetary, and credit matters from national politics.

CONCLUSIONS

A profound contradiction in liberal democracy has emerged in the Americas. Elected governments can stress democracy, majority rule, and the interests of the public (the civil society), but in doing so they would face relentless opposition and sabotage from domestic and international business, leading to eventual ineffectiveness if not outright destabilization. The other, more common course is for governments to stress liberalism and turn their backs on the civil society and rule on behalf of the profit sector. This is what Ralph Nader, speaking of the United States, has labeled a plutocracy. The political cost of this option is very high in the long run: loss of legitimacy and an erosion of the trust between elected officials and the electorate, a central tenet of both governance and institutionalization.[53]

Given the level of political alienation, it is not surprising that there have been popular insurrections in communities confronted with threats to their livelihoods. The civil uprising in Santiago del Estero, Argentina, in December 1993 and the armed revolt in Chiapas, Mexico, led one month later by the Zapatista National Liberation Front (FZLN), are symptomatic. Despite formal differences, both developments have a number of things in common. They resulted from specific local grievances explicitly against orthodox economic policies. Their discourse was at odds with the more traditional leftist ideological slogans associated with guerrilla movements. Moreover, the end of the Cold War and the effective isolation of Cuba made it more difficult to label these movements as threats to hemispheric security. The demands posed by these insurgencies were quite negotiable and specific. Although the Argentine revolt was more spontaneous and middle-class in orientation, the one in Chiapas was firmly rooted in peasant and indigenous grassroots. The rebels presented an articulate grievance mixed with a good dose of Liberation Theology and were apparently well trained and organized. The Chiapas uprising also manifested itself in a military-political strategy that showed an exceptional degree of determination and success. Despite a cosmetic truce brought about by the Mexican presidential election of 1994, a year later the circumstances in Chiapas had returned to those before the crisis, as President Ernesto Zedillo launched an all-out military campaign to wipe out the insurgents and restore business confidence in his government.

Regime responses have also varied considerably. While President Carlos Menem of Argentina sent a special envoy to solve the grievances (mostly unpaid wages, rollbacks, and corruption) right away, the Salinas and subsequently the Zedillo administrations used a two-pronged strategy of negotiation and repression by deploying nearly one-tenth of the Mexican army in the affected zone. Of the two cases, the Chiapas insurrection had the broader national and international implications. It received substantial support from indigenous groups from all over the Americas and was portrayed with sympathy by the North American and European media, largely on account of its native roots and its anti-NAFTA stand. The episode highlights the profound internal malaise of the Mexican political system as well as the reversal of the social achievements attained since the 1917 revolution. These are underscored by a violent power struggle within the country's authoritarian ruling party, the PRI, resulting in the assassinations of both the handpicked official presidential candidate, Luis Colosio, and the PRI's general secretary. Subsequent investigations have revealed involvement by the highest political offices. This political turmoil, combined with wild financial speculation, provided the context for the dramatic monetary collapse of December 1994.

The resurgence of resistance suggests that popular movements and rebellions are still present in the new regional order.[54] They are still political options, and it is likely that we may witness more such developments in the near future. Instability, even under the mask of freer trade, is more than skin-deep. On the other hand, by challenging the legitimacy of the new intra-elite and transnational arrangements, these movements reveal the intrinsic weakness of the current regimes. From a long-range structural perspective, violent upheavals have not withered away altogether, although their manifestations have changed. For many, rebellion is still seen as an alternative to the cycle of poverty, repression, and insecurity that has historically strangled the region's development. But revolution is not the only nor the most common type of violence. For others, repression offers a shortcut to stability and modernity and the prevention of chaos. The partial ending of the Cold War in the hemisphere and the collapse of communism worldwide do not necessarily mean the end of repression and revolts in the region. Compressed tensions and multiple conflicts could erupt at any moment. In this context, rebellion—though muted in the current conjuncture—could evolve into a self-fulfilling prophecy either as the perceived alternative to oppression and hopelessness or as a means for simple protection and survival. The constriction of political options tends to reduce the political process into a simple equation: force equals power, and vice versa.

Despite formally clean and competitive elections and a tapering off of the worst infringements on human rights and refugee flows over the last years, both the political arenas and alternatives for compromise beyond the realm of the political elites remain exceedingly narrow. Consensus building is even more difficult when the heavily indebted economies and the pro-business policies do not have the ability to generate the surplus necessary for effective and legitimate governance. The shrinkage of the state throughout the region under the spell of structural adjustment with neoliberal, exclusionary policies has compounded the crisis of governance and institutionalization. In the context of a crisis of legitimation and as long as the benefits of "modernization" remain elusive for the majorities, no reformist development project or significant human security will be viable. Democratization and progress in the region will remain largely meaningless if these are confined to the upper and middle sectors of society. Profound social conflicts rooted in enduring inequities cannot be deconstructed out of existence by semantic illusions, such as "transition to democracy," "demilitarization," "competitiveness," or "macroeconomic equilibrium."

The preceding analysis strongly suggests that the politics of limited democratization with neoliberal economics, though an improvement over the human rights record of the national security regimes, imposes built-in constraints upon the realization of a truly stable and sustainable democratic project for and by the populace. Nor are limited democracy and neoliberalism a guarantee against expanding corruption or popular alienation; in fact, the opposite seems to be the case. If economic recovery fails to produce a better standard of living for the majorities (as is currently the case) or should the structural crisis deepen, it is likely that these weak and "pragmatic" civilian regimes could be overturned by equally weak yet violently repressive regimes. After all, the national security doctrine is still the ideological "software" (or culture) of the hemispheric security establishments and a staple in the training of special forces in Latin America and the United States. "Communist" subversion is being replaced by a new definition of the internal enemy: "terrorism," "anarchy," or "narco-terrorism," or more broadly anything that threatens the "investment climate."

Poverty alleviation, respect for human rights, and public ethics are important factors to bring about political and economic stability in the area. Unlike other regions of the world, inequity in Latin America—and in North America—is less a function of generalized scarcity than a result of powerlessness. Therefore, good governance, not mere "governability," acquires a cardinal importance. Market-oriented reforms (or any other reforms for that matter) are bound to produce instability when not accompanied by a qualitative improvement of public probity, participation, management, and quality of life. The historical record, despite spates of business optimism (every twenty years or so) such as the one in the late 1990s, shows that socioeconomic progress in Latin America has been neither widespread nor persistent. Rather, it has been weak and unstable and conditioned by exogenous factors. Progress, when it has taken place in any shape or form, has been reversible (witness the Brazilian "miracle" of the 1970s or socialist Cuba's "success record" of the early to mid-1980s or Mexico in the 1990s).

As the entire region becomes more closely integrated, a potentially dysfunctional system of mutual vulnerability[55] is beginning to take shape. Its potential impact on the life of millions throughout the Americas can be dramatic. The present course points toward scenarios where unemployment, poverty, violence, criminality, health hazards, addiction, refugee flows, massive population displacements, repression, and environmental decay feed upon each other. Without profound changes in both the South and the North of the hemisphere, the possibility of arresting or reversing threats to human security will remain minimal. Unless a radical reorganization of the pattern of regional governance, including decisionmaking and regional cooperation (for instance, the OAS system)[56] takes place, multiple and perhaps critical dysfunctions are likely to increase.

Regional security cannot be equated with short-term business confidence nor with the messianic vision of U.S. "Manifest Destiny." A breakdown of democratic development, prosperity, equity, and the increase of tensions in the more volatile countries of the region would have a direct and most deleterious effect upon the well-being and security of North America. The weakness of democratic institutions and their inability to traverse from democratic transition to consolidation of democracy are a critical structural flaw in the security of the hemisphere. It is becoming painfully obvious elsewhere that the end of the Cold War does not automatically translate into a Fukuyama-type scenario of the "end of history," with global prosperity, peace, and democracy.[57] The current democratic transition in the region cannot be equated with either the entrenchment of participatory practices or responsible government, let alone human security. The "safe," "limited," "low-intensity," and meaningless democracy[58] peddled by transition theorists impedes more than facilitates the emergence of a sustainable security community in the Americas.

NOTES

1. See Tom Burns and Walter Buckley, "Meta Power and the Structuring of Social Hierarchies," in Burns and Buckley (eds.), *Power and Control: Social Structures and Their Transformation* (Beverly Hills: Sage, 1976), pp. 224–225.

2. For a comparison between superpower control in (the former) Soviet bloc and the Western Hemisphere, see Terry-Lynn Karl and Richard Fagen, "The Logic of Hegemony: The United States as a Superpower in Central America," in Jan Triska (ed.), *Dominant Powers and Subordinate States: The United States in Latin America and the Soviet Union in Eastern Europe* (Durham, N.C.: Duke University Press, 1986), pp. 218–238.

3. See the classical work by Rodolfo Stavenhagen, "Seven Fallacies About Latin America," in James Petras and Maurice Zeitlin (eds.), *Latin America: Reform or Revolution? A Reader* (New York: Fawcett, 1969), pp. 13–31; also Suzanne Bodenheimer, "The Ideology of Developmentalism: American Political Science Paradigm-Surrogate for Latin American Studies," *Berkeley Journal of Sociology* 15 (1970), pp. 95–137.

4. For instance, Giuseppe DiPalma and Lawrence Whitehead (eds.), *The Central American Impasse* (New York: St. Martin's Press, 1986); Paul Drake and Eduardo Silva (eds.), *Elections and Democratization in Latin America, 1980–85* (San Diego: Center for Iberian and Latin American Studies, Center for U.S.-Mexican Studies, Institute of the Americas, University of California at San Diego, 1986); and Guillermo O'Donnell, Philippe C. Schmitter, and Lawrence Whitehead (eds.), *Transitions from Authoritarian Rule: Prospects for Democracy* (Baltimore: Johns Hopkins University Press, 1986). A critical analysis of the transition literature is contained in Jorge Nef, "The Trend Towards Democratization and Redemocratization in Latin America: Shadow and Substance," *Latin American Research Review* 23, 3 (Fall 1988), pp. 131–153.

5. On "liberal democracies," see Arturo Siat and Gregorio Iriarte, "De la seguridad nacional al trilateralismo," *Cuadernos de Cristianismo y Sociedad* (Buenos Aires), May 1979, pp. 23–24. The themes of "manageability" and, more to the point, "governability" are central to the Task Force Report to the Trilateral Commission, "The Governability of Democracies," prepared by Samuel Huntington, Michel Crozier, and Joji Watanuki for the first plenary meeting of the commission in Tokyo in May 1975. It was subsequently published as the very influential *Crisis of Democracy: Report on the Governability of Democracy to the Trilateral Commission* (New York: New York University Press, 1975). On overparticipation, see Noam Chomsky, "Trilateral's RX for Crisis: Governability Yes, Democracy No," *Seven Days*, February 14, 1977.

6. Chantal Mouffe, "Democracia y nueva derecha," in R. Green (ed.), *Los mitos de Milton Friedman* (Mexico, D.F.: Nueva Imagen, 1983); Clauss Offe, "Ingobernabilidad. El re-

nacimiento de las teorías conservadoras," *Revista Mexicana de Sociología* 42 (Special Issue 1981).

7. Gabriel Almond, "The Development of Political Development," in Myron Weiner and Samuel Huntington (eds.), *Understanding Political Development* (Boston: Little, Brown, 1987), pp. 437–490.

8. David Pollock, "Debt, Development and Democracy: Recent Trends in Latin America," in Peter Blanchard and Peter Landstreet (eds.), *Human Rights in Latin America and the Caribbean* (Toronto: Canadian Scholars' Press, 1989), pp. 119–125.

9. Bodenheimer, "The Ideology of Developmentalism."

10. Stanislav Andreski, *Parasitism and Subversion: The Case of Latin America* (New York: Pantheon, 1967), passim.

11. Frederick Weaver, "Capitalist Development, Empire and Latin American Underdevelopment: An Interpretative Essay on Historical Change," *Latin American Perspectives* 3, 4 (Fall 1976), p. 17.

12. Nineteenth-century instances of such modernizing attempts were numerous: Rosas's unifying dictatorship in Argentina, the Portalean republic in Chile, the Brazilian empire, the two López regimes in Paraguay, and the Porfiriato in Mexico.

13. These include José Uriburu in Argentina, Carlos Ibáñez in Chile, Getulio Vargas in Brazil, Gabriel Terra in Uruguay, Anastosio Somoza in Nicaragua, Maximiliano Hernández-Martínez in El Salvador, Rafael Trujillo in the Dominican Republic, Tiburcio Carías in Honduras, Jorge Ubico in Guatemala, Luis Sánchez-Cerro in Peru, and Enrique Peñaranda in Bolivia.

14. Luis Costa-Pinto, *Pueblo y populismo* (Madrid: Centro de Estudios Constitucionales, 1978), pp. 45–46; also D. L. Raby, "Populism: A Marxist Analysis," *McGill Studies in International Development* 32, passim.

15. Jerome Levinson and Juan de Onís, *The Alliance That Lost Its Way: A Critical Report of the Alliance for Progress* (Chicago: Quadrangle Books, 1970).

16. William Barber and Neale Ronning, *Internal Security and Military Power: Counterinsurgency and Civic Action in Latin America* (Columbus: Ohio State University Press, 1966), pp. 217–245.

17. See Douglas Chalmers, "Developing in the Periphery: External Factors in Latin American Politics," in Yale Ferguson (ed.), *Contemporary Interamerican Relations: A Reader in Theory and Issues* (Englewood Cliffs, N.J.: Prentice-Hall, 1972), pp. 11–34, especially p. 11.

18. Jürgen Habermas, *Legitimation Crisis* (Boston: Beacon Press, 1975), passim.

19. Nelson Rockefeller, *The Rockefeller Report of United States Presidential Mission for the Western Hemisphere* (Chicago: Quadrangle Books, 1969), passim.

20. Donal Cruise O'Brien, "Modernization, Order and the Erosion of a Democratic Ideal: American Political Science 1960–1970," *Journal of Development Studies* (July 1972), pp. 351–378.

21. Mexico, Venezuela, Colombia, Costa Rica, and Communist Cuba.

22. See Jorge Nef, "Redemocratization in Latin America or the Modernization of the Status Quo?" *Canadian Journal of Latin American and Caribbean Studies* 11, 21 (1986), pp. 43–55; especially pp. 43–44 and 53–55.

23. Jean-Louis Weil, Joseph Comblin, and Judge Senese, *The Repressive State: The Brazilian National Security Doctrine and Latin America,* LARU Studies no. 3 (Toronto: Latin American Research Unit, 1978), pp. 36–73.

24. Albert Szymanski, *The Logic of Imperialism* (London: Zed Press, 1981), pp. 444–464.

25. Liisa North, "Development and Underdevelopment in Latin America," in J. Nef (ed.), *Canada and the Latin American Challenge* (Guelph: Ontario Cooperative Program for Latin America and Caribbean Studies, 1978), p. 79.

26. Orlando Letelier, "The 'Chicago Boys' in Chile: Economic 'Freedom's' Awful Toll," *Nation*, August 28, 1976, pp. 138, 142.

27. Louis Lefever, "The Problem of Debt," *International Viewpoints*, supplement of the *York Gazette* (York University), March 2, 1987, p. 2.

28. Commission on U.S.–Latin American Relations (Sol Linowitz, chair), *The Americas in a Changing World* (New York: Quadrangle Books, 1975), passim.

29. Alan Wolfe, "Capitalism Shows Its Face," *Nation*, November 29, 1975, pp. 557–563.

30. Alfred Stepan, *Rethinking Military Politics: Brazil and the Southern Cone* (Princeton, N.J.: Princeton University Press, 1988), passim.

31. Richard E. Feinberg and Ricardo Ffrench-Davis (eds.), *Development and External Debt in Latin America* (Notre Dame, Ind.: University of Notre Dame Press, 1988), pp. 1–11.

32. World Bank, *World Development Report*, 1990, 1991, and 1992, passim, and 1994, pp. 206–207; and *World Debt Tables: External Debt of Developing Countries*, 1987–1988, 1989–1990, and 1991–1992 editions, vol., "Country Tables" (Washington, D.C.: World Bank, 1988, 1989, 1992). Osvaldo Martínez, "Debt and Foreign Capital: The Origins of the Crisis," *Latin American Perspectives* 20, 1 (Winter 1992), p. 65.

33. Since 1982 the Inter-American Dialogue, under the chairmanship of Sol Linowitz, has been bringing together American, Canadian, Latin American, and Caribbean intellectuals and politicians to create a nongovernmental channel of North-South communications. The dialogue has published annual position papers about once a year since 1983 in Washington, under the sponsorship of the Aspen Institute for Humanistic Studies.

34. See Jorge Nef and Remonda Bensabat, "'Governability' and the Receiver State in Latin America: Analysis and Prospects," in Archibald Ritter, Maxwell Cameron, and David Pollock (eds.), *Latin America to the Year 2000: Reactivating Growth, Improving Equity, Sustaining Democracy* (New York: Praeger, 1992), pp. 171–173.

35. Seamus Cleary and George Gerber, "Crushing Burden: Latin America's Foreign Debt," in Cleary and Gerber (eds.), *Poverty and Power: Latin America After 500 Years* (London: CAFOD, 1992), pp. 81–96; also International Development Research Centre, *The Global Cash Crunch: An Examination of Debt and Development* (Ottawa: IDRC, 1992), pp. 26–31.

36. See Nef and Bensabat, "'Governability' and the Receiver State in Latin America," pp. 161–176.

37. Verónica Montecinos and John Markoff, "Democrats and Technocrats: Professional Economists and Regime Transition in Latin America," *Canadian Journal of Development Studies* 14, 1 (1993), pp. 7–22, especially pp. 12–14.

38. Barry Gill, Joel Rocamora, and Richard Wilson (eds.), *Low Intensity Democracy: Political Power in the New World Order* (London: Pluto Press, 1993), pp. 3–34.

39. Huntington, Crozier, and Watanuki, *The Crisis of Democracy*, passim. See Holly Sklar, "Managing Dependence and Democracy—An Overview," in Sklar (ed.), *Trilateralism: The Trilateral Commission and Elite Planning for World Management* (Montreal: Black Rose, 1980), pp. 1–55.

40. United Nations, *World Economic and Social Survey 1994* (New York: United Nations, 1994), p. 42.

41. William I. Robinson, "Central America: Which Way After the Cold War?" *NotiSur* 4, 8 (February 25, 1994), pp. 1–9, especially p. 5. See also Oscar Altimir, "Income Distribution and Poverty Through Crisis and Adjustment," *CEPAL Review* 52 (April 1994).

42. Altimir, "Income Distribution," p. 6.

43. *NotiSur*, January 14, 1994, p. 9.

44. Ibid.

45. Robinson, "Central America," p. 6.

46. David Barkin, *Un desarrollo distorsionado: la integración de México a la economía mundial.* (Mexico, D.F.: Siglo Veintiuno Editores y UNAM-Xochimilco, 1991). Also Julio Boltvinik, "Ciudadanos de la pobreza y la marginalización," *El Cotidiano* 19 (1987), pp. 305–317.

47. William Robinson, citing the 1993 UNDP *Human Development Report*, notes that the wealthiest 20 percent of humanity receives 82.7 percent of the world's income. They also control 80 percent of world trade, 95 percent of all loans, 80 percent of all domestic savings, and 80.5 percent of world investments. They consume 70 percent of world energy, 75 percent of all metals, 85 percent of its timbers, and 60 percent of its food supplies. He noted that in this context the middle classes are tending to shrink considerably, since the 20 percent of what could be called the world's middle class receives only 11.7 percent of the world's wealth. *NotiSur*, February 18, 1994, p. 7.

48. For a historical overview of the Latin American military, see Linda Alexander Rodríguez's introduction to her edited work, *Rank and Privilege: The Military and Society in Latin America* (Greenhill, Del.: Scholarly Resources, 1994), pp. ix–xxii.

49. Between 1985 and 1991, the region's defense budgets declined on the average 24.6 percent, or 4.1 percent per year, and twelve out of twenty countries cut defense expenditures ranging between 59 percent (Chile) and 4.8 percent (Honduras). On the other hand, two rather large countries, Venezuela and Colombia, dramatically increased such expenditures: respectively 23 percent and 275 percent. When the number of troops are examined, the overall trend is a seemingly modest increase of 4.2 percent for the region, or 0.7 percent per year.

50. International Institute of Strategic Studies (IISS), *The Military Balance*, 1987–1988, 1991–1992, and 1992–1993 (London: IISS, 1987, 1991, and 1992), pp. 177–178, 214, 221–222 (1987); pp. 185–186, 220–221 (1991); pp. 166 and 215 (1992).

51. *NotiSur* 4, 5 (February 4, 1994), p. 8. Eighty-four percent abstained in the Guatemalan referendum of 1994 and 50 percent in El Salvador's general election of March 1994. In the Colombian parliamentary elections of 1994, over 70 percent did not vote, while in the Ecuadoran congressional competition the same year, spoiled ballots received the second largest plurality. Colombia and the United States top the list of electoral abstentionism, with roughly 30 percent of the voters casting their ballots.

52. *NotiSur* 4, 10 (March 18, 1994), pp. 2–3.

53. Samuel Huntington, *Political Order in Changing Societies* (New Haven, Conn.: Yale University Press, 1968), pp. 1–92.

54. *Latin America Weekly Report*, January 13, 1994, p. 2; and February 17, 1994, p. 62.

55. See Jorge Nef, *Human Security and Mutual Vulnerability: An Exploration into the Global Political Economy of Development and Underdevelopment* (Ottawa: IDRC Books, 1995), pp. 13-21.

56. Jorge Nef and Ximena Núñez, *Las relaciones interamericanas frente al siglo XXI* (Quito: Facultad Latinoamericana de Ciencias Sociales, 1994), pp. 109–119; also George Wright,

Liisa North, and Yasmine Shamsie, "Reforming the OAS to Sustain Democracy: A Canadian Perspective," working paper, Centre for Research on Latin America and the Caribbean, York University, 1995, passim.

57. Francis Fukuyama, "The End of History?" *National Interest* 16 (Summer 1989), pp. 3–18.

58. Gill, Rocamora, and Wilson, *Low Intensity Democracy,* pp. 3–5.

PART SIX
EXTERNAL RELATIONS

14

INTERNATIONAL RELATIONS IN LATIN AMERICA: CONFLICT AND COOPERATION

JAMES LEE RAY

The battle of Ayacucho in 1824 traditionally marks the end of Spanish rule in South America; Brazil broke its ties with Portugal a couple of years earlier. This chapter will focus on the relationship among the states that emerged from the ruins of Spanish and Portuguese empires in Latin America. The United States has played an important role in those relationships, of course, but the foreign policy of the United States vis-à-vis its southern neighbors will be treated only tangentially (U.S. policy in Latin America is dealt with in Chapter 15). The United States will enter the discussion here, however, to the extent that it has presented challenges and problems with which Latin American states have tried to deal in their foreign policies and in their dealings with each other.

DREAMS OF UNITY, REALITIES OF STRIFE

The Early Years

The Spanish colonies achieved their independence in three more or less separate movements. The first movement originated in Mexico and was joined by Central America. Mexico emerged as an empire under Agustín de Iturbide, who annexed Central America. But that empire lasted only briefly. Central America went its own way in 1823, and by 1824, Iturbide had been kicked out of Mexico by General Antonio López de Santa Anna. Mexico, of course, evolved into a solitary independent nation, but the United Provinces of Central America had fallen apart by 1838, with Guatemala, Honduras, El Salvador, Nicaragua, and Costa Rica emerging as independent nations.

Simón Bolívar led the campaign for independence in the northern part of Spanish America while José de San Martín fought against the Spanish colonialists in the southern part of the continent. The two revolutionary leaders met in 1822 and discussed the possible coordination of their liberation efforts. For reasons that to this day are rather mysterious, they parted company without an agreement. So this early step toward the unification of Spanish America met the same fate as all the numerous succeeding ones to date. It failed.

When Buenos Aires revolted against Spain, the leaders of that movement tried to bring the territory that became known as Paraguay along with them. But a Paraguayan army defeated troops from Buenos Aires who aimed to persuade Paraguayan leaders of the wisdom of unity against the Spanish. Buenos Aires, of course, provided the core of what became Argentina. Chile and Argentina, one can reasonably surmise, were fated to emerge as two countries because of the Andes Mountains, which separate them.

If Simón Bolívar had had his way, the territory that obtained freedom under his leadership would have emerged as two large republics. But Upper Peru, led by Antonio José de Sucre, wanted freedom from both Spain and Peru, and the first great republic of Bolívar's dreams was split into the independent countries of Bolivia and Peru. Bolívar did manage to bring the republic of Gran Colombia into the world in 1819, but by 1830, this republic had also fallen prey to geographical barriers, regional antagonisms, and the ambitions of quarreling political leaders. Gran Colombia dissolved ultimately into the separate countries of Venezuela, Colombia, and Ecuador. Bolívar's death occurred soon after that of "his" republic. Shortly before he died, he mourned the demise of his dreams: "America is ungovernable. Those who have served the revolution have plowed the sea."

Nineteenth-Century Conflicts

Nineteenth-century relations among the newly independent countries in Latin America involved a series of important conflicts and wars, and the impact of those struggles has often been visible in the twentieth century. Conflicts between Brazil and Argentina, for example, evoked the mediation of Great Britain, which managed to arrange the creation of the buffer state of Uruguay in 1830. Peru and Colombia agreed to settle a dispute between them in a process that resulted in the birth of another buffer state at about the same time, i.e., Ecuador. By 1835, General Andrés de Santa Cruz in Bolivia established the Peru-Bolivia Confederation as part of an effort to enlarge his domain. Both Chile and Argentina objected to this confederation for the classical balance-of-power reason that it represented a concentration of power that was dangerous to their continued independence. Argentina declared war against the confederation, but it was the intervention of Chile that effectively brought about its dissolution in 1838.

The 1840s and 1850s were marked by subtle, more or less independent balance-of-power maneuverings among two sets of states: Chile and the other western states comprised the first set; Argentina, Uruguay, Paraguay, and Brazil on the eastern half of the continent made up the second. Major warfare was avoided until a very bloody conflict occurred among the latter set of states beginning in 1864, with Uruguay serving as the pawn over which the other states fought. Both Brazil and Argentina had made repeated attempts to influence the frequently violent political conflict in Uruguay in ways that would benefit their interests. Left to their own devices, it seems likely that Brazil and Argentina might have become involved in a war against each other over Uruguay. But Paraguay managed to get all three of these states into a war against it.

Until the 1860s, Paraguay had been a rather isolated state, ruled by dictators since the days of liberation. The second of these, Carlos Antonio López, did modify this isolation somewhat, but perhaps his most fateful decision was to put his son, Francisco Solano López, in charge of Paraguay's army. In that role, the younger López traveled to England, France, Germany, Italy, and Spain in the early 1850s, picking up a large amount of arms and ammunition, ideas of grandeur from Napoleon III in France, and an Irish mistress, Elisa Lynch (whom he met in Paris), along the way.[1] Solano López became president of Paraguay upon the death of his father in 1862. In the ensuing years, he grew increasingly suspicious of the motives of both Brazilian and Argentine leaders with respect to Uruguay. In 1864, he became so certain of Brazil's imperialistic ambitions vis-à-vis Uruguay that he decided to thwart them forcefully. (This is not to deny that he had imperialistic ambitions of his own.) To do so, he requested permission for his troops to cross part of Argentina en route to Uruguay. Argentina refused to allow this. When Solano López sent his troops into Argentina anyway, he soon found himself at war with Brazil, Argentina, and Uruguay.

Whether little Paraguay had any chance of winning the war is an interesting historical question. During the war, the provisions of a secret treaty signed by Brazil, Uruguay, and Argentina became known; it was obvious that Brazil and Argentina meant to destroy the government of Paraguay and to help themselves to ample slices of Paraguayan territory. It is commonly asserted in standard historical sources that the Paraguayans fought so desperately that something on the order of nine out of ten males, or roughly half the population of the country, perished in the struggle. However, at least one contemporary historical-demographic analysis indicates that "the War of the Triple Alliance actually cost Paraguay between 8.7 and 19.5 percent of its prewar population. . . . The evidence demonstrates that the Paraguayan population casualties due to the war have been enormously exaggerated."[2]

Interestingly, both during and after the war, the nations of western Latin America objected to Brazilian and Argentine plans to dismember Paraguay and limit its sovereignty. This was an important step toward the integration of the two more or less independent balance-of-power systems on the continent.[3] That process was reinforced by rivalries among the western states that were to culminate in the War of the

Pacific between Chile on one side and Bolivia and Peru on the other. They fought over the bleak Atacama Desert and the rich nitrates it contained. By 1870, Chileans, Peruvians, and Bolivians were all exploiting the mineral resources of the area. The Chileans were the most energetic and successful in these ventures. Unfortunately, from their point of view, many of their successes occurred in territories that belonged to Bolivia or Peru. When the Bolivians tried to increase taxes on Chilean operations in their territory and the Peruvians nationalized Chilean nitrate works in theirs, the Chilean government decided to resist these steps by military means.

Chile was eminently successful in this war, which began in February of 1879. By 1883, Chile had won, taking over Antofagasta from Bolivia and the provinces of Tarapacá, Tacna, and Arica from Peru. With the addition of that territory, "Chile entered . . . upon an era of unequaled prosperity from the sale of nitrates, copper and other minerals."[4] Bolivia and Peru, on the other hand, got nothing from the war but grievances, which survived for decades. Bolivia lost its only seaport, at Antofagasta, and despite consistent efforts for the last 100 years, has yet to regain it. Chile promised Peru that a plebiscite would be held ten years after the war in the provinces of Tacna and Arica to determine their permanent status, but that plebiscite was continually postponed. The dispute was finally resolved in 1929, with the help of the U.S. government; as a result of the Washington Protocol of that year, Chile retained Arica while Peru reclaimed Tacna.

THE CHANGING OF THE GUARD

The United States Edges Out Great Britain

The remainder of the nineteenth century in Latin America was most notable, perhaps, for the culmination of a long-term trend. The United States had issued its Monroe Doctrine in 1823, warning other states to refrain from colonizing efforts in the Western Hemisphere. It is widely agreed that the United States lacked the power to enforce the doctrine through most of the nineteenth century. Latin America was not, however, subjected to serious or sustained colonizing efforts for most of that century because Great Britain, in effect, enforced the Monroe Doctrine for the United States. (The most obvious exception to this rule occurred when France set up the empire of Maximilian in Mexico from 1864 to 1867.) Throughout most of the nineteenth century, Great Britain and the United States shared a common interest in keeping other powers out of Latin America. Long-range ambitions by the United States to replace Great Britain as the most influential power in the Western Hemisphere added a measure of conflict to the relationship, but it never became serious until the twentieth century approached.

In 1895, a crisis resulted from the culmination of a dispute between Great Britain and Venezuela over the boundary of British Guiana. President Grover Cleveland insisted on arbitration, and the British ultimately gave in, partly because they were more concerned at the time about the apparent inclination of the German kaiser to stir up trouble for them in South Africa.

Thus, the year 1895 marks the point at which British hegemony in South America began to be challenged seriously by the United States. Further indications of this "changing of the guard" were soon to follow. For example, in 1850, the United States and Great Britain had signed the Clayton-Bulwer Treaty, in which both agreed that neither would attempt to build or exclusively control any canal through Central America. But in 1901, the Clayton-Bulwer Treaty was superseded by the Hay-Pauncefote Treaty, which gave the United States exclusive rights to build and control such an interoceanic canal.

The Era of U.S. Military Interventions

In between the boundary dispute involving Great Britain and Venezuela and the Hay-Pauncefote Treaty, of course, the United States took on and defeated Spain in the Spanish American War of 1898, acquiring Cuba, Puerto Rico, and the Philippines. By 1903, the United States had helped arrange the independence of Panama from Colombia and had signed a treaty with the new Panamanian republic granting to the United States, in perpetuity, a zone in which a transisthmus canal was to be built. A year later, Theodore Roosevelt proclaimed his famous corollary to the Monroe Doctrine, in which he claimed the right to intervene in the internal affairs of other nations in the Western Hemisphere that through "flagrant . . . wrongdoing or impotence" give rise to a need for an "international police power." The United States used this corollary as a rationale for a lengthy series of armed interventions in the ensuing years. For example, the United States militarily occupied Haiti from 1915 to 1934, the Dominican Republic from 1916 to 1924, and Nicaragua from 1912 to 1925 and again from 1927 to 1932. Since these were only the most-prolonged examples among a longer list of interventions, it is not surprising that for the first decades of the twentieth century, one of the primary foreign policy concerns of the Latin American states was to find means of restraining "the colossus of the North."

It is, perhaps, a revealing indication of the desperate and vulnerable position in which the Latin American states found themselves vis-à-vis the United States that the first line of defense to which they resorted was international law. As early as 1868, the Argentine jurist Carlos Calvo had argued that intervention by foreign governments to enforce claims of their citizens residing abroad was illegal because it violated the principle of national sovereignty. In 1902, when Venezuela was the target of a blockade by Britain, Germany, and Italy, the Argentine foreign minister Luis Drago argued that it was also illegal for foreign governments to intervene in attempts to collect public debts (which is what Britain, Germany, and Italy were doing).

The Calvo Doctrine and the Drago Doctrine were originally designed to counter interventions by European states, but the "Roosevelt Corollary . . . and the subsequent U.S. interventions in the Caribbean area based on it, definitely shifted Latin American fears from Europe to the United States."[5] For the first three decades of the twentieth century, Latin American states tried repeatedly, and unsuccessfully, to get the United States to accept the international principle of nonintervention embodied in the doctrines espoused by Calvo and Drago.

Latin American states were only tangentially involved in World War I. Eight declared war, but only Brazil and Cuba played an active role in it. Five other states severed diplomatic relations with Germany, while such important states as Argentina, Chile, and Mexico remained neutral. Since the war cut Latin American countries off from their hitherto major trading partners in Europe, it dramatically reinforced the paramount role of the United States in the Western Hemisphere, and U.S. political pretensions were further reinforced by a burgeoning economic ascendancy. This made the Latin American states even more anxious, of course, to curb the interventionist tendencies of the U.S. government, and many thought they had found a useful instrument in the League of Nations. That organization emphasized the principle of nonintervention and might have provided allies for the Latin American states against any interventionist moves by the United States. It is not surprising, then, that most Latin American countries were disappointed when the United States refused to join the League, even though its covenant explicitly recognized the legitimacy of the Monroe Doctrine.

Since the Latin American states had not been successful in their efforts to restrain the United States within the framework of the League of Nations, they pressed even harder to construct such restraints within the inter-American system. The Pan-American movement had begun with a meeting in Washington in 1889. From that year to 1928, there were six international conferences of American states. Those meetings adhered to a definite pattern. The United States was primarily interested in measures that would facilitate international trade, while the Latin American states preferred to dwell on measures that would secure them against intervention by the United States.

The official attitude of the U.S. government began to change perceptibly in 1929. The new president, Herbert Hoover, ordered a study of the Monroe Doctrine in that year, and by 1930, he had publicly endorsed the results of that study in a move that amounted to a rejection of the Roosevelt Corollary. Franklin D. Roosevelt, of course, adopted the Good Neighbor Policy toward Latin America, the highlight of which was a nonintervention pledge made tentatively at the Seventh Inter-American Conference in Montevideo in 1933 and reaffirmed, with significantly smaller loopholes, at the Inter-American Conference for the Maintenance of Peace at Buenos Aires in 1936. The sincerity with which the Roosevelt administration adopted this new policy was given two significant tests when Bolivia nationalized foreign oil companies in that country in 1937 and Mexico nationalized its oil industry in 1938. Roosevelt resisted pressures to intervene in both cases.

TERRITORIAL CONFLICT IN SOUTH AMERICA

The Chaco War

As the Latin American states were in the midst of their successful effort (albeit only temporarily) to deal with U.S. interventions, two of the countries fought each other in the only really major war between Latin American states in this century. This war was fought between the two big losers of the most important South American wars in the nineteenth century, perhaps not coincidentally. After Bolivia lost its outlet to the sea during the War of the Pacific, some historians argue, its leaders began to look to the Rio de la Plata system and possible ports on the Atlantic. This meant that Bolivia needed access to the Paraguay River, and early in the twentieth century, Bolivia began building forts in the area of that river in order to ensure access to it. Paraguay, in the meantime, according to several accounts, was looking for some way to recover its national honor after its humiliating defeat in the war against Brazil, Uruguay, and Argentina. The emotions evoked in this manner soon focused on the Chaco Boreal, a desolate area near the border between Paraguay and Bolivia. Both countries had made claims to this area as early as the mid-1500s, during the colonial era, and border clashes between the two states occurred as early as 1927. Then rumors of vast oil deposits in the Chaco added fuel to the controversy, so to speak. War finally broke out in 1932.

Bolivia's population at the time was roughly three times that of Paraguay, but Bolivia suffered disadvantages that, in the end, turned out to be more important. Perhaps the most important was the composition of its army. Most Bolivian soldiers were Indians who had been drafted into the army off the 2-mi-high (3-km) plain known as the Altiplano. They were not accustomed to the tropical heat of the Chaco and had no understanding of the conflict (which is not to say that they would have been enthusiastic if they *had* understood the reasons for the war). Paraguayan soldiers, in contrast, were more comfortable in the climate of the area and felt they were defending their homeland.

Even so, the war dragged on for three years, with both sides suffering heavy losses. Estimates of these losses vary widely, of course: One apparently authoritative source concludes that 50,000 Paraguayan soldiers died in the conflict while 80,000 Bolivian soldiers met the same fate.[6] A truce was finally arranged in 1938. In the treaty, Paraguay was awarded most of the disputed Chaco area; Bolivia's reward was further frustration of its quest for an outlet to the sea.

Further Disputes

Two serious border disputes between Latin American states surfaced during the 1930s and 1940s. Both involved Peru. Peruvian troops seized the Amazon River town of Leticia in 1932. Since that town had been awarded to Colombia in 1930, the Colombian government sent troops to Leticia to make its objections known. There was some brief but bloody fighting. After a change of government in Peru, serious negotiations began. It took two years, but an amicable settlement was achieved, with Colombia retaining its hold on Leticia.

Peru was more successful in a dispute with Ecuador, which reached a crisis stage in 1941. Peruvian troops occupied territory claimed by Ecuador north of the Marañón River. That river is important because it allows access to the Amazon River. The dispute did escalate into actual military combat, with each side losing several hundred troops, but a wider war was averted, probably, by the Japanese attack on Pearl Harbor in December 1941. That catastrophe made the United States in particular unwilling to let its neighbors engage in such disruptive activities. So the United States, in cooperation with Argentina, Brazil, and Chile, imposed a peace through the Rio Protocol of 1942. The protocol forced Ecuador to relinquish control over the disputed territory, some 77,000 sq mi (199,000 sq km), to Peru. Understandably, Ecuador has never been happy with this solution. In 1960 the Ecuadoran Senate renounced the Rio Protocol. Open border clashes between Ecuador and Peru occurred in 1981, and even more serious military conflict broke out between Ecuador and Peru in early 1995.

WORLD WAR II AND ITS AFTERMATH

The Latin American countries played a minor role in World War II. With the onset of the conflict, the United States tried to get the Western Hemisphere organized, but this project met with more problems than might have been anticipated. Argentina was least enthusiastic about unification against the Axis powers. The government of Argentina, in fact, did not break relations with Germany until 1944 and did not declare war until 1945. Brazil, on the other hand, did send a significant number of troops to Italy, while Mexican troops served in the Pacific theater. Generally speaking, the effect of World War II on Inter-American relations was to reinforce trends set in motion by World War I. Once again, the Latin American states were cut off from the world outside the Western Hemisphere and became more closely tied to the United States. The United States, of course, emerged from World War II as the most powerful state in the world, regardless of how the controversial concept of power might be defined or measured.

In the years after the war, a controversy about the agenda of relations between the United States and Latin American countries surfaced in a shape that was to remain consistent in the postwar decades. For the United States, the primary issue was communist subversion; the Latin American states, on the other hand, were almost always more interested in policies and strategies that would foster their economic development.

One of the first indications of concern about international economic issues on the part of Latin American states was their proposal to form the Economic Commission for Latin America (ECLA) as a part of the new United Nations organization. The United States was opposed to the idea, but ECLA was created in 1948 in spite of that opposition. In the early 1950s, ECLA proposed the creation of a new inter-American bank and a Latin American common market (the Inter-American Development Bank was established in 1959). The United States was more interested in a collective defense treaty, i.e., the Inter-American Treaty of Reciprocal Assistance (Rio Treaty) signed on September 2, 1947, and the establishment of the Organization of American States (OAS) in 1948. Latin Americans preferred that economic issues be dealt with in ECLA, but "for years, the United States favored the OAS Inter-American Economic and Social Council and regarded the efforts of the competitor ECLA with political disapproval as well as deep distrust."[7]

REGIONAL APPROACHES TO DEVELOPMENT

Economic Integration as a Tool

One of the proposed solutions to the problems of underdevelopment seized on by ECLA and several Latin American economists was economic integration.[8] Integration might provide markets sufficiently large, for example, to make it feasible for Latin American states to manufacture their own capital goods, thus reducing their dependence on the imports of such heavy equipment. Large markets created by the elimination of intraregional tariff barriers, and the construction of common external tariffs that would be part of the economic integration processes, might also allow industries to benefit from economies of scale, which, in turn, could evoke efficiency at levels competitive on the world market.

With these ideas in mind, ECLA and national officials worked toward the creation of two regional integration organizations: the Central American Common Market (CACM) and the Latin American Free Trade Association (LAFTA). The former organization was launched in 1960 with Guatemala, El Salvador, Honduras, Nicaragua, and later, Costa Rica as its members. Ten South American countries, later joined by Mexico, formed LAFTA in the same year. Both organizations were inspired to some extent by the success enjoyed by the European Economic Community (EEC) at the time. Furthermore, both were based on a philosophy of economic integration similar to that utilized in Europe. That is, CACM and LAFTA both sought economic integration on the basis of the functional (or neofunctional) theory of integration. According to that theory, the benefits that accrue to the member states as a result of the activities of the central organization of the integration organization mean that the member states, little by little, become willing to allow that central organization much broader authority until someday (in theory), it is running virtually everything.[9]

Such ideas had seemed to work reasonably well in Europe, and they seemed to work for a time in Latin America. The CACM promoted a marked increase in intraregional trade, and the rate of economic growth of the Central American countries increased. Similarly, the members of LAFTA managed to negotiate numerous reductions of tariffs, and intraregional trade increased 100 percent from 1961 to 1968.[10] But the two organizations soon ran into problems, at least one of which plagued both.

That problem involved the distribution of the benefits of integration among the member states. The founders of both the CACM and LAFTA had anticipated this problem by initially giving special concessions to the poorer member states. In the

CACM, for example, special incentives were adopted in order to lure new industries into the relatively poor states (i.e., Honduras and Nicaragua). Members of LAFTA divided themselves into three categories according to levels of development and size of domestic markets. The countries in the lower categories were given trade concessions and the right to protect some infant industries from competition with similar industries in such relatively developed countries as Brazil, Argentina, and Mexico. Nevertheless, by the end of the 1960s, both organizations were showing signs of strain resulting in part from suspicions by the less-developed members that they were receiving an unequal share of the benefits of integration.

Problems for CACM and LAFTA

In 1969, the CACM was plagued by an even more dramatic problem. Two of its member states, Honduras and El Salvador, fought a war against each other. El Salvador is densely populated, whereas Honduras is relatively underpopulated. Throughout the 1960s, unemployed workers from El Salvador poured into the empty fertile valleys in Honduras. By 1969, the military government of Honduras was faced with considerable internal unrest, and it decided to deal with that discontent with a land reform program that, not accidentally, deprived many Salvadoran squatters of their recently acquired property.

The government of El Salvador responded with a surprise attack in July 1969. The attack failed, and a bloody stalemate resulted. The OAS managed to arrange a truce, which was broken in January of 1970. A prolonged kind of "cold war" between Honduras and El Salvador ensued. Trade between them stopped, and Honduras put an embargo on trade between El Salvador on the one hand and Nicaragua and Costa Rica on the other. All in all, the war was a devastating blow to the CACM.

In the process of resolving the conflict between Honduras and El Salvador, CACM officials and government leaders discovered that other fissures in the organization threatened its existence. Honduras had been dissatisfied with the Common Market in any case, for the eminently predictable reason. Honduras, along with Nicaragua the least-developed country in that area, felt itself the victim of unfair competition. Relief from the burdens of such competition was difficult to arrange in the face of continued antagonism between El Salvador and Honduras. By the end of the 1970s, of course, the CACM faced a new set of problems. The overthrow of Somoza in Nicaragua and serious civil unrest elsewhere, especially in El Salvador, threatened to destroy what was left of the organization.

In the late 1960s, LAFTA also began to fall apart. Bolivia, Chile, Colombia, Ecuador, and Peru made plans to form a common market among themselves, excluding Argentina, Brazil, and Mexico. These five countries, later joined by Venezuela, formed what became known as the Andean Common Market (ANCOM). The members of ANCOM hoped to achieve sufficient economic progress to be able to compete successfully with the larger, more economically developed countries in

LAFTA. Then, according to the plan, the ANCOM countries would rejoin LAFTA, able to share more equally in the benefits of economic integration provided by that organization.

ANCOM aroused a lot of interest in the Third World because of its approach toward foreign investment. By the late 1960s, the evidence arising out of the experience of the European Common Market made it obvious that multinational corporations (particularly U.S.-based ones) could benefit enormously from the new, enlarged, and protected markets resulting from the process of economic integration. There was fear that integration among Latin American states might make them even more vulnerable to penetration and domination by foreign investors than they had been in the past. It was this fear, in part, that led ANCOM to adopt regulations aimed at controlling foreign investment within the boundaries of its member states.

There were rules, for example, concerning which sectors of the economies were open to investors. There were limits on the amount of capital that could be repatriated. Parent companies were forbidden to restrict exports by their subsidiaries. Provisions were also made to ensure that subsidiaries of foreign corporations would become locally owned in time. "Foreign enterprises already established in the Andean region must within three years of the code's adoption work out gradual divestment plans that would give local investors . . . majority control (51%) of the total shares within 15 years. New foreign investors must adopt similar 15-year fade-out schedules two years after production begins."[11]

How well these rules aimed at controlling foreign investments have worked is a controversial question. Some corporations have managed to obtain exceptions to them in important cases. And there are ways in which these kinds of rules can be subverted even if they are ostensibly enforced.[12] Furthermore, there have been obvious differences in the manner in which the rules are enforced by the members. Chile has provided the most spectacular example of these differences. Under Allende, of course, the Chilean government was an enthusiastic supporter of strict controls on foreign investment. The post-Allende government, however, was so desperate to attract foreign investment that it pushed hard for a relaxation of those controls. Even though the other members of ANCOM gave Chile much of what it wanted in this regard, the Pinochet regime withdrew Chile from the organization in 1976.

Peru, in the meantime, underwent a political transformation of its own. The Peruvian "revolution" in 1968 served as an inspiration for many of the innovations adopted by ANCOM with respect to foreign investment. But the new regime experienced a series of economic disasters that helped bring about a change of government and a change of attitude about foreign investment. As a result of this transition, Peru became a less-enthusiastic supporter of some of the innovations adopted by ANCOM. This increased skepticism about the extent to which rules on paper were being enforced in fact. As the end of the 1970s approached, ANCOM could hardly be written off as a failure, but even sympathetic observers admitted that its future was uncertain.[13]

INTER-AMERICAN RELATIONS IN THE 1990S

The road to economic integration continued to be a rocky one as the 1970s turned into the 1980s. The Latin American Free Trade Association gave up the ghost entirely in August of 1980. It was replaced by the Latin American Integration Association (LAIA), but it is difficult not to be skeptical about the fate of this new organization. Its goals are even more vague and distant than those of LAFTA, and the members of LAFTA were forever postponing tough decisions.

However, both intraregional trade and economic integration seemed to get a new lease on life in Latin America in the 1990s. Probably the most successful venture is known variously as the South American Free Trade Area or the Southern Cone Common Market and goes by the acronym of Mercosur. It was formed by Argentina, Brazil, Paraguay, and Uruguay in 1991. By 1994, the *New York Times* declared that "on Rio's bay, two huge Brazilian cannons have been waiting for Argentine warships for decades, monuments to the long enmity between South America's two regional powers. But today the guns are frozen with rust, visited by tourists, many of them Argentines." The story goes on to attribute the decrease in tension between Brazil and Argentina, as well as similar improvements in bilateral relationships around the South American continent, to increased interdependence among these countries, primarily in the form of international trade.[14]

The other major step toward economic integration in Latin America involved Mexico's commitment to the North American Free Trade Agreement. This "constituted an especially interesting experiment from the point of view of international integration theories, because the disparity in average income between Mexico and the United States is greater than that between any other pair of bordering states in the world."[15] NAFTA is designed to eliminate all restrictions on trade in manufactured products and cross-national investment within ten years and to remove all such barriers to trade in agricultural goods in fifteen years. Its launching in 1994 coincided, but certainly not by coincidence, with the launching of a rebellion by disaffected peasants led by the Zapatista National Liberation Army in the southern state of Chiapas. That rebellion, combined with economic policies of questionable wisdom (at least according to defenders of NAFTA) in anticipation of the Mexican election in 1994,[16] combined to bring about a massive devaluation of the Mexican peso toward the end of the year and a downturn in most Mexican economic statistics that reflected widespread suffering for huge numbers of Mexicans. However, if those economic trends are not reversed soon in Mexico, NAFTA will receive a major share of the blame, in Mexico and elsewhere, regardless of the academic or logical merit of arguments in its defense.

The setbacks for NAFTA did not discourage economic integration elsewhere in Latin America. In fact, to some extent, Mercosur can be seen as a competitor with NAFTA, and NAFTA's problems might strengthen integration in the Southern Cone. In addition, "intraregional commerce among the members of the Andean

Common Market . . . has more than doubled in the last four years. . . . During the same period, trade among Colombia, Mexico and Venezuela—known as the G3 group—has risen close to 14%."[17]

At the same time, however, most Latin American states in the 1990s, basing their policies on "neoclassical" or classical liberal, market-oriented strategies, appeared to be experiencing increases in economic inequality, and in a region widely thought to have already some of the most unequal distributions of wealth in the world. These increases, along with a widely reported rise in the proportions of Latin Americans living in official poverty, led to, or at least were joined with, greater unrest in many of the region's newly reborn democratic governments that came into being in the 1980s. The survival of these governments is an official policy aim of the U.S. government, as evidenced most energetically in Haiti, where U.S. troops intervened in the early 1990s directly to reinstate an elected, ostensibly democratic government.

Latin American countries generally have become considerably less suspicious of such U.S. efforts to preserve democracy in the hemisphere, as the "Santiago Commitment to Democracy and the Renewal of the Inter-American System" passed by the General Assembly of the Organization of American States in 1991 and OAS-backed efforts to sustain democracy in Peru and Guatemala as well as Haiti suggest. While autocratic governments in Latin America have certainly not been uniformly successful in pursuit of economic progress, the fate of many democratic regimes in Latin America in the coming decade will probably depend in important part on their ability to deal with such problems as increased levels of inequality and unemployment and the proportions of their populations living in poverty.

Not all economic trends in Latin America are discouraging. In fact, the UN has pointed out that in the developing world in general there has been

> unprecedented improvement in human development in the past 30 years. . . . Life expectancy is now 17 years longer than it was in 1960. Infant mortality has been more than halved. The combined enrollment in primary and secondary school is nearly 1.5 times higher. The human development disparities between North and South have diminished sharply. . . . The South . . . now has a life expectancy that is 85%, and nutritional levels and adult literacy that are 81% of those in the North.

An analysis of the UN's statistics on which such a claim is based reveals that Latin American countries in general, even the most impoverished (such as Haiti, Bolivia, Peru, and Nicaragua), have experienced some improvement in such important quality-of-life statistics as life expectancy, infant mortality, and access to potable water.[18] Whether such improvements can be sustained, and by democratic governments, in the face of an increasingly competitive international economy ever more closely integrated by the forces of "globalization" will surely be one of the most central economic and political issues throughout Latin America as the twenty-first century approaches.

NOTES

1. Mention of the last acquisition might seem out of place in an otherwise somber and proper discussion, but Elisa Lynch reputedly had a significant impact on the policies of Solano López. Pelham H. Box, for example, asserts that "the nature of the influence that for sixteen years the 'lorette parisienne' expressed over the mind of Francisco Solano López has not been adequately investigated. That it was considerable admits of no doubt" (Box, *The Origins of the Paraguayan War* [Urbana: University of Illinois Press, 1927], pp. 181–182).

2. Vera Blinn Reber, "The Demographics of Paraguay: A Reinterpretation of the Great War, 1864–1970," *Hispanic American Historical Review* 68 (May 1988), p. 290. For a standard source making the higher estimate of the Paraguayan casualties of the kind referred to by Reber, see Charles J. Kolinski, *Independence or Death: The Story of the Paraguayan War* (Gainesville: University of Florida Press, 1965), p. 198.

3. Robert N. Burr, "The Balance of Power in Nineteenth-Century South America: An Exploratory Essay," *Hispanic American Historical Review* 25 (February 1955), pp. 40–41.

4. Hubert Herring, *A History of Latin America*, 3d ed. (New York: Alfred A. Knopf, 1972), p. 655.

5. G. Pope Atkins, *Latin America in the International Political System* (New York: Free Press, 1977), p. 323.

6. J. David Singer and Melvin Small, *The Wages of War 1816–1965: A Statistical Handbook* (New York: Wiley and Jones, 1972), p. 67.

7. Minerva M. Etzioni, *The Majority of One: Towards a Theory of Regional Compatibility* (Beverly Hills, Calif.: Sage Publications, 1970), pp. 118–119.

8. This section relies heavily on my earlier discussion of integration in Latin America in James Lee Ray, *Global Politics,* 4th ed. (Boston: Houghton Mifflin, 1990), pp. 429–440, as well as on an updated analysis in James Lee Ray, *Global Politics,* 6th ed. (Boston: Houghton Mifflin, 1995), pp. 392–397.

9. David Mitrany, *A Working Peace System* (London: Royal Institute of International Affairs, 1943), and Ernst Haas, *The Uniting of Europe* (Stanford: Stanford University Press, 1958).

10. Joseph Grunwald, Miguel S. Wionczek, and Martin Carnoy, *Latin American Economic Integration and U.S. Policy* (Washington, D.C.: Brookings Institution, 1972), p. 51.

11. Roger W. Fontaine, *The Andean Pact: A Political Analysis* (Beverly Hills, Calif.: Sage Publications, 1977), p. 19.

12. Thomas J. Biersteker, "The Illusion of State Power: Transnational Corporations and the Neutralization of Host-Country Legislation," *Journal of Peace Research 17* (1980), pp. 207–221.

13. Ricardo Ffrench-Davis, "The Andean Pact: A Model of Economic Integration for Developing Countries," in *Latin America and the World Economy,* ed. Joseph Grunwald (Beverly Hills, Calif.: Sage Publications, 1978), pp. 165–194.

14. James Brooke, "The New South Americans: Friends and Partners," *New York Times,* April 8, 1994, p. A3.

15. Ray, *Global Politics,* 6th ed., p. 394.

16. Moises Naim, "Mexico's Larger Story," *Foreign Policy* 99 (1995), pp. 112–131.

17. Keith Miceli, "Latin America: A Region of Opportunities and Challenges for American Business," speech delivered to the National Technological University's meeting on manage-

ment of technology, January 5, 1996. Available on the Home Page of CIPE: http://www.cipe.org/pr/miceli.html.

18. United Nations Development Programme, *Human Development Report 1995* (New York: Oxford University Press, 1995), p. 15.

SUGGESTED READINGS

Atkins, G. Pope. *Latin America in the International Political System.* 2d ed. New York: Free Press, 1989. A good broad and basic introduction to inter-American relations, as well as to the relationship of the Latin American region with the rest of the world.

Burr, Robert N. "The Balance of Power in Nineteenth-Century South America: An Exploratory Essay." *Hispanic American Historical Review* 25 (February 1955), pp. 37–60. An informative discussion of relations among the South American states in the nineteenth century, with a focus on the impact of the interstate wars in that time period.

Connell-Smith, Gordon. *The United States and Latin America.* New York: John Wiley and Sons, 1974. One of the liveliest historical accounts on U.S. foreign policy toward Latin America.

Davis, Harold Eugene, and Larman C. Wilson, eds. *Latin American Foreign Policies: An Analysis.* Baltimore: Johns Hopkins University Press, 1975. Concentrates on a country-by-country analysis of the foreign policies of Latin American states. Emphasizes recent foreign policy problems and approaches.

de Soto, Hernando. *The Other Path.* New York: Harper and Row, 1989. An English translation of this Peruvian work, which has apparently become a kind of "bible" of advocates of neoclassical reforms in Latin America. There is a rather lengthy introduction by Mario Vargas Llosa.

Domínguez, Jorge. "Consensus and Divergence: The State of the Literature in Interamerican Relations in the 1970s." *Latin American Research Review* 13:1 (1978), pp. 87–126. Interesting discussion of the current trends and competing viewpoints in the academic literature on inter-American relations.

Herring, Hubert. *A History of Latin America.* 3d ed. New York: Alfred A. Knopf, 1972. A very comprehensive, authoritative history of the region with each country discussed in some detail.

Levinson, Jerome, and Juan de Onis. *The Alliance That Lost Its Way.* Chicago: Quadrangle Books, 1970. A penetrating analysis of the Alliance for Progress. Especially good on the problems faced by the United States in its attempts to mold the internal political systems of Latin American states.

Lowenthal, Abraham. "Latin America: Ready for Partnership?" *Foreign Affairs* 72:1 (1992–1993), pp. 74–92. A comprehensive if concise view of the relationship between Latin America and the United States in the 1990s.

Malloy, James M., and Mitchell A. Seligson, eds. *Authoritarians and Democrats: Regime Transition in Latin America.* Pittsburgh: University of Pittsburgh Press, 1987. An analysis of the transition to democracy in several Latin American countries with a general, theoretical discussion of the phenomenon in both the introduction and a concluding chapter.

Smith, Peter H. *Talons of the Eagle: Dynamics of U.S.–Latin American Relations.* New York: Oxford University Press, 1996. An analysis of U.S.–Latin American relations broken down into three periods, from the 1790s to the 1920s, the Cold War era, and the contemporary era.

Szulc, Tad. *Fidel: A Critical Portrait.* New York: Avon, 1986. A very readable biography with lots of interesting tidbits about, for example, how the CIA helped Fidel financially in the 1950s, and how Fidel contacted and developed a close relationship with the traditional Communist Party in Havana almost from the moment he came to town in 1959.

15

THE UNITED STATES AND LATIN AMERICA: INTO A NEW ERA

WAYNE S. SMITH

U.S.–Latin American relations are at a historic turning point. It is not simply that the Cold War is over: That, after all, was a phenomenon of only the past half century. Rather, it is that the basic strategic calculations that shaped U.S. policy over the past 200 years or more—or virtually since the birth of the Republic—are now suddenly obsolete.

The most central of these was what has been called the concept of strategic denial.[1] Simply put, this was the response of U.S. leaders to the calculation that while no state or potential state to the south was powerful enough to threaten the security of the United States, their very weakness rendered them vulnerable to the control of outside powers. The United States had first the Atlantic, and later the Pacific, the two great oceans, between it and those who might intend it harm. The latter, however, might overcome those natural barriers by positioning themselves to the south of the United States. Thus, one of the earliest and most enduring U.S. objectives was to keep other powers out of the Western Hemisphere.

At first, of course, two European powers were already positioned to the south: Spain and Portugal. But Portugal was never viewed as a threat, and by the beginning of the nineteenth century Spain also had come to be seen as the weakling of Europe. So long as the colonies were in their hands, there was little cause for concern. Transfer to a more powerful state, however, was unacceptable, and thus the No-Transfer Resolution passed by the U.S. Congress in 1811 with respect to the Floridas. Obviously, it was this concern also that underlay Secretary of State Henry Clay's assertion in 1825 that "we could not consent to the occupation of those islands [Cuba and Puerto Rico] by any European power other than Spain under any contingency whatever."[2] It was a warning repeated several times over the next few decades.

Indeed, with the Louisiana Purchase, Cuba had come to be seen as the most strategically vital piece of territory outside the continental limits of the United States itself. From 1803 forward, the Port of New Orleans was the window onto the rest of the world for the vast interior of the United States. All trade and communications funneled through that window and out through the Gulf of Mexico. And what sat in the entrance to the gulf, like a cork in a bottle? The island of Cuba. That Cuba not be allowed to fall into the hands of a powerful enemy, which might thus block vital U.S. trade routes, became a maxim for U.S. leaders.

The second basic calculation was that the United States must assert hegemony over the lands to its south. The second in effect flowed from the first, for keeping other powers out obviously required some degree of control on the United States' part. As Gaddis Smith has put it, the Monroe Doctrine was an assertion of a U.S. sphere of influence.[3] Ideas as to the form that might take changed over time. Early leaders tended to assume the U.S. flag was destined eventually to fly over the entire continent, that is, the United States would exercise outright sovereignty. By the end of the nineteenth century, however, it was seen that control was more important—and cheaper—than sovereignty. Thus, Secretary of State Richard Olney could say with satisfaction in 1895 that the United States "is practically sovereign on this continent, and its fiat is law upon the subjects to which it confines its interposition."[4]

One may smile at Olney's statement and others like it (though at the time few Latin Americans found them amusing), for they certainly exaggerated the degree of control actually enjoyed by the United States. It was in fact never "practically sovereign" in the hemisphere (though it came close to it for a time in Central America and the Caribbean). The point, however, is that Americans tended to believe it was and, more important, to believe that their very security required that it be so.

Obviously, that is no longer the case. With the collapse of the Soviet Union, there are now no powers in the world that have the capability to position themselves in Latin America so as to threaten U.S. security. A far more realistic danger lies in the possible clandestine introduction of a nuclear device by terrorists. No Latin American base would be required for that. There are still adversary nations against which the United States must be alert—countries such as Iraq, Iran, and Libya. But those are all regional powers. None has the capability—or the need—to mount a threat from the south.

And indeed the nature of warfare has so changed that the old concepts are now obsolete. One thinks today in terms of intercontinental missiles that reach their targets from the other side of the world in less than forty minutes. The great oceans are no longer much protection and have not been for decades. Having nearby naval bases so as to position a fleet off American shores is a tactic of the past, not of today.

Thus, the entire concept of strategic denial has become invalid. So, too, has the rationale for the Monroe Doctrine, and with it any need for the United States to assert hegemony over the rest of the hemisphere. The problems that face the United States today require a cooperative relationship, not the exercise of hegemony. The

United States needs to rethink its entire position and to base its policies on today's realities, not yesterday's. But old habits die hard. Whether U.S. policymakers can make the necessary mental adjustment and fashion an effective policy for today remains to be seen.

Before turning to an analysis of the post–Cold War situation, however, a historical review would seem to be in order. The future of U.S.–Latin American relations is uncertain. Rationale even for today's policies is confused. To put it in literary terms: The United States is uncertain where it is going or even of the ground on which it now stands; all the more important that we at least be clear as to how it got here.

MANIFEST DESTINY, 1823–1898

As for over a century the Monroe Doctrine has been described as the "great American shibboleth," one would imagine that it was issued with great fanfare and comment. That was not at all the case. Europeans were momentarily irritated by its brashness, but realizing that the United States had little means of enforcing it, they paid it little heed. And even in the United States itself for over two decades there was little further reference to Monroe's statement. If European powers were dissuaded from adventures in the Caribbean Basin, it was largely because of the presence of a powerful British naval squadron, not because of anything the United States said or did. The United States had to grow into the role of protector, had first to become strong. U.S. leaders expected the Stars and Stripes to fly over the rest of the hemisphere, yes, but that was for the future. For the moment, they were focused on consolidating their hold over the vast territory already within U.S. borders.

By 1845, however, the United States was looking beyond those borders. It not only had decided to bring Texas into the Union but was also casting covetous eyes at California and Oregon, areas on which Great Britain and perhaps other European powers had designs as well. President James Polk therefore saw fit to revive the Monroe Doctrine, restating it twenty-two years to the day, December 2, 1845, after President Monroe's famous message to the Congress. The Western Hemisphere, he emphasized again, was not open to colonization by outside powers, though because of the focus of U.S. attention at that point (i.e., Texas, California, and Oregon), he added that this was especially true of North America.

In early 1846, war broke out with Mexico, a short-lived conflict that ended with U.S. troops occupying Mexico City and the United States seizing half of Mexico's territory, including California. It thus became a continental power, with shores on both the Atlantic and Pacific Oceans. Manifest Destiny was on the march. As cargo and passengers bound from one coast to the other now more often than not moved across the Central American isthmus, control of that area took on new importance. It was no coincidence that the United States encouraged William Walker's filibustering expeditions to Central America and his successful efforts to establish himself (briefly) as the ruler of Nicaragua.

As early as 1823, John Quincy Adams had described Cuba as a ripening fruit destined inevitably to fall into the lap of the Union. Guarding as it did one of the approaches to the isthmus, the island took on even greater strategic importance after 1848 and U.S. administrations began a series of efforts to acquire it, beginning with President Polk's attempted purchase that very year. Over the next half century, four other U.S. presidents tried to buy Cuba outright. There were also a number of abortive and certainly less straightforward schemes to transfer the island to U.S. ownership.[5] In addition, there were three major filibustering expeditions against the island. One of these, led by a Venezuelan-born former Spanish army officer named Narciso López, came in 1850 and in many ways was a preview of the Bay of Pigs disaster more than a century later. Just as did the CIA in 1961, López assured his little band of invaders that as soon as they landed, the Cuban people would rise in arms against their government. That turned out to be as wild a dream in 1850 as in 1961.

The acquisitive tendencies that were so much a part of Manifest Destiny were interrupted by the Civil War, that great and bloody conflict that tested the very survival of the nation. Further, while the United States was locked in its own mortal combat, the Monroe Doctrine was challenged more clearly than ever before. Louis Napoleon of France occupied Mexico and imposed an emperor, Maximilian of Hapsburg, to rule it—on the points of French bayonets. Maximilian's reign came to a tragic end, however, as the Civil War ended and the United States warned Louis Napoleon to withdraw his troops. He did, leaving Maximilian defenseless. An honorable man, the latter would not abandon his few Mexican supporters. He fought on and was captured and shot by Mexican patriots led by Benito Juárez. The Monroe Doctrine and Mexican sovereignty (not always easy traveling companions) had been preserved.

At mid-century, it had seemed that more and more territory in Latin America was destined to come under the U.S. flag, but by the end of the century U.S. perceptions of its security needs were changing. Washington wished to assert hegemony and to turn a profit financially, especially in the areas nearest to it, that is, in Central America and the Caribbean, but it had growing reservations about the need, or even the desirability, of bringing these areas into the Union or in some other way incorporating them into the U.S. system. That would require permanent occupying forces and be expensive. That was one objection. Probably a more important one was chauvinistic. As E. L. Godkin, editor of the *Nation* magazine put it, "semi-civilized Catholic states" had no place in the American system.[6]

As the other states were to remain independent, there might even be something to be gained by developing a hemispheric grouping of nations, though with the United States clearly to be primus inter pares. Thus, in 1889 the first Pan-American Conference was held in Washington under the stewardship of Secretary of State James G. Blaine. All independent states attended except for the Dominican Republic. With the Argentine delegation taking the lead, the majority of Latin Americans present made it clear that they were not to be dictated to by the United

States, and a number of U.S. proposals were rejected. Even so, a permanent secretariat was established in Washington that eventually became the Pan-American Union, and a system of arbitration was set up for handling disputes between nations—a system, however, that was all too rarely used. The governments apparently were not prepared to go as far as the delegates to the congress.

Even long-standing U.S. designs on Cuba were altered by this new reluctance to incorporate territories into the U.S. system. Despite all its past efforts to acquire the island, in 1898, just as Cuba's war of independence against Spain was reaching its climax and the United States was on the verge of entering the conflict on Cuba's side, that is, just as conditions seemed most favorable for annexation, the United States stepped back. Under the famous Teller Amendment attached to the declaration of hostilities, the United States vowed not to acquire Cuba as the result of those hostilities. Nothing was said about the Philippines or Guam or Puerto Rico. As a result of the war with Spain, the United States took them all, and in the process became a global power. But Cuba was left with its independence—not fully independent to be sure; rather, under the Platt Amendment, which the United States forced Cuba to attach to its constitution, Cuba became virtually a U.S. protectorate.

The United States in effect supervised Cuba's foreign affairs, including foreign loans, and had the right to intervene whenever it saw fit to preserve peace and stability. "It is not the absolute independence we had dreamed about," mused the embittered old Cuban military leader Máximo Gómez.[7] He nonetheless urged his fellow countrymen to accept the amendment as the price of U.S. withdrawal. It was better to accept limited sovereignty and be rid of the occupying forces, he reasoned. Perhaps in the future, the dream of the republic might be realized. (In 1959 it was.)

GUNBOAT DIPLOMACY, 1898–1929

This was the pattern followed over the next thirty-four years. The United States considered everything to the south to be its sphere of influence, and it often exercised outright control in Central America and the Caribbean Basin. U.S. capital flooded into those same nearby regions. Banks, utility enterprises, and companies such as United Fruit soon virtually controlled the economies of several states. By 1929, for example, over 65 percent of the Cuban economy was in the hands of U.S. owners. It was an age of dollar diplomacy backed up by U.S. gunboats.

The United States did, however, continue to meet periodically with the other governments at Pan-American conferences. The fiction of juridical equality was maintained, and, most important, the United States did not seize outright any more territory, not even to build a canal in Panama, one of President Theodore Roosevelt's overriding priorities. The United States first negotiated with Colombia, of which state Panama was a province. When those negotiations did not prosper, Washington engineered a rebellion in the province, immediately recognized the breakaway rebels as the government of a new Panamanian state, and in 1903 signed an agreement with them to build a canal. U.S. forces made certain Colombia did not intervene. But the new state remained independent (though with a circumscribed form of independence, as in the case of Cuba) and almost eight decades later would itself assume control of the canal.

Elsewhere, U.S. insistence that extra-hemispheric states not meddle in its sphere of influence raised difficulties. It was all well and good for the United States to say that other powers could not intervene, but what, then, if the states of the hemisphere defaulted on their debts or in some other way (in the parlance of the times in the United States) "behaved irresponsibly"? Who was to police them? In his annual message to Congress in 1904, President Theodore Roosevelt gave the answer: The United States would become the policeman of the Western Hemisphere. "Chronic wrongdoing," he said, "or an impotence which results in a general loosening of the ties of civilized society, may in America, as elsewhere, ultimately require intervention by some civilized nation, and in the Western Hemisphere the adherence of the United States to the Monroe Doctrine may force the United States, however reluctantly, in flagrant cases of such wrongdoing or impotence, to the exercise of an international police power."[8]

This became known as the Roosevelt Corollary to the Monroe Doctrine. The United States wasted no time in implementing it. In 1905 it intervened in the Dominican Republic to set up a customs collection operation to pay off that country's debt to several European creditors. It did the same thing in Nicaragua in 1912 and in Haiti in 1915, with marines remaining in occupation of those countries off and on for many years. On various other grounds, it intervened no less than twenty-six times in other states of Central America and the Caribbean. Even President Woodrow Wilson landed marines in Veracruz and sent U.S. troops under General John Pershing into northern Mexico. By 1927, U.S. hegemony over Central America was so complete that Undersecretary of State Robert Olds could say, "Central America has always understood that governments we recognize and support stay in power, while those we do not recognize and support fail."[9]

Old's statement was as direct an assertion of hegemony as one can imagine. Perhaps in part it was the very brazenness of the attitudes behind such statements— a brazenness that clashed painfully with U.S. idealism—that caused opinion in the United States to begin to swing toward a more cooperative relationship. Shifting opinions were pushed also by the growing resistance of Latin America. Offended by the condescending paternalism of the Roosevelt Corollary, they increasingly protested U.S. interventions and high-handed actions. By the Pan-American Conference held in Havana in 1928, the other states were demanding a rectification of U.S. policy. Perhaps to their surprise, the United States listened. There was a greater spirit of equality and cooperation than ever before, and issues such as intervention in the internal affairs of the member states were discussed frankly. In the past, they had not even been on the agenda. As the conference broke up, it was understood that at the next meeting, an anti-intervention resolution would be on the agenda. The stage was set for the Good Neighbor Policy.

THE GOOD NEIGHBOR POLICY, 1929–1953

Many chronologies mark the beginning of the Good Neighbor Policy in 1933, with the inauguration of President Franklin Delano Roosevelt. In fact, however, it was begun under President Herbert Hoover. He deplored U.S. interventionism, and during his presidency, 1929–1933, U.S. Marines were pulled out of every country in Latin America except Haiti. Hoover also ordered a review of the historical rationale for interventionism. In response, a memorandum prepared by Undersecretary of State J. Reuben Clark and published in 1930 held that nothing in the Monroe Doctrine had ever given the United States the right to intervene in the internal affairs of its neighbors. This removed the underpinning from the Roosevelt Corollary, and it was never again cited as the basis for U.S. policy.[10]

The trend away from interventionism was given new impetus during the presidency of Franklin Roosevelt. He stressed strong economic ties with Latin America, not political domination, and favored collective security over unilateral actions by the United States. He abrogated the Platt Amendment, thus removing the protectorate infringement of Cuban sovereignty. And, as promised at Havana in 1928, at the 1933 Pan-American Conference in Montevideo, Uruguay, the United States pledged itself to the principle of nonintervention. The following year, Roosevelt pulled the last marines out of Haiti and, true to his word, did not send them again into any Latin American country during his long presidency (1933–1945).

Good relations were further spurred by World War II. With the exception of Argentina, which tended to sympathize with the Axis powers (until a last-minute change of sides in 1945), all the Latin American states were allies of the United States and made no small contribution to the war effort, assuring natural resources and other needed commodities, providing air and naval bases, and, in the case of Mexico and Brazil, even sending troops. A Brazilian army division fought in Italy, a squadron of Mexican fighter aircraft in the Pacific. As the war ended, U.S.–Latin American relations were more harmonious than they had ever been.

Even warmer, more cooperative relations seemed to lie ahead. Roosevelt's successor, President Harry S. Truman, continued Roosevelt's noninterventionist policy and in 1947 also helped bring into being the so-called Rio Pact, a collective security treaty that made defense of the Western Hemisphere the responsibility of all member states. This was followed in 1948 by the creation of the Organization of American States (OAS), which provided for the adjudication of disputes among members and for collective peacekeeping measures. The OAS, in effect, took the old Pan-American Union to a new level of cooperation and organizational cohesion.

If the hemisphere still had to be defended from outside powers, it was clear that those who had framed the OAS charter and the Rio Pact did not think that was any longer the responsibility of the United States alone. Rather, it now became the duty of all member states. As U.S. political leaders and scholars commented at the time, the Monroe Doctrine was thus to become a multilateral instrument.[11] And so it might have. Unfortunately, as the OAS was being formed, the Cold War between the

United States and the Soviet Union was heating up. Soon it was to become an all-consuming struggle to which all other considerations and objectives were sacrificed.

THE COLD WAR, 1953–1989

In the same year that the Rio Pact was signed, 1949, China fell to the Communists and the Soviet Union exploded its own atomic bomb. The next year, 1950, saw the outbreak of the Korean War. The Cold War was on in earnest. That had little immediate effect on U.S.–Latin American relations, however. Latin America was perceived to be far removed from the Soviet Union and safely within the U.S. sphere of influence. Indeed, Latin American states were perceived as important allies on whose votes in the UN General Assembly the United States could always count. The Truman administration continued its noninterventionist policies. Thus, despite the growing Cold War hysteria in the United States as reflected by McCarthyism, and despite some rumblings in the Policy Planning Bureau of the State Department that a harder line might be in order, it can be said that the Good Neighbor Policy toward Latin America continued until 1953.

In that year, however, with the inauguration of Dwight Eisenhower as president and the appointment of John Foster Dulles as secretary of state, the Cold War came to Latin America full force. The concept of strategic denial now had but one focus: the Soviet Union. Thus, Dulles, on the basis of no hard evidence, immediately warned of increasing Communist influence in the hemisphere that the Soviet Union was determined to exploit. He pointed to Guatemala as a case in point. At the meeting of OAS foreign ministers in Caracas that year, he presented a resolution that stipulated that any hemispheric government under Communist influence represented a threat to peace and security against which the other states would take multilateral action. Dulles made it clear that the other states could either accept the resolution and cooperate with the United States or risk a return to unilateral interventions. The resolution was accepted, but only after it had been changed to provide for "consultations" rather than immediate multilateral action.

Undaunted, the Eisenhower administration moved ahead with plans to oust the "Communist-controlled" government of Jacobo Arbenz with a coup clandestinely organized by the CIA. In June 1954, Colonel Castillo Armas, a disaffected Guatemalan officer, led a group of several hundred armed men in an uprising against Arbenz.[12] The United States could maintain that it was not intervening, that this was a Guatemalan reaction. Few believed it, but all that was needed was a fig leaf. As the Guatemalan army would not fight for the government, the coup quickly succeeded. The Guatemalan Revolution, which might best be described as a liberal reform movement begun in 1944, ended. What followed, thanks to the U.S. intervention, was a long series of bloody military dictatorships, occasionally interrupted by elected governments—governments, however, that served at the sufferance of the military and were rarely allowed even to serve out their terms. Repression was massive. Tens of thousands of Guatemalans were slaughtered by the army in the next fifty years.

Only recently has there been encouraging movement toward democracy and an end to the bloody guerrilla warfare that has plagued the country since the early 1960s.

In retrospect, it is clear that there was no Communist—let alone Soviet—threat in Guatemala. Arbenz himself was not a Communist. On the contrary, though elected by the people, he was a colonel in the Guatemalan army. There were no Communist cabinet ministers in his government and only four Communist Party members in the National Assembly. The Soviet Union had not even bothered to establish diplomatic relations with Guatemala and certainly was providing no assistance of any kind. The government was progressive, however, and was carrying out an agrarian reform. In the process, it nationalized some land belonging to United Fruit. That may have been what really triggered Arbenz's overthrow, especially when we consider that John Foster Dulles's law firm had handled the United Fruit account and that his brother, CIA director Allen Dulles; Henry Cabot Lodge, the United States' UN ambassador; and a series of other senior government officials had all been members of the United Fruit board.

The Eisenhower administration also adopted a policy of supporting any right-wing dictatorship, no matter how repressive, so long as they professed themselves to be "anti-Communist." For eight years, from 1953 until 1961, the United States forgot all about the pursuit of democracy. It seemed to see dictators as more reliable allies. Secretary of State Dulles at one point even described Venezuela under Perez Jimenez, that country's comic-opera military dictator, as pursuing the kind of political and economic policies the United States would wish to see emulated by every Latin American country.[13]

In the Guatemalan case and in most other U.S. interventions in Latin America during the Cold War, the perceived threats of Communist takeovers were more figments of the imaginations of U.S. leaders, fed by Cold War hysteria, than real. Only in the Cuban case was there legitimate cause for concern. Not that Fidel Castro was a Communist when he took power in 1959. But his objectives of sharply reducing U.S. influence in the hemisphere and encouraging the emergence of a whole series of other revolutionary regimes seemed likely to carry him toward an alliance with the Soviet Union. They were objectives, after all, that he could not achieve on his own. By early 1960, the United States concluded that such an alliance was in formation and began preparations to overthrow the Castro government. That effort was made at the Bay of Pigs in April 1961, with disastrous results. The idea that the 1,200 men of the Cuban exile brigade could defeat Castro's army of over 60,000 armed with tanks and artillery was preposterous. They could have succeeded only had they been supported by U.S. troops. President John F. Kennedy, who had taken office in January 1961 and inherited the invasion plan from the Eisenhower administration, had stated flatly that no U.S. forces would be used, but the CIA counted on a change of orders once it became clear that the brigade could not hold the beach. They were wrong. Kennedy stuck by his determination not to commit U.S. forces, and the invasion failed. Its two principal results were the destruction of any internal opposition and the consolidation of a Cuban-Soviet alliance.

The latter led, in October 1962, to the Cuban missile crisis. Suddenly the worst nightmare U.S. policymakers could imagine in Latin America was upon them. For almost 150 years, the Monroe Doctrine had been intended to keep other powers out of the hemisphere and thus prevent them from threatening U.S. security from the nation's southern frontier. Now the United States' principal global adversary, the Soviet Union, was doing just that, and threatening in a most fearsome way, with nuclear missiles. The crisis was eventually resolved through the Kennedy-Khrushchev Understanding, under which the Soviet Union agreed to withdraw its missiles in return for a U.S. pledge not to invade Cuba. Even so, it is fair to say that U.S. policymakers were badly traumatized by the missile crisis and that from 1962 onward they were absolutely determined that there would be no more Cubas.

The Kennedy administration itself followed a two-track policy toward that objective: (1) It moved to contain Castroism by trying to isolate him in the hemisphere and by giving military assistance to the other governments to defend themselves against Castro-backed guerrillas. But (2), to its credit, it also launched the Alliance for Progress, a program of economic and technical assistance. This recognized that revolutionary conditions resulted from economic and social distress and that addressing these problems was as important as military aid. For the same reason, the Kennedy administration also gave greater emphasis to supporting democratic regimes rather than dictatorships.

With Kennedy's death, however, the Alliance for Progress was for all practical purposes abandoned by the harder-line administration of Lyndon Johnson. In 1964 the latter also made it clear to the Brazilian generals that the United States would endorse their overthrow of the democratically elected government of Jango Goulart, who was regarded by the United States as much too far to the left. The generals proceeded to do just that, thus aborting the democratic process in Brazil and ushering in two decades of military rule.

Johnson also sent troops into the Dominican Republic in 1965 when it seemed that political instability there might open the way to "a Castroite take-over." Johnson was able to get OAS cover for the intervention (the grateful Brazilian generals providing many of the troops). What he was unable to do was to come up with any evidence of a Communist conspiracy.[14]

Eight years later, Richard Nixon and Henry Kissinger played a role in Chile similar to that of the Johnson administration in Brazil. Regarding the Popular Front government of Salvador Allende to be under the influence of the Communists, they at the very least indicated to the Chilean military that they would welcome his overthrow, if indeed they did not actively encourage it. True, Allende was a Socialist and the Communist Party was part of the ruling Popular Front. On the other hand, Allende had been democratically elected (in 1970). All the institutions were intact and functioning. Thus, he had either to play within the constitutional parameters or face impeachment. There was no need to overthrow him. He could have been voted out at the polls in the next elections. But neither the Chilean military nor the Nixon administration wanted to wait. On September 11, 1973, the coup was launched—

and not in the cause of democracy. On the contrary, what followed were seventeen years of the bloodiest military dictatorship in Chile's history, a period during which tens of thousands of Chilean citizens were tortured and murdered, often because they simply looked like leftists. Not until 1990 did democracy return to Chile. To its credit, the United States, which must bear some responsibility for those seventeen years of horror in Chile, under the administration of George Bush encouraged Chile's return to democracy.

The last significant Cold War chapter in the hemisphere was played out in Central America—with one small sideshow in Grenada. In Nicaragua, where the Somozas had ruled the country since 1936, the administration of Jimmy Carter found itself in an uncomfortable position. It was glad to see the Somoza dictatorship end in 1979 but concerned that the Sandinista guerrillas who had ousted him were avowedly Marxist and friendly to Fidel Castro, although they quickly vowed to move toward elections and to address U.S. security concerns. The Carter administration, albeit nervously, was prepared to meet them halfway, to handle differences through negotiations and even to provide limited economic assistance as an incentive. Not so the administration of Ronald Reagan, which took office in January 1981. It regarded the Sandinistas as nothing less than instruments of Soviet aggression and was determined to get rid of them one way or another.

Meanwhile, encouraged perhaps by the Sandinista victory in Nicaragua, left-wing guerrillas in El Salvador had launched an all-out effort to topple the government in that country, and with it the traditional control of the landowning elite. The Carter administration focused as much on the need for economic and social reforms as on the need to contain the guerrillas, and the U.S. ambassador, Robert E. White, insisted that the government curb the right-wing death squads (which had been responsible for the murder of Archbishop Romero) as a condition for U.S. assistance.

The Reagan administration had no such qualms. As it came into office in 1981, it in effect told the government and the military to do whatever they deemed necessary to defeat the guerrillas. Atrocities on the government's side shot up at an appalling rate, often carried out by troops or death squads trained by the United States. Equally determined to win in Nicaragua, the Reagan administration eschewed negotiations and other efforts at peaceful solutions. Instead, it armed former Somoza national guardsmen and other anti-Sandinista elements, organized them into a force called the Contras, and launched them as a guerrilla force against the government in Managua. The ensuing conflict raged from 1982 until 1989. During that time, the United States pulled Honduras into the conflict by having the Contras operate from its territory and by training Honduran death squads to go after suspected leftists. In 1984 it also mined Nicaraguan harbors, an act that resulted in a 14–3 decision by the International Court of Justice (ICJ) declaring the United States to be in violation of international law. The United States, having already taken the position that the ICJ did not have jurisdiction in the matter, simply ignored the decision.

In its frantic efforts to do away with the Sandinistas, officials of the Reagan administration also lied to the Congress and then, in their efforts to circumvent congressional restrictions on aid to the Contras, initiated what became known as Iran-Contra-gate, a bizarre operation that began with efforts to divert to the Contras "profits" made by overcharging for arms the United States illegally sold Iran as part of a deal to bring about the release of Americans held hostage by Islamic groups in Lebanon. Eventually, the operation involved secret donations made by a whole series of governments and shady individuals, and all in direct violation of congressional directives.[15] The U.S. Army even trained Central American officers in methods of torture and assassination and wrote manuals advocating those methods that were used in the infamous School of the Americas.[16]

In short, the last chapter of the Cold War was one in which the United States seemed to lose its way or to forget the values on which the country had been founded. As Gaddis Smith has so well put it:

> James Monroe in 1823 had contrasted American principles of candor, self-government, and respect for national independence with the devious, autocratic, imperial ways of Europe. The [Monroe] doctrine was proclaimed as protection of the first against the second. The abandonment after 1945 of its original ideals made the last years of the Monroe Doctrine a history of moral degradation. Sometimes the words and principles of the Monroe Doctrine were embraced openly, enthusiastically, and with complete candor. More often they were muffled in secrecy, tainted by lies, and in conflict with the public creed of democracy and human rights.[17]

In the end, the Central Americans ended the conflict through their own peace process, with little encouragement or support from the United States. Indeed, it would be more accurate to say that until quite late in the day, the United States opposed the negotiations. Certainly, it was U.S. opposition that frustrated the so-called Contadora process, an effort on the part of the Central American and Mexican presidents begun in 1983 to work out solutions to the region's conflicts. As this stood near the verge of collapse, however, it was followed by a new effort begun in 1987 at a meeting of presidents in Esquipulas, Guatemala. The prime mover of this new negotiating effort was Oscar Arias, the new president of Costa Rica and a man of great determination. Over the next two years, agreements were hammered out that eventually led to an end to the civil war in El Salvador, the phasing-out of fighting between the Contras and the Sandinistas in Nicaragua, and the holding of elections in that country in 1990. When the Sandinistas lost, they peacefully turned power over to the opposition.

And so the conflict ended in Central America—no thanks to the United States. Oscar Arias won the Nobel Peace Prize, much to the disgust of some in the Reagan administration who had thought his plan for negotiations simply a means of appeasing "the Communists." Meanwhile, back in 1983, in something of a sideshow performance, the Reagan administration had used U.S. forces to invade the island of Grenada. Relations with Grenada had deteriorated steadily after the New Jewel Movement took power there in 1979. Led by Maurice Bishop, a friend of Castro's, it was considered by both the Carter and Reagan administrations as being much too far to the left. On the other hand, it was a tiny island that threatened no one. Even so, in October 1983 the Reagan administration took advantage of internecine political strife on the island to send in U.S. forces and remove the New Jewel Movement from power. The specific pretexts for the invasion were (1) to assure the safety of U.S. students at a medical school on the island and (2) to prevent the completion of an airfield that President Reagan himself warned was probably intended for use by the Soviets.

In fact, subsequent investigations made clear that the students were in no danger and in any event could have been peacefully evacuated had it not been for the invasion. It also turned out that the United Nations Development Program had recommended construction of the airfield as part of an effort to expand tourism on the island. And once the invasion was over, the U.S. taxpayers forked over $19 million to help the new Grenadian government complete that same airfield—to expand tourism! In other words, the pretexts were phony.

The United States did at least have a legal fig leaf for its invasion, however. The other governments of the eastern Caribbean said they had urged the United States to step in. They said it only after the fact, however, and that was the case also of the alleged invitation from the British governor-general, which no one remembered to mention until the invasion was over. No one was fooled by these after-the-fact invitations. Certainly the British government was not. Prime Minister Margaret Thatcher, friend though she was of President Reagan's, roundly condemned the invasion. Still, by holding to its fig leaf, the United States was at least suggesting that it cared about the diplomatic and legal niceties, and it was sticking to the pattern that had existed since the withdrawal of the last marines from Haiti in 1934 of not intervening unilaterally with its own forces—without, that is, at least some shred of multilateral endorsement.

Strangely, with the Cold War virtually over, President Bush broke that pattern, sending U.S. forces to invade Panama in December 1989 without any invitation from the OAS, the Central American countries, or anyone else. And unlike all other U.S.-organized interventions since 1954, the invasion of Panama was not aimed at thwarting some thrust on the part of the Soviet Union or Cuba. Indeed, it had nothing to do with the dwindling Cold War. Rather, Panama was invaded in order to arrest its president, Manuel Noriega, who was said to be involved in major drug trafficking. Noriega, once a paid asset of the CIA, had made the mistake of courting Cuba's Castro and of thumbing his nose at the United States. He paid the price. In blatant violation of international norms, U.S. forces stormed into Panama, arrested Noriega, and brought him back to the United States to stand trial, much as conquering Roman legions once brought their prisoners back to Rome in chains.

Few shed any tears for Noriega, who had indeed won election by fraud and was something of a thug. The U.S. invasion was nonetheless illegal and was so condemned by near unanimous vote in the OAS. For the first time since 1934, U.S. troops had intervened in Latin America without even an effort to win multilateral approval. Some wondered if the end of the Cold War meant a return to U.S. gunboat diplomacy.

Meanwhile, the Soviet Union was in the throes of cataclysmic change. Mikhail Gorbachev had taken power there in 1985 and tried to revive the sputtering Soviet economy by introducing liberalizing reforms. In effect, he tried to fashion a socialist system with a more democratic face. Some said he went too far too fast. Others held that the system depended on coercion and ground to a halt when Gorbachev removed it. Whatever the case, the Soviet system began to collapse.

Gorbachev had also changed dramatically the thrust of Soviet foreign policy. In the past, it had been geared to the Marxist tenet that worldwide revolution was a historical inevitability. In other words, it had been geared to expanding the socialist system to the extent possible. Quite understandably, the West had perceived this to be aggressive and threatening. But Gorbachev abandoned the whole concept. No more would the Soviet Union try to extend the reach of socialism; rather, it was now strictly up to each country to determine its internal arrangements without outside interference. With that, the Cold War began to wind down.

When an abortive coup by hard-liners in late 1991 failed, the almost seventy-five years of Communist Party rule was swept aside in reaction. The other republics then quickly pulled out of the Soviet Union, and by 1992 the latter had disappeared, replaced by the Russian Republic and a loose grouping of the former union republics. The Cold War was over.

THE POST–COLD WAR PERIOD, 1992 TO THE PRESENT

And as stated at the outset, with the end of the Cold War, the imperatives that had driven U.S. policy for almost 200 years were suddenly rendered obsolete. If the United States had treated the Caribbean as an American lake so as to protect the approaches to the Panama Canal, there was now no other power that wished to hinder those approaches; the canal was virtually in the hands of Panama and in any event no longer of vital importance to the United States. The factors that had once riveted U.S. attention to the Caribbean had gone the way of the 3-mile limit to territorial waters (because that had once been the range of a cannon shot). There was no need to treat the Caribbean as an American lake. There was no need either to assert U.S. hegemony, in the Caribbean or Central America and certainly not in the rest of the hemisphere. The kinds of interests and objectives the United States has in the hemisphere today require the cooperation of the other governments, not their subservience. A new approach geared to vastly changed circumstances is required.

What are those interests and objectives? The most pressing ones, not necessarily in order of priority, are as follows: (1) to halt or at least sharply reduce the flow of drugs into the United States; (2) to keep the populations in place (the United States does not want to receive vast flows of illegal immigrants or refugees from the south); (3) to help protect the environment on which we all depend; and (4) to increase trade, especially U.S. exports.

Is the United States developing a new and more cooperative approach to address these interests? Let us examine them case by case.

Drug Interdiction

The United States cannot reduce the flow of drugs over its borders by sending battleships and marines to the Caribbean and Central American states, and certainly not by landing troops in South America. Further, the drug problem is in fact two-sided: consumption and production, with the former centered in the United States. It is up to the United States to address the matter of demand, for so long as there is a market for any product, it will be produced, no matter how energetic the efforts to turn it off. So far, the United States has done very little to reduce consumption. That would require a major effort and outlay of funds, for which U.S. political leaders have simply not had the stomach. Unless they do make such a commitment, however, their seriousness of purpose is in question, their vows to come to grips with the drug problem not really credible.

As to the second side, neither the United States nor the Latin American governments can eradicate production through legislation and police action, though those are of course necessary components. The result of those efforts over past years has been but to contain production to a 10 percent per year increase![18] The cartels are in fact only part of the problem. By and large, the coca and other narcotics are grown by poor peasants in Bolivia, Peru, Colombia, and other countries. They depend upon their crops of coca leaves, poppies, and marijuana to eke out a meager existence. They have raised these plants for centuries and have little concept of the havoc they cause elsewhere. They are not likely to give up their major source of income just because the United States and their own governments demand it. They must find alternative crops and sources of income, and this will occur only as the result of a major cooperative effort among the United States, individual Latin American governments, and international organizations. Such an effort would require a large-scale input of resources, most of which would have to come from the United States. It would be a small price to pay, however, if, as President Bush told Americans some years back, drugs are the principal threat to national security.[19] So far, the United States has shown not the slightest interest.

Most important of all, the fight against drugs must be a cooperative one, one in which the United States and its Latin American neighbors join as equal partners. That has not yet been the case. At a summit conference of the presidents of Colombia, Peru, Bolivia, and the United States held in Cartagena, Colombia, in February 1990 to discuss the drug problem, Bush did indeed stress the need for a broad multilateral campaign, but he was woefully short on specifics. In fact, he offered no plan at all. Meanwhile, the United States has done all too little to reduce consumption, has put few resources into the fight to reduce production, and instead has tended simply to shift the blame to the Latin American governments. The system of certification imposed by the United States in 1987 was, as many Latin American governments saw it, confirmation that the United States saw itself as judge and jury of whether the efforts of Latin American governments to interdict drugs were adequate. If it deemed them inadequate, then that government was no longer eligible for certain economic benefits. Never mind what the Latin American governments might think of the inadequacy of U.S. efforts and its failure to commit resources. Clearly, this was not a cooperative effort among equal partners.

Protection of the Environment

The United States also needs the cooperation of the Latin American governments in the protection of the environment, or the habitat in which we all live. Yet it has yet to provide the leadership and resources that are required. The so-called Earth Summit in Rio in June 1992 (or, more formally, the United Nations Conference on the Environment and Development) offered a perfect opportunity at least to provide leadership. Rather than that, the Bush administration raised objections to the two major treaties to be signed at the conference even before it opened. In the event, it refused to sign the treaty to preserve the world's plants, animals, and natural resources, much to the disgust of the other delegates and even of many in the U.S. delegation. It signed the other major treaty, dealing with the problem of global warming, but only on the condition that the strict timetable for curbing harmful emissions was deleted. Rather than leading and encouraging cooperation, the Bush administration played an obstructionist role and was almost completely isolated in its position.[20]

The intentions at least of the administration of Bill Clinton have been an improvement over those of the Bush administration. In 1993 Clinton called for "a new covenant for environmental progress." His administration then negotiated a multilateral agreement aimed at halting the depletion of the ozone layer in the upper atmosphere, and in 1996 it began massive negotiations for a worldwide effort to address the critical problem of global climate change. These are steps in the right direction, but unless they are funded, they can achieve nothing tangible. Congress has not cooperated. It has so far refused to put up the funds. The United States has not even been able to come up with seed money for the project to reduce CFCs worldwide and thus reduce the depletion of the ozone layer. And just as the United States has not paid its dues to the United Nations, it is the biggest debtor in the Global Environmental Facility, the principal international funding mechanism for the effort called for by the Climate Change Convention.[21] Unless there are resources to match the challenge, the whole effort will fail. At the moment, the prognosis is not encouraging.

The heart of the matter in the Western Hemisphere is the need to halt the destruction of the Amazon rain forest, often described as the lungs of the world. But halting deforestation is linked to responsible economic development. Alternatives must be offered so that destruction of the forest is no longer profitable, but that requires a carefully coordinated developmental effort and, again, the outlay of resources. As one Brazilian official put it: "We of course want to protect the environment. In the best of all possible worlds, we'd like to preserve the rain forest. On the other hand, we must develop, must offer our people a better way of life. We can't afford to be the lungs of the world if we are also to pay off our foreign debt and finance our development plans."[22] As one might imagine, Congress has shown no interest whatever in funding any projects related to saving the rain forests.

Economic Development: Keeping the Populations in Place

During the Cold War, U.S. representatives often answered Latin American requests for economic assistance by pointing to the United States' huge defense expenditures. Were it not for the need to defend the rest of the world against the aggressive intentions of the Soviet Union, politicians said, the United States would have ample resources to assist the economic development efforts of its neighbors. As it was, those resources had to be diverted to defense.

But now that the Cold War is over, there should be no further need to divert those resources. Defense spending has fallen little, however, and the United States seems no more disposed now than before to make resources available for developmental projects. This is especially difficult to understand given that the interests of the United States would be advanced by those efforts. It is not simply that an economically imbalanced hemisphere is unhealthy and morally unsustainable; it is that such a situation fuels one of Washington's major headaches: the influx of illegal immigrants from the south. There is only one way to encourage unstable populations to the south to remain in place (i.e., not to head for the United States), and that is by giving them some hope of a better future in their own countries. Clearly, this was the reason for the U.S. intervention in Haiti. It had been noticed that during Aristide's brief period in power, the flow of boat people from Haiti had dried up. But once he had been overthrown and the military again began its repression of the Haitian people, the flood resumed. And so, in 1994, the United States returned Aristide to power, arranged for elections, and began some efforts toward economic development. This worked, at least temporarily. The number of boat people dropped off dramatically. Typically, however, while willing to commit troops, at least for a time, the United States was unwilling to commit more than token financial and material resources. The success of the inchoate developmental programs in Haiti remains very much in doubt.

Elsewhere, rather than developmental programs involving even small-scale transfer of public resources, the United States has urged the countries to its south to privatize and to depend upon private investment, both local and foreign. In short, it has urged a neoliberal approach. This was accompanied during the Bush administration by a good deal of rhetoric centering around the "Enterprise for the Americas," a vague program of trade preferences, incentives for private investment, calls for limited debt reduction, and promises of movement toward a hemispheric free-trade zone. While praiseworthy in its concept, very little came of it. Few of the necessary legislative packages were ever even presented. One of the few concrete achievements was that the Bush administration did succeed in negotiating and winning congressional approval for a free-trade agreement with Canada, the first step in putting in place a North American Free Trade Agreement (NAFTA). It initiated the process with Mexico, but it was left to the Clinton administration to complete it. In 1994, at the urging of the Clinton administration, NAFTA was extended to Mexico as well.

Much hoopla attended the so-called Summit of the Americas held in Miami in December 1994. The heads of thirty-four governments met and signed a Declaration of Principles and Plan of Action involving twenty-three separate initiatives on everything from efforts to end corruption to the extension of the free-trade zone to virtually all states of the hemisphere by the year 2005. As in the case of the "Enterprise for the Americas" before it, however, there has been more rhetoric than substance to the promises of the Miami summit. The key initiative was the extension of free-trade arrangements, yet more than two years after the summit, the Clinton administration has done little to get the project on a fast track, and the Congress has shown little enthusiasm for approving the idea even if new agreements were presented tomorrow. Further, given that in March 1996, as discussed below, the Clinton administration signed the Helms-Burton bill, which directly violates the NAFTA, one must question how seriously it takes the whole free-trade effort.

Meanwhile, the results of the new economic policies advocated by Washington are decidedly mixed. Over the first five years of the 1990s, most countries succeeded, with their new neoliberal economic measures, in controlling inflation, reducing budget deficits, attracting foreign investment, and getting growth rates up around a respectable 3 percent (after a near stagnant decade during the 1980s). The downside, however, was that the reforms produced higher unemployment, more people living in poverty, a greater disparity between rich and poor, and declining standards of living for the majority. According to the World Bank, income distribution in Latin America "approaches the most unequal in the developing world."[23]

This was exacerbated by the neoliberal policy of reducing social welfare programs wherever possible. The poor not only got poorer but found even less of a safety net than there might otherwise have been to ease their suffering. Even in Argentina many simply went hungry. Social injustice in Brazil is perhaps the most glaring in the world.

The worst case, of course, was Mexico. Shortly after becoming part of the NAFTA and as a direct result of mistakes in adjusting to the agreement, in December 1994 its economy virtually collapsed. Only a massive bailout led by the U.S. Treasury kept Mexico from going under. By late 1996, it was beginning to recover. That is, growth rates were back up and foreign investment was again beginning to flow into the country. But the disparities were worse than ever. Mexico could boast of fifteen billionaires (only four other countries had more), but 50 percent of the Mexican population was living in abject misery, and more were falling beneath the poverty line every day.[24] Social and political tensions were on the rise, as evidenced by the peasant uprisings in Mexico's southern states. These were not conditions likely to encourage Mexicans to remain in their own country. On the contrary, the flow north is increasing. What else would one expect?

Increasing U.S. Exports

The neoliberal economic policies pushed by the United States and the lack of a concerted developmental program are having a negative effect on another U.S. interest: trade. Countries with growing numbers of impoverished masses are not good markets. Thus, rather than booming trade, with balances in favor of the United States, trade has increased little at all and U.S. trade imbalances with Latin America have worsened dramatically over the past few years. In 1992 the balance against the United States was only $991 million. By 1995, it was almost $9 billion.[25]

Failure of U.S. Policy

What is clear is that the United States has failed to formulate a policy that works in the changed post–Cold War world. What is needed is the cooperation of the other governments in combating the drug problem and protecting the environment. But the United States has provided little leadership and even less in the way of resources. Hence, the problems of drugs and a deteriorating environment have not even been reduced, let alone resolved.

The neoliberal approach to economic development advocated by the United States has fared little better. Growth rates improved somewhat overall but were accompanied by worsening poverty and social instability, exactly the conditions that can be expected to produce an increased flow of illegal immigrants to the United States. Further, the market for U.S. products shrinks as more and more Latin Americans fall below the poverty line.

Obviously, the key to the achievement of all four major U.S. objectives would be a large-scale developmental effort, counting with significant resource inputs from the United States. An economically healthy Latin America would be a far more effective partner in stopping drug trafficking and protecting the environment. Its populations would be far more likely to remain in place and would be able to buy more U.S. products.

Unfortunately, the United States seems unwilling to mount such a joint developmental effort, and certainly unwilling to transfer resources. On the contrary, its leaders seem locked in a Cold War mind-set. They continue to spend almost as much—some might say to waste almost as much—as during the Cold War on defense and intelligence. But they will not spend on projects that would in fact contribute directly to the achievement of today's pressing objectives.

A Return to Unilateralism?

Worse, the United States gives evidence of moving back toward a kind of unilateralism more appropriate to the days of gunboat diplomacy than to the post–Cold War world. During the Cold War, the United States often spoke of committing itself to abide strictly by the United Nations Charter and international law if the Soviet

Union would but do so also.[26] With the Soviet Union having collapsed and its successor state, the Russian Republic, indeed having committed itself to adhere to the charter, it had been hoped that the United States might now go back to the spirit of multilateralism that had so briefly prevailed with the formation of the Rio Pact in 1947 and the Organization of American States in 1948. That spirit had been undermined by the anti-Communist hysteria of the Cold War. Might it now be possible to resuscitate it and to construct a hemispheric system based on rule of law?

As of mid-1997, that seemed unlikely. For one thing, the United States continues to behave as though the Cold War is not over, at least with respect to Cuba. During the 1980s, the U.S. position was that there could be a significant improvement in relations with Cuba if the latter would but (1) remove its troops from Africa, (2) stop fueling revolutionary situations in Central America and elsewhere, and (3) reduce its military ties with the Soviet Union. But as of 1992, all those conditions had been met. Yet rather than moving to relax tensions and improve relations with the island, the United States did exactly the opposite. With passage of the Cuban Democracy Act of that year, it actually tightened the embargo against the island. Congressman Robert Torricelli (D–New Jersey), the act's principal proponent, assured one and all in a television debate in December 1992 that as the result of his legislation Castro would be gone within months.[27]

But three years later, not only was Castro still in power, but the Cuban economy was beginning to recover. Hence, ultraconservative forces in the U.S. Congress came up with even more draconian legislation aimed at forcing other countries to reduce trade with and investments in Cuba. The Helms-Burton Act, signed into law in March 1996, is extraterritorial in nature and violates international law and various international agreements to which the United States is a party, including the NAFTA. It represents nothing less than an effort on the part of the United States unilaterally to dictate to the rest of the world without regard to the rules of the international system.

Not surprisingly, Helms-Burton has been roundly condemned by the international community. At its General Assembly in June 1996, the Organization of American States rejected it by unanimous vote and called on the Inter-American Juridical Committee (IAJC) to rule on the legislation's legality. In a unanimous ruling handed down on August 23, the IAJC found Helms-Burton to be in violation of international law on at least eight counts. In November the United Nations General Assembly condemned the U.S. embargo, including Helms-Burton, by a vote of 138–3. Only Israel and Uzbekistan voted with the United States, and they both trade with Cuba! In other words, no one supports U.S. policy.

Canada, Mexico, and the European Union have all drafted retaliatory legislation under which their companies can sue U.S. entities if the latter take action against them under Helms-Burton. This could lead to disruptions of the whole international commercial system, to say nothing of chaos in the courts. And meanwhile, on October 4, 1996, the European Union also filed an official request for the Dispute

Settlement Body of the World Trade Organization (WTO) to rule on whether Helms-Burton conforms to the WTO's rules of conduct.

One cannot be certain what all this will produce. It points up, however, that Helms-Burton is an irrational act on the part of the United States. With the Cold War over, Cuba no longer represents even a potential threat to U.S. security and certainly not to U.S. economic interests. In fact, in terms of U.S. interests, Cuba is of little importance at all. U.S. commercial ties with Canada, Europe, and Mexico, on the other hand, are vital. That the United States is willing to place at risk that which is important over that which is not is simply illogical.

Unfortunately, Helms-Burton seems to be part of a pattern. If some see the end of the Cold War as providing an opportunity to construct a more stable international system based on international law and adherence to rules of conduct agreed to by all in such international fora as the UN and the WTO, others, such as Senator Jesse Helms (R–North Carolina) (let us call them the unilateralists) see it in quite another light. To them it means that the United States is the only remaining superpower and so can and should order things to suit its own purposes, paying less attention to such abstractions as international law and international organizations. The United States wants to bring down the Castro government and so insists that other governments cooperate with it or face the consequences. It wanted to get rid of Boutros Boutros Ghali as UN secretary-general, and so, acting against the will of the other countries, it forced his resignation. The United States didn't like him, and so he had to go. Senator Helms has made it clear that as far as he is concerned, the United Nations must either carry out the reforms the United States wants (whether or not the rest of the world community agrees with them) or the United States will simply pull out. And of course as of this writing, the United States hasn't paid its dues to the organization in years.

None of this bodes well for the kind of international system many Americans had hoped would emerge in the wake of the Cold War. The imperatives that brought forth the Monroe Doctrine are now but a memory. Rather than grasping the opportunity thus presented to fashion a more cooperative and productive hemispheric system, the United States seems stuck in a time warp. The policies it has followed so far neither advance the cause of an international system based on rule of law, nor do they even serve U.S. interests and objectives.

NOTES

1. See Lars Schoultz, University of North Carolina, "Inter-American Security: The Changing Perceptions of U.S. Policymakers," a paper dated April 1990. See also Wayne S. Smith, "The United States and South America: Beyond the Monroe Doctrine," in *Current History*, February 1991.

2. Quoted in Julius W. Pratt, *A History of U.S. Foreign Policy* (Englewood Cliffs, N.J.: Prentice-Hall, 1955), p. 165.

3. Gaddis Smith, *Last Years of the Monroe Doctrine* (New York: Hill and Wang, 1994), p. 8.

4. Pratt, *History of U.S. Foreign Policy*, p. 348.

5. Wayne S. Smith, *Portrait of Cuba* (Atlanta: Turner Publishing, 1991); see footnote on p. 41.

6. George Black, *The Good Neighbor* (New York: Pantheon Books, 1988), p. 16.

7. Louis A. Perez, Jr., *Cuba Between Empires* (Pittsburgh: University of Pittsburgh Press, 1983), p. 327.

8. Quoted in Black, *The Good Neighbor*, p. 23.

9. Quoted in Wayne S. Smith, "Will the U.S. Again Send in the Marines?" in *World Paper*, November 1983.

10. J. Reuben Clark, *Memorandum on the Monroe Doctrine* (Washington, D.C.: U.S. Government Printing Office, 1930).

11. Ann Van Wynen Thomas and A. J. Thomas, Jr., *The Organization of American States* (Dallas, Tex.: Southern Methodist University Press, 1963), p. 356, conclude that "the Rio Treaty is the final step to date in the multilateralization of the Monroe Doctrine." See also Samuel Guy Inman's account of Republican senator Arthur Vandenberg's conclusion that this would be the effect of the OAS, in *Inter-American Conferences, 1826–1954: History and Problems* (Washington, D.C.: University Press of Washington, 1965), pp. 221–222.

12. See Smith, *Last Years,* pp. 78–84. For perhaps the most penetrating study of the U.S. intervention in Guatemala, see Piero Gleijeses, *Shattered Hope* (Princeton, N.J.: Princeton University Press, 1991).

13. See Stephen G. Rabe, *Eisenhower and Latin America* (Chapel Hill: University of North Carolina Press, 1988), p. 94.

14. Smith, *Last Years,* pp. 122–129.

15. Ibid., pp. 196–199.

16. Dana Priest, "U.S. Instructed Latins on Executions, Torture," *Washington Post,* September 21, 1996.

17. Smith, *Last Years,* p. 7.

18. James Brooke, "Peru Suggests U.S. Rethink Eradication in Land Where Coca Is Still King," *New York Times,* November 18, 1990, p. 3.

19. Ibid.

20. See discussion in the following articles in the *New York Times:* Sanjoy Hazarika, "India Is Facing Ecological Quandary in Plans to Dam River," April 11, 1992, p. 8; Gwen Ifill, "Clinton Links Ecology with Jobs," April 23, 1992, p. 22; Keith Schneider, "U.S. to Reject Pact on Protection of Wildlife and Global Resources," May 30, 1992, p. 1; James Brooke, "U.S. Has a Starring Role at Rio Summit as Villain," June 2, 1992, p. A10.

21. See article by Deputy Secretary of State Strobe Talbott, "Our Mission and the Global Environment," *State Magazine,* December 31, 1996, pp. 15–32.

22. Interview with a senior Brazilian diplomat who requested anonymity, Washington, D.C., May 1990.

23. Molly Moore, "Three Years After Mexico Embraced Free Trade, Rural Poor Still Flock to the Capital," *Washington Post,* December 31, 1996, pp. A12–13.

24. Ibid.

25. Figures are taken from tables 6 and 8 of *U.S. Foreign Trade Highlights, 1995* (U.S. Department of Commerce, International Trade Administration, Office of Trade and Economic Analysis, August 1996).

26. See the interesting debate in Council on Foreign Relations, ed., *Might vs. Right* (New York: Council on Foreign Relations, 1989). See especially the presentation by Jeane Kirkpatrick and Allan Gerson, "The Reagan Doctrine, Human Rights, and International Law," pp. 37–71, in which they make the point that respect for international law is based on reciprocity, that is, if I respect it, so must you.

27. See the transcript of *Crossfire* on CNN, December 30, 1992.

SUGGESTED READINGS

Langley, Lester. *America and the Americans.* Athens: University of Georgia Press, 1989.

Munro, Dana. *Intervention and Dollar Diplomacy.* Princeton, N.J.: Princeton University Press, 1964.

Smith, Gaddis. *Last Years of the Monroe Doctrine.* New York: Hill and Wang, 1994.

Smith, Peter. *Talons of the Eagle: Dynamics of U.S.–Latin American Relations.* New York: Oxford University Press, 1996.

Whitaker, Arthur. *The Western Hemisphere Idea.* Ithaca: Cornell University Press, 1954.

Wood, Bryce. *The Dismantling of the Good Neighbor Policy.* Austin: University of Texas Press, 1985.

_____. *The Making of the Good Neighbor Policy.* Austin: University of Texas Press, 1961.

16

LATIN AMERICA
IN THE WORLD

LARMAN C. WILSON

Latin America's role in the world has undergone extensive change in recent decades: first during the Cold War and then since its end. Though progress was retarded in the 1980s by the oil and debt crises, the area's involvement in global affairs expanded in the 1970s. Among the several factors contributing to change and expansion have been U.S. policy toward Latin America and the response of the area, and of certain countries in particular, to that policy. In an attempt to reduce their dependence on the United States and thereby improve their bargaining positions, a number of Latin American countries have turned to the industrialized countries of Europe and to Japan. Meanwhile, Japan and several Western European states have actively and successfully increased their trade with, investments in, and aid to Latin America. This has not only increased the influence of these countries in the region, but has assured the decline in relative terms of U.S. hegemony. Another reason for the redirection of economic relations has been the change in political and/or ideological orientations of certain Latin American governments, whether by military coup (the Dominican Republic in 1963, Brazil in 1964, Peru in 1968, Chile in 1973, and Grenada in 1983), by revolution or insurrection (Bolivia in 1952, Cuba in 1959, and Nicaragua in 1979), or by election (Chile in 1970, Jamaica in 1972, and Peru in 1985). As a result of political changes, a few new governments joined the Nonaligned Movement and announced that they would pursue an independent foreign policy; Peru, for example, did so in 1968. In addition, a few governments or presidents have aspired to Third World leadership via the Nonaligned Movement (e.g., Luis Echeverría of Mexico, 1970–1976, and Fidel Castro). Reflecting the Latin American preoccupation with economic development, a new approach was adopted in the United Nations Conference on Trade and Development (UNCTAD) and the third UN Law of the Sea Conference (UNLOS III) for bringing about a New International Economic Order. Furthermore, the new states in the Caribbean, the former British territories, had views toward Latin America, and particularly toward Cuba, that diverged sharply from those of the United States. An additional factor contributing to change during the Cold War was the improving economic status of a few Latin American states—Brazil, Venezuela, and Mexico—which became substantial exporters of manufactured goods and/or petroleum.

Second, certain developments near and after the Cold War's end (1989) and the Soviet Union's collapse (1991) also affected the role of the Latin American and Caribbean states. These developments increased the economic dependency of some states and increased the economic dominance of the United States. In the mid-1980s, the International Monetary Fund (IMF) added to its standby arrangement mechanism that of structural adjustment. Both mechanisms established conditions, often harsh ones, that had to be met by a state in difficult financial straits in order to receive credits or loans. An extreme example was provided by Mexico after the late 1994 collapse of the peso. The $50 billion bailout package arranged by the IMF and the United States imposed strict fiscal and monetary controls and required as collateral Mexico's oil exports. The other development was the revival of the regional integration movement and a new free trade movement. Both were signaled by President George Bush's proposed 1990 Enterprise for the Americas (ETA), a hemispheric free-trade zone. In 1991, four states—Argentina, Brazil, Paraguay, and Uruguay—formed a Southern Cone Common Market (Mercosur). And in 1995, the North American Free Trade Agreement (NAFTA) among Canada, Mexico, and the United States became effective. The United States is the prime mover in NAFTA for negotiating the terms of association or entry for other states.

The new position Brazil achieved in the world during the Cold War, particularly its major economic ties with the Federal Republic of Germany, illustrates a number of the above reasons for change. First, in 1975, Brazil turned to West Germany and signed a nuclear treaty with that country, which provided for the sale by West Germany of a complete nuclear fuel cycle. This arrangement was made because of U.S. restrictions on the export of technology and equipment for the enrichment of uranium and the separation of plutonium. The Carter administration applied diplomatic pressure on Brazil in an unsuccessful effort to secure annulment of the treaty. Brazil was antagonized by this pressure as well as by pressure exerted later when the United States announced that it was cutting off aid to Brazil on account of human rights violations. Brazil responded by rejecting U.S. military assistance, thus ending the long "special relationship" that had existed between the two countries. Although private U.S. capital in Brazil is still greater than capital from any other country, that of Germany is substantial: in the early 1980s, 53 percent of West German private capital in Latin America was in Brazil.[1] In terms of trade, one-third of West Germany's Latin American imports came from Brazil, and one-third of its exports to Latin America went to Brazil.[2] (German investment in and trade with Brazil have changed since the early 1980s. Investment has since shifted to favor Mexico, although German investment in Brazil was $5.6 billion in 1990. German exports to Mexico and Brazil among Latin American countries in 1991 were 33 percent and 25 percent, respectively.[3])

Brazil has demonstrated its increasing regional power status in the post–Cold War period, for its leadership led to the 1991 formation of Mercosur. President Fernando H. Cardoso is challenging the United States and NAFTA and is moving toward the creation of a South American Free Trade Area—by the merging of Mercosur and the Andean Pact—as an alternative to NAFTA.

Latin America's changing role in the world highlights two triangular sets of relationships: an older Atlantic triangle linking Latin America with the United States and Western Europe,[4] and a newer Pacific triangle linking Latin America with the United States and Japan.[5] As a result of recent changes, the side of the triangle joining Latin America with Western Europe is being strengthened by the Lomé accords and the activities of the Institute for European–Latin American Relations (IRELA), while the one with the United States is being weakened because of problems negotiating an arrangement of association and parity with NAFTA and the U.S. Cuban embargo. On the other side, the Pacific triangle is experiencing a strengthening of the side joining Latin America (particularly Brazil and Mexico) and Japan and a relative weakening of the Latin American–U.S. linkage. The Japan–Latin American link is overshadowed, however, by the sizable trade between Japan and the United States.

Although focusing primarily on Latin American relations with Europe and Japan, this chapter will also consider Latin American relations with the former Soviet bloc and China. The context for examination will be East-West and North-South—that is, first Cold War competition and then developed or industrialized states vis-à-vis developing ones. There will be no consideration of the limited but increasing relations on the South-South axis.

RELATIONS WITH THE SOVIET UNION AND THE COMMUNIST STATES

Cuba

After Cuba's incorporation into the Soviet system, the Soviet Union supported the Cuban economy not only through trade, but also through furnishing convertible currency for Cuba's trade with the Western states, financing trade deficits, buying Cuban sugar above the world price, providing military equipment, and giving direct credit for economic development.

Cuba's dependency upon the Soviet bloc was well established by 1961, when the bloc accounted for 74 percent of Cuba's exports and 70 percent of its imports. The Soviet Union (USSR) itself accounted for 48.5 percent and 41 percent, respectively.[6] (Trade with the Soviet bloc declined in the late 1970s and early 1980s, but increased to 87 percent in 1987.[7]) While total USSR economic aid exceeded $8 billion by 1976, it was between $4 and $5 billion per year since that time until reduced by Gorbachev in 1986.[8] The sugar subsidy had been paid almost regularly, since the world price had usually been lower than the Cuban cost of production. In 1974–

1975, however, Cuba had a bonanza because the world price was very high. Consequently, Cuba was creditworthy in convertible currency in its trade with the West and received credits in the early and mid-1970s from Canada, England, Japan, France, West Germany, Spain, and Sweden.[9] Soviet trade subsidies for 1961–1986 were at $35 billion, as follows: sugar—$27 billion, oil—$6 billion, and nickel—$555 million.[10] Soviet military aid had been considerable, estimated at $1.5 billion through 1969 and $875 million for the period 1975–1979 and $7.8 billion for the period 1982–1986.[11] Military assistance from Eastern Europe had been in the form of loans, but such aid from the Soviet Union, since 1962, had been in the form of grants.

There is another side to Cuba's foreign policy stance, despite its economic dependency, its endorsement of the 1968 Soviet intervention in Czechoslovakia, and its membership, since 1972, in the Council for Mutual Economic Assistance (COMECON). Some Cuban autonomy in foreign policy was demonstrated by its activism in the United Nations and the Nonaligned Movement, its support for revolutionary movements in both Latin America and Africa, and its strong support of Third World goals. Cuba was the first Latin American country to join the Nonaligned Movement when it was founded in Yugoslavia in 1961. (At various times in the 1970s, Argentina, Bolivia, Chile, Grenada, Guyana, Jamaica, Nicaragua, and Peru were members, although several of these countries have since withdrawn. Most of the Commonwealth Caribbean states joined when they became independent.) Castro was very active in the organization and tried to move it to the left, thus provoking great controversy, e.g., his endorsement of the 1979 Soviet invasion of Afghanistan. Nonetheless, Castro was elected president of the organization for a three-year term; he presided over the conference when it met in Cuba in 1979, the first meeting to be held in Latin America.

Also in the 1960s, Cuba took a strong stand at the Tricontinental (1966) and Latin American Solidarity (1967) Conferences in favor of supporting revolutionary movements, a stance that was opposed by the Soviet Union. Cuba supported various guerrilla organizations both before and after these conferences and into the early 1970s. After a respite, Cuba resumed such support in the late 1970s, and along with several other Latin American states, including Costa Rica, Panama, and Venezuela, provided arms, training, and transport to the Sandinistas in their successful insurrection against Somoza in Nicaragua. In similar fashion, Cuba also helped the left in its rebellion against the government in El Salvador in 1981, an action the Reagan administration considered to be Soviet intervention via Cuba and Nicaragua. The United States thereby justified as counterintervention its increasing economic and military aid to El Salvador and covert activities against Nicaragua. These covert acts—prohibited by the Congress and which undermined the Central American peace process (initiated by Colombia, Mexico, Panama, and Venezuela)—included the mining of Nicaraguan harbors and supporting (arming and provisioning) the Contras, a Nicaraguan exile army operating out of Honduras.[12] President Reagan's Cold War approach and his unilateral policies were opposed by most Latin American governments and members of the EEC and NATO.

What is more important for consideration here, however, is Cuba's support of revolutionary governments in Africa, particularly the sending of combat troops, which was unprecedented. There is great debate about whether Cuba became militarily involved in Africa, first in Angola in 1976, as a surrogate of the Soviet Union or for its own reasons. Whatever the motives, Cuban troops fought to keep the revolutionary government in power in Angola, and they also fought in Ethiopia against Somalia. It has been estimated that in the early 1980s, Cuba had almost 50,000 troops in seventeen African countries.[13] After many years of negotiations—mediated by the United States—to end the civil war in Angola as well as outside involvement by South Africa and the Southwest African People's Organization (SWAPO) in Namibia, agreement was reached and an accord signed in December 1988. The accord provided for the withdrawal of all foreign troops by July 1991: Angolan from Namibia, Cuban from Angola, and South African from Namibia.[14]

Relations between Cuba and the USSR deteriorated after Mikhail Gorbachev became first secretary of the Communist Party in 1985. Although agreements were signed providing new and increased credits of $3 billion for 1986–1990,[15] Gorbachev announced that Soviet aid to Cuba would be cut (oil exports were cut back in 1985). His policies of *glasnost* (liberalization and openness) and *perestroika* (decentralization and modernization) resulted in his criticism of Castro's policies. Castro had criticized Gorbachev's new approaches and the withdrawal from Afghanistan even before his visit to Cuba in April 1989.[16] Castro had also criticized the reforms in the People's Republic of China (PRC) that began in the early 1980s, but he approved the suppression that ended them the summer of 1989.

Other Latin American Countries

The various forms of relations between the Communist states and Latin America—economic and trade, diplomatic, military, and political—reflected common interests as well as the state of Latin American–U.S. and Soviet-U.S. relations. The Communist states, especially the Soviet Union, were striving to enhance their influence—economic, ideological, and political—as well as to improve their economic situation. They attempted to capitalize upon problems between the United States and individual Latin American republics, but in ways that did not involve running serious political risk. Soviet and Eastern European relations with Chile during the period of the Allende government, with Peru during the military governments of Generals Juan Velasco Alvarado (1968–1975) and Francisco Morales Bermúdez (1975–1980), and with Nicaragua under the Daniel Ortega government (1980–1990) are examples. For their part, some Latin American governments have dealt with the Communist states as an offset to the United States—as a means of bargaining for better terms with the United States, to diversify their dependency, and/or to demonstrate their independence from the United States. Argentina's large sale of wheat to the Soviet Union (1980–1982) in defiance of President Carter's embargo was a combination of an independent foreign policy, retaliation against the United

States for its human rights policy, and the need for export income, which was exacerbated by Argentina's inability to sell wheat to EEC countries.

During the presidency of Salvador Allende (1970–1973), Chile experienced an expansion of economic and diplomatic relations with the Communist states, including the People's Republic of China. The Allende government received a number of loans from the USSR and Eastern European countries, but not nearly enough to save the Chilean economy. The total value of loans received from these countries was $656 million: $260.5 million from the USSR and $395.5 million from the other Communist states ($276 million was provided by other Latin American countries, Western Europe, and Japan).[17] Following Allende's overthrow, the Communist states—with the exception of China—broke off or suspended relations with Chile. In 1977, however, the Pinochet government renegotiated the Allende-era debt, which resulted in a resurgence of trade with most of the Communist countries.

In the early 1970s, Argentina began establishing relations with Eastern European countries and permitting them to set up trade offices and/or consulates in Argentina. Thereafter, Argentine trade with the Soviet Union steadily increased, particularly Argentine exports of beef and wheat. Starting in 1978, the USSR began a sales drive to reduce its widening trade imbalance with Argentina. These efforts resulted in contracts for turbines for the Paraná Medio Dam, a $2.5 billion project the Soviet Union had been awarded the contract to design. As already mentioned, Argentina refused to comply with the Carter administration's embargo on grain sales to the USSR and greatly increased its exports of wheat. In 1981, for example, Argentine exports to the Soviet Union were $1.8 billion, 78 percent of the Latin American export total to the USSR and 47 percent of total Latin American exports to all of the Communist states.[18]

Brazil's percentage of total Latin American exports to the Soviet Union increased from 4.6 percent in 1975 to 27 percent in 1979.[19] In 1981, it was 17 percent due to an increase in Soviet imports from Latin America, but the Soviet total decreased thereafter to $2.5 billion and remained there until the mid-1980s. Soviet imports dropped off in the late 1980s, which resulted in Brazil's portion—20 percent in the mid-1980s—increasing later in the decade. All the Communist states had trade imbalances with Brazil because of their heavy importation of food and raw materials. Consequently, they provided credits to stimulate Brazilian importation of their equipment and machinery.[20] In the late 1970s, Brazil accepted its largest single credit from Eastern Europe, $200 million from the German Democratic Republic. China signed its first agreement with Brazil in 1978, which was followed by a contract for exchanging Brazilian iron ore for Chinese oil. In 1982, the Brazilian government proposed an industrial cooperation program with the USSR for manufacturing heavy equipment. At the time of the announcement, the secretary-general of the Brazilian Foreign Ministry stressed Brazil's commitment to increase its bilateral trade with the Soviet Union and thereby diversify its trade patterns. Its import package from the USSR cost $154 million in 1981; this increased to almost $200 million in 1982, but started declining and was below $100 million by 1985, where it remained through the 1980s.[21]

Nicaragua became a recipient of Soviet arms in the 1980s. Once the Sandinista-led insurrection toppled General Anastasio Somoza in 1979 and the Sandinistas came to power, Cuba became the first principal provider of aid. The USSR began making arms available and steadily increased them as the confrontation between Nicaragua and the United States mounted. The arms included artillery, helicopters, and tanks. In the 1980s, Nicaragua received $679 million and $1.6 billion in economic aid from Eastern Europe and the USSR, respectively.[22]

For the 1954–1987 period, economic aid to Latin America from the USSR and Eastern European countries amounted to almost $7 billion, with over 50 percent being furnished by the USSR. The principal recipients were (excluding Cuba and Nicaragua), in descending order, Brazil, Argentina, Peru, Bolivia, Colombia, and Peru, with Argentina and Bolivia receiving more aid from the USSR than Eastern Europe[23] (if the cutoff year is 1979, Chile under Allende was in third place). There was also mounting tension between the USSR and Cuba and Nicaragua due to the critical and restrictive policies of Secretary Gorbachev.

LATIN AMERICA AND THIRD WORLD BARGAINING

Since the 1960s, Latin American initiatives to promote economic development have included the formation of bargaining blocs of developing states, operating on both the regional and the global levels. The contemporary struggle to alter their relations with the industrialized countries resulted in a North-South confrontation. The main channels for bargaining and waging the struggle have been the United Nations, particularly two of its organs, the General Assembly and the Economic and Social Council (ECOSOC); certain conferences sponsored by the United Nations, e.g., UNCTAD and UNLOS III; the formation of commodity agreements patterned after those of the Organization of Petroleum Exporting Countries (OPEC); and the creation of the Latin American Economic System (SELA).

Certain long-run trends involving Latin America's changing place in the world have been clear for some time—although slowed in the 1980s by the debt crisis—and have been accelerated by Third World activism and bargaining. Two good examples concern trade and investment. The trend has been for Latin American exports of food and raw materials to decline, while exports of manufactures have increased, and for U.S. private investment to decline in relative terms in Latin America.[24] Although previously, the Latin American governments bargained on a regional basis with the United States for greater access for their exports to the U.S. market, for greater cooperation in support of commodity arrangements, and for the transfer of U.S. technology to Latin America in the 1970s, these states turned to Europe and Japan in seeking the same goals and bargained more on an international basis. (In the late 1980s, there was a return to regional bargaining as part of regional integration and a free-trade movement, discussed below.) In the 1980s, many Latin American states stressed access to the industrial northern markets rather than higher export prices. Many have also changed their attitudes toward private investment and multinational corporations; now they want the former to increase and the latter to return, subject to local control. (The Reagan administration's 1983 Caribbean Basin Initiative, CBI, still in effect in the late 1990s, was a much later partial response, even though its main goal was to isolate Nicaragua.)

Inspired by the ideas of ECLA, and disturbed by the serious economic problems of the late 1950s and early 1960s as well as by U.S. preoccupation with security, the Latin American republics began to work through certain regional caucusing groups, e.g., the Special Latin American Coordinating Committee (CECLA); the Special Committee for Consultation and Negotiation (CECON); the UN Latin American Group (LAG); and the Group of 77 (G-77, numbering about 120 members in the early 1980s), the caucus of developing states in the United Nations. The Latin Americans were successful in getting many of their regionally developed ideas and positions adopted by the UN General Assembly, by UNCTAD, and by UNLOS III. And some of them were accepted by the developed states (see LOS III below).

The G-77 found UNCTAD to be a very useful forum in bargaining with the industrialized states (once the conference was organized, Raúl Prebisch of ECLA was appointed its executive secretary). At the first three meetings of UNCTAD—in 1964 (Switzerland), 1969 (India), and 1972 (Chile)—the G-77 put forward the following recommendations: that the industrialized countries provide 1 percent of their GNP in the form of aid to the Third World states; that an increased number of commodity agreements be concluded; that the developed countries grant concessions to the developing states without reciprocal concessions; that a compulsory code of conduct be drawn up for regulating transnational enterprises; and that a charter on the economic rights and duties of states be prepared as a major step toward creating the New International Economic Order.

In response, the northern states were willing to accept the 1 percent figure for aid to the Third World, but only on a voluntary basis. The formation of commodity agreements for the purpose of stabilizing prices, especially for food and mineral exports, was also supported, although some of the industrialized nations were opposed. (It is worth recalling that Venezuela initiated the formation of OPEC in 1960.) The developed states responded positively to the proposal of granting trade concessions on a nonreciprocal basis and committed themselves to the concept of granting preferences to the less developed countries (LDCs). This approach was accepted both by the General Agreement on Tariffs and Trade (GATT) and by the European Economic Community (EEC) in the Lomé accords, to be discussed below. The industrialized nations' response to a compulsory code to regulate the multinationals was mixed: They were not opposed to the drafting of such a code by the United Nations but believed that it should be applied on a voluntary basis. In 1974, the United Nations created a commission and a center on transnational corporations for the purpose of monitoring the conduct of such companies.

Latin America in general and certain countries in particular have made major contributions to changing the economic, legal, and political relations between North and South. These contributions are illustrated by Mexican leadership in the drafting of the 1974 economic charter and by Peruvian and Venezuelan leadership during the lengthy UNLOS III (1973–1982). At the 1972 UNCTAD meeting in Chile, Mexican president Luis Echeverría suggested that the United Nations draft a set of economic obligations on the rights and duties of states. His appeal resulted in the UN Charter on the Economic Rights and Duties of States, which was approved by the General Assembly in 1974 as a chapter in the Program of Action on the Establishment of a New Economic Order. Among other things, the charter stressed the right of expropriation of foreign assets, high and stable prices for Third World exports, and preferential treatment without reciprocity. (On a regional basis, the presidents of Mexico and Venezuela initiated the formation of SELA in 1975, a strictly Latin American bloc, including Cuba, to bargain over U.S. economic and trade policies.)

The Latin American contribution to UNLOS III began in the early 1950s when three states—Ecuador, Chile, and Peru—signed an accord in which they claimed a 200-mi (352-km) territorial waters limit for the purpose of regulating the catching of tuna off their coasts. They justified this extension of jurisdiction as a means of protecting an important resource and source of revenue for developing countries. This move was viewed by the United States, in particular, as contrary to international law. U.S. opposition and advice to private fishermen not to comply resulted in the so-called Tuna War, as Ecuador and Peru started seizing and fining U.S. fishing boats in the late 1960s and early 1970s. In the 1960s, however, other Latin American governments followed suit in claiming a 200-mi limit, a claim soon joined by African and Asian states. This was one of many issues that demonstrated the need to negotiate a series of new treaties on the law of the sea.

From the time the second session of UNLOS III began in Venezuela in 1974 until the final session ended in New York in 1982, the Third World countries employed a political bargaining strategy to achieve their goals. By means of bloc caucusing and bargaining, the G-77 was successful in having its positions adopted. One major goal was the acceptance of the 200-mi limit; this, in fact, became the 200-mi exclusive economic zone (EEZ). At the end of the long North-South negotiation process, a few of the industrialized states found the final draft unacceptable, e.g., the Reagan administration, which objected specifically to the deep seabed mining provision. The convention was voted on at the United Nations in 1982 and received overwhelming Third World support. Only four states voted against it—Israel, Turkey, the United States, and Venezuela—and seventeen abstained, including Belgium, the Netherlands, Luxembourg, West Germany, Britain, Italy, Spain, Thailand, and the Soviet-bloc members. Although the convention had the needed sixty ratifications to go into effect in November 1994 (it included those of twelve Commonwealth Caribbean states and seven Latin American states), it did not include those of most developed states and the United States. Since the mid-1980s there had been negotiations about the International Seabed Authority, which finally resulted in an Implementation Agreement in July 1994. Three months later, President Clinton sent the 1982 convention and new agreement with his request for approval to the U.S.

Senate. No action was taken, and ratification remained up to the Senate in the 1997 Congress.

RELATIONS WITH WESTERN EUROPE AND THE EUROPEAN COMMUNITY

The four Lomé accords (1975–1980, 1980–1985, 1985–1990, 1990–2000), which govern economic relations between the EC and many Third World states, mainly in Africa but also some in the Caribbean and the Pacific, follow the model that resulted from the bargaining of the G-77 at UNCTAD. Lomé I was prompted by the 1973 entry into the EEC of Denmark, Great Britain, and Ireland and the decision of several former Commonwealth countries in Africa, the Caribbean, and the Pacific (ACP states) to join the eighteen African states already associated with the EEC via the 1963 Yaoundé Convention.[25] In 1975, there were fifty-seven ACP states associated with the EEC, six of them in the Caribbean (fifteen by 1991).

The European Development Fund contributes to financing the development of ACP projects, which are supplemented by loans from the European Investment Bank. The funds made available have been increased 72 percent by Lomé II. The EC also has a small but expanding aid program to nonassociated states; four Central American states were added in the mid-1980s, and Haiti was added via the 1987 "Comprex" plan to aid the world's least developed nations. In terms of development assistance, the European states—i.e., Germany, Great Britain, France, the Netherlands, and Sweden—have steadily increased their aid since the late 1970s, eclipsing that of the United States.[26]

Although the EEC entered into a trade agreement with the Andean Common Market in 1981, a number of the more developed countries in Latin America have encountered problems of access to the European market. The EEC also entered into a number of nonpreferential trade agreements in the 1970s for three- to five-year periods, subject to renewal, with Argentina, Brazil, Mexico, and Uruguay. Problems have developed, however, over agricultural imports from Latin America in view of the EEC's Common Agricultural Policy. This is one reason why Argentina turned to the Soviet Union as a major buyer of Argentine grain exports, especially wheat. The Latin Americans hoped that the entry into the EEC by Portugal and Spain in 1986—the latter was seen as a "bridge"—would greatly improve the access of their exports. The situation started improving a few years later on account of the activities of the Institute for European–Latin American Relations, established by the European Community in Madrid in 1985. IRELA's expanding activities in the late 1980s and 1990s resulted in EC agreements and regular relations with the Andean Group and Mercosur (there is an EC group that monitors integration in Latin America), the Latin American Parliament, and the Rio Group.

Another area of change was Latin America's increasing purchase of arms from Europe. The arms employed in the 1982 Falklands/Malvinas War between Argentina and Britain indicated the variety of arms sellers. (During this war, sparked by

Argentina's April island invasion, the Latin American states viewed it as a regional matter under the OAS, whereas Great Britain, the United States, and the EC considered it a global one under the UN Security Council. The latter view prevailed, and the Security Council passed an OAS resolution condemning the EC's sanctions against Argentina.[27]) Argentina had combat planes made in England, France, Israel, and the United States; its navy included vessels from England, West Germany, and the United States; and the infantry had weapons from England, Eastern Europe, Israel, and the United States. Until the late 1960s, the United States monopolized the sale of arms, particularly of planes, ships, and tanks, and the provision of military training to Latin America. Because of U.S. congressionally imposed restrictions, bureaucratic delays, and attractive terms offered by European countries, some of the Latin American governments, starting with Peru, turned to Europe. Despite the ending of the U.S. monopoly, the United States is still an important arms supplier. However, Argentina and Brazil have developed their own arms industries, and the latter has become an ambitious arms exporter to its neighbors as well as to other countries.

RELATIONS WITH JAPAN AND CHINA

Since the 1970s, the influence of Japan as a rising economic superpower has resulted in a balancing of commercial power among Japan, Europe, and the United States in Latin America. Japan's exports to Latin America began to mount in the late 1960s and moved from light manufactures to heavy-industrial and chemical products, reflecting the great development of heavy industry in Japan. The former exports were replaced by the latter categories, which increased threefold by 1970 and thereafter came to constitute 80 percent of Japan's total exports to Latin America in the 1970s and 1980s.[28] Japan's exports increased from $8.2 billion in 1987 to $12.2 billion in 1991.[29] Although the composition of Japan's exports changed, the percentage of its total exports to Latin America has not fluctuated very much, remaining in the area of 4–7 percent.

On the other hand, Japan's imports from Latin America continued to increase in the 1970s and included, in descending order of importance, minerals, fuels, foodstuffs, and metal ores. More specifically, Japan imports copper from Chile and Peru; iron ore from Brazil, Chile, and Peru; cotton from Brazil and Mexico; and foodstuffs from Argentina and Brazil.[30] Imports started to decline after the second oil crisis in 1978 as Japan shifted to the Middle East for oil, and they remained around 4.5 percent in the 1980s[31] but increased from $6 to $9.3 billion from 1987 to 1991.[32] Japanese exports greatly increased in the 1970s, especially to Argentina, Brazil, and Chile. The 1987 breakdown of exports (and imports) by country was: Panama—$3 billion ($89 million); Mexico—$1 billion ($1.4 billion); Brazil—$975 million ($1.8 billion); and Venezuela—$492 million ($330 million).[33] (Panama heads the list, receiving 33 percent of total exports, mainly because it buys Japanese ships that are used by third countries under Panama's flag of convenience.)

Concerning the flow of economic cooperation—a composite of aid, export credits, and private funds—Japan's flow to Latin America increased from almost 17 percent in 1971 to 46 percent only two years later, which then exceeded its flow to Asia (39 percent), the country's natural area of economic penetration. Japan's official development assistance (ODA) to Latin American countries amounted to about $118 million; the major beneficiaries were Brazil, Bolivia, and Paraguay.[34] This amount jumped to a $50 billion Japanese government commitment for 1988–1992.[35] What really has elevated the economic cooperation flow figure is direct private investment, for it has increased at a much faster rate than trade. During the period from 1969 until the mid-1970s, Japan's direct investment increased eightfold, thus placing Latin America in fourth place in terms of investment, right after the United States, Asia, and Europe, respectively. However, Latin America moved to third place in Japan's total accumulated foreign investment ($106 billion) by region for the period 1951–1986.[36]

In the early 1970s, Japanese investment in Latin America bypassed that of France, and in the late 1970s, it bypassed that of England. Over one-half of Japan's direct investment has continued to be in Brazil (it was $3.5 billion in 1994), where it ranked sixth in 1973, following that of the United States, West Germany, Canada, England, Switzerland, and France, respectively. Since that time, however, Japan has surpassed the last four and begun challenging Germany, the most important European exporter of capital to Brazil. In the mid-1980s, Japan made an important change while increasing its investment in Mexico (with 7 percent, it was in third place after the United States and Brazil): It began shifting out of its traditional fields of autos, electronics, and steel to Mexico's in-bond, or *maquiladora,* industry in order to compete in the U.S. market.[37] (It was announced during a summer 1989 visit by Prime Minister Toshiki Kaifu that Japan would loan Mexico $1 billion for an air pollution project in its capital.[38] The loan was made and later enlarged.)

A few words are in order about the general magnitude of Latin American economic relations with the People's Republic of China (PRC). The PRC–Latin American volume of trade was almost $3 billion in 1989; Brazil was first with $1.5 billion and Argentina second with a little over $500 million. Since that time, China's trade has been increasing with several Latin American countries, particularly with Mexico and Chile in the early 1990s. In addition, China has organized some joint ventures in the Caribbean and bought an iron ore mine in Peru.[39]

CONCLUSION

This chapter has examined the changing role and place in the world of Latin America in general and of certain major Latin American countries in particular during the Cold War and thereafter. Changing U.S. policies prompted the Latin American countries to look elsewhere for trade and aid, while Europeans and Japanese actively and successfully promoted their trade with, aid to, and investments in Latin America. This promotion has increased their influence in the region and has diminished Latin America's dependence on the United States. Furthermore, occasional changes of political orientation in some Latin American countries have resulted in periods of participation in the Nonaligned Movement and/or attempts to pursue an independent foreign policy. A few governments, such as those of Mexico and Cuba, have aspired to Third World leadership. Latin America's preoccupation with economic development has also been expressed through a new collective-bargaining approach and activism manifested in UNCTAD and in UNLOS III. Another factor in Latin America's changing global stature was the improving economic status of a few Latin American republics, which became exporters of manufactures and, in two cases—Argentina and Brazil—of armaments.

In their drive to become economically developed and to diversify their dependence, many of the more developed Latin American states appear to have come almost full circle. First in the 1960s and into the 1970s, they bargained for higher prices, for access to the U.S. market for their primary goods, and for more aid; then in the late 1970s and the 1980s, they placed restrictions upon private investment, nationalized some foreign companies, and demanded that international control be established over multinational corporations (MNCs). In the late 1980s and the 1990s, these states bargained for access for their industrial goods to the markets of the industrialized countries and are seeking more private investment and the reentry of the MNCs (often participants in privatization), although under effective local control.

Despite the enhanced role of Latin America in general and of certain states in particular in the international system and the changing patterns of dependence, it became clear that one form of dependence had increased in the 1980s: the dependence upon foreign lenders—governments, private banks, and multilateral lending institutions—as evidenced by the oppressive foreign debts and attendant problems suffered by most Latin American countries. This difficult situation started improving in the late 1980s with the refinancing and restructuring plans of U.S. treasury secretaries James Baker and Nicholas Brady. Also at this time there began a new movement— one affecting both the regional and global roles (they are interrelated) of the Latin American and Caribbean states—that stressed privatization (the buyers were mainly European and U.S. companies), regional integration, and free trade. A major indicator of the movement was President Bush's Enterprise for the Americas (ETA) proposal for a hemispheric free-trade association in June 1990. This was followed by the establishment of Mercosur (Argentina, Brazil, Paraguay, and Uruguay) in 1991, the Group of Three (Colombia, Venezuela, and Mexico) in 1993, and NAFTA (Canada, Mexico, and the United States) in January 1995.

To many in the Caribbean and Latin America, NAFTA seemed to be a means for reestablishing U.S. dominance, since it was the prime mover in negotiating the terms of other states' association with or entry into NAFTA. It also raised new fears of dependency and unequal treatment, particularly among the Caribbean/CARICOM and Central American/Central American Common Market states, who were concerned about the access of their exports to the U.S. market and their continued access via the 1984 Caribbean Basin Initiative (CBI). These states requested access parity with NAFTA and formed the Association of Caribbean States (ACS) in August 1995 to enhance their bargaining position. In South America, however, Brazil, the leader of Mercosur, is challenging the United States and overseeing the formation of a South American Free Trade Association (SAFTA)—by merging Mercosur and the Andean Pact members (from Chile to Venezuela)—as an alternative to NAFTA. While this regional competition is shaping up between the United States/NAFTA and Brazil/SAFTA, the Latin American and Caribbean countries are maintaining and strengthening their trilateralism—their relations with both Europe and Japan. Although the future course of this regional North-South struggle and its impact upon the world role of the Latin American and Caribbean states depend upon a number of factors, the leadership role and influence of the United States here as well as globally will continue to be compromised and impaired as long as it maintains the 1960 Cold War embargo against Cuba.

NOTES

1. Wolf Grabendorff, *West Germany and Brazil: A Showcase for the First World–Third World Relationship?* Occasional Papers Series no. 4 (Baltimore, Md.: Center of Brazilian Studies, School of Advanced International Studies, Johns Hopkins University, January 1980), p. 2.

2. *Ibid.* For Brazil's development and increasing status, see Werner Baer and Carlos von Doellinger, "Determinants of Brazil's Economic Policy," in Joseph Grunwald, ed., *Latin America and World Economy: A Changing International Order* (Beverly Hills, Calif.: Sage Publications, 1978), pp. 147–161; Baer, *The Brazilian Economy: Growth and Development,* 3d ed. (New York: Praeger, 1989); and Wayne A. Selcher, ed., *Brazil in the International System* (Boulder, Colo.: Westview Press, 1981).

3. Susan Kaufman Purcell and Françoise Simon, eds., *Europe and Latin America in the World Economy* (Boulder, Colo.: Lynne Rienner Publishers, 1995), pp. 20, 24, 93, 96.

4. Wolf Grabendorff and Riordan Roett, eds., *Latin America, Western Europe and the United States: Reevaluating the Atlantic Triangle* (New York: Praeger, 1985); and Gustavo Lagos Matus, ed., *Las Relaciones entre América Latina, Estados Unidos y Europa Occidental* (Santiago, Chile: Editorial Universitaria, 1980). See also Roett's chapter in Purcell and Simon, *Europe and Latin America.*

5. Barbara Stallings and Gabriel Székely, eds., *Japan, the United States, and Latin America* (Baltimore, Md.: Johns Hopkins University Press, 1993).

6. Jorge I. Domínguez, *Cuba: Order and Revolution* (Cambridge: Harvard University Press, 1978), pp. 149–154.

7. Speech of Ernesto Betancourt, USIA, Radio Martí, at Cuban American National Foundation conference, "The Cuban Revolution at 30," January 10, 1989.

8. W. Raymond Duncan, *The Soviet Union and Cuba: Interests and Influence* (New York: Praeger, 1985), pp. 105, 178.

9. Domínguez, *Cuba,* pp. 149–154. These credits and their sales to and trade with Cuba were all in defiance of the U.S. and OAS embargo against Cuba, by the United States in 1960 and by the OAS in 1964. The latter lifted its embargo in 1975.

10. U.S. Central Intelligence Agency (CIA), Directorate of Intelligence, *Handbook of Economic Statistics 1988: A Reference Aid* (Washington, D.C.: CIA, 1988), p. 181.

11. U.S. Department of State, Bureau of Public Affairs, *Cuban Armed Forces and the Soviet Military Presence,* Special Report no. 103 (Washington, D.C., August 1982), pp. 3–5; and U.S. Arms Control and Disarmament Agency (ACDA), *World Military Expenditures and Arms Transfers, 1987* (Washington, D.C.: GPO, 1988), p. 129.

12. Larman C. Wilson, "Contra Caper: A Secret War on Will of Congress," *Times of the Americas,* July 1, 1987.

13. William M. LeoGrande, *Cuba's Policy in Africa, 1959–1980,* Policy Paper no. 13 (Berkeley: Institute of International Studies, University of California, 1984); and Carmelo Mesa-Lago and June S. Belkin, eds., *Cuba in Africa* (Pittsburgh: University of Pittsburgh Press, 1981).

14. David B. Ottawa. "The Peace Process in Southern Africa: How the U.S. Brokered a Political Settlement," *Washington Post,* December 23, 1988.

15. Richard J. Payne, *Opportunities and Dangers of Soviet-Cuban Expansion: Towards a Pragmatic U.S. Policy* (Albany: State University of New York Press, 1988), p. 9. Since the promised credits were shortly reduced, Cuban imports dropped almost 75 percent from 1989 to 1992: from $8.1 billion to $2.2 billion. U.S. Central Intelligence Agency (CIA), Directorate of Intelligence, *Handbook of International Economic Statistics, 1993* (Washington, D.C.: CIA, 1993), p. 155.

16. *Diario las Américas,* January 7, 1989; and *Washington Post,* July 27, 1988.

17. Timothy F. Olsen, "What Caused the Downfall of the Allende Government?" (M.A. thesis, American University, Washington, D.C., 1979), p. 229.

18. IMF, *Direction of Trade Statistics,* 1982, pp. 46, 48, 66–67.

19. Augusto Varas, "The Soviet Union in the Foreign Relations of Latin America" (Paper presented at the 1982 annual meeting of the International Studies Association, Cincinnati, Ohio, March 24–27, 1982), p. 18.

20. U.S. Central Intelligence Agency (CIA), National Foreign Assessment Center, *Communist Aid Activities in Non-Communist Less Developed Countries 1978: A Research Paper,* ER 79–1041 2U (Washington, D.C.: CIA, 1979), p. 29.

21. IMF, *Direction of Trade Statistics Yearbook, 1988* (Washington, D.C.: IMF, 1988), p. 400.

22. CIA, *Handbook of Economic Statistics, 1988,* pp. 178–179.

23. CIA, National Foreign Assessment Center, *Handbook of Economic Statistics 1980: A Research Aid* (Washington, D.C.: CIA, 1980), p. 108; and CIA, *Handbook of Economic Statistics, 1988,* pp. 178–179.

24. Obie G. Whichard, "Trends in the U.S. Direct Investment Position Abroad, 1950–1979," *Survey of Current Business* 56 (February 1981), pp. 39–56. Total U.S. investment in Latin America declined from 38 percent in 1950 to 20 percent in 1979, and its composition was changed by a decline in petroleum investment and a substantial increase in manufacturing investment (pp. 41, 44). These trends continued in the 1980s. James W. Wilkie et al., eds., *Statistical Abstract of Latin America,* vol. 26 (Los Angeles: University of California, 1988), p. 711; and Purcell and Simon, *Europe and Latin America,* p. 21.

25. Lomé, where the two conventions were signed, is the capital of Togo; Yaoundé is the capital of Cameroon. For the leading works on the subject, see Glenn Mower, Jr., *The European Community and Latin America: A Case Study in Global Role Expansion* (Westport, Conn.: Greenwood Press, 1981), and Christopher Stevens, ed., *EEC and the Third World: A Survey, Renegotiating Lomé,* vol. 4 (New York: Holmes & Meier, 1985).

26. Over half of all development assistance to the Third World comes from Western Europe. In 1980, France gave over half the amount given by the United States, and the Federal Republic of Germany provided half the U.S. amount. Starting in 1970, the European states gave a higher percentage of their GNP than the United States did. Steven H. Arnold, *Implementing Development Assistance: European Approaches to Basic Needs* (Boulder, Colo.: Westview Press, 1982), pp. 2, 4. The Western European industrial states—plus the four Scandinavian states, Israel, Japan, Portugal, Spain, and Yugoslavia—have joined the Inter-American Development Bank.

27. Jack Child, "Present Trends in the Interamerican Security System and the Role of the Rio Treaty," in OAS, *Anuario Jurídico Interamericano 1983* (Washington, D.C.: OAS, 1984), pp. 49–58.

28. Adalbert Krieger Vasena and Javier Pazos, *Latin America: A Broader World Role* (London: Ernest Benn, 1973), p. 119; and Akio Hosono, "Economic Relationship Between Japan and Latin America," *Latin American Studies* 6 (1983), p. 79.

29. Barbara Stallings and Kotaro Horisaka, "Japan and Latin America: New Patterns in the 1990s," in Abraham F. Lowenthal and Gregory F. Treverton, eds., *Latin America in a New World* (Boulder, Colo.: Westview Press, 1994), p. 131.

30. Business International Corporation (BIC), *Business Latin America,* December 24, 1980, p. 414; and Wilkie et al., *Statistical Abstract of Latin America*, vol. 21 (1981), p. 435.

31. IMF, *Direction of Trade Statistics Yearbook, 1988*, p. 400; and Hosono, "Economic Relationship," pp. 76–77.

32. Stallings and Horisaka, "Japan and Latin America," p. 131.

33. BIC, *Business Latin America*, March 28, 1988, p. 99. See Barbara Stallings, "Panama and Japan: The Role of the Panama Canal," in Stallings and Székely, *Japan, the United States, and Latin America*, pp. 210–228.

34. Hosono, "Economic Relationship," p. 82.

35. Stallings and Horisaka, "Japan and Latin America," p. 138.

36. BIC, *Business Latin America,* March 28, 1988, p. 99.

37. BIC, *Business Latin America*, November 7, 1988, pp. 350–351.

38. *Washington Post,* August 30, 1989. See Gabriel Székely, "Mexico's International Strategy: Looking East and North," in Stallings and Székely, *Japan, the United States, and Latin America,* pp. 149–170.

39. Feng Xu, "China and Latin America After the Cold War's End," in Lowenthal and Treverton, *Latin America in a New World*, pp. 159–160.

SUGGESTED READINGS

Official Sources

There are several major sources of information and data on Latin American economic development, finances, and trade, including:

Institute for European-Latin American Relations. *Yearbook of European-Latin American Relations, 1996.* Madrid. Published annually.
Inter-American Development Bank. *Economic and Social Progress in Latin America.* Washington, D.C. Published annually.
International Monetary Fund. *Direction of World Trade.* Washington, D.C.

Organization of American States. *América en cifras.* Washington, D.C. Published annually.

United Nations, Economic Commission for Latin America. *Economic Survey of Latin America and the Caribbean.* Santiago, Chile. Published annually.

————. *Statistical Yearbook for Latin America.* Santiago, Chile. Published annually.

Wilkie, James W., ed. *Statistical Abstract of Latin America.* Published biennially at the University of California, Los Angeles. An invaluable private publication.

Books

Atkins, G. Pope. *Latin America in the International Political System.* 3d ed. Boulder, Colo.: Westview Press, 1995. This leading study in the field is by a political scientist who employs a systems approach in dealing with Latin America as a regional actor.

Calvert, Peter. *The International Politics of Latin America.* Manchester, UK: Manchester University Press, 1994. By a British scholar who uses a neorealist approach.

Davis, Harold E., and Larman C. Wilson et al. *Latin American Foreign Policies: An Analysis.* Baltimore, Md.: Johns Hopkins University Press, 1975. By a historian and political scientist and a group of country specialists who consider each country's relations with Europe, the Soviet bloc, and the Third World.

Ferris, Elizabeth, and Jennie K. Lincoln, eds. *Latin American Foreign Policies: Global and Regional Dimensions.* Boulder, Colo.: Westview Press, 1981. By a political scientist and a sociologist who have brought together an excellent set of articles. Part 2, "Latin American Global Foreign Policies," is especially relevant.

Fontaine, Roger W., and James D. Theberge, eds. *Latin America's New Internationalism: The End of Hemispheric Isolation.* New York: Praeger, 1976. By a political scientist and an economist who have included some very informative essays on Latin American relations with the Communist states, the Third World, Europe, and Japan.

Grabendorff, Wolf, and Riordan Roett, eds. *Latin America, Western Europe and the United States: Reevaluating the Atlantic Triangle.* New York: Praeger, 1985. By a German (director of IRELA in Madrid) and a U.S. scholar who have brought together the papers of leading experts in Europe, Latin America, and the United States presented at conferences held in each region.

Grunwald, Joseph, ed. *Latin America and World Economy: A Changing International Order.* Beverly Hills, Calif.: Sage Publications, 1978. Edited by an economist, and most chapters are by economists. Includes particularly factual and relevant essays in part 1, "Economic Relations with Industrial Countries."

Hellman, Ronald G., and H. Jon Rosenbaum, eds. *Latin America: The Search for a New International Economic Role.* New York: John Wiley and Sons, 1975. By two political scientists who have integrated a series of important essays, mainly by other political scientists. Part 4, "Latin America and the World," is especially pertinent.

Jaguarabe, Hélio. *El Nuevo Escenario Internacional.* Mexico City: Fondo de Cultura Económica, 1985. A Brazilian scholar's analysis of Latin America's place in the new international scene.

Lagos Matús, Gustavo, ed. *Las Relaciones entre América Latina, Estados Unidos y Europa Occidental.* Santiago, Chile: Editorial Universitaria, 1980. An excellent collection of essays on many facets of relations by Latin American experts.

Lowenthal, Abraham F., and Gregory F. Treverton, eds. *Latin America in a New World.* Boulder, Colo.: Westview Press, 1994. Edited by a political scientist and national security specialist, with a number of country and policy studies by leading experts. Chapter on China is first available.

Muñoz, Heraldo, and Joseph S. Tulchin, eds. *Latin American Nations in World Politics.* 2d ed. Boulder, Colo.: Westview Press, 1996. By a Chilean and a U.S. scholar who have assembled valuable essays by leading analysts in Latin America and the United States—and one West German.

Oxford Analytica. *Latin America in Perspective.* Boston: Houghton Mifflin, 1991. A British study team commissioned chapter contributions by European, Latin American, and U.S. specialists. Part on international relations has chapters on relations with countries and regions and on the roles of the IMF and World Bank.

Purcell, Susan Kaufman, and Françoise Simon, eds. *Europe and Latin America in the World Economy.* Boulder, Colo.: Lynne Rienner Publishers, 1995. Edited by two specialists in international economics and finance, this volume includes country studies by leading specialists and chapters on economic relations and integration. A major source of investment and trade data.

Stallings, Barbara, and Gabriel Székely, eds. *Japan, the United States and Latin America: Toward a Trilateral Relationship in the Western Hemisphere?* Baltimore, Md.: Johns Hopkins University Press, 1993. Edited by two political scientists, one U.S. and the other Mexican. Country studies by leading specialists with invaluable economic analysis and figures.

Specialized Works

Blasier, Cole. *The Giant's Revival: The USSR and Latin America.* Rev. ed. Pittsburgh: University of Pittsburgh Press, 1987.

Dent, David W., ed. *U.S.–Latin American Policymaking: A Reference Handbook.* Westport, Conn.: Greenwood Press, 1995.

Domínguez, Jorge. *Cuba: Internal and International Affairs.* Beverly Hills, Calif.: Sage Publications, 1982.

Duncan, W. Raymond. *The Soviet Union and Cuba: Interests and Influence.* New York: Praeger, 1985.

Heine, Jorge, and Leslie Manigat, eds. *The Caribbean and World Politics: Cross Currents and Cleavages.* New York: Holmes & Meier, 1988.

Kryzanek, Michael J. *U.S.–Latin American Relations.* 3d ed. Westport, Conn.: Praeger, 1996.

Lowenthal, Abraham F. *Partners in Conflict: The United States and Latin America.* Baltimore, Md.: Johns Hopkins University Press, 1987.

Maira, Luis, ed. *El Sistema Internacional y América Latina: Una Nueva Era de Hegemonía Norteamericano?* Buenos Aires: RIAL, Grupo Editor Latinoamericano, 1986.

Martz, John D., ed. *United States Policy in Latin America: A Quarter Century of Crisis and Challenge, 1961–1986.* Lincoln: University of Nebraska Press, 1989.

Milenky, Edward S. *Argentina's Foreign Policies.* Boulder, Colo.: Westview Press, 1987.

Purcell, Susan Kaufman, and Robert M. Immerman, eds. *Japan and Latin America in the New Global Order.* Boulder, Colo.: Lynne Rienner Publishers, 1992.

Seara Vásquez, Modesto. *Política Exterior de México.* 3d ed. Mexico, D.F.: Harper & Row Latinoamericana, 1985.

SELA, comp. *Relaciones Económicas Internacionales de América Latina.* Caracas: SELA, 1987.

Selcher, Wayne A., ed. *Brazil in the International System: The Rise of a Middle Power.* Boulder, Colo.: Westview Press, 1981.

Tomassini, Luciano, comp. *Relaciones internacionales de América Latina.* Mexico City: Fondo de Cultura Económica, 1981.

United Nations, Economic Commission for Latin America. *The Economic Relations of Latin America with Europe.* Santiago, Chile: ECLA, 1980.

Varas, Augusto, ed. *Soviet–Latin American Relations in the 1980s.* Boulder, Colo.: Westview Press, 1987.

Watson, Hilbourne A., ed. *The Caribbean in the Global Political Economy.* Boulder, Colo.: Lynne Rienner Publishers, 1994.

Professional Journals

Two Latin American journals with frequent, relevant articles on the global role of certain countries and Latin America are *Estudios internacionales* (University of Santiago, Chile) and *Foro internacional* (College of Mexico).

Two leading journals published in the United States that have occasional articles on the subject are *Journal of Latin American Studies and World Affairs* and *Latin American Research Review.*

Newspapers

The two most useful newspapers in English are *New York Times* and *Washington Post.*

Two very useful English digests reproducing newspaper articles are *Information Services Latin America* and *Keesing's Contemporary Archives.*

PART SEVEN
MEXICO

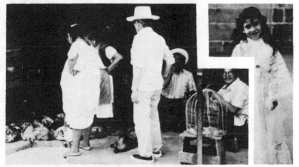

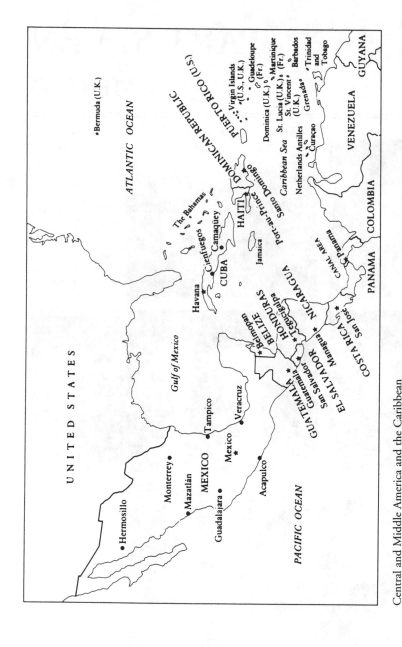

Central and Middle America and the Caribbean

Reprinted, with permission, from Howard J. Wiarda and Harvey F. Kline, eds., *Latin American Politics and Development*, Second Edition (Boulder, Colo.: Westview Press, 1985).

17

MEXICO: HISTORICAL FOUNDATIONS

FRED R. HARRIS

All nations and peoples are, more or less, products of their own history. Mexico and Mexicans are more so than most. Mexican sociologist Raúl Béjar Navarro has shown that studies seeking to prove that there is a unique Mexican "character" are largely impressionistic and unscientific.[1] But there certainly is, in Mexico, such a thing as national experience, a shared history.

History is not only a chronological recording of past events but also an attempt to explain the events. In order to understand a country and a people, then, we must know not only what has happened to them but also what they choose to remember and what they choose to make of what they remember—what they teach.

"To say Benito Juárez is to say Mexico. To say Mexico is to say sovereign nation." Those were the beginning words of a patriotic speaker at the annual Mexico City ceremony on Benito Juárez Day, March 21, 1982—the 176th anniversary of the birth of the Zapotecan Indian who rose to be president of Mexico. Virtually every Mexican town and city has a monument to Juárez or a principal street named for him—this stern "man of law" who stripped the Catholic Church of its property and privileges; reformed Mexican politics; instituted public education; ended the rule of the Mexican dictator Santa Anna; and later, drove the French from Mexico.

Reform. Respect for law. Nationalism and resistance to foreign aggression. Civilian control of the government. The importance of "great leaders." Public morality. Separation of church and state. Pride in Indian history. These are some of the concepts that the memory of Benito Juárez evokes for Mexicans—and is used to evoke. To Mexicans, Juárez was an Indian who became a Mexican, as Mexico was an Indian nation that became a Mexican nation. But it was Indian first.

THE PRE-CORTÉS PERIOD

Within the great sweep of Middle America lies the Valley of Mexico (in which present-day Mexico City is situated). It is 7,000 ft (2,134 m) above sea level and encompasses some 5,000 sq mi (12,950 sq km). The valley is bounded on all sides by snowy volcano mountains. In prehistoric times, much of the valley floor was covered by large shallow lakes. By around 8000 B.C., people had begun farming in the valley. After 1500 B.C., population centers began to develop. Stratifications of power and wealth evolved. Trade flourished over wide areas. Agriculture became highly advanced.

Civilization was already ancient—great cities, like Teotihuacán and Tula, had already risen and then fallen—by the time the Aztecs came into the Valley of Mexico in the thirteenth century. They were an especially industrious, vigorous, and expansionist people. By 1425, they had subjugated, or made alliances with, all the other peoples of the valley. Eventually, their influence reached from the Mexican highlands to the coasts on either side and as far south as present Guatemala. Only the Tlaxcalans to the east, the Tarascans to the west, and some of the Mixtecs to the south remained apart.

By the time Moctezuma II became its principal lord in 1502, the capital city of the Aztecs, Tenochtitlán, was a clean, healthy, bustling metropolis, one of the largest cities of the world, with a population as high as 200,000 people. (By contrast, Seville, the Spanish city from which the conquistadores were later to sail, had a population of around 40,000, and only four European cities—Paris, Venice, Milan, and Naples—had populations of 100,000 or more.) There were some fifty other cities in the Valley of Mexico. Millions and millions of people lived in an area of one of the greatest population concentrations in the world.

THE SPANISH CONQUEST

When Hernán Cortés and the conquistadores came over the snowy pass to the east and first saw Tenochtitlán and the other cities in and around the lake, they could hardly believe their eyes. Bernal Díaz del Castillo, who was in the party, later wrote that "we were amazed and said that it was like the enchantment they tell of in the legend of Amadis, on account of the great towers and cues and buildings rising from the water, and all built of masonry." Within three years thereafter, Cortés was the ruler of all he had at first surveyed—except that, by then, the great city was in ruins.

Why did Moctezuma II, the Aztec ruler, let the Spaniards come freely into Tenochtitlán? Cortés's monstrous use of terrorism as a tactic must have been puzzlingly and terrifyingly different from any kind of war that Moctezuma II had known. Why destroy a huge tribute city like Cholula and the income one could derive from it, as Cortés did? Why kill such great numbers of people for no useful purpose? Moctezuma II must also have let the Spaniards come because he was certain that at any later moment when he wanted to, he could easily defeat and capture Cortés and his army. Moctezuma must have been influenced, too, by Cortés's continued and effusive expressions of friendly intention. And, philosopher and thinker that he was, intellectually curious, Moctezuma must have been intrigued by these strange white men and anxious to know more about their identity and their place of origin.

In any event, Cortés did indeed come in. Once inside Tenochtitlán, he seized Moctezuma and held him prisoner. But Cortés soon had to leave for the Gulf Coast to defeat a rival Spanish army sent by the governor of Cuba. While he was away, the Aztecs at last rose up and attacked the Spaniards. Moctezuma was killed in the bloody fighting. Cortés, with his Tlaxcalan allies, marched back to Tenochtitlán to relieve the embattled Spanish garrison there. But the Aztecs had had enough, and they drove Cortés and the Spaniards from the city.

Then came into play one of the most terrible factors in the success of the conquest—European disease, in this case, smallpox. The European plagues—smallpox, influenza, typhus, typhoid, diphtheria, measles, whooping cough, and others—were unknown in the New World. The native peoples of the Western Hemisphere had built up no immunities to them. Time after time, then, with first contact, one or another of the European diseases decimated whole populations in the Americas. Such was now the fate of Tenochtitlán. Smallpox swept through the city with devastating effect, throwing social and political organization into disarray and shaking religious beliefs. Thousands upon thousands died within the span of a week. Bodies piled up and could not be disposed of rapidly enough. Cuitlahuac, the nephew of Moctezuma who succeeded him, was one of those who died. Cuauhtémoc assumed the leadership. As one historian has written, "Clearly, if smallpox had not come when it did, the Spanish victory could not have been achieved in Mexico."[2] Another historian concurs, writing that "the glorious victories attributed to Spanish arms would not have been possible without the devastation wrought by Spanish disease."[3] Cortés had time to regroup. When he attacked, he fought a weakened enemy. Still, Cuauhtémoc and the Aztecs resisted fiercely until, at last, they were defeated—and Cuauhtémoc captured—in the suburb of Tlatelolco on August 21, 1521. By that time, Tenochtitlán had been destroyed.

As Robert E. Quirk and others have written, one can tell a great deal about a country by the monuments it chooses to erect—and by the monuments it chooses *not* to erect. There are no monuments in Mexico to Cortés. Neither are there monuments to Malinche, the collaborating Indian woman who became mistress of and interpreter for Cortés (indeed, in Mexico today, *malinchismo* is the act of selling out one's country to foreigners). There are no monuments to Moctezuma. Cuauhtémoc is the Indian hero of Mexico history.

SPANISH COLONIALISM

Cortés had cut off the head of the Aztec Empire. In the next years, the body followed. The Spanish captain rewarded his men—and himself—as richly as he had promised. There were great quantities of gold. Cortés took for himself vast estates of rich land and huge *encomiendas* (entrustments or grants of Indians) to work them. He gave land and *encomiendas* to his followers, also.

The first year, Cortés began growing sugarcane. With this and other crops, the plow was also introduced. Soon, great herds of sheep and cattle were imported and set to graze. Slave labor built *ingenios,* or sugar mills. Forests were felled to provide fuel, lumber for building, and charcoal for cooking. Thus began, from the first year of Spanish colonialism, the overplowing, overgrazing, deforestation, and desertification that have continued to plague Mexico to this day.

Gold and silver mines were established, expanded, and worked, under incredibly brutal conditions, by Indian slave labor. *Obrajes,* or sweatshops, were everywhere set up to produce the coarse cloth and other products needed for domestic consumption. When the *encomienda* system and slavery were later made illegal, these monarchical edicts were often ignored, or were replaced by debt peonage, which was just as bad. Brutal treatment and European diseases wiped out more than two-thirds of the native population in the Valley of Mexico between 1519 and 1650!

Spanish colonialism, then, was characterized by exploitation of people and natural resources. It was also characterized by mercantilism—the crown's practice of keeping Mexico a producer of raw materials only and a purchaser of Spain's manufactured goods. Education was a privilege in colonial Mexico, not a right. The Roman Catholic Church was the established church. After a first period of missionary zeal, the Church fell, in many instances, into dissolution. The Church, itself, became a great landholder and exploiter of Indian labor. There were wholesale conversions to Catholicism, but the Indian converts still held on to much of their old religion. The Spaniards built churches on sacred Indian sites. The Virgin of Guadalupe appeared to an Indian convert, Juan Diego, at a site where there had previously been a shrine to an Aztec goddess.

After 1700, the Mexican and Spanish economies, both of which had been depressed, began to revive. The population in Mexico began to grow—mostly among the mestizos. The numbers of the *criollos* (Spaniards born in the New World) also grew, and they began to develop a pride in Mexicanness, which paralleled their increasing resentment of the privileged position of the *peninsulares,* who had been born in Spain.

Spain's wars in Europe meant more taxes in Mexico, more "forced loans" to the crown, and confiscation of Church charitable funds. Then, Napoleon Bonaparte imposed his brother on Spain as its ruler. At this, some *criollos* in Mexico attempted a revolt against the *peninsulares,* but this revolt was put down. Political dissatisfaction was soon joined by economic troubles.

INDEPENDENCE AND EMPIRE

Throughout Mexico, groups of dissidents began to meet in 1809, some to plot. One such group met regularly in Querétaro. Among its members were a young cavalry captain, Ignacio Allende, thirty-five, and a fifty-seven-year-old priest, Miguel Hidalgo y Costilla, whose parish was in the small nearby village of Dolores. Hidalgo, a *criollo,* had been investigated twice by the Inquisition for his political views. When word leaked out about the conspiracy in Querétaro, its members were warned by the wife of the local *corregidor,* or governor (she is celebrated in Mexican history as *la corregidora*). In Dolores, with Allende by his side, Father Hidalgo rang his church bell to summon his parishioners and issued what came to be called the *grito de Dolores,* a call to rebellion, on September 16, 1810. Many *criollos* were alarmed by the excesses of the mestizos and Indians who fought for Hidalgo and independence. Government forces rallied. Hidalgo and Allende were defeated, captured, and killed.

A mestizo priest, José María Morelos y Pavón, took up the sword of leadership, and in the Congress that he called in 1813, he made clear by his stirring speech to the delegates that the sword he carried was meant to cut the *criollo,* as well as the *peninsular,* bonds that had for so long held down the mestizos and Indians of Mexico. The constitution adopted by this Congress was a liberal document. Principles could not stand up to guns, however. *Criollos* and *peninsulares* joined together in opposition to this rebellion, and by 1815, Morelos, too, had been captured and killed. Still, the war—or wars—for independence sputtered on for another five years.

In Spain, Ferdinand VII had been restored to the throne in 1814, but the *criollos* of Mexico felt increasingly separate from Spain. In 1823, led by a conservative military man, Agustín de Iturbide, the *criollos,* backed by the Church, declared Mexican independence—a conservative independence, much different from that for which Morelos and Hidalgo had fought and died. Spain, after years of war, had no alternative but to agree to Mexican independence. The Mexican economy was in shambles. And after all the fighting, the lives of the great mass of the Mexican people had not changed. The identity of their oppressors had changed, but the nature of the oppression remained the same. Iturbide had himself declared emperor of Mexico—the first of its *caudillo,* or strongman, rulers. But the imperial grandeur in which Iturbide lived and ruled lasted only ten months.

Now, there rode onto the Mexican scene one of the most flamboyant and most enduring *caudillos* of Mexican history, the Veracruz military commander, a twenty-nine-year-old *criollo,* Antonio López de Santa Anna. Santa Anna had switched from the Spanish army to support Iturbide. After Iturbide dissolved the Mexican Congress, Santa Anna switched and led the forces that unseated Iturbide. He could be a monarchist or an antimonarchist. He could be a liberal or a conservative. He could be a defender of his country, or he could sell it out. For him, expediency and self-interest were the first principles. In February of 1823, Iturbide was driven into European exile, and his rule was replaced by that of a provisional government, run by a three-man military junta.

Needless to say, there are no statues in Mexico honoring Iturbide. By contrast, both Hidalgo and Morelos had states named after them, and there are many monuments to them. On each anniversary of the *grito de Dolores,* the president of the Mexican republic rings the old bell, now at the National Palace, in commemoration of that important event.

THE MEXICAN REPUBLIC

A new Mexican constitution was promulgated in 1824. It established the Estados Unidos Mexicanos, which consisted of nineteen states and four territories. Patterned after the constitution of the United States and influenced by the writings of the

French philosopher Montesquieu, the Mexican Constitution established a national government of three branches—executive, legislative, and judicial—a bicameral legislature, and a president to be elected by nationwide popular vote. Roman Catholicism was continued as the established religion. Military men and priests were guaranteed their special privilege of the *fuero*—that is, the right to be tried for any offense not by the civil courts but by military or Church courts.

After Manuel Félix Fernández Guadalupe Victoria was elected as the first president, poor Iturbide mistakenly thought he heard a call of the Mexican people—all the way over in Italy. He unwisely returned home, where he was arrested and executed. In 1827, Santa Anna put down another attempted revolt. In 1830, he was called on to defend the country and the government once more. When the second republican president had pushed through legislation expelling all Spaniards from Mexico, Spain had invaded Mexico at Tampico. Santa Anna laid siege to the Spanish forces and eventually forced their surrender. By then, he was easily the most popular figure in Mexico. The president of Mexico was then thrown out of office and executed by his vice-president. Santa Anna rose up and threw this usurper out of office. He was then elected president of Mexico in 1833.

It turned out that Santa Anna was not very much interested in governing. His vice-president, though, began to push through liberal reforms. So the army, the Church, and other conservatives banded together to overthrow the constitutional government and rescind the reforms. And who should lead this revolt but the president of the republic himself, Antonio López de Santa Anna. Now the foremost conservative, Santa Anna abolished the Constitution of 1824 and made the states into military districts. He required that he be addressed as Your Serene Highness. He was to occupy the presidency again and again, off and on, until 1855. During those years, the army became larger and larger, the bureaucracy became ever more bloated, taxes became higher and higher, the economy stagnated, bribery and corruption of officials became outrageous, and there were conflicts with foreign governments—first with the Republic of Texas, then with France, and finally, and disastrously, with the United States.

For years, Mexico had encouraged emigration from the United States to the sparsely settled, vast lands of Texas—provided only that the new emigrants were Catholics, would be loyal to the Mexican government, and would use Spanish as their official language. As the years passed, little was done to enforce these requirements. The flood of emigration swelled. Eventually, people from the United States greatly outnumbered Mexicans in Texas, and they became increasingly critical of the central government, until, at last, they rebelled and declared the establishment of the Lone Star republic in 1836. Santa Anna took personal command of the Mexican army and marched to San Antonio, where, at the Alamo on March 6, 1836, he defeated the Texas defenders there and killed them all. Another part of the Mexican army captured the small town of Goliad, taking 365 prisoners, all of whom Santa Anna had executed. Then, on April 21 of that same year, Santa Anna was himself defeated at the San Jacinto River and was taken captive.

To save himself, Santa Anna promised the Texans that Mexico would not again fight against Texas and that the Mexican cabinet would receive a formal mission from the Lone Star republic. When the cabinet heard of these agreements, they immediately repudiated them and sent Santa Anna back to his estate near Veracruz. Soon, however, the trumpets sounded again for Santa Anna. Provoked by Mexico's refusal—actually an inability—to pay its French debts, France ordered a shelling and invasion of Veracruz. Santa Anna led the Mexican forces that eventually drove the French away.

WAR WITH THE UNITED STATES

Then came the war between the United States and Mexico (1846–1848). U.S. attitudes toward Mexico and Mexicans were highly derogatory, even racist—especially after the war with Texas. Furthermore, the people and government of the United States felt that it was their Manifest Destiny to stretch their country's boundaries westward, all the way to the Pacific. The United States annexed Texas as a state of the Union in 1845. Mexican officials seethed, but were largely powerless to do anything else. Then, without any discoverable basis in law or fact, Texas claimed that its border went, not just to the Nueces River, but much past it to the Rio Grande (which the Mexicans call the Rio Bravo). Not only had Mexico suffered the loss of Texas, but it was now expected to accept the doubling of Texas territory—to include additionally, for example, San Antonio, Nacogdoches, and Galveston in Texas as well as Albuquerque, Santa Fe, and Taos in present New Mexico.

It is known from President James K. Polk's diary that he had made up his mind early to engage in a war with Mexico and was only waiting for a provocation. He sent U.S. troops into the area between the Nueces and the Rio Grande. When they skirmished with Mexican cavalry, Polk went before Congress, declared that he had made every effort at reconciliation, that the Mexicans had invaded U.S. territory and "shed American blood on American soil," and asked for a declaration of war. Congress complied.

The U.S. Army of the West was divided into three attack groups, which rapidly took New Mexico, California, and Chihuahua. The Army of the Center attacked Monterrey, where it was stopped by none other than Santa Anna. The main U.S. attack came from the Army of Occupation at Veracruz, which eventually marched all the way to Mexico City. The last battle there was on September 13 at Chapultepec Castle, the site of a military academy. Young Mexican cadets fought alongside the Mexican regulars, many preferring death to surrender. Mexico was defeated.

Peace was even more humiliating for Mexico than the war had been. According to the Treaty of Guadalupe Hidalgo, Mexico lost half of its territory in return for a payment of a little over $18 million—all of California, some of present-day Colorado, and most of the present states of New Mexico and Arizona. More humiliation was to come. When Santa Anna again came to power in 1853, needing money, he sold the rest of present New Mexico and Arizona (in the so-called Gadsden Purchase) to the United States for $10 million.

Today, one of Mexico's principal national monuments is located in Chapultepec Park. It is dedicated to the *niños héroes* ("boy heroes") of the war with the United States. Similar national monuments commemorating the patriotism and courage of the young cadets have been erected in villages and towns throughout Mexico. There are no monuments to Santa Anna.

THE REFORM

By 1854, the liberals of Mexico had had enough of dictatorial government. Among them was Benito Juárez, the lawyer of Zapotec Indian origin who had been governor of his home state, Oaxaca. They rose up in arms behind the liberal Plan of Ayutla. Santa Anna was driven into exile in 1855. Thus began what is called La Reforma (the Reform). Benito Juárez, as secretary of justice in the new government, was instrumental in having promulgated three important new reform laws: *ley Juárez, ley Lerdo,* and *ley Iglesias.* The first law abolished the *fuero,* the right of priests and military men to be tried in their own courts. The second law prohibited the Church and public units (including *ejidos,* the communal landholdings of Indian villages) from owning more property than was necessary for Church or governmental functions. The extra lands were not divided among the people. They were put up for sale. The unfortunate result was that large landholdings went to those who had the money. The third law struck again at the Church—making registration of births, deaths, marriages, and adoptions a civil, not a Church, responsibility; giving control of cemeteries to civil authorities; and prohibiting priests from charging high fees for administering the sacraments.

The Constitution of 1857 incorporated these and other reforms. Pope Pius IX declared any who followed the constitution heretics. The lines were sharply and bitterly drawn between the liberals on one side and the conservatives and supporters of the Church on the other. The War of the Reform broke out in 1858. Conservative forces overran the capital. Benito Juárez, who had earlier been elected chief justice and was, therefore, next in line for succession to the presidency, took over that office when its occupant resigned. Juárez eventually made his capital in Veracruz.

The conservative government in Mexico City renounced the Reform laws and swore allegiance to the pope. The Juárez government, on the other hand, issued even stronger decrees against the Church. The Church and the state were formally separated. Monastic orders were outlawed. All Church properties and assets were nationalized. Taking advantage of dissension within conservative circles, the liberal forces began to win some battles. Finally, on January 1, 1861, Mexico City fell to them.

FRENCH INTERVENTION

Juárez entered Mexico triumphantly in March and was officially elected president. But before 1861 was over, foreign troops invaded. Mexico owed debts to France, Spain, and Great Britain, which it had not been able to pay. Napoleon III of France persuaded the other powers to join with him in an invasion of Mexico. The Spanish and British withdrew after they learned that Napoleon III was bent on conquest. The French troops were then reinforced, and they began to march toward Mexico City. On the *cinco de mayo* ("the fifth of May"), the French troops were defeated near Puebla by the Mexican army. After this victory, Juárez, incensed by the fact that many priests had urged their parishioners to support the French, issued a decree prohibiting priests and nuns from wearing distinguishing garments and from speaking against the government.

The *cinco de mayo* victory was short-lived. Juárez retreated northward, eventually all the way to El Paso del Norte (later to be renamed Ciudad Juárez). Now began one of the most bizarre and tragic episodes in Mexico's political history—the imposition in 1864 by Napoleon III of the Hapsburg prince from Austria, Ferdinand Maximilian, as emperor of Mexico. Poor Maximilian and his wife, Carlota, believed the Mexican conservative, monarchist, and pro-Church emissaries who came to urge Maximilian to accept the Mexican throne. They were told that the people would welcome them with warm enthusiasm. They also believed Napoleon III when he said he would finance Maximilian's rule and sustain him on the Mexican throne with French troops as long as necessary. They also believed their Mexican advisers who told them that Juárez was defeated and had fled to the United States. These things were not true.

When the U.S. Civil War ended, the United States again turned its attention to Mexico and began to pressure France to withdraw. At the same time, the U.S. government began to furnish munitions and other supplies to Juárez. In late 1865 and early 1866, the French troops were called home, and Napoleon III announced that he could no longer pay the costs of Maximilian's government. Carlota went to Rome to secure the pope's help; when this effort was unsuccessful, she lost her mind. Maximilian began a final and hopeless resistance to the republican army—being soundly defeated and captured in Querétaro on May 15, 1867. Despite a great number of petitions by numerous heads of state, Juárez denied clemency for Maximilian and had him executed. Juárez entered Mexico City once more, reinstituted the Constitution of 1857, and in December of 1867, was elected to a third term as president. During this "restored republic," Juárez reduced the size of the army, instituted economic and educational reforms, and began construction of a railroad system to pull Mexico together as one nation.

Mexico had developed a strong sense of nationalism—and significantly, this nationalism had flowered in struggles against foreign powers. There are, of course, no monuments in Mexico to Maximilian. There are many monuments dedicated to Juárez, and Mexico City's principal boulevard is named the Paseo de la Reforma.

THE PORFIRIATO

Perhaps Juárez stayed in office too long. There were complaints that he centralized too much authority in the presidency, manipulated and dominated the Congress, caused the alienation of *ejido* land, and increased the power of the national government, to the detriment of state and local governments. Nevertheless, Juárez announced for election to a fourth term in 1871. There was a three-way contest, and no candidate received a majority of the vote. The election was thrown into the Congress, which chose Juárez. One of the other candidates, a military hero of the battles with the French, Porfirio Díaz, attempted a revolt under the slogan of No Reelection. The attempt failed. The revolt was quashed. But, in July of 1872, before he could take office, Juárez died.

The chief justice, one of the other candidates, Sebastián Lerdo de Tejada, succeeded to the office and in special elections in October of that year, was elected president. Lerdo continued the basic policies of Juárez and then announced for reelection to a second term. Porfirio Díaz took to the field with his military supporters again. This time, his No Reelection slogan caught fire. By force of arms and general support among those who counted, Díaz took over the presidency in 1876. This Mexican *caudillo* was to rule Mexico for over a third of a century. True to his No Reelection theme, Díaz did not seek reelection in 1880. After the undistinguished administration of his successor, Díaz became president again in the election of 1884. Thereafter, he remained in office until he was forced out in 1911.

The Porfiriato, as the Díaz reign is called, was a time of stability, law and order, and overall economic growth. It was dominated by men whom detractors later came to call *científicos*—followers of French positivism (a belief in progress through scientific knowledge and the scientific method), pragmatism, and social Darwinism. Chief among the *científicos* was the son of a French emigrant, José Ives Limantour, who became secretary of the treasury. Porfirio Díaz and his backers believed, among other things, that Mexico needed a period of "administrative power"—a nice way to say dictatorship—if the country was to be transformed from a backward nation into a modern one.

Díaz created a powerful political machine, run from the top. He practiced a shrewd politics of conciliation and coalition. There were great political and economic benefits for those who joined up—jobs and positions, land, subsidies, concessions. Constitutional local government continued in theory, but real local power was vested in some 300 *jefes políticos* ("political chiefs"), named by Díaz. The military was also a part of the Díaz coalition. Key generals were allowed to dominate their states. Government policies encouraged bigness in agriculture, as in everything else. New laws allowed surveying companies to keep a portion of any idle, unclaimed, or public lands they surveyed. Great land grabs resulted. Four surveying companies, for example, were able to obtain two-thirds of all the land in the northern state of Sonora, territory equal to the size of England and Wales combined!

The *científicos* believed that Mexico's economic development depended upon attracting foreign capital through special subsidies and concessions. By 1910, U.S. interests controlled 75 percent of Mexican mines, 72 percent of the metal industry, 68 percent of the rubber business, and 58 percent of oil production. Other foreigners—mostly British, French, German, and Dutch—controlled 80 percent of the rest of Mexico's industry.

The theme of the Porfiriato was "peace, order, and progress." A modern railroad network was built. This helped to double cotton production. Mining flourished; so did industrialization. Some ports were modernized and others opened. Exports mushroomed—and Mexico became dependent upon them. Mexico's population doubled.

But the costs were exorbitant. The great majority of Mexicans lived in misery or in otherwise intolerable conditions. The Indians, who Limantour believed were biologically inferior, were considerably worse off by 1910 than they had been a hundred years earlier, prior to independence. The rural *peones,* or laborers, were also worse off. The *peones,* as well as the miners, were paid, not in money, but in scrip or special coins, which could only be spent at the *tienda de raya,* the company store, and they were perpetually behind in what they owed. *Rurales* ("rural police") hunted down and brought back anyone who tried to escape. Debts were passed on from one generation to another. Because Mexico's agriculture had increasingly been converted to cash crops and to the cattle and sheep business, especially for export, Mexico was producing less corn and beans in 1910 than it had produced in 1867—and was a large importer of food.

Railroad, mining, and industrial workers became increasingly hostile to the owners, to foreigners, and to their own government. Labor agitation and attempts at organization began in the 1880s—some of it encouraged by the Catholic Church following the issuance of a papal encyclical in 1891 that called for greater recognition of the rights of labor. Between 1881 and 1911, there were 250 strikes. In the worst of these, against French- and U.S.-owned companies, federal troops were used to break the strikes.

A growing Mexican middle class was also increasingly unhappy with the government. The economic policies and the educational programs of the Díaz regime had helped to create this middle class. But, as Porfirio Díaz and his administration aged, they turned more and more to a politics of exclusion. Liberal intellectuals began to speak out against the undemocratic practices of the government and the exploitation of Mexican labor. Two Flores Magón brothers, Jesus and Ricardo, started a liberal publication, *Regeneración,* to call for change. The publication was closed down by the government, and the Flores Magón brothers fled to the United States, where their writings and calls for action became increasingly radical.

On top of all this came bad economic times. The year 1907 was one of both severe drought in Mexico and severe economic problems in the world. A financial panic in the United States cut off credit to Mexico. The worldwide economic problems deprived Mexico of its export market, upon which it had come to depend so heavily. Mines were shut down. The economy stagnated. The prices of food and clothing rose rapidly—the costs of flour, beans, wheat, corn, and chile nearly doubling.

Then, in an interview with a U.S. magazine in 1908, Porfirio Díaz announced— and this was widely publicized in Mexico—that he felt the time had come for Mexico to choose its own president in the elections of 1910. Díaz himself eventually became a candidate for reelection. In the meantime, Francisco Ignacio Madero, the son of a Coahuila *hacendado* who had studied for five years in France and eight months at the University of California in Berkeley, wrote a very important book, *The Presidential Succession of 1910,* in which he called for political reform (although he said virtually nothing in regard to land, labor, or other economic or social reforms). Madero formed an Anti-Reelection Party and began to expound his views in well-attended meetings around the country. Actually doubtful that Díaz would really allow a free election, Madero nevertheless announced as a candidate for president. Madero's doubts were well founded. He was arrested and jailed. Díaz was declared the winner in the 1910 elections; Madero went into exile in San Antonio, Texas.

THE REVOLUTION

With this latest usurpation of power by Porfirio Díaz, Madero's frustrations at last rose to a level that matched Mexico's. In October of 1910, he issued his Plan of San Luís Potosí, reiterating his call for political reform and asking Mexicans to rise up in arms against the Díaz regime on November 20. Rise up they did! This moderate man, with his moderate plan, became the lightning rod that attracted all of the dissident elements of the country. Some who joined him were more conservative than Madero; many were more radical. Some joined him to secure a share of the power and wealth, others to fight for social and economic, as well as political, reforms.

There was an uprising in Yucatán. The Flores Magón brothers led an uprising in Baja California. In Chihuahua, Pascual Orozco, Jr., a muleteer disgruntled by the political and economic stranglehold of the *hacendados,* raised an army and began to achieve significant victories over the federal forces. Among his lieutenants was a man who called himself Francisco "Pancho" Villa. Born Doroteo Arango into a poor family living on a hacienda, Villa had spent most of his life as a bandit and a cattle rustler.

In February of 1911, Madero returned to Mexico and took command of the revolutionary army. In the state of Morelos, Emiliano Zapata, a charismatic and dedicated leader for land reform, announced his support for the Madero revolution. It turned out that the federal army had become as debilitated by power and corruption as the government itself. It could not stop Zapata in the state of Morelos nor Orozco and Villa in the northern states. Zapata took Cuautla; Orozco and Villa captured Ciudad Juárez. It became clear to Díaz and those around him that after a third of a century, his government had lost its legitimacy and, with it, control of the country. Limantour went to Ciudad Juárez and negotiated a transfer of power. Díaz abdicated on May 25 and left for Europe, never to return. The Porfiriato had ended. Madero thought that the Revolution had also ended, but it had only begun.

The war was to continue for another decade. Countless Mexicans, including Madero himself, were to be killed by other Mexicans. The country was to be ravished, the economy devastated. The population of Mexico, which had been rapidly growing, was to suffer a decline of nearly 1 million people between 1910 and 1920. But all that was somewhere in the future when a triumphant Madero boarded the train for Mexico City. The troubles to come were presaged, though, by a harsh confrontation Madero had with Orozco and Villa just before he left Ciudad Juárez. In Mexico City, Madero made a strategic mistake. A stickler for legality, he allowed an interim president to serve until Madero could be formally elected in October of 1911. By then, perhaps, his moment had passed. Madero was to govern for only thirteen months. His meager and timid reforms did nothing to satisfy labor and land-reform demands. He continued the fiscal policies of Díaz and retained many of the Porfiriato's high officials.

Orozco took to the battlefield again. Zapata issued his Plan of Ayala, which demanded immediate land reform; denounced Madero; and recognized Orozco as the true leader of the Revolution. Now, Madero made another mistake, this one literally a fatal mistake. He called upon a Porfiriato general, Victoriano Huerta, a mestizo from the state of Jalisco, to head the federal army against Orozco and Zapata. Huerta was successful against Orozco (who later, opportunistically, joined forces with him), and he began to put pressure upon Zapata. Then came another challenge—from the right. Felix Díaz, a nephew of the former president, rose in arms in Veracruz against the Madero government. Again, Huerta was successful. This rebellion, too, was quashed, and Felix Díaz was brought to Mexico City and jailed. Soon, however, other conservative forces freed Díaz and threatened the government again. There then ensued what is called in Mexican history the *decena trágica* ("the ten tragic days"). The killing and destruction wrought by the Díaz and the Huerta forces, fighting against each other, were horrible. It appears now that Huerta might have been going through a sham in order, purposely, to cause the decimation of his own government army, because he was, at the same time, opening secret negotiations with Díaz. These negotiations culminated in an agreement, which was reached under the direction and guidance of the U.S. ambassador, Henry Lane Wilson. Huerta switched sides and the U.S. ambassador supported him. Herta immediately took over the government, arrested Madero, and had the president's brother killed. Madero was imprisoned. Despite the pleas for help by Madero's wife to Wilson, the ambassador did nothing, and Madero and his vice-president were taken out and cruelly murdered.

In the United States, President Woodrow Wilson refused to recognize the Huerta regime. But, in Mexico, most state governors did. Zapata, of course, did not recognize Huerta. Neither did Villa, and he was joined in arms by Alvaro Obregón, a former schoolteacher and *cacique* ("political boss") in Sonora, and a former revolutionary commander. The leadership of these constitutionalist forces was assumed by Venustiano Carranza, nearly sixty years old, the governor of Coahuila, and the patriarch of a distinguished *criollo* family there. Carranza took as his title First Chief. He issued his Plan of Guadalupe, a moderate plan, promising, again, only political reforms. As the fighting worsened and widened, as villages were taken first by one side and then another, many people began to wonder what it was all about. Even the soldiers—in both the federal and constitutionalist armies—were not agreed among themselves on what they were fighting for.

Although, interestingly, Huerta probably achieved more in the way of reforms and in support of education than did Madero, he also severely suppressed the press, jailed opponents, countenanced the use of assassination as a political tool, and practiced harsh repression generally. Huerta also initiated forced conscription to supply his army with soldiers—producing an inferior army and depleting the Mexican work force, adding injury to the Mexican economy. President Wilson possessed a moralistic zeal for democracy. He replaced Henry Lane Wilson and, using the pretext of a Mexican affront to some U.S. sailors, sent an armed force to capture the port of Veracruz in 1914. This caused a new wave of severely anti-U.S. feeling in Mexico. The vigor and successes of the constitutionalist army, augmented by the facts that Huerta had to divert troops to Veracruz and that his outside sources of supply had been cut off by the U.S. occupation of that port, brought down the Huerta government in July of that same year. Huerta resigned, blaming the United States for his fall (he later died in a Texas jail in 1916, still plotting to return to Mexico).

The First Chief, Venustiano Carranza, took control of the Mexican government. Partisans of social and economic reform soon found out that he was not one of them. To consolidate his position, Carranza called a military convention in Aguascalientes in 1914. *Carrancistas, Villistas,* and *Zapatistas* met to pull the country together and to decide upon a provisional president until elections could be held. But the convention soon got out of hand. Led by the *Zapatistas,* a majority of the delegates, in a burst of revolutionary fervor, elected a provisional president who was opposed by Carranza. The First Chief disowned the convention and called for his representatives to withdraw from it. Fatefully, as time would show, one of those who decided to obey this order was Alvaro Obregón.

The troops of Villa and Zapata marched on Mexico City. Carranza withdrew his headquarters to Veracruz (from which, incidentally, the U.S. occupation forces were eventually evacuated). The provisional president chosen by the Aguascalientes Convention was installed in office. But Obregón was a student of the new tactics of war being used at the time in Europe. At Celaya, in April of 1915, he met an old-style massed cavalry charge with a deadly stationary defense. Thousands of Villa's men were killed and wounded, and Villa himself withdrew northward. Zapata thereafter confined himself and his forces to the state of Morelos.

Carranza returned to power in Mexico City. His government was recognized by President Woodrow Wilson. The First Chief then called another convention, this one a constitutional convention in Querétaro. To avoid his earlier mistake, he decreed that none of the delegates to be elected could include anyone who had fought with Huerta, Villa, or Zapata. But when the convention met, these restrictions proved unavailing. A majority of the delegates quickly rejected the moderate model constitution that Carranza had sent them. Instead, they wrote an organic law—still in effect in Mexico—which was a radical document for its day. It limited the president to one four-year term. Its Article 3 was vigorously anti-Church, incorporating all such earlier restrictions and prohibitions and, further, taking primary education away from the Church (making education purely secular as well as mandatory and free). Article 27 incorporated the basic philosophy and provisions of the Plan of Ayala in regard to land reform, made private ownership a privilege subject to the public interest as the government might define it, and restricted the right to exploit Mexico's water and mineral resources to Mexican nationals. Article 123 mandated extensive labor reforms—an eight-hour day, a six-day week, equal pay regardless of sex or nationality, and a minimum wage. The right of labor to organize and to strike was guaranteed.

Shocked as he was by the product of this second runaway convention, Carranza nevertheless accepted the constitution, although he made it clear that he had no intention of following it. He was elected president in March of 1917. Carranza distributed very little land. His labor reforms were also minor, although he did permit the organization of Mexico's first nationwide union, the Regional Confederation of Mexican Labor (CROM). In the north, Villa was relatively quiet—and wealthy—on his hacienda. But from Morelos, Zapata wrote a defiant open letter to Carranza, calling on him to resign and charging that Carranza and his friends had only fought in the Revolution for "riches, honors, businesses, banquets, sumptuous feasts, bacchanals, orgies." Carranza had tried direct military action against Zapata, to no avail. Now he decided upon treachery. On Carranza's orders, an officer of the federal army in Morelos, indicating that he wanted to defect to Zapata, led Zapata into a trap and killed him in 1919. Carranza rewarded the assassin with an army promotion and a generous cash prize.

But things were far from settled in Mexico, and the battered country had not seen the last of political violence—nor of political assassinations. General Obregón, the one armed hero of the constitutionalist forces, had gone back to his native Sonora after Carranza's government had been firmly put in place. As a *hacendado,* a grower and "merchant of garbanzos," a cattleman and an exporter of beef and hides, and an all-around entrepreneur, Obregón had grown very wealthy. But power interested him as much as wealth. So, when he thought Carranza had passed over him in choosing the "approved" presidential candidate for 1920, Obregón led a military revolt against Carranza—a successful one. Sadly, Carranza was killed while retreating toward Veracruz. Obregón's subsequent election as president in 1920 was not the last time a presidential election would ratify a result earlier achieved by military means. But Obregón's revolt was the last successful revolt against the government.

The Mexican Revolution was over, and it was soon enshrined forever—with a capital *R*—in Mexican history. With time, the Mexican Constitution came to be regarded as a nearly sacred document—though it was a long way from actually being implemented. Time did not improve the image of Huerta, whom Mexican history remembers as "the bloody usurper." No Mexican monuments were erected in memory of Porfirio Díaz (although, ironically, a street in El Paso, Texas, still bears his name). But plenty of Mexican monuments and street names, today, pay homage to Madero, Carranza, and Zapata. Mexican history makes Madero "the apostle" of the Revolution and of Mexican democracy, Carranza "the father of the constitution," and Zapata the heroic fighter for the Mexican masses.

THE NORTHERN DYNASTY

Alvaro Obregón and his fellow Sonoran, Plutarco Elías Calles, who had fought with Obregón, apparently soon worked out an arrangement by which they agreed to pass the presidency back and forth between them in the years that were to follow.

Obregón was elected president in 1920. He was a charismatic leader and a dynamic orator, and he gathered power into the presidency. Obregón was also a conciliator. He made a kind of peace with the Church and with his former foes. He had another rich hacienda bought for Pancho Villa, and the mellowing revolutionary of the North settled down (and was later assassinated in 1923). The economy recovered. Mexico became the world's third largest producer of oil. The first national system of education was established, and rural schools were built. Obregón allowed some cautious labor advances to be made and endorsed some cautious land reform. A sense of what came to be called revolutionary nationalism began to develop in the country— in its writings, in its music, and in its art. In the United States, Warren G. Harding, a friend of big oil, became president in 1921. He pressured Mexico to recognize the U.S. oil holdings there, and Obregón yielded.

Calles became president in 1924—after an attempted rightist rebellion was put down by military force. Taking office, Calles became the strongest—and, as it turned out, the longest-lived—president and *caudillo* since Díaz. He put down his enemies without mercy. He built up Mexico's economy, pushed health programs, expanded education, helped make labor more powerful, and established a cooperative relationship with CROM. He also vigorously enforced, as Obregón had not, the anti-Church provisions of the constitution. Militant Catholics rose up in a bloody rebellion, their cry being "Viva Cristo Rey!" ("Long live Christ, the King!"). Calles dealt very harshly with this *cristero* rebellion and, after much shedding of blood on both sides, eventually suppressed it.

Calles also confronted the United States in regard to oil. It was decreed that all interests that predated the Constitution of 1917 would have to be renegotiated with the government—and these new concessions were to be limited in duration. The United States sent a Wall Street investment banker, Dwight Morrow, to Mexico as its ambassador. His quiet negotiations eventually worked out a compromise. The oil interests were allowed to continue their concessions without the duration lid.

Calles caused the presidential term to be changed from four years to six years. He then prepared to turn the government back over to Obregón in the 1928 presidential election. There was a rebellion, again, and it was again put down. The election ratified the earlier military victory. But before Obregón could take office, he was killed by a religious mystic. Calles assumed power again—ruling through puppets as the *jefe maximo* ("maximum chief") until 1934. During this period, called in Mexican history the *maximato,* Calles established Mexico's ruling party in order to institutionalize his political control, since he was not charismatic or dynamic enough to rule by power of personality. Calles shifted the Revolution to the right. Powerful leaders of labor, business, and government became immensely wealthy during the Calles *maximato.* Calles, himself, seemed to own property almost everywhere.

THE CÁRDENAS *SEXENIO*

With the end of the 1928–1934 *sexenio,* the *maximato* had run its course. Calles was the last survivor of the great revolutionary *caudillos*—Madero, Zapata, Villa,

Carranza, and Obregón had all been assassinated—and he was now to lose control. But Calles did not know that that was about to happen when he chose the populist and popular governor of Michoacán and his former minister of war, Lázaro Cárdenas, as the National Revolutionary Party (PNR) presidential candidate in the elections of 1934. Elected, Cárdenas turned out to have a mind of his own. Once he had cut down the strength and influence of the military and had bolstered his own political position with labor, the peasants, and other elements in the country, he confronted Calles and exiled him from the country.

Cárdenas undertook more land reform—mostly by delivering land to *ejidos*—than all of his predecessors put together. He instituted socialist education in the schools and expanded education generally. He reorganized the national labor union into the Confederation of Mexican Workers (CTM) and made this organization a much more aggressive and representative body. The minimum wage was raised. The old hacienda system was broken. A limited peace was achieved with the Church. The railroads were nearly all nationalized. Nationalistic artists were encouraged. A cultural nationalism blossomed. The ruling party, PNR, was reorganized to make it much more broad based and more truly representative of the people to the government, rather than, as it had been, from the government to the people. The name of the party was changed to Mexican Revolutionary Party (PRM).

Then, in 1938, came the major decision of the Cárdenas *sexenio*, the confrontation with big oil. Oil workers had gone on strike. By modern standards, their demands in regard to wages, hours, and working conditions were modest. But the oil interests, chiefly based in the United States and Great Britain, were adamant in their rejection of the demands and in their intention to crush the strike. When the companies showed their arrogance toward the president himself and, thus, toward Mexican sovereignty, Cárdenas invoked Article 27 of the constitution and nationalized the oil industry. He did not turn the industry over to the workers as they wanted, but he did create a public corporation, Petróleos Mexicanos (PEMEX), to run it. He saw to it that this public company dealt generously with the *petroleros,* or oil workers, as it has done ever since.

In the United States, the powerful oil industry called upon the United States to take action—from economic sanctions to outright invasion—to protect their oil holdings and businesses. The U.S. government, and the government of Great Britain, were only too happy to back the companies. They boycotted Mexican oil and sought to isolate PEMEX from oil-production and exploration technology and technical assistance (thus, it turned out, forcing Mexico to build what is today a first-rate oil industry of its own).

Cárdenas had spent a great part of his term walking among the ordinary people of Mexico. Unannounced, he would visit small villages and, on the spot, sign orders for irrigation projects, for distribution of land, for clinics, and for other responses to local petitions that were humbly presented to him. The people of the country saw Cárdenas as one of their own. Now, with the expropriation of oil, the people—including even leaders of the Church and many conservatives—stood up with Cárdenas and with their country against the "greedy" oil companies and against foreign powers—particularly *el coloso del norte* ("the colossus of the North"), the United States. Never had there been such an outpouring of popular support for a president and his government.

Today, Cárdenas remains the greatest hero of Mexico's modern history. The anniversary of his birth and the anniversary of his expropriation of Mexico's oil are national holidays (by contrast, Calles is not considered to have been one of the "revolutionary family"). Under Cárdenas, Mexico's political system became more firmly institutionalized—in the presidency and in the official party (later renamed Institutional Revolutionary Party, PRI).

MEXICO SINCE 1940

Mexico's history since 1940 can best be capsulized by considering a series of "lasts" and "firsts" among its presidents during that period and earlier. Calles was the last presidential exemplar of *continuismo,* continued control past one term. Cárdenas (1934–1940) was the last of the openly and consistently leftist and populist presidents. After his *sexenio,* the Mexican government increasingly focused its attention and efforts on rapid economic growth—the *milagro mexicano* ("Mexican miracle")—to the detriment of economic equity.

Avila Camacho (1940–1946), chosen by Cárdenas to succeed him, was the last military man to serve as president. Interestingly, it was he who disbanded the military arm of the official party (though this action by no means eliminated the influence of the military on government and policy). Miguel Alemán Valdés (1946–1952) was the first civilian president. He allowed new parties to form (some had formed earlier, too). But the PRI's monopoly was not seriously challenged. Alemán was the first Mexican president to exchange visits with a U.S. president. Trade with the United States flourished, as did U.S. private investment in Mexico. Alemán was the last president to devote a really substantial portion of Mexican public investment to agriculture. After his term, the trends toward rapid industrialization and urbanization were accelerated, and Mexico eventually became an urban nation and a net importer of food.

Gustavo Díaz Ordáz (1964–1970) was the last Mexican president to come from outside the metropolis of Mexico City, and he was the last president to have held prior elective office. His political experience did not protect his popularity, though, when economic conditions worsened. The legitimacy of the Mexican political system was seriously strained when students at the national university and other protesters mounted huge demonstrations against government policies and were brutally attacked, with many killed and imprisoned, at Tlatelolco. Still, Díaz Ordáz was the last president under whom Mexico's foreign debt was below double-digit billions of dollars. He was the last president, too, during whose administration the rate of inflation remained at tolerable levels and the value of the peso continued to be stable.

Luís Echeverría Alvarez (1970–1976) was the first of four "insider" presidents— Echeverría, José López Portillo, Miguel de la Madrid Hurtado, and Carlos Salinas de

Gortari; each came from the Federal District, had built his career in federal-government positions, and had served in the cabinet of his predecessor. Echeverría was also the first president since 1954 to devalue the peso. He was the first president to lead Mexico into an activist role in foreign affairs, particularly in regard to its own region and Third World countries, and this role increasingly diverged from U.S. policy. Echeverría was the first Mexican president to institute government-backed family planning—none too soon, since Mexico's population had gone from 16.5 million in the 1930s to around 51 million by 1970 (and over 80 million and growing by 1987).

José López Portillo (1976–1982) was the first Mexican president to expropriate Mexican private banks. He did so after hopes had soared at the beginning of his term, when new oil was discovered, only to plummet with a drop in world oil prices. This drop in prices, coupled with skyrocketing federal deficits, inflation, foreign borrowing, and two devaluations, as well as reports of widespread corruption, produced a crisis of confidence for his government.

Miguel de la Madrid Hurtado (1982–1988) was the first president to institute a *sexenio*-long austerity program, causing increased Mexican unemployment and poverty. Pressured to follow this course by the International Monetary Fund and the foreign banks that held Mexico's mammoth $100 billion foreign debt, he was the object of increasing public criticism and opposition during his term.

Carlos Salinas de Gortari (1988–1994) was the first modern president to take office with questioned legitimacy, his victory having been clouded by serious charges of widespread election fraud, as were previous PRI-claimed victories in certain northern state elections. He was the first president to face heavy parliamentary opposition and the first president whose inaugural ceremony in the great hall of the Chamber of Deputies was marred by a raucous demonstration and a protest walkout. Improvement in economic conditions and restoration of the legitimacy of the Mexican system—these were the fundamental challenges Salinas de Gortari had to confront. The economy was at first restored, and Salinas de Gortari signed the North American Free Trade Agreement. But after a *Zapatista* rebellion in Chiapas exploded and the handpicked PRI presidential candidate, Luis Donaldo Colosio, was assassinated, a severe financial crisis and economic depression ensued.

The succeeding PRI nominee and president, Ernesto Zedillo (1994–), was truly elected but took office when the legitimacy of the system and the hegemony of PRI were being challenged as never before. The brother of Carlos Salinas de Gortari was imprisoned for complicity in political assassination and for unlawful enrichment, and the former president himself fled into exile. President Zedillo struggled to restore political and economic stability.

CONCLUSION

Mexican politics and government are products of—and are to some degree constrained by—Mexican history. The role of the "great leader" is still highly important. Authority is still concentrated in the national government and, within it, in the president. Mexicans have a justified cynicism about government and a skepticism about the revolutionary rhetoric of candidates and officials. Still, candidates and officials know that they must make the obligatory obeisance toward the principles of the Revolution and the constitution. They would act in substantial and open opposition to these principles at their peril—although, obviously, they can fail to act in pursuance of these principles. And at the beginning of each *sexenio*, there is hope anew (tinged, of course, with some skepticism). Each new president becomes the symbolic leader of the country as well as its official leader, the repository of national authority and national honor, and the focus of Mexican aspirations. For more than fifty years, the Mexican system was stable, and the country's governmental system generally was seen as legitimate by Mexicans—despite gross inequities that have existed, and still exist, and a good deal of misery. The "institutionalization" of the Revolution and the legitimacy of the "official" PRI government faced serious questioning and challenge during the *sexenio* of Ernesto Zedillo.

NOTES

1. Raúl Béjar Navarro, *El Mexicano: Aspectos culturales y psicosociales* (Mexico City: Univérsidad Nacional Autónoma de México, 1979).

2. William C. McNeill, *Plagues and People* (Garden City, N.Y.: Doubleday, Anchor Press, 1976), p. 207.

3. John Duffy, "Smallpox and the Indians in the American Colonies," in Roger L. Nichols, ed., *The American Indian, Past and Present,* 2d ed. (New York: John Wiley and Sons, 1981), p. 64.

SUGGESTED READINGS

Barry, Tom, ed., *Mexico: A Country Guide.* Albuquerque, N.M.: Inter-Hemispheric Education Resource Center, 1992. A detailed and very good report and analysis of Mexico's politics, government, and economy.

Grayson, George W. *The United States and Mexico: Patterns of Influence.* New York: Praeger, 1984. This is an excellent history and assessment of relations between Mexico and the United States, with particular emphasis on key issues, including marketing of oil and gas, policy toward Central America and Cuba, and illegal immigration of Mexicans to the United States.

Hellman, Judith Adler. *Mexico in Crisis.* New York: Holmes and Meier, 1979. An important study of Mexican politics from a leftist perspective, this book is also very useful because of its treatment of the history of the Mexican Revolution, its institutionalization, and the formation of the ruling political party.

Levy, Daniel, and Gabriel Székely. *Mexico: Paradoxes of Stability and Change.* 2d ed. Boulder, Colo.: Westview Press, 1987. An outstanding brief text, this book discusses Mexican politics and government from precolonial days to the time of President de la Madrid.

Meyer, Michael C., and William L. Sherman. *The Course of Mexican History.* New York: Oxford University Press, 1979. This is a highly readable and well-researched history of Mexico from pre-Cortés times to the election of President José López Portillo.

Pastor, Robert A., and Jorge Castaneda. *Limits to Friendship: The United States and Mexico.* New York: Knopf, 1988. A U.S. and a Mexican authority have written alternating chapters in this illuminating book about U.S.-Mexican relations and the misperceptions that have hampered their greater cooperation.

Raat, W. Dirk, and William H. Beezley. *Twentieth Century Mexico.* Lincoln: University of Nebraska Press, 1986. This highly worthwhile anthology contains chapters that usefully explain Mexico "from Porfirio Díaz to petrodollars."

Ruíz, Ramón Eduardo. *The Great Rebellion: Mexico, 1905–1924.* New York: W. W. Norton, 1980. This is a well-researched and fully footnoted study of the events, conditions, and leaders that made the Mexican Revolution. It concludes that the Revolution was a bourgeois revolt, led by middle-class dissidents, that did not produce the social and economic justice some of its rhetoric promised.

Wilkie, James W., and Albert L. Michaels. *Revolution in Mexico: Years of Upheaval, 1910–1940.* New York: Knopf, 1969. This excellent sourcebook reprints a large number of works of various authors, as well as some original documents, and contains several useful chronologies.

Wolf, Eric. *Sons of the Shaking Earth.* Chicago: University of Chicago Press, 1959. Written by an anthropologist, this history of Mexico is particularly useful in regard to the pre-Cortés and colonial periods.

Womack, John, Jr. *Zapata and the Mexican Revolution.* New York: Random House, 1970. This is a detailed, step-by-step account of the Mexican Revolution and the part played in it by the heroic fighter for agrarian reform.

18

MEXICO: THE PERMANENT CRISIS

MARTIN C. NEEDLER

More U.S. political scientists consider themselves specialists on Mexico than on any other Latin American country. Of course Mexico and Canada are the nearest neighbors of the United States and its partners in the North American Free Trade Agreement (NAFTA); Mexico is its third or fourth largest trading partner, the destination of millions of U.S. tourists annually, and the ancestral home of other millions of inhabitants of the United States. But there are other reasons for paying special attention to Mexico. Mexico is the largest Spanish-speaking country, with more than twice the population of Argentina or Colombia and almost twice the population of Spain itself. And Mexico is now the fourth or fifth largest world producer of that most valuable strategic commodity, petroleum.

The present time—the last few years of the twentieth century—is a difficult time in which to try to understand Mexican politics and economics. Today is a time of fundamental shift in the system's parameters, and it is not clear, even to the major participants themselves, what directions change will take.

The system that is undergoing change might have been difficult to characterize, but it was not hard to understand. It was established after the Mexican Revolution had stabilized. Behind the façade of a constitutional democratic system similar to that of the United States, it was dominated by a hegemonic political party growing out of the coalition of those who had fought successfully for the Revolution. In this respect it was similar to other dominant parties that claimed origins in a national revolution, such as those in the developing countries of Africa and Asia, and even those in the Communist countries of Eastern Europe. Like them, its social and economic policies reflected in part its revolutionary and nationalist rhetoric. But after a period of experimentation the ruling elite had come to terms with the facts of the world capitalist system and Mexico's position as a neighbor of the dominant country in that system: Although the economy was mixed, with some government ownership of basic utilities and major industries and with central government guidance and planning, the bulk of the economy was in private hands, and foreign investment was encouraged.

The rules that were supposed to protect Mexico's independence from foreign control by carefully stipulating the areas in which foreign investment was allowed, and the circumstances in which only state investment or investment by private Mexican nationals was to be tolerated, could often be evaded. Indeed, evasion of the law was widespread, political figures became wealthy by one means or another, and the various police forces of the republic were notorious more as a cause of crime than as a deterrent to it. But Mexico was not simply a kleptocracy, a government that existed only so that its rulers could steal; the ideals of the Revolution lived on and were frequently embodied in policy, and many government officials were capable and progressive servants of the public interest.

THE POLITICAL SYSTEM

The formal political system resembles that of the United States in its major structural features, but it has been modified in major respects to meet objections raised by opposition parties to the fact that the same party, the Institutional Revolutionary Party, or PRI, has occupied the presidency and dominated the legislature and the state governments since its founding in 1929.

There is a constitutional separation between the president and the two houses of the legislature, that is, they are elected independently of each other and each has powers specified in the constitution. The president is directly elected by the voters for a single six-year term and can never be reelected. Members of the Senate, now four from each state—the number increased from two to make it easier for the opposition parties to elect senators—are now not elected for staggered terms, as formerly, but all at the same time as the president. Members of the Chamber of Deputies are elected for three-year terms by a method similar to that pioneered by the German Federal Republic but increasingly adopted elsewhere; under it 300 members represent individual districts, but another 200 are chosen by proportional representation on party lists—again, so that opposition parties have a better chance of electing representatives.

It is a federal system, with each state having its own constitutional structure and elections for governor and a single-chamber legislature. However, his leadership of the ruling party gives the president a powerful position vis-à-vis the governors, most of whom are also from the PRI. President Carlos Salinas (1988–1994), especially, used to treat governors as though they were his political appointees, moving them into cabinet or party positions or ordering them to resign if he thought the local political situation required it.

President Ernesto Zedillo (1994–2000) found himself in a much weaker political position than Salinas, however. Not the most popular or politically able of the possible successors to Salinas, Salinas picked him—behind the formal procedures, the outgoing PRI president in effect designates his successor—after the popular nominee, Luis Donaldo Colosio, was assassinated in a crime that has still not been satisfactorily explained. Zedillo has not been able to impose his authority on a disciplined PRI, and local party machines have resisted his attempts to comply with promises to fully democratize and constitutionalize Mexican political life by guaranteeing honest elections, impartial media, and an uncorrupt police and judiciary.

Nevertheless, Zedillo—no matter what his personal views, which are hardly relevant—has made a virtue of necessity and has adopted a posture of leadership with respect to democratizing and constitutionalizing measures he has in effect been forced to adopt by the strength of opposition protest. The 1996 reform in a series of such reforms was supposed to eliminate any possibility of political manipulation of election results by establishing an electoral tribunal independent of the executive branch (along with providing for the direct election of the governor of the Federal District, which includes Mexico City).

The strongest opposition party is the PAN, the Party of National Action. Its leadership core has traditionally consisted of those educated in Catholic secondary schools and active in Catholic lay organizations, working in the professions and small business, but as its access to local- and state-level political power has grown, it has attracted some big-business support and the votes of opponents of the regime from across the class and income structure. Its national organization is uneven, being stronger in the northern border states and some other specific regions, such as Yucatán, but its recent presidential candidates have begun to look like serious contenders for power.

As the policy positions of the PRI have shifted to the center-right of the political spectrum, with acceptance of neoliberal economic theory, the PRI has come closer to the PAN, and the two parties have formed an implicit alliance on some policy issues in the legislature, especially when two-thirds of the votes have been required to pass a constitutional amendment, more than the PRI could muster on its own.

Such cooperation has been directed against the third party in strength, the PRD, or Democratic Revolutionary Party. The PRD developed out of a secessionist movement from the left of the PRI loyal to the nationalism, agrarianism (support of land reform), and semisocialism that had characterized the PRI's rhetoric and to some extent its policy, before the shift to the right that began under President Miguel de la Madrid (1982–1988) and was carried further by Carlos Salinas. That movement managed to attract substantial support for its 1988 presidential candidate, Cuauhtémoc Cárdenas, the decidedly uncharismatic son of the leftist revolutionary general who served from 1934 to 1940 as probably the most popular president of Mexico ever. While Salinas may well have received more votes than Cárdenas, the actual official results announced were universally regarded with skepticism. Cárdenas's incompetent campaigning and indecision on policy questions, however, together with the apparent success of Salinas's economic policies and a strong showing by a dynamic PAN candidate, put him in a weak third place in the 1994 presidential elections. The disgrace into which Salinas fell after the end of his term, however, led to an upswing in support for the PRD and the election of Cárdenas, then vindicated, as governor of the Federal District.

Opinion polls today show that a plurality of Mexicans still prefer the PRI over the PAN, with the PRD slightly behind. Nevertheless, the opposition parties—including two groupings, the Environmental Party (PVEM) and the Labor Party (PT), currently represented in the Congress—have been able to win local-level elections, and the PAN has recently won several governorships. Salinas also let the PAN have two governorships they may not have won in the vote, rather than face drawn-out campaigns of demonstrations and civil disobedience over contested election results.

EXTRA-SYSTEM OPPOSITION

The movement of the PRI to the right, and especially its abandonment of the principles of the land reform, under which land expropriated from large owners was owned in common (but usually farmed individually) by *ejido* collectivities, provided the occasion for a revolt of rural workers who had been mobilized through Catholic Liberation Theology grassroots organizations by activists left over from the student movements of the late 1960s. Taking the name of the great agrarian reformer of revolutionary days, Emiliano Zapata, the movement was catalyzed in the southern border state of Chiapas by the collapse in coffee prices and competition from immigrant Guatemalan agricultural workers. As notoriously mistreated people espousing noble goals, the Chiapas Indians who made up the Zapatista forces that took up arms on January 1, 1995, and especially their ironic and quotable leader, Marcos, aroused general sympathy among the Mexican public. Although the Zapatista forces were too weak to win any military victories, the government correctly perceived that to attempt to wipe them out would create an endless Vietnam War in southern Mexico, with all the political costs that would entail, and instead settled down to an indefinite process of slow-motion negotiations that could hope at least to defuse the situation even if it did not resolve it.

The mountainous state of Guerrero, which lies west and south of Mexico City, has always been home to bandit and even guerrilla forces. During the middle of 1996, a new guerrilla force, the People's Revolutionary Army (EPR), abruptly made its presence known there in attacks on army units, subsequently appearing in Oaxaca and Chiapas states as well. It is out of the question that a guerrilla movement of this kind could come to power by force. The country is too big, too complicated, and too sophisticated; as weak as the government may be, it is stronger by many orders of magnitude than any conceivable guerrilla army.

Yet such a movement is a symptom of how Mexico's "civil society" is beginning to crumble and how people have lost faith in the ability of PRI governments to rule wisely and well. It may also be the cause of further deterioration, as governments feel more insecure and therefore become more oppressive, or as armies take the classic route of striking out at innocent peasants in the attempt to reach the guerrillas. It seems only too likely that armed political dissent and growing criminal activity will create in Mexico the kind of permanent endemic violence made familiar to us by Colombia.

ECONOMIC STRUCTURE AND
PERFORMANCE UNTIL 1980

The economic performance of the country was very impressive until the early 1980s. The long-term rate of growth in the gross national product between 1940 and 1980 was 7 or 8 percent annually. Industry grew, producing both for the domestic market and, under special tariff arrangements, for export; but today about 8 million Mexicans still work on the land. Commercial farmers in the north of Mexico grow a great many specialty crops, such as winter vegetables, which are exported to the United States and are a valuable source of foreign exchange.

Since the middle of the 1970s, Mexico's major industry and major export has been petroleum. Early in the century, before the coming of the automobile era, when demand for the product was small, Mexico was the world's leading producer of petroleum. The international oil companies were active in Mexico until 1938. They played the obstreperous role they have often played elsewhere, mixing in the country's politics to try to keep down their tax payments and labor costs and making themselves generally disliked. The 1938 expropriation of the oil companies by Lázaro Cárdenas was thus very popular in Mexico and was looked upon as a kind of economic declaration of independence. After the expropriation, the international corporations got their crude elsewhere, however, and Mexican production declined to the level necessary simply to supply the domestic market. The state oil corporation, now called Petróleos Mexicanos (PEMEX), contented itself with producing mostly from already established wells, lacking the incentive or the funds for serious exploration.

However, over the years, PEMEX built up the technical capabilities necessary for all phases of the industry—exploration, production, refining, and marketing—except for offshore drilling. With the development of an adverse balance of payments and the sharp rise in world petroleum prices that took place in the early 1970s, PEMEX undertook explorations that established Mexico's possession of huge reserves; in mid-1997 proved and potential reserves exceeded 300 billion barrels. Yet this figure represents the exploration of only a fraction of the sedimentary basins that could contain hydrocarbon deposits. Mexico advanced to fourth place among the world's petroleum producers and became the third largest exporter after Saudi Arabia and Venezuela.

The ambiguity of the economic system, which combined capitalism with a strong dose of nationalism and socialism, paralleled the ambiguity of the political system, whose democratic institutions were belied by its underlying authoritarian character. In foreign policy, similarly, Mexico combined a wariness of its giant neighbor that reflected a long history of intervention, insult, and loss of territory, with a lively appreciation of the relative political and economic power of the two countries, which meant that defiant confrontation was not a viable option. Thus, equally well-informed observers believed that Mexico had a nationalist foreign policy behind a façade of cooperation with the United States or that it had a policy of subservience to the United States behind a nationalist facade.

Despite its revolutionary rhetoric and the many social welfare and economic projects undertaken by the government, twentieth-century Mexico fell a long way short of meeting the goals of the Revolution. Although Mexico's economic growth was undeniable, the benefits of that growth were concentrated in the upper and middle ranges of the income distribution. Moreover, privilege and corruption were widespread, and the country never came close to achieving full employment. Nevertheless, by the relative standards appropriate to an imperfect world, on the whole most observers accounted the Mexican experiment a success until late in the century.

Political stability was underwritten by economic growth. For most of the period, the economy grew steadily—indeed Mexico had more years of continuous uninterrupted economic growth than any other country. The political system remained stable, and since 1920 the constitutional succession has been unbroken, although perhaps bent a few times. The possibility of a military seizure of power, a daily worry in many of the Latin American countries, has long been a thing of the past in Mexico.

There was room for steady expansion of the domestic market as remote rural areas and indigenous populations that had been self-sufficient were progressively incorporated into the national market. In a country that lacked so much, government expenditure on infrastructure—communications, social investment, or the provision of basic utilities—was bound to generate a substantial return. Mexico's geographic position next to the United States guaranteed a constant inflow of capital and income from tourism and border transactions, providing a steady stream of convertible currency that normally made unnecessary the fiscal austerity to avoid inflation that put brakes on economic growth elsewhere.

THE INEVITABILITY OF CHANGE

When democracy triumphed with the collapse of the Soviet Union, so did the world capitalist system, which flexed its muscles and decided it no longer needed to tolerate socialist- or nationalist-inspired restrictions on its ability to seek maximum profits across state boundaries. So the classic Mexican mixed economy would have been under pressure to change in any case. However, the change in the Mexican economic model, like most major events in history, was overdetermined—that is, several factors were working in the same direction to make it happen.

It had been clear to students of development that the political and economic model that characterized the middle years of the century could not last indefinitely. For one thing, the social changes that were occurring would clearly put intolerable strains, sooner or later, on the single-party system. As the country developed socially, more students went to the university, more illiterates learned to read, more peasants moved to the city. A nation of illiterate peasants may believe that their government always does everything right and public officials are invariably competent and public-spirited. A nation of sophisticated urban dwellers led by a large university-trained elite is likely to be more skeptical. A growing managerial class is likely to chafe at government controls, and it is not possible to provide comfortable, well-paying positions for all members of a rapidly growing educated elite.

Mexico's steady economic growth was based on the gradual incorporation into the market of hitherto marginalized Indian peasants, gradually growing foreign earnings, and a stable exchange rate of the peso to the dollar. In the late 1970s, however, a volatile new factor was introduced into this equation when the rise in international petroleum prices made it worthwhile for PEMEX, the national oil monopoly, to incur the costs involved in exploring for new sources of petroleum. The tremendous reserves that were then found made it possible for Mexico to earn huge amounts of money on the international oil market. But the sudden affluence brought by oil exports, like the touch of King Midas, proved in the long run a curse rather than a blessing. Corruption grew to new levels; the ready availability of foreign exchange made it easier to import everything than to produce it in Mexico, and Mexico's own factories closed down; government employment mushroomed; and growing inflation hurt the standard of living of everyone not in a position to benefit from oil revenues.

When the inevitable downturn in oil prices came, the government of President José López Portillo (1976–1982) refused to adjust and instead borrowed abroad to cover the government's inflated expenses, hoping that prices would quickly rebound. When that didn't happen, Mexico's international creditors forced a drastic retrenchment in expenditures, so that all available resources could be devoted to paying down the debt. The result was that it was precisely those who had benefited least from the oil boom who were forced to bear the brunt of the policies of austerity that became necessary in its wake.

The abandonment by the governments of de la Madrid and Salinas of the distinctive Mexican mixed economic model, as they moved to align Mexico with the norms of the world capitalist economy, was thus presented as a painful but necessary process of adjustment that would get the economy on a sound footing and make renewed growth possible. During Salinas's presidential term, it appeared that the formula was successful. The value of the currency stabilized, economic growth resumed, and for a while the ruling PRI seemed to have regained the legitimacy it had lost with the economic crisis.

The shift in the economic model was drastic, involving not only changes in the laws governing the freedom of action of foreign capital but also a colossal sell-off of industries that had been in the public sector and the introduction of private-enterprise norms into the reformed sector of agriculture, whose collectivist principles had until then been viewed as sacred cows of revolutionary ideology. Out of the profits of the privatization program (which would have been greater if state property had not been sold to the president's friends and family at bargain prices), Salinas managed to mount a significant poverty-reduction program, called Solidarity, which softened the blow that structural reform dealt to Mexicans of lower income. It also contributed to the president's popularity and looked for a time as though it could provide a new generation of political activists Salinas would use to replace the "dinosaurs" of the PRI party organization.

However, the economic stabilization successes of the Salinas administration were based in part on a sort of confidence trick. Long-term monetary stability and economic growth were financed by short-term and potentially volatile investment funds, much of them attracted into high-interest government bonds. Not wanting to damage his image as a financial wizard, which he thought would help him win the post of secretary-general of the new World Trade Organization, Salinas did not devalue the peso when it would have been appropriate to do so. His successor, Ernesto Zedillo, then mishandled the overdue devaluation, when it finally came, with the result that capital fled the country, the value of the peso dropped, and a new wave of foreign borrowing, "structural reform," and decline in standards of living became necessary.

SOCIAL STRUCTURE AND PROBLEMS

During the years of steady economic growth, before the borrowing, inflation, and austerity of the 1980s and 1990s, things gradually got better for most Mexicans. Life expectancy at birth, a good general measure of well-being, increased from forty-eight years in 1950 to sixty-eight years in 1986. Literacy climbed during the same period from about 66 percent to about 90 percent of the population. The high rate of annual population increase—which made social problems more difficult to resolve—dropped from 3.2 percent in the 1960s to 2.9 percent in the 1970s and 2.4 percent in the 1980s.

Thereafter, however, social indicators stopped improving and indicators of economic well-being deteriorated as gains in income were nullified and the average standard of living in the mid-1990s dropped back to about where it was in the 1960s. Income inequality increased. By 1995 the top 10 percent of Mexicans received 41 percent of national income, while 3.2 percent went to the 20 percent at the bottom of the scale. As many as half of the urban population lacks regular paid employment and makes do with occasional temporary work, street vending, marginal and dubiously legal activity. In the rural areas, about half of those engaged in agricultural are landless laborers, while most of the rest have small plots that provide hardly more than a subsistence living.

PROBLEMS OF MEXICO CITY

Even if the rate of population increase should decline further, however, it will come too late to avoid the onset of some major problems. The combination of population growth and migration to the cities has made Mexico City the largest urban agglomeration in the world. This has meant the loosing of an avalanche of problems—in the areas of housing, employment, transportation, sanitation, and so on. Government performance has fallen short of a satisfactory resolution of these problems, which were worsened by the effects of the 1985 earthquake. Unemployment and underemployment are acute; standards of housing are uneven, ranging down to very poor in the satellite city of Netzahualcoyotl; and pollution has reached health-threatening proportions. Surface transportation can be a nightmare; a worker may have to travel as much as two hours each way to get to work and back each day. Construction of a subway system has alleviated the situation, but only in part.

CHANGE IN THE POLITICAL SYSTEM

The political effects of these economic developments reinforced tendencies in the political arena that grew out of other causes. The general strategy adopted by the ruling PRI for dealing with the political pressures arising from the changes going forward in Mexican society was to negotiate a long-drawn-out strategic retreat that kept opposition political forces engaged in the political game and willing to channel their opposition into constitutional means within the system, by delivering a phased series of concessions. These were enough to enable the opposition parties to feel they were gaining ground but not enough to affect the substance of power at the national level. From time to time, electoral laws were reformed so as to enable opposition parties to win a few more legislative seats; some opposition victories in municipal elections were recognized. Over time, the concessions became greater: Opposition victories were recognized for governorships, and senators from opposition parties were seated.

To put it another way, the current political drama in Mexico can be regarded as the resultant of the working-out of two sets of political dynamics. *In the long term,* Mexican politics will have to adjust somehow to the changes that have been taking place in Mexican society—urbanization, higher literacy and levels of education, greater popular participation, and the growth of what has been called "civil society" in general. This implies greater autonomy in social institutions and in the infrastructure of politics—unions, interest groups, and the media—and thus the increasing constitutionalization of the political system. *In the short and medium term,* however, the dominant force shaping the country's politics is the will of the ruling elite to stay in power. The resulting dynamic is that the ruling party conducts its strategic retreat: Various features of a fully democratic constitutional system are introduced gradually, with the party gaining enough time between each concession to adapt to the changed circumstances and to find ways to retain its monopoly on power nevertheless.

The danger for the opposition in this scenario is that the strategy of the PRI will be successful: Participation of the opposition parties in the process will lend it legitimacy, but the coming of the opposition to power will be postponed indefinitely. On the other hand, the danger exists for the ruling group that some concession that was thought to be trivial or purely cosmetic may turn out to be significant, and that the PRI will be riven by splits as the more traditional sectors of the party refuse to go along with some concession the leadership is willing to make. This is especially the case since a concession that seems trivial to the national leadership may well be a matter of life or death for a state or regional leadership group. In fact, much of the significant drama in Mexican politics today lies in the conflict within the PRI over the acceptability of reform, as much as between the PRI and the opposition parties, and many believe that the assassinations and political violence of recent years have actually been the work of hard-line PRI elements unwilling to modernize.

CONCLUSION

Although eventually the democratic façade of Mexico's political system must surely acquire greater and greater reality until Mexico becomes a "normal" country of the developed world, politically speaking it should not be assumed that that result is just about to happen: The obituary of the PRI has been pronounced prematurely many times. There are still many tricks left in the bag. It should be remembered, moreover, that even where electoral machinery functions the way it is supposed to, elected leaders must take into account economic realities that mean that policies reflect more the interests of wealth than those of poverty.

Ironically, in any case, as the country's democratic façade acquires more reality by virtue of concessions from the PRI and the development of a pluralist institutional infrastructure, this newer, more democratic character of the system is being undermined from a different direction. All too predictably, Mexico has begun to follow the path of Colombia in suffering the increased domination of its institutions by the lords of the narcotics traffic. This problem will grow worse as the ineffectual antidrug policy of the United States continues to make the trade profitable without being able to end it, while the domestic social policies of the United States continue to provide a pool of unemployed people needing relief from despair and some income, legal or not. In Mexico the judiciary is acquiring independence from domination by the executive branch only to fall under the influence of drug dealers, expressed through the double offer one cannot refuse: the megabribe to say yes, the assassin's bullet if one says no ("silver or lead"). The envelopes stuffed with pesos that journalists have long been accustomed to receiving from the government ministries they cover are increasingly being supplemented by other envelopes with different fingerprints on them.

Mexico's revolutionaries followed the path of nationalism because they knew that otherwise their policies and their politics would necessarily fall under the dominance of the concentrated power of money, which they identified with the government of the United States. Today, money calls the tune most places in the world—and within the United States, too; but it may be money that originates in back alleys, not on Wall Street. Mexico's distinctiveness will remain, of course—in its culture, its food, its music, its traditions—but less and less in its politics and its economics.

SUGGESTED READINGS

Basáñez, Miguel. *El Pulso de los Sexenios: 20 años de crisis en México.* 2d ed. Mexico City: Siglo XXI, 1991. An account of the shifts in popular attitudes as revealed in opinion polls.

Collier, Ruth Berins. *The Contradictory Alliance: State-Labor Relations and Regime Change in Mexico.* Berkeley, Calif.: International and Area Studies, 1992.

Hellman, Judith Adler. *Mexico in Crisis.* 2d ed. New York: Holmes and Meier, 1983. A good critique of Mexican political practice from the left.

Informe. This annual report by Mexico's president is one of the most valuable sources on Mexican politics and policies. It consists of a compendium of figures, a review of the previous year's performance (hardly an impartial one, of course), and a prognosis of what is to come. The report is reproduced in the major newspapers, and it is usually made available as a separate document by the office of the president (and sometimes in translation by the U.S. embassy).

Lustig, Nora. *Mexico: The Remaking of an Economy.* Washington, D.C.: Brookings Institution, 1992.

Needler, Martin C. *Mexican Politics: The Containment of Conflict.* 3d edition. New York: Praeger, 1995. This general book covers the country's history, geography, economy, and social structure—as well as its politics—from the same point of view as this chapter.

_____. *Politics and Society in Mexico.* Albuquerque: University of New Mexico Press, 1971. Interpretive essays, generally optimistic and favorable in tone.

Paz, Octavio. *The Labyrinth of Solitude.* Translated by Lysander Kemp. New York: Grove Press, 1961. A brilliant discussion of the national character of Mexico by one of the country's leading men of letters.

Philip, George. *The Presidency in Mexico.* New York: St. Martin's Press, 1992. Examination of the terms of the recent presidents that takes into account psychological as well as political and economic factors.

PART EIGHT
CENTRAL AMERICA
AND PANAMA

19

CENTRAL AMERICA: BACKGROUND TO THE CRISIS

RICHARD MILLETT

After decades of relative obscurity, Central America emerged in the 1980s as a major focus of world attention. Long seen as the backyard of the United States, a region where North American companies raised bananas and U.S. Marines deposed and installed governments, Central America now experiences the benefits and the pains of involvement by a multitude of governments and political organizations. Even Israel and the Palestine Liberation Organization (PLO) have found in Central America a new arena for their ongoing rivalry. Reluctantly, and at an appalling cost, this traditional backwater area has been dragged into the world of late-twentieth-century power politics. Old social and political structures are collapsing, but what will succeed them is still unclear.

For most North Americans, the result of this forcible intrusion of Central America upon their public consciousness has been a series of confused impressions. Violent clashes and presidential visits, coups and elections, murdered nuns and Cuban-trained guerrillas combine to form a chaotic montage of a region apparently gone mad. Explanations of this situation frequently center on simplistic responses of "Communist subversion" or "U.S.-supported repression." An adequate analysis, however, requires an understanding of Central America's tortured past and a critical examination of its violent present.

The first step in this task is to define the area under consideration. Historians have generally defined Central America as the five nations that were originally part of the Spanish colonial Captaincy General of Guatemala: Guatemala, El Salvador, Honduras, Nicaragua, and Costa Rica. Since these same nations make up the Central American Common Market, economists also generally accept this definition. Geographers, however, usually include Panama and the newly independent nation of

Belize, formerly British Honduras. In recent years, this latter approach has gained growing support from some political scientists as the interactions between Panama and Belize and the five traditional republics have steadily increased. The focus of this chapter will be something of a middle course: Emphasis will be placed on the traditional republics, but some attention will be paid to Panama and Belize, especially in regard to their involvement in regional politics.

Compared to the United States or such Latin American nations as Brazil and Mexico, the five Central American republics are small. But on a world scale they look somewhat different. Three of them (Guatemala, Honduras, and Nicaragua) are larger than East Germany, and the combined area of the five republics exceeds that of both Germanies and Austria combined. Their combined population is also small, but it has grown rapidly in recent years. In 1916, the combined population was under 5 million; by 1960, it had passed 10 million; and by 1982, it was approximately 22 million.

The cultural and ethnic patterns of Central America are varied and quite distinct from those of Mexico. Half of Guatemala's population is Indian. Descendants of the ancient Maya, they speak a wide variety of indigenous languages, still wear traditional dress, and, where the violence of the last few years has not yet reached them, live much as they did centuries ago. The predominant ethnic element in El Salvador, Honduras, and Nicaragua is mestizo, but even among these nations there is little uniformity. Diet, work habits, even some aspects of physical appearance differ from nation to nation. In addition, the Caribbean coastal areas contain a heavy concentration of black and black-Indian peoples, especially in Nicaragua, Costa Rica, and Belize. They frequently speak English as their primary language. They enjoy strong Caribbean cultural influences, and have traditionally played a limited role in national politics. Except for this coastal area, Costa Rica's ethnic composition is largely European, especially in the central plateau area. If Belize and Panama are included in this panorama, the variety becomes even greater. Belize is English speaking, the dominant culture is that of the Commonwealth Caribbean, and its politics is based on the Westminster model. Panama (see Chapter 21) has the most complex cultural pattern of any nation in the region.

This ethnic and cultural variety has played a major role in the differing national histories of the region, and it helps explain the wide variations in literacy rates, political systems, and racial attitudes. In Guatemala and El Salvador, less than half of the adult population is literate whereas in Costa Rica, the literacy rate is nearly 90 percent. In Guatemala, the Indian majority has been victimized by the prejudice of the ruling elites for centuries. One result has been the failure to integrate the Indian into Guatemalan society; a more recent product of this situation has been the growing influence of radical-left guerrilla movements among the Indian population. In Costa Rica, the predominant European population has long felt superior to the mestizos of neighboring nations and to their own country's Caribbean black minority. Until World War II, blacks from the coast were even prohibited from settling in the central part of the country. By contrast, neighboring Nicaragua, even during the decades of the Somoza family dictatorship, has been almost a model of racial toleration and integration.

For most of its history, Central America has been a rural, overwhelmingly peasant society, dependent on one or two basic crops for foreign exchange. This pattern, though, has changed greatly in recent years. Today, over half the populations of Nicaragua and Panama live in urban areas, and Costa Rica is rapidly approaching 50 percent urbanization. Export diversification and industrial development have proceeded rapidly in the region during the last quarter of a century. In 1981, manufacturing contributed more than agriculture to the GNP of Costa Rica, and the amounts were roughly equal in Nicaragua and Panama. In these areas, as in virtually every other, Central America is a region of increasing diversity and change, an area experiencing all the trauma of attempting to leap from the mid-nineteenth to the late twentieth century in a few decades.

SPANISH CONQUEST AND COLONIZATION

The history of Central America is a depressing mixture of violence, exploitation, and neglect. That pattern extends back to pre-Columbian times. Conflict more than cooperation characterized relations among the varied indigenous groups. Most developed were the Maya of Guatemala, Honduras, and northern El Salvador. They reached a relatively high level of civilization from the fourth through the ninth centuries, but a combination of civil conflicts, natural disasters, and agricultural failures led to their decline and fragmentation. In the last centuries before the Spanish conquest, Aztec influence from Mexico became an important factor, but Central America remained divided into a host of disparate tribal groups with distinct languages and cultural patterns.

The arrival of the Spaniards had a generally disastrous effect on the peoples of Central America. Slave raiding along the Honduran coast and a smallpox epidemic spreading down from Mexico preceded the actual arrival of the conquistadores. The divided nature of the indigenous populations, the difficult terrain, and divisions among the Spaniards all combined to make the conquest period a prolonged and destructive one. Actual occupation began in 1524, but parts of highland Costa Rica and Honduras were not effectively controlled by Spain until the latter half of the century. The last Mayan city held out until 1697, and some of the Caribbean lowlands were never effectively controlled by Spain.

Long before they had completely subdued the indigenous populations, the new conquerors began fighting among themselves. Meanwhile, enslavement and diseases brought by the Spaniards decimated the indigenous population. Over 200,000 Indians were shipped from Nicaragua to Panama and Peru, and tens of thousands of others were sent from Honduras and Guatemala to the Caribbean. In the 1520s, the Spanish estimated the Indian population of Nicaragua as in excess of half a million; in 1548, a census could locate only 11,137 Indians.

Both the political situation and the population began to stabilize in the second half of the sixteenth century. At the same time, other trends emerged that were to become long-term features of Central American life. One was the development of monocultural export agriculture, beginning with the cacao industry. The collapse of this export industry after a few decades also established a boom-and-bust cycle for the region's economy, a pattern reinforced a few decades later when a similar fate overtook indigo exports and Honduran silver mining.

The seventeenth century witnessed the beginnings of international rivalry and conflict in Central America, a development that would plague the region from then until the present. English and Dutch adventurers began to attack along the Caribbean coast, and in some areas, English log cutters began to establish settlements. This disrupted commerce, contributed to the general seventeenth-century economic depression in the region, and laid the basis for British control over Belize and claims to influence over the Miskito coast of Nicaragua and Honduras. During the eighteenth century, Spain's alliance with France led to increased conflicts with the English, who began to use the coastal Miskito Indians as allies for forays into the settled highlands.

By the start of the nineteenth century, the outline of present-day Central America had begun to take shape. Although overall administration was handled from Guatemala City, provincial divisions, generally corresponding to present national boundaries, were firmly established. The British were developing their own government for Belize, Panama was administratively and economically separate from the rest of the region, and the Caribbean coast, though claimed by Spain, was developing a cultural identity tied to the British Caribbean. Guatemala's population was largely Indian while 84 percent of the people living in Nicaragua were classified as ladinos, the Central American equivalent of mestizos. In the region as a whole, 65 percent of the population was Indian, 31 percent was ladino, and 4 percent was of European descent. Blacks were still rare in Spanish Central America.

INDEPENDENCE AND
THE CENTRAL AMERICAN REPUBLIC

Independence came to Central America with a minimum of actual conflict. In 1821, following news of Mexico's independence, Guatemala declared its independence from Spain. Early the following year, all of Central America was joined with the new Mexican Empire of Agustín de Iturbide. When Iturbide fell in 1823, Central Americans moved rapidly to sever their links with Mexico. After some confusion all but the province of Chiapas, which remained under Mexican control, joined the United Provinces of Central America, a federated republic with a three-member executive. This union lasted only until 1838, but it left a lasting mark upon the Central American political consciousness. Union as a political ideal has been a continuing force in the region.

Unfortunately, the union period also left two other, equally enduring, heritages. One was a pattern of conflict and jealousy among the Central American states; the other, a deep division between Liberal and Conservative political factions within each state and across state lines. The net result is that Central Americans have found it almost impossible to live with or without each other. Efforts at union have been constantly disrupted by war. Since 1837, the Central American nations have fought more than twice as many wars among themselves as have all other nations of Latin America combined. Except in Costa Rica, the ongoing conflicts led to a tradition of strong-man leadership and the involvement of the military as the ultimate arbiter of the political process.

COFFEE CULTURE AND FOREIGN INTRIGUE

The mid-nineteenth century witnessed two developments that would be basic to Central America's future. The first was the rise of coffee as a primary export crop. It created a new class of landowning elites, export oriented, interested in scientific agriculture, and increasingly conscious of common interests. Conversely, it meant the displacement of peasants from communal or subsistence plots (though not to the extent that occurred with the spread of cotton plantations in the mid-twentieth century). The primacy of coffee also led to foreign immigration and investment, with Germans and Britons being the most prominent. Finally, as commerce expanded, so also did government revenues.

The other major development of this period was the rise in foreign, especially U.S., interest in the region. In 1849, a group of U.S. investors, headed by Cornelius Vanderbilt, began operating a transportation system across Nicaragua. This produced a potential conflict with British interests, so in 1850 the United States and Great Britain concluded the Clayton-Bulwer Treaty, which provided that neither nation would seek to control the transit routes through Central America or "exercise any dominion" over any part of the Central American republics. In the years following the signing of the treaty, British influence in the region declined while that of the United States expanded. British presence on the Miskito coast, however, continued until the end of the century.

The increased North American presence was all too frequently violent. In 1854, U.S. Marines burned San Juan del Norte in retaliation for an alleged insult to the U.S. minister to Nicaragua. In 1856, marines landed for the first time in Panama, a process they repeated in 1860. But the most notable intervention was unofficial. Beginning in 1855, a Tennessee adventurer, William Walker, began a series of filibustering expeditions designed to establish his personal control over Nicaragua and, perhaps ultimately, much of the rest of Central America. He succeeded in making himself Nicaragua's president for a brief time, but the efforts of a combined Central American army, financed in part by Cornelius Vanderbilt, finally defeated him. A later effort in Honduras also failed. Walker surrendered to a British naval commander, who promptly turned him over to a Honduran firing squad. Walker's death ended serious filibustering efforts in Central America but left behind a heritage of suspicion of U.S. motives in the area.

In the 1860s, the Civil War diverted U.S. interest away from Central America, which entered upon a relatively stable and prosperous period. In the 1880s, Costa Rica began its tradition of one-term, elected presidents, a tradition that, despite brief interruptions in 1917 and 1948, has endured ever since. Strong, Liberal Party dictators emerged in the region, with Presidents Justo Ruffino Barrios in Guatemala (1873–1885) and José Santos Zelaya in Nicaragua (1893–1909) being the most influential.

In the late nineteenth century, bananas also became a major Central American export. Unlike coffee, this new trade was overwhelmingly concentrated in foreign hands. The United Fruit Company and, to a lesser extent, the Standard Fruit Company represented major U.S. business involvement in the area.

THE ERA OF DIRECT INTERVENTION

The Spanish American War signaled a greatly increased U.S. interest in the Caribbean and Central America. A new treaty with Great Britain (Hay-Pauncefote) abrogated the Clayton-Bulwer Treaty and cleared the way for the United States to build a transoceanic canal. After considerable debate, the Nicaraguan route was rejected and a site through Panama was selected. Panama was then part of Colombia, but it was liberated in 1903 with considerable help from the U.S. Navy.

Marines landed in Panama, Honduras, and Nicaragua several times during the early twentieth century, culminating in a major intervention in Nicaragua in 1912. A force of marines remained in Nicaragua until 1925, ensuring that no government at all unsympathetic to U.S. interests took power in that nation. During this period, Nicaragua agreed to the Bryan-Chamorro Treaty, which gave the United States exclusive rights over canal construction through the nation. In reality, the effect of this treaty was to ensure that no canal would be built through Nicaragua, thus protecting Washington's strategic and economic interests in Panama.

During the first three decades of the twentieth century, the U.S. government and North American banana companies exercised dominant influence over most of Central America. U.S. pressures played a major role in governmental changes in every nation but El Salvador. The overall thrust of U.S. policy during this period was summed up in 1927 by Under-Secretary of State Robert Olds, who wrote:

> The Central American area down to and including the Isthmus of Panama constitutes a legitimate sphere of influence for the United States if we are to have due regard for our own safety and protection. . . . Our ministers accredited to the five little republics stretching from the Mexican border to Panama . . . have been advisors whose advice has been accepted virtually as law . . . we do control the destinies of Central America. . . . There is no room for any outside influence other than ours in this region. . . .
>
> Until now Central America has always understood that those governments which we recognize and support stay in power, while those which we do not recognize and support fall.

These attitudes and actions produced a nationalistic backlash in much of Latin America. Opinion in El Salvador and Costa Rica was especially critical of U.S. policy, but the most effective protest came in Nicaragua. The marines had left that nation in 1925, but returned the following year when renewed civil conflict seemed to threaten U.S. dominance. A peace treaty—providing for general disarmament, supervised elections, and a prolonged marine occupation during which a new, supposedly nonpartisan National Guard would be created by marine officers—was imposed on the warring Liberal and Conservative factions. One Liberal general, however, refused to accept the terms and began a guerrilla war against the marines and the National Guard that would last until 1933. His name was Augusto César Sandino, and be became a heroic symbol to thousands of Latin Americans because of his resistance to North American intervention.

DEPRESSION AND DICTATORSHIP

The era of overt U.S. interventions came to an end in the 1930s, and a quartet of strong military dictators enforced stability in every Central American nation except Costa Rica. Maximiliano Hernández Martínez in El Salvador, Jorge Ubico in Guatemala, Anastasio Somoza García in Nicaragua, and Tiburcio Carías Andino in Honduras all began long terms in power in the 1930s. All but Somoza lost this power in the 1940s—the Somoza family was destined to retain its control of Nicaragua until 1979—but each left a deep imprint upon his nation.

The first to gain power was Martínez in El Salvador. After helping to unseat an elected civilian president, he moved rapidly to consolidate his control over the military and the rest of society. The economic rigors of the depression had combined with rising population pressures and the activities of Central America's strongest Communist Party to generate a major uprising by rural, largely Indian, peasants. Badly planned and executed, the uprising was quickly put down with only a few casualties. Afterward, however, the military, urged on by a frightened rural oligarchy, massacred between 10,000 and 30,000 peasants, decimating what remained of the nation's indigenous population. This slaughter, known as the *matanza,* left a heritage of class fear and hatred that has persisted up to the present. But it also solidified General Martínez in power. Despite such personal eccentricities as hanging colored lights across streets in the capital to avert a smallpox epidemic, he managed to prolong his rule until 1944.

General Jorge Ubico ruled Guatemala from 1931 until 1944. He was a strong supporter of the United States and especially of the United Fruit Company, which reached its peak of influence during this period. Indian labor was ensured by a law that made unemployment a crime. This was accompanied by another Ubico innovation, a maximum wage law for rural Indians. Other Ubico "reforms" included the abolition of independent local government, the expansion and strengthening of the armed forces, and during World War II, the confiscation of all German landholdings. The United States provided rather bizarre assistance in this last case, interning Germans from Guatemala, El Salvador, and other parts of Central America in Texas and then shipping them back to Germany, where many of them had never lived, late in the war.

In Honduras, the rule of General Tiburcio Carías Andino was less colorful than that of his Salvadoran or Guatemalan contemporaries, but it endured even longer. He took power in a relatively honest election in 1932, then through a variety of maneuvers, maintained himself in office until the end of 1948.

Nicaragua's Somoza Dynasty

By far the most enduring of these dictatorships was that established by General Anastasio Somoza García in Nicaragua. Unlike the other dictators, Somoza had begun his career as a politician, not as a military officer. He had studied in the United States and then married into a prominent political family. General Somoza learned early in life that the path to power in Nicaragua ran through Washington, and he made a career out of cultivating ties and influence with North Americans. He served as an intermediary between Nicaraguan President José María Moncada and the U.S. Marines and State Department during the 1926–1933 intervention, somehow persuading each side that his real loyalties lay with it. This role made him an acceptable candidate to most factions for the post of commander of the new National Guard when the marines left Nicaragua in 1933.

The guerrilla leader Sandino had fought against the intervention until it ended, but once the marines left Nicaragua, he rapidly agreed to a truce with the government. The following year the National Guard, with Somoza's support, murdered Sandino and scattered his remaining followers. After two more years of maneuvering, Somoza overthrew his wife's uncle and, supported by the guard, installed himself as Nicaragua's president. With one brief interruption, he retained control over the country until he was assassinated in 1956. By then, the system he had established proved so strong that his two sons, Luis and Anastasio Somoza Debayle, were able to keep the family in power until 1979.

The keys to the Somoza dynasty's success were numerous. Most basic was absolute control over the U.S.-created National Guard, a mixed military-police force that monopolized armed power within Nicaragua. This control was achieved through massive corruption, personal favoritism, ruthless purging of any officer who showed signs of personal ambition or loyalty to anything but the Somoza family, and a long tradition of always having a family member in command.

Other factors that made the family's long rule possible were a constant cultivation of U.S. support, creating the image in Nicaragua that Somoza was Washington's choice for president and that no effort to overthrow him would be tolerated, and the conversion of the traditional Liberal Party to a compliant instrument of Somoza ambitions. The Somozas were also able to co-opt much of the traditional opposition in the middle and upper classes by offering them some share in the spoils of power, usually guaranteeing their lives and property even when they tried to overthrow the family, and constantly presenting themselves as the only sure bulwark against the left. In all of this, General Somoza García combined an uncanny political skill with a blatant disregard for the real interests of the nation. The Somozas became the richest as well as the most enduring family in Central America's political history, corruption became the dominant national institution, and the military became a private guard.

The Tumultuous Aftermath of World War II

World War II accelerated the modernization process in Central America. U.S. training and equipment helped modernize the armed forces, and a massive propaganda campaign, which portrayed the war as a fight of democracies against dictators, caused some officers to begin to question their own national political systems. In 1944, massive popular uprisings, with some military support, toppled Generals Ubico in Guatemala and Martínez in El Salvador. In the latter case, reform efforts proved short-lived, and a form of institutional military rule was established. In Guatemala, however, more fundamental changes were begun.

Guatemala: Abortive Revolution and Counterrevolution

After some infighting, a group of young, reform-minded officers gained control of the revolution in Guatemala. They promptly set about writing a new, liberal constitution and holding elections for president and Congress. The presidential elections were won by Dr. Juan José Arévalo, a scholar who had been exiled for years. Under President Arévalo, numerous major reforms were initiated. Compulsory labor for the Indians was abolished, illiterates (the vast majority of the population) gained the right to vote, and education, especially in rural areas, was expanded. Even more notable was the government's encouragement of labor unions and the passage of a liberal labor code. This, combined with the establishment of a rudimentary social security system, gained considerable support for the government but, at the same time, produced growing alarm among traditional elites.

Controversy within the military over the pace of reforms and over the presidential succession led to bitter conflict, which culminated in 1949 when the leader of the more conservative faction, Colonel Francisco Arana, was assassinated. His chief rival, Colonel Jacobo Arbenz Guzmán, was then able to consolidate his own power and assure his election as Arévalo's successor.

Urged on by his wife, Arbenz was determined to accelerate the pace of change in Guatemala. In this process, he found Guatemala's Communists to be eager allies. Although relatively small, Guatemala's Communist Party had the advantages of organization, discipline, and external support, elements that the democratic left usually lacked. Party members were also hardworking, relatively honest, and anxious to take on the entrenched Guatemalan power structure. The result was a rapid polarization process. The upper classes and the Roman Catholic Church were quick to denounce reforms, such as the forced reduction of rates by the private electric company, as "Communist inspired." For their part, the Communists, aided by their increasing role in the media, were quite content to take credit for reforms in which they had actually played a limited role.

It soon became clear that the chief issue was the Agrarian Reform Law, Decree 900, of 1952. This provided for the expropriation of uncultivated landholdings in excess of 665 acres (269 hectares). Members of the rural oligarchy were furious because this law threatened their economic and political power and because compensation was to be paid on the basis of tax-assessed value, something they had long notoriously underdeclared. The giant United Fruit Company (UFCO) felt at least equally threatened. Already engaged in a bitter dispute with the government over taxes on the national railroad system, which UFCO controlled, the company now saw the Agrarian Reform Law as threatening its survival in Guatemala. Labor disputes and popular resentment over UFCO's power and arrogance all contributed to growing tension and hostility.

Unfortunately for Arbenz, the Dulles family was closely connected with UFCO, and in 1953, John Foster Dulles was the U.S. secretary of state and his brother, Allen, was head of the CIA. They were easily convinced that Guatemala was on the verge of a Communist takeover. At the Tenth Inter-American Conference of Foreign Ministers, held in Caracas in March 1954, the United States, over bitter Guatemalan opposition, pushed through a resolution declaring that communism was a threat to inter-American security.

While the diplomats were arguing in Caracas, the CIA was organizing and training Guatemalan right-wing exiles in Honduras and Nicaragua. U.S. arms shipments to both of these nations were sharply increased, and many of the arms were passed directly to the exiles. Plans for an invasion of Guatemala were accelerated in the spring of 1954 as strikes began to hit the U.S. banana plantations in Honduras and as Arbenz began seeking arms from the Soviet bloc. With CIA support, especially air support, the exiles, led by Colonel Carlos Castillo Armas, crossed the border. Actual fighting was limited, as the Guatemalan army showed little desire to defend the Arbenz government. Under strong U.S. pressure, the army ultimately forced President Arbenz to resign and go into exile; then, after some additional maneuvering, it yielded to the U.S. ambassador's demands and allowed the installation of Castillo Armas as president.

The new Guatemalan government promptly set about reversing many of the reforms of the previous decade. United Fruit and other large landowners got much of their land back, labor unions were purged of Communists and other leftist leaders and their influence was greatly reduced, and political parties on the left were brutally suppressed. For a brief period, the Eisenhower administration pumped aid into Guatemala in a demonstration of support for the new government, but as time passed and the "Communist menace" faded, this assistance was gradually reduced. Castillo Armas was assassinated by one of his own bodyguards in 1957, but after some confusion, another right-wing officer, General Miguel Ydígoras Fuentes, was installed as president, and the policy of maintaining the status quo continued.

The U.S.-sponsored overthrow of the Arbenz government represents a watershed in Central American history. The exact degree of Communist influence in that regime remains a matter of some dispute, but it now seems clear that the Communists were never in control and that the Eisenhower administration reacted in a heavy-handed, arrogant manner to an essentially nationalistic reform movement.

Costa Rica: The Rise of the National Liberation Party

Costa Rica's electoral campaign of 1948 was marred by violence, and the returns, which seemed to give victory to the opposition candidate, Otilio Ulate, were disputed. The moderately reformist administration of Teodoro Picado Michalski used its control over the Congress to annul the elections and, shortly thereafter, arrested Ulate and several of his supporters. These actions gave José ("Pepe") Figueres, leader of a new social democratic party, an opportunity to rebel against the government. Actual fighting was limited, but by Costa Rican standards, surprisingly bloody. Ultimately, former President Rafael Calderón Guardia, the government's candidate, and Picado fled to Nicaragua and a junta, headed by Pepe Figueres, was installed. In a few months, the junta held elections, won by Ulate; nationalized Costa Rica's banks; outlawed the Communist (Vanguardia Popular) Party; and dissolved the Costa Rican army. The army was replaced by a constabulary force known as the Civil Guard. What distinguished this force from constabularies in Panama and Nicaragua was the nonprofessional nature of the higher officers who were appointed by each new administration.

Figueres, who for a time had concentrated his energies on trying to bring down dictators in the Caribbean area, won the Costa Rican presidential election in 1953, representing his National Liberation Party. In 1955, Figueres's archrival, Somoza, sought to topple the Costa Rican government. Costa Rican resistance, strengthened by U.S. and OAS support, defeated this movement. Somoza was assassinated the following year, but the dictator's sons, Luis and Anastasio Somoza Debayle, succeeded their father in power and maintained the feud with Figueres.

ECONOMIC GROWTH AND POLITICAL FERMENT

The late 1950s and early 1960s saw relative calm and progress in Central America. In Costa Rica, the National Liberation Party and its more conservative opponents regularly succeeded each other in power, beginning a pattern in which the party in power has lost every subsequent presidential election but one from 1948 through 1982. In Nicaragua, after a brief wave of repression following General Somoza García's assassination, Luis Somoza, who succeeded his father as president, began a slight liberalization: He even allowed a non-Somoza to serve as president for the 1963–1967 term. Real power, however, including command of the military, remained firmly in Somoza family hands.

In El Salvador, a period of extreme corruption was ended in 1960 by a junior officers' coup, but their moderately leftist government lasted for only a few weeks before other officers, responding to pressures from the oligarchy and the United States, staged a countercoup and installed Colonel Julio Adalberto Rivera as president.

Rivera initiated a series of limited reforms, mostly in urban areas, and began to allow opposition parties to function openly.

Even Honduras enjoyed a brief period of reformist, democratic government under Liberal Party President Ramón Villeda Morales (1957–1963), but this was brought to an end by yet another military coup, led by Colonel Osvaldo López Arellano. Guatemala remained the most depressing nation, at least from a political standpoint, with fraudulent elections, military coups, and an increasingly bitter conflict with left-wing guerrillas in the 1960s. One reasonably honest election was held in 1966, and the victorious civilian candidate actually managed to complete his term. But real power remained with the military, which launched a particularly brutal campaign in 1966, decimating the several hundred rural guerrillas along with several thousand uninvolved Indian peasants.

Two broader trends overshadowed domestic political developments during the 1959–1968 period. The first was the growing preoccupation of regional elites and the United States with the Communist regime in Cuba. The Cuban exiles who attacked Fidel Castro in the 1961 Bay of Pigs invasion had been trained in Guatemala and launched their invasion from Nicaragua. In 1965, Honduras, Nicaragua, and even Costa Rica contributed units to the U.S.-sponsored Inter-American Peace Force sent to the Dominican Republic. Castro, for his part, began to offer some assistance and training to left-wing guerrilla groups in Central America, most notably to the newly organized Sandinista National Liberation Front (FSLN) in Nicaragua. All these events contributed to a growing climate of repression in much of the region and to increased U.S. concern with military assistance and training. During the Kennedy administration, there was also considerable emphasis on economic and political reforms to undercut the appeal of the Cuban model, but as the Johnson administration got bogged down in Vietnam, this emphasis was replaced with an overriding concern for stability and order.

The other, more positive development was the rapid economic growth of the region, a trend spurred on by the establishment of the Central American Common Market, formalized by treaty in 1961 (Costa Rica did not join until 1963). During this same period, a Central American Development Bank was established, and several other regional organizations, including a U.S.-sponsored defense pact (Central American Defense Council, CONDECA), were created.

As the Common Market developed and prices for basic exports such as coffee and cotton rose, the economies boomed. This economic growth was partly offset by rapid population growth, which at times, especially in Costa Rica and El Salvador, was as great as anywhere in the world, but when this was taken into account and allowance also made for inflation, actual per capita income still increased by well over 40 percent during the period.

This growth produced important alterations in the region's social and economic patterns. One obvious effect was a rapid increase in urbanization, accelerating the growth of the middle class. Previously a small and weak buffer between the landed elite and the poor rural mass, the middle class by the early 1970s had become a significant force in the region, especially in Costa Rica and El Salvador. Members of this class wanted to curb the power of the military and the traditional elites, and they often sought to forge alliances with the more upwardly mobile sectors of the working poor.

Perhaps the most significant change in Central America during the 1950s and 1960s, however, was the revolution in communications. At the end of World War II, the average Central American was a peasant who could expect to spend his entire life as an isolated illiterate, never venturing more than 20 mi (30 km) from the place of his birth. By the early 1970s, the growth of the economy had produced a boom in road building, followed by the creation of a network of rural bus services. The great majority of Central Americans could now get up in the morning and be in a major city before dark.

Increased education and mobility and such technological innovations as the transistor radio led to greatly expanded access to information about the outside world. The net effect of all these factors was to greatly increase the number of individuals involved in national politics, or at least beginning to question the inevitability and justice of existing structures and to be aware of competing political and economic philosophies and the possibility of change.

There were other, less desirable results of Central America's economic development. In many rural areas, land concentration increased as large landowners began to convert plots formerly used by the poor for food production into plantations for commercial, export-oriented agriculture. Cotton, sugar (after the elimination of Cuba's quota in the U.S. market), and cattle began to rival the traditional dependence on coffee and bananas. While the GNP increased, the nutritional level of many Central Americans actually declined as food production failed to keep pace with population growth.

Two natural results of the situation in the countryside were accelerated migration to urban centers and the growth of belts of poverty within and surrounding the principal cities. This contributed to rising crime rates and greatly increased the level of class tension. As long as the economy continued to grow at a steady, relatively rapid rate, these pressures could be controlled, but beginning in 1969, the Central American economic miracle began to falter.

ECONOMIC CRISIS AND POLITICAL REPRESSION

A slowdown in the world economy contributed to the crisis of 1969, but the major issue was the brief war that summer between El Salvador and Honduras. In an effort to shore up his sagging popularity and deal with the weakened economy, Honduran dictator Osvaldo López Arellano began expelling tens of thousands of illegal Salvadoran immigrants. This led to a rapid escalation of tensions between the two nations, and in July, following a bloody clash at a soccer match, El Salvador invaded Honduras. In less than a week of fighting, El Salvador managed to seize large chunks of Honduran territory, but its air force was decimated, and a combination of U.S.

and OAS pressures soon forced El Salvador to withdraw from most of the captured territory. An OAS mission was set up to control the remaining pockets of disputed territory, known as *bolsones,* and to prevent further outbreaks of fighting. Until 1981, formal diplomatic relations remained suspended, and trade was virtually shut off between Honduras and El Salvador, with disastrous consequences for both nations.

An even greater blow to the region's economy was the rapid rise in petroleum prices beginning in 1973. Guatemala would begin limited petroleum production in the late 1970s, but in 1973 all of the Central American nations were totally dependent on imported oil. This dependence had been increased by the economic growth of the preceding years, not only because of the considerable increase in automobile and truck traffic, but because of the heavy use of petroleum-based fertilizers and pesticides in the production of new export crops such as cotton. The increased energy costs not only slowed economic growth, they also led to increased government borrowing to cover current accounts deficits. By the late 1970s, service on debts and payments for imported petroleum products were consuming the bulk of Central America's export earnings.

Polarization in El Salvador

While the economy was slowing down, the apparent progress toward more democratic structures in the region was being reversed. By the late 1970s, only Costa Rica and the British self-governing colony of Belize (formerly British Honduras) had functioning democratic governments. The worst changes had taken place in El Salvador. There, during the 1960s, the military, ruling through the National Conciliation Party (PCN), had allowed opposition parties to function and even gain a large number of congressional seats and local offices. The Christian Democratic Party (PCD) profited most from this apparent liberalization. Its leader, José Napoleon Duarte, had been elected mayor of the capital city, San Salvador; with Social Democrat Guillermo Manuel Ungo as his running mate, Duarte appeared to have a good chance of winning the 1972 presidential election. Blatant fraud, however, was used to give the victory to the army's candidate, Colonel Arturo Molina. A subsequent revolt by part of the army was crushed, Duarte was arrested and exiled, and right-wing paramilitary groups began to attack Christian Democratic and other opposition leaders throughout the country.

The fraud of 1972 damaged both the Christian Democrats and the legitimacy of the entire electoral process. Two results were the growth of mass organizations further to the left and the slow resurgence of both urban and rural guerrilla conflicts. In 1975, several labor and peasant organizations joined with the national teachers association (ANDES) to form the Popular Revolutionary Block (BPR). Other coalitions, even further to the left, also came into existence, providing a powerful set of opponents to the continued rule of the military-oligarchy alliance. By the time of the 1977 elections, violence was growing, and the government had little legitimacy left. Its international image was further eroded when the army's chief of staff was arrested and convicted in the United States for attempting to sell weapons to organized crime syndicates. The battered democratic opposition parties united again for the 1977 elections. Realizing that the military would not permit a civilian to win the presidency, this coalition nominated a retired military officer, Colonel Ernesto Claramount. But the military resorted to even more blatant fraud to secure the victory of the official candidate, Colonel Carlos Humberto Romero, then brutally crushed popular demonstrations of protest.

Guatemala's Official Terrorism

In Guatemala, too, the military strengthened its stranglehold over politics in the early and mid-1970s. Colonel Carlos Arana, chief architect of the bloody counterinsurgency campaign of the mid-1960s, was elected president in 1970 and continued his efforts to crush all opposition from the left. The guerrillas responded by turning to urban terrorism, murdering the U.S. ambassador in 1968 and the German ambassador in 1970. But guerrilla ranks were steadily decimated, and by 1973 they no longer appeared capable of offering a serious challenge to the government.

The real challenge to oligarchic rule now came from moderate reformist parties such as the Christian Democrats, the Social Democrats (led by former Foreign Minister Alberto Fuentes Mohr), and after 1974, the United Revolutionary Front (FUR) led by Guatemala City's mayor, Manuel Colom Argüeta. In 1974, these parties backed the presidential candidacy of General Efrain Ríos Montt. In classical Central American fashion, Ríos Montt apparently won the election but lost the official count to the government's candidate, General Kjell Laugerud García.

Costa Rica: The Price of Prosperity

While elections in El Salvador and Guatemala were dominated by fraud and violence, Costa Rica managed to continue its tradition of open democracy. "Pepe" Figueres was elected to a second presidential term in 1970. Growing tourism, high coffee prices, and foreign investment fueled a steady economic growth, which gave Costa Rica a gross domestic product per capita of $1,311 in 1979, fifth highest in Latin America. Economic progress was translated into such social benefits as Latin America's fourth highest literacy rate, second longest life expectancy, and, along with Cuba, lowest infant mortality rate.

These favorable statistics, however, masked growing problems. The administration of President Daniel Oduber Quirós, who succeeded Figueres in 1974, responded to economic pressures by promoting tourism, the settlement of retired North Americans in Costa Rica, real estate sales to foreigners, and, increasingly, borrowing abroad to cover deficits in current accounts. As a result, the nation's external debt, which was only $277 million in 1970, had reached $1,869,000,000 in 1979. Debt service that year cost Costa Rica $255 million, more than the entire national debt nine years earlier.

Honduras: Corruption and Military Musical Chairs

While Costa Rica continued to develop in the 1970s, Honduras continued to stagnate. Severe hurricanes, economic mismanagement, and internal political conflict added to the devastation of the 1969 war with El Salvador. In a rigged election, marked by massive national indifference, the military had allowed the civilian leadership of the conservative National Party to return to the Presidential Palace in 1971, but the new president, Ramón Ernesto Cruz, proved inept and, after a year and a half in office, was unceremoniously removed by the armed forces and replaced by General López Arellano.

To the surprise of most outside observers, the new military government actually promoted some modest reforms, including a limited agrarian reform program. Peasant and labor unions also grew in the mid-1970s, and clashes with the entrenched landed oligarchy increased. These clashes were particularly acute on the north coast, where the military and local landowners murdered numerous peasant leaders and even killed two missionary priests. In this latter case, again in contrast to Honduran tradition, the military officer responsible for the killings was actually tried, convicted, and imprisoned.

Corruption, however, remained rampant; even President López Arellano was eventually detected taking large bribes from the United Fruit Company in order to keep Honduras from joining other banana-exporting nations in levying an export tax on bananas. This was too much even for the Honduran military, which dumped its erstwhile president and replaced him with another officer, Colonel Juan Alberto Melgar Castro. As compensation, López Arellano assumed control of both Honduran national airlines.

The new president found himself sharing power with a Superior Council of the Armed Forces, a group of twenty-five or more officers who assumed control over internal army functions and could exercise a de facto veto over most major areas of national policy. This situation inevitably led to conflicts, and in 1978 the Superior Council removed Melgar Castro from office, installing army commander-in-chief General Policarpo Paz García in his place. Known neither for his personal ambition nor for his sobriety, General Paz was to prove a more compliant instrument of the wishes of the officer corps.

Nicaragua: Prelude to Revolution

On the surface, Nicaragua seemed to be experiencing little change during the first two-thirds of the 1970s. Presidents came and went in the other republics, but the Somozas remained Nicaragua's overwhelmingly dominant political force. Anastasio Somoza Debayle, the younger and less able of the two legitimate sons of the dynasty's founder, took his turn as president in 1967. He set about using the office of president to further increase his already enormous fortune and to reward his relatives and the National Guard. As long as the economy continued to grow and the traditional elite and the opposition parties were allowed to share in the profits, though not in the power, they largely accepted this situation.

This intra-elite accord, along with most of Nicaragua's capital city of Managua, collapsed in the devastating earthquake of December 1972. For a brief period, the destruction of the quake and the near-total disintegration of the National Guard in the subsequent confusion appeared to threaten Somoza dominance, but thanks in part to the energetic support of the U.S. ambassador, the system survived. General Somoza declared martial law and began using the misery of this natural disaster to further enrich himself and his supporters. He also expressed his gratitude to the U.S. ambassador for his support by placing the latter's picture, along with his own, on Nicaragua's twenty-cordoba bill.

All of this increased popular discontent with Somoza rule and damaged what remained of the family's international image. It even alienated the business community, which found the Somozas now intruding in areas of the economy, such as banking and construction, that they had previously left to the private sector. Seeking to take advantage of this situation, the Sandinista National Liberation Front (FSLN) guerrillas increased their activities. In 1974, they staged a spectacular raid on Managua itself, seizing several cabinet ministers and Somoza relatives as hostages. This action resulted in considerable publicity for the Sandinistas and revealed the extent of popular disaffection with the regime, as crowds of loudly cheering Nicaraguans ignored government orders and demonstrated their support for the guerrillas. At the time, however, the FSLN still did not seem able to seriously threaten Somoza rule.

ESCALATING CONFLICT

By late 1977, tensions were rising throughout Central America, and with the exception of Costa Rica, existing political systems became subject to increasing strain. Several factors, in addition to growing economic and social problems, contributed to this. The Roman Catholic Church, especially in Nicaragua and El Salvador, was becoming increasingly vocal in its condemnations of existing inequalities and repression. The victory of Jimmy Carter in the 1976 U.S. presidential elections weakened right-wing influences in Washington and led to a greatly increased emphasis on human rights by the U.S. State Department. As hopes for peaceful, democratic change in the region were increasingly frustrated by electoral fraud and political violence, guerrilla groups and other organizations of the radical left began to gain influence. Alarmed by these developments, the anachronistic power structures of most of the nations turned increasingly to military force and private right-wing terrorist groups to maintain their grip on power.

Revolution in Nicaragua

El Salvador's situation appeared to be the most explosive at the start of 1978, but the collapse of the old order actually began in Nicaragua. The Sandinistas had increased their activities in 1976 and 1977, but the Somozas and their National Guard appeared up to the challenge, even managing to kill the FSLN's founder, Carlos Fonseca Amador, in a late 1976 encounter. Then, in January 1978, assassins, connected with business associates of President Somoza, killed Nicaragua's leading newspaper publisher and opposition political leader, Pedro Joaquín Chamorro. The result was an explosion of national defiance and international indignation. Mass popular demonstrations were followed by a prolonged national strike, with employers actually paying their employees not to work, and by scattered popular uprisings, most notably in the city of Masaya. A group of twelve business, political, and intellectual leaders, known as *Los Doce,* began issuing calls for Somoza's resignation and for the inclusion of the FSLN in the government of post-Somoza Nicaragua.

These developments alarmed both the Somozas and the Carter administration. The United States began pressuring Somoza to end the state of siege and open up the political system. Other nations, notably Panama and Venezuela, were much blunter in their condemnation of the Nicaraguan government. They even established contacts with the Sandinistas, which gave them much greater legitimacy than that provided by their traditional Cuban connection.

In an effort to defuse both domestic and international opposition, the Nicaraguan dictator, who had only recently recovered from a heart attack, adopted a series of somewhat contradictory actions. On the one hand, he lifted the state of siege; ended press, but not radio, censorship; allowed the members of *Los Doce* to return to Nicaragua; and pledged not to be a candidate for reelection in 1980. At the same time, he increased the use of force by the National Guard against the Sandinistas, raised his son to the rank of lieutenant colonel and placed him in charge of the military's best combat unit, and stubbornly resisted all suggestions that he step down before 1981.

By mid-summer of 1978, it appeared that the Somozas had successfully weathered another crisis. The general strike had collapsed, the Sandinistas seemed unable to seize major towns, and even the United States had modified its opposition as President Carter sent General Somoza a letter expressing his appreciation for the "improvement" in internal conditions. Then, in August, the situation underwent a dramatic change.

The immediate cause was the seizure of the National Palace by a Sandinista commando group headed by Edén Pastora (known as Comandante Cero). The Congress and several cabinet members were held hostage until Somoza agreed to free Sandinista prisoners (including Tomás Borge, the last surviving founder of the FSLN), publish and broadcast an antigovernment manifesto, and allow free passage to Panama for the commandos and the freed prisoners. This humiliation was rapidly followed by others. A plot against the dictator by moderate guard officers was discovered and crushed, but a series of popular uprisings that broke out shortly thereafter proved much more difficult to deal with. Several cities were taken over for days or even weeks by the FSLN and were returned to government control only after bloody fighting, during which National Guard tactics caused thousands of civilian casualties. A national strike further compounded the dictator's problems, as did the rising tide of international opposition to his continued rule. Costa Rica began openly to provide a haven for the FSLN, and Venezuela and Panama began funneling arms to the anti-Somoza guerrillas. Even the Carter administration apparently decided that the longtime U.S. ally had outlived his usefulness and had to go.

The method chosen by Washington to remove Somoza, and at the same time prevent a Sandinista military victory, was international mediation under OAS auspices. Both the dictator and the traditional opposition were persuaded to agree to this process. The FSLN refused to participate directly, but was at first represented by *Los Doce*. When it became apparent, however, that Somoza hoped to use the process to hang on to at least a major share of power, *Los Doce* withdrew, as did other leftist elements. The United States and the moderate, traditional opposition continued the effort to negotiate Somoza's departure until the start of 1979 when the entire mediation process collapsed. Convinced that the United States would not use significant economic or military force to remove him and still believing that he could force the middle and upper classes to resume their support for, or at least acceptance of, his rule in order to keep the Sandinistas out of power, Somoza had used the time of the mediation to expand his armed forces for a showdown with the guerrillas.

By early 1979, Nicaragua was on the verge of collapse. The economy was in a shambles. The gross domestic product had declined 7.2 percent in 1978 and would decline an additional 25.8 percent in 1979. The international debt was soaring past the $1.4-billion mark, and the currency had to be devalued. Tens of thousands of Nicaraguans had been killed or wounded, and many had become homeless refugees within Nicaragua or had fled to neighboring countries. General Somoza seemed quite willing to destroy his own nation in order to postpone his fall from power.

Sandinista strength increased dramatically following the collapse of the mediation. With U.S. policy apparently adrift and the traditional opposition discredited by its participation in the mediation effort, the FSLN appeared to offer the only hope of bringing down the dynasty. Previously divided into three competing factions, the FSLN now forged a unified national directorate of nine individuals and undertook a coordinated military strategy. Meanwhile, *Los Doce* did an effective job of mustering international support for their cause in Europe and Latin America and in further isolating the tottering Somoza regime.

In May, the FSLN began an all-out offensive. Operating openly from Costa Rica, it soon managed to seize several major towns and even staged uprisings within the capital. OAS delegates, in an emergency meeting called to deal with the crisis, refused to go along with a U.S. proposal to send a peacekeeping force to Nicaragua to end the fighting. Instead, with only two dissenting votes, the OAS called for Somoza's replacement.

Following this meeting, the United States concentrated its efforts on removing Somoza, ending the fighting, and preserving some elements of the National Guard. The Sandinistas established a provisional government, including many moderates and non-Sandinistas, which was quickly granted belligerent status and even recognition by many Latin American governments. As the national uprising continued to spread, the guard began to run out of fuel and supplies. Now anxious to get himself and his leading supporters out of Nicaragua, General Somoza finally agreed to resign and hand over power to an interim government, which would then turn it over to the Sandinista-appointed junta. But, in private, the dictator urged his supporters to continue the war, promising that once he had departed, the United States would join the fight against the guerrillas. When he fled to Miami on July 17, 1979, his hand-picked successor, Dr. Francisco Urcuyo, therefore announced his determination to hang on to power. The United States immediately denounced this move, and the Sandinistas stepped up the military pressure. In a matter of hours the National Guard dissolved. On July 19, the Sandinistas entered Managua in triumph, bringing to an end the longest-lasting family dictatorship in Latin American history.

Spreading Hopes and Fears

With the end of the civil war, large credits were provided by other Latin American nations to the virtually bankrupt new government of Nicaragua, and President Carter requested $75 million in aid from the U.S. Congress. In addition, Washington stepped up its pressures on Honduras, El Salvador, and Guatemala to move toward more representative government and, in the latter two cases, to cut down on widespread human rights abuses.

For a while it appeared that there was some reason for optimism in regard to Central America's future. The military rulers of Honduras scheduled elections for a civilian Constituent Assembly for April 1980. In Nicaragua, the Sandinistas had imprisoned thousands of ex-guardsmen and confiscated the holdings of Somoza and his supporters but had avoided the predicted bloodbath after the dictator's fall; they had included numerous prominent moderates and even several priests in their new government, and they were allowing a high degree of individual freedom. The economy was in terrible condition, but the government and the private sector appeared to be trying, with the help of massive foreign assistance, to put it back on its feet.

Guatemala and El Salvador remained the major problems. In the former case, the military had arranged the election of General Romeo Lucas García as president in 1978 but had allowed a moderate civilian reformer, Dr. Francisco Villagrán Kramer, to become vice-president. The Sandinista uprising and ultimate triumph in Nicaragua, however, had led to a growing polarization within Guatemala and had drawn the army into an ever-closer alliance with the extreme right. Prominent civilian politicians, including Social Democratic leader Alberto Fuentes Mohr and FUR head Manuel Colom Argueta, were assassinated by the far right. In response, guerrilla violence began to spread in the countryside.

While options were being closed in Guatemala, they appeared to be opening up in El Salvador. In October 1979, an internal military coup ousted the corrupt and incompetent Romero government and installed a mixed military-civilian regime, including a relatively moderate young colonel, Adolfo Majano; the head of the small Social Democratic Party (MNR), Guillermo Manuel Ungo; and former Catholic

University rector Ramon Mayorga. The cabinet included representatives of almost every imaginable sector from conservative urban businessmen to the Salvadoran Communist Party (UDN). Reforms, an end to repression, and free elections were promised; U.S. aid was resumed and increased; and prospects for avoiding a Nicaraguan-style civil war seemed fairly good. The year seemed to be ending on an optimistic note.

The hopes of late 1979 soon dissolved into the tragic realities of 1980. Except for Honduras and Belize, conditions deteriorated notably throughout Central America during that year. In a surprisingly honest election, the Honduran Liberal Party managed to gain a small majority in the Constituent Assembly over the promilitary National Party. Economic growth, however, slowed from 6.7 percent in 1979 to only 2 percent in 1980, and rising debt also caused concern.

In Costa Rica, the administration of President Rodrigo Carazo proved unable to cope with the mounting burdens of rising debt, regional turmoil, and stagnant exports. The GDP increased by only 3.3 percent in 1979 and 1.9 percent in 1980. Inflation climbed past 18 percent and the government's deficit rose to 12 percent of the total GDP.

Bullets, not ballots, were Guatemala's answer to political problems in 1980. The year opened with a massacre of antigovernment protesters who had seized the Spanish embassy, and conditions deteriorated steadily thereafter. Guerrilla activity grew, with large numbers of Indians joining guerrilla ranks for the first time. Church-state relations became increasingly tense; the army even exiled the president of the National Bishop's Conference. Relations with the United States also reached a nadir as the Lucas government, anticipating a Reagan victory in the fall, refused to accept the Carter administration's choice for ambassador. Despairing of any chance for political progress, Vice-President Villagrán Kramer fled abroad and resigned.

In Nicaragua, the highlight of 1980 was a massive literacy campaign, which mobilized national energies in a largely successful effort to deal with the heritage of adult illiteracy left by the Somozas. Other developments, however, were less positive. As it became clear that all real power in Nicaragua lay with the nine-member, self-appointed National Directorate of the FSLN, not with the provisional Government of National Reconstruction, moderates began to leave the government. The most notable defections were those of junta members Alfonso Robelo and Violeta Barrios de Chamorro, widow of murdered opposition leader Pedro Joaquín Chamorro. *La Prensa,* the nation's leading newspaper, became increasingly critical of the regime and of what it perceived as growing Cuban influence over the government. Relations with the United States also began to deteriorate, despite final approval of the $75 million aid package, as the Carter administration charged that Nicaragua was supporting the growing insurgency in El Salvador.

The Salvadoran Tragedy

It was in El Salvador that the tragedy of 1980 was most profound. Caught between growing pressures from mass organizations on the left and the intransigence of the increasingly murderous right, the first junta collapsed because of the military's inability or unwillingness to halt repression. The Christian Democrats joined a second civilian-military junta, but it, too, proved unable to deal with the situation, and several of its members quit. Thanks, in part, to U.S. efforts, right-wing plots to overthrow the government—often linked to a former army major, Roberto D'Aubuisson—failed, but the military refused to arrest the major or his supporters. Under pressure from Washington, the government did decree a sweeping agrarian reform program, but its implementation was slow and subject to widespread official abuse. In a desperate effort to gain credibility, the military installed Christian Democratic leader José Napoleón Duarte in the junta, but gave him little real power.

The growing disarray in politics was paralleled by increasing violence throughout the country. In March, Archbishop Oscar Romero, who had supported the first civil-military junta but had become increasingly critical of the government's failure to curb right-wing violence, was assassinated by elements of the extreme right. His funeral degenerated into a bloody confrontation between the mass organizations of the left and government security forces. Civilian leaders, such as ex–junta member Guillermo Ungo, now joined an umbrella left-wing opposition group, the Democratic Revolutionary Front (FDR), while the guerrillas, openly linked to the front, formed their own united command, the Farabundo Martí National Liberation Front (FMLN). Efforts to call a national strike in the fall failed in the face of growing government resistance and the decimation of the leadership of the left's mass organizations by officially tolerated, if not supported, death squads. In November, six FDR leaders were seized in San Salvador and murdered. The following month, three U.S. nuns and a religious worker were killed by elements of the security forces, and a few weeks later, the head of the agrarian reform program and two U.S. government advisers were assassinated with the complicity of elements of the military.

This produced a major dilemma for the outgoing Carter administration, a problem compounded by the ousting of moderate Colonel Majano from the junta and the rise to real power of Defense Minister Colonel José Guillermo García. Aid was suspended briefly, until the junta was reorganized with Duarte installed as provisional president. But in January 1981, the guerrillas launched a massive offensive. Washington hurriedly resumed aid and even began shipping lethal military equipment to El Salvador, the first case of such open assistance in Central America since the mid-1970s.

THE EARLY YEARS OF THE REAGAN ADMINISTRATION

Right-wing elements in Central America joyfully celebrated the election of Ronald Reagan as president of the United States, believing that he would abandon the country's concern about human rights and provide massive military assistance for their struggles against the guerrillas and all other elements working for meaningful changes in their societies. At first, the rhetoric, if not the deeds, from Washington seemed to measure up to right-wing expectations. Military assistance to El Salvador and Honduras was quickly increased while economic assistance to Nicaragua was suspended. Secretary of State Alexander Haig talked of "drawing a line" against Communist expansionism in Central America and of "going to the source" of subversion, a source that he identified with Cuba and Nicaragua rather than with the decades of domestic misrule and foreign exploitation.

Unfortunately for the Reagan administration, it soon became obvious that it was easier to propound slogans in Washington than it was to implement effective policies in Central America. In El Salvador, the guerrilla offensive failed, but the government could not regain control of guerrilla strongholds in rural areas, nor did it seem capable of controlling abuses by its own security forces. Investigations into the murders of the U.S. citizens dragged on without visible progress, and the economy continued to decline at an alarming rate. In Guatemala, efforts to open a dialogue with the Lucas regime, which would lead to some amelioration of the murderous internal repression in return for a resumption of U.S. assistance, succeeded only in convincing some elements of the Guatemalan right that Ronald Reagan, too, was soft on communism. As the government's slaughter of its opponents mounted, so too did support for the numerous far-left guerrilla organizations. Guatemala seemed to be heading down the road of violent civil conflict already taken by El Salvador and Nicaragua.

Efforts to intimidate Nicaragua's Sandinista rulers also backfired. At first, they had shown signs of willingness to make some compromises, reducing their support for El Salvador's guerrillas and making gestures toward an accommodation with internal opposition forces. But as the months passed and pressures from Washington continued, they began to crack down on internal dissent and to move closer to Cuba and the Soviet Union in international arenas. In 1981, Arturo Cruz left the government, and Eden Pastora left Nicaragua. Conflicts began developing along the Honduran border with ex-guardsmen and even some former Sandinistas now launching guerrilla attacks against the Sandinistas. The rising tensions served to short-circuit efforts at economic recovery and produced a growing climate of hostility between the private business sector and the government. Church-state relations also became strained, and finally, open clashes broke out on the isolated Atlantic coast over government efforts to forcibly relocate thousands of Miskito and Suma Indians. By 1982, Nicaragua seemed to be heading for another civil war, especially after Pastora announced that he would fight against the regime.

In Honduras and Costa Rica, democratic institutions managed to survive, despite the pressures of rapidly declining economies. In late 1981, presidential and congressional elections in Honduras resulted in victories for the Liberal Party and its presidential candidate, Dr. Roberto Suazo Córdova. A new constitution was also adopted, basically democratic in character but carefully drawn to ensure the autonomy of the armed forces. In Costa Rica, elections in early 1982 swept the discredited Carazo administration from power and brought the National Liberation Party, with its candidate, Luis Alberto Monge, back into office. In both cases, the new presidents inherited bankrupt treasures, monumental debt burdens, soaring inflation and unemployment, and deteriorating relations with Nicaragua.

The dreary pattern of escalating violence and collapsing economies established in 1981 continued through 1982. Despite the inauguration of new civilian administrations in Costa Rica and Honduras, the achievement of full independence for Belize (over Guatemalan threats and objections), and the apparently successful holding of Constituent Assembly elections in El Salvador, the basic problems confronting the region remained unresolved. In March, Guatemalan junior officers ousted the corrupt government of General Lucas. The Lucas regime had just staged a rigged election, which had been won by General Aníbal Guevara, Lucas's handpicked successor. Seeing no hope under such conditions of reversing the growing strength of the guerrillas, curbing the rampant corruption that was weakening the army, or restoring access to badly needed U.S. assistance and military supplies, junior officers took over the government. To head their movement, united only in its dislike of Lucas and Guevara, they seized on a retired army general, Efraín Ríos Montt. Now a "born-again" Christian pentecostal, Ríos Montt at first had to share power with two other generals, but in June he ousted them and took control himself. He purged the most corrupt members of the government, ended right-wing terrorism in the cities, and restored some measure of fiscal integrity. He also began a rapprochement with the United States and offered some concessions to Belize, publicly dropping Guatemala's traditional claim to that nation's entire territory. But he was unable or unwilling to stop the slaughter of Indians and other peasants by the military, and he tolerated little criticism from the press or from traditional political leaders. As for the guerrillas, he offered them a limited amnesty, but when that offer was rejected, he made it clear that death was the only fate they could expect at the hands of his government.

In El Salvador, the Reagan administration at first hailed the 1982 elections as a popular rejection of the guerrillas and the left, since the left had urged the population to boycott the elections and had tried to disrupt them. But the elections had produced a victory for a far-right coalition, led by Major D'Aubuisson, which undercut the agrarian reform, resisted efforts to curb human rights abuses, and even tolerated or encouraged attacks on Christian Democratic leaders in rural areas. Government infighting increased steadily, and guerrilla strength once again began to increase.

In Nicaragua, the government continued to drift to the left, and conflicts with domestic critics and armed exile factions increased. The revelation of the Reagan administration's support for armed opposition groups, mostly operating from Honduras, and of other efforts to destabilize the Sandinista government helped revive the government's sagging prestige and served to discredit its opponents. This also served to justify the Soviet- and Cuba-supported internal arms buildup and new restrictions on domestic critics.

While failing to produce any notable weakening of the Sandinistas' grip on power in Nicaragua, Washington's policies did undermine the newly installed civilian government in Honduras. The increasing involvement of that nation in the civil conflicts of both Nicaragua and El Salvador and the growing power of the Honduran military, led by General Gustavo Alvarez (a highly conservative, ambitious graduate of Argentina's military academy), fueled growing domestic dissent and international criticism. Human rights abuses, especially against resident aliens, increased, and at times, the nation seemed on the verge of war with Nicaragua.

Meanwhile, Costa Rica's declining economy, burdened by a monumental debt, produced high unemployment, declining living standards, and increased labor unrest. U.S. emergency economic assistance, much of it funneled through the new Caribbean Basin Initiative, served to avert complete national bankruptcy in Costa Rica, El Salvador, and Honduras but did nothing to cure the underlying causes of the economic crisis. By the start of 1983, Central America was caught in a vicious circle. Economic problems contributed to political instability, which, in turn, aggravated the economic situation. Moderate political solutions proved ineffective, strengthening the extremes of both left and right. Service of the enormous regional debt, rapidly approaching the $10 billion mark, combined with the cost of imported energy, consumed the overwhelming bulk of the region's foreign currency earnings. The 1981 regional deficit in balance of payments exceeded $2 billion, and by late 1982, regional monetary reserves were a negative $840.7 million. Optimists believed that if the violence could be reduced and stability and trade restored, Central America could regain its 1978 standard of living by 1990; pessimists felt that a return to 1978 levels was unlikely in this century.

CAUSES OF THE CONFLICT

The transformation of Central America from a relatively quiet, stagnant backwater area of "banana republics" to an arena of violent conflicts with international involvement can be attributed to five basic, interrelated factors. The first of these is the accumulated burden of the region's history. In Central America, social and political debts were postponed, not paid. In El Salvador, Guatemala, and Somoza's Nicaragua, entrenched, inflexible oligarchies refused to give up any of their control and met pressures for change with increasingly violent repression. When the Church supported the status quo, these oligarchies were supporters of the Church, but when the Church began to criticize conditions, ruling elites unleashed their hired killers on lay workers, priests, and in El Salvador, even the archbishop. They used money, flattery, and fear of communism to enlist the military in their support, at times undertaking "dirty tasks" that the military preferred to avoid. Reform was equated with subversion; criticism, with treason; and national security, with the interests of their own small class. When threatened, the ruling elites sent their money and their families to Miami but reserved part of their wealth to finance death squads, military coups, and any other available means of postponing the inevitable death of their anachronistic social order.

The military institutions of Central America also bear a heavy responsibility in this area. Their increasing professionalization in the post–World War II era did not produce greater loyalty to the nations as a whole or a commitment to defend the rights of the majority of their citizens; rather, it produced a growing concern with the power and survival of the military institutions. In El Salvador, loyalty to classmates from the military academy frequently overrode any concept of allegiance to the government or the nation. Military careers were frequently viewed as a road to personal enrichment. Corruption became totally institutionalized in Nicaragua, where the National Guard served as the personal bodyguard of the Somoza family and functioned more as an occupying force than as a national army. But corruption also weakened military efficiency and undermined potential popular support for the governments of Honduras, Guatemala, and, especially, El Salvador. The situation in the last nation was further complicated by the division of the security forces into separate, but closely linked, organizations performing both police and military functions. The net result of all these factors was that the military in Central America was at least as much the source of violence and disorder as it was the promoter of order and stability.

A second destabilizing factor in the region is the nature of the economic structures that developed during the post–World War II era. Economic growth was rapid for much of this period, but the rewards were unevenly distributed, and the economic structures that emerged were extremely vulnerable to both internal and external pressures. The rapidly growing cities were service oriented, producing little and consuming much of the wealth from the countryside. Their biggest source of employment for newly arrived rural dwellers was in construction, but this industry was exceptionally vulnerable to downturns in the economy.

The industrial growth that did occur was largely designed to serve the Common Market. Much of it was dependent on imported raw materials and was relatively inefficient. When violence disrupted the Common Market and economic conditions made foreign exchange increasingly unobtainable, many of these industries were forced to reduce operations or to shut down entirely.

The emphasis on new and expanded export-crop production also reduced food production, accelerated rural to urban migration, and increased the economies' vulnerability to price and demand fluctuations in the world market. In summary, the economic growth of earlier years produced few lasting benefits, inflated middle-class consumer appetites, and forced governments to engage in excessive borrowing to maintain existing structures when world conditions deteriorated. Far from contributing to greater stability, the economic changes of the 1960s and 1970s actually set the stage for increased instability.

A third factor in Central America's current crisis is the failure of the moderate, reformist parties, notably the Christian Democrats and the Social Democrats. These parties were frequently believed to be the wave of the future in the 1960s and early 1970s. They remain influential political actors in many areas and continue to exercise power in Costa Rica. But they have been unable to resolve the area's basic problems and have proved ineffective in dealing with the extremes of both left and right. In Guatemala and El Salvador, moderates joined in coalitions with far-right, antidemocratic elements in the hopes of modifying conditions or gaining influence. As the cases of Francisco Villagrán Kramer in Guatemala and José Napoleón Duarte in El Salvador demonstrate, the moderates were simply being used to lend legitimacy to the right while being denied any real influence over basic developments. Many moderate parties were also too dependent on foreign support, especially that emanating from the United States. In Nicaragua, they stuck with the U.S.-sponsored mediation effort until the bitter end, discrediting themselves in the process and making themselves largely irrelevant in the final struggle for power between Somoza and the Sandinistas.

Whereas the first three factors are largely domestic, the remaining two basic causes of Central America's problems relate to external influences. The most obvious of these is the impact of world economic conditions. Beginning with the 1973 rise in energy costs, these conditions have had an increasingly negative impact. In recent years, the rise in the costs of imported manufactured goods has been paralleled by declines or, at best, stagnation in the prices received for regional exports. An even greater impact was brought about by the rapid rise of interest rates in the early 1980s, which made service on the huge new debts virtually impossible. Finally, the world economic recession of the early 1980s reduced demand for Central America's exports; cut the region's sources of available foreign assistance, especially from Mexico; and contributed, along with the insecurity generated by the spreading violence, to drying up most sources of new investment capital.

As harmful as external economic influences have been, the effects of foreign political involvements have been even worse. Cuban involvement in Central America has encouraged guerrilla activities and provided right-wing forces with a convenient excuse for increased repression. But the greatest destabilizing factor has been the inconsistent policies of the United States. For decades, U.S. concern with stability served to lend support to a series of corrupt, repressive regimes. Nicaragua's civil conflict of 1978–1979 clearly had its roots in the U.S. intervention of the late 1920s and early 1930s and the subsequent U.S. support of the Somoza dynasty. Many aspects of Guatemala's current conflict can be traced to the CIA-sponsored exile invasion of 1954. Activities of both U.S. government and U.S. private businesses, especially the United Fruit Company, have contributed also to Honduras's problems. The pattern of manipulation there was continuing in early 1984 as the United States was attempting to use Honduras as a base for operations against Nicaragua. This action was threatening the tenuous civil-military balance in that nation and even raising the possibility of a regional war. In El Salvador, U.S. efforts have done more to prolong the current conflict than to resolve it. If anything, far-right intransigence has been increased by the perception, based on statements emanating from Washington, that a victory by the left would not be allowed.

Part of the basic contradiction in U.S. policy toward Central America is Washington's determination to maintain regional control coupled with an unwillingness to assume the responsibilities of or to pay the price associated with such control. While activities of the left are frequently ascribed to Cuban and Soviet influence, no responsibility is admitted for the brutality or corruption of past or present allies on the right. Rightist factions have learned how to play the Cuban card to get Washington's attention and support. They constantly strive to force the United States to choose between supporting them and accepting the armed triumph of a left violently denied any peaceful access to power. They also promise cheap stability in exchange for military assistance rather than acknowledging the high costs of dealing with the social and economic roots of Central America's problems.

Finally, U.S. policy toward the region is inconsistent and often confusing. Central American politicians have to constantly strive to keep abreast of the latest nuances from the north, embracing human rights, economic development, anti-communism, or whatever other panacea is currently being promoted by Washington. Conflicts between the U.S. Congress and the executive branch and even changes within the executive, such as those produced when George Shultz succeeded Alexander Haig as secretary of state, add to the confusion. Frequently, the United States seems to act like a petulant, fearful child with a limited attention span, a capacity for throwing occasional public tantrums, and a constant demand for attention and control. In a situation already made desperate by other factors, the ultimate impact of U.S. involvement in Central America has usually been to make things worse.

Central America is likely to remain all too frequently in that part of U.S. news coverage reserved for wars, murders, and other disasters. The region retains the economic and human potential for considerable development and progress, but it also contains the potential for conflict and destruction beyond that experienced to date. The situation was summed up by Costa Rican President Luis Alberto Monge in May 1982 when he said: "The political crisis that afflicts our region has internal roots, of old injustices and lost hopes, which are jumbled together with the intervention of foreign interests. There will be no peace in Central America and the Caribbean while the infernal game of hegemonic interests continues in our region. In the cruel conflicts of our peoples, the Central Americans provide the bodies and others gather the advantages."

SUGGESTED READINGS

There is no truly adequate history of Central America in English. The best available, although already somewhat dated, work is Ralph Lee Woodward, Jr., *Central America: A Nation Divided* (New York and London: Oxford University Press, 1976). Colonial history is covered by Murdo J. MacLeod, *Spanish Central America: A Socioeconomic History, 1520–1720* (Berkeley and Los Angeles: University of California, 1973). The subsequent century can be traced in Miles L. Wortman, *Government and Society in Central America, 1680–1840* (New York: Columbia University Press, 1982). The best survey of the modern situation is Thomas P. Anderson, *Politics in Central America* (New York: Praeger, 1982), but this study for some reason omits Costa Rica.

No scholarly history of U.S.–Central American relations is yet available. The problems for the first third of this century were covered in two volumes by Dana G. Munro in *Intervention and Dollar Diplomacy in the Caribbean, 1900–1921* (Princeton: Princeton University Press, 1964). And *The United States and the Caribbean Republics, 1921–1933* (Princeton: Princeton

University Press, 1974). Varied views of the current situation are surveyed in Richard E. Feinberg, ed., *Central America: International Dimensions of the Crisis* (New York: Holmes and Meier, 1982).

Two specialized studies contribute important insights into the regional situation. The first is Patrick Cotter and George Bowdler, *Voter Participation in Central America, 1954–1981* (Washington, D.C.: University Press of America, 1982). The other is William Cline and Enrique Delgado, *Economic Integration in Central America* (Washington, D.C.: Brookings Institution, 1978).

The amount of material available on individual nations varies widely. By far the least studied nation in the region is Honduras. William Stokes, *Honduras: An Area Study in Government* (Madison: University of Wisconsin, 1950), remains the basic work in English despite its notable weaknesses and the fact that it is very badly outdated. Thomas P. Anderson, *The War of the Dispossessed: Honduras and El Salvador, 1969* (Lincoln: University of Nebraska, 1981), sheds important light on the 1969 conflict with El Salvador.

In recent years El Salvador, not surprisingly, has come in for considerable attention. Basic to any understanding of that nation's problems is Thomas P. Anderson, *Matanza* (Lincoln: University of Nebraska, 1971), a scholarly study of the 1931 peasant uprising and the subsequent government massacre. Additional background, this time on El Salvador's Christian Democratic Party, is found in Stephen Webre, *José Napoleón Duarte and the Christian Democratic Party in Salvadoran Politics, 1960–1972* (Baton Rouge: Louisiana State University Press, 1979). Among the host of studies on recent developments, the most readable and useful is probably Cynthia Arnson, *El Salvador: A Revolution Confronts the United States* (Washington, D.C.: Institute for Policy Studies, 1982).

There has also been a wave of writing on Nicaragua in recent years. Background to the Revolution can be found in Neill Macaulay, *The Sandino Affair* (Chicago: Quadrangle Books, 1967); Richard Millett, *Guardians of the Dynasty: A History of the U.S. Created Guardia Nacional de Nicaragua* (Maryknoll, N.Y.: Orbis Books, 1977); and Bernard Diedrich, *Somoza and the Legacy of U.S. Involvement in Central America* (New York: Dutton, 1981). Among the host of available volumes on the Revolution and its aftermath, the best to date is probably John A. Booth, *The End and the Beginning: The Nicaraguan Revolution* (Boulder, Colo.: Westview Press, 1982).

Guatemala has been of greater interest to anthropologists than it has been to political scientists or historians. Richard Adams, *Crucified by Power* (Austin: University of Texas, 1970), is still the best introduction to the basic realities of that nation. Important aspects of Guatemalan history are covered in Kenneth Grieb, *Guatemalan Caudillo: The Regime of Jorge Ubico, Guatemala, 1931–1944* (Athens: Ohio University Press, 1979), and Stephen Kinzer and Stephen Schlesinger, *Bitter Fruit: The Untold Story of the American Coup in Guatemala* (New York: Doubleday, 1982).

Belize has been the subject of a surprising number of studies, the most up-to-date of which is William D. Stetzkorn, *Formerly British Honduras: A Profile of the New Nation of Belize* (Athens: Ohio University Press, 1981). Costa Rica has long been a favored topic of research by North Americans, probably because of its tradition of peace and democracy. Among the most useful books in English on that nation are Charles Ameringer, *Don Pepe: A Political Biography of José Figueres of Costa Rica* (Albuquerque: University of New Mexico, 1977), and Mitchell Seligson, *Peasants of Costa Rica and the Development of Agrarian Capitalism* (Madison: University of Wisconsin, 1980).

20

CENTRAL AMERICA: FROM REVOLUTION TO NEOLIBERAL "REFORM"

THOMAS W. WALKER

The short period from the victory of the Sandinista Front for National Liberation (FSLN) in Nicaragua in 1979 to the mid-1990s was a time of truly kaleidoscopic change for Central America. In the realm of politics, Nicaragua experienced revolutionary rule and a bloody and costly U.S.-orchestrated counterrevolution for almost eleven years before its people elected a conservative government more compatible with the whims of Washington. Elsewhere, prolonged armed struggle between revolutionary insurgents and elite-dominated regimes led eventually to a comprehensive peace settlement in El Salvador (1992) and protracted negotiations and a peace settlement in Guatemala (1996). Finally, though they avoided armed struggle, Honduras and Costa Rica were both strongly buffeted by events taking place in neighboring countries.

There were other changes, too. For one, the political debate spilled over into religion. At the beginning of the period, progressive priests, nuns, and Catholic laypersons were moved to action in behalf of the poor through their understanding of Jesus' original message and example as a cry for social justice. These were the practitioners of Liberation Theology.[1] Not surprisingly, conservative forces in Central America and elsewhere were alarmed by this progressive approach to religion, which they saw as playing into the hands of an international "Communist" conspiracy. Accordingly, conservative religious groupings in the United States, with the encouragement and support of the U.S. government, raised vast sums of money to promote the growth of conservative charismatic Protestantism in the region as an antidote to Liberation Theology. At the same time, a fervently anti-Communist, Polish-born pope, John Paul II (elected in 1979), used his influence and power to counter

Liberation Theology within the Church and to discredit what he and the conservative hierarchy derisively labeled the "Popular Church."

On a more secular plane, government troops and right-wing death squads in El Salvador and Guatemala killed progressive priests and nuns (including Archbishop Oscar Romero of El Salvador in 1980) or, particularly in Guatemala, drove them out of rural parishes where conservative Protestants then became the only religious personnel present. The end result of all this was that, by the mid-1990s, Liberation Theology was largely in eclipse; the Catholic Church itself had become increasingly conservative, extraworldly, and, some would say, out of touch with the impoverished majority; and there were Protestant temples and chapels in even the poorest urban neighborhoods and most remote villages throughout the region.

Equally important, in most of these countries in the same short period, national economic policy based on a belief in the government's responsibility to manage the economy to ensure social justice gave way to a more market-driven approach in which the impoverished majority would be asked to wait to receive their "fair share" until some ill-defined future after the national economic "pie" had been allowed to grow "naturally." When the period began, Costa Rica could already boast a viable "welfare state" dating from the 1940s, Nicaragua was embarking on sweeping social reform orchestrated by a revolutionary government, and U.S. advisers were pushing state-run social and economic reform in El Salvador as an essential counterinsurgency technique. By the mid-1990s, however, Nicaragua and El Salvador (and to a lesser extent Costa Rica) were undergoing a downsizing of government bureaucracy and social services, the privatization of former government enterprises, the redirection of credit away from the peasantry into large private export activities, and a variety of other socially regressive policies designed to stimulate export, earn foreign exchange, and ultimately service the region's enormous foreign debt. Since many of these policies were reminiscent of the laissez-faire, agro-export measures promoted by the region's liberal politicians of the late nineteenth and early twentieth centuries, they were frequently dubbed "neoliberal."

CONTEMPORARY DIFFERENCES AND THEIR HISTORICAL DETERMINANTS

Within this matrix of sweeping change, however, there were significant differences among the countries that deserve examination and explanation. Why, for instance, did Nicaragua, El Salvador, and Guatemala experience violent upheaval while Costa Rica and Honduras remained relatively peaceful? The answer, as John Booth and I suggest elsewhere,[2] probably lies in five centuries of historical formation. Put in very simple terms, the large native populations of what would become Guatemala, Nicaragua, and El Salvador were quickly conquered by invading Spaniards at the beginning of the sixteenth century, thus forming a vast, racially distinct underclass that could be exploited for the enrichment of a small European ruling class. In those countries the foundations of very inegalitarian societies were already firmly set within decades of the arrival of the conquistadors. In Costa Rica, in contrast, the native population resisted fiercely and, for their troubles, were largely exterminated or driven out of the fertile highlands where the Spanish eventually settled. With no racially distinct underclass to exploit, the society created by the Spanish settlers in Costa Rica was always relatively more egalitarian. For its part, Honduras until the twentieth century was so underpopulated and such an economic backwater that a self-confident and exploitative ruling class was slow in developing.

By the 1970s, as a result of these distinct social histories, Costa Rica had developed a functioning democracy and welfare state; Honduran governments, though not always democratic, were normally willing at least to pay lip service to grassroots demands; and the dictatorships in the other three countries had become accustomed to responding with violence to growing demands for social justice from the impoverished majority. While social problems existed throughout the region, they had been allowed to build to explosive levels only in Nicaragua, Guatemala, and El Salvador. It was primarily this built-up pressure rather than some sort of sinister "Communist" conspiracy—as the U.S. government would claim[3]—that led to the armed revolts of the 1970s and 1980s.

The Revolutionary Three

Though Nicaragua, El Salvador, and Guatemala share the experience of prolonged armed revolt, only in Nicaragua did the insurgents actually seize power. It is interesting to ask why insurgents succeeded there and not in the other two countries. A number of single-factor explanations have been offered: Somoza was corrupt; the peasants were exploited; the FSLN had the right strategy; the United States failed to act effectively to block the rebel victory.

Perhaps the best explanation is given by Timothy Wickham-Crowley.[4] Rejecting single-factor theories, he argues that four conditions were met in Nicaragua that were not fully met elsewhere in Latin America except Cuba two decades earlier: Nicaragua (and Cuba) had the right social conditions (an impoverished and exploited rural population living in very precarious circumstances); an intelligent and flexible guerrilla movement; a target regime so despicable that it had alienated most of its political base; and the right international environment (i.e., a temporary lapse in U.S. support for the local dictator).

Guatemala and El Salvador met only the first two conditions. In both of the latter countries, military and eventually civilian presidents succeeded each other at relatively short intervals. Though brutal and certainly not democratic, these governments were hardly *caudillo*-dominated "mafiacracies" of the type run by Fulgencio Batista in Cuba or Anastasio Somoza in Nicaragua. As a result, much of the Salvadoran and Guatemalan upper and middle classes remained loyal to their respective regimes. In addition, alarmed by the Sandinista victory in Nicaragua, the United States—which had been immobilized by the contradictions inherent in trying to promote human rights in Somoza's Nicaragua—now focused on preventing leftist victories in the other two countries, often with little regard to human rights.

Therefore, with the backing of the United States and privileged domestic group-ings, Salvadoran and Guatemalan regimes were able to ward off rebel takeovers. But their victories and the rebels' failures were certainly not absolute. Even though they did not come to power, the rebels in both countries achieved some measure of suc-cess in that they eventually forced their foes to accept major changes in historically repressive systems as their price for peace.

Nicaragua

The Sandinista Period. From July 19, 1979, to April 25, 1990, Nicaragua had an avowedly revolutionary government. However, sobered by an awareness of the weakness of the socialist model of the Soviet Union and the Eastern European coun-tries[5] and some obvious excesses of the Cuban experiment (the cult of personality, overnationalization of the economy, etc.), the Sandinistas developed policies that were actually quite moderate and pragmatic.

The Sandinista revolution can be divided into two periods: transition and recon-struction (1979–1984) and the constitutional period (1985–1990). The first was a time of innovation, experimentation, some excesses, yet a number of successes. In the second, the U.S.-orchestrated Contra war, though never a military threat, inflicted such heavy economic and human damage that the revolution began to unravel and was eventually voted out of office.

The Period of Transition. The economic policy adopted during the period of transition and maintained thereafter was one of a mixed economy. Confiscation of property was confined mainly to land and enterprises owned by ousted dictator Anastasio Somoza and his henchmen. Though these were turned into public enter-prises or cooperatives or parceled out to the poor, around 60 percent of the produc-tive capacity of the country remained in private hands throughout the revolution. Indeed, though very nervous about the intent of the Sandinistas, the private sector was actually encouraged, through favorable exchange rates and other measures, to re-main productive.

Complementing these domestic economic policies, the Sandinistas pursued inter-national policies—renegotiating and servicing the national debt and writing liberal foreign investment laws—designed to maintain Nicaragua's credit in Western circles. These policies paid off. From 1979 through 1983, Nicaragua's gross domestic prod-uct per capita grew a total of 7 percent, while Central America as a whole suffered a decline of 14.7 percent.[6] It was only in the wake of the full impact of the Contra war and a U.S.-orchestrated international credit boycott that the Nicaraguan economy began to decline (1984) and then plummet (1985 onward).

The new government also oversaw innovative and highly successful social projects during this period. Inexpensive, grassroots-based programs for literacy (1980) and health (beginning in 1981) brought such positive change that by 1984 even President Reagan's Kissinger Commission had to admit that "Nicaragua's govern-ment has made significant gains against illiteracy and disease."[7]

There was also much innovation and some success in the area of politics and gov-ernment. First, the government encouraged the creation or strengthening of massive grassroots organizations representing neighborhoods, women, youth, urban and rural workers, and peasants. These groupings in turn were given the responsibility of articulating the interests of their constituencies and delegated the task of implementing programs designed to help the people (the literacy crusade, health work days, neighborhood watch, etc.). By 1984, an in-house U.S. embassy report placed membership in these organizations at 700,000 to 800,000, the equivalent of about half of the population aged sixteen or over.[8]

The Revolution also moved during this time from transitional to elected constitutional government. The first institutions of government were a multiperson executive, or junta; a corporative legislature (Council of State); and a judiciary composed of the usual lower and higher courts plus People's Anti-Somoza Tribunals set up to process Somoza-era war criminals but later used to deal with Contras. By 1983, however, the Council of State was writing election and party laws (designed with the advice of the Swedish Electoral Commission and modeled after Western European practices) that would enable the holding of a clean, competitive, internationally monitored[9] election in November 1984 and the swearing-in of a Constituent Assembly and an elected president, Daniel Ortega, in 1985.

Finally, in the area of human rights, Sandinista performance, though not perfect, was better than that of most other contemporary Latin American governments—and strikingly good compared with that of U.S. client regimes in northern Central America. There were restrictions of civil liberties, as take place almost anywhere when a country is under siege, but freedom of religion was generally respected, there were no death squads, and extralegal deprivation of life was relatively infrequent.[10]

The worst problems Nicaragua encountered during the early 1980s were in foreign affairs, particularly with the United States. Though the Sandinistas repeatedly expressed their interest in having good relations with the superpower to the north, the victory of revolutionaries in Nicaragua—and the specter of a "second Cuba"— had alarmed Washington from the very beginning.[11] While the Carter administration was frigid but correct in its relations with the new government in Nicaragua, the Reagan administration, inaugurated in January 1981, set out immediately to destroy what it portrayed as a dangerous extension of Soviet and Cuban influence into Central America. Almost immediately, it began training, equipping, and directing a Nicaraguan exile counterrevolutionary ("Contra") army to fight against its own government; used its influence to block normal World Bank and Inter-American Development Bank loans to the upstart state; and orchestrated a massive propaganda campaign and program of dirty tricks to discredit the Sandinistas.[12]

The Constitutional Period.   The second half of the Sandinista period was marked both by significant achievements and serious economic, social, and political setbacks. Respect for human rights continued at a relatively high level. New governmental institutions were created by the Constituent Assembly elected in 1984. After much open public debate, a new constitution was promulgated in 1987. That same year, an innovative autonomy law for the peoples of the Atlantic Coast was formalized. Later, new parties and electoral laws were passed (1988) and amended (1989) laying the groundwork for a second clean, internationally supervised election in February 1990. Two months later, the losing FSLN turned over the reins of power to the victorious opposition.

But this was also a time of hardship that ultimately led to the defeat of the FSLN at the polls. The cost of the Contra war, U.S.-orchestrated international economic strangulation, and some Sandinista mismanagement combined to produce such a collapse of the economy that by 1988 hyperinflation had reached over 33,000 percent annually. Though the Sandinistas implemented structural reforms that year and the next that would cut inflation to 1,690 percent by 1989,[13] the unemployment and social pain these early neoliberal policies caused was enormous. Added to this, cutbacks in government social programs and the tremendous human cost of the war (almost 31,000 dead[14] and many more wounded and maimed) created an environment in which the U.S.-organized, -managed, and -funded National Opposition Union (UNO) was able to defeat the Sandinistas handily in the 1990 election.[15]

The Post-Sandinista Period.[16]   Violeta Barrios de Chamorro, elected president with 55 percent of the vote, was inaugurated in April 1990 for a term of office that would expire almost seven years later. Though a political novice with only a high school education, Chamorro would eventually score some important successes. Her economic policies cut inflation to relatively low levels and by the mid-1990s actually led to modest overall growth for the first time in over a decade.

Her greatest achievements, however, lay in the area of peacemaking and reconciliation. After months of negotiation, the Contra war was brought to an end in mid-1990. By cleverly allowing Sandinista general Humberto Ortega to oversee that otherwise difficult task, Chamorro was able to bring the size of the Sandinista People's Army down from over 80,000 to under 15,000. Finally, Chamorro steadfastly eschewed pressure from the United States (until 1993) and right-wing members of UNO to engage in a vengeful "desandinization" program for the country. As a result, a new political "normalcy" gradually developed. Negotiations in the National Assembly led to the promulgation of a new "Military Code" (1994) and some revisions in the 1987 Constitution (1995). And elections on the Atlantic Coast (1994) and nationwide (1996) were carried out without a major hitch. In January 1997, Chamorro passed the reins of office to Arnoldo Alemán of the National Liberal Alliance.

There were also notable failures in this period. The most glaring were in the social area. The neoliberal economic policies urged on Nicaragua by Washington and the international financial community and enthusiastically implemented by the Chamorro administration pummeled the poor majority. The downsizing of government, cutbacks in social services, privatization of state enterprises, the credit emphasis on agro-export rather than peasant production of domestic foodstuffs, and so on combined to exacerbate the misery of ordinary people. Unemployment, underemployment, crime rates, drug addiction, domestic violence, homelessness (especially among children) all soared. Gone was the sense of optimism about the future that most people had felt a decade earlier.

In addition, there was a growing sense of cynicism about politicians and most government institutions. It was widely reported that top Sandinista leaders had appropriated large amounts of property in the last months of their administration and that both Arnoldo Alemán and Antonio Lacayo (Chamorro's son-in-law) had increased their fortunes through corruption while serving, respectively, as mayor of Managua and minister of the presidency before launching their presidential campaigns in 1996. Thus, ironically, while Nicaraguans retained an almost touching faith in elections and the electoral process, many by the mid-1990s were bitterly skeptical about politicians, parties, and most institutions of government.

El Salvador

Insurgency and Counterinsurgency: 1979–1992.   The 1970s had been a time of tremendous mobilization in Salvadoran society. Social democratic and Christian democratic parties as well as segments of the Catholic Church and even USAID and the U.S. Peace Corps had promoted development projects and grassroots participation. Salvadoran elites and the military regimes they supported, however, viewed this phenomenon with alarm and responded to it with repression. Apparent opposition victories in both the 1972 and 1977 elections were overturned as increasingly brutal military regimes used security forces and associated death squads to kill party, interest group, and religious leaders working with the masses. Responding to this repression, groups of various political affiliations fielded small guerrilla armies that in 1980 would unite into the Farabundo Martí National Liberation Front (FMLN).

The Sandinista victory in Nicaragua alarmed the forces of the status quo and heartened popular organizations in El Salvador. Convinced that it was now possible to topple the dictatorship, the FMLN began preparing for its (unsuccessful) "final offensive" of early 1981. At the same time, sobered by events in Nicaragua, the Salvadoran elite and the U.S. government took measures to prevent a repetition. Within days of the Nicaraguan victory, planners in Washington had decided that in order to justify beefing up the Salvadoran military, the existing regime would have to be replaced with a cosmetically more acceptable government run by a junta combining both progressive military and civilian members.[17] On October 15, 1979, a military coup by "moderates" essentially implemented this objective.

For the following twelve years, the forces of the status quo would pursue a two-pronged strategy for containing revolution. On the one hand, until the end of the Cold War, Washington would insist on military victory over the insurgents. In these years it would give its ally in the war against "communism" over $6 billion in aid—much of it military aid to security forces that were responsible for killing most of the 75,000 people (mainly civilians) who died during the conflict. Though Salvadoran regimes, especially in the late 1980s, would occasionally go through the motions of negotiating, no serious effort to arrive at an accord was made.

On the other hand, in order to get a reluctant U.S. Congress to provide the arms necessary to implement the overall military strategy, it was also necessary for Salvadoran governments to appear both democratic and progressive. Accordingly, after several years of civilian-military juntas in which civilians had no real power, elections for a Constituent Assembly (1982) and then president (1984) were held. Staged against a background of state-sponsored terror and in the absence of a free press, these elections—in which voting was obligatory and the sequentially numbered, translucent ballots were deposited in clear plastic ballot boxes—produced the presidencies of conservative Christian Democrat José Napoleón Duarte in 1984 and right-wing Nationalist Republican Alliance (ARENA) Party member Alfredo Cristiani in 1989.

At the same time, government social policy took an apparently more humane turn. Immediately after the Sandinista victory in Nicaragua, Salvadoran regimes (under tremendous pressure from the United States) actually seemed to be competing in the social realm with the Nicaraguan revolution.[18] The first junta, like the Sandinista government, implemented sweeping agrarian reform programs and nationalized the banking industry. Though some of this reform was stillborn and much of the rest was reversed after a right-wing victory in the 1982 Constituent Assembly elections, heavy aid from the United States allowed various civic action and other programs to continue throughout the period.

Meanwhile, responding to international reality, the FMLN modified its objectives in the early 1980s. By 1982 the guerrillas had come to realize that an all-out victory would, in the words of their civilian ally Rubén Zamora, "be ashes in our mouths."[19] They had seen what the United States was already doing to the Nicaraguan Revolution. And though they still had confidence that they could win militarily, they had decided instead to fight only until the regime agreed to a peace treaty instituting major changes in the military, political, and social character of the system.

The war dragged on, with Washington and the Salvadoran military pushing for all-out victory and the guerrillas fighting to achieve a negotiated settlement. By the end of 1989, it looked as if the stalemate was beginning to break. Early that year the government refused an opposition request to delay the national election in order to institute democratic safeguards so that FMLN candidates might participate. That November, in response, the FMLN staged a massive assault on the city of San Salvador, taking over and holding whole neighborhoods for weeks at a time. In addition, under the cover of the turmoil of that period, the U.S.-trained Atlacatl Battalion (under orders of the Army High Command) entered the grounds of the Central American University and executed six prominent Jesuit intellectuals, their maid, and her daughter.

As a result of all this, it was now very clear that (1) the FMLN was still alive and effective and (2) the regime was still badly in need of reform. Thus, when the Soviet Union collapsed a little over a year later, the Bush administration decided to cut its losses in El Salvador by reversing its position on negotiations. As a major report on El Salvador prepared for the U.S. Defense Department put it, with the end of the Cold War, "'Winning' in El Salvador no longer matters much. A negotiated solution, or even 'losing,' would no longer carry the same ominous significance."[20] Now, with the full backing of Washington and even such right-wing Salvadorans as Roberto D'Aubuisson, the United Nations could move ahead and broker a formal peace.

The Imperfect Peace: 1992 Onward.   The peace accords of January 1992 encompassed most of the reforms and changes the FMLN had proposed almost a decade earlier. Under UN supervision, the government was to depoliticize and drastically reduce the size of its army. It was obliged to abolish "rapid deployment" forces (such as the Atlacatl Battalion), the Treasury Police, and the National Guard. The hated National Police would be replaced by a Civil Police in which veterans of the conflict would be drawn equally from both sides and, together, would constitute less than half of the force. An Ad Hoc Commission was to be named to provide a list of war criminals to be purged from the armed forces. Once that purging had taken place, a Truth Commission was to make a report on war crimes committed by both sides and by civilians. On another plane, there were to be significant reforms of electoral mechanisms and of the judiciary. And land and resources were to be set aside to resettle former combatants from both sides. In return, the FMLN was to demobilize.

The peace accords were in fact implemented, if imperfectly and slowly. The FMLN demobilized, if a bit behind schedule, and turned over most—but apparently not all[21]—of its weapons. The Ad Hoc and Truth Commissions performed their duties bravely. The armed forces were reduced, reorganized, and purged, though at an extraordinarily slow pace and not as fully as stipulated. Sweeping changes were made in the police forces, though not to the extent envisioned in the accords. Limited changes were made in the corrupt judicial system. Land was distributed to some, though not most, of the demilitarized combatants from both sides. And in 1994 a much-observed national election took place in which the FMLN was allowed to participate—but on a far from "level playing field."[22]

As a result of the 1994 election, the candidate of the ruling ARENA Party, Armando Calderón Sol, was inaugurated president on June 1. Though ARENA had also won the largest block of seats in the Chamber of Deputies (thirty-seven out of ninety-seven), the FMLN had established itself as the country's second political force with a respectable twenty-one deputies. The Christian Democrats, discredited by corrupt and ineffective rule in the 1980s, had slumped to third place with eighteen seats.

The first two years of the Calderón presidency were marked by the declaration of sweeping neoliberal reform (the reduction of trade barriers and the government payroll, the imposition of a regressive value-added tax, and the dollarization of the economy) followed by some backpedaling when the economy, which had been strong in 1994, began to stagnate a year later. By mid-1996, the government was being accused by the FMLN of having brought "economic recession, poverty, tragedy and social abandonment" and "increasing organized crime, citizen insecurity, corruption, tax evasion, impunity, authoritarianism," and so on.[23] In all, however, though the economic and social situation in El Salvador left a lot to be desired, political and human rights conditions had improved markedly since the dark days of the early 1980s.

Guatemala

The Guatemalan experience in the same period bore both striking similarities to and important differences from that of El Salvador. There, too, bloody civil war raged throughout the late 1970s and 1980s and the possibility for real peace emerged only after the end of the Cold War and a change in policy in Washington. And as in El Salvador, the guerrilla strategy of fighting to force reform of a previously brutal system seemed by 1996 to pay off. However, unlike the case in El Salvador, the U.S. role in the conflict—though very real—was somewhat less visible, and the Guatemalan military appeared to be a bit more autonomous. In addition, the peace settlement would be negotiated (and implemented) in a step-by-step fashion over a period of more than half a decade rather than all at once as in El Salvador.

By the late 1970s, Guatemala had already experienced almost two decades of bloody civil war. Frustrated by the destruction of the democratic revolution in 1954 and by a U.S.-approved military coup that blocked the return to elected civilian rule in 1963, some Guatemalans had turned to armed insurrection. In response, the United States had trained the Guatemalan army and security forces in the methods of counterinsurgency and "counterterror." By 1966, death squads had begun to operate and the term "disappeared" was first used as a noun to refer to victims of these tactics. By 1979, thousands of people—mainly civilians—had already been killed and a long series of military dictatorships had ruled the country.

As in El Salvador, U.S. policy toward Guatemala was often two-tracked.[24] On the one hand, there was the primordial need to "stop Communism." On the other, it was always important to appear concerned with human rights and democracy. Early in his administration, Jimmy Carter's criticism of Guatemalan human rights violations had led to a rupture in the flow of military aid to that country. Though Washington obviously hoped for a Salvador-type coup that would justify a resumption of such aid, the military clung to power until the mid-1980s, thus making it impossible to get such assistance approved by Congress. To some extent, the Reagan administration got around the problem by relabeling as "civilian" such obviously military items as helicopters; by successfully pressuring Israel—the world's leading recipient of U.S. assistance—to increase arms assistance to Guatemala;[25] and by continuing both covert CIA assistance and the U.S. military's counterinsurgency advisory role.

But by the early 1980s things seemed to be getting out of hand. President/General Lucas García (1978–1982) sharply increased already high levels of repression. As a result, the divided guerrilla opposition came together in one organization, the Guatemalan National Revolutionary Unity (URNG), in 1982. Replacing Lucas in a coup d'état that same year, President/General Efrain Ríos Montt increased the repression even more. Altogether, in a scorched-earth war that lasted from 1981 through 1983, between 100,000 and 150,000 civilians were killed, hundreds of villages were destroyed, and over 1 million persons were displaced.[26]

Though the United States had approved of Guatemala's dirty war, it eventually became the better part of wisdom to push for the emergence of a more cosmetically acceptable system. The vehicle for this policy was General Oscar Humberto Mejía Victores, who overthrew Rios Montt in 1983. Though the brutality did not cease, a new constitution was written, an election was held, and a civilian president, Christian Democrat Vinicio Cerezo, was inaugurated in 1986.

It would be hard to argue that democracy in Guatemala was born again in 1986. Though the constitution was a reasonably good one and the elections were fairly clean from a procedural standpoint, the fact that the former was frequently violated, that the latter had been held against a background of state-sponsored terror, and that the military, rather than the new president, continued to hold real power obviated such claims. Nevertheless an atmosphere of "possibility" began to emerge. For its part, the URNG—by now convinced that outright military victory was neither possible nor desirable for the guerrillas—began calling for a negotiated settlement. In August of the following year, President Cerezo and the other four presidents of Central America signed the Esquipulas Peace Accord, which, after the end of the Cold War four years later, would serve as a rough framework for peacemaking in Guatemala.

With its ally's surface "democratization" in the mid-1980s, the Reagan administration was able to get Congress to approve military aid for Guatemala. The war dragged on, and not much was done to promote a general settlement throughout the rest of the Cerezo administration.

However, as the Cold War was winding down, the Catholic Church and then important civilian groups began to establish a dialog with the URNG. Finally, in 1991, shortly after his election, conservative president Jorge Serrano began negotiating directly with the guerrillas. In 1992 an agreement on democratization and some discussion of human rights took place. The following year, after Serrano tried (and failed) to seize dictatorial powers, he was removed from office by the military and replaced with former human rights ombudsman Ramiro de León Carpio. Though negotiations stalled for a while, they picked up again in January 1994 and resulted in a framework accord for the negotiation of a settlement to be brokered by the United Nations. This was followed in rapid succession by a global human rights accord in March and two accords in June, one dealing with the resettlement of displaced populations and the other with the creation of a Truth Commission. In March 1995, a landmark identity and rights of indigenous peoples accord was signed—very important for a country in which over 60 percent of the population is indigenous.

In November 1995, the possibilities of a comprehensive peace moved forward even farther as Alvaro Arzú, a conservative who understood that civil war is bad for business, was elected president. Negotiations were accelerated. In March 1996, the URNG declared an open-ended cessation of hostilities, and the army soon followed suit. This was followed in September by the landmark "Accord on the Strengthening of Civilian Power and the Function of the Army." Finally, in December, the two sides signed a "definitive cease-fire," an "Accord on Constitutional and Electoral Reforms," "Bases for the Incorporation of the URNG into Legality," and, at the end of the month, the final comprehensive peace settlement. All said, these appeared to constitute a truly revolutionary end to the war. Indeed, as the leading U.S. authority on Guatemalan politics commented to the author, "This is the completion of Guatemala's democratic revolution—interrupted by the U.S. intervention of 1954."[27]

The "Tranquil Two"

Honduras

Having experienced decades of military rule, Honduras was certainly no democracy as it entered the period examined in this chapter. However, its military was different from that of the three neighboring republics in that it believed in responding to grassroots mobilization with reform and co-optation rather than with repression.[28] As a result, tiny guerrilla groups that appeared in the 1960s and 1970s never gained legitimacy or support.

In the late 1970s, as part of its policy of promoting human rights, the Carter administration began pressuring Honduras to return to democratic forms. The regime of President/General Policarpio Paz García responded by holding Constituent Assembly elections in 1980 and full national elections in 1981. The winner of the presidential race, Liberal candidate Roberto Suazo Córdova, was inaugurated early in 1982.

As it turns out, Suazo Córdova would be president in name only. By the time he donned the sash of office, the United States was deeply involved in containing "Communism" in El Salvador and programming the Contra war in Nicaragua. Honduras, nestled between the two, was seen as an ideal base of operation for many aspects of these two projects. Salvadoran military personnel would be trained in Honduras to circumvent a ceiling Congress had placed on the number of U.S. military advisers to be sent to El Salvador. Honduran and Salvadoran forces would perform pincer operations on the border to annihilate Salvadoran civilian populations thought loyal to the guerrillas. Nearly continuous joint U.S.-Honduran military "training" exercises—designed to intimidate the Sandinistas—would be conducted on Honduran territory close to the Nicaraguan border. Several U.S. military bases would be built. And Honduran troops and civilians would be moved out of some territory bordering Nicaragua to allow the Nicaraguan Contras sanctuaries out of which to operate against their own government.

To do all of these things, the United States worked closely with the Honduran military while essentially ignoring the weak civilian government. In the early 1980s, Honduras received hundreds of millions of dollars in U.S. aid, much of it military. CIA asset General Gustavo Alvarez became the head of the military and virtual dictator of the country in 1982. For the first time in Honduran history, "death squads" became active, as opponents to the military were murdered or disappeared by the hundreds. Meanwhile, Alvarez and his clique reportedly "embezzled over $30 million of public funds."[29]

By 1984, Alvarez, who had gone beyond bounds acceptable even to the military, was replaced in an internal military coup by another general with CIA connections,

Walter López Reyes. From then until the end of the Cold War, a growing segment in Honduran society would call for a return to real civilian rule, an end to human rights abuses, and greater U.S. respect for their country's sovereignty. Nominal civilian presidents came and went as Suazo Córdova was succeeded in 1986 by fellow Liberal José Azcona Hoyos, who in turn passed the presidential sash to Nationalist Leonardo Callejas in 1990.

In August 1987, Honduras agreed to the Esquipulas peace framework for Central America. However, under pressure from the United States (which was still pursuing the dream of military victory over the "Communists" in Nicaragua and El Salvador), it failed to fulfill its obligations—most important, that of not allowing its territory to be used by irregular troops (the Contras) attacking the government of a neighboring country (Nicaragua). Widespread dissatisfaction with U.S. and Contra troop presence in Honduras simmered throughout the 1980s. On April 7, 1988, after the United States engineered the illegal extradition of an accused drug trafficker from Honduras, thousands of enraged students set fire to the U.S. consulate building in Tegucigalpa. It is probably significant that the Honduran police took over two hours to respond to calls for assistance from the embassy.

In the long run, the Honduran people would have to wait until the end of the Cold War and the demobilization of the Contras for their country to return to some form of normalcy. Even then, Rafael Leonardo Callejas in the early 1990s would refuse to reform the military, and human rights abuses, a legacy of the early 1980s, would continue at high levels. To make matters worse, as part of an overall package of neoliberal reforms, an Agricultural Modernization Act would be passed in 1992 that would partially dismantle Honduras's earlier agrarian reform laws, thus threatening the interests of members of agricultural cooperatives.

Understandably, the inauguration of human rights lawyer Carlos Roberto Reina of the Liberal Party as president in 1994 was cause for hope for many Hondurans. The new president, while pursuing generally neoliberal economic policies, was at least willing to negotiate with those sectors of society (peasants, workers, etc.) upon which these policies had the biggest negative impact. In addition, he moved decisively to curb the inordinate power of the military. Obligatory military service was ended. Plans to place a civilian defense chief at the head of the armed forces and to replace the militarized police force with a civilian police were announced. And trials of military officers charged with atrocities during the early 1980s were held and their outcome was upheld by the Supreme Court—despite three amnesty laws passed during previous, more subservient administrations. As of 1996, Honduras still had a long way to go to reverse the dark legacy of the 1980s, but it seemed to be moving in that direction.

Costa Rica

The country with the strongest democratic traditions and most egalitarian society in 1979, Costa Rica was still the leader in 1997. Its formal democratic system functioned without a major hitch throughout the period. Conservative Unity (Unidad) president Rodrigo Carazo (1978–1982) was followed in office by Party of National Liberation (PLN) presidents Luis Alberto Monge (1982–1986) and Oscar Arias (1986–1990), Social Christian Unity Party (PUSC) president Rafael Angel Calderón (1990–1994), and PLN president José María Figueres (1994–).

Similarly, at least until the 1990s, Costa Rica's relatively more egalitarian social structures also appeared to be holding their own. In the period 1980 to 1990, even though population grew from slightly less than 2.3 million to over 3 million and gross domestic product per capita declined slightly from $2,032 to $1,829, the frequency of households in poverty stayed constant at 19 percent, infant mortality actually dropped from nineteen per thousand to fifteen, and life expectancy increased from 72.6 to 75.6 years.[30]

But even for Costa Rica, all was not well in this period. First, the Cold War struggles to the north during the 1980s inevitably had their impact on the region's most democratic republic. Attempts by the Reagan administration to involve Costa Rica in the U.S. crusade against Sandinista Nicaragua caused serious problems. During the presidencies of Rodrigo Carazo and Luis Alberto Monge, the United States operated a Contra "southern front"[31] out of Costa Rica. At the same time, it built a military airstrip and subverted Costa Rica's tradition of not having a military by pouring tens of millions of dollars into that country's "civil guard." Meanwhile, the CIA carried out dirty tricks and disseminated anti-Sandinista propaganda via segments of the Costa Rican media that it came to influence. There were even credible charges that CIA planes carrying weapons for the Contras were off-loading in Costa Rica and returning to the United States with drugs to help pay for the Contra war.[32]

All of this offended the national sensibilities of many Costa Ricans and led to the February 1986 electoral victory of Oscar Arias, who had promised to bring such affronts to his country's sovereignty to an end. Almost immediately the airstrip was shut down for fear that "it was being used by counterrevolutionaries or by drug traffickers."[33] Arias also defied the will of the United States—at the time still bent on outright military victory over its chosen enemies—by working on a comprehensive peace plan for Central America. The Esquipulas Peace Accord of August 1987 won Arias that year's Nobel Peace Prize. Apparently annoyed by Arias's disloyalty, the United States would subsequently channel large sums of money through the National Endowment for Democracy into the conservative Costa Rican Association for the Defense of Democracy and Liberty, whose executive director, Rafael Calderón Fournier, would win the 1990 presidential election.

Though Costa Rica's Contra war–related problems would fade by the late 1980s, economic difficulties would quickly take their place. A growing government deficit and foreign debt combined with intensified pressures from international lenders would cause the country's leaders to implement neoliberal economic reforms in the late 1980s and 1990s that would threaten the relatively egalitarian nature of the country's social system. Social spending would drop in 1989 to 1992 from slightly under 22 percent to slightly under 19 percent of gross domestic product.[34] By the mid-1990s, the full gamut of neoliberal policies was in play as José María Figueres was downsizing the government payroll and reducing social services, selling state enterprises, lowering tariffs, raising taxes, and "reforming" Costa Rica's unique state pension system.

CENTRAL AMERICA AS IT ENTERS THE TWENTY-FIRST CENTURY

As of 1997, it was clear that the previous two decades had brought advances as well as tragedy and problems to Central America. The insurrectionary wars, and especially the U.S.-coordinated reaction to them, had cost the lives of between 250,000 and 300,000 people, mainly innocent civilians. Other people had been wounded and maimed, and vast amounts of property had been destroyed. But all had not been in vain: The political systems in Nicaragua, El Salvador, and Guatemala, though not perfect, were far more democratic and respectful of human rights in 1996 than they had been two decades earlier. The political culture of Honduras, though damaged in the 1980s, was recovering, and that of Costa Rica remained resilient.

The big question by 1997 was whether or not economic neoliberalism and real democracy could coexist into the future. Could an economic model that normally achieves growth at the expense of social justice be compatible with government of, by, and for the people? If not, which would give way first, democracy or neoliberalism?

NOTES

1. See Edward L. Cleary, *Crisis and Change: The Church in Latin America Today* (Maryknoll, N.Y.: Orbis Books, 1985).

2. John A. Booth and Thomas W. Walker, *Understanding Central America* (Boulder, Colo.: Westview Press, 1993).

3. Washington's point of view was articulated in the Kissinger Commission Report of 1984: National Bipartisan Commission on Central America, *Report of the National Bipartisan Commission on Central America* (Washington, D.C.: Government Printing Office, 1984). While mentioning social injustice, the report stresses the Communist conspiracy explanation.

4. Timothy P. Wickham-Crowley, *Guerrillas and Revolution in Latin America: A Comparative Study of Insurgents and Regimes Since 1956* (Princeton, N.J.: Princeton University Press, 1992).

5. In fact, Daniel Ortega once argued, if immodestly, that "it is the Sandinista Revolution which invented perestroika." In his first meeting with Mikhail Gorbachev in April 1985, he claims to have informed the new Soviet leader—who had not yet gone public with his reformist ideas—that Nicaragua was following a path very different from that of the Soviet Union with its command economy. To his surprise, Gorbachev had responded with approval. (From an Ortega interview with Pierre Hurel, "Ortega ne rend pas les armes," *Paris Match*, March 22, 1990, pp. 78–81).

6. Michael E. Conroy, "Economic Legacy and Policies: Performance and Critique," in Thomas W. Walker, ed., *Nicaragua: The First Five Years* (New York: Praeger, 1985), pp. 219–244.

7. National Bipartisan Commission on Central America, *Report of the National Bipartisan Commission*, p. 30.

8. This information was revealed by an official of the U.S. embassy to a group of which I was part on June 25, 1985.

9. For a discussion of that election and citation of the pertinent British Parliament and House of Lords, Irish Parliament, Dutch government, and other observer reports, see Thomas W. Walker, *Nicaragua: The Land of Sandino* (Boulder, Colo.: Westview Press, 1991), pp. 50, 51, and footnotes 23 and 25 on p. 64.

10. Michael Linfield, "Human Rights," in Thomas W. Walker, ed., *Revolution and Counterrevolution in Nicaragua* (Boulder, Colo.: Westview Press, 1996), pp. 275–294.

11. On August 2, 1979, less than two weeks after the Sandinista victory, I had the unusual experience of being one of three academics to deliver short presentations at a dinner seminar on Central America hosted by CIA director Admiral Stansfield Turner in his executive dining room. (By prior agreement, my presentation consisted of a sharp criticism of U.S. policy in Central America.) Turner, who had just left a long meeting with President Carter, set the tone of the evening with his first six words: "There can be no more Nicaraguas."

12. See Thomas W. Walker, ed., *Reagan Versus the Sandinistas: The Undeclared War on Nicaragua* (Boulder, Colo.: Westview Press, 1987).

13. Both inflation figures are from United Nations ECLAC, "Balance Preliminar de la Economía de la América Latina y el Caribe, 1990," *Notas Sobre la Economía y el Desarrollo* 500/501 (December 1990), p. 27.

14. This figure is from eight pages of charts on the human cost of the war provided me by the Ministry of the Presidency in January 1990.

15. William I. Robinson, *A Faustian Bargain: The U.S. Involvement in the Nicaraguan Elections and American Foreign Policy in the Post–Cold War Era* (Boulder, Colo.: Westview Press, 1992).

16. For coverage of this period, see Thomas W. Walker, ed., *Nicaragua Without Illusions: Regime Transition and Structural Adjustment in the 1990s* (Wilmington, Del.: Scholarly Resources, 1997).

17. In fact, that solution was openly discussed at the August 2, 1979, CIA dinner seminar mentioned in note 11.

18. Indeed, State Department official James Cheek, addressing a plenary session of the Latin American Studies Association congress in Washington on October 18, 1980, argued passionately—if unconvincingly—that Salvador's was the "real" revolution.

19. As part of the Presbyterian Task Force on Central America, I had the opportunity to interview both Rubén Zamora (once) and several official spokespersons of the FMLN (twice) in Managua in November 1982.

20. Benjamin C. Schwarz, *American Counterinsurgency Doctrine and El Salvador: The Frustration of Reform and the Illusion of Nation Building* (Santa Monica, Calif.: Rand Corporation, 1991), p. xii.

21. A large cache of FMLN weapons exploded in Managua in March 1993.

22. For good coverage of the implementation of the Salvadoran peace accords, see Hemisphere Initiatives, *Justice Impugned: The Salvadoran Peace Accords and the Problem of Impunity* (Cambridge, Mass.: Hemisphere Initiatives, 1993); Jack Spence and George Vickers, with Margaret Popkin, Philip Williams, and Kevin Murray, *A Negotiated Revolution: A Two Year Progress Report on the Salvadoran Peace Accords* (Cambridge, Mass.: Hemisphere

Initiatives, 1994); and Jack Spence, David R. Dye, and George Vickers, with Garth David Cheff, Carol Lynne D'Arcangelis, Pablo Galarce, and Ken Ward, *El Salvador: Elections of the Century: Results, Recommendations, Analysis* (Cambridge, Mass.: Hemisphere Initiatives, 1994).

23. As quoted in "El Salvador: ARENA Government's Second Year: Economic Woes and Internal Disputes," *Central America Report* 23, 22 (June 13, 1996), pp. 6, 7.

24. See Susanne Jonas, "Dangerous Liaisons: The U.S. in Guatemala," *Foreign Policy* 103 (Summer 1996), pp. 144–160.

25. For lengthy documentation, see Booth and Walker, *Understanding Central America*, p. 208, note 26.

26. Jonas, "Dangerous Liaisons," p. 147.

27. From a phone conversation with Susanne Jonas, December 12, 1996.

28. Rachel Sieder, "Honduras: The Politics of Exception and Military Reformism (1912–1978)," *Journal of Latin American Studies* 27, part 1 (February 1995), pp. 99–127.

29. James D. Cockcroft, *Latin America: History Politics, and U.S. Policy* (Chicago: Nelson Hall, 1996), p. 191.

30. Proyecto Estado de la Nación, *Estado de la nacion en desarrollo humano sostenible* (San Jose, Costa Rica: Estado de la Nación, 1996), p. 4.

31. Former U.S. ambassador Lewis Tambs as quoted in Cockcroft, *Latin America,* p. 240.

32. Martha Honey, *Hostile Acts: U.S. Policy in Costa Rica in the 1980s* (Gainesville: University of Florida Press, 1993).

33. Costa Rican minister of public safety Hernán Garrón Salazar, as quoted in Cockcroft, *Latin America,* p. 240.

34. Proyecto Estado de la Nación, *Estado de la Nación,* p. 68.

SUGGESTED READINGS

Booth, John A. *Costa Rican Democracy.* Boulder, Colo.: Westview Press, 1997.

Booth, John A., and Thomas W. Walker. *Understanding Central America.* Boulder, Colo.: Westview Press, 1993.

Jonas, Susanne. *The Battle for Guatemala: Rebels, Death Squads and U.S. Power.* Boulder, Colo.: Westview Press, 1991. A good overview of Guatemala in the twentieth century.

Montgomery, Tommie Sue. *Revolution in El Salvador: From Civil Strife to Civil Peace.* Boulder, Colo.: Westview Press, 1995. An insightful and current study of Salvador's troubled history.

Seligson, Mitchell A., and John A. Booth, eds. *Elections and Democracy in Central America.* Chapel Hill: University of North Carolina Press, 1995. A good collection of essays by important authorities on the subject.

Walker, Thomas W., ed. *Nicaragua Without Illusions: Regime Transition and Structural Adjustment in the 1990s.* Wilmington, Del.: Scholarly Resources, 1997. A comprehensive overview of Nicaragua in the first half of the 1990s.

_____. *Revolution and Counterrevolution in Nicaragua.* Boulder, Colo.: Westview, 1991. A systematic examination of Nicaragua's eleven-year experience with revolution and counterrevolution.

21

PANAMA AND THE CANAL

STEVE C. ROPP

Panama is a country that should be well known to every citizen of the United States because the United States was literally present at the creation. Panama gained its independence in 1903 largely because the United States, under President Theodore Roosevelt, was interested in constructing a canal across the isthmus. After independence, U.S. citizens in large numbers journeyed to Panama to dig "the big ditch." Upon completion of the canal in 1914, many chose to stay, becoming permanent residents of the Canal Zone. In subsequent decades, the U.S. political and economic presence on the isthmus was massive, and it was not until the 1978 signing of the Carter-Torrijos treaties that the United States recognized Panama's sovereign rights in the Canal Zone.

During the 1980s, Panama remained in the public eye because of the confrontation between the U.S. government and General Manuel Antonio Noriega. The administration of President Ronald Reagan at first supported Noriega and the Panamanian Defense Forces (PDF) in exchange for the help Noriega provided in dealing with the crisis in Central America. But a policy shift began to occur in 1986 for a number of reasons, including increasing national concern about the drug problem. Beginning in 1987, both the Reagan and Bush administrations used economic sanctions and other means in an attempt to unseat Noriega. When these policies failed to remove him, President Bush launched a military invasion in December 1989 that resulted in Noriega's capture and transport to the United States to face drug trafficking charges.

And yet, in spite of the United States' historical and contemporary involvement in isthmian affairs, there is little understanding in the United States of Panama and its people. Ironically, the very presence of the canal and the associated zone enclave seems to have led to a general belief that the canal is all (or most) of what there is to Panama. Scholarly studies have concentrated more on relations between the United States and Panama than on Panama as an independent country with a political and social system worthy of study on its own terms.

With these thoughts in mind, we turn to a closer examination of the country called Panama. This chapter consists of four parts. In the first, we examine the historical setting. In the second, we look more closely at some of the specific ways in which Panama's socioeconomic structures have been shaped by the country's unique development as a transit area. The third section focuses on the changes in government structure and policy substance that have taken place during the 1990s following two decades of military rule. Finally, we take note of Panama's relationship with the United States and its changing place in the world.

HISTORICAL SETTING

Although geography is not always destiny, Panama has been influenced more than most countries by its location. Panama is an isthmus, a narrow strip of land 420 mi (676 km) long, which joins Central and South America. As both the narrowest and the lowest point in the Southern Hemisphere, the isthmus has historically served as a transit route from the Atlantic Ocean to the Pacific. The first Europeans to take advantage of Panama's location were the Spaniards, who occupied the isthmus soon after Vasco Núñez de Balboa discovered in 1513 that it linked the Atlantic to the great "south sea." With the Spanish discovery and conquest of the Incan Empire after 1532, Panama became a major transit route for treasure shipped back to Spain and for slaves and foodstuffs flowing to Peru.

The social and economic system that emerged on the isthmus during colonial times reflected Panama's importance as a strategic "bridge." A small urban elite developed that derived its influence from the ability to control isthmian trade. The political and economic position of this urban elite was quite strong until the middle of the eighteenth century because the Spanish crown had made Panama City one of only three ports in all of Latin America through which trade with the home country could be conducted. However, Panama City (and hence the urban elite) lost its favored position in the Spanish Empire during the seventeenth and eighteenth centuries when the Spanish trade monopoly in Latin America began to erode. By 1655, the British had established a military and trading base in Jamaica from which they began rapidly to expand their reach. The final blow to Panama's favored economic position came in 1739, when the British destroyed the forts protecting the isthmian trade route.

Termination of Panama's port monopoly seriously undermined the economic base of the urban commercial and bureaucratic elite. Some members of this elite managed to maintain their power positions, but on greatly reduced sources of income. Although they no longer controlled the port, they were able to turn to contraband trade with the British or to provisioning military garrisons that continued to occupy the isthmus under Spanish, and later Colombian, rule. Most important, termination of Panama's port monopoly led to diversification within the social and economic system. Although many of the high-ranking Spanish-born administrators returned to the metropole or found bureaucratic posts elsewhere in Latin America, the locally born Creoles were forced to find other local sources of income, particularly in the countryside. There they could invest in cheap rural land. Because there was no large indigenous labor force like that found in the Andes, the major rural activity became cattle-raising. Termination of the port monopoly and the attendant decline in trade thus led to the creation of a new economic class of small property owners in the interior.[1]

During the nineteenth century, those who remained on the isthmus had to adjust to a new set of relationships with outside powers. On November 28, 1821, Panama declared its independence from Spain. After considerable debate, a decision was made to affiliate with the former viceroyalty of New Granada. This led in turn to Panama's becoming a province of Colombia when Colombia went its separate way.

As a small but strategically important province of a weak Latin American country, Panama was tugged in a number of directions. Lacking any strong historical allegiance to Colombia, Panamanians made numerous attempts to achieve either outright independence or increased autonomy within the Colombian political system. Both Great Britain and the United States were interested in the isthmus because of its central importance to the existing and potential hemispheric transportation network. As the United States expanded across the North American continent, the isthmus came to be viewed as a major component of the "domestic" transportation system, linking the industrialized cities of the East Coast to the rapidly expanding settlements in the West.[2] In 1851, U.S. financiers underwrote the construction of a railroad across the isthmus. To forestall any possible conflict over future canal rights, the United States and Great Britain had signed the Clayton-Bulwer Treaty in 1850. This treaty guaranteed that any canal constructed by either country anywhere in Central America would not be exclusively fortified or controlled.

The social and economic consequences of Panama's new relationship with these outside powers during the nineteenth century cannot be overestimated. Renewed attention to the transit function restored the economic vitality of the urban transit area and even led to the creation of an entirely new city, called Colón, on the Atlantic side of the isthmus. Panama City once again became an economic magnet, drawing workers from the interior to construct the railroad and later to work on the canal project undertaken by the French in 1878. A second major effect of these new external relationships was to change the composition of Panama's urban lower class. Until the middle of the nineteenth century, the urban lower class consisted largely of Hispanicized blacks who had come to Panama as slaves during the colonial period to work in the transit area. Beginning with construction of the railroad, English-speaking black workers were imported in great numbers from the Caribbean islands. At the height of the U.S. canal-building efforts in 1910, the Panama Canal Company employed over 35,000 such workers. Many remained in urban Panama after the canal was completed in 1914. Their English language and Protestant religion set them apart from preexisting Panamanian culture and society.

Growing U.S. interest in constructing a canal across the isthmus led to Panama's independence from Colombia in 1903. President Theodore Roosevelt gave tacit encouragement to Panamanian nationalists intent on liberating the isthmus from Colombian rule. The result was an uprising on November 3, 1903, that led to the creation of the Republic of Panama.

It is not surprising that U.S. influence in early Panamanian politics was extensive. Article 136 of the new constitution granted the United States the right to "intervene in any part of Panama, to reestablish peace and constitutional order if it has been disturbed."³ Panamanian politicians frequently called upon U.S. officials in the Canal Zone for help in restoring order when it suited their purposes. Additionally, many high-level positions in the Panamanian bureaucracy were held by U.S. citizens. The United States also exercised overwhelming economic influence in the new republic. The primary source of such influence was the Canal Zone, the 10-mi-wide (16-km) strip of U.S.-controlled land that cut the isthmus in half. Employing a large number of U.S. and Panamanian workers, it was both a major source of jobs and a market for Panamanian products. Furthermore, large banana plantations established by the U.S.-owned United Fruit Company in the interior employed many Panamanians and served as a primary source of export income for the new nation.

As in a number of other Latin American nations, the highly visible U.S. political and economic presence eventually caused a strong national reaction, particularly in the 1920s and 1930s. During this period, a number of factors worked to seriously undermine the economy. There was a massive reduction of the canal workforce after completion of the locks in 1914, and heavy debts were incurred by the national government, leading to a cutback in public-sector employment after 1916.

On August 19, 1923, a semisecret nationalist group was formed that embodied much of the resentment Panamanians felt toward the United States as well as toward the Antillean blacks who held many of the jobs in the Canal Zone. Called Community Action, it espoused Hispanic nationalism. Although not the founder of Community Action, Arnulfo Arias soon became its natural leader. Born on a small cattle ranch in the interior in 1901, Arias graduated from Harvard Medical School and returned to Panama, where he practiced medicine and began to dabble in politics. Elected president on three separate occasions (1940, 1949, and 1968), he was never allowed to complete a full term.

The popular political movement led by Arias was partially displaced by another emerging political force beginning in the 1950s. After Panama achieved independence in 1903, the army was disbanded because of the threat it posed to the political elite and to the United States. Only a small police force was retained. However, during the 1930s the National Police gradually began to gain political influence under the guidance of José Antonio Remón. By the late 1940s, Colonel Remón and his police organization had become important arbiters in the feuds among leaders of the traditional political parties. Using the police as a springboard, Remón won the presidential election in 1952. Several years later, the National Police was converted into a National Guard and given a new, expanded military role.

With the rise in the power and influence of the National Guard in the 1950s, the base was laid for several subsequent decades of military government. Although the government returned to civilian hands after Remón's assassination in 1955, the National Guard retained much of its political influence. During this period, the guard became increasingly professionalized as more officers with academy training entered it. Because of the Cold War, the United States greatly expanded its military assistance programs during the 1950s, and many Panamanian soldiers were trained at U.S. installations.

On October 11, 1968, the civilian government of President Arnulfo Arias was overthrown by a military coup. The young lieutenant colonel who soon emerged as the central figure in the National Guard was Omar Torrijos. He quickly moved Panamanian policy in a symbolically anti-U.S. direction and restored diplomatic relations with Castro's Cuba. Although Torrijos and the National Guard never displayed the same degree of anti-U.S. sentiment that existed in the early days of Community Action, the restoration of the armed forces to a central position in Panamanian politics created an important new institutional base from which nationalist sentiments could be voiced.

TRANSIT AREA GROWTH AND SOCIOECONOMIC STRUCTURES

Panama's social and economic structures are largely the product of its unique development as a transit area. The perceived need by the United States for hegemonic control of this transit area led to the creation in 1903 of an enclave (the Canal Zone) in the heart of urban Panama. Although foreign-controlled enclaves have been common elsewhere in Latin America, the economic importance and geographic centrality of the Canal Zone were such that they largely determined not only the rate and direction of national economic growth but also the nature of the domestic class structure. Urban commercial groups and rural cattlemen depended heavily on the Canal Zone as a market for their products. Perhaps most important, the existence of the zone played a determining role in the evolution of Panama's urban working class.

In many Latin American countries, the urban working class has served as an important base of support for political leaders intent on restructuring internal relations between elites and masses or relations between the nation and outside powers. However, in Panama the working class has remained quite dormant except for a brief spurt of activity while the military governed during the 1970s. This dormancy has come about because workers have operated within the context of an alliance between Canal Zone and Panamanian elites that actively worked to limit the workers' influence since 1903. During the early years of the republic, repression of working-class interests was often brutal and exercised through the direct use of military force. For example, when canal workers living in Panama City went on strike in 1925 to keep rents from being raised, Panamanian slumlords called on U.S. troops from the zone to quell the rioting.

The ease with which working-class demands were historically repressed was due to two rather unique features of the transit area that negatively affected labor's bargaining power. First, Canal Zone workers were organized into unions that had their primary ties to the United States rather than to Panama. Second, the Canal Zone workforce was largely composed of English-speaking blacks who enjoyed little sympathy among the Spanish-speaking Panamanian population. That Canal Zone workers historically received higher wages by national standards led to the general perception that they were a "labor elite," privileged and culturally distinct from Panamanians elsewhere in the republic.

Rapid growth of economic activities in the transit area during the 1960s and 1970s led to the mass migration of people from the interior provinces. As in many other Latin American countries, Panama's urban population grew very rapidly, increasing from 36 percent of the national total in 1950 to 48 percent by 1970.[4] The result of this massive internal migration was the creation of a large, culturally and economically heterogeneous class of urban poor living in numerous squatter settlements around Panama City.

The magnetic attraction of the transit area during the 1960s and 1970s served in turn to reinforce the historic marginality of the countryside. The interior provinces continued to be neglected by urban civilian politicians representing the interests of commercial elites, so that neither the rural cattlemen nor the peasants really prospered. However, the structure of the rural economy was significantly altered during these two decades. Traditionally, the Panamanian peasant engaged in subsistence farming on small plots of land that were owned by the government. The expansion of commercial cattle-raising activities greatly reduced the amount of land available to peasants. In addition to forcing many of them off the land and into the cities, this development increased the tension between cattlemen and peasants.

The military regime that controlled politics from 1968 until 1989 came to power partly because of the above-mentioned marginality of those living in the countryside and related changes in the structure of the rural economy. Power was taken from the hands of the urban economic elite who had held sway since 1903. In contrast to members of this elite, General Torrijos was born and raised in the interior. And although his anti-urban biases were not as strong as the smoldering antagonism of the marginalized cattlemen who had supported Arnulfo Arias, his concern for the culture and economy of rural Panama was just as real.

Industrial growth after World War II created an economy that consisted by the 1960s of three major parts. Supplementing the traditional service and agricultural activities was an expanded industrial light manufacturing sector, which led to growth of the industrial working class. The most important economic development in the 1970s and 1980s was the dramatic change in the overall importance of these three sectors. Although the service economy continued to expand at a rapid rate, industrial manufacturing activities began to level off. The same was true for the agricultural sector, which experienced a number of problems related to international competitiveness, marketing, and farm technology.

Panama's transit area and related service sector continue to play a central role in determining the fundamental structure of the economy and the distribution of various activities within it. Growth of this sector has been largely the result of Panama's continuing development as a service center for global multinational corporations. Initially during the 1970s and 1980s, U.S., European, and Japanese corporations used Panama as a location for servicing their regional financial transactions with a minimum of red tape, as well as for a variety of transportation, communication, and warehousing activities. More recently, large corporations in the rapidly growing East Asian newly industrialized countries (South Korea, Taiwan, Singapore) have been using the transit area for service-related regional activities in the context of NAFTA, as well as for a certain amount of low-level manufacturing production.

The importance of this continued rapid growth of the service sector for Panamanian social and political development is difficult to assess. However, it may result in a further reduction in the political influence of urban laborers engaged in manufacturing activities. Not only has the growth of the industrial labor force slowed, but the nature of the "new" service sector (with its close ties to the multinational corporations) would seem to suggest impediments to the further organization of the urban workforce. One of the attractive features of service-sector workers, as perceived by multinational corporations, is their current lack of organization.[5]

GOVERNMENT AND POLITICAL DYNAMICS

For some two decades (1968–1989), Panama was dominated by the military.[6] During these years, government structures were altered in order to give the military more of a role in policy formulation and implementation. The substance of policy also changed because military officers viewed themselves as representing previously marginalized rural and urban working-class groups. Military leaders used heavy state intervention in the economy and enlarged governmental structures to pursue economic development strategies aimed at improving the lot of their class allies.

Following the U.S. military invasion of 1989, there were major changes in government structure associated with Panama's return to civilian democratic rule. And just as important, there were changes in the substance of policy. Two successive civilian administrations, one dominated by the old urban commercial elite and the other by civilian allies of the previous military government, have both moved in the direction of reducing the role of government and implementing neoliberal economic reforms.

Although there was considerable modification of the Panamanian government structure after the military seized power in 1968, it is important to note that the fundamental characteristics of government under *both* military and civilian leaders have been heavily influenced by the nation's Iberian political heritage. When Panama declared its independence from Colombia in 1903, a new constitution was drafted that was based on Colombian law. Provision was made for a centralized unitary government composed of three branches: executive, legislative, and judicial. The president was to be elected for a four-year term and to be ineligible for immediate reelection.

The legislative branch historically centered around a unicameral National Assembly, whose members were elected for four-year terms at the same time as the president. Assembly representatives were elected from circuits corresponding to the nine provinces into which the country was divided. This traditional political system was eminently "presidential," since the chief executive normally dominated both the legislative and judicial branches. Through his power to appoint provincial governors, the president's authority extended into the countryside and influenced administration on the local level. Although the municipalities theoretically possessed more autonomy than the provinces, this autonomy was seldom manifest in practice.

After the military coup in 1968, the dominance of the executive branch became even more pronounced, but power was concentrated in military rather than civilian hands. A new constitution promulgated in 1972 made General Omar Torrijos "maximum leader of the Panamanian Revolution." As for the legislative branch, this new constitution substituted a system of representation based on the nation's 505 municipal subdistricts for the National Assembly. Members of this reconfigured legislature were elected for longer terms in a process that was tightly controlled by the executive branch, and traditional parties played no role.

The military's domination of these civilian political institutions remained contingent upon its ability to both circumvent legal mechanisms designed to curb military power and maintain strict discipline with the military institution itself. Prior to the 1968 coup, the president of the republic was commander-in-chief of the armed forces as specified by the 1946 Constitution. As such, the president had the right—if not always the power—to appoint and remove military personnel. Under provisions of the 1972 Constitution, the president (appointed, in fact, by the military) had no such powers. Furthermore, article 2 stated that government agencies were to act in "harmonic collaboration" with the armed forces.

General Torrijos and his successor, General Noriega, maintained control of the military through a highly centralized administrative apparatus. Lines of authority ran directly from the commander-in-chief to all military units without being channeled through the General Staff. Torrijos maintained direct control over all seven of Panama's infantry companies, and no officer assignments were made, even at the lieutenant level, without his express approval.

One important additional change following the 1968 coup was that the traditional political parties were banned, largely because they were perceived as representing the interests of the traditional elites. In 1978 the Democratic Revolutionary Party (PRD) was formed to incorporate and guide the various groups that supported the military regime. According to its declaration of principles, the PRD was to be democratic, multiclass, unitary, nationalistic, revolutionary, popular, and independent.[7] In many respects, it resembled other Latin American political parties historically established by military leaders to give civilian institutional form to their ideas. As with Mexico's existing Institutional Revolutionary Party (PRI), the PRD attempted to ensure, through close collaboration among military, government, and party leaders, that participation of opposition groups would be carefully channeled.

In sum, a form of "guided democracy" existed in Panama for two decades. Military leaders adopted economic policies that were tailored to improving the lot of their multiclass popular constituency and relied on heavy state intervention to implement them. During this period, the government bureaucracy experienced considerable growth, organized labor gained more influence, and the social safety net was expanded to include a large number of new and previously marginalized social groups.

When civilians returned to power in Panama following the U.S. invasion, most of the country's traditional democratic institutions were reestablished, including the unicameral National Assembly. At the same time, problems of democratic governability soon emerged that related to three major factors. First, some Panamanians remained unconvinced that the urban commercial elite that had been returned to power on the backs of U.S. tanks was fully legitimate and that it would govern in the best interests of all the people. Second, there were serious political divisions within this elite governing coalition. And finally, changes in the global economy forced civilian governments to undertake neoliberal economic reforms that were perceived as possibly having a negative impact on certain social groups and classes.

Guillermo Endara, Panama's first postinvasion civilian president, was sworn into office on a U.S. military base. A longtime supporter of Arnulfo Arias, he headed an alliance of political parties that had been kept from assuming power by General Noriega following fraudulent 1989 elections. From the very beginning, this alliance was plagued by internal disagreements and bickering. The roots of this problem can be traced to the fact that General Noriega had not permitted Endara's political party to participate in the 1989 elections. This forced many of the party's numerous supporters to vote for the candidates of several smaller coalition parties, giving these smaller parties an exaggerated impression of their postelection importance.

With regard to the economy, Endara's administration initially focused its attention on efforts to restore the government's credibility in international financial circles. As a consequence, it made some rather halfhearted and unsuccessful attempts to reduce the size of the public sector in order to allow for larger payments on the country's substantial national debt. More important, his administration began reacting to the sea change in global economic thinking that had taken place during the late 1980s with regard to the most appropriate national strategies for promoting growth. The new neoliberal economic model that gained ascendancy following the collapse of Soviet Communism emphasized the lowering of national tariff barriers, reduction in the size of the public sector through the privatization of state-owned companies, coupled with a shift from the traditional import-substitution growth strategy to one that emphasized promotion of industrial exports.

While Endara was president of postinvasion Panama, the nation made some headway with regard to making major policy changes that would be required for genuine productive restructuring. However, it was only following the election of Ernesto Pérez Balladares in 1994 that the government began to make serious and sustained efforts to implement economic reform. The curious aspect of this situation was that

Pérez Balladares represented the old party of military rule, the Democratic Revolutionary Party. As the party that had been largely responsible in previous decades for doubling the size of the government bureaucracy and calling for increased state economic intervention, it seemed a most unlikely candidate to lead such neoliberal reform efforts.

When Pérez Balladares took office in the fall of 1994, he moved quickly toward the pursuit of his major economic goals. These included joining the General Agreement on Tariffs and Trade (GATT) and reducing the size of the public sector. Another centerpiece of this neoliberal reform process was the effort to alter the progressive labor legislation that had been enacted in 1972 during the early years of military rule. Economics minister Guillermo Chapman argued that some changes in the labor code would be necessary in order to create a more modern and efficient state.

Although some of Panama's governability problems are not as serious as they appeared to be in the early 1990s, there are still major disagreements concerning the process of neoliberal economic reform. Although the Pérez Balladares administration did make some initial attempt at being broadly consultative, it soon became clear that his administration was intent on imposing these reforms at almost any cost. The absence of a traditional military "populist" dimension was indicated by the lack of attention given to creating a safety net for the poverty-stricken groups that would presumably stand to lose the most through the implementation of the reforms.

By 1995, the battle lines had been drawn between the neoliberal reformers who dominated government thinking and some sectors of the public who opposed their policies. When the National Assembly attempted to revise the labor code in August, there were strikes and riots in Panama City that left an estimated four people dead and hundreds detained by the police. Some forty-nine labor unions went on strike and received broad support from business professional associations, students, and opposition political parties.

COOPERATION AND CONFLICT
WITH THE UNITED STATES

Because of Panama's small size and unique geographical position, its foreign relations have been heavily influenced by outside powers.[8] By 1903, the United States had emerged as the dominant outside power with multiple sources of influence over Panama's foreign initiatives. The large U.S. troop presence in the Canal Zone and the strategic importance of the isthmus to the United States limited the contacts the Panamanian government was allowed to develop with global adversaries of the United States, such as the Soviet Union. In addition to this military presence, U.S. dominance of the economy meant that independent foreign policy initiatives had to be cautiously pursued. During the Cold War, Panama's economic reliance on the U.S. government and private companies was probably greater than that of any other country in the world.[9]

Because of the dominant position of the United States throughout most of the twentieth century, Panama's foreign policy was largely bilateral. The commercial elites who controlled the foreign ministry were primarily interested in extracting the maximum economic benefits from their relationship with the United States. A secondary concern was to modify the worst colonial aspects of the U.S.-Panamanian relationship, particularly as it related to the Canal Zone. According to terms of the original 1903 treaty, the United States could act "in perpetuity" in the Canal Zone "as if it were the sovereign of the territory . . . to the entire exclusion of the exercise by the Republic of Panama of any such sovereign rights, power, and authority."[10] Numerous attempts were made over the years by leaders of various political persuasions to negotiate treaties that did not so egregiously violate the country's sense of sovereignty.

In spite of these attempts, the major provisions of the 1903 treaty remained unchanged until 1978. In that year, the U.S. Congress ratified two completely new treaties, the Panama Canal Treaty and the Treaty of Neutrality. The former recognizes Panamanian sovereignty over the Canal Zone and specifies that U.S. troops will be withdrawn completely from this area by the year 2000; the latter guarantees that the waterway will remain permanently neutral in time of peace or war.

Ratification of the canal treaties led to a period of greater cooperation between Panama and the United States. And yet, there were storm clouds on the horizon. That the Carter administration had placed so much faith in a military strongman (General Omar Torrijos) during the treaty negotiations meant that it was difficult thereafter for the United States to distance itself from the military regime. The Reagan administration inherited these close U.S. ties to Panama's military and built on them to serve its own strategic purposes of fighting Communism in Central America.

The long honeymoon in U.S.-Panamanian relations that had been created by the new canal treaties and by General Noriega's cooperation in Central America during the early 1980s ended abruptly in 1986. In that year, Seymour Hersh published a scathing account of Noriega's activities in the *New York Times*. Quoting high U.S. government officials, he accused the general of involvement in the torture-killing of a Panamanian dissident, drug trafficking, and covertly supporting left-wing guerrilla movements.[11]

In February 1988, Noriega was indicted by two Florida grand juries on charges of drug-money laundering. With drug trafficking increasingly viewed as a major security threat to the United States, the Reagan administration moved quickly to force Noriega from office. A series of economic sanctions were implemented that succeeded in devastating the economy but not in removing the general. For the remainder of the year and on into 1989, the United States and Panama hurled invectives at each other. This three-year struggle ended in December when President George Bush sent U.S. troops into Panama in Operation Just Cause.

With the end of the Cold War and the demise of Panama's military regime, U.S.-Panamanian relations have once again improved. The dominant issues in these relations during the final years of the 1990s will be those related to transfer of the canal in the year 2000. Particularly sensitive is the question whether any of the various military facilities that the United States still controls will be allowed to remain in U.S. hands. Although the Panama Canal Treaty stipulates that all these facilities will revert to Panama, there has been considerable speculation about a deal that would allow the United States to retain de facto control of a few key military bases through creation of a regional counterdrug center.[12]

CONCLUSION

Panama's geographical location has been of considerable importance in defining its global function as a transit area, shaping the country's socioeconomic structures, and influencing related political dynamics. For most of the twentieth century, the United States exercised near-hegemonic control over Panama and maintained a close bilateral relationship in the context of hemispheric struggles with other great world powers.

Now that the twentieth century is drawing to a close, it is time to take a closer look at Panama's evolving place in the world and to assess the consequences of this evolution for the country's future political and economic development. Such a task is beyond the scope of this chapter, but we can note three important facts. First, the U.S. invasion of Panama in 1989 vastly reduced the voice in Panamanian politics of those highly nationalistic groups who gave priority to the maintenance of a culturally and economically autonomous state. Second, with the reversion of the canal and associated military facilities to Panama, there will be less concern on the part of the United States about the country's future political status. Finally, the rapid globalization of production and financial markets is simultaneously creating new sources of external influence and eroding central government authority.

In such a twenty-first-century context, what becomes problematic is not just the nature of Panamanian politics and society but the very nature of the state itself. Panama can be described as a historically weak and fragmented new state that formed around a transit area. It was created and maintained as a territorial entity largely by hegemonic external factors (U.S. security interests) until the Panamanian military became strong enough to give the country a more independent global voice.

Will Panama retain its essential characteristics as a nation state into the twenty-first century? Or will it once again become something akin to a "deterritorialized" global city, floating freely within the new geometry of globalized economic activity?

NOTES

1. Omar Jaén Suárez, *La Población del Istmo de Panamá del siglo XVI al siglo XX* (Panama City: Impresora de la Nación, 1978), pp. 187–190, 301.

2. Walter LaFeber, *The Panama Canal: The Crisis in Historical Perspective* (New York: Oxford University Press, 1979), p. 8.

3. Juan Materno Vásquez, *Teoría del estado Panameño* (Panama City: Ediciones Olga Elena, 1980), p. 122.

4. Panamá, Dirección de Estadística y Censo, Contraloría General, *Panamá en cifras: 1973–1977* (Panama City, n.d.), p. 38.

5. Steve C. Ropp, *Panamanian Politics: From Guarded Nation to National Guard* (New York: Praeger, 1982), pp. 60–61.

6. For an attempt to explain this long period of military rule, see Steve C. Ropp, "Explaining the Long-Term Maintenance of a Military Regime: Panama Before the U.S. Invasion," *World Politics* 44, January 1992, pp. 210–234.

7. Partido Revolucionario Democrático, "Documentos fundamentales" (Panama City, 1979), pp. 16–17.

8. Jan Black, "The Canal and the Caribbean," in Richard Millett and W. Marvin Will, eds., *The Restless Caribbean: Changing Patterns of International Relations* (New York: Praeger, 1979), pp. 90–91.

9. Neil R. Richardson, *Foreign Policy and Economic Dependence* (Austin: University of Texas Press, 1978), pp. 103–106.

10. U.S. Congress, Senate, Committee on Foreign Relations, *Hearings on the Panama Canal Treaties*, 95th Cong., 1st Session, September 1977, pt. 1, p. 588.

11. "Panama Strongman Said to Trade in Drugs, Arms and Illicit Money," *New York Times*, June 12, 1986.

12. Steve C. Ropp, "Panama: Tailoring a New Image," *Current History* 96, 607 (February 1997), p. 59.

SUGGESTED READINGS

Biesanz, John, and Mavis Biesanz. *The People of Panama*. New York: Columbia University Press, 1955. This is a classic book on Panamanian politics and society. It offers insights that are still valuable.

Jorden, William J. *Panama Odyssey*. Austin: University of Texas Press, 1984. A former ambassador to Panama, Jorden presents a fascinating and detailed description of the behind-the-scenes negotiations leading to passage of the 1978 canal treaties.

McCullough, David. *The Path Between the Seas: The Creation of the Panama Canal, 1870–1914*. New York: Simon and Schuster, 1977. An epic book dealing with the French and U.S. efforts to build the Panama Canal.

Ropp, Steve C. *Panamanian Politics: From Guarded Nation to National Guard*. New York: Praeger, 1982. A short introductory examination of Panamanian politics from the nineteenth century through the period of military rule.

Scranton, Margaret. *The Noriega Years: U.S.-Panamanian Relations, 1981–1990*. Boulder, Colo.: Lynne Rienner Publishers, 1991. Very good analysis of the factors explaining the tension between the United States and Panama during this period.

Ward, Christopher. *Imperial Panama: Commerce and Conflict in Isthmian America, 1550–1800*. Albuquerque: University of New Mexico Press, 1993. Solid on Panama's colonial period.

Zimbalist, Andrew, and John Weeks. *Panama at the Crossroads*. Berkeley: University of California Press, 1991. An excellent overview of Panama's early economic development and its implications for the current distribution of political power.

PART NINE
CUBA AND THE CARIBBEAN

22

THE CUBAN REVOLUTION

NELSON P. VALDÉS

A social revolution is a radical, abrupt, thorough, and systematic alteration of the so-cial relations, the patterns of behavior, and the institutional structures that exist in the economic, political, cultural, and social life of a country. By definition, a social revolution touches every facet of interaction in society. It often attempts a total break with tradition. But even revolutionaries cannot escape their material and historical contexts.

The agendas of social revolutions have changed through time. From the seven-teenth century on, Western Europe dealt with a series of critical problems, ranging from nation building (the creation of national institutions, a central system of au-thority, and a national economy) to the creation of representative political institu-tions and industrialization. This process of becoming modern capitalist nation states took centuries to unfold and was often plagued with social conflict at home and war abroad. During this century, the countries of the Third World (including most of those in Latin America) have confronted some of the same difficulties (nation build-ing, economic development, the problems of citizenship) as well as new ones (na-tional self-determination and ending foreign control and neocolonial institutions and practices).

In general, revolutionaries have defined their tasks in such a manner that their aims are, to say the least, awesome. Social revolutions are supposed to bring about the full blossoming of national sovereignty, fight foreign influence, develop national resources, distribute the economic benefits of growth, centralize political power while increasing the sense of citizenship and the degree of political participation, and carry out a total transformation in the major institutions of the country. And all of these tasks are to be done in a short period of time with the few resources the coun-try may have at its command.

The Cuban Revolution is worthy of study because it presents us with an example of what a revolutionary state has tried to do, how it has gone about it, and what has resulted from the effort. Also, this Revolution, although multifaceted and complex, has been a unique phenomenon that a number of countries have attempted to emulate. Finally, the very fact of the Revolution has placed this small island in the center of the struggle between the superpowers. The impact of the Cuban Revolution, in other words, has been felt not only within its own borders but beyond its shores as well.

THE HISTORICAL CONTEXT

Social revolutions occur in particular places and times. They cannot escape either of the two. The fact that Cuba is an island in a very strategic location has made it a crossroads of trade and cultures. And the fact that it lies only 90 mi (145 km) from the U.S. mainland has preoccupied U.S. as well as Cuban authorities, particularly since 1959.

Yet the islanders have been somewhat isolated from most of Latin America. There is a certain attitude of self-containment and self-sufficiency in the culture. Moreover, Cubans are not sufficiently aware of the dramatic differences between a country that developed a plantation economy very early in its history and the agrarian, peasant, and other traditional forms of social interaction found elsewhere in the hemisphere. This has led some Cubans to consider their experience a model that could be emulated elsewhere—a vanguard rather than an exception.

Social revolutions do not occur in a historical vacuum; they are shaped and bound by history. History, as such, is a dynamic, ever-changing process. How that process unfolds and how it is interpreted do not have to coincide. Yet the interpretation that a society or a portion of a population gives to that process may have a power all its own. Historical interpretation may be a tool for understanding as well as a call to action. Revolutionaries know this well.

Spanish Colonial Period

The history of Cuba has been quite different in its basic pattern from that of most of Latin America. From the onset of the Spanish conquest, the island became a springboard for the conquest of Mexico, Central America, and even portions of South America. Lacking mineral wealth and a large native labor force, Cuba offered little incentive for settlement. The population was fairly small, and the economy was geared toward servicing the fleet system that visited the port of Havana once or twice a year. Most of the population tended to concentrate in the small towns. Colonial institutions were not as strong as in Peru or Mexico, and the Catholic Church held sway only in the urban milieu.

From the 1760s on, Cuba experienced dramatic changes in its economic, social, and political organization. These changes were initiated by the development of the sugar plantation economy and, with it, of a cohesive class of sugar planters (referred to in Cuba as the *sucarocracia*). As sugar production rose, the demand for labor also increased. Since this shift in production occurred just as the British began their industrial revolution, the steam engine was soon introduced into the refining of sugar.

This generated a greater demand for sugarcane and thus for the labor force that cut it. Hence, with the sugar plantation and the modernization of production, black slaves arrived in ever-larger numbers. Sugar production was essentially for profit, although dependent on slave-master relations. The sugar economy dominated the western part of the island, particularly around Havana. In the eastern region, however, a small farming class, mainly white, produced coffee, tobacco, and cattle—a significant portion for barter or direct use.

The sugar areas were held by people born in Spain (*peninsulares*), and the rest of the land was essentially in the hands of poor farmers who had little contact with the Spanish colonial system. The latter were, in a sense, the early *criollos;* the first indications of a Cuban national identity would be found in the eastern part of the island. The differences between the two economic regions, with their distinct modes of production, gave rise to tensions between the Spaniards and the Cubans. The latter, of course, were barred from political power.

The early nineteenth century witnessed independence struggles throughout most of Latin America. Cuba, however, remained under Spanish control. This was due to three factors. First, economic prosperity brought about by sugar cultivation kept much of the population contented. Second, the defeats suffered by the Spanish military forces throughout the hemisphere meant that a large proportion of the defeated personnel ended up in Cuba—thus fortifying colonial rule there. Finally, the sugar planters, as well as many other whites who were not directly connected to the sugar economy, were afraid that a war of independence would be transformed into a slave revolt, as had been the case in Haiti after 1791.

In 1868, Cuba began a war of independence led by the independent, small, white farming class of eastern Cuba. The war went on for ten years but ended in defeat for the rebels as well as in the total destruction of the nonsugar economy. The plantation became ever more powerful and began to expand to the east. The class system, at the same time, was simplified: A basic tension surfaced between the slaveowners and the slaves. In this confrontation, the Catholic Church sided with the plantation and the colonial system. Thus, sugar-plantation slaves and colonial rule became one side of the equation, while the emancipation of the slaves, the reduction of the dominance exerted by the plantation, and Cuban independence became united themes. It is in this period that one begins to find the antisugar mentality that has dominated the thinking of Cuban revolutionists ever since.

In 1895, the war of independence broke out again, this time led by the Cuban Revolutionary Party (PRC) under the guidance of Cuba's most important poet, national hero, and thinker: José Martí. The PRC was a unique development. No other independence war in Latin America was organized by a political party. The party had political and military control of the entire struggle. This was new as well. But the PRC went even further. José Martí had studied the conditions of Latin America and concluded that even though many countries had attained political independence, the laws, traditions, practices, and institutions of colonialism had survived. The PRC therefore had a decolonization program. In that respect, the party foretold a process that would take root throughout the Third World in the second half of the twentieth century.

The American Protectorate

But the war of independence did not achieve its goal. The international situation was far different from what it had been when the rest of Latin America became free of Spain. Late in the nineteenth century, the United States was emerging as a major power in the hemisphere. Manifest Destiny had numerous adherents in Washington, D.C., and the Caribbean was considered an American lake. The Cuban war of independence was lost when the United States and Spain went to war in 1898. U.S. military intervention in the island brought to an end Spanish colonial rule, but only to initiate a new period of U.S. hegemony.

The island became an integral part of the U.S. economy. The culture and education of the Cubans became ever more Americanized. The United States imposed a new economic arrangement, new trade partners, and a new political system. The U.S. dollar became the main currency. From 1899 to 1902, the U.S. military ruled over Cuba, restructuring its socioeconomic system so as to meet U.S. needs. U.S. investors began to control the strategic sectors of the Cuban economy (sugar, transportation, utilities, trade). All communal lands were lost, passing into U.S. ownership.

An amendment to the Cuban Constitution, dictated by U.S. military authorities, allowed the U.S. government to pass judgment on the acceptability of Cuban public policy. And should that judgment be negative, the United States asserted, through the Platt Amendment, the right to intervene militarily to ensure that its dictates were honored.

A new regime in Cuba, ushered in by the so-called sergeants revolt, unilaterally repudiated the Platt Amendment in 1933. Other progressive and nationalistic reforms that had followed the sergeants revolt were soon undermined as the leader of that revolt, Fulgencio Batista, assumed dictatorial powers and curried favor with the United States. But that revolt, which elevated noncommissioned officers of lower-class background to command positions, had severed the tie between the traditional Cuban elite and the officer corps, a factor that later worked to the disadvantage of the military.

The Cuban Revolutionary Party, which had spearheaded the struggle for independence from Spain, had disintegrated after the death of its leader, Martí. But in 1944, a new populist party, of the same name and inspiration, was elected and allowed to rule until 1952, when Batista displaced it and again established a dictatorship.

From 1953 to 1958, the opposition to Batista clustered around the 26th of July Revolutionary Movement. This was a movement formed by ex-members of the Cuban People's Party (PPC), a splinter of the PRC, many of whom remained committed to populism, nationalism, and general concepts of social justice. Under the leadership of a young lawyer, Fidel Castro, they successfully carried out a guerrilla war that managed, for the first time in Latin America, to overthrow a military regime. The United States apparently misunderstood the degree to which these revolutionaries were committed to thorough and rapid social change. But it soon became obvious.

From Nationalism to Socialism

The young revolutionaries sought control over the major economic decisions affecting their country in order to redistribute wealth and promote development. There is no evidence that they had envisioned either a complete break with the United States or a thorough socialization of the economy. But the U.S. government and business community equated the nationalist policies of the Revolution in regard to foreign investments and the reformist policies, beginning with land reform, with communism. U.S. countermeasures, including the slashing of Cuba's sugar quota and, later, the economic embargo, pushed the Cubans to further expropriations.

By late 1960, the state owned a significant portion of the means of production in Cuba. No one had planned this. Through a process of confrontation and nationalist actions and reactions, the capitalist economy of Cuba had been socialized, even though the Cuban state did not have the personnel to run all the enterprises. At issue had been the right of Cuba to make decisions within its own borders, and failure to reply to the U.S. challenge would have amounted to forfeiting sovereignty.

It was the identification with, and the defense of, nationalism that led the Cuban revolutionaries, in practice, to socialism. The United States had come to represent capitalism as well as imperial power, and Cuban nationalism and socialized property were integrated into the new revolutionary ideology. The Bay of Pigs invasion, organized and financed by the CIA, captured the dichotomy well.

On April 15, 1961, airplanes piloted by Cubans hired by the CIA bombarded the airports at Santiago de Cuba and Havana. This was the softening-up period prior to a Cuban-exile invasion. Seven persons died. Speaking at the burial ceremony the next day, Fidel Castro said that a counterrevolutionary invasion, seeking to return capitalism, was imminent. And on that day, he characterized the Cuban Revolution as socialist. The invasion began on April 17, but within two days it had been defeated. Again, just as the cutting of the sugar quota led to the socialization of the basic means of production, the Bay of Pigs invasion made Cuba's identification with socialism the only possible reaction that a radical nationalist movement could take.

This turn of the Revolution surprised the United States as well as the USSR. In fact, the Cuban experience defied some basic tenets of orthodox Marxist theory. Communists, following the views of Lenin, had believed for quite some time that without a revolutionary theory (i.e., Marxism-Leninism), there could be no revolutionary party or movement. And without the party, there could be no revolutionary practice—seizing political power and socializing the means of production. In Cuba, the formula was reversed. Power was seized without a revolutionary theory or party.

The state took over a significant part of the economy and months later called the outcome socialism. Only much later, on December 2, 1961, was there a formal adoption of Marxism-Leninism. It was only in early 1962 that a revolutionary party began to be formed, and it held its first party Congress thirteen years later. Thus, the Cuban experience has been unique in many ways.

THE POLITICAL SYSTEM

During the first sixteen years of revolutionary rule, Cuba's leaders successfully merged charisma with patrimonialism and a high degree of mass mobilization. The Communist Party did not play an important role during that first phase of the Revolution because the very nature of a political party runs counter to charismatic authority. Until 1970, political and organizational work was concentrated on the growth and development of mass organizations (Cuba has six mass organizations: Cuban Confederation of Labor, Federation of Cuban Women, National Association of Small Farmers, Federation of Secondary School Students, the Union of Young Pioneers, and the Committees for the Defense of the Revolution).

The institutionalization of the Revolution, after 1975, redefined the role of the Communist Party. It was to coordinate, control, lead, and supervise the tasks of the state and the mass organizations, without administering. But to assume such roles, the party had to grow, train its cadres, develop efficient methods of leadership, establish internal discipline, and improve its political training as well as the educational level of its members.

In 1965, the Communist Party had just 45,000 members; ten years later, the number had increased to 211,642, and in 1980, the membership numbered 434,143. The educational level has changed as well. In 1970, 33.6 percent of the members did not have a sixth-grade education; nine years later, that proportion had declined to 11.4 percent. The proportion of members with higher education has also been rapidly increasing, from 2.8 percent in 1970 to 6.2 percent in 1979. Party cadres have shown an even greater improvement, with 16 percent having had a high school education in 1975 and 75.5 percent five years later. Meanwhile, membership in the mass organizations has ceased to grow. Since the 1970s, the revolutionary leadership has been preparing the party to play the "leading role" that Marxist-Leninist theory had claimed for it.

Communist Party Organs

The present system of government is characterized by a complex web of interlocking power relations. The Communist Party, the state, and the government are functionally differentiated, although some individuals occupy more than one post in each of these three centers of power. The Communist Party, at present the locus of political power, is highly structured. At the base, the party membership is organized in cells, or *nucleos,* 26,500 of them in 1980. The party is organized on a territorial basis (local, municipal, provincial, and national).

On the national level, the party Congress is the highest authority, but only in a formal sense since it meets only once every five years. Delegates to the party Congress, elected from subordinate territorial levels, in turn elect (really ratify) from among themselves the members of the Central Committee (CC). Because of its size, and the fact that its members have other responsibilities, the CC has only about two one-day plenums annually. At these meetings, the CC selects the members of the Political Bureau (PB) and the Secretariat.

The PB makes policy between congresses and plenums on behalf of the CC and the party. Its task consists of translating general principles and aims into more precise policy, and its decisions are binding.

The Secretariat is also a powerful institution. To some it has appeared that the PB is much more powerful than the Secretariat because the latter has to answer to the former (just like the PB answers to the CC, and it, in turn, responds to the party Congress). However, it would be more useful to see the PB and the Secretariat as functioning in different arenas.

The Secretariat is responsible for the maintenance of the party apparatus. It decides who may join or who is expelled. It also takes care of internal political education and promotion within party ranks. The Secretariat also transmits to the institutions of the state, government, and mass organizations the guidelines of the PB.

The internal organization of the Communist Party parallels that of the administrative and political divisions of the island, with fourteen committees representing the provinces and 179 representing municipalities. Below the municipal committees are the party cells, organized at work centers, schools, and military barracks. At the base, then, the party is organized by function rather than by territory (which discriminates against people who are not employed, do not study, or are not in the military).

The functions and hierarchical lines of the CC, the PB, and the Secretariat are clearly demarcated, but in practice, the demarcations seem to be insignificant. Many of the same individuals can be found in all three bodies. The Secretariat has nine members—five are full members of the PB, and two are alternates. Political power is interlocked for the simple reason that the same person can have two entirely different statuses and roles. On the basis of that web, it can be stated that in 1982, thirty men and one woman comprised the core of revolutionary power in Cuba (what in Mexico has been called "the revolutionary family").

The Communist Party makes decisions but does not execute them, guides but does not administer. The implementation of policy—that is, practical day-to-day decision making and policy formulation—is carried out by a different set of institutions. From 1959 to 1975, the people who had political power and those who held key government posts were the same; there was no distinction of roles. In 1976, however, a constitution was issued proclaiming the socialist nature of the Cuban state and establishing the rules of government. Executive, legislative, and judicial powers were separated. Granted, the executive still had some legislative prerogatives, but nothing similar to those of the 1959–1975 period.

In the 1980s a number of changes took place within the Communist Party. Some of these were due to the internal dynamics of the revolution itself. The party grew from just 50,000 persons in 1965 to 523,639 members in 1986. There was some fluctuation in the growth; however as a whole, party recruitment increased faster than population increase. In the period 1975–1980, it grew almost 21 percent; in the 1980s it dropped to 4.1 percent (1980–1986). After 1986 there was a greater effort to gain members again, particularly young ones. Tied to the reduction in membership age was an improvement in educational level. In 1975, 19.6 percent of the members had a ninth-grade education or more; in 1986 the figure was 72.4 percent. This shift reflects the overall improvement in the educational level of the population at large.

There have been some changes in the internal organization of the party over the years. The Central Committee membership can be divided into full members (who actually participate in decision making) and alternates (who may take the place of full members due to death, promotion, etc.). There were 100 full members in the CC in 1965. As the PCC membership grew, new members were incorporated into leadership positions. The PCC avoided demoting CC full members, however, by inventing the concept of alternates. By 1986 the Central Committee had 146 members and seventy-nine alternates.

The Political Bureau had also expanded. Whereas it had eight members when the party was organized in 1965, it had thirteen full members and fourteen alternates in early 1990. Eleven of the fourteen alternates had assumed their positions since 1986.

At the 1986 Party Congress, Fidel Castro noted that "we had to renew or die." Thus, he went on, "we must trust our youth." Indeed a policy of affirmative action that targeted women, the young, and blacks began from the 1986 Congress on. At previous Congresses the party stressed the recruitment of workers and peasants. In other words, class had priority. By 1980 special attention was being given to having more women in the PCC. The same theme was repeated at the Third Congress, but the PCC went further this time, enunciating a policy of affirmative action for women, blacks, and the young. The Main Report read by Fidel Castro stated, "The mechanisms that ensure the correct selection, permanence and promotion of cadre must be improved constantly on the basis of thorough, critical, objective and systematic evaluations and with appropriate attention to development and training. Women's representation in keeping with their participation and their important contribution to the building of socialism in our country must be ensured, along with the existence of a growing reserve of promising young people born and tempered in the forge of the Revolution."

In 1986 women accounted for 21.5 percent of party membership. (The number of women in the CC had increased to 18.8 percent of the combined CC membership.) Ethnicity has become an important issue in the party, perhaps related to the growing influence, education, and expectations of the black population. A Communist Party document stated that "in order for the Party's leadership to duly reflect the ethnic composition of our people, it must include those compatriots of proven revolutionary merit and talents who in the past had been discriminated against because of their skin color."

Fidel Castro has noted that the "rectification of historical injustices" such as racial discrimination "cannot be left to spontaneity." By 1986, only 28.4 percent of the CC membership was black or mulatto. But the affirmative action policies adopted by the revolutionary leadership suggested that the failures in this area were acknowledged and steps were to be taken to address them.

The Communist Party internal organization was also confronted by the changes begun in 1985 in the Soviet Union, and then taken up by Eastern Europe in the late 1980s, as well as by Communist Parties throughout the rest of the world. Thus, in mid-February 1990, the Communist Party leadership announced new plans to transform itself. The promised changes, however, did not imply the abolition of the one-party state. A party document stated, "What we are talking about is the perfecting of a single, Leninist party based on the principles of democratic centralism." (This happened precisely as the Soviets abandoned a constitutional monopoly on power.)

In 1990 the ten-member Secretariat was reduced to six persons. No explanations were given. As a consequence of the changes, the labor movement no longer had a representative (the peasant/farmer sector had no direct voice either). The representative of the labor movement (former head of the Cuban Confederation of Labor) was also dropped from the Political Bureau at that time.

In summary, while the permanent full-time membership of the Political Bureau remained fairly constant throughout the 1980s, the alternate membership experienced drastic change. However, the alternates have little power as long as they remain in that position. In a sense, the increasing number of alternates suggests that rising stars within the revolutionary ranks have been promised power and authority, but they have not been given enough of it to shape decisions within the Political Bureau and the Secretariat. True, the alternates have power vis-à-vis the society at large. They participate in controlling key social, economic, and governmental institutions; but since the core of power resides within the party, they merely implement the significant decisions made elsewhere.

At the 1991 Communist Party Congress, the Congress announced that religious persons could become members of the Communist Party and outlined the major policy changes that would follow—among them: opening major areas of the economy to foreign investments, developing a mixed economy under the guidance of the state, allowing a greater role to private enterprise, and establishing party cells at the neighborhood level (until that time, party cells were found only at the workplace).

The Communist Party was supposed to have another Congress in 1996, but none was held. It is possible that one will take place in 1997 and that some changes in the

Cuban political system may be introduced, particularly in the area of transferring a greater say to the party membership over political matters—since most of the decisions have remained in the hands of the political leadership.

There has been a significant leadership change at the municipal, provincial, and even national levels of the Communist Party, and even some of the "historical" figures have been replaced, although control remains in the hands of much older members. Nonetheless, a growing number of cabinet posts and state and administrative leaders are now under the age of fifty.

The National Assembly

In 1977, a National Assembly (NA) with formal legislative powers was established for the first time. The NA is a representative institution whose members are elected for five-year periods. Election is indirect, delegates being chosen by provincial assemblies. (Provincial elections are popular and direct.) The NA has 481 delegates and meets twice a year, usually for less than a week. It can generate legislation as well as approve it, but laws must be consonant with the general guidelines of the Communist Party. How much real power the NA possesses is debatable. Sessions are so short that there is little time to study, analyze, and debate. Recently, some delegates have tried to represent their respective local constituencies, but the NA is not receptive to that idea. In general, the NA serves to legitimize decisions made elsewhere.

The real work of the NA is done by standing work committees and the Council of State (CS). Committee members are appointed. Chosen for their specialized knowledge rather than for their political credentials, they need not be delegates to any legislative body. The NA has fifteen committees, fourteen commissions, and nine departments. It should be noted that the persons elected to the assemblies, whether on the national, provincial, or municipal level, do not run on a particular political platform. They have no individual set of policy proposals; instead, they are chosen for their personal characteristics. It is a given that a candidate's political platform will be that of the Communist Party.

The National Assembly has come under criticism by the general population, its members, and members of the Communist Party. The population, at meetings with their elected representatives, have expressed dismay at the institution's lack of power and its incapacity to deal with substantive issues. The members of the municipal and provincial assemblies, on the other hand, have begun to lobby their own constituencies as well as the National Assembly, in order to acquire a greater role in making policy decisions, particularly in the area of economic and social policy. Finally, National Assembly members have complained that they ought to be able to work for a longer period of time, taking for themselves the powers enjoyed by the executive committees. They also have demanded a say in determining budgetary priorities, the size of the budget, and real control over matters of foreign policy.

At the Communist Party Congress in 1991, these matters were addressed, and in 1992 the Cuban constitution was drastically changed in order to provide more power and influence to the National Assembly. The 1993 elections of the National Assembly produced a major overhaul of the elected members; new people entered the scene, most of them in their thirties.

When the NA is not meeting, its functions and prerogatives are assumed by its executive committee, the Council of State, which is selected by the NA from its own ranks. The CS carries out the decisions of the NA as well as tasks outlined in the 1976 Constitution. The CS, in 1982, had forty members. Its most important power is that of issuing laws when the NA is not functioning (in a sense, the CS is the country's real legislature). The CS also interprets the law, exercises legislative initiative, declares war or makes peace, removes or appoints members of the Council of Ministers, gives instructions of a general nature to the office of the attorney general and to the judiciary, supervises the diplomatic corps, vetoes ministerial decisions as well as those made at any other level, and exercises any other power that the NA may give it.

The president of the CS is expected to control and supervise the activities of all government ministries and administrative agencies. He could take over any ministry or government post and propose to the NA the members of the Council of Ministers. He is also commander-in-chief of the armed forces. The president, first vice-president, and five vice-presidents of the CS are all in the Political Bureau. The president and the first vice-president also head the Secretariat. The other thirty-three members of the CS are either in the PB, the CC, or the Secretariat.

The Council of Ministers

The government proper is the Council of Ministers (CM), whose members are appointed by the president of the Council of State and ratified by the NA. The CM has one president, one first vice-president, twelve vice-presidents, thirty ministers, forty-eight commission members, eight advisers, one deputy-secretary, and one minister-secretary. The CM administers the state apparatus, executes the laws, issues decrees in accordance with existing laws, develops and administers the national budget, carries out foreign policy, and organizes and directs social, economic, cultural, scientific, and military matters. The CM's Executive Committee (comprising the president, first vice-president, and the twelve vice-presidents) is the real power in government. In 1982, of the fourteen persons on the Executive Committee, nine were in the PB, two were in the Secretariat, five were full members of the CS, and six others were alternates.

Before 1976, the same individuals performed numerous functions although they had one role: They were revolutionaries with power—revolutionary leaders assumed both political and administrative functions. Political leadership and administration are now separate. Charismatic authority is being transformed into a legal-rational system of authority, but during that transition, which may take years, the rules and regulations of the new political structure are elaborated, defined, and given content as well as life by the charismatic authority.

Fidel and Raúl Castro have a tremendous amount of power and control over the key institutions of Cuban society. But this is to be expected. A charismatic system of authority transfers legitimacy to a legal-rational type of authority by placing the representatives of the previous system in key positions. As time goes on and the charismatic leaders play by the new rules, the institutions themselves gain legitimacy. Of course, it remains to be seen whether such a process will continue to unfold in the future. In 1982, Fidel Castro held the following posts: first secretary of the Political Bureau and the Secretariat; member of the Central Committee; deputy to the National Assembly; president of the Council of State, the Council of Ministers, and the Executive Committee of the Council of Ministers; and commander-in-chief of the armed forces. Raúl Castro was the second secretary of the Political Bureau and the Secretariat; member of the Central Committee; deputy to the National Assembly; first vice-president of the Council of State, the Council of Ministers, and the Executive Committee of the Council of Ministers; and minister of the Armed Forces. Thus, the answer to the perennial question, What will happen when Fidel Castro dies?, has to be—on the basis of the institutionalization of authority and the resources that Raúl Castro commands—that Raúl would succeed his brother.

The succession question, a problem confronted by any political system based on charismatic authority, has become more acute as the revolution and its leaders have gotten older. To the concerns with a gerontocracy should be added the international situation as of late. The Communist movement is in disarray. In the Soviet Union as well as Eastern Europe the one-party state monopoly has disappeared; electoral politics are now accepted as a matter of political necessity, and Communists everywhere no longer claim to have all the answers. Elections in Nicaragua, the dissolution of Communist parties in Eastern Europe, the revamping of NATO, and the rediscovery of Western political "democracy" have imposed tremendous pressure on the Cuban political system.

The European Parliament, as well as traditional leftist friends of the Cuban Revolution, are demanding the establishment of a more open political system in the island. To these pressures should be added the very success of the revolution: It has created a more sophisticated political culture, a more educated population, and a more generalized belief that the people can rule themselves. The period of charismatic rule, in other words, confronts its major crisis. It has one option: to transfer authority from the charismatic leader to representative institutions that enjoy legitimacy.

How this will be accomplished has not yet been resolved. Nor is there a consensus within Cuba that this should be done. Many people still identify solely with Fidel Castro, the charismatic leader ("el original," the man who conceived, organized, made, consolidated, and maintained the revolution for over thirty-eight years). In fact, those who wish to preserve the charismatic type of political regime note that "in the face of the crisis of socialism and the aggressive euphoria of North American imperialism" it is impossible to play with Western political models. Their reasoning suggests that the United States is now ready to attack Cuba, as the revolution becomes one of the few surviving socialist/revolutionary regimes in the world. In their view the only possibility for survival is to be in a permanent state of readiness, which only the mass mobilization qualities of charismatic authority can assure. Perhaps this reasoning would be easily dismissed if the revolutionaries thought that the United States had no intention of attacking the revolution, but U.S. policymakers, in a sense, have contributed to the fear of attack. (See "U.S.-Cuban Relations" below.)

From 1989 to 1992, the Cuban revolutionaries returned to the methods of earlier years. Mass mobilization and calls to nationalism have become a daily occurrence. The revolutionary leadership asserts that Cuba's independence and the very future of socialism depend on the survival and durability of the revolution. Thus, political reforms have been defined as concessions that could lead to revolutionary defeat. According to Fidel Castro, in a number of speeches given in late 1989 and early 1990, Cuba's independence, national sovereignty, and the defense of "socialism" are inexorably linked. The battle cry "Fatherland or Death" of earlier years has been transformed into "Socialism or Death."

After the 1991 Communist Party Congress and the 1992 constitutional reform, the political picture changed again. The nationalist theme was replaced by stress on economic efficiency and reorganization. One heard less talk of socialism as seminars on management, quality circles, and profitability became the order of the day. The regime had begun building a state capitalist economy without private capitalists.

Calls to emulate the experience of Eastern Europe are dismissed by Cuban revolutionaries as another form of "intellectual and political colonialism." Cuba's realities, they say, are different from those of Europe. Cuba, and the rest of Latin America, must find their own answers on the basis of their own material and cultural conditions. Moreover, the recent return to power by electoral means of socialists and even Communists in Eastern Europe had given cause for hope to those in power in Havana.

REDISTRIBUTION AND ECONOMIC EXPERIMENTATION

Cuba is a poor and underdeveloped country. When the Cuban revolutionaries attained power, the country confronted serious economic problems. Foremost among these was dependence on one crop—sugar—and one buyer—the United States. How much sugar the United States bought was determined by the U.S. Congress and the Agriculture Department. The sugar harvest lasted, at best, four months; thus, Cuba also faced serious unemployment and underemployment.

Prior to the Revolution, the unemployment rate averaged 16.4 percent of the available workforce. However, when the sugar harvest ended, it could climb to 20–21 percent. In 1957, only 37.2 percent of the labor force worked the entire year. Social inequality was also a problem. According to a Labor Ministry report issued in 1957, 62.2 percent of the employed received an average monthly salary of less than 75 pesos (peso value was then equal to the dollar). Only 38 percent of the male workers earned more than $75 per month. In 1956, 34 percent of the total population of Cuba received 10 percent of the national income, and only 7.2 percent of the employees earned more than $1,000 a year. A family of six, on the average, had a yearly income of $548.75 and could spend about $0.17 per person for food on a daily basis. In the first year of the Revolution, 73 percent of all families had an average income of $715 per year. Poverty was widespread, particularly in the rural areas.

Land was unequally distributed. A small portion of the landowners owned most of it. In 1959, 8.5 percent of all farms comprised 71.6 percent of the land area in farms; on the other hand, 80 percent of all farms comprised 13.8 percent of the farmland. At the time, 94.6 percent of the land was privately owned; the state controlled just 5.4 percent. Only 32.2 percent of the landowners worked their own land; 25.5 percent of the farmland was administered on behalf of the landowners, and 42.3 percent was rented out or sharecropped. One-quarter of the best agricultural land was owned by U.S. companies, while 63.7 percent of the agricultural workforce had no land of its own. Most of those who owned their land were usually engaged in production for family use since their parcels were very small. Altogether, U.S. corporate interests controlled 2 million acres (810,000 hectares) of land in the island, out of a total surface of 23 million acres (9.3 million hectares)—that is, 8.7 percent of the national territory. In Camagüey Province, six companies controlled 20.7 percent of the land.

U.S. interests could be found elsewhere as well. Total U.S. investments had reached a little over $1 billion when the revolutionaries took power; this was the equivalent of 40 percent of the GNP. U.S. capital dominated 90 percent of the utilities, 50 percent of the railways, 40 percent of the production of raw sugar, 25 percent of all bank deposits. U.S. interests controlled more than 80 percent of mining, oil production, hotels, pharmaceuticals, detergents, fertilizers, auto dealerships, tires, imports, and exports. Of 161 sugar mills, U.S. companies owned 36. U.S. capital was shifting away from traditional investments (sugar, utilities, mining) and moving toward new areas (loans, imports, exports, light industry). The reported rate of return on U.S. investments was 9 percent, but Cuban revolutionary authorities have estimated that the real rate was about 23 percent. From 1952 to 1958, U.S. companies repatriated an average of $50 million yearly (new investment during the period was $40 million yearly).

In 1958, the United States supplied 72 percent of Cuban imports and bought 69 percent of Cuban exports. Cuba's balance of trade from 1948 to 1958 was positive with most of the world, except the United States. It has been estimated that the rate of economic growth from 1945 to 1958 averaged 4.3 percent per year while the per capita income growth was 1.8 percent.

When the revolutionaries seized power, they found an economy that relied on sugar production, primarily controlled in its numerous facets by U.S. capital, as well as an economy that was unable to generate sufficient jobs in the primary or secondary sector to absorb the surplus labor. The Cuban economy was essentially capitalist in nature, with a large proletarian labor force in the countryside (over 64 percent of the rural laborers were wage earners).

In the first two years of the Revolution two major trends developed. On the one hand, a progressive redistribution of income took place.

- February 2, 1959: all debts owed to the Cuban state were suspended
- March 10, 1959: house rents lowered 50 percent
- May 17, 1959: Agrarian Reform Law began redistribution of land
- December 23, 1959: social security made available to all workers
- October 14, 1960: Urban Reform Law established procedure by which renter will use rent payments as amortization in order to purchase home
- June 7, 1961: free universal education established
- August 1, 1961: transportation costs lowered
- September 21, 1961: child care centers subsidized by the state
- March 12, 1962: rationing introduced, price of all food items frozen (remained frozen until the early 1980s)

The second trend was a radical change in prevailing property relations. By the end of 1960, the critical areas of the Cuban economy had been taken over by the state: All of banking, export-import operations, energy, and utilities were owned by the state. More than three-quarters of industry, construction, and transportation was also in the hands of the government. Only the bulk of agriculture was in the hands of the private sector, and that was primarily the result of the redistribution of land.

During the period 1959–1960, there was no talk of socialism on the part of the authorities. Economic thinking revolved around the ideas of rapid industrialization, import substitution, and reducing the role of sugar while diversifying agriculture. There were no real controls of an economic nature. The capitalist market was not replaced; it disappeared, and nothing took its place. No one seemed to pay attention to capital accumulation. The central idea was simply to establish greater equality by increasing the income and resources of the lower classes. This was the distributionist phase of the Revolution. As the state moved into the private economy, it found that it lacked the personnel to run the new enterprises; often those who were considered loyal were put in command. They had to learn their jobs while performing them. Consumption improved altogether, but it led to shortages because no effort was made to increase stocks.

In 1961, after the revolutionaries discovered that they had socialism, they began looking for a model to emulate. The Czechoslovakian model was copied, and industrialization was stressed; sugar was set aside. From 1961 to 1963, some problems developed with the emerging rural middle class. Since the revolutionary regime had little use for sugar and industry seemed more appealing, a second agrarian reform was issued that abolished the remaining medium-sized landholdings. During this period, the state further socialized the means of production so that it controlled 70 percent of the agricultural sector and more than 95 percent of industry, transportation, and construction. The private sector could sell only to the state. The Cuban economy had the highest index of state control in the world. A generalized process of centralization of economic decision making took root, led by Ché Guevara from the Ministry of Industries.

It should be noted that this is the period when Cuba and the United States had reached the equivalent of a state of war (in 1961, the Bay of Pigs; in 1962, the October missile crisis). Within Cuba, the revolutionaries continued their distributionist policies. Health care, for example, became free in this period. Unemployment disappeared—primarily because the productivity of labor declined and more people were hired to do a job that in the past had been performed by one person. Also, many of the previously unemployed were absorbed by the service sector. From 1961 to 1962, sugar output dropped from 6.8 million tons to 3.8 million. Yet, few sectors were growing or generating the necessary foreign exchange. This led to a rectification of the economic policy.

In 1963, the revolutionary authorities abandoned their stress on industrialization; sugar was to be the pivot of Cuba's economic development. The new economic strategy was to be based on modernizing Cuban agriculture, introducing more up-to-date forces of production, while improving the skills of the workers. The effort would be centered on the state farms. At the time, two entirely different economic models for constructing the future socialist society were being discussed.

Meanwhile, the United States had imposed an economic blockade on the island in 1962, and except for Mexico, no country in the hemisphere traded with the Cubans. Moreover, Cuba's terms of trade deteriorated from 1964 to 1966 due primarily to the drop in the price of sugar (in 1963, the price was 8.3 cents per pound; by 1966, it had dropped to 1.8 cents). So the cost of imports increased greatly.

In 1966, Cuba's most original phase began. It lasted until 1970. The goal was to produce ever-larger amounts of sugar, regardless of the world market situation. Moreover, since the country did not have the material resources to reward effort, moral (i.e., political) incentives were to be used to motivate the workers. The highly centralized economic plans of the previous period were replaced by sectoral, independent, decentralized plans. The plans (and enterprises) received money allocated through a central budget. Enterprises did not engage in mercantile relations with one another, and they did not have to show a profit. Cost accounting was disregarded altogether. Efficiency depended merely on meeting output goals, regardless of cost. During the period, a concentrated effort was made to avoid bureaucratic rigidity and to discourage criticism of the approach. Revolutionary consciousness and commitment, it was believed, would do the trick.

At the same time, the state took over complete control of industry, all of construction, 98 percent of transportation, and every single retail business. The labor force involved in harvesting sugar was militarized in 1969. Sugar output went through cycles. From 1966 to 1967, it went up from 4.5 million tons to 6.2 million; then it dropped to 5.1 million in 1968 and to 4.4 million in 1969. The 1970 harvest was the largest in the history of the country, but it had a tremendous negative impact on the larger economy since most of the national resources were concentrated on meeting the goal of producing 10 million tons of sugar.

There was an abrupt drop in economic efficiency during this period. Economic growth averaged just 0.4 percent. The revolutionary authorities had ended the connection between output and salaries; that is, workers got paid regardless of production. Moreover, during this period, the state distributed, free of charge, water, public phone service, and child care, among other things. Gratuities were on the increase, and labor productivity declined. An excess of money in circulation ensued; purchasing power exceeded goods available, contributing to labor absenteeism. During the period, the country invested up to 30 percent of its material product on economic growth, which forced it to rely more than ever on imports. The economy did not fare as poorly as one might have expected because the price of sugar consistently climbed during these years (in 1966, the price was 1.8 cents per pound; 1967, 1.9; 1968, 1.9; 1969, 3.2; 1970, 3.68).

In 1970, the revolutionary authorities reconsidered their strategy and revised it, shifting from the budgetary system of finance to what is called *calculo economico*, or self-finance system. The new system stressed centralized economic planning, cost accounting and enterprise profitability, material rewards, mercantile relations among enterprises, and contracts between enterprises and labor unions. Productivity and efficiency came to be measured on the basis of the rate of return (connected to the cost of production). Managerial expertise on the administrative level began to take precedence over revolutionary zeal. The role of sugar was de-emphasized somewhat, as more attention was paid to the diversification of agriculture and the development of mineral resources. The *cálculo económico* had become nationwide in its application by 1977. Thus, 1971 to 1976 were years of transition. It should be noted that the shift away from the budgetary system coincided with the move toward institutionalization. This was not coincidental. Cuba's economic and political organizations are highly interrelated. Charismatic authority went hand in hand with moral incentives and mass mobilization to achieve economic goals; rational-legal authority now permeates the political as well as the economic spheres.

The new economic and political organization seemed to pay off very well. The gross material product (GMP)—that is, the gross value of production from agriculture, industry, and construction—has shown some remarkable developments; for example, the GMP growth rates for the 1970s were as follows.

1971:	4.2%
1972:	9.7
1973:	13.1
1974:	7.8
1975:	12.3
1976:	3.5
1977:	3.1

1978:   8.2
1979:   2.4

The improvement and subsequent deterioration of the economy in the 1970s, however, were not due to internal conditions. Rather, the price of sugar in the world market affects the general performance of the Cuban economy. Sugar prices rose from 4.5 cents per pound in 1970 to 29.6 in 1974 and 20.3 in 1975 before they began to drop, reaching 7.4 cents in 1982. The cycle was reflected in the Cuban economy because, more than twenty years after the Revolution, the export of sugar has remained crucial to the overall functioning of the economy. Sugar accounts for 80 percent of foreign earnings.

It should be stressed, however, that the revolutionary government has worked out an arrangement with the Soviet Union that has allowed the island to escape, to some extent, the cycles of the capitalist economy as far as sugar is concerned. Since the 1960s, the Soviets have paid a much higher price for Cuban sugar than the price in the open world market. Only on three occasions (1963, 1972, 1974) were world market prices higher than those paid by the Soviets. By 1979, when the world price had reached a low point of 9.6 cents, the Soviets were paying 44 cents. The treatment that the revolutionary government has received from the Soviet Union has been positive and extraordinary. In 1972, the USSR agreed to postpone until 1986 the payment of Cuba's debt. The debt covered a period of twenty-five years during which Cuba paid no interest.

Approximately 20 percent of Cuba's trade in the early 1980s was with the capitalist market economies. The terms of trade were such, however, that while the price of sugar declined, the prices of the products Cuba had to buy to process the sugarcane and produce sugar went up. (A metric ton of urea in 1972 sold for $76, but by 1980 the price was $303. The same situation occurred with ammonia nitrate: Its price changed from $206 to $506.) In constant 1970 prices, a pound of sugar in 1982 sold for 2.8 cents. In order to import the same amount of goods, then, Cuba had to export much more.

Cuba's economic performance in the first five years of the 1980s was significantly better than that of the rest of Latin America (see Table 22.1). But the Cuban situation started to change in 1986, the year that Fidel Castro announced the initiation of the "rectification" campaign in the economy. The campaign denounced and took steps against private enterprise (the free peasants' market created in 1980, the appearance of private urban businesses, and the reliance on profitability as an indicator for the allocation of resources). The rectification campaign, in other words, put political decisions rather than "economic logic" in command. The overall performance of the economy suffered as a result.

Moreover, events in Eastern Europe and the Soviet Union damaged external trade. The Eastern European countries shifted toward convertible currency transactions, and the democratization of the Soviet political system led to a greater demand for consumer goods just as the situation produced tremendous uncertainty in the sup-

Table 22.1
Annual Growth Rates of Latin American and Cuban Per Capita Gross Domestic Product, 1982–1988

	Latin America	Cuba
1982	−3.5	3.3
1983	−4.7	4.3
1984	1.4	6.5
1985	1.4	3.9
1986	1.6	0.3
1987	0.3	−4.7
1988	−1.5	1.0

Source: ECLAC, *Preliminary Overview of the Latin American Economy,* Document LG/G 1536 (Santiago, Chile: ECLAC, 1988), p. 18.

ply of goods from abroad. Cuban economic planning and performance hence suffered. The revolutionary government, with little foreign exchange in hand, adopted a policy of more import substitution. The strategy was accompanied by greater stress on export diversification.

In early 1990 Fidel Castro told the Cuban people that very difficult years could be expected and that rationing might be extended to new products. At the same time, the Cuban authorities contacted Mexican, Brazilian, and Japanese investors and made new offers to transnational corporations in the hope that the shortage of capital could be overcome. Cuban foreign reserves in 1988 and 1989 were less than $100 million.

In 1991–1992, Cuba's traditional economic allies disappeared, and so did all aid, credit, suppliers, and buyers. The Cuban economy suffered an almost overwhelming blow. From 1992 to 1993, imports collapsed, as did exports. The absence of supplies and raw materials meant that economic output declined between 30 and 35 percent in just two years. By 1994, the economy touched bottom. The following year it grew by about 3 percent, and in 1996 it achieved a growth of 7.8 percent. Bouncing back, however, has not meant that the overall standard of living of the population has improved in a major way. In the late 1990s, Cuba still produced at a level below that of 1985. Yet the positive turn in the economy has been quite extraordinary. Foreign investments, tourism, and nickel exports are the three major contributors to the recovery. Not long ago most foreign analysts considered Cuba's economic prospects rather dim. The trend now appears to be moving in the opposite direction.

Table 22.2 shows the major changes that have taken place in the economy since 1958. Despite Cuba's limited economic resources, the revolutionary government has been able to distribute social services in a manner that has produced profound positive results. The population of Cuba is about 10 million. The country is highly urban (in 1958, 58.7 percent of the people lived in cities; by 1983 the figure was 64.5 per-

Table 22.2
Cuban Economic Indicators, 1958–1980

	1958	1980
Gross social product		
(1965 current pesos)	6,013[a]	22,358[b]
Exports (f.o.b.)		
(million pesos)	733	3,967
Imports (c.i.f.)		
(million pesos)	771	4,509
Trade balance		
(million pesos)	−37	−542
Per capita income		
(pesos)	365	2,016[c]
Sugar output		
(million metric tons)	5.8	8.2[b]
Tobacco		
(thousand metric tons)	51	51[d]
Citrus fruits		
(thousand metric tons)	7	250
Rice		
(thousand metric tons)	253	384
Eggs		
(thousand metric tons)	315	2,018
Coffee		
(thousand metric tons)	30	19
Bread		
(thousand metric tons)	–	417
Fish		
(thousand metric tons)	21	193
Nickel		
(thousand metric tons)	18	37
Cement		
(thousand metric tons)	748	2,645
Electricity		
(million kw)	2,550	9,391
Oil refining		
(thousand metric tons)	3,600	6,371
Fertilizers		
(thousand metric tons)	159	872
Steel		
(thousand metric tons)	24	327

[a]1962
[b]1982
[c]1981
[d]1976

cent). The mortality rate is 5.6 per 1,000 inhabitants, and life expectancy increased from 58 years in 1959 to 73.5 years in 1981. The infant mortality rate, a major index of how much poverty and inequality a society has, has been radically changed—from a high of 33 it dropped to 19 in 1983. The age distribution of the population has changed as well. Before the Revolution, 36.2 percent of the population was younger than fifteen; in the early 1980s the figure was 32 percent. At the same time, the percentage of people over sixty-five increased from 4.2 percent in 1958 to 7.3 percent in 1980.

Illiteracy has been reduced to less than 4 percent, and almost the entire population has received a primary education. At present, 96–97 percent of all the children of primary school age go to school. More than a million people have received a secondary education since 1959. One out of every 2.83 Cubans studies today. Full employment was achieved, although in the last few years unemployment has begun to grow (it is estimated that it was 2–4 percent of the male labor force in 1982). The social benefits that the population receives in the form of old-age pensions; workers' compensation; and maternity, illness, and social security allowances place Cuba at the forefront of all Latin American countries. It is by this means that the popularity and legitimacy of the Revolution have been maintained. The distributionist policies of Cuba's revolutionary government have been far more successful than its economic policies. It remains to be seen whether the tremendous investment in human capital will pay off in the foreseeable future. The next few years, however, will be difficult ones for Cuba.

U.S.-CUBAN RELATIONS

From 1959 to 1961, relations between the United States and Cuba progressively deteriorated. From 1961 to 1965, the two countries were in a state of semiwar. After 1965, the situation relaxed somewhat, but the two had no contact with one another. This situation continued until the last years of the Nixon administration, when some unofficial talks began. Finally, when Carter was elected president of the United States, relations began to thaw. Diplomatic relations were renewed on the section level (as opposed to the embassy level), but no steps were taken toward restoring trade relations. The U.S. economic embargo was relaxed somewhat, as well as travel restrictions between the two countries. When Reagan arrived at the White House, however, every major social upheaval in Latin America was interpreted as the work of Cuban subversion. Consequently, the United States returned to policies reminiscent of the Eisenhower administration. There were even claims from the Cubans that the Reagan administration attempted to assassinate the leaders of the Revolution.

After eight years of the Reagan administration, the Cuban government assumed that President George Bush would improve bilateral relations. But relations, in fact, deteriorated. The dramatic changes in world communism led the White House to conclude that Cuba would be one more "domino" and that there was no need to take any initiatives that would change the island's isolation. Rather, the White House began to broadcast television programs to the island and tightened the economic embargo, while attempting to link improvement in the relations between the United States and Eastern Europe with the severance of their ties with the Revolution.

In 1992, an election year, both Democratic and Republican Parties ended up supporting the Torricelli Bill, which imposed stricter U.S. government policies on Cuba and, moreover, shifted policymaking away from the executive branch and placed that power in the hands of the U.S. Congress. Presidential candidate Bill Clinton campaigned in support of a harder line against the Cuban government. Once Clinton was elected president, the government in Havana adopted a wait-and-see policy but soon discovered that the new administration addressed Cuban policy on the basis of domestic political needs. The Clinton administration took a fairly aggressive approach of supporting human rights activists and political opponents, and the Cuban government reacted by imposing even harsher restrictions on anyone considered a political enemy. During the summer of 1994, as the standard of living deteriorated and political repression augmented in Cuba, the number of boat people leaving the island climbed. As the U.S. government continued to welcome the so-called *balseros,* the Cuban government opted to allow anyone who so wished to leave the island by sea in order to reach the United States. The initiative forced the White House to begin negotiations with Havana. The end result was a break with past migration policy on Cuba: The United States no longer would allow any Cuban to enter the country unless proper procedures were followed, including the granting of a visa.

Throughout 1995 there were hints and indications that perhaps relations between the two longtime adversaries would improve. Tension between the White House and the conservative exile organizations was manifested on many occasions. The conservative victory in congressional elections in 1994 meant that new forces pushed for a tougher stance on Cuba in U.S. politics. Exile organizations believed that the time was right to manufacture a crisis. In the fall of 1995 and early 1996, conservative exiles initiated a series of ventures against the Cuban government, the best known led by Brothers to the Rescue, a Miami group that began to fly over Cuban territory to drop political leaflets. In early 1995, two of the planes were shot down by the Cuban air force. This incited the Congress to adopt the Helms-Burton Bill, which President Clinton rapidly signed. The legislation signified a return to the worst days of U.S. interference in the domestic affairs of Cuba, at the same time creating the mechanism to attempt to impose a policy of economic isolation by third countries on Cuba. Thus, the policy of extraterritoriality was made into law and applied against Cuba and other countries as well.

Such a policy has reinforced the "besieged fortress" mentality in Havana. Thus the revolutionary authorities have initiated a worldwide campaign to break away from their isolation. At present, however, there is little prospect of improvement in the relations between the United States and Cuba.

Regardless of what anyone may think, the Cuban Revolution is there to stay. It has radically affected every facet of Cuban life as well as of the country's international relations. What will happen as the population becomes better educated and the political system further institutionalized, no one knows. It is clear, nonetheless, that internal developments—as is the case with other social revolutions—will be affected by the international context.

SUGGESTED READINGS

Periodical Literature

Following are a number of very useful periodical sources that can help the student of Cuba to keep up with events.

Bohemia. This major Havana weekly covers social, economic, cultural, and political events.
Cuba internacional. A glossy monthly portraying achievements of the Revolution.
Cuba Resource Center Newsletter. The main English-language publication presenting a friendly view of revolutionary Cuba. Published in New York City.
Cuban Studies. The best scholarly journal published on Cuba. Published in Pittsburgh, it concentrates on the post-1959 period. Each issue contains the best bibliography available on publications dealing with Cuba.
Foreign Broadcast Information Service. Daily translations of Cuban radio and television broadcasts monitored by U.S. intelligence agencies. Available on microfiche.
Translations on Latin America. Translations of the documents and articles that are considered most important by the U.S. intelligence community. Deals with all of Latin America and has a section on Cuba. Is published at least twice a week.

Books

Domínguez, Jorge I. *Cuba: Order and Revolution.* Cambridge: Harvard University Press, 1978. This is a massive, thorough, and encompassing book covering the period 1902–1978. Functionalist in approach, it concentrates on politics.
MacEwan, Arthur. *Revolution and Economic Development in Cuba.* New York: St. Martin's Press, 1981. A friendly Marxist presentation dealing with the problems of building socialism.
Mesa-Lago, Carmelo. *The Economy of Socialist Cuba: A Two-Decade Appraisal.* Albuquerque: University of New Mexico Press, 1981. A most important work tracing the different stages of the Revolution, its accomplishments, and its failures. Essentially an institutional-economist approach.
United Nations, Economic Commission for Latin America. *Cuba: Estilo de desarrollo y políticas sociales.* Mexico City, 1980. Provides an overview of the Cuban economy and the Revolution's social accomplishments.

23

THE CARIBBEAN: THE STRUCTURE OF MODERN-CONSERVATIVE SOCIETIES

ANTHONY P. MAINGOT

In a geopolitical sense, it is best to define the Caribbean in terms of all the countries that border on that sea. This includes the islands as well as the countries of the mainland whose eastern coasts form the western perimeter of the Caribbean. Together, they make up a "basin" of which the sea is the crucial geopolitical feature.

Geographical definitions, however, are ultimately arbitrary. Their validity depends on the purpose or ends pursued, that is, on their utility. So El Salvador, which has no border on the Caribbean Sea, is regarded by some as a Caribbean Basin country, whereas Mexico, Colombia, and most Central American countries are two-ocean countries yet look more toward the Caribbean than toward the Pacific. A simple explanation lies in the fact that colonization and subsequent trade and cultural contacts developed as part of the Atlantic expansion, first of Spain and later the rest of Europe.

For the purpose of this chapter, "the Caribbean" is considered to be the islands plus those mainland territories that, until recently, were part of the British, Dutch, and French colonial empires. Clearly, it is difficult to generalize on any level about countries as varied as these. Haiti has almost six times more land and five times the population of Trinidad and Tobago but only one-fifth the gross domestic product (GDP). Haitians speak Creole, and a liberal estimate is that 50 percent of them are illiterate; Trinidadians speak English, and 96 percent are literate (see Table 23.1). The former has been governed by dictators throughout most of its 180 years of independence; the latter had a functioning parliamentary system even before it became independent in 1962.

Table 23.1
Independent Caribbean Nations: Selected Data

Country (by Date of Independence)	Area (sq miles)	Estimated Population 1992 (millions)	Life Expectancy	Adult Literacy Rate	GNP Per Capita	HDI[a] Rank	U.S. Direct Investment ($ million), 1991	Democracy[b] Ranking (1992)
French-speaking								
Haiti (1804)	10,714	6.6	55.7	53.0	933	137	25	14
Spanish-speaking								
Dominican Rep. (1844)	18,700	7.3	66.7	83.3	2,404	97	605	5
Cuba (1902)	44,000	10.7	75.4	94.0	2,200	75	Undisclosed	14
English-speaking								
Jamaica (1962)	10,411	2.4	73.1	98.4	2,979	69	667	4
Trinidad/Tobago (1962)	1,980	1.3	71.6	96.0	6,604	31	526	2
Barbados (1966)	166	0.3	75.1	99.0	8,304	20	405	2
Guyana (1966)	83,000	0.8	64.2	96.4	1,464	105	Undisclosed	6
Bahamas (1973)	5,382	0.25	71.5	99.0	11,235	32	3,319	3
Grenada (1974)	133	0.084	71.5	96.0	4,081	59	3	3
Dominica (1978)	289	0.085	76.0	97.0	3,910	51	1	3
St. Lucia (1979)	238	0.15	70.5	93.0	3,470	72	Undisclosed	3
St. Vincent (1979)	150	0.115	70.0	84.0	3,647	76	4	3
Antigua (1981)	108	0.064	72.0	96.0	4,000	60	19	6
Belize (1981)	8,864	0.2	69.5	95.0	3,000	82	–10	2
St. Kitts/Nevis (1983)	104	0.08	67.5	92.0	3,300	79	–1	2
Dutch-speaking								
Surinam (1975)	63,227	0.48	69.5	94.9	3,927	65	102	6

[a]The Human Development Index (HDI) combines indicators of real purchasing power, education, and health.

[b]Ranking scale developed by the think tank Freedom House, *Freedom in the World Annual Survey, 1992–1993* (New York: Freedom House, 1993). Countries with 2–5 ranking are considered "free," countries ranked 6–11 are considered "partly free," and 11–14 countries are considered "not free."

Sources: United Nations Development Program, *Human Development Report, 1993* (Oxford: Oxford University Press, 1993), pp. 135–137; Survey of Current Business, Department of Commerce (February 2, 1993), cited in United States Agency for International Development, *Latin America and the Caribbean: Selected Economic and Social Data* (Washington, D.C.: USAID, 1993), p. 198.

As with any other geographical region or expression ("Africa," "Latin America," "Asia"), each unit in the region deserves to be studied individually. And yet, there is also value in an understanding of the broader continuities and similarities that make any region a culture area. Keep in mind, as Melville Herskovits reminds us, that the concept of culture area does not denote a self-conscious grouping. Rather than focusing on the details, it points to the broad lines of similarities and differences between cultures. In the Caribbean, these continuities and similarities result from a blending of modern and conservative features in the composition of major institutions as well as in social and behavioral dynamics. It is useful to call Caribbean societies modern-conservative systems.

THE CONCEPT OF MODERN-CONSERVATIVE SOCIETIES

Like all concepts or heuristic devices in the social sciences, the concept of modern-conservative societies is used to explain complex social structures and social processes. This is especially important in a region as varied as the Caribbean. The point is that the concept appears to describe Caribbean social structure well, and we conclude therefore that it will also help explain the political manifestations of that social structure.

It is important to note that we are not talking about traditional societies: those relatively static, passive, and acquiescent societies generally resistant to change. They approximate rather what Michael Oakeshott calls societies underpinned by "skeptical conservatism," a peculiar mixture of political conservatism and radical individualism and skepticism. The modern-conservative society is not only capable of social change, it is often prone to dramatic calls or movements for change. Several cases from the English-speaking Caribbean illustrate the latent explosive character of the modern-conservative society.

In 1970, the island state of Trinidad and Tobago was suffering from both a decline in oil production and low world prices for oil. OPEC had not yet managed to control the market; it would do this in 1972. The economy had been radically changed by oil. The production of sugar, cacao, and other agricultural commodities was now subsidized; the state became the largest employer. By 1970, there was 22 percent open unemployment and 23 percent hidden unemployment, while the unemployment among moderately educated youth (more than eight years of schooling) was 40 percent higher than the average. Additionally, since 80 percent of the women indicated no desire to work outside the home, the problem was squarely centered on the young males. These youth were integrated into the modern sector: urban, educated, organized, and in close contact with the outside world.

With the Black Power Movement in full bloom in the United States and Canada, two events outside Trinidad lit the spark of Trinidad's own Black Power uprising. One occurred in Jamaica, where authorities prohibited a Guyanese university lecturer, Walter Rodney, from reentering Jamaica from Canada. The so-called Rodney affair stirred the university students in Trinidad, as did the "riot" of a dozen

Trinidadian students in Canada claiming racial discrimination. Racial grievances, unemployment, unrest among the professional military men, and accusations of graft and corruption against certain government ministers all came to a head in a massive movement against "the system." And yet, the motor, the driving force, was not class conflict but a deep sense of righteous indignation. The target of the movement, Prime Minister Eric Williams, was repeatedly invited to join the moral crusade for black identity and ownership. Clearly, he had lost his moral authority but not his political legitimacy.

In 1970 in Trinidad, righteous indignation took on psychological and cultural dimensions: a return to history, to a purer and more integral past as a means of collective and individual cleansing and redemption. African names and apparel were adopted and modern European ways rejected to such an extent that the movement's leadership soon began to alienate large sectors of the Indian and colored populations as well as the black middle class. A reorganized police force put an end to the armed phase of the movement, and when ten years later the same leaders competed in a free election, they were soundly defeated. Had the problems of the society been solved by the massive influx of oil revenues since 1973? Not at all. Fully 83 percent of those who in 1981 felt that life was getting worse on the island attributed that deterioration to corruption.

Although the incumbent party won a sizable electoral victory in 1981, race again showed its strength: The victorious People's National Movement (PNM) won the safe "black" seats; the opposition United Labour Force (ULF), the safe "Indian" seats. As in 1970, a deterioration in the economy could again spark unrest, but it will have to play on certain moral chords and generate a sense of indignation among both leaders and followers, with totally unpredictable outcomes.

The case of St. Lucia in early 1982 illustrates this aspect of political behavior in modern-conservative societies. On January 16, 1982, the prime minister of St. Lucia resigned under pressure. This forced the dismissal of Parliament and mandated the calling of elections within a few months. The caretaker government was led by a member of a radical party, the smallest of St. Lucia's three main parties. It was not this party, however, that had led the antigovernment movement, nor were the issues in the movement ideological ones in the political sense. That movement was headed by the chamber of commerce and other middle sectors, protesting what they regarded as official corruption and abuse of government authority.

The upheaval in St. Lucia was very similar to that which had occurred in Grenada three years earlier: Incompetence, corruption, and abuse of authority had engendered a massive sense of indignation among a multiplicity of sectors. In Grenada, the opposition movement was called the Committee of 21, indicating the number of groups involved in the opposition to Prime Minister Eric Gairy. The difference between Grenada in 1979 and St. Lucia in 1982 was that a small clique managed to wrest power by force of arms in the former, teaching a lesson to the middle classes in the latter. Although all groups participated in the 1982 elections in St. Lucia, the moderates won every seat in the House of Assembly. Similar defeats of radical parties had already occurred in Dominica, St. Vincent, St. Kitts, Jamaica, Barbados, and Trinidad. Elections in the Dominican Republic in mid-1982 also indicated a tendency toward the center in political-ideological terms; it appeared to be a Caribbean-wide phenomenon.

A decade later, similar moderate responses were evident in Trinidadians' response to an armed insurrectionary attempt. In 1991, a Black Muslim group, the Jamaat al Muslimeen, played on the deep sense of malaise among the urban masses. After assaulting police headquarters, taking the prime minister and most of his Cabinet hostage and taking control of the television station, the rebels called on the populace to rebel. They did no such thing, and the terrorists had to surrender to the still standing authorities. Although 60 percent of a national poll expressed sympathy with the Muslimeen's grievances, fully 75 percent rejected the use of force to achieve redress of these.

These illustrations allow us to identify some of the characteristics of the modern-conservative society. It should at the outset be understood that to speak of "structures" does not imply anything static: It merely means that certain underlying factors or interrelationships are more durable, more tenacious and retentive, than many of the immediate and observable manifestations of those relationships suggest. Such ideas or concepts as history, life, being, and essence are central to this conservative view of life and are logical products of ex-colonial, multiethnic, and deeply religious societies, as we shall see. As Karl Mannheim has noted, these patterns of thought, far from becoming superfluous through modernization, tend to survive and adapt themselves to each new stage of social development.[1] Because it has a real social basis, conservative thought is functional and useful as a guide to action.

The modern conservative society, then, tends to mobilize politically around issues that strike chords of a conservative type, issues that engender a collective sense of moral indignation. Mobilization occurs, however, through modern mechanisms and institutional arrangements. The most conservative of values, if widely shared and if the spokespeople have access to modern institutions and mechanisms, can have impacts that have revolutionary manifestations though something less than revolutionary goals—if "revolutionary" implies a complete overthrow of the existing sociopolitical structure, not merely the regime.

The myth of the modern, revolutionary nature of Caribbean societies stems from a misunderstanding of the nature of many of the movements that brought revolutionary elites to power. Even in modern-conservative societies (as Lenin theorized and demonstrated), a determined elite can bring about a designed outcome. This is so because after the initial mobilization, the movement tends to enter into a qualitatively new phase. This phase has dynamics of its own, dynamics that tend to represent a combination of the unpredictability and complexity of all mass actions and the more predictable—or at least understandable—actions of revolutionary cadres and elites. The latter can turn the movement in a revolutionary direction even in modern-conservative societies; they are less capable, however, of initially generating a revolutionary mobilization in such societies.

This explains why the Surinam Revolution (1980) and the Grenadian Revolution (1979), like the Nicaraguan Revolution, had to coexist with strong private sectors, established churches, and other aroused but hardly revolutionary sectors. These regimes were confronted with the complexity of the modern-conservative society, which explains as much about the failure of revolution as does the implacable opposition of Washington (which certainly played its part).

Understanding the nature of political change in these societies, then, requires an analysis not only of the immediate political happenings in the area—the political landscape—but also of what might be called the structural or enduring aspects of Caribbean political dynamics: the political substructure. What is required, thus, is a political economy approach to the area in which demographics and economics are central, though not exclusive, topics of analysis.

The central questions, however, remain. Who reacts, why, and over what? What do the answers tell us about the ongoing and therefore relatively predictable aspects of Caribbean political culture and dynamics? Some answers might be forthcoming from an analysis of the ideology and behavior of a few of the major political leaders in recent Caribbean history.

POLITICAL-IDEOLOGICAL LEADERSHIP

The career of Trinidad's prime minister Eric Williams, who governed from 1956 until his death in 1981, illustrates the complexity of style and orientation of the region's leadership. Much has changed in the Caribbean since 1956, when Williams first came to power as a celebrated scholar-administrator. His Ph.D. thesis at Oxford, "Capitalism and Slavery," had become the standard radical interpretation of European industrialization (made possible by the triangular slave trade) and emancipation (made necessary by the very success of that industrialization). He was living proof that a man of color was indeed capable of great achievements in a mother country's highest centers of learning.

This success and his later "telling off" of the English, Americans, French, and Dutch in the Caribbean Commission—an agency set up by the colonial powers to assist in Caribbean development—were proof sufficient to make him the man to lead the island's decolonization movement. "Massa day done" became Williams's battle cry, a welcome prospect to the black and colored middle and working classes who followed his charismatic leadership. The psychic scars of colonialism had found their soothing balm. But where to turn for models?

Asia and Africa were also going through the pains and pleasures of decolonization, and those continents—more than neighboring Latin America—provided some, but not all, of the models. It was in the paths of Nehru, Nkrumah, Sukarno, and Kenyatta that Williams saw represented the post–World War II, nonwhite decolonization process. Like those leaders, Williams understood very early that decolonization had both racial and political connotations. The very concept of empire had been based on ideas of racial superiority and inferiority. These men had to give living rebuttals to the imperial myths that people of color could not govern themselves and that non-Western societies could never be viable nations. Not only did they have to prove their people's capacity by leading the political struggle, they also had to prove their personal worth through exceptional achievement. In colonial situations, the burden of proof is always with the colonized.

It is no surprise, therefore, that more often than not these decolonizers began to perceive themselves as the very—if not the sole—embodiment of their countries. This perhaps was the genesis of their eventual sense of indispensability. Williams acted for twenty-five years on that belief. Repeated victories at the polls did little to dispel the illusion.

But Trinidad, like the rest of the English-speaking West Indies, was in the Western Hemisphere, where the majority of the independent countries were Spanish speaking and most were far from being democratic models. Surrounded by dictators who enjoyed warm relations with Washington and London, Williams understood that the decolonization of the English-speaking Caribbean was to be a lonely process in the Latin American setting. The parliamentary system adopted by the West Indies differed from the executive system of Latin America, and Williams always felt that the former suited the West Indies better.

This belief was shared by an array of truly exceptional West Indian leaders: Alexander Bustamante and Norman Manley in Jamaica, Grantly Adams and Errol Barrow in Barbados, and Cheddi Jagan in Guyana (a true constitutionalist despite his Marxist rhetoric). By the mid-1960s, these leaders had laid the foundations of West Indian constitutional democracy, thereby giving the lie to colonial racists and modern ideologists who argued that only authoritarian one-party states fit the Caribbean reality.

Williams governed long enough to deal with two elected Manleys (father and son) and two elected Adamses (father and son), to see the OPEC-created explosion in revenues from gas and oil, to see the collapse of the West Indian Federation and the rise of the Caribbean Common Market, and to see the decline of Britain and the rise of Cuba and Venezuela as regional powers. He lived long enough to see the rise and fall of Michael Manley's "democratic socialism" in Jamaica (1972–1980), and he appeared ready to deal with Jamaica's new leader, Edward Seaga, who emphasized the role of the private sector.

By the time of Williams's death in 1981, the Caribbean had witnessed many a social and economic experiment and was quite a different area. Although there were some governments "for life" (Cuba, Haiti, and probably also Guyana), there were now democratic governments in virtually all the other Caribbean island states, making the Caribbean the largest area governed by democratically elected regimes in the hemisphere. The parliamentary system was working in the West Indies.

The first generation of postindependence leaders in the English-speaking Caribbean had sown well and, in so doing, left their marks on the immediate post-colonial era. By the mid-1980s, there were indications that the passing of that era meant not only generational change but also the passing of the charismatic, "indispensable" leader as a part of the political culture. This change was demonstrated by a trend in the region's politics: the emergence in the 1980s of the less-than-charismatic "manager" political type: Edward Seaga of Jamaica, Mary Eugenia Charles of Dominica, Tom Adams of Barbados, George Chambers in Trinidad, and Antonio Guzmán and Jorge Blanco in the Dominican Republic all fit this mold.

What explains this shift in leadership? Certainly there is some truth to the view that the trend is partly reactive: a response to the dismal administrative performance of some of the area's most celebrated charismatic leaders of the 1960s and 1970s—Fidel Castro of Cuba, Michael Manley of Jamaica, and Forbes Burnham of Guyana, for example. But a fuller explanation would bring us closer to the issue of complexity that was posited earlier, that dual process involving enduring, underlying relationships, values, and interests (substrata) and the changing political landscape. The careers of Caribbean leaders of Marxist or non-Marxist socialist persuasion, that is, the secular modernizers, are illustrative.

One such case is Aimé Césaire, mayor of Fort-de-France, Martinique, and Communist *député* to the National Assembly in Paris for over thirty-five years. When Césaire resigned from the French Communist Party in 1956, it was a sensational event. "Thinking of Martinique," he wrote, "I see that communism has managed to encyst us, isolate us in the Caribbean Basin." To Césaire, there was an alternative path: "Black Africa, the dam of our civilization and source of our culture." Only through race, culture, and the richness of ethnic particulars, he continued, could Caribbean people avoid the alienation wrought by what he called the "fleshless universalism" of European communism.[2]

This return to history, to culture, and ultimately to race has been a fairly consistent response to many Caribbean socialist modernizers—who never stop referring to themselves as socialists—faced with the difficulties of attempting secular revolutionary change in large, nonrevolutionary and conservative societies. The counterpoint between a rational secular universalism and a particularism of "being" has resulted in some original and dynamic West Indian ideological modifications to Marxism and non-Marxist socialist thought. In Césaire's case, it led to his fundamental contributions to negritude, a literary-political movement highlighting African contributions to contemporary society, as well as to an accommodation with continued French-Caribbean integration (though not assimilation) into the French system. None of this is new.

Trinidad's first major socialist activist in the 1920s, Andrew Cipriani, yearly paid his homages to Fabian thought and the British Labour Party, but after decades of militancy he withdrew in the face of two challenges to his basic conservative view of the world: the divorce bill, which he saw as a threat to the family, and the use of violence in strike action. Those who used violence (such as Uriah Butler, the "spontaneous" leader in Trinidad's 1937 labor movement and uprising) themselves ended up turning to religion (quoting biblical passages) and to English history (studying the rule of Henry VIII). The "pull" on the leadership of the conservative values and norms of the masses has been powerful. Even Eric Williams, whose early historical writings were gems of Marxist thought and careful documentation, would eventually abandon what one admirer called "the infinite, barren track of documents, dates and texts" to write "gossip . . . which experience had established as the truth."

A review of Trinidadian C.L.R. James's five decades of thought on Trotskyite socialism and revolution indicates that he never resolved the universalism-particularism counterpoint. In his *Black Jacobins* (1938), perhaps the most influential West Indian work of the twentieth century, James vacillates and hedges but ends up on the side of the Dessalinean Black Revolution as distinct from the universalist experiment of Toussaint.

It is not at all evident that there can be in practice a working and productive relationship between racial or ethnic populism and a program based on premises of secular modernism, whether socialist or not. Even in theory, the reconciliation appears improbable. A case in point is the work of the Martinican Frantz Fanon. Like Césaire—whom he knew and greatly admired—Fanon wished to be liberated from the "fleshless shacks" of European thought; thus he searched for a key to what he called the "psycho-affective equilibrium" of the angry Third World intellectual. This search is central to an understanding of the dynamics of modern-conservative societies. Fanon felt compelled to describe and explain what he perceived as the relentless determination of revolutionary elites to return to history: to "renew contact once more with the oldest and most pre-colonial springs of life of their people." Fanon understood the enduring consequences of the racial hurts and angst inflicted during colonialism. "This state belief in national culture," he wrote, "is in fact an ardent despairing turning toward anything that will afford him anchorage."[3] Even such a lifelong and dedicated Marxist as Guyana's Cheddi Jagan finds a practical and perhaps even psychological need to blend his Marxism with an ongoing devotion to Hinduism. Clearly, then, race and desire for a return to history have been powerful forces blocking a universalist and secular approach to politics.

The rational and secular view of the world that is necessary for modern (especially socialist) revolution is not easily sustained in these societies. In the cases of Césaire, Williams, Norman Manley, Forbes Burnham, and others, Marxist or socialist thought was mediated by pressures from the multiethnic, religious, and conservative societies they led—and which eventually forced them to succumb to the particularistic note in the particularism-universalism counterpoint. It is a fundamental characteristic of a conservative society that views of the world and of social change resist any notions of dealing with problems in any way other than in terms of their historically perceived uniqueness. This characteristic has been, more often than not, part of the Caribbean experience.[4]

The experience explains how a Dr. François Duvalier ("Papa Doc") could come into power in Haiti in 1957 advocating a radical Black Power revolution but revert to a very traditional form of political barbarism. He played the most retrograde chords of a deeply conservative society to entrench himself—and then his son, Jean Claude—in power.

CARIBBEAN POLITICAL ECONOMY

In part because it involves modern societies with relatively skilled labor and a high degree of unionization, and thus high wages, the development process in the Caribbean has tended to be industrial and capital intensive. The overflow of available labor (because of reduced migration) has tended to be absorbed by the public sector. The financial and economic retrenchments made necessary by the energy crisis (and consequent balance-of-payments difficulties) have forced a slowing down of this public employment. The result is not merely unemployment but rather a process that is creating a whole generation of "never employed." The vast majority of this group has attained at least some high school education and has aspirations and some skills. Alas, they tend not to be the skills that are in demand nor the aspirations that would encourage needed activities such as agricultural enterprises. Only the latter, with its labor intensity, could in fact absorb the large numbers of people who annually enter the labor market.

Such an agricultural orientation and direction is to be found nowhere in the Caribbean except Haiti, which is still 80 percent rural. The decline of the agricultural sector is a fundamental fact of Caribbean political economy. The movement is toward the urban areas and, critically, migration abroad. In the English-speaking Caribbean, migration accounted for a 46,000-person decrease in the labor force during the 1960s. Because of a slowdown in migration, this labor force is calculated to have increased by about 400,000 during the 1970s, two-thirds of the increase being among young adults.

On every one of the Caribbean islands, youthful adults make up an ever-increasing percentage of the total population, and everywhere they share the restlessness of youth the world over. But the "complexity" approach cautions that it would be a terrible mistake to associate a priori all this modern political ferment and activity with a state of social revolution. Such an association might preempt a close look at the substratum—the political economy—of Caribbean society. Although the configurations and expressions of this conservatism vary, the following aspects of Caribbean society show great similarities from one country to another.

Throughout the area, there is a deep and dynamic religiosity, even though the intensity and pervasiveness of religion—as doctrine and as institutions—do vary. One situation is that of the dominant church in the central plaza being attended by women and children once a week; such was the case in Cuba before the Revolution and is the case in Puerto Rico today.[5]

Another situation is that of the English-speaking West Indies, where one finds multiple denominations and many churches scattered throughout neighborhoods, urban and rural. This case illustrates a living presence of religion rather than a ceremonial one and is typical also of countries such as Haiti, where Christianity combined with West African religions to create a syncretism called Voodoo (also called *santería* in Cuba and *Shango* in Trinidad). This religiosity impinges on other spheres of life.

One attitudinal spin-off from the doctrines of the major religions in the area is the belief in private property, especially land. There is an intense love and respect for the land and a desire to own a piece of it. The popular Haitian saying *Se vagabon qui loue kay* ("Only vagabonds rent their homes") expresses the desire for ownership, for full possession. On Nevis, 80 percent of the homeowners own their house lot; on St. Vincent, the figure is 75 percent. Although the figure is only 46.8 percent on Barbados, travel around that island reveals that even the smallest house has a name; the name represents the emotional dimension of property ownership. The little picket fence around the house is the physical expression of the emotional dimension. That picket fence (or cactus fence in the Netherlands Antilles) also expresses another characteristic of Caribbean peoples. In the midst of their gregariousness, they like their privacy, an expression of their intrinsic independence. This characteristic, usually identified as a rural phenomenon, is pervasive even in urban areas. This explains the living presence in West Indian language of old English sayings such as "A man's home is his castle" or, as used with an additional meaning in Creole, "Two man rat can't live in same hole."

This latter saying expresses the idea that in any house only one of the partners can wear the pants. It is taken for granted that the male partner does. And yet, these societies are fundamentally matriarchal and matrilocal: Because of the very high illegitimacy rate among the working class, it is the mother who raises the child, and the child lives where the mother (as well as the maternal grandmother) lives. As the 1981 study by Gary and Rosemary Brana-Shute demonstrates, there is a deep underlying conservatism in the socialization processes and aspirations of even the hard-core— and angry—unemployed youth in the area.

And yet, as Caribbean history has repeatedly shown, these generally moderate and family-oriented societies, and especially the youths, are capable of sudden, quite unpredictable political and social outbursts. This was very evident in Curaçao, in the Netherlands Antilles, in 1969 when a minor industrial strike exploded into a class and race attack on the system. Half of the buildings in the main commercial sector of the island were burned to the ground.

The basically conservative substrata of Caribbean societies also sustain very modern and highly mobilized societies and their corresponding agencies. Note in Table 23.1, for instance, the following dimensions and configurations of that modernity— with certain exceptions, such as Haiti, the populations are literate and schooled. On island after island, from 90 to 100 percent of the children of primary school age are in school, and literacy rates everywhere are above 85 percent. Although there is some evidence that conservative attitudes are positively correlated with greater degrees of education,[6] the fact is that a population that participates in the articulation of grievances and wishes and that can utilize the modern techniques of communication is one that has an increased capability for mobilization. Throughout the Caribbean, people are politically mobilized. There are everywhere political parties and interest groups with capacities for extensive articulation of interests and aggregation of these into policy options. No government today, of the left, middle, or right, can ignore the demands of the groups. Literacy and education also make the labor union system more effective in the West Indies since 30 to 50 percent of the workforce is unionized, and historic ties with political parties give unions additional leverage in the bargaining processes.

Another of the modern agencies that a literate and schooled population makes possible is the state bureaucracy, which, according to Max Weber, is the most "rational" of all forms of organization. Such state bureaucracies are found throughout the Caribbean in the form of a relatively skilled public or civil service. In Trinidad, there are three and a half times more people with diplomas or degrees in the public service than in the private sector, and in Jamaica the institutionalization and legitimacy of the public service are evident in its capacity to survive dramatic shifts in political party fortunes. The top echelons of these bureaucracies are now being educated in the area. The University of the West Indies (UWI), with campuses in Jamaica, Trinidad, and Barbados, now makes university education accessible to a much broader sector, as do the universities in Guyana, Martinique, Surinam, Curaçao, and elsewhere. Whereas in 1957 there were 2,632 West Indians studying at universities abroad compared to only 566 at UWI, by 1982 the number abroad had doubled, but the number of students at UWI had increased twelvefold.

Caribbean modernity is reflected also in other areas. That Caribbean working people have largely developed both the habits and the skills required of labor in modern societies has made them very desirable as immigrant workers. This explains the long tradition of migration, and return, of Caribbean workers; they are and always have been a mobile population. Whether building the Panama Canal and Central America's railroads and ports or running the London public transportation system, Caribbean workers have had the attitudes and skills of urban workers. They return with new skills, but also with the hope of buying that house or piece of land for which they have saved. In Haiti, the "Bahamas" house was built with remittances from Haitians working in the Bahamas, whereas the newer "Miami" house points to the new destination of Haitian migrants and the source of their remittances.

While abroad, Caribbean workers are able to communicate with their compatriots. Mailboxes stand along every road; there is widespread use of radio and newspapers and direct-dialing telephones from the United States to many islands, and in the French West Indies, Netherlands Antilles, Jamaica, Trinidad, and Barbados, the widespread use of television. Modern communications assist both in modernizing the Caribbean and in preserving ethnic attachments. Literacy in one or more of the major languages of the world (English, Spanish, and French) gives Caribbeans access to the main currents of ideas and technology, while their native variations on those languages (Creole in Haiti, papiamento in Curaçao, taki-taki in Surinam) strengthen the sense of *Volk*, or nation, of gemeinschaft, or community.

If one adds the fact that any particular sector of the islands is within, at most, a two-hour bus ride of some urban center, one understands something of the modernity of the society as well as its continued proximity to rural village life. Ties to the land and to tradition are not broken by a move to the city; rather, those links provide something of the underpinnings of the conservative values and orientations of the urban residents even as the diversification of memberships and involvements (churches, sport clubs, unions, political parties, service clubs) contributes to and expresses the society's modern dimensions. The glue that holds all together is the Caribbean family, both the nuclear and the extended family with its *compadres* (godfathers), *comadres* (godmothers), "cousins," and "aunties."

These, then, are some of the native aspects of these modern-conservative societies. Yet, an analysis of the substrata also has to take into account the external factors affecting change. Although on balance internal factors tend to carry more weight in any causal analysis of social change, the small size of the Caribbean states makes external factors somewhat more important than they would be for most states.

There can be no question that smallness makes them vulnerable to a host of problems. One of these is national insecurity, as was illustrated by the extraordinary 1981 attempted invasion and subversion of the government of Dominica by U.S. mercenaries in league with local politicians. Furthermore, securing a degree of national representation abroad is costly. But such representation is important not only to facilitate contact with foreign nations through traditional diplomatic ties but also to attract attention from the ever-increasing number of international and multilateral banking or lending agencies.[7]

Also contributing to the vulnerability are the cleavages created by the race and ethnic divisions that characterize the politics of nations such as Trinidad and Tobago, Guyana, and Surinam. In each of these countries, Indians (originally from British India) compose half or more of the population. Predominantly Hindu in religion (some 20 percent are Muslim), these sectors are in themselves prototypical modern-conservative groups. Reconciling Hinduism with secular ideologies such as Marxism is a difficult task in itself; to do so in a context in which major elements of that Indian population are capitalists, landowners, and merchants (as in the case of Guyana and Surinam) is an even more complex proposition. Whether the cleavage is black versus white, Indian versus black, or black versus mulatto, race and race conflict contribute to social division and to the vulnerability of Caribbean societies.

Understanding and awareness of the vulnerabilities resulting from smallness have led to many attempts at regional or subregional integration. Dreams of a united Caribbean are not new. They were expressed in José Martí's theme that Cuba and Puerto Rico were wings of the same dove; in Haitian president Jean Puerre Boyer's dream of liberating all the slaves, first of neighboring Santo Domingo (which his armies occupied from 1822 to 1844), then of other islands; and in the West Indies Federation, which lasted from 1958 to 1961. The repeated failures of such attempts, however, created skepticism about the viability and indeed the desirability of such union.

Despite constant talk about "integration," such as the mid-1990s creation of the thirty-five-member Association of Caribbean States, the mini–nation state is now a reality of the Caribbean scene, and we probably have not seen the last of the newly independent entities. By the 1990s, the area was limiting itself to attempts at economic integration through such instruments as the Caribbean Common Market (CARICOM) and the Caribbean Development Bank. Even the Association of Eastern Caribbean Community[8] emphasizes the economic aspects of association, leaving politics, including foreign policy, to each individual member.

Unfortunately, while insularity gathers strength on each island, globalization, impelled by international politics and transnational forces (including multinational corporations), presses for a reduction in state sovereignty. And today, as in the past, size and isolation make these territories targets for international expansion. During the Cold War (the 1960s through the 1980s), escalating ideological competition among international forces made the Caribbean a cockpit, the modern-day equivalent of the European battlegrounds of the seventeenth and eighteenth centuries. Marxism-Leninism, the Socialist International, the Christian Democrats, and international labor organizations as well as new regional actors such as Cuba, Venezuela, and Mexico all joined the battle for the minds of Caribbean peoples. The United States has long been engaged in the competition. To these may be added many proselytizing religious and semireligious groups, from Islam to the Seventh-Day Adventists to the Rastafarian Movement (now of Pan-Caribbean character). Since the foreign offices and intelligence services of the major states never left the area, the ideational scene in the Caribbean was a bewildering panorama of competing radio broadcasts; roaming sports, cultural, and scientific missions; state visits; and sojourning consultants from international aid agencies—and these activities were only the overt ones. By the 1990s, with the end of the Cold War, the "taming" of Cuban internationalism, and the shocks of the denouements of the Grenadian and Surinamese revolutions, all that changed. The new Caribbean geopolitics have more to do with economics: In the search for markets and foreign investment capital, import-substitution economies have been opened up (i.e., "liberalized") and forced to become export-driven. The private sectors, not the state, have been given the responsibility for economic development. It is all too recent to say whether this will prove to be a more productive strategy of development. It certainly is global in application and strongly pushed by the single power whose influence now stands unchallenged in the region, the United States.

The structural elements revealed in this bare-bones sketch of the internal nature and dynamics of Caribbean societies dispute the generalized idea that these societies were invariably or structurally revolutionary in nature. To be sure, these societies were never static; they often reacted violently when the sense of moral indignation and the collective democratic sensibilities were challenged. These were the responses of modern-conservative societies.

By the late 1990s, a new and arguably greater threat faced these vulnerable states: the threat of organized international crime, pushing every form of illegal activity from drugs to guns to money laundering to financial scams of every conceivable type. Accompanying these structural changes are new sources of threat: the fear that the greatest menace to these small states comes from the internationalization of crime, corruption, and violence. International criminal cartels are quite capable of corrupting whole states, subverting their electoral, legal, and police systems. Formal sovereignty does not mean much under such circumstances. The question is whether the moral conservatism that was so instrumental in withstanding the totalitarian temptation will also serve as a bulwark against the onslaught of organized crime. I conclude by addressing this question, the central challenge at the end of the twentieth century.

CONCLUSION

The first thing to keep in mind in analyzing the "new" Caribbean is the degree of social change, both in speed and in kind. These changes can be illustrated by the cases of Haiti and the Dominican Republic. Both had been governed for decades by dictatorial dynasties, both experienced U.S. military interventions, and both were governed in the late 1990s by former political radicals. In Haiti, both president René Preval and his prime minister, Rosmy Smarth, had been members of their country's Communist Party. In the Dominican Republic, president Leonel Fernández had long espoused the radical platform of the Partido de Liberación Dominicana and its leader, Juan Bosch. And yet, all governed with decidedly moderate programs, closely coordinated with the dictates of the multilateral lending agencies and the exigencies of the U.S.-dominated market. There appear to be few dissenting voices from the emphasis on private-sector-driven, export-oriented policies. The cases of Puerto Rico and Cuba serve to further illustrate the nature of this change.

In contrast to the self-satisfaction of earlier years, in the 1990s there appears to be a sense of ennui with what is perceived to be Cuba's and Puerto Rico's inability to deal successfully with their particular problems, political and economic. Neither of these two Caribbean experiments is any longer perceived as a model. Like all other countries in the region, they both have had to become acquainted with the strategic value of political and economic pragmatism, small countries attempting to sort out what this post–Cold War period, with its globalization of trade and the formation of free-trading blocs, portends. Cuba still operates under an onerous—and quite evidently futile—U.S. embargo that denies it the one privilege the rest of the region enjoys: the regular lobbying that takes place in Washington, the world's largest market and source of investment capital. This Cuba-U.S. confrontation is the last vestige of the Cold War and is being left behind by a host of fundamental changes in the international relations of the area. So fast is the actual pace of change that there is a perceptible cultural gap between the new economic realities and much of the intellectual and scholarly literature on the region, which in too many cases is still statist in proclivity. In much of the Caribbean, the cultural lag extends to important sectors of the population, accustomed after three decades to the protections and subsidies provided by centralized economic arrangements. Cuba is a classic case in point. "The conceptualization of the partial reforms of the Cuban economy," note two reform-minded Cuban economists, "finds itself well behind the actual changes which are taking place."[9] Be this as it may, it is widely accepted that neoliberal economics have superseded statist practices on every island, including—in its own way—Cuba.

Despite the triumphalist posture of the apostles of neoliberalism, there are no ironclad guarantees that this new doxa will bring the region to the promised land. The difficulties of a transition involving the downsizing of state employment, reducing the state's social net, and opening up the economy should not be minimized. The political costs have been all too evident as one government after another has been punished at elections or even come close to being overthrown, as was the case with Trinidad in 1990. Selwyn Ryan illuminates the issue for the Caribbean when he notes that the critical problem is "whether the Caribbean masses, weaned as they have been on state dispensed patronage," will accept the new policies of downsizing the state and eliminating subsidies. Whatever the answer, says Ryan, "the age of innocence may indeed be over."[10] Given the drastic nature of the restructuring and the decline in standards of living for many, it is remarkable and to some even "surprising," therefore, that these systems continue to enjoy pluralist democratic practices.[11]

In the final analysis, however, the interpretation of Caribbean societies presented here does provide some grounds for optimism. The wide acceptance of democratic forms is but one expression of political cultures that are at once very conservative about basic social and political issues and yet modern and adaptable in their capacity to adjust and even innovate. Such predispositions to incorporate the new without discarding what has worked historically will surely come in handy in the new era.

The future will not be without its dilemmas. The "U.S. dilemma" will have its own Caribbean counterpart. The desire of Caribbeans for modernity draws their attention to the United States, yet their yearning for liberation and economic justice for themselves (and their African brothers and sisters) turns their eyes occasionally toward Cuba. Both sentiments have as context societies with deep attachments to organized religions, private property, and highly diversified and plural social structures. The result is ambivalence and unpredictability. And yet, in many ways the ebb and flow of Caribbean politics and social change can be illustrated through the metaphor of the counterpoint between the desire and capacity for modernization and change and the strength of conservatism. Each tendency has well-developed idea systems, as well as institutional and organizational representation. Not surprisingly, both tendencies can be found in the vast majority of Caribbean peoples. Thus, it is useful to characterize Caribbean societies as modern-conservative societies, an ideal-type construct that helps us understand what otherwise might appear to be contradictory or even unintelligible in the behavior of this multilingual, multiracial, and multistate area.

NOTES

1. Karl Mannheim, "Conservative Thought," in Paul Kecskemeti, ed., *Essays on Sociology and Social Psychology* (New York: Oxford University Press, 1953), pp. 77–164.

2. Aimé Césaire, "Lettre à Maurice Thorez," *Présence Africaine* (Paris) (1956), p. 15.

3. Frantz Fanon, *The Wretched of the Earth* (New York: Grove Press, 1968), p. 217.

4. One interesting exception is the New Jewel Movement, which came to power in Grenada in 1979, attempting to portray that experience as an extension of a Caribbean decolonization process begun in Cuba. It was deposed through U.S. military intervention in 1983.

5. Cuba and Puerto Rico were perhaps the least structurally conservative of the Caribbean societies, in large measure because of the considerable influence of secular North American values and interests.

6. See Selwyn Ryan, Eddie Greene, and Jack Harewood, *The Confused Electorate* (St. Augustine and Trinidad, 1979); and Anthony P. Maingot, "The Difficult Path to Socialism in the English-Speaking Caribbean," in Richard R. Fagen, ed., *Capitalism and the State in U.S.–Latin American Relations* (Stanford: Stanford University Press, 1979).

7. This is not only a question of asymmetry of power but also a question of commanding respect and dignity.

8. Antigua, St. Vincent, Dominica, St. Lucia, and Grenada.

9. Pedro Monreal and Manuel Rúa, "Apertura y reforma de la economía cubana: Las transformaciones institucionales, 1990–1993" (paper delivered at the conference "Cuba in the International System," Carleton University, Ottawa, Canada, September 23, 1993), p. 1.

10. Selwyn Ryan, "Problems and Prospects for the Survival of Liberal Democracy in the Commonwealth Caribbean," *Caribbean Affairs*, 6:60 (January–March 1992).

11. See Jorge I. Domínguez, "The Caribbean Question: Why Has Liberal Democracy (Surprisingly) Flourished?" in Jorge I. Domínguez, Robert A. Pastor, and R. Delisle Worrell, eds., *Democracy in the Caribbean* (Baltimore, Md.: Johns Hopkins University Press, 1993), pp. 1–25.

SUGGESTED READINGS

A good general treatment of the Caribbean as a whole is Franklin W. Knight, *The Caribbean: The Genesis of a Fragmented Nationalism,* 2d ed. (New York: Oxford University Press, 1980). Knight also edited, with Margaret E. Crahan, *Africa and the Caribbean: The Legacies of a Link* (Baltimore, Md.: Johns Hopkins University Press, 1979). On the English-speaking Caribbean, Gordon K. Lewis, *The Growth of the Modern West Indies* (New York: Monthly Review Press, 1968), is somewhat outdated but contains excellent insights and analysis. David Lowenthal's *West Indian Societies* (New York: Oxford University Press, 1972) is especially strong on race relations and the analysis of the "plural society." On the development of socialist politics and the region's conservative responses, see Anthony P. Maingot, *The United States and the Caribbean* (Boulder, Colo.: Westview Press, 1994).

Contemporary affairs are best followed through the newsletter from London *Caribbean Insight* and the magazine *Hemisphere* (Florida International University).

PART TEN
THE ANDES

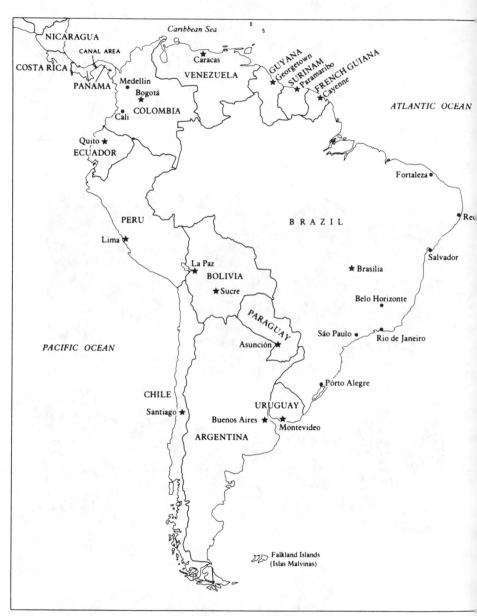

South America

Reprinted, with permission, from Howard J. Wiarda and Harvey F. Kline, eds., *Latin American Politics and Development,* Second Edition (Boulder, Colo.: Westview Press, 1985).

24

VENEZUELA, COLOMBIA, AND ECUADOR

JOHN D. MARTZ

"America is ungovernable. Those who have served the revolution have plowed the sea." Such was the embittered disillusionment of Simón Bolívar by the time of his death on December 17, 1830. Not the least of his disappointments was the dissolution earlier that year of his cherished Gran Colombia, a political union of today's Venezuela, Colombia, Ecuador, and Panama. From 1819 until 1830, this fragile creation had survived periodic insubordination to the central authorities in Bogotá. Resentment in both Venezuela and Ecuador mounted until the former withdrew in April and the latter in May of 1830. The Bolívar-enforced union had been unnatural, destined for inexorable failure. Yet there were commonalities that went well beyond sheer geographic contiguity, and even today the tradition of the Bolivarian ethos lends justification to collective consideration of the three republics.

In recent and contemporary times, these countries have collaborated with Peru and Bolivia in the Andean Pact. In 1990 all three enjoyed elected civilian governments and were outspoken hemispheric champions of democracy, freedom, and human rights. Within the Latin American context, each constitutes a multiracial society in which enlarging middle sectors are breaking down historic class rigidities. And to varying degrees, each possesses sufficiently diverse natural resources to provide a basis for economic growth and modernization.

Venezuela in 1958 ousted the dictatorship of General Marcos Pérez Jiménez and inaugurated a constitutional, party-based regime, which stands today as the most vigorously open and competitive system in all Latin America. Seven successive presidents have abided by the rules of the game while guiding economic modernization fueled by vast petroleum and other natural resources. A shaky multiparty system evolved into one dominated by the social democratic Democratic Action Party (AD) and the social Christian party (Committee for Independent Political and Electoral Organization, COPEI). Political legitimacy has thrived as four of the last five governments have been defeated at the polls and have yielded power to the victorious opposition. More recently, however, attempted military coups and the political "impeachment" of a president have shaken the nation to its democratic roots.

The year 1958 also marked the ouster of military authoritarianism in Colombia, with General Gustavo Rojas Pinilla being replaced by a carefully engineered alliance between the Conservatives and Liberals. The two historic rival parties agreed upon a constitutional pact whereby for sixteen years they shared political power equally. An informal variation since 1974 has allowed traditional elites to maintain control over the pace and character of change and modernization. Although far less representative or responsive than that of Venezuela, the Colombian leadership has nonetheless been able to draw on varied economic resources to meet the more pressing priorities of society. The scandal over financing of the 1994 electoral campaign by the drug industry, however, has weakened the legitimacy of Colombia's democratic system.

Ecuador, by all indices the least progressive or modern of the three countries, falls less neatly into a chronological category. The unparalleled succession of three elected governments from 1948 to 1960 then gave way to more typical instability. During the next twelve years, Ecuador was ruled by two elected presidents, two provisional presidents, one military junta, and a vice-president who ousted his erstwhile superior. In a sense, the contemporary experience parallels the advent of Ecuador's petroleum era, which began in 1972. Seven years of military rule yielded to an elected government in 1979 under the reformist leadership of Jaime Roldós Aguilera. A new generation of political leaders also came to power and has undertaken to implement socioeconomic change supported primarily by income from oil. Social distance and hierarchical rigidities remain far greater in Ecuador than in the other two countries and will prove far less susceptible to modernization.

By the decade of the 1990s, then, both similarities and differences among the three countries were pronounced. To understand them more fully, we will undertake a brief excursion into the Spanish colonial legacy and the evolution of political and socioeconomic patterns during the following century and a half.

HISTORICAL SETTING

With the arrival of the conquistadores early in the sixteenth century, Spain moved to implant its colonial system of control and domination. Personifying the king in the New World was the viceroy, whose role as spokesman of the distant monarch enhanced his powers. The primary viceroyalties were New Spain and Peru until the creation of New Granada in 1717. Although dismantled seven years later, the last was reinstituted in 1740. With the capital in Bogotá, it bore responsibility for today's Venezuela, Colombia, and Ecuador. New Granada received relatively low priority during the first two colonial centuries and was largely isolated from the major imperial centers of power. With creation of the viceroyalty, it gradually received more attention, yet by the final years of Spanish rule, it was still of only marginal concern to

Madrid. It was not coincidental that early cries for freedom came from such backwaters of the empire.

Among the greatest precursors of independence was Francisco de Miranda, born in Caracas in 1750. By the turn of the century, he was renowned throughout Europe as an advocate of freedom, and in 1810, he had returned home as dictator of the newly independent junta. Defeated and captured by royalist forces two years later, he was imprisoned and transported to Spain, while leadership fell to another Caracas-born figure, Bolívar. It was the Liberator who brought about the ultimate victory over royalist forces in Venezuela, Colombia, and Ecuador. After 1810, there was periodic collaboration and communication among rebel leaders in the three future countries, and in December 1819, Gran Colombian unity was proclaimed by the Congress of Angostura. Francisco de Paula Santander, as vice-president, directed the affairs of government while Bolívar continued to lead the armed struggle.

As time passed, differences between Bolívar and Santander were aggravated while in Venezuela, the illiterate *llanero* ("plainsman") José Antonio Páez, a brilliant military leader, plotted secession from Gran Colombia. There was similar restiveness in Ecuador, far removed from the government in Bogotá. So it was that with the ailing Bolívar's final retirement in May 1830, Gran Colombia disintegrated, giving way to three separate countries. In Caracas, Páez became Venezuela's first president; he was to rule with the support of Caracas's conservative oligarchy until 1848. Colombia began its independent existence under Santander, who ruled until 1837. In Ecuador, Venezuelan-born General Juan José Flores was proclaimed president, and he succeeded in perpetuating his power until 1845.

The nineteenth century was a period of civil strife, turbulence, and sporadic anarchy in all three countries. In Venezuela, which had an eminently rural population dominated by merchants and coffee growers, the relative prosperity and peace of the Conservative oligarchy under Páez eventually yielded to heightened conflict between Conservatives and Liberals. Intermittent civil war and governmental instability in 1870 led to the rule of the Liberal Antonio Guzmán Blanco. Until 1888, he ruled either from the presidency or through puppets while bringing efficiency to government, suppressing opposition, and glorifying his own image. Following his overthrow, renewed Conservative-Liberal conflict raged until a band of revolutionaries descended upon Caracas from the Andes in 1899. This introduced authoritarian rule under a succession of Andean military figures, which, with one brief interruption, would endure until 1958.

The central figure of Andean hegemony was Juan Vicente Gómez, "the tyrant of the Andes," who exercised despotic rule from 1908 until his death in 1935. It was during the Gómez era that pastoral Venezuela underwent its transformation to an industrial, petroleum-based society. The first major oil strike came in 1922, and Gómez capitalized upon the discovery to strengthen the economy, develop a basic infrastructure, centralize governmental authority, and preserve his personal hegemony. The oil multinationals arrived with a vengeance, while foreign investment acquired central importance to the economy. Yet it was also under Gómez that student rebellion planted the seeds of the contemporary party-based system.

During the decade following Gómez's death, a youthful Rómulo Betancourt created and built the Democratic Action Party (AD), Venezuela's first modern, mass-based party. Its initial exercise of power, from 1945 to 1948, saw the party undertake massive and far-reaching changes throughout the polity and society. The AD introduced major reforms that were radical within the context of the times, meanwhile enhancing its organizational base and national popularity. Impatient, arrogant, determined to remake Venezuela overnight, the AD eventually overreached itself and was deposed by the military. Beginning in 1948, the country experienced a bleak decade of harsh repression, political persecution, and profligate corruption under Pérez Jiménez and his collaborators. With his flight from power in the face of massive protests in January 1958, the stage was set for the return of political leaders and creation of the system that has endured to the present.

To the west, in Colombia, regional rivalries and strife emerged soon after Santander's departure from power. The Conservative-Liberal conflict was more profound in Colombia than in Venezuela. Divided over the character of government authority, the role of the Church, and economic policies, the combatants alternated in power throughout the first century of independence and beyond. The 1860–1862 Federal War resulted in a Liberal victory, enhancing that party's advocacy of states' rights and anticlericalism. The pendulum later swung back to the Conservatives under Rafael Núñez, president in 1880–1882 and 1884–1894. The 1886 Constitution enshrined centralized authority and restored the preeminence of the Church through an 1887 concordat with the Vatican. The bloody War of a Thousand Days (1899–1902) left Colombia under Conservative domination as it entered the twentieth century, and a year later, the loss of Panama further shattered both the economy and national morale.

From 1904 to 1909, Rafael Reyes presided over a period of authoritarian reconstruction. While Conservative elites reestablished unchallenged dominion, the rise of coffee production stimulated the economy. Not until 1930 were the Liberals to regain power, aided by the repercussions of the world depression and a division of the Conservative elites. In time, the Liberals themselves split between reformist and traditionalist forces, ultimately permitting the election of a minority Conservative government in 1946. Increasing bitterness between both elitist and rank-and-file Conservatives and Liberals introduced a rising wave of rural violence. When the charismatic and controversial Liberal leader Jorge Eliécer Gaitán was assassinated in the streets of Bogotá on April 9, 1948, an unprecedented wave of lawlessness and urban destruction—the infamous *bogotazo*—spread across the country. For more than a decade, the *violencia* ("violence") raged at a high pitch of intensity and intemperance. By conservative estimates, some 250,000 lives were lost.

Increasingly repressive Conservative rule eventually led to the first military regime in decades, but General Gustavo Rojas Pinilla failed to end the *violencia* while assuming increasingly dictatorial authority. Toppled from power in May 1957, he was succeeded by an interim military junta, which led in August 1958 to the so-called National Front. Negotiated by Conservative and Liberal leaders, the front sought to minimize partisan conflict and revive the stagnant economy while assuring continuation of rule by national socioeconomic and political elites. *Paridad* ("parity") divided legislative seats and cabinet posts equally between Conservatives and Liberals, while *alternación* ("alternation") provided for the rotation of four-year presidencies between the two parties. Thus, it was the National Front that introduced the arrangement that has explicitly or implicitly characterized the political dynamics of contemporary Colombia.

The nineteenth-century Ecuadoran experience with independence was also marked by instability, civil unrest, and periods of hegemony under either Conservatives or Liberals. By the time of Juan José Flores's departure in 1845, the familiar issues between the two groups had become well established. During the 1850s, the Liberals restricted the Church, expelled the Jesuits, and abolished slavery. Their replacement by the Conservatives in 1860 was accompanied by perhaps the most theocratic regime known to Latin America. While establishing civilian control, promoting public works, and achieving fiscal soundness, President Gabriel García Moreno (1861–1865 and 1869–1875) directed a regime of fanatical religious absolutism. The Jesuits were readmitted, a concordat with the Vatican negotiated, and education virtually handed over to the Church. In 1873, the republic was officially dedicated to "the Sacred Heart of Jesus," while Liberal opponents were ruthlessly persecuted.

Successful beyond all his predecessors in fostering a spirit of national identity, García Moreno created a system that survived his 1875 assassination by some two decades. Only in 1895 did the Liberals, under Eloy Alfaro, regain power. With minor interruptions, their control was to endure a full half century. While a number of both military and civilian governments were ousted by unconstitutional means, the country was ruled by the banking and commercial oligarchy that grew up in Guayaquil. The booming cacao market generated economic wealth until its collapse in the 1920s, but the subsequent decline in agricultural productivity left political power largely unchanged. Only military defeat and humiliating capitulation to Peru in the 1941 border war created the conditions necessary for the ouster of the Liberals. This defeat also contributed to the prominence of the erratic, charismatic, and demagogic José María Velasco Ibarra, whose figure cast the dominant shadow across national politics for over four decades.

A self-styled populist of great oratorical skill, Velasco governed on five different occasions, only once completing his constitutional term. Waging war against both Conservatives and Liberals, vacillating between rhetorical radicalism and opportunistic collaboration with the oligarchy, he lacked a well-defined program. Elected to his fourth term in 1960 with an unparalleled popular mandate, he was replaced by his vice-president only fifteen months later. After a succession of provisional civilian and military governments, he again won election in 1968. Two years later, he suspended the constitution and assumed dictatorial powers, which were maintained until military intervention in 1972. Only with Velasco's death in 1979 at the age of eighty-six was Ecuador to pursue its political evolution free from his extraordinary omnipresence. And it was in that same year that the military turned over power to a new generation of civilian leaders, whose responsibility it was to capitalize upon the petroleum era, which had been initiated in 1972.

SOCIAL AND ECONOMIC STRUCTURES

Despite geographic proximity and historical similarities, the socioeconomic characters of the three Gran Colombian republics are markedly varied. Venezuela's multiracial society enjoys an openness of attitude and class mobility encouraged by its contemporary political system and supported by oil income and its rich resource base. In Colombia, mestizo ethnic diversity overlies social rigidities and class distinctions, which took root in colonial days. The social aristocracy retains its preeminence in politics, as illustrated in 1974 by the presidential competition of three offspring of former presidents. An increasingly diversified economy continues to benefit largely the wealthy and a portion of the urban middle sector. Unlike its two sisters, Ecuador continues to have a large Indian population—40 percent at the very least. This includes the Andean descendants of the Incas, primitive Amazonian tribes, and the distinctive coastal *montuvios*. No more than 15 percent are of European ancestry, although this group remains the dominant one in national life. Traditional social and economic structures are resistant to modernization, and the impact of petroleum on deep-seated rigidities cannot yet be assessed.

Turning first to Venezuela, we encounter an estimated population of 22 million, to which at least 2 million illegal immigrants from Colombia should be added. Society is increasingly youthful, mobile, and urbanized. Over half the population is too young to vote (under eighteen); some 40 percent no longer live in or near their birthplace; the urban population has risen from 30 percent in the 1940s to 80 percent today; literacy has doubled during the same period of time. Ethnically, Venezuela is at least 70 percent mestizo, with its Indian component largely in the southwestern Andean region and the people of African ancestry scattered along the Caribbean coast. Racial discrimination, although not unknown, is not a serious barrier to advancement. During the contemporary era, mestizos and mulattoes have been among those to achieve prominence in politics, business, and commerce. Mobility between social classes and subgroupings is also common, and Venezuela has little of the white Hispanic aristocracy that survives in Colombia and Ecuador.

While social opportunity therefore exists, the number of marginals remains large. The influx to the cities has aggravated the condition of those living in the slum barrios, and easily one-third of the population lives in abject poverty, many of whom are at least underemployed if not unemployed. In rural areas, small farmers, who initially benefited from the 1960 agrarian reform, have often been pushed aside by large, mechanized agribusiness interests, ultimately seeking refuge by flight to the cities. An enlarging middle sector has been more conservative than social minded in its determination to reap the benefits of an affluent society, further its own interests, and discount the needs of the dispossessed. Despite the powerful reformist currents of the post-1958 political system, social inequalities remain a major challenge to Venezuela's leadership.

The modernization and diversification of economic structures have been predicated upon the application of petroleum earnings to other sectors of activity. To "sow the oil" (*sembrar el petróleo*) has been an unchallenged slogan since the 1940s, while the potential for growth has been dramatically expanded as the result of rich deposits of iron ore, nickel, coal, aluminum, and bauxite, further enhanced by the availability of massive hydroelectric power. During the 1960s, Venezuelan governments stressed import substitution within a context of protective tariffs and government subsidies. This policy was to be followed by the expansion of new export-oriented activities, and in the decade of the 1970s, government emphasis was placed upon a massive expansion of economic infrastructure and public works, accompanied by the promotion of heavy industry. President Carlos Andrés Pérez (1974–1979) in particular followed this developmental strategy, with high priority being accorded to an integrated iron and steel industry, to petrochemicals, and to modernized transportation and communications facilities.

Although the effectiveness of this strategy cannot yet be adequately judged, there is little debate about the country's inability to modernize the agricultural sector after years of effort and a massive infusion of government funds. The 1960 agrarian reform directed attention to a peasant-oriented strategy with land redistribution at the core. Relative success with this phase did not, however, lead to broader sectoral productivity. By the 1970s, both COPEI and AD had turned toward the promotion of mechanized agriculture in response to periodic shortages of basic foodstuffs and expensively subsidized imports. The consequence has been a strengthening of the rural entrepreneurial sector at the cost of implicit abandonment of small farmers and marginal producers. By the early 1980s, the country was importing some $1 billion of food supplies annually, nearly 20 percent of its total imports. The decline of international petroleum prices, which had set in by 1982, also forced a reduction in government programs and expenditures. Economic conditions also suffered as the foreign debt grew, reaching some $35 billion by 1989, when major demonstrations protested the austerity program of a new government. By the mid-1990s, economic problems were even more serious, with the rates of unemployment and inflation the highest on the continent.

Notwithstanding such problems, the long-range outlook for the Venezuelan economy remains bright. Although traditional reserves of petroleum stand at some 18 billion barrels, exploration by the state-owned Petróleos de Venezuela is identifying additional subsoil deposits. More important, the vast Orinoco Tar Belt is in the early stage of exploitation. Although modern technology can presently recover only some 10 percent of this oil, advances can be expected to render a higher yield, and estimates of these deposits run from 700 billion to a staggering 2 trillion barrels. Given the impressive performance of the industry since nationalization in 1976, income from petroleum should remain substantial well into the twenty-first century. In the meantime, the wealth of other minerals and the fertility of the land provide further potential for the country. Thus, the long-range obstacles are constituted not by natural resources but by the underdevelopment of human capabilities.

Venezuela is not lacking in technicians and experts of great skill and sophistication, but the quantity of such personnel is wanting. Despite progress in recent years, the country still lacks sufficient managerial ability, technological competence, and labor productivity. Education, traditionally humanistic, has only belatedly turned toward scientific and technical fields. In a characteristic effort to ameliorate conditions through lavish government funding, the Pérez administration in 1974 created the Gran Mariscal de Ayacucho fellowships, whereby thousands were sent abroad for training in areas of critical need.

In neighboring Colombia, the predominant ethnic character is also mestizo. With the population low, now above 30 million, an estimated 20 percent is of European ancestry, with Indians and blacks together numbering no more than 5 percent. Over 60 percent of Colombians are now urban, and the urban growth rate is more than double that of the rural. Unlike many Latin American countries, the urban population is dispersed. Although metropolitan Bogotá is over 4 million, there are ten cities with more than 200,000 inhabitants. The ruggedly mountainous topography, with three Andean chains dividing Colombia into sometimes isolated valleys, has limited somewhat the physical mobility of the population. Regionalism has consequently been an enduring national phenomenon, one that until contemporary times retarded the growth of national consciousness and of socioeconomic integration. It has also slowed the modernization of class structures and the unifying of social attitudes and values.

Unlike Venezuela, Colombia retains a social structure heavily dependent upon Hispanic cultural traditions. Attitudes toward authority and religion are largely inflexible, and the improvement of transportation and communications has opened society only marginally. At the pinnacle stands an upper class erected on generations of intermarriage, economic cohesion, and shared values of political elitism. Kinship in the Hispanic Catholic tradition is deeply embedded in socioeconomic and political life, the upper class grudgingly permitting only those mild reforms necessary to maintain its hegemony. Such is the social-rank distinction between elites and masses that only limited mobility is available to the middle and lower sectors. Education and urban migration provide the more favorable avenues to self-advancement, yet the infrastructure is insufficient to respond to more than a small number. One-third of the children of primary school age never see the inside of a classroom. As migration from country to city has grown, unemployment has exceeded the growth of the urban labor sector, and increasing numbers live amid devastating slum conditions.

Since the early 1970s, industry has outstripped agriculture as the major sectoral contributor to the economy, although much of Colombia's wealth remains agricultural. Coffee has long stood as the foundation of the export trade, in recent years earning over half the country's legal foreign exchange. Much of the crop is produced by small independent farmers, although the owners of large plantations largely control its production and export. Most rural Colombians follow the traditional pattern of subsistence farming of food staples for local markets. Land distribution is still dominated by the large hacienda, while nearly one-third of the rural parcels are too small to be economically viable. Recent governments have achieved relative success in developing a variety of commodities for export, with the diversification reducing somewhat the past dependence on the international price of coffee. This trend has been accompanied by greater emphasis upon industrialization as a key to economic growth and modernization.

Manufacturing of consumer goods, notably food products and textiles, has strengthened the economic base. To this has been added the expansion of heavy industry, iron and steel in particular. Known deposits of minerals have increased, including largely untapped supplies of coal, the Cerro Matoso nickel reserves, and newly developed fields of petroleum and natural gas. Both the state-owned Empresa Colombiana de Petróleos and multinational corporations are increasing their explorations, suggesting the possibility that Colombia may become an exporter on a small scale. Not appearing in many official reports, but increasingly crucial to the economy, is the illicit trade in drugs, which has helped to swell Colombia's foreign exchange reserves to record highs.

In recent years, the major economic difficulties have been inflation and unemployment. The former has been running above 20 percent, and the flourishing drug traffic has now magnified the problem. The spiral of prices presses on the middle class, and many basic staples have been priced beyond the means of the poor. As capital-intensive industrialization continues to receive high priority from both public and private sectors, the workforce cannot fully absorb the swollen urban population. Rising foreign investment, encouraged by recent governments, contributes to overall economic growth but does not respond to the needs of the unemployed and underemployed. The contemporary Colombian profile therefore reveals a growing economy, increased fiscal reserves, expanding industry, and agricultural diversification— yet little of this progress benefits the bulk of the people or encourages social justice and individual mobility.

Ecuadoran society, as already noted, presents a sharp contrast to its neighbors because of its Indian component. Its population of some 12 million is divided almost equally between the coast and the highlands (*costa* and *sierra*). The regional contrasts are central to an understanding of Ecuador and are epitomized by the rivalry between the port city of Guayaquil and Quito, the highland capital. Its population having now reached 1 million, Guayaquil has been the center for banking, commercial, and export-import interests since the early 1900s. Despite massive unemployment, economic opportunities do exist for the poor, who can rise from the lower to the middle class. Elites have acquired their wealth in recent generations, and the basic outlook is sympathetic to modernization. There are linkages to the international system, and the cultural outlook on the coast is Western rather than Indian. There is a spirit of independence and individual freedom, which encourages social mobility, economic activity, and political volatility.

In the sierra, in contrast, the Indians live in accord with attitudes dating from colonial times. Indentured, at least until 1964, to the *hacendado,* many now divide their time between farming tiny, almost vertical plots and doing seasonal wage labor on coastal plantations. Others have joined the migration to crowded city slums and an urban subsistence existence. Unable to achieve mobility or improve their economic lot, the impoverished of the highlands remain tied to ancient values, dominated by traditional elites as deeply entrenched as those in Colombia, yet less enlightened socially. The expansion of highland industry has touched only lightly the lives of the masses, while conservatism and an affinity for the status quo endure. In the wake of expanded petroleum production since 1972, job opportunities have gradually expanded, but far too slowly to accommodate those flocking to the cities in the vain hope of an oil bonanza and its rewards. Although urbanization has come later and less dramatically than in Venezuela and Colombia, it has transformed Ecuadoran society from two-thirds rural in 1960 to over 50 percent urban today.

Ecuadoran economic structures have been predominantly agricultural. Cacao provided the first important export commodity late in the nineteenth century and continued to be an important export until being ravaged by witchbroom disease in the 1920s. Bananas, long a staple of the coastal economy, received a major government impetus after World War II. Acreage grew tenfold between 1948 and 1954, making Ecuador the world's leading banana exporter. This boom also was to ebb, and by the 1970s, the banana trade was characterized by the stagnation that existed for cacao, coffee, and sugar. Agricultural productivity has been slumping for years, and such basic commodities as milk, barley, and corn are periodically imported in order to compensate for inadequate domestic supplies. As the agricultural growth rate barely held even with population increase in the 1970s, the economy has rested primarily on increased earnings from petroleum.

After four decades of modest oil production, Ecuador contracted with a Texaco-Gulf consortium in 1964 to explore in the northeastern Amazonian area. Resultant discoveries led to the initiation in 1972 of what many anticipated would be an oil-induced "dance of the millions." A refinery was constructed, a pipeline laid across the Andes to the Pacific, and production facilities increased. In 1973, the government created the state-operated Corporación Estatal Petrolera Ecuatoriana (CEPE) and initiated its own participation in the industry. Joining OPEC the same year, Ecuador eventually raised production to over 350,000 barrels per day. By way of comparison, Venezuelan production is running slightly below 2 million barrels per day. Moreover, Ecuador's known reserves have been drawn down to slightly over 1 billion barrels.

Several years of nationalistic policies induced Gulf to withdraw, and Texaco has been reluctant to undertake any major exploration. With CEPE lacking much of the necessary technical expertise, the oil industry has therefore been stagnating. In the meantime, inflation has exceeded 20 percent, the price of foodstuffs has increased sharply, and the civilian government inaugurated in 1979 was forced to adopt unpopular austerity measures. Massive expenditures by the military rulers between 1972 and 1979 created additional burdens on the economy, generating the highest foreign debt in the country's history. As Ecuador passed through the 1980s, it was confronted by dwindling oil reserves, an expanded but inefficient industry, fiscal imbalances, an agricultural sector stubbornly resistant to stimulation and growth, and the same weakened petroleum market that was plaguing Venezuela. The Durán administration responded in the 1990s by reopening the petroleum industry to the multinational corporations and privatizing important sectors of CEPE.

GOVERNMENTAL AND POLITICAL DYNAMICS

The institutional profiles of the three governments bear much in common: a highly centralized system under which local and regional power is limited; a dominant executive with extensive constitutional and ad hoc authority; a vocal, even vociferous, legislature, which nonetheless is more often obstructive than constructive; a judiciary that exercises limited influence on national politics; and a vast array of state-related organs and agencies with responsibility extending into many areas of social and economic activity. From a less formal perspective, the political parties are central to the operation of the system, while ever sensitive to the views and interests of a politicized military. Major economic and commercial interests enjoy well-established access to the political leadership, generally espousing policies opposed by organized labor and by student activists. The role of the Church varies considerably in the region, as do the form and extent of popular participation in politics. In this latter regard, Venezuela stands out among the three.

Perhaps no other nation in Latin America enjoys the level of popular participation and the political centrality of organized mass-based parties that distinguish Venezuela. Beginning with the storied student uprising against the despotic Gómez by the generation of '28, young activists undertook a lengthy task of organization, from which came the Democratic Action Party under Rómulo Betancourt in 1941. It was during the AD-dominated *trienio* that the social Christian COPEI emerged under the guidance of Rafael Caldera. With the return to Venezuela of long-exiled party leaders in the wake of Pérez Jiménez's 1958 ouster, a concerted effort was concentrated upon the building of democracy and creation of a fully competitive party system. In the 1958 Pact of Punto Fijo, AD and COPEI were joined by the Democratic Republican Union (URD) of Jóvito Villalba in pledging civic collaboration as the means of nurturing the fledgling democratic system. The electoral victory of Betancourt and the AD led to a coalition government for five years. Although the URD withdrew in 1960, COPEI remained a staunch partner throughout Betancourt's term.

Despite episodic assaults by recalcitrant right-wing officers, an assassination attempt on Betancourt directed by the Dominican dictatorship, and both rural and urban terrorism from Cuban-inspired revolutionary leftists, the administration completed its term and transferred power to the AD's Raúl Leoni in 1964. Five years later, a division of AD opened the door to electoral victory for COPEI and Rafael Caldera. For the first time in Venezuelan history, a government party accepted defeat and transferred the reins of power to the opposition. As democratic practices and values grew more commonplace, the opposition party was to win elections in 1973, 1978, and 1983. Thus the AD under Carlos Andrés Pérez replaced Caldera, only to give way once again to COPEI when the latter won the presidency with Luis Herrera Campins in 1978. The AD regained the presidency in the elections of December 1983 with the victory of Jaime Lusinchi over Caldera. It retained office when Pérez won a second term in December 1988. After he was forced out in 1993, Venezuelan democratic traditions survived with the election of former president Rafael Caldera (now separated from COPEI).

The Venezuelan party system underwent marked change during these years. In 1958, there were only four organizations—AD, COPEI, URD, and the Communist Party of Venezuela (PCV). A proliferation of parties soon dotted the political landscape, however, reaching a zenith when twelve candidates contested the presidency in 1973. In popular reaction, the electorate that year cast 85 percent of the vote for the AD and COPEI candidates. Five years later, the percentage was 89, leaving the two parties virtually unchallenged. Given their organizational strength, wealth of leadership, rank-and-file support, and access to financial resources, the two parties appear likely to maintain their hegemony over the party system. The greatest threat would come from internal disunity or division, which only COPEI successfully avoided through the years. And even this was dissipated when party founder Rafael Caldera left after losing the 1988 presidential nomination, only to win the presidency five years later at the head of his personalistic, jerry-built Convergencia Nacional.

In addition to several small, personalistic, ad hoc organizations—"microparties" in the Venezuelan political vernacular—the country has seen the rise and fall of numerous organizations centered about popular independent leaders. None has won the presidency, but several have polled a large number of votes. Perhaps more important, the return to constitutionality of once-proscribed Marxist parties has produced a vigorous sector on the left of the political spectrum. Although the left consistently suffers from a lack of unity and incessant factional squabbling, the Movement to Socialism (MAS) appeared to be the major Marxist organization by the 1980s. Not yet capable of amassing 10 percent of the presidential vote, it has nonetheless won congressional seats, and it participates vigorously in congressional debate, where its votes are sometimes necessary to achieve a majority. It was also challenged in the early 1990s by the rise of Causa R, which sought to become the major voice of Venezuela's political left.

Organizational activity has been the hallmark of success for both AD and COPEI. Ceaselessly active on the local and regional levels, and deeply involved in the governing of the country, the parties have vigorously championed popular participation. Electoral turnout is consistently over 90 percent of the electorate, and survey data amply document the commitment of the people to democratic politics. At the same time, there is also evidence of disillusionment with party politicians and with government performance. The realization of economic democracy and social justice is a goal far more difficult to achieve than political democracy, and party leaders themselves recognize the increasing urgency of the challenge.

The potential for military intervention is ever present, notwithstanding over twenty years of judiciously sympathetic and cautious treatment by civilian leaders. The Herrera government, less skillful than its predecessors in this regard, was seriously threatened by military rebellion in mid-1979 and again in late 1980. Only the personal persuasiveness and moral authority of the two principal founders of the democratic system—Betancourt and Caldera—discouraged a military seizure of power; thus, the attitudes of the armed forces cannot be discounted. An increasingly professionalized officer corps, well educated and knowledgeable about socioeconomic policy matters, also expresses the popular disenchantment with a rise in corruption and public immorality. Betancourt himself, who died in September 1981, spoke out forthrightly on the subject. As a consequence, the survival of the present democracy cannot be assumed, notwithstanding its accomplishments since 1958 and the strength of civic approval. Two attempted military *golpes* against the government in 1992 reminded Venezuelans not to assume that the armed forces were untouched by internal economic and social problems.

Colombia's democracy is qualitatively different from that of its neighbor. Characterized by Alexander Wilde as an oligarchical conversation among gentlemen, it is a system built upon a tradition of political compromise devoted to maintenance of elitist control. Resurrected by Conservative and Liberal leaders in response to *la violencia* and to the military incursion under Rojas Pinilla, the system sought to restore oligarchical hegemony through a collaborative sharing of power. The Liberal Alberto Lleras Camargo, an architect of the system and the first of its presidents (1958–1962), viewed Colombia as insufficiently mature to enjoy truly competitive democracy. Thus, a sixteen-year period would be required to reunify the republic, modernize the economy, and consolidate the attitudes and practices requisite for constructive partisan competition. For critics, the National Front also provided the vehicle for a solidification of control by the upper bourgeoisie while clouding the lack of meaningful difference between Conservative and Liberal leaders.

Unlike Venezuela's, the Colombian system more closely approaches the two-party model. Although third parties have appeared periodically, none has survived, and the Marxist left is severely divided among its several contending groups. More important has been a tendency toward factionalism within the two major parties since the introduction of the National Front. With interparty competition effectively stifled from 1958 to 1974 by the front arrangement, competition turned inward for both Conservatives and Liberals. More often reflecting rival personal ambitions than genuine policy disagreements, it has continued to be waged among members and/or representatives of the traditional Colombian elites. Rare indeed have been popular leaders of the masses, such as Gaitán during an earlier era.

Contrary to early predictions, the National Front ran its entire course. The Conservatives' Guillermo León Valencia served as president from 1962 to 1966, the Liberals' Carlos Lleras Restrepo from 1966 to 1970, and Misael Pastrana for the

Conservatives from 1970 to 1974. Legislative bodies remained equally divided between the parties, as were the cabinet and other high administrative posts. The front officially ended with the August 1974 inauguration of the Liberal Alfonso López Michelsen, who polled 56 percent of the vote in the first competitive elections in more than a quarter century. Yet López maintained virtual parity between the two parties throughout his term, as did Liberal Julio César Turbay Ayala, who was elected in 1978. The same pattern was also followed by the first two presidents of the 1990s, César Gaviria and Ernesto Samper.

The party system nonetheless seems likely to continue the emphasis on compromise and collaboration. Internal disunity still plagues both parties, as former presidents, ex-candidates, and would-be aspirants divide into personalistic cabals linked by family, business, and social ties. At the same time, neither Conservatives nor Liberals are mass based in organizational dimensions comparable to those of the Venezuelan system. On the other hand, family allegiances to one or the other party are often permanent, dating back for generations. Yet the constant recruitment and proselytizing found in Venezuela are more the exception than the rule in Colombia. Policy differences are now modest at best, as the historic issues that divided Conservatives and Liberals in the nineteenth and early twentieth centuries have dissipated.

A by-product of the party system and its performance is a profound dissatisfaction on the part of the citizenry. Voter abstention during the years of the National Front was usually more than 50 percent of the eligible population, prompting the explanation that the lack of meaningful competition discouraged the voter from casting a ballot. Since 1974, the figure has not increased markedly, however, suggesting that the negativism reported in public opinion surveys has not been mitigated by recent events. With grassroots preferences frequently ignored by the party elites, decisions about candidates and presidential aspirants reflect the inner dynamics of leadership circles rather than mass support. Thus, the system remains faithful to the intentions and interests of the oligarchy.

Developments since the late 1970s further diminished the extent of popular support. The congenital lawlessness in urban areas, combined with sporadic if small-scale guerrilla activity in the countryside, has enforced a climate in which civil liberties and freedoms do not engender a sense of personal security. Wealthy businessmen live behind high walls, travel to work with bodyguards, and fear for their safety; for the masses, crime is an everyday peril. Underworld activity linked to the drug traffic has aggravated the situation, and state security forces are increasingly active. Although the armed forces have shown little present inclination to seize power, they have exerted strong pressure for repressive powers while frequently violating individual freedoms in the pursuit of guerrillas and leftists.

President Betancur sought, with some success, to reverse the trend toward polarization and to interrupt the cycle of escalating insurgency and repression. After ending the state of siege in 1982, he granted amnesty to political prisoners and to the active guerrillas who would lay down their arms. To the surprise of most observers, many accepted the offer. Unlike its predecessors, the Betancur government stressed respect for human rights. It also launched investigations into the fate of the "disappeared" and into the activities of right-wing death squads. The progress achieved by Betancur, however, proved temporary, and under Barco the level of violence again escalated. In 1989 the drug lords assassinated the Liberal Party's presidential candidate, who had pledged a campaign against them. Since that time, increasingly determined government action has resulted in the capture of leaders of both the Medellín and Cali cartels. However, the so-called drug war continues, while President Ernesto Samper was deeply involved in charges that his 1994 presidential campaign had been corrupted by drug money.

If Colombian democracy is portrayed as a structured manifestation of oligarchical control, that of Ecuador is still more artificial. Jaime Roldós Aguilera, the first elected president in a decade, said that his country has never experienced true popular democracy. Rather, it has been merely formalistic at best, honoring appearances rather than substance. Such had been the case when three consecutive elected governments held office from 1948 to 1960. The facade of democracy was stripped away by the events of succeeding years. Only Velasco won national elections (1960 and 1968)—failing to complete either term—until the restoration of constitutional government under Roldós in 1979. The armed forces remained the ultimate political authority, twice assuming direct government responsibility (1963–1966 and 1972–1979). And whether the regime was military or civilian, traditional socioeconomic elites continued to wield decisive influence on policymaking.

While the clash for power between the coastal oligarchy and dominant highland interests continued unabated, the armed forces departed from their usual role as constitutional arbiter to undertake a remolding of development policies. The effectiveness of military rule, however, was severely constrained by a lack of internal unity and by disagreement over procedures and objectives. The 1963–1966 military junta adopted certain moderate reformist policies, including Ecuador's first agrarian reform. At the same time, it was incapable of resisting the pressures from traditional economic elites and exhibited virtual paranoia over alleged threats from the left. Repression of opposition and extreme sensitivity to criticism created a climate of popular resentment, which ultimately led the junta to despair of its task and to resign in frustration.

When the military terminated the fifth Velasco government in 1972 and resumed power, General Guillermo Rodríguez Lara characterized the new regime as "revolutionary and nationalist." For two years, the so-called *peruanista* reformist elements held the upper hand, and although there was more rhetoric than substance to the government, nationalistic interests were sometimes promoted. With petroleum becoming the prime source of economic strength, the minister of natural resources, Vice-Admiral Gustavo Jarrín Ampudia, devised a vigorously independent policy. Contracts were renegotiated with multinational corporations on relatively more favorable terms; the state petroleum agency, CEPE, was created; and Ecuador became a member of OPEC. Official decrees pledged more favorable treatment to the agricultural worker, and commitments to amelioration of social injustices were extended. Organized labor for a time supported the regime, and even the Communist Party offered guarded approval.

The military had never reached consensus on the nationalistic approach, however, and hard-line *brasileño* officers stiffened their resistance. By 1974, the balance of power within the leadership had shifted. General Rodríguez deftly responded to the pressures, policy emphases were revised, and such figures as Jarrín were forced out of government. As popular sympathies waned and official repression became more pronounced, traditionalist officers secured the resignation of Rodríguez in January 1976, established a three-man Council of Government, and announced the intention of restoring constitutional government and withdrawing to the barracks. The agonizingly slow and complex process took a total of forty-three months, during which the military remained divided over the desirability of yielding power. It was the continuing disunity within the armed forces that ultimately permitted the inauguration of Roldós, whose candidacy had been at best unpopular with the military.

As civilian forces reorganized for electoral competition beginning in 1976, the party system remained disorganized and fragmented. The single party with significant popular support was the Confederation of Popular Forces (CFP), led by its irascible, autocratic, and impetuously demagogic *caudillo* Asaad Bucaram. Atypical of Ecuadoran political leaders, he was a largely self-educated man of modest origins whose parents had immigrated from Lebanon. Mistrusted for his unpredictability and scorned for his humble background, Bucaram was anathema to both civilian and military leaders. When his presidential candidacy was barred on a specious legal technicality, Bucaram chose the party's leading thinker and political tactician—and also the husband of his niece—Roldós. Following a national plebiscite to choose a new constitution, Roldós unexpectedly won a six-candidate race by polling 29 percent of the vote. In the subsequent runoff against the rightist Sixto Durán Ballén, he won by 69 percent, while the CFP also led the congressional race.

Representing a new generation of political leadership, the thirty-seven-year-old Roldós worked closely with his electoral allies, Popular Democracy. This Christian democratic force under Vice-President Osvaldo Hurtado provided effective support in seeking to realize campaign promises of economic progress and social reform. The outbreak of border conflict with Peru in early 1981 was followed in May by the death of Roldós in a plane crash. His Christian democratic vice-president succeeded to power and attempted to maintain legitimacy while pursuing Roldós's reformist objectives. In the meantime, it is significant that in the 1980s past leaders and parties were displaced by a younger generation.

The presidential elections of January 1984 saw two candidates emerge from the pack and pull ahead in a close and indecisive race. They were Rodrigo Borja of the Democratic Left (ID), a relatively new but rapidly growing party having philosophical and organizational links to European socialists and social democrats, and León Febres Cordero, a leader of populistic style and liberal, laissez-faire economic persuasion whose vehicle is the conservative Social Christian Party. As neither candidate won an absolute majority of the vote, the two front-runners competed in a runoff election in May. The winner was Febres Cordero.

The next four years proved hectic as the fiery Febres undertook free-market policies in vigorous but erratic fashion. Despite early successes, the economy soon worsened. Official corruption and ineffective policymaking combined with declining oil prices and a costly earthquake to wreck government plans. The atmosphere was worsened by presidential scorn for the rights of the opposition, while meddling with the military provoked both an attempted *golpe de estado* and, in 1987, a brief kidnapping of Febres by Air Force commandos. Leaving office on a wave of unpopularity, he also assured a weak showing by conservative forces in the 1988 elections. The victor was Rodrigo Borja of the Izquierda Democrática, or Democratic Left. Borja's social democratic government was confronted by a large foreign debt, an ailing economy, and the unenviable necessity of applying stringent austerity measures. Thus he was frustrated in carrying out intended reforms. The election of Sixto Durán Ballén in 1992 brought to office a former Febres ally and previous presidential candidate. The grandfatherly Durán presided loosely over an administration committed to neoliberal policies, and these were to continue until the August 1996 inauguration of the populist Abdalá Bucaram. A popular protest movement in February 1997 led to his forced resignation. Fabián Alarcón, the president of Congress, was named interim president until the May 1998 elections.

FOREIGN RELATIONS

The three republics have not historically been hemispheric leaders, although Colombian diplomats have long enjoyed a reputation for professionalism. In more recent years, however, their presence in inter-American circles has been increasingly noticeable. The prestige of democratic regimes, the collective ambitions of the Andean Pact, and a greater concern about international relationships have all encouraged heightened activity in foreign affairs. This situation is particularly true in Venezuela, with its wealth of petrodollars providing economic legitimacy to its energetic initiatives. During the earlier years of its democratic period, Venezuela under Betancourt and Leoni established its credentials as a staunch bastion of liberty in the conflict with authoritarianism of both right and left. By the beginning of the 1970s, the internationally minded Caldera had extended Venezuelan influence through his own hemispheric stature as guided by Christian democratic principles. When Pérez took office at the time of soaring oil prices, the nation's role was even further enhanced.

In conjunction with Mexican president Luis Echeverría, Pérez championed creation of the Latin American Economic System (SELA), with its seat located in Caracas. The windfall of profits from petroleum permitted contributions of $500 million each to the World Bank, the Inter-American Development Bank, and the International Monetary Fund; $60 million to the Andean Development Corporation; and $25 million to the Caribbean Development Bank. There was a flurry of activity in the Caribbean, including major impetus in the elaboration of trade and economic agreements with newly independent English-speaking countries. As private interests followed increased government investment, some people even charged Venezuela with launching a new imperialist campaign toward the islands—most notably Trinidad and Tobago's Prime Minister Eric Williams.

Luis Herrera Campins maintained Venezuela's high profile. His Christian democratic government did not continue the uncritical Pérez approval of Nicaragua's Sandinistas; it provided instead strong encouragement to the much criticized junta in embattled El Salvador. Despite the deterioration of the Salvadoran situation and charges that Venezuela was acting in part as surrogate for the United States, the Herrera government continued with both moral and material support. It worked sympathetically with the quasi-Christian democratic Costa Rican government and in 1980, joined with Mexico in a plan to supply oil at less than market price to Central American and selected Caribbean countries. Venezuelan anger at the United States over the latter's position toward the Malvinas/Falklands conflict in 1982, however, stimulated a rethinking of policy in Caracas. Since then, on Central American and other issues, Venezuela has been disinclined to follow the lead of the United States. With the 1989 return to power of Carlos Andrés Pérez, moreover, Venezuela swiftly assumed a position of leadership among the Latin American democracies. This was seriously weakened, however, with the advent of domestic political crises in the 1990s.

Notwithstanding its hemispheric visibility, Venezuela has yet to resolve basic disputes with its neighbors. To the east, the border disagreement with Guyana, reopened by Betancourt in 1962, continues to resist resolution despite periodic negotiation. The relationship with Colombia is also still marred by multiple disputes. The estimated annual toll of 200,000–300,000 head of cattle smuggled into Venezuela has continued. More seriously, the migration of illegal Colombians in search of Venezuelan employment and wages unavailable at home had become a growing problem to the Caracas government by the 1980s. Reliable figures do not exist, but 2 million to 3 million *indocumentados* ("undocumented workers") are estimated to be living in Venezuela. Equally grave is the contested Gulf of Venezuela boundary, lying as it does in an area of offshore oil deposits. A series of border incidents in 1995, in which Colombian guerrillas were involved, worsened relations between the two nations, although their trade has increased greatly following a series of reciprocal trade arrangements.

Colombia in part has shared recent Venezuelan efforts to promote and encourage democracy and civilian government, although at a reduced level of commitment. The government concurred with Pérez's efforts on behalf of the canal treaty negotiations between Panama and the United States and also favored the overthrow of the Somoza dictatorship in Nicaragua. Through the Andean Pact, it expressed opposition to the military disruption of the electoral process in Bolivia in mid-1980. Greater attention, however, centered on continued haggling with the United States over the drug traffic. North American charges that the Colombian government was unconcerned were met with the retort that the thriving demand in the United States bore primary responsibility. Disturbed by the charges of drug lord contributions to the Samper presidential campaign, the Clinton administration decertified Colombia in early 1996, threatening disruption of trade and aid.

When Ecuador returned to democratic rule in 1979, Jaime Roldós stressed the importance of hemispheric freedom and elected government. His championing of such principles as a manifestation of national sovereignty was overshadowed in early 1981 by the unexpected renewal of border hostilities between Ecuador and Peru. Vice-President Osvaldo Hurtado followed the same patterns during his portion of the constitutional term, but León Febres Cordero shifted emphases through his pronounced friendship with Ronald Reagan. Rodrigo Borja pulled back from Washington's embrace, but both of his successors courted the United States assiduously. This remained the case following the renewal of border clashes with Peru in 1995 over the long-unresolved conflict.

SUGGESTED READINGS

Baloyra, Enrique A., and John D. Martz. *Political Attitudes in Venezuela: Societal Cleavages & Political Opinion.* Austin: University of Texas Press, 1979. The second of two volumes on Venezuelan mobilization and political attitudes; based on extensive survey data.

Berry, R. Albert, Ronald G. Hellman, and Mauricio Solaún, eds. *Politics of Compromise: Coalition Government in Colombia.* New Brunswick, N.J.: Transaction Books, for the Center for Inter-American Relations, 1980. A multiauthored review based on a conference discussing recent and contemporary events in Colombia.

Conaghan, Catherine A. *Restructuring Domination: Industrialists and the State in Ecuador.* Pittsburgh: University of Pittsburgh Press, 1988. Examines Ecuador's industrialists within the context of national development.

Dix, Robert H. *Colombia: The Political Dimensions of Change.* New Haven: Yale University Press, 1967. Although dated, this analysis is still rich in historicopolitical patterns.

_____. *The Politics of Colombia.* New York: Praeger, 1987. An insightful reinterpretation twenty years after his earlier book, again stressing political factors.

Fitch, John Samuel. *The Military Coup d'Etat as a Political Process: Ecuador, 1948–1966.* Baltimore: Johns Hopkins University Press, 1977. An excellent and well-documented study of the armed forces that ties their role to the evolution of contemporary Ecuadoran politics.

Gil Yepes, José Antonio. *The Challenge of Venezuelan Democracy.* Trans. by Evelyn Harrison I., Lolo Gil de Yanes, and Danielle Salti. New Brunswick, N.J.: Transaction Books, 1981. The work of a Venezuelan sociologist that builds on the literature of administrative decision-making in studying the Venezuelan business sector and its impact on national politics.

Hartlyn, Jonathan. *The Politics of Coalition Rule in Colombia.* Cambridge: Cambridge University Press, 1988. A careful study that stresses both formal and informal aspects of two-party collaboration.

Herman, Donald L. *Christian Democracy in Venezuela.* Chapel Hill: University of North Carolina Press, 1980. A detailed treatment of COPEI through the Caldera administration and including the 1978 election of Luis Herrera Campins.

_____, ed. *Democracy in Latin America: Colombia and Venezuela.* New York: Praeger, 1988. Well-known authorities on both countries collaborated for this comparative study.

Hurtado, Osvaldo. *Political Power in Ecuador.* Trans. by Nick D. Mills, Jr. Albuquerque: University of New Mexico Press, 1980. Historical and sociological analysis of Ecuadoran politics by the subsequent president of the republic. The book includes a brief epilogue discussing the withdrawal of the military and the 1979 Roldós-Hurtado victory.

Martz, John D. *Acción Democrática: Evolution of a Modern Political Party in Venezuela.* Princeton: Princeton University Press, 1966. A detailed study of Venezuela's original mass-based party; includes attention to the genesis and emergence of the party system.

_____. *Ecuador: Conflicting Political Cultures and the Quest for Progress.* Boston: Allyn and Bacon, 1972. Now dated, but the first political overview of Ecuador in over two decades.

_____. *The Politics of Petroleum in Ecuador.* New Brunswick, N.J.: Transaction Press, 1987. Contrasts in policymaking characteristics of respective military and civilian regimes over the past two decades, especially as regards petroleum. Also incorporates extensive treatment of parties and elections.

_____. *The Politics of Clientelism in Colombia: Democracy and the State.* New Brunswick, N.J.: Transaction Press, 1996. An extended analysis of national politics over the past four decades.

Martz, John D., and David J. Myers, eds. *Venezuela: The Democratic Experience.* 2d ed. New York: Praeger Publishers, 1986. A multiauthored work examining major aspects of Venezuelan politics and economy.

Schodt, David W. *Ecuador: An Andean Enigma.* Boulder, Colo.: Westview Press, 1987. A succinct review by a knowledgeable political economist.

25
PERU AND BOLIVIA

JOSÉ Z. GARCÍA

The widest, most massive chunk of the Andean Cordillera straddles the boundary between southeastern Peru and northwestern Bolivia. In this region, on a huge plain the size of Colorado and about 12,000 ft high, surrounded by high mountains and punctuated by steep valleys, lies the Altiplano, the cultural core of both countries. The ruggedness of the Andean terrain makes communication and transportation difficult, a factor that for many centuries gave rise to the development of powerful regional jealousies. When combined with ethnic and linguistic diversity, this has made social unification difficult, especially across linguistic boundary lines. Only extremely well organized societies have been able to govern diverse populations in the Altiplano. Nevertheless, some of the most advanced civilizations in the Western Hemisphere—the Tiahuanaco, the Aymara, and finally, the Inca—forged empires over the disparate tribes that populated the area long before the arrival of Spaniards. The descendants of these tribes still deeply influence the ethnic, linguistic, and political makeup of both Peru and Bolivia.

The Spaniards captured the Incan Empire by destroying the royal family and its institutions in a process that was completed in four decades. By then, diseases imported from Europe and the psychological damage associated with defeat and enslavement had shrunk the native population, as in Mexico, by 90 percent. A complex, multilayered caste system, in which indigenous communities provided what amounted to slave labor for white masters, replaced local social and political organizations. This, in turn, led to a rapid destruction of indigenous cultural production. A magnificent tradition of artistic pottery production—Nazca, Chavin, Mochica, and Chimu, to name only a few examples—was diminished within a half century after conquest to a pitiful, shriveled parody of what it had once been, even though major indigenous language groups, and hence cultural remnants, survived.

Today, nearly two centuries after the end of the Spanish Empire, the failure of the Bolivian and, especially, Peruvian states to forge viable national cross-ethnic identities or interethnic alliances has encouraged nonstate, antistate, and transnational actors, such as guerrilla groups, drug merchants, indigenous ethnic associations, and transnational members of the "informal sector" of the economy, to compete for the loyalties of large portions of the population. This situation has greatly weakened the effectiveness of the state to govern outside a rather narrowly defined coalition of social and economic interests. In Bolivia, the Revolution of 1952 gave full citizenship rights to Indians and also provided an institutional framework for indigenous people to compete for access to government support. Since 1985, however, new political coalitions and ideologies have rendered these institutions less effective, leaving large portions of the population relatively more adrift than before and forcing many into the transnational "informal" (contraband trade) or "black" (drug) economies. In Peru, the failure to create a positive national identity for millions of indigenous people in cultural transition during the past few decades has left the society vulnerable to many kinds of social tensions, reflected in two full-fledged guerrilla movements, an expanded indigenous movement, severe economic contraction, internal divisions over control of coca production, and soaring crime rates. While these ills cannot be attributed solely to questions of internal identity, it is difficult to imagine successful resolution until fundamental issues of national integration are addressed.

HISTORICAL SKETCH OF BOLIVIA: FROM CONQUEST TO THE END OF THE CHACO WAR

Early in the conquest, Spaniards distinguished between what they called Upper Peru, or Charcas, roughly the area now comprising Bolivia, and Lower Peru, site of contemporary Peru. Upper Peru (Bolivia) was subordinated to governments in Lower Peru throughout the colonial period, although geographic isolation permitted considerable autonomy for Upper Peru. In 1545 a phenomenal silver deposit was discovered at Potosí, the exploitation of which transformed Chuquisaca (today Sucre), capital of Charcas, and Potosí, the site of the mines, into some of the richest cities in the world. Although these cities developed an outstanding tradition of colonial religious painting and two superb universities during the sixteenth and seventeenth centuries, the wealth that made these possible flowed from the forced labor of indigenous populations. Silver production gradually declined because of rising import costs (especially mercury) essential to mining operations, periodic weaknesses in the international silver market, and depletion of silver supplies. By the early nineteenth century, the cycle was reversed and Bolivia was one of the poorest areas in Latin America.

When independence came to the region in 1825, the Bolivian state was created in part as a buffer between Peru and Argentina, to separate what were believed to be two emerging regional powers. As traditional trade routes were severed by the independence movement, the mining industry nearly collapsed. The decline in silver produced a shift in power away from silver producers, who had dominated political life for centuries, to a landed aristocracy. As land became more valuable, the state began to take measures to acquire land owned by nonprivate holders. First the government confiscated Church-owned lands, which were sold or rented for the state. Then the government began to confiscate communal lands—some held by Indian communities from the time of the conquest—forcing Indian residents to purchase individual plots and destroying part of the foundation of Indian society. Many peasants were reduced to semiserf status. Mariano Melgarejo, a *caudillo* who ruled from 1862 to 1871, abrogated land titles of more than 100,000 peasants, about 10 percent of the Bolivian population.

Melgarejo is also known in Bolivian history as the ruler who sold the country to the highest bidder. Within a few decades after independence, Bolivia had lost one-half of its territory to its neighbors: Brazil, Argentina, Chile, Peru, and later, Paraguay. Melgarejo ceded territory to Brazil in 1867 for questionable commercial advantages; a war with Brazil in 1903 resulted in further losses of land. In 1879 Chile occupied Bolivia's small coastal strip on the Pacific Ocean between Peru and Chile. Bolivia, with the support of Peru, declared war against Chile. In 1884 a truce was declared. Bolivia lost its coastland and has been landlocked ever since, a fact Bolivians have never fully accepted and which creates a potential vulnerability in international trade.

Bolivia's economy was revived during the 1870s with the discovery of huge tin deposits near the old silver mines. Tin prices remained high on world markets for several decades thereafter. Wealth generated by large-scale tin mining paid for the repair of silver mines and for the modernization of the country as a whole. Three new railroad lines were built, which connected Bolivia with the rest of the world for the first time, and highways integrated large areas of the country. A new era of prosperity began.

The tin boom forced the landed aristocracy to share power once again with mineral entrepreneurs. In short order, three families—Patiño, Hochschild, and Aramayo—emerged to monopolize most of the booming tin-mining industry. These powerful families encouraged the development of a professional army and a middle class to improve the government bureaucracy after decades of neglect. University students, eager to join these rising groups, began to organize for the first time as a political force. Traditional silver-mining interests also organized and formed a conservative political party. The landed aristocracy maintained its position. In short, a powerful set of new economic elites was emerging while, at the same time, several soon-to-be-powerful middle-sector groups were expanding and gaining strength.

Although competition for the presidency remained intense and sometimes violent during this period, there was widespread agreement on economic policy, which remained remarkably consistent. The middle class prospered with the boom in tin, which paid for contracts to build railroads, highways, and other infrastructural projects that required an increase in the national stock of professional skills. Government policy encouraged middle-class education and paid for development projects. Serious structural problems in the political system, however, began to emerge. These had to do with the impact of Bolivia's dependence on the world market price of tin and on the relationship between the upper and middle classes on the one hand and the middle and lower classes on the other.

During periods when the price of tin dropped severely on the world market, the shrinking revenue base was felt most markedly by the middle classes, as government and owners adjusted downward. The middle classes, however, had tasted power through their shared control of military, financial, and bureaucratic institutions. They were unlikely passively to accept high rates of unemployment or drastically lowered status during periods of economic bust. But they could maintain their social and economic position during a depression only if they could acquire control of the private-sector mining revenues through outright confiscation or seize more control over the government's ability to tax the rich. Thus, the mutual dependence of upper and middle classes on a commodity with unstable prices created a strong potential tension between the two.

When the poor began to organize, with strong middle-class assistance after the Great Depression and after the Chaco War with Paraguay (1932–1935), the instrument for middle-class acquisition of the major economic enterprises through the state was created. If the tin-mining enterprises provided a potential economic base for the middle-classes, the organization of the lower classes gave them the potential power to acquire it. The alliance forged between certain sectors of the working and middle classes, consummated in 1952, would produce one of the few social revolutions in Latin American history.

HISTORICAL SKETCH OF PERU: FROM COLONIAL RULE TO THE GUANO BOOM

The Spanish located Peru's capital city, Lima, on the coast. Lima's port, Callao, became one of the two primary ports in the Americas (the other was Veracruz, in Mexico) to which trade with Spain was directed. The relative frequency of contact with the outside world, the relative wealth of the area (some of which was generated in the administratively subordinate region of Upper Peru), and the opportunities provided by the strategic and administrative importance of the city combined to make Lima and its neighboring valleys and mountains a prestigious area for permanent settlement by large numbers of Spaniards. The Upper Peruvian economy, on the other hand—based on extraction of minerals, at high altitudes, through forced labor of Indians—caused Bolivia to become an exploitation colony. Relatively few Spaniards considered Bolivia a permanent place of residence, and Spain paid little attention to the development there of autonomous and resilient civil institutions. In Peru, in contrast, a settlement colony developed, based on landownership. Black slaves were imported to work coastal and sierra estates, and a diversified economy emerged with adaptable institutions and endless bureaucratic controls to ensure a multilayered caste system roughly based on skin color. Peru's institutions were therefore more robust, with a conservative strain that persists today. By the seventeenth century, Peru had a thriving economy, producing local wines, olives, sugar, rice, wheat, livestock, cotton, and wool and had simple manufacturing, some mining, and a brisk trade with Spain. The aristocracy was cosmopolitan in outlook and extremely self-assured. Bolivia remained tied to mineral production, its inhabitants subject to the vagaries of boom or bust.

By the end of the eighteenth century, immigration to Peru had reduced the Indian proportion to less than 60 percent of the total population of around 1 million, with whites, blacks, and "half-castes" accounting for the remainder. Since nearly half the white population lived in three main cities (Lima, Cuzco, and Arequipa), Indians vastly outnumbered whites in rural areas, and their treatment varied considerably. A major Indian rebellion led by Tupac Amaru, a descendant of the Inca royal family, lasted for nearly two years, with much bloodshed, before it was put down. Thereafter, in spite of halfhearted reforms designed to reduce the threat of further violence, the imperial hold over the native population began to weaken, in part because of a gradual decline in Spain itself. Peru's internal institutional fabric, however, was so strong and conservative that Peruvians accepted independence rather reluctantly, after José de San Martín, an Argentinean, wrested control from Spanish royalists with the aid of Simón Bolívar and Antonio José de Sucre, both Venezuelans, during the early 1820s. For the next two decades, Peru was wracked by bloody civil wars and power struggles, the unfortunate legacy of an independence movement with few internal roots.

The chaos produced by the sudden amputation of economic, social, and political relations between Peru and Spain ended abruptly with the growth of the guano trade at mid-century. Bird droppings discovered in large quantities on islands off the coast were found to be superior as fertilizer. Guano was shipped throughout the world from these islands. The government handled the guano trade as a state monopoly. Revenues from these exports financed the modernization of the state bureaucracy and infrastructural improvements for the city of Lima.

TWENTIETH-CENTURY POLITICAL DYNAMICS: APRA IN PERU AND THE BOLIVIAN REVOLUTION OF 1952

The Rise and Fall of APRA in Peru

Later in the nineteenth century, a handful of families began acquiring large tracts of land in the northern coastal valleys of Peru, converting these into sugar plantations with refining mills. Very quickly these families, in alliance with older, more traditional sierra hacienda owners, began to dominate the political, social, and economic life of the country. The way in which the sugar plantation owners acquired their land had profound consequences for the Peruvian political system.

Wealthy entrepreneurs bought out large numbers of middle-class landowners, often using deceptive means and questionable legal tactics. Their aggressiveness and often ruthless style caused considerable disgruntlement among the middle-class owners who suddenly found their power and status fading. By 1923 a young north coast intellectual, Víctor Raúl Haya de la Torre, channeled the discontent festering in the north to forge an alliance between frustrated northerners and young middle-class university students and labor union members in Lima. Within a decade, the American Popular Revolutionary Alliance (APRA) founded by Haya was the largest in Peru. APRA combined an anti-imperialist ideology with grassroots organization of trade unions. The anti-imperialism of APRA responded to growing nationalist sentiment among middle classes in Peru. After all, most mining interests in Peru were foreign. Guano prices had long been dictated by a take-it-or-leave-it attitude on the part of foreign contractors. Foreign capital had assisted in the consolidation of sugar plantations in the north. Some of the growing manufacturing industries were controlled by foreigners. The organizational genius of Haya lay in his ability to merge various types of discontent into the first mass political party in Latin American history. Other leftist intellectuals in Peru, such as Carlos Mariátegui, stressed the need to adapt Marxism to the ethnic realities of Peru. As he saw it, discrimination against Indians—at that time a majority population heavily engaged in (precapitalist) peasant activities—in a society with only a weak industrial base required modification of traditional Marxist strategies for gaining power; he emphasized raising Indian consciousness. But his appeal was intellectual, hence limited. Meanwhile, Haya was building a non-Indian-based, multiclass urban organization with strong political capabilities.

As APRA became increasingly powerful, traditional upper-class parties took steps to prevent its leaders from gaining power. The party was outlawed, its leaders exiled. But it continued to organize urban masses and succeeded in infiltrating portions of the armed forces. Pro-APRA and anti-APRA officers contended for power within the military. For more than three decades (late 1930s to late 1960s), national politics was dominated by this power struggle, with anti-APRA officers usually victorious. In 1948 a failed APRA conspiracy to overthrow a conservative government resulted in an eight-year military dictatorship by General Manuel Odría, a period in which APRA moderated its program while younger military officers began playing increasingly important roles in government. In 1962 the high command of the armed forces prevented Odría, by then retired, from becoming president, in part because his election depended on an alliance with APRA. After a year of military government, a reformist, Fernando Belaúnde, became president through elections in 1963.

By the late 1960s, a small but powerful sector within the armed forces had come to accept much of the philosophy of the earlier, more radical APRA. The APRA, in turn, had lost a good deal of dynamism, struggling more to win votes without offending the entrenched oligarchy and military than to fight without power for the masses. The radical officers in 1968 were able to take advantage of a corruption scandal near the end of Belaúnde's term to overthrow him and, in an ironic reversal, implement much of the original APRA program that the military had blocked in years past. One of the first steps the officers took was to nationalize the sugar plantations of the north coast, resolving a long-festering problem that had stimulated the creation of APRA in the first place. APRA leaders, who had become more conservative than their military governors, spent the next few years observing the armed forces adopt their former program.

The Rise and Fall of the Bolivian Revolution of 1952

Most countries in Latin America suffered severely throughout the Great Depression, and Bolivia was no exception. The added factor of the Chaco War with Paraguay, which Bolivia lost, culminated in 1952 in the rise to power of a civil-military movement that would affect Bolivian politics for the remainder of the century.

Conservative president Daniel Salamanca began building a powerful army during the depression, at the expense of other government services. During a border skirmish in the disputed Chaco border region, Salamanca ordered his army to invade Paraguayan territory—even though his military advisers warned that such a move would have disastrous consequences. Paraguay mobilized fully and eventually invaded Bolivian territory and routed its army. A peace treaty was signed in 1935, in which Bolivian territory in the Chaco was ceded to Paraguay.

Several groups were embittered by this experience. The officer corps were outraged that a civilian president had instigated an unwinnable war on an unprepared military. For two decades, military officers dominated politics. In addition, the war effort mobilized more than 10 percent of the population of Bolivia, at that time one of the least mobilized countries in Latin America. Groups that most directly participated in the war—Indian and mestizo peasants and labor union members—played major political roles in the country's politics thereafter. The organization of the Chaco War army into three castes—white officers, mestizo subofficers, and Indian soldiers—would further create caste and class consciousness as it became known that Indians suffered most of the casualties. Finally, a hitherto largely ineffectual left-wing intellectual group galvanized the general outrage against the political system that had produced needless destruction and defeat. Its goal was to undo the power relations of the previous half century.

From the end of the Chaco War to 1939, young military officers destroyed the political system that emerged from the tin boom of 1880. Standard Oil Company was nationalized without compensation, the first such confiscation in Latin American history. An interventionist constitutional convention created an activist state for the first time. A far-reaching labor code, favorable to the laboring classes, was written. Large mining concerns were required to turn over their foreign exchange to the national bank, which could then tax corporations more effectively. The mines themselves, however, were not nationalized, and a period of political uncertainty followed until 1952.

ORIGINS OF THE MNR IN BOLIVIA

As a result of the social ferment that followed the Chaco War, several new political parties were formed, including three socialist parties and two pro-fascist parties, all responding to middle-class interests. The most talented leadership came from the National Revolutionary Movement (MNR), initially a fascist party. The leader of the MNR, Víctor Paz Estenssoro, was also highly pragmatic. He allied himself with the leader of the Trotskyist party, Juan Lechín, who had organized mine workers into a powerful force. The MNR did not come to power until several successive presidents tried in vain to consolidate the reforms of the late 1930s. The party finally experienced a period of co-government with a young military officer, Major Gualberto Villarroel, who took over in a military coup in 1943 and combined reformism (he encouraged unionization of tin miners) with brutal repression. Villarroel was murdered, burned, and hanged from a lamppost by an angry mob in 1946. Six years of conservative government followed, during which Paz Estenssoro was exiled to Argentina. In 1952, after years of repression against the middle class from right-wing rulers, a revolt against the regime was organized by the MNR, with portions of the armed forces. Peasants and labor union members were armed. Paz returned to Bolivia and the MNR was in power.

Two major things happened during the revolt. First, Indians took control over many haciendas and distributed the land among themselves. Once in power, the MNR formalized the takeovers through land reform law and granted Indians full citizenship rights for the first time since the conquest. Peasants who armed themselves during the revolt were allowed to keep their weapons. Second, tin miners had occupied the mines. The MNR nationalized the tin mines and reduced the size and political power of the armed forces. Thus, a coalition of lower- and middle-class groups took power in Bolivia.

The Revolution, headed by the MNR, unified several major political forces in the country: the miners, who had been a force since their organization in the early 1930s; the armed forces, which the MNR infiltrated; and large sectors of the middle classes. After the Revolution, a fourth group emerged, the peasants, who rapidly organized themselves once it became clear that lands were available for distribution. This coalition, however, was short-lived. If the Revolution had altered the power structure of Bolivia by enabling new players to sit at the political table, it had not changed the precarious, boom-and-bust nature of the Bolivian economy. The legitimation of new social forces increased competition for scarce resources, sometimes creating even more political instability. Within a few years, internal divisions within the MNR, the armed forces, and the middle classes led to new, more complex patterns of political alignment.

At the time of the revolution, four of the top leaders, each with an independent power base, forged a pact by which they would rotate the presidency among themselves every four years until 1964. The revolution was so popular and its alliance structure so strong it seemed reasonable to assume the men who led it would be able to withstand electoral challenges to their rule. Víctor Paz Estenssoro was the first president for the MNR from 1952 until 1956. He pledged he would support Hernán Siles Zuazo from 1956 to 1960; Siles would be followed by Walter Guevara Arce until 1964, when labor leader Juan Lechín would become the candidate. The intrigues and betrayals of these four men dominated much of Bolivian politics for the next four decades.

Siles Zuazo indeed followed Paz as the presidential candidate in 1956. He was elected and served out his term. But in 1960 former president Víctor Paz intervened in MNR party affairs to block the agreed-upon candidacy of Walter Guevara in favor of his own. Paz became president again, but at the cost of splitting the MNR coalition. Paz acted swiftly to fortify and woo the armed forces, which were severely weakened under Siles. Then, as the 1964 presidential elections approached, Paz used his influence in the legislature to amend the constitution to permit him to run for another term in office, betraying his pledge to back Trotskyist labor leader Juan Lechín for president. In this effort, he was assisted by elements of the U.S. government and by large portions of the armed forces, both concerned about the potential implications of a government headed by an avowed Marxist during the Cold War.

The armed forces accepted the ploy by Paz, but only after insisting that the MNR candidate for vice-president be a member of the armed forces. Paz was duly elected under these circumstances. But a few months later the armed forces overthrew him, allowing Vice-President (General) Rene Barrientos to become president. Barrientos, a truly popular leader who tried to create a multiclass power base of his own, independent of the MNR, was killed three years later in a helicopter crash that some thought related to jealousies within the armed forces. A succession of military governments followed. The most bizarre was the regime of General Juan José Torres, which allowed students, labor unions, and left-wing activists to form a Popular Assembly (which elected Juan Lechín its president) but did not permit them to arm themselves against the inevitable right-wing reaction. General Hugo Bánzer, with the support of the Santa Cruz regiment, ousted Torres from office in less than a year. Bánzer remained in office for several years, forging a strong power base among the Santa Cruz oligarchy, enjoying an economic boom in the western part of the country.

By the late 1970s, international pressure—especially the prodemocratic foreign policy orientation of U.S. president Jimmy Carter—forced Banzer to hold elections in 1978. These pitted former president Siles Zuazo against General Juan Pereda Asbún, a candidate publicly favored by President Bánzer. Several other candidates also ran. Siles denounced electoral fraud on behalf of Pereda during the vote count, and the tally eventually revealed neither received enough votes (the minimum requirement is 50 percent plus one of the valid votes cast) to be elected outright, throwing the election to the legislature, where Siles had enough votes to be elected. Pereda then staged a coup d'état and assumed dictatorial powers. He in turn was ousted a few months later by General David Padilla, who held elections in 1979.

The major candidates were former presidents Siles and Paz. Again, neither candidate received enough votes and again the election was handed to the legislature, which was gridlocked on the issue for days. It finally selected Walter Guevara Arce, whom Paz had betrayed in 1960 and who was then president of the Senate. Guevara had not been a candidate in the 1979 elections, and the constitutionality of his selection is still disputed. His election, however, was widely viewed as an effort to correct an injustice committed two decades earlier. He was overthrown a few months later by General Alberto Natusch Busch, who had links to international cocaine traffickers. Facing strong opposition, Natusch stepped down. The legislature was reconvened to elect a new president. Lydia Gueiler, the first woman to serve as president of Bolivia, was chosen interim president until new elections could be held in 1980; these pitted Paz and Siles against each other again. Siles won a plurality of votes, but once again not enough for election. Before the legislature could convene to settle the issue, General Luis García Meza, connected to drug trafficking, toppled the government. He was ousted in a coup a year later. Unable to contain growing labor unrest, the armed forces in 1982 reconvened the legislature, which, completing the electoral process of 1980, chose Siles as president.

Thus, of the four men who agreed to alternate their candidacies, three eventually became president; all were deposed at one time or another, and all were active politically through the 1980s. The fourth, Juan Lechín, remained an outsider; but as undisputed leader of the labor movement he remained a force to be reckoned with throughout the period.

By 1982 Bolivia had plunged into a free-falling economic collapse characterized by a heavy international debt, declining prices and production from tin and other exports, declining agricultural production, negative national growth, and because the government began printing excess money, hyperinflation. Siles was unable to moderate severe competition among labor unions, government workers, and private business groups, all seeking favorable treatment from government in the economic crisis, and a period of great instability followed, including a moment in which a group of military officers connected to drug traffickers kidnapped the president for several hours. Siles retired voluntarily from the presidency in 1985, a year before the expiration of his term. New elections were held and Víctor Paz Estenssoro was elected president once again.

President Paz alleviated the economic crisis with a mixture of economic austerity, severe repression of labor, and martial law. Moreover, in an ironic twist Paz, leader of the Revolution of 1952, took the first steps toward dismantling the institutions and political understandings that emerged from the Revolution. In 1985 he introduced the "neoliberal model" to Bolivia: rapid privatization of government corporations; reduction in state subsidies; a diminished role for government in social investments such as education, health care, and welfare; and a toleration of income redistribution favoring the wealthy. These policies stabilized the economy, but at the expense of those who were the major beneficiaries of the 1952 Revolution: peasant organizations, tin miners, labor unions, and the poor in general, creating serious unrest among labor and peasant unions. Expenditures for education dropped from nearly 20 percent of the national budget to less than 10 percent. Rates of illiteracy and infant mortality began to rise significantly as expenditures on social programs plunged.

Paz's nephew, Jaime Paz Zamora, was elected president in 1989 by the legislature after he failed to receive a majority of votes in the general election, which he contested with General Hugo Bánzer. His party, the formerly leftist Movimiento de Izquierda Revolucionaria, formed an alliance with General Bánzer's Acción Democrática Nacionalista (ADN) to share cabinet positions in a National Unity government that continued the neoliberal policies begun by Paz. In 1993 the MNR returned to power, electing Gonzalo Sánchez de Lozada president until 1997, again with the election determined by the legislature. Once more, General Bánzer came in second and a coalition government was formed. Hugo Cárdenas, an Aymara Indian and leader of the Tupac Katari Revolutionary Movement of Liberation, was elected vice-president, reflecting the growing power of the indigenous movement in Bolivia. Within weeks after becoming president, Sanchez announced his intentions to sell 49 percent of the government-owned oil company to private interests and to transfer the tin-mining industry to the private sector.

For more than a decade, Bolivia's political system has remained relatively stable while governments pursued conservative policies designed to promote steady growth in the economy, control inflation, seek support from international financial institutions such as the World Bank and Inter-American Development Bank, and undermine the egalitarian assumptions of government action during the previous decades. For the entire period, these policies were resisted by labor unions, peasant groups, and other players who were given a voice in the nation's affairs following the Revolution.

RECENT POLITICAL MOVEMENTS

The Rise and Fall of the Peruvian Military Regime of 1968–1980

By 1968 the aging leaders of APRA had mellowed to the point of bland advocacy of the status quo. Younger members of the party in the 1960s had even joined Marxist guerrilla groups fighting in the highlands, as they became convinced that legal reform through party participation was unlikely. But in 1968 a small group of officers led by General Juan Velasco Alvarado overthrew President Belaúnde, replacing him with a governing junta and cabinet composed entirely of active-duty generals in the three branches of the armed forces. Their first official act was to expropriate the holdings of the U.S.-owned International Petroleum Company, which had been accused of collaborating with government officials to lower the price they paid for Peruvian oil. This popular act was followed six months later by the expropriation of the sugar haciendas in the north, a massive redistribution plan for agricultural lands in the highlands, a profit-sharing program covering industrial workers, and a series of regulations designed to control the influence of foreign investors. Within a few years, expropriations had increased the share of the economy derived from state-owned enterprises from about 1 percent in the mid-1960s to 20 percent a decade later.

Internal dissension within the armed forces made full implementation of these policies impossible, and eventually conservative forces within the military were able to wrest power away from the original group of reformist officers. But the government that followed soon became mired in economic problems, corruption scandals, and political opposition from both right and left. Following the trend in Latin America, the armed forces retired from power in 1980, and the public elected as president Fernando Belaúnde, who had been overthrown by the armed forces twelve years earlier.

The Collapse of Peruvian National Coherence During the 1980s and 1990s

The centrist governments of Belaúnde (1980–1985) and APRA leader Alan García (1985–1990) grappled without success with economic problems as Peru entered a period of severe decline. From 1975 to 1990, there were only two years of positive economic growth. García's unorthodox economic policies (increased public borrowing, wage and price controls to curtail skyrocketing prices, debt moratorium on some foreign loans) led the wealthy to disinvest in Peru's economy and caused the international financial community to shun Peru. As the economy began to collapse during the early 1980s, a terrorist group known as the Partido Comunista del Peru en el Sendero Luminoso de Carlos Mariátegui (often abbreviated Sendero Luminoso, or Shining Path) began to challenge the government. Its leadership rejected most Western Marxist strategies for taking power and instead followed the thinking of Mariátegui, who decades earlier had suggested adaptation of Marxism to Peruvian ethnic conditions, and Maoist (Chinese) models for a long-term struggle.

In the early 1960s, a small group of Marxist university professors in the ancient Inca stronghold of Ayacucho—the poorest region in Peru—split into competing pro-Soviet and Maoist-oriented factions. After controlling the university for a number of years, the Maoist faction, led by Abimael Guzmán, eventually went underground for a period of apparent self-study and emerged only in 1980, announcing the beginning of the People's War. Within three years, Sendero had effective organizations both in large urban centers and in the rural highlands. Their methods were sometimes bizarre, often astonishingly successful. Before moving to control a village, they would sometimes hang dead dogs from nearby trees or posts as a warning sign to keep villagers from resisting—the same technique the Incas had used in conquests centuries earlier. Once, on the birthday of their leader, Abimael Guzmán Reynoso, they blew out the lights of the entire city of Lima, with 8 million inhabitants, leaving only one huge torchlit symbol, a hammer and sickle glowing in the dark on the side of a hill.

Sendero grew in strength from a fighting force of perhaps 100 in 1980 to more than 10,000. By 1990 Sendero violence caused the government to declare one-half of the provinces of Peru to be in a state of emergency. That same year Sendero retook control of much of the Huallaga Valley, where most of Peru's coca plants are grown, and helped finance its activities through an arrangement with peasants and drug lords. While experts disagreed on the exact nature of the appeal the movement had among its adherents, support for Sendero derived in part from sheer intimidation, in part from centuries of alienation of *cholos* from the political system, and in part from its characterization of Peru's governmental system as thoroughly corrupted. Another guerrilla group, the Tupac Amaru Revolutionary Movement (MRTA), emerged in the 1980s, named after the eighteenth-century Indian leader who rebelled against Spanish rule. Guerrilla-inspired violence during the 1980s and 1990s and military counterinsurgency campaigns caused 30,000 deaths and $25 billion in property damage. By the early 1990s, Peru's economy was near collapse, its political system under severe assault from terrorist organizations bent on destroying its major institutions.

But at about that time middle sectors began to regroup. In 1990 an unknown political novice, Alberto Fujimori, head of a party that had not existed six months earlier, won an astonishing victory over his major opponent, the novelist Mario Vargas Llosa, who had spent much of his life writing in Europe but who was backed by the country's major conservative groups. Fujimori would spend the next few years implementing neoliberalism in Peru. He promptly restored ties to the international financial community and began an economic stabilization plan that ended hyperinflation, encouraged private investors to repatriate capital, and produced positive economic growth. These measures forced extreme belt-tightening for the vast majority of Peruvians, as the government fired hundreds of thousands of workers and cut expenditures drastically. During Fujimori's first two years in office, the income level of Peruvians dropped 30 percent, after having fallen during the 1980s to less than half what of what it had been during the 1970s. The situation caused serious hardship; more than 60 percent of the population fell below the poverty level. But the measures created a positive growth rate for the first time in many years in 1993 and Peruvians appeared to accept them.

In April 1992, impatient with the legislature (his own party had very few seats in a legislature dominated by more traditional parties) and supported by the armed forces, Fujimori dissolved the legislature and suspended constitutional guarantees. As a result, the United States suspended aid, and the international community held up rescheduling of the large international debt Peru owed until democracy was restored. In November 1992, a constitutional congress was elected, which restored many parts of the 1979 Constitution. Foreign assistance resumed. Two of the new features of the constitution that was eventually ratified in October 1993 were provisions for a unicameral legislature and for possible reelection of the president.

In spite of the severity of the economic measures, Fujimori maintained high popularity during his first term in office. In part this may have been because of the government's success in September 1992 in capturing Abimael Guzmán and other top leaders of Sendero Luminoso, crippling, though not eliminating, the movement. Much of the MRTA leadership was captured. Remaining members of both groups split into competing factions. Fujimori was reelected president in April 1995, and his party received a comfortable majority of seats in the legislature. But in spite of these victories for the government, neither Sendero nor MRTA was defeated. And the Peruvian economy, which grew exceptionally well during 1994 and 1995, stagnated in 1996, causing Fujimori's popularity to sag somewhat. In December 1996, MRTA was able to take hundreds of guests hostage at the residence of the Japanese ambassador in a spectacular drama that was reported worldwide.

CONTEMPORARY SOCIAL AND ECONOMIC STRUCTURES

Peru

Peru, with a population of 24 million, is socially and economically more complex than Bolivia, because of greater geographic and economic diversity. Although the proportion has dropped gradually since the 1970s, 35–45 percent of the population can be classified as Indian. Precise data on Indians are difficult to obtain, since the definition of an Indian in Peru is more cultural than racial. As Indians make efforts to acculturate into white society (by changing from native to Western clothing and leaving traditional occupations), they become known as *cholos,* a term that also signals low social status. During the past half century, *cholification* has reduced the Indian population, which is located primarily in the sierra; Indians are usually employed as farm workers, peasants, or small merchants.

Economic and social opportunities for upward mobility in recent decades have been greater on the coast than in the sierra, precipitating a mass migration of *cholos* from their traditional homeland in the sierra to the coast. This has altered Peruvian society. Huge congregations of *cholos* in slum areas in and around Lima have outstripped the ability of the city to provide them with city services. The population of Lima has quadrupled in four decades, largely through in-migration of *cholos.* Urban *cholos* face difficult conditions: As they lose traditional identities and values, they are simultaneously stigmatized with negative new identities imposed by the more powerful white minority. And in recent years the economy has not provided adequate employment. These difficulties are reflected in part by high rates of alcoholism and crime. Social decomposition has also left millions in an anomic state, vulnerable to appeals from religious or magical cults and sects, political creeds, or other value-substituting mechanisms. Sendero Luminoso has been extremely successful in recruiting a terrorist cadre from this population in neighborhoods that have not already been well organized by political parties, government penetration, or religious organizations.

Indians or *cholos* provide most of the country's manual labor. The middle classes tend to identify more closely with the nation's upper class, which has assiduously avoided contact with indigenous Peruvian society for several centuries. An exclusive Creole culture has developed, complete with its own musical tradition (the most popular is the *marinera* dance), literature (from Ricardo Palma to Mario Vargas Llosa), and cuisine. The long-standing habit of importing European cultural traditions—bullfights, music and drama, literary fashions, dress, ideologies—persists, although it now comes from the United States as well. Legislative efforts were made during the early part of the Velasco regime (1968–1975) to limit the foreign content of radio and television programming and advertising, but these were not enforced. Popular urban culture today responds more to Western norms than to native traditions. It is in part against these norms that Sendero Luminoso based its appeal, and that helps account for a strengthened nativist movement during the 1990s.

Peru's highly exclusive traditional oligarchy, accustomed to a near-monopoly of power, was effectively weakened by the reforms of the Velasco regime and the two subsequent governments, which redistributed land and acquired many large industries. The oligarchy was replaced by a new class of urban entrepreneurs with strong international connections, but it is too early to tell what the political future might be for this new elite; the Fujimori period, however, is clearly characterized by a concentration of wealth.

Peru's economy during the late 1990s was reasonably well diversified, with about 12 percent of GDP derived from agriculture (which employs about one-third of all workers), about 11 percent from mining, 20 percent from manufacturing, 7 percent from construction, and 43 percent from services. Government expenditures accounted for 7 percent of GDP. The nongovernment service sector has been expanding rapidly since the economic policies of President Fujimori have resulted in large cutbacks of government workers and employment in the industrial sector. Peru's GDP was around $45 billion in the mid-1990s, but it decreased by an average of about 0.5 percent per year from 1980 to 1993, leaving per capita income at 70.7 percent of what it had been in 1980. Peru's exports were also diversified in the mid-1990s, with about 44 percent derived from sales of mining products (nearly half of which is copper), 16 percent from fishmeal, 9 percent from textiles, 9 percent from manufactured goods, 7 percent from fisheries, and about 7 percent from agricultural products.

While the economy of Peru grew during the mid-1990s, for the first time in a sustained fashion since the late 1970s, inflation-adjusted salaries in Lima (where statistics are most reliable) had fallen to about one-half of what they had been in the mid-1980s, and underemployment rates had doubled to about 75 percent. Real wages for government workers had fallen even more drastically, to about 20 percent of what they had been in the mid-1980s. Increasing numbers of persons participate in the "informal" service sector, relying on sales of consumer items often smuggled from abroad.

Bolivia

About 55 percent of Bolivia's population of about 8 million is Indian, the proportion slowly declining during the past half century with *cholification*. About 30 percent of the population speaks Quechua, while another 25 percent speaks Aymara; both languages, in addition to Spanish, are official languages. Only 5–15 percent is European in origin; 25–30 percent of the population is mestizo. Two of every three Bolivians live on the Altiplano in the western part of the country; the rest live at lower altitudes in the south or east, many new settlers having been attracted there by recent economic development. Migration to the Santa Cruz area and the region of Cochabamba, where coca leaves are grown, has been especially rapid. Moreover, nearly one million persons have recently migrated to El Alto, the plain above La Paz (which lies in a large canyon), at an altitude of nearly 14,000 ft.

Although still confined largely to the lower class, Indians enjoy more positive identities in Bolivia than in Peru. For more than two generations, Bolivian Indians have organized politically and have participated in most of the major political events of the nation. National political awareness began with mass conscription during the Chaco War and grew with unionization of tin miners during the 1940s, armed participation in the Revolution of 1952, and the agrarian reform that followed. Indians have voted since 1954.

The traditional upper class largely disappeared after the Revolution, but it has been replaced by a new class of entrepreneurs engaged in nontraditional economic ventures, including new agricultural products, financial services, commerce, and since the early 1990s, management and ownership of formerly state-owned enterprises. Middle sectors include labor union members, military officers, government bureaucrats, and professionals. Before the Revolution, these were highly dependent on the upper classes. After the Revolution, they were dependent on government. In the post-Revolution period that began in 1985, middle groups have struggled to survive, and they may end up dependent on the upper classes once again. They have, however, shared power with other social classes, including the lower classes, and have highly developed political skills. In this respect, Bolivia is different from Peru, where little political mingling has taken place between the middle and lower classes.

Bolivia has undergone a major economic transformation during the past three decades, leading to a dramatic diversification of resources. From the turn of the century until the 1960s, Bolivia's exports of unrefined tin and silver accounted for an average of over 90 percent of export value. Today these minerals account for about 20 percent of exports, as zinc and natural gas have replaced tin as the leading exports. Brazil has overtaken Bolivia as the world's leading exporter of tin, Bolivian exports only accounting for about 6 percent of world production. Minerals now account for less than half of all exports. Agriculture contributes to about 18 percent of GDP and employs 47 percent of the workforce. Mining now accounts for only 11 percent of GDP, surpassed by manufacturing (15 percent) and trade, transportation, and other services (46 percent). Government expenditures account for about 10 percent of GDP.

The Bolivian economy grew at an average rate of nearly 2 percent annually from 1986 to 1996, representing about $6 billion GDP in 1996, about $750 per capita. Real wages have kept pace with economic growth, and official unemployment figures dropped during the early 1990s from over 10 percent to about 7 percent. The economy is not robust enough to provide satisfactory employment for all Bolivians, however, many of whom have tended to drift into the "informal," or contraband, sector, including the drug trade, which thrives in large urban areas.

The Cocaine Trade in Peru and Bolivia

Over 90 percent of the world's supply of coca leaves is grown on the Altiplano of Peru and Bolivia. Until the 1970s, most coca leaves were grown for local consumption by peasant farmers for other peasants. A slight narcotic effect (it numbs the mouth and stomach) is activated when one inserts a small sandy stone (known as *llucta*) into the mouth while chewing on coca leaves. Virtually all peasants on the Altiplano have been chewing coca leaves legally for centuries, and it remains legal today. As the demand for the more powerful coca-derived chemical cocaine grew in the United States to staggering proportions in the 1970s and 1980s, peasants accommodated by vastly increasing acreages. The Upper Huallaga Valley in Peru today produces more than half of the world's supply of cocaine. Much of the rest comes from Bolivia.

It is difficult to calculate the effects of coca production on the national economies of Peru and Bolivia, but they are large. In Peru estimates range from $300 million to $1 billion in foreign exchange, up to nearly 3 percent of Peru's GDP; in Bolivia estimates are up to $600 million, almost as much as the value of all exports, or 10 percent of GDP. Revenues from much coca traffic, which are not recorded by national statistical gathering agencies, have contributed heavily to the economic health of both countries. For this reason, and since the most negative effects of cocaine consumption are visible principally in the slums of northern cities far away, it is sometimes difficult for Andean people to understand why U.S. policymakers seem so intent on destroying this lucrative source of hard currency. But under heavy pressure from the U.S. government, incentives for peasants to grow alternative crops; U.S. assistance to military and police forces to destroy excess crops, smash laboratories, and interdict drug shipments; and other measures have been adopted—all with little success.

In Bolivia many high-level officials have been implicated in drug-trafficking scandals, and powerful coca producers' organizations were able to pressure the government to curtail coca-eradication programs. Violent clashes between government drug-control troops (UMOPAR) and coca farmers took place in 1995 in the Chapare Valley of Cochabamba, where UMOPAR units began to destroy coca crops to meet the U.S. eradication target of 5,400 hectares. In Peru, after allegations of military involvement in illegal trafficking, responsibility for fighting the drug trade was passed in 1996 to the national police, and President Fujimori began a new program, declaring coca-producing areas to be under a state of emergency, placing transportation under direct police control.

EXTERNAL RELATIONS

Since independence, both Peru and Bolivia have faced periods of extreme tension with their neighbors. Bolivia lost territory to all of its neighbors—Brazil, Paraguay, Chile, Peru, and Argentina—most painfully during the War of the Pacific (1879–1883), when Chile seized Bolivia's only coastal territories, and during the Chaco War with Paraguay. Peru, too, lost territory to Chile during the War of the Pacific. In the twentieth century, Peru has engaged in numerous border skirmishes with its northern neighbors, Ecuador and Colombia. In 1932 a border flare-up in the Amazon region near Leticia led to hostilities with Colombia. During a border conflict in 1941, Peru forcibly seized a large portion of lightly populated and unused Amazonian territory claimed by Ecuador. A team of mediators, including a delegation from the United States, fixed the present boundaries largely in accordance with the status quo after the seizure. Ecuador remained dissatisfied with the terms of the protocol signed at the time, and border tensions between the two countries have flared up occasionally since then. A border crisis in 1981 led to open hostility and temporary mobilization of troops on both sides of the border. In early 1995, fighting between the two countries broke out along a 48-mile stretch of undemarcated border. Although Peru's military is more than double the size of Ecuador's, Ecuadoran military forces did surprisingly well for several weeks. A formal peace accord was signed in Brasília on February 17, 1995, providing for international observers to supervise a demilitarized region.

Both Peru and Bolivia have made efforts to cooperate with their Andean neighbors (Ecuador, Colombia, and Venezuela) in creating an Andean free-trade area through a gradual reduction in tariffs and other trade barriers. Peru withdrew from the Andean Group in 1992 but in March 1996 signed an agreement to join a restructured Andean Community that will establish a common external tariff. Bolivia also signed a free-trade agreement with Mexico in 1994. During the 1990s, Bolivia's foreign policy focused on securing access both to Pacific Ocean and Atlantic Ocean ports. In 1993 Bolivia signed an agreement with Peru, granting Bolivia free access to the Peruvian port of Ilo on the Pacific. And in 1995, Bolivia strengthened its access to the Chilean port of Arica. In 1990, Bolivia began to open river ports connecting to the Amazon River near Manaus, Brazil, and in 1994 an agreement was signed to provide a waterway linking Bolivia with the Atlantic coast in Uruguay.

Overall, during the latter half of the twentieth century, Peru has maintained a more nationalist foreign policy, especially with respect to the United States, than has Bolivia. Peru has nationalized foreign enterprises, curtailed the power of foreign investors, declared unilateral debt moratoriums with foreign creditors, and experimented with purchases of Soviet military equipment. Recently, however, Peruvian governments have been more concerned about their standing among the wealthier nations. Bolivia has been more closely associated with U.S. foreign policy.

CONCLUSIONS

Peru and Bolivia have recently implemented "neoliberal" economic reforms that unraveled decades of government experience with state ownership of many large enterprises, including airlines, petroleum resources, mineral production, and telecommunications—ventures that many had considered the culmination of years of political struggle by the APRA and MNR parties, among the most important mass parties in Latin America. The scope of governmental action has now been significantly reduced. In both countries these changes followed on the heels of serious economic crises in which governments were pressed by demands made by private-sector, labor union, bureaucratic, and other groups, some of which had only recently been accepted within the polity as equal members. These crises were complicated by grievances against military governments—often corrupt, insensitive, and arbitrary—that had interrupted democratic rule, often with civilian compliance. "Neoliberalism" thus represents a repudiation not only of the post–World War II era of "big government," as it does in the United States, but also of the capriciousness of military government.

In Bolivia, where a social revolution provided greater respect as well as powerful political institutions for Indian peasants, tin miners, and the lower classes in general, "neoliberalism," albeit hard on these groups, takes place in an atmosphere of relative inclusion. While the institutions that support these groups may not fare as well as those of the higher classes, their representatives are nevertheless sitting at the table where distributional issues are being discussed. Ethnic issues are not completely resolved, as evidenced by a growing indigenous movement, but these are likely to be contained within nonviolent political arenas. In Peru, in contrast, where attitudes toward Indians and lower-class *cholos* have not improved and where institutional mechanisms to incorporate these populations effectively into the polity have not prospered, the appeal to violence is still attractive to groups that feel excluded. Guerrilla groups formed two decades ago under very different circumstances have been able to evolve, transform, and survive. Moreover, the social discomposition in large cities such as Lima—in large part the product of negative attitudes—creates a formidable obstacle to political development.

SUGGESTED READINGS

Pre-Columbian history of the Altiplano region has been studied intermittently for several centuries; at present such study is flourishing. A comprehensive but dated summary of this literature can be found in Luis G. Lumbreras, *The People and Cultures of Ancient Peru* (Washington, D.C.: Smithsonian Institution, 1974). A more recent summary is found in Richard Keatinge, *Peruvian Prehistory* (London: Cambridge University Press, 1988). An excellent reference is Helaine Silverman, *Ancient Peruvian Art: An Annotated Bibliography* (G. K. Hall, 1996). William H. Prescott wrote *The Conquest of Peru*, describing the early Spanish period, in 1874. A newer volume is Susan Ramirez, *A World Upside Down: Cross-cultural Contact and Conflict in Sixteenth Century Peru* (Stanford: Stanford University Press, 1996).

Recent surveys of the entire range of history of Peru and Bolivia can be found in Herbert S. Klein's *Bolivia: The Evolution of a Multiethnic Society,* 2d edition (New York: Oxford University Press, 1992), and in Orin Stern, C. Degregori, and Robin Kirk, *The Peru Reader: History, Culture, Politics* (Durham, N.C.: Duke University Press, 1995).

In a more specialized vein, Peter F. Klaren, *Modernization, Dislocation, and Aprismo: Origins of the Peruvian Aprista Party* (Austin: University of Texas Press, 1973); Robert J. Alexander, *The Bolivian National Revolution* (New Brunswick, N.J.: Rutgers University Press, 1958); David Scott Palmer's second edition of *Shining Path of Peru* (New York: St. Martin's Press, 1994); Linda Seligman, *Between Reform and Revolution: Political Struggles in the Peruvian Andes* (Stanford: Stanford University Press, 1995); Ricardo Godoy, *Mining and Agriculture in*

Highland Bolivia (Tucson: University of Arizona Press, 1990); and Paul Gootenberg, *Between Silver and Guano: Commercial Policy and the State in Postindependence Peru* (Princeton: Princeton University Press, 1991), deal with major themes.

Works dealing with coca production and U.S. efforts to limit it in recent years include Sewell H. Menzel, *Fire in the Andes: U.S. Foreign Policy and Cocaine Politics in Bolivia and Peru* (Lanham, Md.: University Press of America, 1996); Felipe MacGregor, *Coca and Cocaine: An Andean Perspective*; and Joseph Gagliano, *Coca Prohibition in Peru: The Historical Debates* (Tucson: University of Arizona Press, 1994).

PART ELEVEN
THE SOUTHERN CONE

26

CHILE: THE DEVELOPMENT, BREAKDOWN, AND RECOVERY OF DEMOCRACY

J. SAMUEL VALENZUELA AND ARTURO VALENZUELA

Chile, a country of 12 million people isolated by the formidable Andes mountains on a narrow and elongated strip of land running 2,650 mi into the far southern reaches of the earth, developed early on a distinctive political system that set it apart from its Latin American neighbors. Soon after independence from Spain, conservative leaders were able to establish a national government that successfully resisted armed challenges to its authority, thereby avoiding the instability that plagued most of Spanish America. Through successive reforms in a pattern reminiscent of British history, Chile toward the end of the nineteenth century had built a democratic regime, although suffrage in national elections was limited to literate males until 1949. The regularity of electoral contests led to the rise of strong parties that have dominated political life during the twentieth century. Running the full range of the ideological spectrum from a communist and socialist left to a conservative right, the Chilean party system has more in common with those of Latin Europe than of Latin America.

This unusual history and party system permitted the election in 1970 of President Salvador Allende, whose leftist government tried to lead the nation to socialism within its constitutional and democratic framework. Allende's experiment attracted world attention and was observed with particular interest in Italy and in France where the left was attempting to follow the same political path. It ended on

This chapter is a revised and expanded version of the authors' chapter, "Chile and the Breakdown of Democracy," in Howard J. Wiarda and Harvey F. Kline, eds., *Latin American Politics and Development,* Second Edition (Boulder, Colo.: Westview Press, 1985).

September 11, 1973, when General Augusto Pinochet staged a bloody military coup that destroyed Chile's democracy and inaugurated a sixteen-and-a-half-year eternity of harsh authoritarian government. Within the context of Chilean history, such military rule was highly exceptional. Prior to Pinochet's regime, Chile had only once before, for less than five months in 1924, been governed by a strictly military junta. The crisis years of 1891 and 1932 produced juntas with military and civilian figures that lasted only a few weeks. The great majority of Chilean presidents had been regularly replaced by their successors following constitutional procedures. The national Congress, an institution that played a crucial role in Chilean political history, was also closed by the military for the first time since independence.

With the inauguration of President Patricio Aylwin on March 11, 1990, in highly emotional ceremonies attended by delegates from sixty-seven countries, including sixteen heads of state, Chile began the recovery of its more than centennial democratic tradition. A new phase in the nation's history has opened, full of possibilities as well as great and difficult challenges.

This chapter examines the origins, evolution, characteristics, and breakdown of Chile's democratic system. It also reviews the main features of the recently terminated military regime and analyzes the difficulties faced in the reestablishment of the nation's democracy.

AN OVERVIEW OF CHILEAN POLITICAL HISTORY, 1818–1970

Phase 1: The Founding of an Oligarchical Proto-Democracy (1818–1850)

As elsewhere on the continent, the defeat of Spanish and Chilean royalist forces after the wars of independence (1810–1818) did not lead to an easy transition toward autonomous rule. The break with Spain did not alter the socioeconomic order. The predominantly rural population, located mainly between Valparaíso and Concepción, continued to live on large estates without sharing the fruits of a weak economy based on exports of animal products, grain, and copper. The break, however, clearly disrupted the political system. Gone was the omnipresent and complex colonial administration as well as the legitimating power of the Crown, the final arbiter of all conflicts. The nation became engulfed in political anarchy as different family, regional, and ideological groups fought each other only to produce unsuccessful dictatorial governments and a series of paper constitutions.

Political anarchy ended in the early 1830s, but it is a mistake, often made in Chilean historiography, to look to those years for an explanation of the subsequent stability of government. Surely the defeat of what were viewed later in the nineteenth century as the liberal factions in the Battle of Lircay (1830), the skillful political and financial maneuvers of ministers Diego Portales and Manuel Rengifo in the administrations of President Joaquín Prieto (1831–1836; 1836–1841), and the adoption of a centralizing constitution in 1833 were important steps in establishing new authority structures. But there is a difference between *establishment* of such structures and their *consolidation*. Consolidation involves the acceptance of the viability and legitimacy of new institutions by the political elites. It is a lengthy process, subject to continuous challenges and reversals. It took many years and was aided by several factors.

The first was the victory of Chilean forces over those of the Peru-Bolivia Confederation. Though the confederation led by General Andrés Santa Cruz had sought to extend its dominion southward, the real spark that ignited the Chilean war effort was the assassination of Portales in 1837. Portales's policies, repressive measures, and advocacy of the war had made him the target of great enmity in Chile. Ironically, because it was rumored that he had been assassinated by agents of Santa Cruz, his death stirred a wave of patriotic emotions that were channeled to military preparations. For the first time Chilean elites mounted a joint endeavor to fight a common enemy, since the war of independence had been as much a civil war as a struggle against colonialism. Plots against the government were forgotten, and victory led to internal amnesty and to a restitution of pensions and ranks for the defeated forces of the 1829–1830 civil war. It also led to the election of the first truly national hero, Manuel Bulnes, to the presidency in 1841. A Chilean defeat in the war would have magnified factional disputes and threatened the stability of fragile institutions. The clear-cut victory, with no parallel in Latin America, created common symbols and a new sense of unity and led to the inauguration of an elected government with unprecedented support.

The second factor was the decisive control of the military by civilian authorities. As leader of the victorious army, Bulnes did not experience much opposition from the military in his first years in office. However, under his leadership the government deliberately reduced support for the regular army, so that by the end of Bulnes's term there were fewer soldiers than at the beginning and the budget for the regular military was severely curtailed. In place of a regular army, the executive encouraged the development of a highly politicized National Guard. Led by loyal government supporters (leadership positions became patronage devices for the president), the part-time guard was composed mainly of lower-middle-class civilians such as artisans, shopkeepers, and small proprietors. It numbered ten to twenty-five times the size of the peacetime army. The outbreak of a revolt against the government in 1851 was partly the reflection of the discontent of regular army officers, based in Concepción, with military policy. Bulnes himself led National Guard forces to suppress the uprising aimed at preventing his elected successor from taking office, even though his cousin was the rival leader. A similar revolt in 1859 was put down by mobilizing loyal army and National Guard forces.

As illustrated by Bulnes's decisive 1851 action, the third factor in the consolidation of the regime was the deliberate support he gave to the fledgling institutional system during his two five-year terms in office (1841–1851). Indeed, Bulnes's role in the consolidation process was, contrary to assertions in Chilean historiography, much greater than that of Portales, whose actual ministerial tenure was short. A written constitution, fixed terms of office, and impersonal authority based on suffrage, however limited, were revolutionary precepts at the time. Bulnes was certainly in a position to ignore those precepts and draw on his prestige and military strength to impose personal rule as did his counterparts in Argentina, Mexico, and Venezuela. Instead, under his leadership the broad outlines of the formal rules of the Republican Constitution of 1833, with its separation of powers between the executive, the Congress, and the courts, became a reality.

The most important single element contributing to this process was the president's refusal to rule autocratically. Following the example of his predecessor, he relied on a strong collegial body, the cabinet, to carry out the main tasks of government. But, unlike those of his predecessor, Bulnes's cabinets drew from different sectors of public opinion, and its members were periodically changed to reflect new pressures and interests.

Though the executive took the initiative, Congress had to approve all legislation. The legislature gradually became more assertive and a platform for dissenting views. As early as the 1840s the Congress resorted to delaying approval of the budget law in order to extract government concessions. Rather than defying this challenge to his authority, Bulnes sought compromise with the legislature. The legitimacy of Congress was therefore not questioned, even if cabinet officials manipulated the electoral process in favor of the official list of congressional candidates. This set the rudiments of the political game for the rest of the century.

Throughout the nineteenth century all relevant factions gained representation in the cabinet or in the legislature, and diverse opposition groups had to learn to collaborate within the shared institutional base to further their interests. It is noteworthy that every nineteenth-century head of state, with the exception of Jorge Montt, who became president after the 1891 civil war, had extensive prior experience as an elected representative in Congress. And the five presidents who succeeded Bulnes until 1886 began government service as young men in his administration.

The fourth factor contributing to regime consolidation was economic prosperity. The break with the colonial trade limitations opened the country to the international market, and Chilean exports thrived. Mining, primarily of silver and copper, expanded with the opening of new mines, and the new markets of California (after the gold rush), Europe, and Australia led to a boom in agricultural sales, mainly of wheat. The state played an important role in encouraging economic development based on external markets: It obtained foreign credit, improved dock facilities, opened new ports, began railway lines, and established a merchant marine. From 1844 to 1864 Chilean exports increased five times, and foreign creditors were quick to take note as Chilean issues brought higher prices on the London market than those of any other Latin American country.

Underlying the success of the government in promoting economic growth, and indirectly the success of the consolidation process itself, was the broad elite consensus on the merits of an "outward-oriented" development policy. Landowners in the central valley, miners in the north, and merchants in Santiago and in port cities all benefited from and promoted an economy based on the export of primary goods in the production of which the country had a decisive advantage. Most manufactured products were imported. There was no protectionism for domestic industry and no effective political force to press for it. The potential internal market for Chilean industry was small, and many obstacles, including the long distances from Europe and the United States and the latter's tariff barriers, discouraged manufacturing for export. However, an incipient industrialization did begin around textiles and iron works in the 1850s and 1860s. It supplied the military and produced materials used in mining, construction, and railways. Chilean artisans also built most of the boats that made their way up and down the long coast.

In sum, by mid-century, Chile had laid the foundations for constitutional republican rule based on the separation of powers. Victory in an international war, the control of the military by the constitutionally established authorities, political leadership respectful of the formal rules, and economic growth had contributed to this result that set Chile on a unique course in Latin America. The Congress had, in particular, taken its place as a basic arena for political accommodation, compromise, overview of the executive, and opposition. And although the franchise was limited and subject to intervention, it became the only mechanism for selecting political officeholders.

Phase 2: State Expansion and Elite Reaction (1850–1890)

Sharp political differences developed among nineteenth-century elites. The differences stemmed from the reaction of local and national notables, particularly those close to the Church, to the expansion of the state. When state institutions began to expand into the local level, rationalize taxes and duties, invest in public-works projects, and reduce church influence over national life, they generated bitter opposition. Our perspective is different from that of many historians, who have interpreted nineteenth-century controversies as a struggle between a Conservative rural aristocracy with a firm grip on the state and a rising group of miners, bankers, merchants, and professionals seeking political control. That view presupposes that political differences were the product of a fundamental, economically based cleavage among the elite. In fact, as already suggested, there was broad consensus on the merits of free-trade policies and on the pursuit of a development model based on primary goods exports. Moreover, socioeconomic divisions among the dominant sectors were not so clear-cut: The wealthiest families often had cross-investments in all areas of the economy. It is also clear that the Conservatives, whose political bases were largely among landed elites (although not all landed elites were Conservative), were far from controlling the government. Quite to the contrary, they were driven into opposition at an early date and remained so for most of the century.

Moreover, by mid-century the state was not simply a tool of economic elites but had a considerable degree of autonomy. An entirely new profession of urban-based government officials and politicians had appeared on the political scene. Like

President Manuel Montt (1851–1856; 1856–1861) himself, they relied on the state for their positions and had a real stake in the expansion of governmental authority. By 1860 over twenty-five hundred persons worked for the state, not counting thousands of workers hired by municipalities and government-financed public-works projects or the many individuals associated with the National Guard and the armed forces.

State autonomy was in part a function of growing governmental institutionalization and of the ability of state officials to manipulate the verdict of the electorate. But it was also the product of a system of revenue collection tied to an export economy. Reliance on customs revenues in a time of export expansion meant an incremental and automatic infusion of larger sums of money into state coffers without imposing large-scale domestic taxation. From 1830 to 1860 government revenues from customs duties, representing about 60 percent of all revenue, increased seven times. State revenues enabled the construction of numerous public-works projects, including the second railroad system of Latin America and the first to be operated by a government. In the fifteen-year period 1845–1860, expenditures on education alone quadrupled.

Given the encroachment of the state on the localities, it is not surprising that control of the state and its expenditures became the most important political issue of the time. Were urban or rural areas to be favored by state resources? Which port facilities should be improved? Where were the railroad lines to be built? Should local officials remain subordinated to the national government's decisions and largess, or should they be autonomous from it? And most importantly, should the state or the Church control the expanding educational system, civil registry, cemeteries, and hospitals?

The Conservative party became the foremost expression of elite discontent over the decreasing autonomy of rural areas and the challenge to the Church's monopoly over educational, cultural, and family life, the maintenance of which it viewed as essential to the preservation of the traditional social order and thus of elite privilege. The party was originally formed by a group that split away from the Montt government as Manuel Montt pressed further to enhance the role of the state. In opposition, the Conservatives soon made alliances of convenience with some ideological Liberals who, while supporting the concept of a secular state, wanted more decentralization of political authority and an expansion of electoral participation. The unsuccessful 1859 uprising reflected the seriousness of the political controversies as a few Liberal, Conservative, and regional elements attempted to prevent Manuel Montt's closest associate from succeeding him to the presidency. Though the government forces, known as the Nationals, controlled the rebellion, Montt's associate wisely withdrew his candidacy. The new National president, José Joaquín Pérez (1861–1866; 1866–1871), saw the political wisdom of granting amnesty to the rebels and, following the Bulnes precedents, of incorporating both Conservatives and Liberals into cabinets of national unity in what became known as the Liberal-Conservative Fusion.

A few measures were adopted during the Pérez administrations to curb the power of executive authority. The president was restricted to one term, armed personnel were barred from voting booths, and other electoral reforms were made. However, the basic character of the state remained unchanged. With Pérez's support, the Liberals outmaneuvered their Conservative allies and continued the basic policies of the preceding National governments. State power transformed the Liberals, not vice versa. State authority expanded further, state-sponsored projects increased, and the secularization of public institutions continued.

By the midpoint of the administration of Liberal president Federico Errázuriz (1871–1876), the Conservatives had had enough. They left the government determined to oppose the drift toward a secular society and the continued encroachment of the state over national life. Ironically, the Conservatives once again made an alliance of convenience with another opposition group, the anticlerical Radical Party, which upheld the Liberal principles its government colleagues had seemingly abandoned. This unlikely alliance held a majority in Congress, since the Conservatives had formed part of the official candidate lists in the 1872 election. The Conservatives took advantage of this majority to press for a dramatic liberalization of the electoral system in 1874. As a result the electorate tripled from 50,000 to 150,000 by 1878, as suffrage was extended to all literate males.

The 1874 reforms were not sufficient to counteract the strong intervention of local agents of the executive in the electoral process, an intervention that became more blatant and violent as the government's control over the electorate diminished. Hence, the Conservatives demanded genuine local autonomy, in which full control of elections (going beyond certain 1874 provisions) would be given to elected local governments independent of the executive. To electoral reforms they added the cry for municipal reform.

The Conservatives stood to gain from these reforms. Given the failure of armed conspiracies, their only hope of curbing state authority and of gaining control of government resources lay in the expansion of suffrage and in the reduction of government manipulation of the voting process. Like their counterparts in northern European countries, the Conservatives knew that their dominant position in small towns and in rural areas gave them the upper hand in capturing the ballot box. The more urban-based Liberals and Radicals stood to lose, since only 12 percent of the population lived in cities over twenty thousand and 26 percent in towns over two thousand. The key role played by the Conservatives in suffrage expansion (which, surprisingly, has been attributed to the Liberals and Radicals by most historians) meant that the principal party of the Chilean right became committed to expressing its power capabilities *through the electoral system,* not, as in other countries, through conspiracies within the armed forces or by gaining the allegiance of the central bureaucracy. It also meant that Church opposition to republican electoral democracy, typical of Latin Europe until at least the 1890s, would not develop in Chile. The use of the electoral system as a mechanism for national leadership selection was reinforced by these circumstances.

The stakes involved in the control of the executive increased dramatically with the Chilean victory in the War of the Pacific (1879–1883), again against Peru and Bolivia. In the 1860s and 1870s customs duties as a percentage of government revenue had declined to as low as 40 percent. After the war, with the incorporation of Peruvian and Bolivian land with enormous nitrate wealth into Chilean territory, customs duties once again climbed to over 70 percent of government income, eventually eliminating the need for internal property taxes. Though a majority of nitrate fields fell into the hands of foreign interests, the Chilean state was able to retain close to 50 percent of all profits through taxation. From 1870 to 1890 government revenues climbed over 150 percent, leading to a new wave of public-works projects and other government expenditures.

The struggle over the role of the state in society finally resulted in the civil war of 1891, during the closing months of José Manuel Balmaceda's government (1886–1891). With burgeoning nitrate wealth, his administration embarked on the most ambitious effort yet to channel governmental resources into massive public-works projects. Though some of his detractors objected to his hostile attitude toward British nitrate interests, opposition to Balmaceda crystallized over the perennial issue of the nineteenth century: control over state resources. The anti-Balmaceda forces included a wide spectrum of political opinion ranging from dissident Liberals to Conservatives and Radicals, not to mention the British nitrate entrepreneurs. The defeat of Balmaceda led to the long-awaited liberalization of electoral registration and counting processes and to a significant change in the character of the political system.

Phase 3: The Party System and Incipient Participation (1890–1925)

After 1891 the center of gravity of the Chilean political system shifted dramatically from the center to the locality. Municipal autonomy and electoral reform finally gave local notables control over suffrage and, therefore, over congressmen and senators. Acting as agents of their local sponsors, the legislators sharply reduced the role of the executive and of the cabinet through constitutional reforms. Politics in the so-called Parliamentary Republic (1891–1925) became an elaborate logrolling game in which legislative factions jockeyed for influence. Budget laws were carved up to please local supporters, and public employment became a primary source for congressional and party patronage. Central government employees increased from 3,048 in 1880 to 13,119 in 1900 and 27,479 in 1919, and the monolithic character of the state changed as its structures were permeated by different political elites. The incredible ministerial instability of the period, with its constant coalition shifts and complex electoral pacts, must be seen in this light.

A key organization of twentieth-century politics, the political party with extensive local bases, developed principally during the Parliamentary Republic. An unanticipated consequence of the liberalization of suffrage was the transformation of elite factions and protoparties into large-scale party organizations and networks. Buying of votes and the manipulation of the electorate became a complex and demanding job, and much of the day-to-day party activities shifted from the hands of notables to those of professional politicians and brokers of lesser status. A new political class began to take shape.

The Conservative rural notables gained influence with local suffrage control. But other forces were not left out of the political game. This resulted partly from the profound socioeconomic transformations set in motion by nitrate production, which gave political groups new potential electoral clienteles. Nitrate fields soon employed 10 to 15 percent of the active population and by expanding the internal market generated a host of other activities, including metallurgical works, clothing industries, and transportation. Rural areas and their commercial networks also experienced changes, as agriculture sought to meet the demand for food in the arid north. The urban population increased dramatically from 26 percent of the total in 1875 to close to 45 percent by the early 1900s, and the Radicals as well as a new group of Social Democrats assured themselves an increased role in politics with their skillful organizational efforts in changing cities, towns, and nitrate areas.

Political parties with direct access to the legislative process developed simultaneously with the establishment of a large-scale government bureaucracy. The growth of the public sector in this period was thus shaped by organizations whose primary goal was electoral success and accountability, organizations that continued to exert a major influence over state institutions and the policy process until the military coup of 1973. Where, as in Brazil or Argentina, the bureaucracy emerged before the structuring of strong party networks, the latter could not become, as they did in Chile, a fundamental linkage mechanism between society and the state.

Parties were not the only important organizations with local bases to appear in this period. Labor unions mushroomed, as nitrate, dock, railway, and industrial workers and artisans sought to improve their lot. However, labor unions were restricted and repressed. Dominant government and business elites thought labor militancy threatened the viability of the whole system. Since nitrate revenues were the lifeline of the state and of the economy, any cut in export revenues because of strikes would have devastating repercussions. The army was repeatedly used to put down strikes, often with great brutality, as in the Iquique massacre of 1907 when (depending on the account) between five hundred and two thousand workers were killed. Repression of labor union activities created a radical union leadership, since radical workers were more likely to assume the great personal risks involved.

Ironically, the openness of the political system, a product of the intense conflict among established elites, meant that industrial repression was not accompanied systematically by political repression. Working-class leaders were allowed to publish newspapers, create cultural associations, lobby Congress, and create political parties. Despite their intensely radical outlooks, they soon realized that their cause could best be advanced politically through alliances of convenience with traditional parties eager to maximize their fortunes. Thus in 1921 the founding father of the labor movement and of the Communist party, Luis Emilio Recabarren, and one of his comrades were elected to Congress through an electoral pact with the Radical Party. This repeated earlier successes in local elections in which pacts had been forged with either Radicals or Democrats. The repression of the working class therefore contributed to the formation of a Marxist labor union and party leadership, and the relatively open and representative character of the political system meant that the Marxist parties soon turned to traditional political strategies to advance their positions.

The freewheeling and free-spending Parliamentary Republic could not survive the decline in nitrate exports with the discovery of synthetic nitrate during World War I and the inability of the complex logrolling process to come up with solutions to many of the social pressures spawned by a changing society. The challenge from reform sectors was matched by a challenge from more traditional groups, which resented excessive democratization. President Arturo Alessandri's (1920–1924) populist politics violated many of the norms of political accommodation and led to demands to do away with politics and to obtain order. Though young army officers had reformist objectives in mind, their intervention in politics in late 1924 marked the end of the Parliamentary Republic and opened the way for the election of a "nonpolitical" figure, Col. Carlos Ibáñez. During his government (1927–1931), Congress lost influence and the president resorted to heavy-handed tactics in an attempt to reduce the role of parties and the strength of the Communist-controlled labor federations, which represented a majority of organized workers.

Ibáñez expanded the bureaucracy, revised the budgetary system, and "purified" the civil service. Liberal parliamentary politics were to be replaced by a more corporatist conception of the state. Interpreting the comprehensive labor laws approved in 1924 to suit his own end, Ibáñez established legal unionism only where his agents could find leaders who agreed to support his government. But the military president failed. Party politics were too entrenched to be easily purged or manipulated from above. His use of the 1924 labor laws only delayed their full and correct implementation until the late 1930s. With the catastrophic effects of the Great Depression (in which Chilean exports dropped to less than a fifth of their value by 1931), a political crisis erupted, forcing Ibáñez to resign. And after a short interval of unrest, Arturo Alessandri was reelected president by a large margin.

Phase 4: Polarization and Mass Participation (1925–1970)

The collapse of the Parliamentary Republic produced constitutional reforms that strengthened the presidency and established the separation of Church and state. However, the so-called 1925 Constitution does not represent the most important political change of the 1920s, which is surely the rise of the left. The Communist party was officially founded when the Socialist Workers' party convention of December 1921 voted to adhere to the Third International. By the end of the decade, a Trotskyite splinter had been expelled from the party, and various Socialist groups had been created. After Ibáñez's resignation, all these organizations emerged from their underground work to produce a confusing array of political groups on the left. However, in April 1933 a core of highly popular leaders formed the Socialist party of Chile by bringing together some of the preexisting Socialist and Trotskyite organizations. The new Socialist party quickly gained significant working-class bases by attracting the support of the country's legal unions, with which the Communists had refused to collaborate because of their origins. Thus by the early 1930s two major parties claiming to represent the workers had emerged on the political landscape, leading to a complex relationship of competition and/or cooperation between them that continues to this day. And with the rise of the Marxist left, the party system became highly polarized, covering the full range of the ideological spectrum.

Following the Popular Front strategy adopted in late 1934 by the Third International, the Communist party agreed to a previous Socialist initiative designed to unite the labor movement and to coordinate political strategies. With an eye on the next presidential elections, the by-then-historical Radical Party decided to withdraw its support of the conservative second Alessandri administration (1932–1938) and to join the left's discussions. These resulted in the merger of the labor movement into a single federation in 1936 and in the creation of a Popular Front coalition that elected the Radical Pedro Aguirre Cerda to the presidency in December 1938. This electoral victory over the candidates of Liberals and Conservatives marked the success, for the first time, of a center-to-Marxist left coalition, which would govern the country until 1947. The coalition government expanded state social services in areas such as health, education, and social security. It also encouraged the rise of legal unionism, including Communist-led unions, within the framework of the 1924 labor laws that shaped Chile's elaborate industrial-relations system. And the Popular Front government created a State Development Corporation (CORFO) in order to plan and direct an industrialization process aimed at substituting imported consumer goods with locally produced articles.

The creation of CORFO was symptomatic of a change of direction in the Chilean economy and economic policy. The depression had dealt the final blow to the crippled nitrate industry, and by the late 1930s copper had become Chile's principal export, representing roughly 55 percent of export earnings in the 1940s and 80 percent by 1970. With the drastic decline of the capacity to import in the early 1930s, policymakers became convinced that the nation should not rely on imported consumer goods to satisfy most of its needs. They sought to encourage industrial growth by establishing new lines of credit, protectionism, direct and indirect subsidies, price controls, and state investments in key areas such as steel and energy, which required large capital outlays. As a result, by the late 1960s Chile's industrial sector produced a broad range of consumer goods, if not always at internationally competitive levels of efficiency.

One of the Popular Front government's objectives in fostering industrialization was the creation of jobs in urban areas, which were urgently required because of the decline of the labor-intensive nitrate industry and of the influx of new migrants into

Table 26.1
Distribution of the Labor Force and Gross Domestic Product (at Market Prices),
1940, 1955, and 1970 (rounded to nearest percentage)

	1940		1955		1970	
	Labor Force	GDP	Labor Force	GDP	Labor Force	GDP
Primary sector	35	15	29	14	24	7
Secondary sector	30	38	33	39	33	48
Service sector	35	47	38	47	43	45

Sources: Estimated from Instituto de Economía de la Universidad de Chile, *La Economía de Chile en el Periodo 1950–1963*, and ODEPLAN figures.

the cities. By 1940, 53 percent of the population lived in urban areas, a figure that increased to 76 percent by 1970. The population in cities with more than twenty thousand people increased at an even faster rate. The new industrialization, however, in the long run did not generate employment at a faster rate than the increase in urban population. The secondary sector (including for present purposes mining, construction, transport, and particularly manufacturing) absorbed roughly the same proportion of the economically active population in 1970 as it had in 1940, even though its proportion of the gross domestic product increased from 38 percent in 1940 to 48 percent in 1970. As illustrated in Table 26.1, it was the service sector that absorbed increasing shares of total employment while contributing a smaller share of the GDP, while the primary sector (agriculture, forestry, and fishing) declined on both counts.

The Popular Front coalition broke down in part because of bitter internecine squabbles among Socialists and between Socialists and Communists and in part because of the fear of both Socialists and Radicals (particularly after the 1947 municipal election) that the Communists were making too much electoral progress. The onset of the cold war and U.S. pressures also played a role in the Radicals' decision not only to expel the Communists from the cabinet but also to declare the party illegal in 1948. The disarray of the left and the unpopularity of the Radicals after so many years of opportunistic bargaining with both the left and the right finally led the electorate including of Chilean politics, who once again promised progress at the margin of party politics. Gen. Carlos Ibáñez (1952–1958) was easily elected to the presidency by a surge movement ranging from the far right to the Socialist left.

Ibáñez's heterogeneous movement did not become a durable political force. As he began his term, the economy entered a recession and inflation increased sharply, finally reaching a high of 86 percent in 1955. Ibáñez abandoned the populist appeal of his campaign and early programs and attempted to apply an austerity economic program. One of Ibáñez's play.

The disintegration of the Ibáñez movement might have allowed the Radicals to move once again to fill the center of Chilean politics. However, they were challenged in that role by the emerging Christian Democratic (DC) party, whose candidate,

Eduardo Frei, outpolled the Radicals in the 1958 presidential contest. But the real surprise of that election was the showing of Salvador Allende, the candidate of the Communist and Socialist parties. With 28.9 percent of the vote in the sharply divided contest, he failed by a fraction (2.7 percent) to defeat the winner, Jorge Alessandri.

In office, Alessandri (1958–1964), a businessman supported by the right and occasionally by the peripatetic Radicals, applied a new set of austerity measures and obtained increased foreign aid to attempt economic stabilization. In the wake of the Cuban Revolution, the United States became determined to prevent a growth of leftist influence in the rest of the hemisphere. Chile, with its large Marxist parties, became a priority of the Kennedy and Johnson administrations' foreign-aid programs and covert intelligence operations.

During the 1964 presidential election, the Chilean center and right as well as the U.S. government sought to prevent what almost occurred in 1958—an Allende victory. As a result the right decided to support the centrist Frei candidacy, which promised a "Revolution in Liberty," and the CIA contributed $1.20 per Chilean voter to the antileft propaganda effort, over twice as much as the $.54 per U.S. voter that Lyndon Johnson and Barry Goldwater jointly spent in their own presidential campaigns that year. Frei was elected with an absolute majority of the votes. His government, that of his successor, and the breakdown of democracy will be discussed after reviewing the principal aspects and actors of the political game of twentieth-century Chilean politics.

POLITICAL GROUPS AND THE STATE: THE POLITICAL SYSTEM AT MID-CENTURY

By mid-century the Chilean state had evolved into a large and complex set of institutions. Even before the election of Salvador Allende to the presidency in 1970, total state expenditures represented about 24 percent of the GDP. The state also generated over 55 percent of gross investment and roughly 50 percent of all available credit. About 13 percent of the active population worked for the state, not counting the employees of the thirty-nine key corporations in which CORFO owned majority shares or the forty-one other enterprises where its participation was substantial. Government agencies were responsible for health care and social-security benefits, for the regulation of prices and wages, and for the settlement of labor disputes. Indeed, the dominant role of government in regulatory, distributive, and redistributive policies meant that private groups were constantly turning to state agencies and to the legislature, at times through elected local government officials, to gain favorable rulings and dispensations.

Over the years, myriad interest groups developed, closely paralleling the expansion of the state. They ranged from professional societies and business organizations to student unions, trade and pensioners' associations, youth and church groups, mothers' clubs, and neighborhood councils. Workers were represented by industrial, craft, and peasant unions (the latter legalized only in 1967), which were subjected to a series of state regulations and restrictions, although their leadership was democratically chosen by the rank and file. Civil servants were organized into a series of associations that, though acting as unions, were never officially recognized as such. Most groups sought to maximize their political clout before the state by organizing national associations with national headquarters. Large industrial, agricultural, and commercial interests were, for example, respectively organized into the Society for Industrial Advancement (SOFOFA), the National Agricultural Society (SNA), and the Central Chamber of Commerce. Professional societies were grouped in the Confederation of Professional Associations. Roughly 60 percent of all unionists were affiliated directly or indirectly with the Central Labor Federation (CUT). Some categories of specialized workers, small industrialists and retail merchants, truck owners, and so on also had national confederation offices.

Following the 1925 Constitution, the president—elected for a six-year term—was the source of major initiatives in the political process. Yet the president was far from an all-powerful figure. The most important checks on executive authority came from the competitive party system, which will be described in the next section. But presidential authority was also checked by the differentiation of governmental institutions and the marked autonomy of agencies even within the executive chain of command.

The legislature was no longer the focal point of the system, as it had been in the Parliamentary Republic. Nevertheless, the Chilean Congress remained the most powerful in Latin America, with the ability to modify and reject executive proposals. The Congress was the main arena for discussion and approval of budgetary matters as well as for the all-important issue of wage readjustments for public and even private employees.

In the final analysis, legislative politics was party politics, and presidents could cajole and bargain with allied as well as with adversary political groups for mutual advantage. By contrast the two other branches of government, the court system and the comptroller general (Contraloría), were well insulated from both presidential and legislative scrutiny. Judicial promotions were determined by seniority and merit, and though the president retained some power of appointment, his candidates had to come from lists prepared by the judges themselves. Equally independent was the comptroller general, who, like the Supreme Court judges, was appointed for life. His agency was charged with auditing public accounts and ruling on the legality of executive decrees. The comptroller's rulings on financial matters were final; on other matters, the president could, with the concurrence of his cabinet, overrule the comptroller. However, because of the prestige of the latter's office, this could be done only at the risk of considerable controversy, and until the Allende years presidents rarely overruled the comptroller.

Even within the executive branch presidential authority was circumscribed. Forty percent of public employees worked for over fifty semiautonomous agencies that, though nominally under government ministries, enjoyed significant managerial and even budgetary autonomy. As elsewhere, the web of private interests affected by a particular agency soon learned to develop more or less workable relationships of mutual benefits with it. Vested interests often made it difficult for a new administration to abolish old programs and bureaus, and innovations often required the creation of new agencies to administer the new projects, thus contributing to the progressive expansion of the state apparatus. Civil-service organizations and professional associations anxious to place their members in the expanding state sector further complicated the picture. Some state agencies became virtual fiefdoms of architects, civil engineers, lawyers, or doctors.

Though many agencies actually had formal interest-group representation on managing councils, such representation never became as important as the more informal and fluid constituency ties. Chilean politics never became corporative politics. Most private groups did obtain legal recognition. But that was a routine procedure and hardly meant that the government was officially sanctioning particular associations with exclusive rights to represent functional segments of society before the state. Indeed, most claims on the state were made by highly competitive groups, often representing interests drawn from the same horizontal or class lines.

If Chilean politics was not corporative, neither was it praetorian. Despite the vast and disarticulated state apparatus and the claims of a multiplicity of interests jockeying for advantage, Chilean politics did not involve the naked confrontation of political forces each seeking to maximize its interests through direct action in the face of weak or transitory authority structures. The key to the Chilean system, which discouraged both corporatist and praetorian tendencies, was the continuing importance of political parties and a party system tied to the legislature, the principal arena for political give-and-take. From the turn of the century on, the norm in Chile was not the direct link between government agencies and interest associations or the unmediated clash of organized social forces. Rather, party structures, permeating all levels of society, served as crucial linkage mechanisms binding organizations, institutions, groups, and individuals to the political center. Local units of competing parties were active within each level of the bureaucracy, each labor union, each student federation. Parties often succeeded in capturing particular organizations or in setting up rival ones. Once an issue affecting the organization arose, party structures were instrumental in conveying the organization's demands to the nucleus of the policy-making process or in acting as brokers before the ubiquitous bureaucracy.

As the historical discussion noted, the Chilean party system was fragmented and very competitive. With the exception of the Christian Democrats in the mid-1960s, no single party received more than 30 percent of the votes in congressional or municipal elections from 1925 to 1973. The party system was also highly polarized. During the 1937–1973 period, the vote for the left (Socialists and Communists) averaged 21.5 percent (or 25.7 percent if one excludes the 1949, 1953, and 1957 elections in which the Communists were banned from participation), and the vote for the right averaged 30.1 percent. Since neither the right nor the left could obtain an effective majority on its own, center groups, especially the Radical Party, played a very important if little-appreciated role in the polarized system: By dealing with both extremes, they were essential elements in most legislative majorities or in winning presidential coalitions—all of which permitted the political system to muddle through despite the sharp ideological divergences. And yet the center movements could not succeed in establishing themselves as a majority force, although they occasionally eroded the strength of either the left or the right. For example, supported by voters on the right, the Christian Democrats scored a dramatic gain in the 1965 congressional election, obtaining 42.3 percent of the vote. But the Liberals and Conservatives, having merged to form the National Party in 1966, regained much of their historical strength by 1969, and their candidate outpolled the Christian Democratic nominee in the 1970 presidential election. Table 26.2 summarizes the electoral strength of the three tendencies in the 1937–1973 period.

Given the fact that no single party or tendency could capture the presidency alone, coalitions were necessary. These were either formed before the election and resulted in winning an absolute majority, as was the case in 1964, or they had to be put together after the election in order to obtain the constitutionally mandated congressional approval of a candidate receiving only a plurality of the vote, as occurred in most cases. But, invariably, coalitions tended to disintegrate shortly after the election. The president could not succeed himself, and party leaders scrambled to disassociate themselves from the difficulties of incumbency in order to maximize electoral fortunes in succeeding contests. This meant that presidents had to compromise often with new supporters in the legislature, to salvage part of their programs and to govern.

Despite the polarization of the party system, politics did not revolve around only ideological and programmatic discussions. Obtaining benefits for groups and even favors for individuals, the essence of politics during the Parliamentary Republic, continued to be an important part of party activities. In fact, officials from all parties spent most of their time acting as political brokers—processing pensions for widows, helping Protestant ministers qualify for the white-collar social-security fund, interviewing the labor minister on behalf of a union leadership, seeking a job for a young schoolteacher, obtaining bridges and sewer systems for communities, and so forth. Legislators had particular access to state agencies because of congressional influence over purse strings, promotions, and programs affecting the bureaucracy.

An important political issue that led to extended bargaining in the legislature and to a flurry of demands and pressures from organized groups was the yearly discussion of the wage readjustment law. The law was intimately related to the budgetary approval process and gave the legislators (and therefore the parties) an input into the economic policy planning process. The state-controlled wage scales in the public sector were used as guidelines for the private sector, and therefore the readjustment laws, which also regulated social-security benefits, were of direct concern to the various party constituencies. In an economy averaging over 25 percent inflation with sharp yearly variations, a fundamental demand would be readjustments that would exceed, or at least match, the rate of inflation. Occasionally, amendments favoring specific groups or unions, but not all in the same category, would be approved as the legisla-

Table 26.2

Percentage of the Vote Received by Parties on the Right, Center, and Left in Chilean Congressional Elections, 1937–1973

	1937	1941	1945	1949	1953	1957	1961	1965	1969	1973	Mean
Right[a]	42.0	31.2	43.7	42.0	25.3	33.0	30.4	12.5	20.0	21.3	30.1
Center[b]	28.1	32.1	27.9	46.7	43.0	44.3	43.7	55.6	42.8	32.8	39.7
Left[c]	15.4	33.9	23.1	9.4	14.2	10.7	22.1	22.7	28.1	34.9	21.5
Other	14.5	2.8	5.3	1.9	17.5	12.0	3.8	9.2	9.1	11.0	8.7

[a]Conservative and Liberal Parties, and National Party after 1965.
[b]Radical, Falangist, Christian Democratic, and Agrarian Laborist Parties.
[c]Socialist and Communist parties.
Source: Dirección del Registro Electoral, Santiago, Chile.

tors in the majority group sought to pay off political debts or favor their party comrades in positions of leadership. And yet the political ramifications of class cleavages in the society would become apparent as the left would, in the middle of dense and legalistic discussions over specifics, normally press for higher wages and benefits for working-class sectors, and the right would generally favor the restrictive readjustments tied to fiscal and economic austerity policies.

There were no giants in the Chilean political system. No single group could win a complete majority or totally impose its will on the others. In fact, since there was no ideological or programmatic consensus among the polarized political forces, the Chilean polity was in many respects a stalemated one, in which each decision led to extensive debates and long processes of political accommodation—or to lengthy protests by the dissatisfied groups. In such a setting, change could only be incremental, not revolutionary. Though upper-class sectors were favored by existing arrangements, the intricate stalemate reflected a situation in which each group derived benefits from participating in the system and thus had real stakes in its preservation. It is therefore not surprising that there was such a strong consensus over procedure, over the expression of power capabilities through elections. But as the left gained positions through the commonly shared political process, the right and the sectors it represented began to question the validity of the process itself.

THE BREAKDOWN OF DEMOCRACY

Chile Under Eduardo Frei

The election of Eduardo Frei to the presidency in 1964 marked a significant shift in the center of Chilean politics. Unlike the Radical Party or the Ibáñez movement, the Christian Democrats (DC) claimed to be a new and cohesive ideological center, intent on breaking the political stalemate. They argued that their reformist strategy would lead to genuine economic and social progress and that it represented a viable third way between the right and the Marxist left. The Christian Democrats therefore ignored the fact that they had achieved the presidency with official endorsement from the rightist parties and that their unprecedented 1965 majority in the Chamber of Deputies was obtained with the support of traditionally right-wing portions of the electorate. They tried to govern as if they had become a majority party that would monopolize the presidency without coalition support for decades to come. Thus they refused to "lower themselves" to share in the distribution of patronage to satisfy electoral clienteles. The Radicals, rather than being cultivated as a potential ally in the political center, were maligned as pragmatic opportunists and were forced to relinquish some of their hold over the state bureaucracy. With the exercise of rigid party discipline in the Chamber of Deputies, which prevented the legislature from overruling presidential initiatives, the lower house became more and more a rubber stamp and the Senate a negative force.

The animosities created by the DC's disdain for coalition politics were compounded by the reforms it set in motion. These were ostensibly designed to raise the living standards and political participation of lower-class sectors as well as to modernize the social and economic systems. Two new groups, in particular, were mobilized as never before: the urban shantytown dwellers and the peasants. The first were encouraged to set up neighborhood councils and a variety of self-help organizations with cultural and community-development ends. The second rapidly became unionized once the peasant unionization law was approved in 1967 or were included in the peasant cooperatives that were set up in the lands expropriated under the government's new agrarian-reform program. Small landholding peasants were also encouraged to form cooperatives. As a result, roughly half the peasant labor force had become organized one way or another by 1970. Many new (particularly craft) unions were also formed among urban workers. Training programs were begun for both workers and peasants to increase their skills, and an educational reform increased the minimum number of mandatory schooling years.

The reforms, especially those in the countryside, engendered great opposition on the right, which traditionally had a strong political base among the landowners, who were threatened with expropriations and peasant unionization. The reforms also caused resentment and bitterness on the left. As the many young Christian Democrats in charge of the new programs spread throughout the country using modern techniques and displaying new equipment, it became clear that the DC was attempting to build a strong political base among popular sectors, precisely those sectors that Communists and Socialists considered their own natural base of support. This led to an intense effort by the left to compete with the DC in the creation of the new popular organizations. As a result sharp party conflicts were extended to broader sections of the population, creating sectarian divisions and feelings at the grass roots as never before. The threat to the left and the overall party competition for popular support were enhanced by the rise of an extreme left movement that also sought to organize its following.

The popular mobilization of the 1960s should therefore be seen as the result of party competition, with primarily political consequences. It cannot be said that the process got out of hand, either in terms of the capacity of party elites to control it or in terms of its having overburdened the nation's economy. In fact, during the Frei administration the general economic situation improved and state income increased, thereby generating greater economic capacity to increase the income of the newly mobilized popular sectors as well as a larger government capability to finance new programs. Though state income rose with better tax collection, the economic and fiscal improvements of the period were largely due to a rise in the price of copper during the Vietnam War and to foreign credit, mainly from U.S. government and private sources. The latter caused an increase in Chilean external debt to US$3 billion by the end of Frei's term and debt-service payments equivalent to roughly a third of export earnings.

Despite all its efforts, the DC vote in the 1969 congressional elections was reduced to 29.8 percent. And given the events of the previous six years, it proved impossible to have anything but a three-way race in the 1970 presidential elections. The right would have nothing to do with the Christian Democrats and decided to rally behind the candidacy of former president Jorge Alessandri. The Radicals and other small centrist and leftist groups joined the Socialists and Communists in forming the Popular Unity (UP) coalition, which presented Salvador Allende as candidate. Allende obtained 36.2 percent of the vote, Alessandri came in a close second with 34.9 percent, and the Christian Democratic nominee trailed with 27.8 percent. It must be noted that the result was not the expression of heightened electoral radicalism. Allende, in fact, received a smaller percentage of the vote than in 1964, when he was supported by only Socialists and Communists, and fewer new voters than his conservative adversary. Moreover, although the Christian Democratic candidate ran on a leftist platform, it is clear from survey and electoral data that his voters would have gone to the right rather than the left.

Following constitutional procedure, the Congress had to elect the president from the two front runners, since none of the candidates received an absolute majority of the vote. In the most flagrant foreign intervention in Chilean history, U.S. president Richard Nixon ordered the CIA to do everything necessary to prevent Allende from coming to power, including economic sabotage and provoking a military coup. The Christian Democrats, unable to vote for their own candidate, held the key swing votes in the legislature, and President Frei and his colleagues were subjected to numerous internal and external pressures to get them to vote for Alessandri. When it appeared that they would reluctantly honor tradition by selecting the front runner, the CIA helped to organize an attempt to kidnap the chief of staff of the armed forces to provoke a military coup. Gen. René Schneider was killed and the coup attempt backfired. It was the first assassination of a major Chilean leader since that of Portales in 1837.

The Allende Years

Allende's inauguration as president represented the first time that a coalition dominated by the Marxist parties took control of the executive. The coalition had campaigned on a program designed to initiate a transition to socialism while preserving Chile's traditional democratic freedoms and constitutional procedures, and the new administration moved swiftly to implement it. With the unanimous consent of the Congress, U.S. interests in the copper mines were nationalized. Resorting to executive powers, some of which were based on admittedly obscure though never repealed legal statutes, the government purchased or took over a broad range of industries as well as the private banking sector and, using Frei's agrarian-reform law, accelerated expropriations of farmland. Some industry and land takeovers were instigated by their workers or peasants, led in most cases by leftist or extreme leftist militants, who began sit-in strikes demanding the expropriations. This phenomenon was aided by the overall political climate created by the Allende inauguration, one that favored rather than repressed working-class actions, even when they contradicted government policies.

The government also quickly set in motion a plan to raise wages, salaries, and benefits, particularly for the lowest-paid workers, and to increase the social services in poor communities. These measures were taken in part to stimulate the economy by increasing demand and in part as an attempt to strengthen the government's electoral support as well as to satisfy the expectations of the left's working-class bases, for whom socialism principally meant a better standard of living. The policies were apparently successful, as the economic growth rate during 1971 was the best in decades, and the Popular Unity obtained roughly 50 percent of the vote in the 1971 municipal elections.

The initially favorable economic trends were, however, quickly reversed. Reflecting the poor's needs, the rising demand was disproportionately channeled to a greater consumption of basic consumer items such as food and clothing, areas of the economy that were least able to respond with rapid production increases. Inflationary pressures were therefore strengthened, particularly since government spending increased without a proportional rise in tax receipts, partly as a result of greater tax evasion. By the end of 1972 inflation had reached 164 percent and currency emissions accounted for over 40 percent of the fiscal budget. Moreover, the economy was clearly hurt by politically motivated cutbacks in credits and spare parts from the usual U.S. private or governmental sources. Foreign-exchange reserves dwindled rapidly as Chile imported more food and equipment with less recourse to credit and as it sought to meet payments, though partly rescheduled, on the foreign debt. The price of copper dropped to record lows, adding to the difficulties.

Early political success also proved short-lived. In 1972 the UP suffered reverses in key by-elections as well as in important institutional elections, such as those of the University of Chile or of labor federations. The courts, Contraloría, and Congress also objected increasingly to government initiatives. And most importantly, the early tacit support of the Christian Democrats turned into active opposition, leading to congressional censorship of ministers and to attempts to limit presidential authority.

The process that led to the brutal 1973 military coup that ended the Allende experiment is a highly complex, multidimensional, and dialectical one. It cannot be reduced to a simple set of causes that are easily construed with the benefits of hindsight. Surely the government made many unwise decisions or proved indecisive at important turning points; the sabotage and conspiracies of foreign and domestic interests seeking to preserve privilege at all costs helped to create an acute economic and political crisis; the actions of revolutionary groups both within and without the government coalition contributed to the exacerbation of an atmosphere of extreme confrontation that strengthened the disloyal and reactionary opposition; elements in the armed forces proved to be less than totally committed to the constitution and the democratic system; the capacity of the state to control and direct civil society disintegrated; taking a longer view, the dependency of the economy made the Allende experiment excessively vulnerable. All these are important factors, but they are not sufficient to explain the final result if viewed apart from a historical process in which contingent events played an important role. The breakdown of the regime was not preordained. It is a mistake to view the middle sectors as hopelessly reactionary, the workers as so radicalized that they would not stop short of total revolution, the army so antidemocratic that it was only waiting for its opportunity, the economy so dependent and the United States so single-handedly powerful and intransigent that the only possible denouement was full-fledged authoritarianism. There was room for choice, but with each unfolding event in the historical process that choice was markedly reduced.

If a single factor must be highlighted, the breakdown of Chilean democracy should be viewed as the result of the inability and unwillingness of moderate forces on both sides of the political dividing line to forge center agreements on programs and policies as well as on regime-saving compromises. The UP could not obtain a workable majority on its own, and the option of arming the workers as demanded by revolutionary groups was not a realistic alternative. The Chilean left was organized to compete in elections, not fight in battles; to change strategy would not have been easy, and any attempt to do so would have provoked an even earlier coup d'état. Without support from centrist forces, principally from the Christian Democrats who had made Allende's election possible in the first place, the UP government would remain a minority government without sufficient power to carry out programs, given the vast and unwieldy character of the Chilean institutional system.

The failure of center agreements resulted from political pressures originating in the extremes of both sides of the polarized party system. The government coalition was in fact sharply divided, the basic disagreements being those separating the Communists from the majority faction in the Socialist party. The latter wanted to press as fast as possible to institute the UP program and felt that support for the government would increase only insofar as it took decisive action to implement a socialist system. Compromise with the DC would, in the Socialists' view, only divert revolutionary objectives and confuse the working class. They therefore sought to undermine UP-DC collaboration and agreements. The Communists were much more willing to moderate the course of government policies in order to consolidate a narrower range of changes and to broaden the government's legislative base by resolving differences with the Christian Democrats. Both Socialists and Communists were pressured by the non-UP extreme left, which sought to accelerate changes through direct action outside constitutional procedures. Their influence in the UP coalition was magnified by the proximity of their positions with those of elements in the Socialist party majority; therefore, the extreme left was not marginalized at the fringe of the political process.

Allende shared the Communists' position but did not wish to cause a break with his own Socialist party. He therefore projected an ambivalent image and at times failed to take decisive action—for fear of alienating his party—without the certainty of receiving consistent support from the center forces in exchange. These political differences affected the daily operations of government agencies; employees, for example, often would not take orders from superiors belonging to other parties. The president and the ministers were so often involved in tending to these daily crises that they had little time to structure long-term policies, analyze the consequences of short-term ones, or develop a coherent strategy to deal with the moderate opposition.

The Christian Democrats were also torn by internal differences: The party was divided into left- and right-leaning factions of approximately equal strength. The 1971 party leadership came from the left-leaning group, and it sought to maintain a working relationship with the government, while the right-wing faction pressed for the adoption of a tougher opposition stand. However, the party leadership was at first rebuffed by an overly confident UP government exhibiting the same arrogance the DC had shown previously, a situation that only strengthened the position of the right-wing sector within the party. Ironically, constitutional reforms adopted in 1970 by the DC and the right had diminished the role of the legislature, thus reducing the executive's need to reach agreements with the opposition. The right-wing faction was also strengthened by the vehement attacks on prominent DC leaders in the leftist media and by the assassination of a former Frei cabinet minister. Though this killing was the action of a small leftist fringe, the DC blamed the government for tolerating a climate of violence that, it argued, led to such incidents.

As a centrist opposition force, the DC was also extremely vulnerable to pressures from the right of the party system. If the DC leadership could not show that its tacit support for the government had resulted in moderating UP policies, the party stood to lose the anti-UP vote to the right without gaining greater support from the left. Therefore, the DC was soon forced to work with the right in opposition. The turning point came in mid-1971 with the first special by-election to fill a vacant congressional seat in which, given the winner-take-all nature of the contest, a UP victory was certain if the opposition fielded separate candidates. Consequently, the DC approached the government suggesting an agreement that would have led to a joint UP-DC candidacy, an offer that Allende accepted but the Socialist party vetoed. In view of this rejection, the DC turned to the right, and the joint opposition candidate won decisively. As a result of this experience, a leftover splinter group decided to leave the Christian Democratic party, which strengthened further the right wing within it. The DC alliance with the right-wing National Party continued in future elections, adding to the polarization of forces.

In February 1972 the DC obtained congressional approval of legislation severely limiting the president's ability to intervene in the economy, thereby challenging the essence of the government's program and marking the beginning of a fundamental constitutional confrontation between the president and the Congress. Interpreting 1970 constitutional amendments differently from the president, the opposition argued that Congress required only a simple majority to override a presidential veto of the new legislation, while the UP maintained, in fact more correctly, that a two-thirds majority was needed. It then became clear to moderates on both sides that accommodation was essential. On two separate occasions government and DC representatives met in an attempt to reach a compromise that would have allowed the government to keep a substantial public sector of the economy while giving the private sector certain guarantees. But the talks collapsed. The Nationals suggested a DC sell-out, while the Socialists and other leftist groups stepped up factory expropriations in order to present the DC with a fait accompli. They thus undermined the negotiating position of the moderate Radical splinter group entrusted by Allende with conducting the discussion, and as a result this group left the UP coalition to join the opposition. Again, this only polarized the political forces further, reducing the potential success of a center agreement.

By mid-1972, the critical situation of the economy and the growing aggressiveness of the opposition led the government to try once again to hold talks with the Christian Democrats. This time Allende was strongly committed to reaching a compromise, and the UP made substantial concessions leading to agreement on a broad range of issues. However, the more conservative faction within the Christian Democratic party maneuvered successfully to prevent the negotiators from finishing their work. By that point, most sectors within the DC felt that the government was clearly on the defensive and thought that by concluding an agreement with it the party would surely lose support among the increasingly discontented middle sectors, thereby running the risk of being routed by the Nationals in the March 1973 congressional elections. Considerations of short-term party interest thus carried the day.

Toward the end of 1972, qualitative changes had begun to take place in Chilean politics. The parties had repeatedly called the mass rallies that characterized the Allende years not only to increase their bargaining stakes but also to prove actual power capabilities. Nonetheless, the nature of this mobilization soon changed. Business and professional associations increasingly took matters into their own hands, and before long the DC and the Nationals were falling over each other not to direct but to pledge support for the independent action of a whole range of groups. These demonstrations culminated in the massive October 1972 strike and lockout by hundreds of truck owners, merchants, industrialists, and professionals. The government parties countered by mobilizing their own supporters, also engendering a significant organizational infrastructure that could operate at the margin of party leadership directives. These demonstrations and counterdemonstrations by a vast array of groups, the numbers of which had continued to increase during the Allende years, were partly stimulated by a vitriolic mass media giving at least two totally different interpretations of every event, generating a dynamic in which the symbolic became the real, falsehoods turned into hysterically believed truths, and perceived threats were taken as imminent. The climate of agitation was also increased by the CIA funds that flowed to opposition groups, strengthening them significantly as political actors independent of party control. For government leaders the decreased capacity of party elites to control group mobilization and confrontation was more serious than for the opposition. It meant that the government lost an important measure of authority over the society, that the state itself would be bypassed as the central arena for political confrontation, and that the legitimacy of the regular processes of bargaining was undermined. In this crisis atmosphere, Allende turned to a presumably neutral referee who would ensure institutional order until the March 1973 congressional elections could clear the political air. Military men were brought into the cabinet, and the chief of staff was made the minister of the interior.

The incorporation of the military into the government ended the strikes of October 1972 and freed the political forces to concentrate on the congressional elections, which party leaders saw as the decisive confrontation. But in serving as a buffer between contending forces, the military itself became the object of intense political pressures. The left within the UP criticized it for slowing down government programs and initiatives, while the more strident elements on the right accused it of helping a government that would otherwise fall. Other sectors went out of their way to praise the military, a tacit recognition that they were the only force with real power. These pressures politicized an institution that had largely remained at the margin of political events. Though it was hardly perceived at the time, a cleavage began to appear within the military between officers supporting the government because they saw it as the constitutional government and those more receptive to the increasingly louder voices of opposition elements calling for the government's downfall.

The March 1973 elections symbolized the final polarization of Chilean politics as the government and the opposition faced each other as two electoral blocs. Not surprisingly, the elections did not help resolve the political crisis. The opposition failed to gain the two-thirds majority it needed to impeach Allende, and the government failed to obtain majority control in either house of Congress. Given the massive inflation and serious shortages of basic goods as well as the climate of political uncertainty, the government's showing was commendable since it managed to win seats at the expense of the opposition. And yet the final results were not dramatically different from those that the two blocs had obtained as separate parties in the previous congressional contest. The electorate did not provide the magic solution. Their task done, the military left the cabinet.

Soon after, a decisive event initiated the final stage in the breakdown of the regime. On June 29, 1973, a military garrison revolted. Though the uprising was quickly put down, President Allende and his advisers realized that it was only a matter of time before the *golpista* (pro-coup) faction of the armed forces consolidated its strength. They again dismissed the far left's counsel to arm the workers, arguing that the creation of a parallel army would only accelerate the coup. Ironically, military officers were quicker to believe, or to make believe, not only that the workers could be a potent force but that sectors of the left had already structured a viable military force. But the well-publicized efforts of military commanders to find secret arms caches uncovered nothing of importance, although they attempted to convey the impression that they had.

To the consternation of the leadership of his own Socialist party, Allende once again called for talks with the Christian Democrats. And despite the vocal opposition of many of their followers, the Christian Democratic leaders, urged to do so by the cardinal, agreed to the new negotiations. However, an agreement at that point was unlikely. The hard-line faction of the Christian Democrats had replaced the more moderate leadership, and Allende was thus obliged to deal with the group most hostile to his government and policies. Moreover, the country was once again in the throes of massive lockouts, strikes, and civil disobedience campaigns led by business and professional associations (with considerable CIA funding), all demanding the president's resignation. By that time significant working-class groups, such as the copper miners, had also staged strikes to express their discontent with specific government policies, which only reinforced the confidence of the opposition. Any form of support for the government junta by the Christian Democrats would therefore have been seen as a sellout by the opposition. The political arena had been reduced to a few men attempting to negotiate a settlement. Even though these men no longer had the kind of control over social forces they once had, a dramatic announcement from the talks would still have placed the nation's largest parties and most respected leaders on the side of a peaceful solution and would have seriously undermined the subversive plans of military officers.

But agreement was not forthcoming. The Christian Democrats did not trust Allende's word that he really wanted a settlement, believing instead that he merely sought to buy time in order to force an armed confrontation. However, it is clear from the president's actions that he sought an agreement. He kept moderate leaders in his cabinets, even though they were severely attacked by the left within and outside the UP, and he virtually broke with his own party. Furthermore, Allende finally did agree to the Christian Democratic demand of bringing the military back into the government. In combating to the end the dubious prospect of "Marxist totalitarianism" and in constantly increasing bargaining demands, the DC leaders failed to realize how much stake they had in the political order they thought they were defending. By not moving forcefully to structure a political solution, they undermined the fragile position of the president and his advisers, who were seeking accommodation. Instead the DC supported a Chamber of Deputies declaration calling on the military to safeguard the constitution and declaring that the government had lost its legitimacy.

Two weeks later, prominently displaying the chamber's resolution as evidence of the legality and broad-based support for their action, the top military leadership led the brutal revolt against the government. Air force jets bombed and strafed the presidential palace, in which Allende himself, after offering resistance, committed suicide. Thousands of government supporters, or presumed government supporters, were arrested, mistreated, tortured, or killed in the months that followed.

Some prominent Christian Democrats condemned the coup in the initial moments. But others, including the leadership, welcomed it as inevitable and blamed the government for all that had transpired. Little did they realize what the "saving" action of the military would mean for the country's and their own future.

THE MILITARY IN GOVERNMENT

The September 11, 1973, coup marked the most dramatic political change in Chilean history. A military junta headed by the commanders of each of the services and the national police took power and argued at first that they had overthrown the Allende government in order to protect democracy and restore constitutional government. But the new authorities soon defined the Chilean crisis as one of regime rather than of government. They placed the blame for the breakdown of Chile's institutions not only on the Popular Unity government but also on liberal democracy itself. Democracy had permitted divisive party competition and the rise of Marxist political leaders intent on defining the nation's politics in class terms. It had also generated demagogic politicians who contributed to economic mismanagement. Government was best left, in their view, in the hands of "technicians" who could formulate the "best" policy choices with administrative efficiency until the people had the necessary "maturity" to exercise better judgment.

The goal of the new junta thus became one of transforming the Chilean system, creating a "new" democracy and a "new" citizen, devoid of the "vices" of the past. The Congress was closed, local governments disbanded, and elections banned. Newspapers, radio stations, and magazines were shut down, and those allowed to publish were subjected to varying degrees of censorship. Officials and leaders of the Popular Unity government and parties were arrested, exiled, and, in some cases, killed. Within months of the coup, Christian Democratic leaders, unwilling to accept an indefinite military regime, saw their activities severely curbed as well.

The military authorities sharply restricted the activities of traditional political parties and ignored the strong pressure of right-wing supporters to create a massive progovernment party or "civic-military movement." For this reason it is inappropriate to label the Chilean regime as fascist. The military regime sought political demobilization.

Neither is it appropriate to view the regime as corporatist. Despite early pronouncements that the junta intended to draw on Catholic integralist doctrine to structure corporative institutions, all of the country's major interest groups, including employers and professional associations and trade organizations (many of which had supported the coup with enthusiasm), saw their influence markedly diminished. The new authorities were simply not interested in bringing into the decision-making process any expression of societal interests. They were convinced that through disciplined administrative management and the advice of qualified experts they would be able to govern and modernize the country without the advice of "interested" or "partisan" groups. They thus sought to replace party politics and interest-group politics with technoadministrative solutions imposed by fiat. The governing style for the country as a whole paralleled the internal governing style of the military institution itself.

The Chilean military regime was extraordinary in the extent to which General Pinochet succeeded in concentrating power in himself. Since he commanded the largest and most important service, his fellow officers named him the first president of the junta, but early suggestions called for the rotation of this position among its four members. Both executive and legislative power rested in the junta. Within a year, Pinochet had acquired greater power than his colleagues. With the adoption of a "Stature of the Military Junta," a protoconstitutional document, together with declaring himself "Supreme Chief of the Nation," Pinochet assumed control of executive power, although it still formally remained in the junta, which had to approve all cabinet and ambassadorial nominations. Half a year later a new constitutional decree named him "President of the Republic of Chile," the traditional designation of Chilean presidents, in addition to preserving the prior titles of "President of the Governmental Junta" and "Supreme Chief of the Nation" and stated unambiguously that he exercised executive power. General Pinochet's position as "President of the Republic," and the junta's as the "legislative power," was reaffirmed in the so-called transitory articles of the constitution adopted in 1980. Pinochet also changed his military title in order to emphasize a position of preeminence over his colleagues in the other services, who then became his subordinates in rank. In 1979 he adopted the designation of "Generalissimo of the Armed Forces" and later that of "Captain General." He effectively positioned himself to control all military promotions and retirements, carefully overseeing in particular those in his own service, the army.

This concentration of power had no parallel in other military regimes in Latin America. Pinochet was not a retired military officer, like most of his Argentine counterparts, nor did he serve at the behest of the corps of generals, like Brazilian military presidents. Policy decisions never originated among high-ranking officers and were never reviewed by them. Pinochet stressed repeatedly that the armed forces were not to deliberate political matters. In this sense, their relation to the executive power was one of subordination just as it had been, in the past, to the Chilean presidents. Military officers occupied a majority of all positions in the government, but they reported to their superiors, be they military or civilian, within the government. General Pinochet led a military regime, but it was not, strictly speaking, of the military. It is best described as a dictatorship of the commander-in-chief. As such, it was a curious, personalized regime in which power derived from occupancy of the top office of a military bureaucracy.

This type of dictatorship was made possible by the highly professional, obedient, and hierarchical nature of the Chilean military. Paradoxically, these were qualities that stemmed from Chile's democratic past. The military was not involved in politics, and Chilean politicians did not expect it to be the source of political instability or coups. It is highly symptomatic that the coup against President Allende did not break the military line of command: The president had appointed General Pinochet to the top position in the army shortly before.

Policy Initiatives of the Military Government

The Pinochet government undertook more far-reaching changes than any of those that preceded it over the last fifty years. The repressive apparatus of the state increased enormously, as did the jurisdiction of military courts over offenses by civilians. But in other respects the size of the state and its role in national life were drastically reduced.

The government pursued an aggressive policy of privatization. All land held under the agrarian reform program was turned over to individual property holders. Only a handful of industries remained in the public sector (aside from the railways and utilities, the most important of these is the copper company controlling the principal established mines; new investments in copper have come from the private sector, mainly in the form of foreign/Chilean joint ventures). The rest of the industries were sold to national and foreign private investors, often at bargain prices. As part of debt-for-equity swaps to reduce an external debt that increased to $20 billion by 1986, many formerly Chilean firms have been denationalized.

The authorities put in place a radical program of privatizing state services in social security and health, which meant dismantling long-standing publicly funded institutions. The public housing development program was also turned over to the private sector. Labor legislation was extensively revamped, making it more difficult for workers to pressure employers through collective action. The size of the unionized workforce declined by about 60 percent compared to its highest membership point in the last two years of the Allende government. Wages and salaries declined in real terms by as much as 50 percent with respect to their levels in 1970, and did not recover fully—even during the years of strong growth—during the whole period of military government. The combination of the incomes and welfare policies led to a significant regression in the distribution of income.

The government also undertook educational reforms. Public, primary, and secondary schools were turned over to municipal administrations (led by mayors appointed by the government), and new legislation encouraged the formation of private schools and even universities.

The economy was opened up to external competition by drastic cuts in import duties, resulting in numerous bankruptcies as industries were unable to adjust to the shock. Except for a few years in the late 1970s and early 1980s in which the government's economic team greatly overvalued the national currency with catastrophic results, economic policies generally sought to stimulate growth through the development of new exports. These policies were successful and reduced the reliance on copper exports from about 85 percent of export earnings in the early 1970s to about 45 percent in the late 1980s.

Economic growth rates were very spotty during the sixteen years of military government. There were severe recessions in 1975 and in 1982 (in each of those years the economy declined by about 14 percent) and periods of significant growth (or recovery) with positive rates of between 5 and 9 percent in the late 1970s and late 1980s. Given this zigzag pattern of growth, the per capita income of Chile by the end of the 1980s was roughly equivalent to its 1970 level measured in constant dollars. And yet the military government prided itself on its economic management, given the fact that the economy registered strong growth in the last three years of authoritarian rule; moreover, inflation was low, the external debt shrunk by $3 billion, and unemployment dropped significantly. Chilean businessmen also developed a new confidence in their abilities and in the economic future of the country, which they associated with the free-market and open-economy policies of the regime. This sense of success was magnified by the disastrous economic performance of Latin America during the 1980s.

Economic and social policy initiatives were in the hands of a team of young economists who came to be known as the Chicago Boys due to their free-market and monetarist approaches. They appealed to Pinochet because of their lack of identification with Chilean parties and their technical competence. Their belief that Chilean underdevelopment could be attributed to an overbloated state that restricted private initiative corresponded well with the effort to drastically restrict state institutions for political reasons, given the association of those institutions with party-sponsored clientelistic politics in the democratic past.

Opposition to the Military Regime

Many authoritarian rulers think that they can drastically reduce support for their oppositions through a combination of repression and political, social, and economic changes. This goal proves to be elusive in countries, like Chile, with strong party systems. Citizens by and large retain their political predilections, and these are passed on from one generation to the next supported by family and community ties creating a collective political memory. Party militants are also able to retain at least the rudiments of their organizations, and they often remain active as leaders in social groups and associations whose activities are allowed by the regime.

Chile was no exception to this rule. The parties retained their organizations despite the severe repression directed especially at those of the left. Many party militants remained in positions of leadership in the same social groups where they found an audience before, be it the labor movement, student federations, or community associations. Supporters of the military government rarely won the internal elections of these groups when they were held freely. The Catholic Church assumed a very important role in the overall opposition to the regime. It continually called for national reconciliation and for a return to liberal democracy and refused to lend any credence to the attempts by the authorities to use Catholic social doctrine—in its most conservative interpretation—as a formula to legitimize the regime. The Church also took decisive steps to challenge the regime for its many abuses of human rights and protected the lawyers and other professionals who actively documented such abuses and defended their victims in court. Moreover, the Church gave legal cover and other forms of support to many groups, such as social science researchers, journalists, unions, and popular community associations through which opposition views were expressed and organizing took place. It was through such Church-sponsored activities that the Christian Democrats and the left gradually came together in the first years of the military regime, leaving behind their bitter divisions from the Allende period.

Through a combination of social mobilization, calls for negotiations, and international pressures, the opposition continually tried to force the military to abdicate and accept a transition to democracy. Militants on the extreme left, some associated with the Communist party, also attempted to organize armed resistance to the regime. All actions undertaken by such groups, including a failed assassination attempt against Pinochet himself, were sharply criticized by the rest of the opposition, on grounds of both morality and expediency. The bulk of the opposition condemned all forms of violence, and such incidents—some of which were of very dubious origins—seemed to play into the hands of the regime by lending credence to its claims that the country, suffering terrorist threats, was not ready for democracy.

The opposition's attempts to mobilize people against the regime were at times enormously successful in the major cities. There was a series of massive "protests" for several years beginning in May of 1983. The movement, called by labor leaders initially, consisted of banging pots at a certain hour in the evening, boycotting classes, staging work slowdowns, and refraining from using public transportation and from shopping. The military regime eventually met such protests, which were initially held monthly, with massive displays of force and random, brutal repression by the army and police. The protests increasingly led to violence, which the government tried, with characteristic aplomb, to blame entirely on the opposition. Labor and political leaders were arrested and tried under security laws, some in military courts.

The moderate opposition eventually called the protest movement off in order to break the increasing cycle of violence. And yet, the movement served an important function. It demonstrated both to the government and to the opposition itself that after ten years of military rule, in which the government, controlling television and most of the rest of the mass media, relentlessly diffused a single interpretation of all events, the opposition could still generate a massive demonstration against the authorities. This emboldened the parties to seek new forms of exercising political leadership, and it convinced many civilian politicians on the right that the military government's long-term project was not entirely viable. Such politicians, whose concerns were dismissed high-handedly by Pinochet, began to organize a new political party of the right, taking some distance from the military regime. This eventually generated a new and quite bitter split on the right of the Chilean party spectrum between those who identified closely with the military regime and those who did not.

While the moderate opposition continually expressed its willingness to negotiate with the military regime over forms of transition to democracy, Pinochet himself steadfastly refused to entertain any such discussions. The personalized Chilean military regime had a very narrow and tight inner circle of power, allowing no space for the development of moderate but influential segments of political leadership within the ruling circles. If such segments had existed, it is conceivable that the opposition could have found a willing partner in the regime to search for a suitable transition formula. But all dissenters from Pinochet's leadership who emerged within the regime were simply excluded from it, and the opposition's attempts to press the government and the armed forces to negotiate came to nothing.

Throughout the military regime, the opposition enjoyed many expressions of international solidarity. The international community repeatedly condemned the government's violations of human rights. When the AFL-CIO threatened to boycott the unloading of Chilean exports in the United States in 1978, the government prepared labor legislation that allowed a significant reactivation of Chile's unions. And arms sales to the Chilean military from major American and European manufacturers were significantly curtailed. Given the orthodoxy of its economic management and commitment to its debt obligations, the Chilean government was well received only in international financial circles.

The Transition to Democratic Government

The opposition was finally able to force the military government into a transition to democracy by using the procedures Pinochet himself had put into the 1980 Constitution.

The origins of this document go back to the immediate post-coup period. The new military authorities were in a juridically untenable position. They justified their seizure of power in part by noting that the Allende coalition had violated the 1925 Constitution, but they themselves were violating it daily through their de facto exercise of power and by not reverting—as many early supporters of the coup expected—to constitutional procedures in order to reconstitute the government. The junta therefore argued that the existing constitution was inadequate to "protect" democracy and announced that a new one would be written. A committee of civilians identified with the right and the extreme right was charged in 1974 with the task of preparing the draft of a new charter.

After writing the "Statute of the Military Junta" to establish some formal procedures, the committee ran into disagreements between its extremist and more moderate members. Eventually, as head of a "Council of State," former president Jorge Alessandri took a leading role in drafting the constitution, which he presented to General Pinochet in 1978 for his approval. The document adhered to a very large extent to Chilean constitutional traditions. It also called for a transition period of five years in which General Pinochet would continue to govern as president, but would share legislative responsibilities with a Congress whose members would initially be designated.

Pinochet changed the draft in significant ways, strengthening the power of non-elected and military officials and extending the presidential term of office to eight years. Moreover he added twenty-nine "transitory articles" that suspended the application of the bulk of the constitutional provisions until the beginning of a second presidential term after the enactment of the constitution. One of these articles named Pinochet to the presidency for a first term, which was to begin on March 11, 1981, and others assigned the legislative power to the junta. The transitory articles therefore permitted Pinochet to extend his personalistic regime for another eight years.

What was to prove decisive for the transition to democratic government were the stipulations Pinochet added to the transitory articles for the presidential succession at the end of the first term. At that point the commanders in chief of the armed services (including Pinochet himself) would select a new presidential candidate, whose name would be submitted to the voters in a plebiscite. If that individual won the plebiscite, congressional elections would be held within a year, and the constitution would be fully applied. If the candidate lost the plebiscite, within a year there would be open presidential as well as congressional elections. It is safe to assume that Pinochet had every intention of running for a second term, and he had no difficulty, when the time came, in obtaining the nomination from his colleagues. Pinochet felt confident of his ability to win plebiscites. He did so by a large margin in 1978, and he obtained what was announced as 65 percent approval in the plebiscite held on September 11, 1980, to approve the 1980 Constitution and his own "first presidential term" along with it.

But both of these plebiscites were held in highly irregular manners, and the opposition had little difficulty in contesting their validity. This rejection of the plebiscites' legitimacy, especially of the one that presumably had approved the constitution and Pinochet's own "presidential term" along with it, struck a raw nerve in ruling circles. Hence, Pinochet and his supporters took pains continually to stress the "constitutionality" of the government. Moreover, adherence to the 1980 Constitution became the centerpiece of the government's political program, replacing the earlier emphasis on building a new Chile that became untenable in the context of the severe economic crisis of 1982–1983 and the rise of the protest movement. The authorities also turned the defense of the "institutionality" enshrined in the constitution into one of the principal missions of the armed forces.

Since by late 1986 the opposition had exhausted all its efforts to force the government into a transition through social mobilization and other forms of pressure, it began to look forward to the 1988 plebiscite as a possible mechanism to defeat the government. Recalling its criticisms of the prior plebiscites, the opposition stipulated a series of conditions that would have to be met for the new plebiscite to be considered a valid expression of the voters' will. These included the reestablishment of a proper electoral registry (the previous one had been burned by the military), a sufficient amount of time for the registration process to ensure that large numbers of citizens actually registered, television access for advocates of the "no" ("no" to another term for Pinochet), the necessary voting procedures to ensure secrecy, and assurances that opposition delegates would be able to observe the balloting and vote-counting processes. The American ambassador in Santiago, Harry Barnes, made it very clear to the members of the military junta that the United States agreed with all these conditions and that it would not consider the plebiscite valid unless they were all met. Given its sensitivity to charges of illegitimacy, the government explicitly or tacitly agreed to all of them.

As the campaign preparations began, the opposition organized a broad coalition for the "no" that included all groups except the Communist party, whose leaders only very belatedly saw any value in the process. The opposition used the half-hour segment the authorities gave it on television very cleverly, with a message focused on future happiness and reconciliation that was developed by social science researchers using political marketing techniques. It also organized poll watchers in every single locality of the country and an alternative vote-counting system that would give it the possibility of checking the veracity of official figures. Citizens were to vote "yes" or "no" to Pinochet's continuing in the presidency, and when the votes were counted on the night of October 5, 1988, 54.7 percent had voted "no," and 43 percent "yes." Over 90 percent of registered voters cast ballots, and over 90 percent of those eligible to register had done so.

Pinochet was shocked by this result. Yet there was little he could do to set it aside. The plebiscite was a procedure that he introduced into the constitution himself, and he could not easily turn against the "institutionality" he had for years urged the armed forces and his civilian supporters to uphold. The opposition also gave the regime no excuses to suspend the plebiscite or the vote count. From beginning to end, it conducted an orderly campaign, refraining from staging demonstrations that might be construed as provocations, especially on the day of the plebiscite. The night of the vote count some government officials did seek to tamper with the results. But while this effort was under way, the commander-in-chief of the air force freely admitted to a journalist that the figures released by the opposition were correct, thereby undermining any tinkering with the results.

The outcome of the plebiscite meant that within a year, open presidential and congressional elections were to be held. The opposition parties agreed to support a single presidential candidate, Christian Democrat Patricio Aylwin, and to present basically a single list (with a parallel list including some Communist and other leftist candidates running in a few districts) for the Senate and the Lower House. The opposition also demanded that the constitution be revised, and the government agreed to some changes. Since the amendments were submitted to a new plebiscite, which the opposition was bound to approve, the government could claim that the constitution had been backed by the voters and thereby had received indisputable democratic legitimation.

The presidential and congressional elections were held on December 14, 1989. Aylwin won 55.2 percent of the validly cast vote, defeating two candidates of the right, and his democratic coalition obtained 56.5 percent of the vote for seats in the Lower House of Congress.

REBUILDING THE DEMOCRATIC REGIME

President Aylwin's term in office was shortened to four years as part of the agreement with the military regime that altered the Constitution in mid-1989. The right and even the military thought that they could recapture the presidency after four years, because they assumed that the incoming opposition would prove to be incompetent in office. Pinochet even created a virtual shadow cabinet with thirty-five advisers in charge of covering developments in all areas of public policy. Supporters of the military regime assumed that labor conflicts over long-standing grievances would emerge; leftist insurgencies and terrorism would expand; demands for accounting of human rights violations would magnify tensions; the political alliance of Christian

Democrats, Socialists, radicals, and others would soon break up; and the economy, already overheated as a result of the military government's overspending for electoral purposes, would deteriorate as investments dried up in a climate of uncertainty. Such perceptions were buttressed by the experience of democratization in neighboring countries, where it had been accompanied by adverse economic results. However, these predictions proved to be grossly incorrect. And after his term in office ended in 1994, President Aylwin turned the government over to Eduardo Frer Ruiz Tagle, another Christian Democrat, who was elected in December 1993 by the same coalition that had won the plebiscite against Pinochet.

The favorable result was a product of the great skill of the new team that took office with Aylwin and of the widespread support the government continued to enjoy among the broad segments of organized Chilean society who opposed military rule. Although the first year of the Aylwin government required an economic adjustment that reduced growth to 3 percent, since then the economy has enjoyed average growth rates of about 7 percent with ever lower rates of inflation (since 1995 in single digits per annum). The rate of savings and investment increased by the mid-1990s to about 27 percent of GNP, a level nearly equal to those of the high-performing Asian economies, and there has been a yearly fiscal budget surplus of 2–3 percent of GNP. Social spending in education, health, and housing has increased by 10 percent in real terms per year since 1990. The lowest pensions and the minimum wage rose about 50 percent in four years, and after a slow start, by 1996 real wages reached their highest levels ever. And despite an increase in labor conflict, including public-sector workers and teachers, the new levels are very low by international standards and minimal when compared to those of the late 1960s and early 1970s in Chile. These low levels of labor conflict reflect some changes in labor laws favoring workers, a drop in unemployment to a 5–6.5 percent level, and a solid recovery of levels of unionization to about 24 percent of the labor force (including associations of public employees). Foreign investors have flocked to place their money in Chile, international credit agencies have given Chilean paper investment grade, and the nation's business sector has begun to invest heavily in neighboring economies. Free-trade agreements negotiated bilaterally with many countries or with groups of countries such as the Mercosur further facilitate the trade and overall economic integration of Chile into the world economy. The main deficiency has been that income distribution continues to retain the regressiveness it reached under the military regime, although more than 1 million Chileans of working age increased their incomes above the poverty line during Aylwin's term in office.

Aylwin personally took charge of handling the difficult issue of human rights violations, and did so skillfully. He initiated a review of the 384 political prisoners who remained in jail when he took office, most of whom were rapidly released. The last handful of prisoners had their sentences changed to exile abroad. Aylwin also appointed a Truth and Reconciliation Committee with representatives of all segments of opinion that documented over 3,000 cases of disappearances and produced a general report providing the country with a common interpretation of the recent and very conflictual past. Only the military took objection to that interpretation. The families of the disappeared persons were compensated by the state, including lifelong pensions for parents, widows or widowers, and stipends or scholarships for children; by 1993 there were about 4,100 beneficiaries. The evidence that was gathered was made public and could be used by the families for prosecuting the perpetrators of human rights violations. The government initiated a new interpretation of Pinochet's 1978 amnesty law stating that unless the body of a disappeared person was found the amnesty could not be applied; this opened the way for judicial inquiries into these human rights violations. It also reduced the jurisdiction of military courts over crimes involving civilians. As a result of all these measures, many cases were re-opened, and by mid-1996 there were still about 250 of them under active review by the courts. Moreover, about two dozen military and police officers have served or are serving sentences for crimes committed during the dictatorship but not covered by the amnesty law. These include the former head of the military regime's intelligence service during the worst period of human rights violations, Gen. Manuel Contreras. In addition, the government assisted the return of about 40,000 political exiles who applied for repatriation.

The human rights policies of the Aylwin government led to sometimes severe tensions with the military. Following a transitory article in the constitution that is still in force, General Pinochet remained as head of the army with an extraordinary term that did not lapse until 1997, although Aylwin twice urged him to resign. Led by Pinochet, officers demonstrated, producing serious incidents. Responding to the second of these demonstrations, Aylwin agreed in mid-1993 to sponsor a bill that would facilitate closure of the pending cases of human rights investigation and prosecution by the courts. However, this bill was not approved by the Congress, given the opposition of deputies of the left and by some Christian Democrats.

The military has opposed any further changes to the 1980 Constitution, which contains important provisions that are incompatible with a fully democratic constitutional framework. Both the Aylwin and the Frei governments have sponsored constitutional reforms that would correct these anomalies, but opponents of the right in Congress have agreed with the military and successfully blocked all such reforms.

Until these changes are enacted, the Chilean democratic transition cannot be said to have been completed. The Chilean Senate still reserves nine seats for unelected senators, all of whom during the years since the reestablishment of democratic government have joined forces with the pro-military right. The constitution stipulates that two of these senators are designated by the president, three by the Supreme Court, and four by the National Security Council, drawing all of them from certain designated pools of people, including former military and police commanders. This means that even the designations due in 1997 will most probably contain a majority of votes for the anticonstitutional-reform right.

Moreover, the 1980 Constitution prevents the president from dismissing the commanders-in-chief of the armed forces and police and from dismissing any high-ranking officer from his post outright. The only way a president can force an officer to retire is by refusing to sign a promotion decree for that officer, which eventually forces him out after completing the maximum number of years in his grade. The president cannot have any direct influence either on military doctrine or on the curriculum in the military academy. The military and police commanders also have half the seats in a National Security Council that is entitled to examine any issue it sees fit to discuss and that also participates—in addition to its designation of former military and police commanders as senators—in selecting one member of a Constitutional Court with considerable power of review over all legislation. The constraints on presidential authority over the military and these formal institutions to channel its influence run counter to democratic constitutionalism, but the necessary reforms have not been approved in Congress, in part because of the votes of the designated senators who are opposed to the abolition of their own seats.

The electoral system inherited from the Pinochet dictatorship is also an anomaly in the annals of democracy. The system favors the election of the runner-up list of candidates, which needs only to obtain slightly over one-third of the vote to win 50 percent of all seats. As the right generally obtains a little more than the requisite third in most districts (the design of which greatly overrepresents the small towns and rural areas where the right is strongest), it benefits from an overrepresentation in Congress even without the added support of the designated senators.

Important constitutional reforms have been enacted, however, since the return to democratic government. One of these re-created elected municipal governments and initiated a process of administrative decentralization. The electoral system adopted for the municipal elections permitted voters to choose between candidates of all parties with a proportional system similar to the one employed before 1973. The results of the first municipal election, held in mid-1992, showed clearly that Chilean voters were still split into right, center, and left tendencies in about the same proportions as before. There are some important differences, however, in the composition of the current party system when compared to the pre-dictatorship past. The right is presently divided into two main parties, one of which is closer to the military regime's legacy than the other. For the first time in Chilean history, the right includes a component that identifies closely with the military. The left currently includes an electorally much weaker Communist Party—the Chilean manifestation of a worldwide phenomenon—and two groups claiming the Social Democratic mantle: the Socialist Party and the Party for Democracy, whose leaders and most members trace their political lineage to the Allende government—whether they were (if they are old enough) in the Christian Left, the Radical, Communist, or other smaller parties. The new party system is also quite different from that of the past. It is no longer sharply polarized, as there is now a considerable consensus over socioeconomic policies. And the current pattern of alliances pits the center and the left, now in government, against the right. In this sense, the coalitions are reminiscent of those in the 1940s, except that the Christian Democrats and not the Radicals are the main centrist group.

In sum, despite its constitutional drawbacks, the transition to democracy in Chile has so far been more uneventful than most observers had predicted, and the country's economy, benefiting from skillful fine-tuning by the governments' economic teams, is experiencing its best and most sustained period of growth in the twentieth century. Chileans look to the future with greater optimism now than they have at any time in living memory.

SUGGESTED READINGS

Angell, Alan. *Politics and the Labour Movement in Chile.* Oxford University Press, London, 1972.

Arriagada, Genaro. *Pinochet: The Politics of Power.* Unwin Hyman, Winchester, Mass., 1988.

Bauer, Robert J. *Chilean Rural Society from the Spanish Conquest to 1930.* Cambridge University Press, London, 1975.

Blakemore, Harold. *British Nitrates and Chilean Politics, 1886–1896: Balmaceda and North.* Athlone Press, London, 1974.

Boorstein, Edward. *Allende's Chile: An Inside View.* International Publishers, New York, 1977.

DeShazo, Peter. *Urban Workers and Labor Unions in Chile, 1902–1927.* University of Wisconsin Press, Madison, 1983.

De Vylder, Stefan. *Allende's Chile: The Political Economy of the Rise and Fall of the Unidad Popular.* Cambridge University Press, Cambridge, 1974.

Drake, Paul W. *Socialism and Populism in Chile, 1932–52.* University of Illinois, Urbana, 1978.

Foxley, Alejandro. *Latin American Experiments in Neoconservative Economics.* University of California, Berkeley, 1983.

Galdames, Luis. *A History of Chile.* Translated and edited by Isaac J. Cox. University of North Carolina Press, Chapel Hill, 1941.

Garretón, Manuel Antonio. *The Chilean Political Process.* Unwin Hyman, Winchester, Mass., 1989.

Gil, Federico. *The Political System of Chile.* Houghton Mifflin, Boston, 1966.

Gil, Federico, Ricardo Lagos E., and H. A. Landsberger, eds. *Chile at the Turning Point: Lessons of the Socialist Years, 1970–73.* Institute for the Study of Human Issues (ISHI), Philadelphia, 1979.

Kaufman, Robert R. *The Politics of Land Reform in Chile 1950–1970: Public Policy, Political Institutions, and Social Change.* Harvard University Press, Cambridge, 1972.

Loveman, Brian. *Chile: The Legacy of Hispanic Capitalism.* Oxford University Press, New York, 1979.

Mamalakis, Markos J. *The Growth and Structure of the Chilean Economy: From Independence to Allende.* Yale University Press, New Haven, Conn., 1976.

Moran, Theodore. *Multinational Corporations and the Politics of Dependence: Copper in Chile.* Princeton University Press, Princeton, N.J., 1974.

Petras, James, and Morris Morley. *The United States and Chile: Imperialism and the Overthrow of the Allende Government.* Monthly Review Press, New York, 1975.

Pike, Fredrick. *Chile and the United States.* University of Notre Dame Press, Notre Dame, Ind., 1963.

Roxborough, Ian, Philip O'Brien, and Jackie Roddick. *Chile: The State and Revolution.* Holmes & Meier Publishers, New York, 1977.

Scully, Timothy R. *Rethinking the Center: Party Politics in Nineteenth and Twentieth Century Chile.* Stanford University Press, Stanford, Calif., 1992.

Sigmund, Paul E. *The Overthrow of Allende and the Politics of Chile, 1964–76.* University of Pittsburgh, Pittsburgh, 1977.

Smith, Brian H. *The Church and Politics in Chile: Challenges to Modern Catholicism.* Princeton University Press, Princeton, N.J., 1982.

Stallings, Barbara. *Class Conflict and Economic Development in Chile, 1958–1973.* Stanford University Press, Stanford, Calif., 1978.

Valenzuela, Arturo. *Political Brokers in Chile: Local Politics in a Centralized Polity.* Duke University Press, Durham, N.C., 1977.

_____. *The Breakdown of Democratic Regimes: Chile.* Johns Hopkins University Press, Baltimore, 1978.

Valenzuela, Arturo, and J. Samuel Valenzuela, eds. *Chile: Politics and Society.* Transaction Books, New Brunswick, N.J., 1976.

Valenzuela, J. Samuel, and Arturo Valenzuela, eds. *Military Rule in Chile: Dictatorship and Oppositions.* Johns Hopkins University Press, Baltimore, 1986.

Valenzuela, J. Samuel, and Erika Maza Valenzuela. *Religion, Class, and Gender: Constructing Electoral Institutions and Party Politics in Chile.* University of Notre Dame Press, Notre Dame, Ind., forthcoming.

Winn, Peter. *Weavers of Revolution: The Yarur Workers and Chile's Road to Socialism.* Oxford University Press, New York, 1986.

Zeitlin, Maurice, and Richard Earl Ratcliff. *Landlords and Capitalists: The Dominant Class of Chile.* Princeton University Press, Princeton, N.J., 1988.

27

ARGENTINA: DECLINE AND REVIVAL

PETER CALVERT

Argentina, the eighth largest country in the world, presents a series of paradoxes. With an area of some 2,767,000 km² it has a population of only 34 million. It is incredibly rich in agricultural land: The vast pampa, stretching westward between Buenos Aires and the Andes, makes Argentina one of the world's few grain-exporting nations and the only one in the Southern Hemisphere. Yet some three-fifths of the population live and work in the sophisticated urban environment of Greater Buenos Aires. Argentina is also self-sufficient in oil and natural gas and wealthy in mineral resources. Although comparable in size with Australia, however, it has not only failed to develop along the same lines but in 1930 entered on a long period of decline. In 1930 Argentina was the seventh richest country in the world. By 1980 it was seventy-seventh, and its rulers, it seemed, were resigned to permanent membership of the Third World. A literate and sophisticated people had been subjected to an exceptionally brutal military dictatorship. "Argentina," people said, "is the land of the future, always has been and always will be."

The jury is still out on whether the transformation of its prospects brought about since the return of democracy in 1983, and especially since 1989, under the leadership of President Carlos Saúl Menem, is permanent. But there can be no doubt that it has already gone far to rid Argentina of the legacy of two generations of political infighting punctuated by increasingly savage periods of military rule.

BUENOS AIRES VERSUS THE PROVINCES

In colonial times, Argentina lay on the furthest edges of the Spanish Empire. The first Spanish settlers in what is now Argentina came from Peru, and until 1776 the region remained backward and neglected. Founded in 1580 and a fine natural port, Buenos Aires long stagnated while all trade had to be channeled through Lima. Direct trade between Buenos Aires and Spain (notably in hides and in silver from what is now Bolivia) only later stimulated the growth of the town. In 1776 the Viceroyalty of the River Plate (Río de la Plata) was established. Buenos Aires began to grow rapidly. In 1807 the bold attempt of Sir Home Popham to seize the city for the British Empire taught its inhabitants that they could defend themselves. With Spain in the hands of the French emperor Napoleon Bonaparte's forces, the city freed itself from Spanish rule in 1810, and its Cabildo (town council) governed on behalf of the Spanish king, Ferdinand VII, even though he was at the time a captive of Napoleon. It was only in 1816, when the Spanish moved to recapture Buenos Aires, that the independence of what were then called the United Provinces of South America was declared at Tucumán.

Buenos Aires in 1810 was already bigger by far than the other main towns scattered along the River Plate and in the west and northwest, in the lee of the Andes. The colony was underpopulated for its size, although the vast and largely treeless plains, the hinterland of Buenos Aires known as the Pampas, still contained a substantial native American population. In the vast, flat, rural plain of the Province (as opposed to the City) of Buenos Aires roamed the Argentine cowboy, the *gaucho,* who opened up the interior and gave Argentina its national myth.

Argentina remained disunited for much of the nineteenth century, owing to the rivalry between Buenos Aires and the other provinces. The former favored a centralized structure, with Buenos Aires dominant, whereas the latter wanted a federal structure with provincial autonomy. Buenos Aires derived its revenues from the port, whereas the prices of provincial manufactures, such as textiles, were undercut by cheaper foreign imports. Buenos Aires did not share its wealth with the other provinces and, moreover, grew more European in its outlook and amenities; the provinces remained backward, dominated by autocratic, often savage leaders (*caudillos*). The struggle between federalists and centralists was overshadowed after 1835 by the dictatorship of Juan Manuel de Rosas, *caudillo* of Buenos Aires. He ignored the national problem, giving the provincial rulers complete freedom of action in return for recognizing him as national leader. Paradoxically, this helped create the national unity he opposed. In 1852 he was deposed by a coalition of his political opponents and died in exile on his farm just outside Southampton, England, in 1877.

In 1853 a federal constitution was created for the new Argentine Republic. Buenos Aires seceded from the federation but in 1859 was defeated in a military confrontation with the other provinces. In 1861 its forces were victorious and it joined the union in order to dominate it. In 1880, three centuries after its founding, the city of Buenos Aires replaced Rosario as the national capital. A new capital for the old Province of Buenos Aires was built at La Plata. The provincial *caudillos* made the transition to being more conventional politicians, though it was the great landowners, the *estancieros,* who dominated national life.

The next four decades were years of economic transformation as the combined impact of British investment, European immigration, the expansion of the railways, and the beef, grain, and wool of the Pampas made Argentina by far the most advanced of the Latin American states. These developments first benefited the cattle barons and big landowners who dominated politics, but two new classes emerged to challenge their hold on power: professionals such as bankers, brokers, and lawyers and an urban working class composed largely of recent immigrants. In any one decade from 1880 to 1950, there were proportionately three times as many immigrants to Argentina as to the United States.

MODERN PARTIES AND AN OLD-FASHIONED MILITARY

The first challenge came in the 1890s with the foundation of the Radical and Socialist Parties, but fraudulent elections kept the oligarchy of landowners, merchants, and bankers in power. In 1912, however, President Roque Sáenz Peña, though a conservative, insisted on the adoption of a law introducing secret ballots, to reduce electoral corruption. As a result, in 1916 Hipólito Yrigoyen, nephew of the founder of the Radical Party, the Unión Cívica Radical (UCR, Radical Civic Union), became Argentina's first popularly elected president and began a six-year term of office. The economy was still growing strongly and manufacturing industry developed under Yrigoyen's Radical successor, Marcelo T. de Alvear. The Radicals by then dominated government, and in 1928 Yrigoyen was elected to a second term, causing a split in the party in opposition to Yrigoyen's personalism. Before the effects of the 1929 depression were felt, Yrigoyen's reclusiveness and society's lack of perception with regard to the threat of a military takeover made it possible for a small band of armed cadets led by a retired general, José E. Uriburu, to seize power in 1930.

From 1932 to 1943, a period known as the Infamous Decade, the oligarchy resumed power in the form of a loose coalition (the Concordancia) of Conservatives and antipersonalist Radicals, supported by the armed forces. It was their friends and supporters who benefited from the economic recovery and from Argentina's role in supplying the Allies with meat and grain during World War II. But the war divided Argentine society further. Some leaders were strongly pro-Allies, but a suspicious isolationism had become the norm, and important elements in the armed forces, admiring German military prowess, were openly pro-Axis. When in 1943 it seemed that the civilian politicians would install a pro-Allies president, the army intervened again.

The year 1943 was a turning point. Col. Juan Domingo Perón, secretary of the army lodge that planned and executed the coup, became minister of war and secretary for labor and social welfare in the military government. He promoted labor reforms and encouraged unionization, becoming immensely popular with the masses, though not with the oligarchy. In 1946, in a free election, he won the presidency decisively. In 1949 he amended the constitution to permit his reelection in 1951; he held power until 1955.

Perón's populistic and personalist regime had many of the marks of a dictatorship. The media were controlled, dissent suppressed, a single ruling party established, the cult of personality encouraged. However, it was based on an alliance with the trade unions and mobilized the popular support of the urban underprivileged, the *descamisados* (shirtless ones). Large welfare programs not only brought Perón a devoted following but yielded real benefits to the poor, dramatized from the Ministry of Social Welfare by Perón's charismatic wife, Eva Duarte de Perón ("Evita"), who came to be regarded virtually as a saint.

A staunch nationalist, Perón bought out the British-owned railways and other public utilities, greatly accelerated industrialization under strong government control, and increased the role of the state in the economy. In his foreign policy he sought a "third position," later to be termed nonalignment, and the leadership of South America. However, he neglected the agricultural sector, formerly the basis of Argentina's export trade. Rural migration increased, and serious economic imbalances developed. As inflation rose and agricultural output fell, the economy's growth slowed down. Evita Perón died in July 1952, depriving her husband of his strongest ally with the masses. However, though the armed forces had been alienated by her prominence and some officers were already tired of Perón himself, support for Peronism remained strong despite the waning radicalism of the leader.

During his second term, from 1951, after surviving an attempted military coup, Perón tempered his policies. He resisted workers' wage demands, supported the farmers, and as of 1954 encouraged foreign capital in the petroleum industry. Such changes alienated many former supporters. Discontent with both the repressive nature of the regime and the large and overzealous bureaucracy grew. Attacks by his supporters on the Roman Catholic Church compounded Perón's problems. Finally, in September 1955, the armed forces intervened and Perón went into exile in Spain. However, his legacy and his political movement survived to form the fundamental divide in Argentine politics for the next three decades.

THE PERONISTS, THE MILITARY, AND THE GUERRILLAS

The critical factor was the antagonism between the armed forces and the Peronists, the former seeking in vain to exclude both Perón and his supporters from national politics and the latter trying hard to return to power and forming a permanent threat to any alternative government. The leader of the coup of 1955, Gen. Eduardo Lonardi, was prepared to work with the Peronists but was soon deposed by the more uncompromising Gen. Pedro Aramburu. For three years (1955–1958), Aramburu attempted to suppress all vestiges of Peronism. Elections from which the Peronists were barred installed a left-wing Radical, Arturo Frondizi (1958–1962), under whom economic development accelerated. Promising fifty years of development in five years, he delivered forty years of inflation in four. Inflation became an endemic problem. When Frondizi, too, proposed to allow the Peronists (though not Perón himself) to stand for election, he was deposed by the army.

New elections were held in 1963, and Arturo Illia, another Radical, was elected. However, in 1966 the military ousted him as well, claiming that he had been ineffective. The new military government headed by Juan Carlos Onganía (1966–1970) made it clear that it intended to stay in power as long as was "necessary" to revive the economy. Supported by authoritarian controls, his minister of economy and labor, Adalberto Krieger Vasena, produced a viable but austere recovery plan. But Krieger Vasena was forced to resign in May 1969 in the wake of a massive demonstration in the city of Córdoba (the "Cordobazo"). Further strikes and protests followed.

Meanwhile, under the influence of the Cuban Revolution and its aftermath, younger Peronists had adopted revolutionary tactics. Two main urban guerrilla movements emerged, a pro-Cuban organization called the Revolutionary Army of the People (ERP, Ejército Revolucionario del Pueblo), and a Peronist group known as the Montoneros. The Montoneros kidnapped and murdered former president Aramburu, thereby undermining Onganía, whose colleagues deposed him in June 1970. An unknown general, Roberto Levingston, was appointed to head the government but was replaced in March 1971 by Gen. Alejandro Lanusse, the organizer of the 1970 coup, who took over the presidency himself.

Lanusse inherited an impossible situation. With guerrilla violence growing and with the economy suffering from such frequent political changes that long-term, consistent policies could not be implemented, he took the ultimate gamble of holding fresh elections in March 1973 and allowing the Peronists to take part for the first time in twenty years. Perón's candidacy was disallowed (he had now been in exile for eighteen years), but his proxy, Héctor Cámpora, was allowed to stand and was duly elected. Cámpora's presidency lasted only a few weeks. Having offered freedom to captured guerrillas, he resigned in order to force Perón's return. The military, internally divided, yielded to the demand for new elections. Perón's return to the country in June 1973 was marred by violence at Ezeiza Airport in which many died. In September, nevertheless, he was returned to the presidency, with his third wife, María Estela ("Isabelita") Martínez de Perón, as vice-president.

However, the hopes of Perón's supporters were soon dashed. Perón, by then a sick man of seventy-eight, was unable to meet the many conflicting demands made on him during his short third term as president, though much was said and planned along the social democratic lines he had seen working well in Europe. He tried to distance himself from the leftist fringe that had infiltrated the movement during the last years of military proscription, only to find that political violence originating from both the left and the right increased. The two major insurgent movements, the Peronist Montoneros and the Marxist ERP, battled openly for power with kidnappings, bombings, and assassinations.

At Perón's death on July 1, 1974, his widow, Isabelita, assumed the presidency in a situation of increasing chaos, becoming, by an irony of history, Latin America's (and indeed the world's) first woman executive president. The Peronist movement was not only divided, but its extreme wings were in fact at war, and rightist death squads appeared, controlled by Isabel Perón's chief confidant, the influential minister of social welfare, José López Rega ("El Brujo," or "the Sorcerer"). The country slid into anarchy. Violence increased as inflation rose to 364 percent in 1976, and the government did little to stop it. In March 1976 the armed forces again seized power.

THE JUNTA AND THE DIRTY WAR

The governing junta of service chiefs chose the commander of the army, Gen. Jorge Videla, as the new president. Under their leadership, there began what the government termed euphemistically the "process of national reorganization." The period has since become better known abroad as the dirty war (*la guerra sucia*).

The process of national reorganization was a concerted attempt to eradicate terrorism by the use of terror. Tens of thousands of "suspects" were arrested, tortured, and murdered. People were arrested simply to fulfill the quotas imposed on provincial agencies. The most conservative estimates put the number of people killed, or who "disappeared," at over 10,000; 15,000 is a more realistic estimate. Such a wholesale purge inevitably included some genuine terrorists, and by 1978 the capacity for disruption by the Montoneros and the ERP had been drastically reduced by the death, exile, or imprisonment of their known leaders.

Meanwhile, massive borrowing and the overvaluation of the currency led to a rapid growth in consumer spending, giving the middle classes a false sense of prosperity. Videla, who had retired from the army and junta in August 1978, was succeeded as president in a quasi-constitutional fashion by Gen. Roberto Viola in March 1981, just at the start of a new economic recession. Ill health and the opposition of military conservatives to his relatively conciliatory policies forced Viola out of office in November. A right-wing nationalist, Gen. Leopoldo Fortunato Galtieri, took over in December as president and head of the junta.

THE FALKLANDS/MALVINAS WAR

At the beginning of 1982, there was a series of labor demonstrations and strikes, culminating on March 30 in a violent confrontation between demonstrators and government forces in Buenos Aires. From the moment of his seizure of power, however, Galtieri had prepared a plan that, he believed, would guarantee his position. On April 2, Argentine forces seized the British-ruled Falkland Islands (Islas Malvinas) in the South Atlantic, title to which had been disputed by Argentina since British occupation in 1833. The tiny British garrison was rapidly overwhelmed by 10,000 Argentine soldiers, and Argentine sovereignty was proclaimed. Initially the seizure of the islands was a resounding success for the government—the Peronists had always supported it. However, the final defeat of the Argentine forces by British troops on June 14 was a catastrophe and a national humiliation. The military government of Galtieri, inept politically and economically, had failed in the one professional field in which lay its claim to national preeminence, that of war. Galtieri was abruptly replaced and a retired general, Reynaldo Bignone, selected to head an interim government under which the military could retreat from power without having to pay the penalty for their misdeeds.

Bignone, having established a dialogue with the political parties, called elections for October 30, 1983, in an atmosphere of deep economic crisis and national confusion, fueled by growing civilian demands for the investigation of human rights abuses committed by the services. The UCR (Radicals) and the Partido Justicialista (Peronists), the two main parties, chose, as their respective presidential candidates Raúl Alfonsín and Italo Luder. The former, a fifty-seven-year-old lawyer who had courageously opposed the war and had a record of defense of human rights, obtained a massive victory over Luder, who lacked charisma and whose party, bereft of Perón himself, was deeply divided.

A HALTING REDEMOCRATIZATION

Inaugurated as president in December 1983, Alfonsín faced massive problems. Of a foreign debt of $40 billion left by the military government, one-quarter at least had been wasted and another quarter was never traced. Meanwhile, hyperinflation and economic stagnation combined to impede the task of fulfilling the hopes that Alfonsín's victory had aroused. For fifteen consecutive years, Argentina had triple-digit inflation, a world record. The trade unions, still largely in Peronist hands, reacted to the new government's imposition of austerity measures by staging a one-day general strike in May 1985, while the military carefully watched the progress of trials of former leaders of the armed forces. During the first year of Alfonsín's presidency, after very protracted negotiations, he managed to renegotiate the foreign debt, maintain political stability, and reach some accord with the Peronists. Equally significant, he finalized with Chile a long-standing dispute over possession of three islets in the Beagle Channel at the extreme south of Tierra del Fuego, which had almost brought the two countries to war in 1978.

MILITARY RESISTANCE

Two issues dominated Alfonsín's government: relations with the military and the resuscitation of the economy. In theory committed to eradicating the military from Argentine politics and to establishing a working democratic system, Alfonsín soon had to temper his policies with reality. The Falklands/Malvinas debacle provided the opportunity to restructure the military high command; Alfonsín removed antidemocratic senior officers and replaced them with more cooperative ones. The defense budget was drastically reduced, for economic as well as for political reasons, and in the 1986 defense budget a start was made on reducing the traditional significance of the armed forces in the nation's economic life.

But complicating the issue was the popular demand for the trial of service personnel for gross abuses of human rights during the so-called dirty war against the guerrillas. Ostensibly an asset to Alfonsín, public pressure on this issue was in fact a two-edged weapon. Alfonsín was sensitive to the dangers of isolation of the armed forces from civilian society and sought to maintain national unity. National revulsion at military behavior had to be taken into account, but at the same time a line had to be drawn between the most culpable and those simply obeying orders. Few objected—even within the reconstituted services—to the court-martial in 1985 of the first three military juntas to rule Argentina after the 1976 coup, for offenses that included abduction, torture, and murder. (In December four of the accused were acquitted, but sentences were passed on the remaining five, including sentences of life imprisonment for General Videla and Adm. Eduardo Massera.) Nor did many complain at the prosecution of the high command that had held office during the South Atlantic conflict.

However, as evidence of military atrocities increased, so, too, did the claims of the military that the dirty war was a just war and that a general amnesty should be enacted. Alfonsín attempted to resolve this conflict in December 1986, when Congress approved a law, known popularly as the "Punto Final" (Full Stop) Law, which established a sixty-day deadline for new indictments. The government had expected that only some seventy such cases might be presented. However, by March 1987, owing to the zeal of the civil courts, over 250 indictments had been accepted. Moreover, for the first time, serving officers as well as retired ones were accused.

In April 1987, military rebellions broke out in Córdoba and later at the Campo de Mayo itself. There the rebels included veterans of the Falklands campaign in full service camouflage and painted faces (*carapintadas*). Although there were popular demonstrations in support of democracy, concessions were made to the military, despite the ensuing controversy. A new army chief of staff was appointed, and Alfonsín submitted to Congress legislative proposals that came to be known as the "Obediencia Debida" (Due Obedience) Law, whereby most military officers accused of human rights violations were to be absolved of their crimes. Out of some 370 members of the armed forces due to be tried for human rights offenses, only between thirty and fifty were left to face charges. Even this number was too many for some sectors of the military, and there were insurrections in January 1988 at Monte Caseros and in December near Buenos Aires. These were firmly suppressed by the government, although there were accusations that Alfonsín subsequently made concessions to the military that resembled some of the rebels' demands.

In January 1989 the army claimed to have successfully defeated an attack by forty left-wing activists on a military base at La Tablada, 25 km west of Buenos Aires. The alleged guerrillas, thirty-nine of whom were already dead, were said to have been members of a hitherto unknown organization, Movimiento Todos por la Patria (All for the Country Movement, or MTP). Alfonsín publicly congratulated the military on its swift suppression of the uprising and reestablished their official right to act against "subversion" by creating a National Security Council. Opposition groups (including the Peronist presidential candidate, Carlos Saúl Menem) accused government and military bodies of having deliberately provoked the attack in an attempt to discredit all opposition factions. But it has since been confirmed to have been a real, if doomed, attempt to resuscitate the guerrilla conflict on the part of Enrique Gorriarán Merlo and a small group of former members of the ERP.

ECONOMIC CRISIS

The second major imponderable for Alfonsín was the Argentine economy. After pursuing gradualist policies to reactivate the economy in 1984 and the first half of 1985, the government turned in June 1985 to the fashionable doctrine of the "heterodox shock." This involved the introduction of austerity measures, under the Austral Plan, named after the new currency that was to end inflation, then running at an estimated annual rate of 1,129 percent. The government's action led to labor unrest, with the Peronist-dominated trade unions holding a series of one-day strikes. Hence, despite its initial promise, the plan was effectively abandoned while the midterm elections took place.

With the elections out of the way and inflation again soaring, in February 1987 a new economic program, the second Austral Plan (the "Australito"), was implemented. Old devices, such as the pegging, or linking, of wage increases to price rises; devaluation of the new currency; and lower interest rates were introduced. Again the government's attempts at achieving economic stabilization were unsuccessful; the deficit on the public-sector account worsened, and inflation continued to spiral upward. These problems led to a deterioration in relations with foreign creditors and pushed the currency to the edge of collapse. In early 1989 the World Bank, which until that time had, like most other multilateral lending agencies, supported Alfonsín, suspended all its financing in Argentina. Negotiations with international creditors were deferred indefinitely. Despite the efforts of two new finance ministers in as many months, no credible economic strategy emerged, and control over inflation was abandoned while the elections of May 1989 were held.

A NEW KIND OF PERONIST

With his economic policy in ruins, Alfonsín's sole remaining aim at the end of his presidency was to be succeeded by another democratically elected president. Despite the crisis the elections were both peaceful and orderly. The candidate of the UCR, Eduardo César Angeloz, proposed widespread privatization and economic austerity in order to combat the economic crisis but was saddled with the burden of Alfonsín's failure. Unlike Alfonsín in 1983, he was unable to add to the UCR's traditional 25 percent of the vote. Victory went to the Peronist candidate, Carlos Saúl Menem, the flamboyant former governor of the inland province of La Rioja. In his campaign, Menem captured the popular vote and a Peronist majority in the Senate with the promise of a "production revolution" based on wage increases and significant aid to industry. Yet long before he was due to take office, the seriousness of the economic crisis led Alfonsín to try to reach an agreement with the Peronists on economic strategy. This Menem wisely declined, and all attempts at accommodation between the incoming and outgoing governments failed. Instead, food riots, looting, and bombings in several Argentine cities forced Alfonsín to impose a state of siege and to hand over presidential power to Menem five months early, on July 8, in order to avoid a total breakdown of public authority.

When Menem succeeded Alfonsín, it was the first time since 1928 that an elected president had handed over the office to his successor without military pressure. Democracy, even in the midst of the greatest economic crisis of the century, was immensely popular. It was immediately clear, moreover, that Menem's economic strategy, to turn Argentina into what he called a "popular market-capitalist country," was much closer to that of the Radicals than his campaign had suggested. The intention was not to revolutionize the system but to bring together a corporate capitalist coalition, containing businesspeople, foreign creditors, the unions, the armed forces, and the Church. This policy marked an immediate departure from the interventionist approach associated with early Peronism, though it was closer to the many pragmatist elements in Perón's thought and policies. Menem first entrusted the conduct of his anti-inflationary policies to economists of Argentina's only native multinational company, Bunge y Born. The attempt failed, and the association with Bunge y Born ended in December 1989, after only five months. Meanwhile, a widespread lack of confidence was reflected in the collapse of the currency and a second hyperinflationary wave.

Menem's relaxed use of presidential authority, divisions in the cabinet, and reluctant support for policies so different to traditional Peronism increased the difficulty in reducing state expenditure and in selling state-owned enterprises. The government's troubles were further exacerbated by the public airing of the president's marital problems. However, the president's personal position was strengthened when on August 10 he was finally elected chairman of the Justicialist (Peronist) Party and his brother, Senator Eduardo Menem, vice-chairman, following the resignation of Governor Antonio Cafiero.

With regard to the military, Menem, who had spent the entire period of the military regime under house arrest, from the outset advocated conciliation, despite strong resistance from among his own supporters. After weeks of rumor, a series of pardons affecting 277 individuals, some of them guerrillas and including members of the military junta responsible for the Falklands debacle, was issued in October 1989. However, the pardons left unresolved issues such as the status of former commanders of the armed forces, while pressure on the president to use his prerogative to pardon again continued to resurface. In other ways, Menem was firmer; the leaders of the rebellions against Alfonsín were dismissed by Menem's chief of staff, Gen. Isidro Cáceres. At the end of 1990, however, military discontent reemerged. The government was taken by surprise when some supporters of Col. Mohammed Ali Seneildín, leader of the December 1988 revolt, rebelled on December 3 and seized the military headquarters, with the loss of at least three lives. Any question of negotiation was speedily rejected; the headquarters were stormed and the leaders charged with insurrection. They were sentenced to indefinite imprisonment and discharge from the service. The price was Menem's irreversible decision to issue, on December 29, his long-heralded pardon of Gen. Jorge Videla, Adm. Emilio Massera, Gen. Roberto Viola, Gen. Ramón Campos, and others convicted (or, in the case of Gen. Guillermo Suárez Masón, extradited but not yet tried) for human rights crimes during the dirty war.

At the same time, the relative strength of the armed forces continued to decline. In February 1990, Menem took the personal decision to resume diplomatic relations with the United Kingdom, keeping the issue of the sovereignty of the disputed islands, as he put it, "under an umbrella." In June 1991 the government announced that the armed forces would be reduced from 75,000 to 55,000 in number and the period of conscription reduced from one year to six months. The final cancellation of the Condor missile project was confirmed. On October 31 the army chief of staff, Gen. Martín Bonnet, resigned in protest against these measures and was replaced by his deputy, Gen. Martín Balza.

Meanwhile, in January 1991 a series of ministerial changes improved the country's economic prospects. The new minister of the economy, Domingo Cavallo, proceeded to implement a far-reaching program of economic stabilization. This had three main aims. The first was the so-called dollarization of the economy, whereby the Argentine economy was linked to the U.S. economy by the establishment of a fixed exchange rate of 10,000 australes to the U.S. dollar. The second was a program of privatization that would reverse forty years of Peronist policy. The third aim was to improve government finances by raising revenue and eliminating tax evasion, by means such as the "fiscal pact" with a highly influential agricultural development association, the Argentina Rural Society (SRA, Sociedad Rural Argentina). By the time of Menem's state visit to the United States in November, he was celebrated as Latin America's leading free-market reformer and U.S. ally. As a result, in March 1992 Menem secured a promise of debt reduction under the Brady Initiative. Argentina's accumulated debt to the United States was reduced from over $60 billion to some $48 billion.

At the same time, support for the ruling Peronist party strengthened. In the provincial elections, the Peronists won fifteen of the twenty-one governorships at stake, including that of the Province of Buenos Aires, where Vice-President Eduardo Duhalde won 47 percent of the votes cast. Although their opponents were in disarray, the Peronists were not free of problems, of which the two main ones were the persistent accusations of corruption leveled against them and their inability to agree on a successor to President Menem. Thus, in February 1993 a campaign was begun among the executive of the Partido Justicialista for an amendment to the constitution to permit Menem's reelection. The project was supported by declarations from fourteen provincial governors and, conditionally, by the Peronist wing of the General Confederation of Labor. The gathering momentum was hardly checked when Menem underwent an emergency operation on a blocked carotid artery in August.

In legislative elections held on October 3, 1993, the Peronists won 42.3 percent of the votes cast, which resulted in their holding 123 seats of the 254-seat parliament. The UCR obtained 30 percent of the votes cast and held eighty-four seats. The right-wing Movimiento por la Dignidad y la Independencia (Modin, Movement for Dignity and Independence), led by the former *carapintada* Aldo Rico, made small but significant gains, receiving 5.8 percent of the ballot. The Peronists were not guaranteed the two-thirds majority necessary in the lower house to approve the constitutional amendment the president sought. However, the Senate did approve the reform proposal in late October.

Fearing that the UCR would be excluded from negotiations on constitutional reform and anxious to avoid another humiliating defeat for the party in a national referendum on the question of constitutional reform, former president Alfonsín, who was elected to lead his party in November 1993, entered into a dialogue with President Menem. The terms of the agreement were endorsed by a UCR national convention in early December. The main proposals detailed in the agreement were allowing a president to seek a consecutive term in office; the creation of the post of coordinating minister to fulfill a prime-ministerial function; an increase in the number of seats in the Senate and a reduction in the length of mandate of all senators; and reform of the procedure for judicial appointments. This last proposal was important in securing UCR support, as the Supreme Court was Peronist dominated. President Menem immediately declared his intention to seek reelection in 1995.

CONSTITUTIONAL REFORM

Elections to a 305-seat constituent assembly, which was to draft and approve the proposed constitution, took place on April 10, 1994. The Peronists won 37.7 percent of the votes cast and 136 seats in the assembly, which left them without the majority that would guarantee the passing of the constitutional amendments. The UCR gained only 19.9 percent of the votes cast, the party's worst election result since Argentina's return to democracy in 1983. The Frente Grande, a left-wing coalition formed in mid-1993 that opposed the proposed reforms, came in third, receiving an unexpected 12.5 percent of the ballot and thirty-one seats. However, on August 22 the assembly approved the new constitution, which allowed for the possibility of presidential reelection for a second term. The constitution came into force on the following day. Other constitutional amendments included the reduction of the presidential mandate from six years to four; the creation of the post of chief of cabinet; a runoff election for presidential and vice-presidential candidates when neither obtained 45 percent of the votes cast, or 40 percent when the nearest candidate gained less than 30 percent of the ballot; the establishment of an autonomous government in the City of Buenos Aires with a directly elected mayor; the extension of congressional sessions to nine months; an increase in the number of senators from two to three from each province; and the creation of a Council of Magistrates and other judicial reforms. In the event, the presidential elections of 1995 were overshadowed by the impact on the economy of the Mexican economic crisis (the "tequila effect"). Unemployment, which rose between April and July from 12.5 percent to 18.6 percent of the economically active population, was the subject of a $1.5 billion initiative. Yet it was not Governor Horacio Massaccesi of Río Negro, candidate of the UCR, who made the running but a dissident Peronist, Senator José Octavio Bordón of Mendoza; his center-left Front for a Country in Solidarity (Frepaso) picking up support from both Radicals and dissident Peronists. Despite this, President Menem won reelection decisively, gaining 49.8 percent of the votes cast in the only round of balloting to 29.2 percent for Governor Bordón. Governor Massaccesi obtained only 17.1 percent, the worst result for the UCR since 1916. The president had carried every province, and his party, the PJ, gained an overall majority of three seats in the 257-seat Chamber of Deputies, the result being: PJ 130; UCR 70; Frepaso 28; others (mostly provincial parties) 29. Among the consequences was that on July 2, the right-wing former general Antonio Domingo Bussi was elected governor of Tucumán. In the aftermath of his victory, President Menem, who was inaugurated on July 8, confirmed his intention to retain Cavallo as economy minister, though later in the year tension grew between the two as Cavallo complained publicly of resistance to reform among entrenched interests in government. Eventually, in 1996, Cavallo was dismissed, but his legacy of free-market reform remains and capital continues to flow back into the country.

The improvement of relations between Argentina and the United States continued in the 1990s under U.S. president Bill Clinton's administration. In exchange for dismantling its Condor II rocket program, it was agreed in early February 1994 that Argentina was to receive two squadrons of Skyhawk A-4M bombers from the United States. President Clinton was also requested to intervene in order to facilitate agreement between Argentina and the United Kingdom over the future of the Falkland Islands, which had been delayed owing to disagreements over measures to protect the islands' fish stocks. In late August 1994, Argentine-British relations became more strained after the reiteration in the new constitution of Argentina's claim to sovereignty over the Falkland Islands. However, Argentine and British troops together patrolled the "green line" in Cyprus, and the visit to Buenos Aires of the British foreign secretary in January 1993 confirmed that relations between the two countries were generally good.

Following his reelection, the president reaffirmed his goal of recovering the Falkland Islands by the year 2000 by peaceful negotiation. Meanwhile, however, with the excuse of economic constraint, the military budget was cut; the army's strength reduced by a further 15 percent, to 23,000, in 1995; and conscription officially ended. With the issue of sovereignty still "under an umbrella," talks led to an agreement signed in New York on September 27, 1995, on joint exploitation of the Malvinas Basin oil deposits, which enables oil companies to bid for licenses in the disputed area without incurring penalties. If the area is as rich as many believe, Argentina stands to gain handsomely from rising world prices.

Menem has decisively rejected the Radical policy of seeking leadership of the Third World and has taken Argentina out of the Nonaligned Movement. The country has reemerged as a candidate member of the First World. At the same time, it has rejected its traditional posture of suspicious isolationism and come out as a strong ally of the United States and an example to the world of the success of the free market. By signing the Treaty of Tlatelolco, sending a naval force to the Persian (Arabian) Gulf in 1990, and supporting UN operations in Bosnia-Herzegovina and in Haiti, President Menem signaled his country's intention of playing a new and wider role in the "new world order" and of being an active participant in UN peacekeeping operations. With every year that passes, it becomes more likely that the profound changes that have taken place in recent years will become permanent and that for Argentina the future has now come.

SUGGESTED READINGS

Alexander, Robert J. *Juan Domingo Perón: A History.* Boulder, Colorado: Westview Press, 1979.

Argentina, Republic of. Comisión Nacional sobre la Desaparición de Personas. *Nunca Mas: Informe de la Comisión Nacional sobre la Desaparición de Personas.* Buenos Aires: Editorial Universitaria de Buenos Aires, 1986.

Calvert, Susan, and Calvert, Peter. *Argentina: Political Culture and Instability.* London: Macmillan, 1988.

Crawley, Eduardo. *A House Divided: Argentina 1880–1980.* London: C. Hurst & Co., 1984.

Di Tella, Guido. *Argentina Under Perón, 1973–76: The Nation's Experience with a Labour-based Government.* London: Macmillan, 1983.

Falcoff, Mark, and Dolkart, Ronald H. (eds.). *Prologue to Perón: Argentina in Depression and War 1930–1943.* Berkeley: University of California Press, 1975.

Fraser, Nicholas, and Navarro, Marysa. *Eva Perón.* London: André Deutsch, 1980.

Graham-Yooll, Andrew. *A State of Fear: Memories of Argentina's Nightmare.* London: Eland, 1986.

Imaz, José Luis de. *Los que mandan.* Buenos Aires: Editorial Universitaria de Buenos Aires, 1964.

Kirkpatrick, Jeane. *Leader and Vanguard in Mass Society: A Study of Peronist Argentina.* Cambridge: Massachusetts Institute of Technology, 1971.

Mallon, Richard D., and Sourrouille, Juan V. *Economic Policymaking in a Conflict Society: The Argentine Case.* Cambridge: Harvard University Press, 1975.

Martínez Estrada, Ezequiel (trans. by Alain Swietlicki). *X-Ray of the Pampa.* Austin: University of Texas Press, 1971.

Milenky, Edward S. *Argentina's Foreign Policies.* Boulder, Colorado: Westview Press, 1978.

O'Donnell, Guillermo. *Modernization and Bureaucratic-Authoritarianism: Studies in South American Politics.* Berkeley: University of California Press, 1973.

Page, Joseph A. *Perón: A Biography.* New York: Random House, 1983.

Platt, D.C.M., and di Tella, Guido (eds.). *Argentina, Australia and Canada: Studies in Comparative Development, 1870–1965.* London: Macmillan, 1985.

Potash, Robert A. *The Army and Politics in Argentina 1928–1945: Yrigoyen to Perón.* Stanford, California: Stanford University Press, 1969.

_____. *The Army and Politics in Argentina 1945–1962: Perón to Frondizi.* London: Athlone Press, 1980.

Rock, David. *Argentina 1516–1982: From Spanish Colonization to the Falklands War.* Berkeley: University of California Press, 1985.

Schoultz, Lars. *The Populist Challenge: Argentine Electoral Behaviour in the Postwar Era.* Chapel Hill: University of North Carolina Press, 1983.

Scobie, James R. *Argentina: A City and a Nation.* New York: Oxford University Press, 1971.

_____. *Buenos Aires: Plaza to Suburb, 1870–1910.* New York: Oxford University Press, 1974.

Snow, Peter G. *Political Forces in Argentina.* Boston: Allyn & Bacon, 1971.

Tamarin, David. *The Argentine Labor Movement, 1930–1945: A Study in the Origins of Peronism.* Albuquerque: University of New Mexico Press, 1985.

Timmerman, Jacobo (trans. by Tony Talbot). *Prisoner Without a Name, Cell Without a Number.* Harmondsworth, Middlesex: Penguin, 1982.

Turner, Frederick C., and Miguens, José Enrique (eds.). *Juan Perón and the Reshaping of Argentina.* Pittsburgh, Pennsylvania: University of Pittsburgh Press, 1983.

Wynia, Gary W. *Argentina in the Postwar Era: Politics and Economic Policy Making in a Divided Society.* Albuquerque: University of New Mexico Press, 1978.

28

URUGUAY AND PARAGUAY: AN ARDUOUS TRANSITION

DIEGO ABENTE BRUN

Uruguay and Paraguay, two of the smallest nations of South America, are often confused one with another because their names are so similar. However, their differences are probably among the greatest between any two single countries in Latin America and can be traced back as far as the beginning of the Spanish conquest in 1536.

Both countries developed around a city; Asunción in the case of Paraguay, Montevideo in the case of Uruguay. The former, established in 1537, is the oldest city in the Rio de la Plata Basin. It remained the center of the Spanish domain in the area until the end of the seventeenth century, when it lost its supremacy to the port city of Buenos Aires due to the administrative partition of the province of Paraguay. Yet it was not until 1680 that the Portuguese established the first settlement, the Colonia del Santísimo Sacramento, in what is now Uruguayan territory. Some forty-five years later, the Spaniards expelled the Portuguese and in 1726, established the city of Montevideo.

Asunción was for several reasons a suitable center for the Spanish domain. It was located on a bay overlooked by the hills of Lambare and therefore easy to defend from nearby Indian populations. Furthermore, the Spaniards were able to work out a political alliance with the Indians living in that particular area, a factor that in time contributed to some of the unique features of the Paraguayan nation. As an aspect of the alliance, the Indians gave to the Spaniards some of their women, whose brothers, in turn, were because of that very link obliged to work certain days a week for the *cuñados* ("brothers-in-law"). This hastened the process of racial integration, or *mestizaje,* and made Paraguay one of the most homogeneous mestizo countries in Latin America. The practice also contributed to the preservation of the Indian language, Guaraní, because the mestizos learned the Indian tongue from their mothers and Spanish from their fathers. Although with heavy racial overtones, this bilingual situation persists to the present.

In the area surrounding Montevideo, by contrast, there were but a few Indians; they did not enter into close contact with the Spanish settlers, who were mostly cattle ranchers. As a result, the country was populated basically by *criollos* (Hispanic Creoles), and *mestizaje* was almost unknown. In addition, the waves of European, especially Italian and Spanish, immigrants in the second half of the nineteenth century and the first decades of the twentieth ultimately made of Uruguay a country racially European.

Paraguay, having acquired through the colonial years some sort of cultural, linguistic, and economic identity, proclaimed its independence from Spain in 1811, but at the same time rejected the domination of Buenos Aires, the city to which it had been administratively linked before the breakdown of the Spanish Empire in the Americas. Soon after independence, José Gaspar Rodríguez de Francia was appointed dictator in 1814 in a truly Roman fashion—first for a two-year term and then for life. Ruling until his death in 1840, he succeeded in completely isolating the country and in defeating the pro–Buenos Aires tendencies. He tolerated no political activity at all and instituted an all-embracing repressive state.

Uruguay, meanwhile, was invaded and annexed by the Portuguese-Brazilian Empire in 1816 and became the Cisplatine Province until 1828. In 1830, it became an independent republic, probably the first buffer state in Latin America, created after long negotiations between Brazilians (Portuguese) and Argentineans with the important intermediation of the British envoy, Lord Ponsonby.

In Paraguay, Francia was succeeded by Carlos Antonio López, who followed some of Francia's policies but opened the door to greater commerce and allowed some very limited political liberalization. Nevertheless, he secured total power for himself and his family, particularly for his son Francisco Solano, who was made brigadier general of the Paraguayan army at the age of eighteen. In quasi-monarchic fashion, Francisco Solano López succeeded his father, who died in 1862. Solano López had been in Europe in 1852–1853 and was heavily influenced by the France of Napoleon III as well as by European geopolitical doctrines. Thus, in 1864, arguing that a partial invasion of Uruguayan territory by Brazilian troops constituted a threat to the equilibrium of the nations of the Rio de la Plata, he declared war on Brazil. Later he declared war against Argentina because of its refusal to let Paraguayan troops cross Argentine territory to engage the Brazilian army. Finally, Uruguay itself declared war on Paraguay, although its participation was minor. The war ended five years later with the almost total destruction of Paraguay and the death of Marshal López, who, true to his previous statements, heroically accepted death but not surrender.

URUGUAY

DEMOCRACY: PRACTICE AND TRADITION OF COPARTICIPATION

Until 1973, Uruguay was considered one of the most stable democracies of Latin America, a model of freedom and progress. Although such enthusiastic claims were somewhat exaggerated, it is certainly true that until the late 1960s Uruguay had a relatively stable polity and ranked among the most democratic regimes in Latin America. Let us therefore examine how this situation came into being.[1]

Early in the nineteenth century, the Uruguayan *caudillos* (later the political elites) came to a conclusion that was to be of foremost importance in the future: that institutionalized compromises were necessary. Thus, since 1830, the history of Uruguay is one of compromises among *caudillos*—broken from time to time but replaced soon thereafter by other compromises reflecting the characteristics of the new situation and the relative forces of the contending parties. This process led to the institutionalization of a practice known as coparticipation, a constant in Uruguayan history and the ideological and practical framework within which Uruguayan politics evolved until the late 1960s. Hence, regardless of which of the two traditional parties, the Blancos (Whites, conservatives) or the Colorados (Reds, liberals), was in power, there was always room, a coparticipative role, for the opposition.

The first half of the twentieth century was dominated by the figure of the Colorado populist leader José Batlle y Ordóñez. Batlle, president during the 1903–1907 and 1911–1915 periods, represented the most advanced and progressive wing of the Colorado Party, and his influence in Uruguayan politics had far-reaching consequences. Under his leadership, Uruguay underwent a rapid process of modernization financed, in part, by rising export revenues. However, it is in the fields of economic and social reforms that his influence was paramount and most lasting. Among other things, he nationalized foreign banks and the public service companies, enacted a law concerning pensions and retirements, established provisions for rest days and workmen's compensation for industrial accidents, and legalized the eight-hour working day. His policies also opened the door for the newly mobilized social and political forces of Montevideo, most of them immigrants or sons of immigrants, to enter the political arena. These new forces, representing the middle and working classes, in turn generated support for the party and faction that implemented such reforms. If one considers that by the turn of the century the population of the capital city of Montevideo already represented 30 percent of the population of the country and that 47 percent of that population was composed of immigrants, one can understand how deeply Batlle's policies changed the map of the country. In electoral terms, his reforms meant that the total number of voters jumped from 31,262 in 1910 to 299,017 in 1928.[2]

As a result of Batlle's influence, the situation in Uruguay changed drastically in the 1920s and 1930s. Two elements were of particular importance. First, the power and role of the state were greatly enhanced through state intervention in the economy. Public and semipublic corporations (*entes autónomos*) were created, necessitating a tremendous expansion of the state bureaucracy. By the 1930s, the budget of the state *entes* represented 62 percent of total national expenses, and the total number of public employees had reached 52,000—approximately 5 percent of the national population.[3] Second, through the reforms promulgated by Batlle, the middle and working classes of Montevideo gained a position as participants in the political system. This gain was also facilitated by the expansion of the industrial sector. For example, the number of industrial establishments increased from 714 to 7,403 between 1901 and 1930.[4]

This new situation did not supersede coparticipation, the old and resilient political tradition; in fact, a new collegial system (*colegiado*) was introduced for the exercise of executive power. The first *colegiado* (1917–1933), a personal triumph for Batlle, consisted of a dual executive power. On the one hand, the president was in charge of foreign affairs and defense, political, and police matters, while on the other, the National Council of Administration, composed of six members representing the majority party and three the largest minority party, was in charge of all other administrative matters. The second *colegiado* (1952–1966) went further and eliminated the figure of the president. It vested all powers in the council, which, like previous ones, had one-third of its seats reserved for the first minority party.[5]

Two factors are of particular importance in explaining the long-lasting success of coparticipation. The first is the country's steady rate of economic growth in the first half of the twentieth century. That growth allowed the political system to respond quite successfully to increasing political and economic demands from different social sectors and to foot the bill for a semiwelfare state. The 1900–1930 period, considered the period of *crecimiento hacia afuera* ("outward-looking growth"), was characterized by an export boom based on meat, wool, and hides. The total value of exports increased from 29.4 million pesos in 1900 to 73.3 million pesos in 1915 and 100.9 million pesos in 1930. By the 1930s, that model of growth had been gradually replaced by a model of *crecimiento hacia adentro* ("inward-looking growth"), though exports, particularly wool, continued to provide the hard currency that ultimately financed the model. The internal dynamic of growth, however, was provided by an industrial process of import substitution. The number of industrial establishments increased from 6,750 in 1930 to 23,080 in 1952, and the number of jobs provided by them jumped from 54,000 to 141,000 in the same period.[6] The proportion contributed by industrial production to the GDP grew from 12.5 percent in 1930 to 20.3 percent in 1950.[7] The fact is that, either through exports or through import substitution, the rate of growth increased steadily, thus providing the government with the necessary resources to accommodate social, economic, and political demands and therefore maintain its political efficacy.

A second important factor in explaining Uruguay's democratic stability until the late 1960s is its peculiar legal-constitutional framework. That framework, by accepting the political reality of a highly fragmented political scene and a machine-type political party system, institutionalized a stable and mutually accepted formula for resolving political disputes. An important part of this framework of practical and legalized coparticipation was the electoral law, passed in 1910, whereby parties were able to withstand fractionalization without losing electoral strength. The law, known as the *ley de lemas* (law of party designations), established a system in which the voter, in national elections, chose, simultaneously, the party of his preference and, within that party, the candidate of his preference. In U.S. terms, that would be tantamount to having the primaries and the national elections held on the same day, the winner being the most popular candidate of the most popular party.

BREAKDOWN OF DEMOCRACY AND
EMERGENCE OF THE MILITARY DICTATORSHIP

The decade of the 1950s signaled the beginning of the end of the economic bonanza and of the political model that this bonanza helped to sustain. The excessive dependence on exports, particularly on a few products, and the nature of an industrialization process that relied too heavily on protectionist measures and on foreign currencies generated by a depressed export sector brought about a series of crises of increasing gravity. Total exports dropped from US $254.3 million in 1950 to US $129.4 million in 1960. Recurrent balance-of-payments problems forced the continuing devaluation of the peso, from 1.90 to the dollar in 1950 to 11.30 to the dollar in 1960 to 250 to the dollar in 1971.[8] The average annual rate of growth declined from 4.8 percent in the 1945–1955 period to 0.9 percent in the 1955–1970 period while the per capita rate of growth for the last period was – 0.3 percent.

The industrial sector lost the dynamism of the earlier period. The number of people employed by industries dropped from 200,642 in 1960 to 197,400 in 1968. The annual rate of growth of the industrial sector decreased from 6 percent for the 1945–1954 period to 1.6 percent for the 1960–1970 period.[9] The inflation rate, which had been 9.8 percent in 1955 and had never before surpassed the 15 percent mark, reached a record high of 125.4 percent in 1968.[10] There was also a dramatic decline in the real wages of workers and employees, especially after 1970. The index of real wages dropped from a base of 100 in 1957 to 76.5 in 1967[11] and from an index of base 100 in 1968 to 66.2 in 1979.[12] This last figure means that workers in 1979 earned an average of 33.8 percent less than in 1968.

This economic panorama of stagnation combined with high rates of inflation and continued balance-of-payments deficits provoked strong reactions from all economic sectors, but particularly from the landed upper classes. In the 1958 elections, the landowning elites threw their most active support to the conservative Blanco Party, which won its first national election in the twentieth century. In order to reverse what the landed elites considered a virtual confiscation of their export earnings through the mechanism of multiple exchange rates, the Blanco government passed in 1959 the Exchange Reform Law, which heavily favored the landowning class. The government was also forced to enter into a number of agreements with the International Monetary Fund (IMF) to regularize the constant balance-of-payments deficits. The crisis, however, continued to deepen. The *colegiado* system of government, implanted by the 1952 Constitution, was blamed for many of the difficulties, and in 1966, concurrent with the national election, a new constitution that restored the presidential system was approved.

The elections were won by retired general Oscar Gestido of the Colorado Party, but he died less than a year after taking office and was replaced by his vice-president, Jorge Pacheco Areco. By the time Pacheco replaced Gestido, the Tupamaro National Liberation Movement, an urban guerrilla group, had become very active. The Tupamaros, who aimed to overthrow the capitalist regime, were mainly young members of the petite bourgeoisie—intellectuals, students, and salaried members of the middle class. They established a highly efficient organization and were able to carry out some spectacular coups de main, including the kidnapping of the British ambassador, the Brazilian consul, and the U.S. police adviser, Dan Mitrione. Mitrione was later killed when the government refused to accept the Tupamaros' conditions for his release. Pacheco was thus forced to employ increasingly greater violence, and the general level of repression gradually rose.

Hence, the 1971 elections took place in a tense climate. The Uruguayan left coalesced in the Frente Amplio (Broad Front), composed of Christian Democrats, Socialists, Communists, and independent leftists. Its presidential candidate was retired general Liber Seregni, a prestigious and widely respected military man. The Broad Front, as expected, did well in Montevideo, where it captured 30 percent of the votes, but it fared poorly in the countryside. Colorado candidate Juan M. Bordaberry, with the support of his party's conservative *pachequista* faction, became the new president. Whereas Pacheco was from the upper classes of Montevideo, Bordaberry was closely associated with the even more conservative landowning classes.

The truce declared by the Tupamaros during the preelectoral and electoral periods, designed to help the Broad Front, was soon over, and a dialectic of increasing repression and rising guerrilla activities began to escalate. The army, which had been called in September 1971 to lead the antisubversive campaign, prepared a full-scale offensive. The killings of a frigate captain and an army colonel (the brother of General Gregorio Alvarez, who became president in 1981) enraged the military, and by September 1972 they had almost completely wiped out the Tupamaro Movement. Simultaneously, a whole array of right-wing terrorist, counterguerrilla movements—death-squad-type organizations—succeeded in generalizing an antileftist persecution. The army's success was based not only on its military superiority but also on the extensive and undiscriminating use of torture against anybody suspected of having any type of connection with the Tupamaros.

Once the process of overt military intervention in the political life of the country was set in motion, it became increasingly difficult, and ultimately impossible, for civilian political leaders to reverse it. Thus, although the antiguerrilla campaign was almost completely successful by the end of 1972, the military gradually assumed a larger role in the decision-making process. With documents seized from the Tupamaros, the military launched a campaign against "corruption" and demanded a greater role in the management of state corporations and other state agencies. President Bordaberry caved in to virtually every demand, and by early 1973 he was a puppet of the military.

The first stage of the final crisis began in February 1973 when the army and the air force resisted Bordaberry's designation of a new defense minister. They further demanded the establishment of a National Security Council (COSENA), composed of officers and civilians, to deal with security and economic matters.

Parliament, in trying to stop the military from completely taking over the government, conducted a series of investigations into the extensive use of torture in army detention centers. On June 27, 1973, the generals retaliated by closing Parliament and replacing it with a Council of State, composed of forty-six members handpicked by the military. Political parties and activities were banned, the National University closed, workers' organizations outlawed, and the most terrible political persecution in Uruguayan history unleashed. From that time on, the only significant changes were in the degree and scope of repression. In 1976, Bordaberry was forced to resign and was replaced by a civilian handpicked by the military, Aparicio Méndez, who was never more than a figurehead.

Early in the 1980s, the military started essaying some kind of political institutionalization of the dictatorship. Following the Brazilian model of changing presidents without changing the regime, the National Security Council elected a new president, General Gregorio Alvarez, in 1981. Soon after assuming power, Alvarez called a national referendum to approve a new constitution greatly restricting political activities—particularly those of the nontraditional parties—and perpetuating a growing role for the military. The plebiscite was a crushing defeat for the military as 54 percent of the voters, ignoring official intimidation, rejected the constitution. The process of controlled liberalization continued, however, and the military promised to hold free presidential and congressional elections in November 1984. Late in 1982, the Colorado and Blanco Parties were allowed to organize internal elections, and the antigovernment factions scored a major victory, winning over 70 percent of the votes. In mid-1983, the government-opposition talks regarding the transition collapsed, due to the intransigence of the military in its attempt to secure control over the decision-making process even after the elections. The government responded by increasing the levels of political repression and press censorship, but the result was a series of mass rallies (the first public gatherings in Montevideo in years) demanding the immediate return to democracy.[13]

Finally, after a prolonged period of negotiations, the military retreated to the barracks in 1984 and Colorado candidate Julio María Sanguinetti was elected president. Sanguinetti led the first postmilitary government through rough waters, particularly because of the adamant refusal of the military to allow officers to stand trial for human rights violations and political crimes. Sanguinetti, however, managed to consolidate the restored democratic system. In the elections of November 1989, Luis A. Lacalle Herrera of the Blanco Party won the presidency.

Meanwhile, the economic situation improved in some respects in the late 1970s. Inflation was relatively controlled at the tremendous social cost of a drastic reduction in the living standards of wage earners, especially industrial workers. International prices for some traditional Uruguayan exports rose, with a consequent improvement of the balance of payments. The most significant change, however, was in the composition of Uruguayan exports. The nontraditional exports share of total exports increased from 25 percent in 1972–1973 to 64 percent in 1978, thanks to increasing tax rebates for these items. In the early 1980s, however, Uruguay plummeted into one of its worst recessions with negative rates of growth of − 1.3 percent in 1981, − 10.0 percent in 1982, and − 8.5 percent in 1983. Inflation, on the other hand, returned to a high of 57.5 percent in 1983, and remained hovering around 60 percent thereafter.

The sectors that benefited most from the policies of the military dictatorship were precisely those linked to the export of nontraditional goods, along with bankers. The landowning classes benefited too, especially to the extent that they provided the raw materials for most of the nontraditional export industries, such as tanning and leather goods. The sectors that suffered most were industrialists producing for domestic consumption, because of the contraction of the market, and salaried workers and employees, because real wages and salaries declined 35 percent in the 1972–1979 period. Labor unions were all but destroyed, and workers were left absolutely defenseless against the military dictatorship.

THE U.S. ROLE

U.S. private investment in Uruguay has never been substantial. In 1960, it totaled only $47 million.[14] By 1980, total U.S. investment in Latin America was more than $38 billion, but Uruguay, Paraguay, and Bolivia shared less than 2 percent of that amount. Nor has U.S. economic aid been significant. U.S. loans and grants (excluding military programs) grew from $10.1 million in 1972 to $13 million in 1975 but declined sharply thereafter to $0.2 million in 1978, reflecting the general deterioration of U.S.-Uruguayan relations in the 1977–1980 period. This deterioration was due to the Carter administration's human rights policy and the failure of the Uruguayan dictatorship to take positive steps toward stopping the systematic violation of human rights and civil liberties.

U.S. military aid, however, has been a different matter. The total extended to Uruguay during the 1950–1966 period was $33.2 million. The figure for 1969 was $1.6 million, increasing to $5.2 million in 1971. Thereafter, it decreased somewhat until 1973 and then jumped to a high of $8.2 million in 1975.[15] In 1977, Secretary of State Cyrus Vance announced that because of the pattern of gross violations of human rights by the Uruguayan government, the United States was suspending all military aid to that country. That policy was reversed by President Reagan in 1981.

It is clear that regardless of the specific amount of money appropriated for military aid to Uruguay each year, there was some sort of U.S. involvement during the heyday of the repression, i.e., the 1970–1975 period. The role of U.S. police adviser Dan Mitrione, for example, killed by the Tupamaros on charges of training Uruguayan policemen in torture methods, has never been adequately explained.

FROM DEMOCRACY TO DICTATORSHIP: A REASSESSMENT

The history of the rise and fall of democracy in Uruguay permits us to draw some interesting conclusions. The uninterrupted economic growth from 1900 to 1950 allowed the political process to become relatively autonomous from the pressures of the dominant classes. The extent to which these classes were able to function normally and make a satisfactory profit was related to their willingness to maintain a low profile in the political arena and to give a free rein to the politicians. The landowning elites, for example, may have considered that their earnings were being confiscated by exchange laws, but the continuing rise in the price of products they sold allowed them to prosper anyway. In fact, it was not until almost a decade after the crisis in the export sector began that they became directly involved in purely political matters.

The relative autonomy of the political process from economic pressure by the dominant classes was also favored by the development of a system of political machines that promoted the "welfarization" of the country. Hence, whereas the economically active population represented some 39 percent of the total population, the number of people on the government payroll plus the passive groups (i.e., retirees and pensioners) represented, in 1969, almost 20 percent of the total population.[16] The state thus became a tremendous source of patronage for whose control parties developed increasingly larger political machines. The machines, in turn, restricted the ability of party leaders to implement sound policies because the parties were virtually mortgaged to the interests of the clientele that had helped them to gain power.

When the crisis emerged in the late 1950s, due to depression of the export sector and decline in the growth rate of the domestic industrial sector, it became increasingly difficult for any government to respond to the contradictory demands of various classes and economic sectors. The emergence of an armed challenge to the regime, the Tupamaros, aggravated the situation. Both the dominant classes—particularly the landowning elite—and the military felt that their interests were threatened. The process that followed the military defeat of the Tupamaros, however, suggested that the army had plans of its own—plans that presupposed the maintenance of a capitalist system but that were not necessarily inspired by the economic elite.

An external factor that may have heavily influenced the Uruguayan process is the involvement of more powerful neighboring states in internal power struggles. One should not forget that the three most powerful countries in the area—Brazil, Argentina, and Chile—were also suffering military dictatorships (except for the 1973–1976 Peronist parenthesis in Argentina) at the time of the militaristic drive in Uruguay. The influence of Brazil, especially, appears to have been quite strong. Likewise, when the winds of liberalization began to blow in Southern Cone countries, it became increasingly difficult for the military to continue refusing the domestic demand for democratization.

URUGUAY IN THE 1990S: A REBIRTH

As elsewhere in Latin America in the 1980s and 1990s, the retreat of the military has been halting and incomplete and the return of elections has not meant the return to full-blown class- or sector-interest competition or to constituency representation and accountability. Even so, the vitality of the born-again democratic system is impressive in light of the repression suffered in the 1970s and the constraints on resource allocation in the 1990s.

The general elections of 1984, heralding a return to civilian rule, were marred, to say the least, by prohibition of the candidacy of two very popular antimilitary leaders, Wilson Ferreira Aldunate of the Nationalist (Blanco) Party and General Liber Seregni of the Broad Front (Frente Amplio). Military intimidation forced the parliamentary adoption, at the end of 1986, of a measure granting amnesty to all military personnel accused of human rights violations.

Military restiveness on a lesser scale continued into the early 1990s, but it was popular opposition to the austerity measures upon which foreign credit was conditional that forced the major traditional parties into a National Accord. That accord carried over with respect to economic strategy from the tenure of the Colorado Party's Sanguinetti to the Blanco Party government of Luis Alberto Lacalle, elected in 1989, and to the subsequent government of Sanguinetti, returned to office in 1994.

The fact that the traditional parties had moved right and become almost indistinguishable opened political space to the left. Occupying the space on the political spectrum where factions of the Colorado Party were found in mid-century is the Ecuentro Progresista (EP, Progressive Alignment), led by former mayor of Montevideo Tabaré Bázquez.

In the 1994 elections, the traditional parties and the EP essentially divided the electorate into thirds. The EP portion, centered in Montevideo, coincided more or less with the constituency of the previously "subversive" Broad Front. Its tempered program calls for sparing from privatization those government services that are being frugally and efficiently run.

The economy, by all counts a disaster as transition to civilian rule got under way, has made something of a comeback. Recovery has followed a zigzag course but without the dramatic setbacks of the 1970s and early 1980s.

"Offshore-style" banking confidentiality and beachfront resort development, among other things, attracted major investments in the late 1980s and early 1990s. GDP growth registered an impressive 7.5 percent in 1992, dropping to 1.7 percent in 1993 and leveling off at about 4 percent in 1994. Foreign debt, inflation, and unemployment remained high in the mid-1990s, though they were generally edging downward, in part because of increasing agricultural exports and industrial production. The country confirmed its commitment to the Southern Cone Common

Market (Mercosur) by implementing the custom union's common external tariff on most tradable goods at the beginning of 1995.

PARAGUAY

A SOCIETY IN CONFLICT: 1870–1940

The War of the Triple Alliance (1864–1870) left Paraguay reduced to ruins, the economy in bankruptcy, the physical infrastructure destroyed, the population decimated, the national territory reduced by some 60,000 sq mi. In 1870, a liberal constitution was approved, but it was a dead letter. The two traditional parties, the Conservative, or Colorado (Red), and the Liberal, or Azul (Blue), were founded in 1887, but the former remained in power until 1904, not precisely through democratic means. Widespread corruption among government officials made things even worse. The enactment in 1883 and 1885 of the Laws of Sale of Public Land and *Yerbales* (maté plantations) brought about not only the beginnings of the great latifundio but also the eviction of poor peasants who had occupied those lands for generations. One Spanish-Argentine capitalist alone bought 14 million acres (5.7 million hectares) of land in the Chaco. In general, most of the 74.1 million acres (30 million hectares) of public lands were absorbed by private claimants.[17]

At the end of the nineteenth century, the situation could not have been worse. A few *estancieros* ("ranchers") owned most of the land. A few foreign enterprises had a quasi-monopoly of tannin and yerba maté, two of the main export products. Poverty and backwardness were widespread. The violation of political and civil rights was routine, and the political elite was unresponsive. With public indignation aroused by this situation, the Liberal Party organized a successful revolt that quickly won widespread popular support. The 1904 Revolution, however, promised much but accomplished little. The main sources of wealth, including the newly developed *frigoríficos* (meat packing and processing plants), continued to be in foreign hands.[18]

By the 1920s, tensions with Bolivia regarding the territory of the Chaco quickly escalated to a point of no return, and in 1932 war broke out. The Paraguayan victory heightened social and economic mobilization, generating demands that existing institutions could not meet. On February 17, 1936, President Eusebio Ayala was overthrown and replaced by Colonel Rafael Franco, a Chaco War hero. Although the *febrerista* (after the month of the revolution) movement was quite heterogeneous, its ranks filled by Nazi-fascists, social democrats, and Marxists alike, it set in motion some of the major social and economic reforms in Paraguayan history.

In August 1937, a military uprising toppled the *febreristas*. The provisional government held elections in 1939, and the candidate of the Liberal Party, another Chaco War hero, General José F. Estigarribia, ran unopposed. In 1940, Estigarribia assumed dictatorial powers and replaced the 1870 Constitution, but he died shortly thereafter in an airplane crash.

THE RISE OF MILITARISM

The army, which between 1936 and 1939 had been playing the role of arbiter, slowly moved toward assuming permanent and direct control of power. When Estigarribia died in 1940, his successor, General Higinio Morínigo, was selected by the military with little—if any—civilian influence. He assumed dictatorial powers and became the first strictly military dictator in Paraguayan history.

Morínigo found his military support in a Nazi-fascist lodge known as the Frente de Guerra (War Front) and, among civilians, in a group known as the *tiempistas* (after their newspaper *El Tiempo*), which had an ambiguous, conservative Christian-corporatist ideology. Fortunately for him, World War II helped to keep exports at high levels and to increase foreign exchange reserves. Besides, although Morínigo's sympathies for the Axis powers were never a secret, he astutely managed to "sell" his hemispheric loyalty to the United States, thus securing a U.S. offer of some $11 million in lend-lease military aid as well as $3 million in economic aid.[19]

Morínigo's economic policies were characterized by the increasing intervention of the state—a trend that started in the early 1930s leading to the creation of public corporations. Among them were COPAL (now APAL) in the field of alcohol production and sale, COPACAR in meat commercialization, and FLOMERES, the state merchant fleet. The cost of living increased dramatically from an index of 110 in 1940 (base: 1938 = 100) to 432 in 1948, an average annual increase of 41.5 percent.[20]

Morínigo's regime was far more repressive than had been any of its predecessors. His corporatist and authoritarian views were well expressed in the motto of his "revolution": Discipline, Hierarchy, Order. In 1942, he decreed the dissolution of the Liberal Party. With a Colorado-military coalition, Morínigo returned to harshly repressive policies, which prompted the rebellion of the Concepción military garrison in March 1947 and, with it, the outbreak of a bloody five-month civil war. With the majority of the army and the officer corps against the dictator, the Colorados turned for help to the United States. They needed it—the petition said—"to protect hemispheric security from the bloody designs of Stalinist imperialism," but the U.S. State Department, after sending a CIA man to check on that claim, concluded that the rebellion was "far from being communist-dominated," and the request of the Colorados was turned down.[21] The Argentine president, Juan D. Perón, though, viewed a similar petition sympathetically and secretly provided the weaponry that permitted the Paraguayan government finally to defeat the rebels in the outskirts of Asunción. Morínigo's victory, however, was a Pyrrhic one, for the Colorados grew stronger and, fearing that Morínigo would not turn over power to their presidential candidate, Natalicio González, overthrew him in February 1948.

THE ERA OF STROESSNER

The period that followed the 1947 government victory was marked by the increasing "Coloradization" of the country. Civil service positions and access to and promotion within the army were contingent upon having a proven Colorado background. Meanwhile, the Korean War helped keep exports at high levels from 1949 to 1953. Monetary reserves, which had dropped from $11 million in 1946 to $3.1 million in 1949, jumped to $17.7 million at the end of 1953. In spite of that, the internal economic situation deteriorated rapidly. Inflation grew at an annual average rate of 67 percent in the 1947–1953 period and reached a record high of 157 percent in 1952. The value of the local currency, the guaraní, decreased by more than 700 percent in the 1946–1954 period.[22]

The worsening internal economic situation coupled with the intense conspiratorial activities of almost every *presidenciable* politician submerged the country into one of the most unstable periods of its history. There was, indeed, a brief but full-scale return to praetorianism, for the Colorados themselves were bitterly divided by factional struggles, each faction seeking the support of some key army officers to advance its particular goals. As a result, the public mood—which in 1936 had favored change—in 1954 called for peace and order.

On May 4, 1954, taking advantage of that situation, forty-two-year-old General Alfredo Stroessner staged a coup that overthrew the Colorado president, Federico Chávez. Three months later, replacing a provisional president, Stroessner assumed power as the victorious candidate in a one-man presidential election. Although he was believed to be a transitional figure, Stroessner quickly proved that all forecasts were wrong. He skillfully played military and civilian sectors against each other, and in 1959, after almost a year of increasing labor and student unrest, he consolidated his position by closing the Colorado Parliament and expelling from the country almost one-half of its members. By the beginning of the 1960s, he had become the unquestionable leader; few *políticos* ("politicians") or military men dared to challenge him.

THE SOCIOECONOMIC STRUCTURE

Between 1954 and the early 1970s, the Paraguayan economy was characterized by very low rates of growth within the framework of a traditional social structure with widespread precapitalist forms of production in the countryside. Vast sectors of the peasantry were virtually excluded from the monetary economy and were devoted to subsistence crops on lands they did not own. By the end of the 1950s, for example, 1,549 landowners controlled some 85 percent of the land, and only 0.9 percent of the territory was dedicated to agriculture.[23] In addition, Paraguay did not undertake import substitution, like most other Latin American countries; the industrial sector, therefore, was quite underdeveloped. By 1963, for example, out of a population of some 1.9 million, only 35,000 were employed by industrial establishments, and nearly half of them, 17,482, worked in plants employing fewer than ten workers; there were only thirty-one industrial firms that employed more than 100 persons each.[24] Foreign investment, mostly British and Argentine, was concentrated in a few relatively dynamic sectors, particularly the meat packing and processing industry, lumber, banking, and, more recently, cottonseed-oil manufacturing.

The economic situation in general was one of quasi-stagnation. The GDP increased between 1954 and 1969 at an annual rate of 3.7 percent, while the GDP per capita increased at an annual rate of only 1.3 percent.[25] The government, nevertheless, was successful in regard to two goals: controlling inflation and developing infrastructure. The former was achieved through an extremely tight monetary policy; the latter, through foreign loans and grants. The government also achieved some equilibrium in the balance of payments thanks to standby agreements signed with the IMF and to U.S. economic aid, especially the U.S. PL-480 program that allowed Paraguay to import wheat with credit granted on favorable terms.

Economic stagnation was accompanied by highly unequal income distribution. Although there are no reliable studies for that period, economist Henry D. Ceuppens estimated that 5 percent of the population had an income share of 50 percent of GNP; 15 percent, an income share of 20 percent of GNP; and 80 percent of the population shared the remaining 30 percent of GNP.[26]

The 1970s witnessed the most rapid and thorough process of modernization in recent Paraguayan history. Two basic factors account for the dynamics and characteristics of this process. First is the Itaipú hydroelectric dam, a project jointly undertaken by Paraguay and Brazil at a cost of $15 billion—almost five times the GNP of Paraguay in 1980. In full operation, the dam is the greatest in the world, producing 12.6 million kilowatts per hour.

The second factor was an agricultural boom associated with a shift to commercial export agriculture, particularly soybeans. The construction of the Itaipú dam and the agribusiness boom brought about a massive influx of foreign capital. As a result, foreign exchange reserves increased dramatically from $18 million in 1970 (the same level as 1953) to $781 million at the end of 1981. The process was also marked by a decline in the importance of Anglo-Argentine investments in relation to Brazilian, U.S., European, and Japanese investments. Meanwhile, there emerged a powerful commercial agricultural sector, dominated by multinational companies, which dramatically transformed the countryside.

The rate of GNP growth increased from an average of 6.4 percent for the 1970–1975 period to an average of 10.2 percent for the 1976–1978 period. In 1979, the rate was 10.7 percent and in 1980, it reached a record high of 11.4 percent. In 1981, it dropped to a more modest 8.5 percent,[27] and 1982 and 1983 witnessed a deep recession and negative growth rates. The commercial deficit increased dangerously and reached a record high of $545 million. Moreover, the factor allowing substantial balance-of-payments surpluses in spite of increasing commercial deficits over the previous five years—the influx of foreign capital, mostly related to the Itaipú project—started to decline in 1981. The foreign debt, on the other hand, increased from $98 million (16.7 percent of the GNP) in 1970 to $2.2 billion (52 percent of the GNP) in 1988.[28]

The modernization process has had other negative consequences, too. Inflation reached a high of 28.1 percent in 1979; it decreased to 22.4 percent in 1980 and to 13 percent in 1981, but the real rate may have been much higher than these official figures. The government reacted with tough monetary restrictions, so tight that the country was thrown into one of its worst recessions. The real minimum wage fell by some 17 percent between 1964 and 1980. Although the GNP per capita in 1980 was $1,131, 62 percent of the urban population had an income of between $150 and $440.[29] In Asunción, the capital city, 13 percent of the population, or 68,000 people, live in eighty-nine *villas miserias* ("shantytowns") scattered around the city.[30]

The most important consequence of the rapid process of economic modernization, however, is the parallel process of social mobilization that is, in turn, greatly increasing social and economic demands on the political system.

The completion of the Itaipú project and the cutoff of the capital influx associated with it placed a considerable strain on the government. The approximately 12,000 Paraguayan workers employed in the project were gradually laid off in the early 1990s, and with continual delays in the start-up of the Paraguayan-Argentinean Yacyreta hydroelectric project, there was no new project big enough to absorb them.

THE POLITICAL PROCESS

By the early 1960s, Stroessner was able to consolidate a power structure based on three pillars: Stroessner himself, the army, and the Colorado Party. He was able to erect and sustain this structure first by demonstrating his ability to remain in power against all odds; second, by harshly repressing people opposed to him; and third, by co-opting the rest, particularly army officers and members of the Colorado Party. Corruption and contraband for the benefit of a small clique became widespread and were part of the arsenal of payoffs at the regime's disposal. Officially, it was considered *el precio de la paz* ("the price of peace").

The dominant economic classes readily and happily "exchanged the right to rule for the right to make money," to borrow Barrington Moore's phrase. In actuality, they had never quite governed, and therefore the transaction was most favorable. Their pressure groups, chronically weak, were satisfied with the "peace" that few other rulers had been able to deliver over such an extended period of time. Important sectors of the population, discouraged by the high level of political repression from any type of political activity, also accepted the situation as an unchallengeable fait accompli.

During a first period (broadly 1954–1962), the regime relied heavily on massive repression and coercion. That approach gradually gave way to an authoritarian model that, without renouncing repression as an occasional necessity, placed increasing emphasis on limited co-optation. Co-optation in Paraguay, however, did not involve access to public offices. Because of the very rigid structure of power, it implied only the absence of politically motivated harassment or repression of individuals as long as they stay away from the political arena. However, the regime continued to unleash periodic waves of repression to remind the real and potential opposition, as well as its own followers, that should they opt for a change in the status quo, they would have to pay a very heavy price. The elements of psychological terror and latent threat therefore remained very effective.

The turning point in the transition from a naked dictatorship to an authoritarian regime was the legal recognition, in 1962, of a splinter Liberal group. In exchange for recognition, the group participated in the 1963 presidential "elections," thus providing a token opposition. Soon afterward, the participationist groups within the opposition prevailed over those proposing an insurrectionary strategy. In 1964, the Febrerista Party was legally recognized, and most of the exiled Liberal leaders were allowed to return. The municipal elections of 1965 witnessed the participation of a Lista Abierta (Open List) registered by the Febreristas but headed by a distinguished independent physician and supported by the mainstream of the Liberals. The "elections," as usual, were plagued by widespread official fraud, but they demonstrated that the majority of the Liberals did not support the Liberal minority splinter group recognized in 1962. That helped the leaders of the majority to win legal recognition as the Liberal Radical Party, the word "radical" being added to distinguish the group from the one legalized in 1962. In 1962 and again in 1967, as well as in the 1964 recognition of the Febrerista Party, U.S. pressure for liberalization played a significant role.

In 1967, with the participation of four opposition parties, a national convention was held to amend the 1940 Constitution. In reality, the only important issue was the addition of an article allowing Stroessner to run for reelection two more times. He did so, in 1968 and 1973, winning easily in elections characterized by widespread fraud.

Participation, however, proved to be a one-way street: All the benefits accrued to the government. Legal opposition parties, though not openly repressed, had their activities restricted to such an extent that they gained very little political ground. An office-seeking elite within those parties remained satisfied to the extent that they had access to some thirty seats in the Senate and Chamber of Deputies, with the corresponding salaries and benefits. Soon, however, it became clear that there were too many politicians and too few sinecures. Politicians began to fight fiercely for the spoils that the regime put at their disposal. Such party infighting further debilitated the legal opposition, already perceived by the public as a highly ineffectual ornamental device.

It was in this context of the debilitation of the legal opposition that student and peasant movements rose to prominence in the late 1960s and early and middle 1970s. Both groups had become disenchanted with the legal opposition, not only because of its chronic inefficacy but also because it failed to provide a real ideological alternative to the right-wing regime. In a few years, they succeeded in organizing some of the largest mass movements in recent Paraguayan history. As a result, peasants and students were harshly repressed. The persecutions unleashed in the 1975–1980 period were of such magnitude that the mass movements were badly crippled.

Other sources of opposition to the regime were the Catholic Church and Church-related groups. Since the late 1960s, the Catholic hierarchy had steadfastly opposed and denounced abuses of the regime as a matter of public posture. The Church, however, did not perceive itself as being an opposition force and therefore did not have a clear political strategy.

Hence, the decade of the 1970s was characterized by the increasing strength of the government vis-à-vis the opposition. The general improvement in economic conditions and the Itaipú-related boom of the late 1970s further reduced the ability of the opposition to draw support from wide sectors of the population. In 1977, the government succeeded in further dividing the legal opposition by isolating those sectors that refused to go along with a 1977 constitutional amendment devised to allow Stroessner to run for reelection indefinitely. Splinter groups of the Liberal Party took advantage of the government search for potential "opposition" parties. At one moment, there were five Liberal parties, four of them bidding for recognition from the government to participate in the 1978 elections. Two of them were finally selected, thus assuring for themselves the highly contested parliamentary seats and for the government the continuation of the democratic façade.

Strengthened by its political and economic success, the regime continued to harass the nonparticipationist opposition. In the late 1970s, these sectors succeeded in articulating a joint opposition front, the Acuerdo Nacional (National Accord), uniting the Liberal Radical Authentic Party, the Febrerista Party, the Christian Democratic Party, and the Popular Colorado Movement (MOPOCO), a Colorado group expelled from the country by Stroessner in 1959. The Acuerdo was born under and encouraged by international, and particularly U.S., pressures against the Stroessner regime for its violation of human rights. It grew stronger as this pressure grew stronger during the Carter administration years. But as international pressure decreased, particularly after the election of Ronald Reagan in November 1980, the importance of the Acuerdo gradually diminished. Its activities, in any case, had been confined to public condemnation of the regime, but it did attain high visibility and have significant public impact.

For the government, nevertheless, there were problems. The international criticisms of its human rights violations were translated into actual sanctions when the U.S. government almost terminated its military assistance program and greatly reduced its economic aid. Moreover, the country was unable to obtain some loans from international institutions on the preferential terms it was accustomed to because of the U.S. refusal to vote favorably on those credits. Internally, the government faced some of its most severe domestic problems since the late 1950s. Within the Colorado Party, there were numerous confrontations among sectors competing for control of the party organization, particularly local branches or sections (*seccionales*) and student organizations. Furthermore, discontent among the youth whose potential role was being postponed while the ruling old guard refused to leave them room for upward mobility increased significantly. Moreover, growing politicization of student and labor sectors resulted in mounting pressures for liberalization. The transition to democracy in neighboring Argentina and Brazil further undermined the Stroessner regime.[31]

But the final blow to the thirty-five-year-old Stroessner dictatorship came as a result of the military ramifications of a major split in the ruling Colorado Party. In August 1987, an aging Stroessner moved virtually to expel from the party a sizable part of its leadership. That group became known as the traditionalists and was believed to be considering ending the automatic endorsement of the Stroessner candidacy for president. The attack on the traditionalists was led by a group of extreme right-wing zealots and diehard Stroessner loyalists known as militants.

Upon seizing control of the party, the militants moved to secure their positions in the state apparatus and the military. When Stroessner underwent major surgery in late August 1988, and his health became increasingly worrisome, the militants sped up their moves and sought to position Stroessner's eldest son, a just-promoted air force colonel, next in the line of military succession. To do so, a large number of generals and colonels had to be retired or reassigned, a move that began in early January 1989. But when, on February 2, Stroessner sought to retire General Andrés Rodríguez, his major military rival and First Army Corps Commander, Rodríguez struck back and with widespread support from all units overthrew Stroessner on the morning of February 3, 1989, after ten hours of bloody battles.

General Rodríguez became provisional president and called for elections within ninety days as the first step in a process of transition to democracy. He ran as the candidate of the Colorado Party. Adopting a strong prodemocracy message, Rodríguez won the elections of May 1 by a landslide; he captured slightly more than 70 percent of the votes, against 20 percent for his closest competitor, PLRA leader Domingo Laíno. Opposition parties complained that they could not organize for elections in such a short period of time after three decades of repression. While the pre-electoral campaign allowed parties full political freedoms, and although General Rodríguez became a very popular candidate who would have won anyway, the elections were marred by many irregularities and systematic and widespread, although not massive, fraud.[32]

Upon assuming the presidency, General Rodríguez began to move decisively in the direction of greater liberalization and the incorporation of opposition or independent leaders into positions of leadership, including the Supreme Court and some ambassadorships. Nevertheless, much remained to be done before a true democratic system might emerge.

THE UNFINISHED TRANSITION

In 1989 few believed that Paraguay could experience a transition to a democratic system along the lines followed by other countries in the region. Guided by deterministic and historic dogmas, many could not understand the present but as the endless repetition of the past. Yet, neither the historic legacy of Paraguay nor the specific nature of the Stroessner regime constituted insurmountable obstacles to a transition to democracy. The coup of February 3, 1989, began a process of transition from above and within that, once unleashed, gradually assumed a dynamic of its own and is now approaching a successful conclusion.

In the early stages of the process, General Rodríguez sought to gain the support of the international community by committing himself to democratize the country but without jeopardizing the old basis of political power of the Colorado Party: its privileged and incestuous relation with the armed forces, its unlimited and exclusive ac-

Table 28.1
Paraguay: Results of the 1993 National Elections

	Presidential		*Senatorial*	
	Votes	*%*	*Votes*	*%*
Wasmosy/ANR	473,176	40.09	498,586	42.3
Laíno/PLRA	378,353	32.06	409,728	34.76
Caballero Vargas/EN	271,905	23.04	203,213	17.24
Others[a]	8,198	0.66	20	

[a]Includes six candidates of small parties from the right and left.

cess to state patronage, and its thorough manipulation and control of the electoral process. Democratization thus in reality meant liberalization. To legitimize this, elections were called for May 1, at which time Rodríguez was elected president and a Colorado-controlled Congress was installed.

The process of liberalization, though, strengthened the opposition and allowed it gradually to gain bargaining power. Simultaneously, it fostered the fragmentation of the Colorado Party, as different factions vied for control of the party. As a consequence, political power became more dispersed and major political decisions began to require the give-and-take that characterizes coalition building. And inasmuch as power became less centralized and concentrated the chances for furthering the process of liberalization and acceleration, that of democratization improved.

It was in this context that a convention to write a new constitution to replace Stroessner's 1967 chart met in the first semester of 1992. The new document neatly reflected the political reality. A presidential system but with a very strong Congress was adopted as its framework. Important principles such as decentralization and many programmatic statements about agrarian reform, social justice, and workers' rights were also incorporated. But the most far-reaching clauses were those concerning the transfer of power.

To begin with, the Constitution banned all forms of reelection and included, in its transitory part, an article tailor-made to impede a possible Rodríguez bid for reelection. This caused considerable tension, and generals loyal to him subtly threatened a coup. Rodríguez refused to swear allegiance to the new constitution, but the ceremony was held nonetheless before Congress and the document entered into effect on June 20, 1992.

Within less than a year, on May 9, 1993, the first relatively competitive elections were held. Three candidates, Juan Carlos Wasmosy for the Colorado Party, Domingo Laíno for the Authentic Radical Liberal Party, and Guillermo Caballero Vargas for the newly formed Encuentro Nacional competed, and Wasmosy won with some 39 percent of the vote, as shown in Table 28.1.

The elections brought into sharp relief both what had been achieved in terms of democratization and what remained to be done. On the one hand, the hotly contested primary elections within the Colorado Party threw a shadow of doubt over the legiti-

Table 28.2
Paraguay: Seats in Congress After the 1993 Elections

	ANR[a]		PLRA	EN	Total
Senate	20	(12)	17	8	45
Deputies	38	(22)	33	9	80
Total	58	(44)	50	17	125

[a]Numbers in parentheses represent the Colorado congressmen who support the government; the rest are dissidents.

macy of Wasmosy's candidacy, as most observers believed his opponent, Luis María Argaña, won the election only to be deprived of it by means of the manipulation of the vote-counting process. On the other hand, the failure of both opposition candidates to join forces reflected the inability of political actors to develop effective mechanisms of coalition building. But perhaps more important, extensive political manipulation was exhibited throughout the electoral process. In fact the Colorado-run Electoral Board thoroughly controlled the process and excluded the opposition from any meaningful oversight of elaboration of registration rolls, distribution of polling places, and appointment of electoral officers, not to speak of the thorough utilization of the state apparatus and resources to support the campaign of the official candidate. Furthermore, there was open intervention of a sector of the military establishment, led by Major General Lino Oviedo, in support of Wasmosy's candidacy.

Considering all these problems part and parcel of the transition process, and taking into account that in spite of them the opposition parties, combined, had won a majority in Congress, both the Authentic Radical Liberal Party and the Encuentro Nacional formally recognized the results as valid and lent legitimacy to the Wasmosy government. Table 28.2 shows the outcome of the 1993 elections as validated by the Congress.

As expected, the first four years of Wasmosy's term were characterized by his constant inability to muster the support of his own party for his program. Much of the backing needed to weather the difficulties was provided by the opposition parties in the belief that it was fundamental for the success of the transition process that Wasmosy complete his term without interruption. In exchange, the opposition won some very important concessions, including the reorganization of the judiciary and the appointment of a more balanced nine-member Supreme Court. Of equally fundamental importance was the establishment of a three-member Supreme Electoral Tribunal, which promises a true reform of the electoral process.

A major military crisis erupted in April 1996 when Wasmosy dismissed the commander of the army, General Lino Oviedo, and he refused to step down. Oviedo had become a sort of power behind the throne, and there was the general perception that Wasmosy could not adopt major decisions without his agreement. Thanks to the prompt reaction of the Congress, the youth, political parties, the international community, and the institutionalist sector of the armed forces, Wasmosy stood firm, and within twenty-four hours Oviedo resigned. This outcome represented the removal of the last obstacle to the complete subordination of the military to the constitution and civilian control.

In this context, the first truly clean and competitive municipal elections were held in November 1996. The results demonstrated an almost even distribution of votes between the Colorado Party and opposition forces. Even though the logic of local elections does not always reflect the national one, this means that if the Colorado Party manages to unite behind a strong candidacy, enjoying widespread consensus, and the opposition cannot do the same in 1998, chances are the Colorados will continue to rule for another five years. The years until the next election, thus, will be key in determining whether the Colorado Party, like Mexico's PRI, retains its fifty-year hegemony within a competitive and democratic system or whether the forces of change are strong enough to bring about a major renewal of the political system.

NOTES

1. For an elaboration on the theme of coparticipation as a framework to study Uruguayan politics see Martin Weinstein, *Uruguay: The Politics of Failure* (Westport, Conn.: Greenwood Press, 1975), whose general approach this section follows.

2. Juan E. Pivel Devoto, "Uruguay independiente," in Antonio Ballesteros, ed., *Historia de America y de los Pueblos Americanos*, vol. 21 (Barcelona: Salvat Editores, 1949), pp. 628–632, and Martin H.J. Fynch, *A Political Economy of Uruguay Since 1970* (New York: St. Martin's Press, 1981), pp. 11–13.

3. Weinstein, *Uruguay*, p. 69.

4. Luis Macadar, Nicolas Reig, and José E. Santías, "Una Economía Latinoamericana," in Luis Benvenuto et al., *Uruguay Hoy* (Buenos Aires: Siglo 21, 1971), pp. 50–52.

5. Victor Pastorino, *Itinerario del colegiado* (Montevideo: Agencia Periodística Interamericana, 1956).

6. Walter Luisiardo, *Reflexiones sobre aspectos de la historia económica del Uruguay: Período 1900–1979* (Montevideo: Comisión Coordinadora para el Desarrollo Económico, 1979), pp. 12–24.

7. Fynch, *Political Economy of Uruguay*, p. 171.

8. Luisiardo, *Reflexiones*, pp. 44–48, 69.

9. Fynch, *Political Economy of Uruguay*, pp. 220–223; Luisiardo, *Reflexiones*, p. 68.

10. James W. Wilkie and Peter Reich, *Statistical Abstract of Latin America* (Los Angeles: University of California Press, 1979), p. 332.

11. Weinstein, *Uruguay*, p. 119.

12. Luisiardo, *Reflexiones*, p. 95.

13. For an excellent analysis of this complex process, see Charles G. Gillespie's "Uruguay: Transition from Collegial-Technocratic Rule," in *Transitions from Authoritarian Rule*, edited by Guillermo O'Donnell, Philippe Schmitter, and Laurence Whitehead (Baltimore: Johns Hopkins University Press, 1986), II, pp. 173–195.

14. Fynch, *Political Economy of Uruguay*, pp. 183–184, 264.

15. Wilkie and Reich, *Statistical Abstract*, pp. 144, 518.

16. Macadar, Reig, and Santías, "Una Economía Latinoamericana," p. 102. The estimation goes as follows: 213,000 public employees + 346,000 pensioners = 559,000, which of a population of around 2.8 million is 19.96 percent.

17. Domingo Laíno, *Paraguay: De la Independencia a la Dependencia* (Asunción: Ediciones Cerro Corá, 1976), p. 171, and Harris G. Warren, *Paraguay and the Triple Alliance: The Post-War Decade 1869–1878* (Austin: Institute of Latin American Studies, University of Texas Press, 1978), p. 286.

18. U.S. Department of Commerce, *Commerce Yearbook* (Washington, D.C.: Government Printing Office, 1928–1932), and *Foreign Commerce Yearbook* (Washington, D.C.: Government Printing Office, 1932–1950).

19. Michael Grow, *The Good Neighbor Policy and Authoritarianism in Paraguay* (Lawrence: Regents Press of Kansas, 1981), p. 115.

20. U.S. Department of Commerce, *Investment in Paraguay: Conditions and Outlook for United States Investors* (Washington, D.C.: Government Printing Office, 1954), pp. 15–17, 84.

21. Grow, *Good Neighbor Policy,* pp. 63, 118, 146–147, n 27.

22. U.S. Department of Commerce, *Investment in Paraguay,* pp. 84–85.

23. Carlos Pastore, *La Lucha por la tierra en el Paraguay* (Montevideo: Editorial Antequera, 1972), p. 422.

24. Censo Industrial 1963, cited in Henry D. Ceuppens, *Paraguay Año 2,000* (Asunción: Editorial Gráfica Zamphirópolos, 1971), p. 61.

25. Wilkie and Reich, *Statistical Abstract,* p. 262.

26. Ceuppens, *Paraguay Año 2,000,* pp. 37, 124–126.

27. Banco Interamericano de Desarrollo (BID), *Progreso económico social en America Latina: Informe 1980–1981* (Washington, D.C., 1981), pp. 358–360. *ABC Color,* "Suplemento económico," July 25, 1982, pp. 4–5.

28. Ricardo Rodriguez Silvero, "Paraguay: El Endeudamiento externo," *Revista Paraguaya de sociología* 17:50 (January–May 1980), p. 81. *Ultima Hora,* February 26, 1989, p. 12.

29. Fernando L. Masi, "Paraguay: Analysis of the Socio-Economic Evolution" (Manuscript prepared in Washington, D.C., at the American University, 1982), p. 21.

30. Study done by the *Comité de Iglesias,* cited in *ABC Color,* "Actualidad profesional," March 5, 1982, pp. 2–3.

31. An extended discussion of these issues can be found in Diego Abente, *Stronismo, Post-Stronismo and the Prospects for Democratization in Paraguay,* Working Paper No. 119, Kellogg Institute, University of Notre Dame, 1989, and "Constraints and Opportunities: External Factors, Authoritarianism, and the Prospects for Democratization in Paraguay," *Journal of Interamerican Studies and World Affairs* 30:1 (Spring 1988), pp. 73–104.

32. For a discussion of the elections, see the Report of the Latin American Studies Association International Commission to Observe the Paraguayan Elections, "The May 1, 1989, Elections in Paraguay: Toward a New Era of Democracy?" *LASA Forum XX,* 3 (Fall 1989), pp. 39–48.

SUGGESTED READINGS

Uruguay

Benvenuto, Luis, et al. *Uruguay Hoy.* Buenos Aires: Siglo 21, 1971. Uruguay as seen by the Uruguayans; interesting perspectives.

Fynch, Martin H.J. *A Political Economy of Uruguay Since 1970.* New York: St. Martin's Press, 1981. An excellent analysis of the Uruguayan economic process until the late 1970s; a must.

Handelman, Howard. *Military Authoritarianism and Political Change in Uruguay.* AUFS Report. Hanover, N.H.: American Universities Field Staff, 1978. A good short analysis of contemporary trends and events.

_____. *Economic Policy and Elite Pressures in Uruguay.* AUFS Report. Hanover, N.H.: American Universities Field Staff, 1979. A good short study on recent changes regarding the decision-making process.

Kaufman, Edy. *Uruguay in Transition.* New Brunswick, N.J.: Transaction Books, 1979. An interesting, up-to-date work on Uruguayan politics.

Pivel Devoto, Juan E. "Uruguay independiente." In Antonio Ballesteros, ed., *Historia de America y de los Pueblos Americanos,* Vol. 21: 405–638. Barcelona: Salvat Editores, 1949. One of the many good and short historical introductions to Uruguay.

Quijana, José M., and Guillermo Waksman. "Las Relaciones Uruguay–Estados Unidos en 1977–1979." In *Cuadernos semestrales* 6 (2° semestre, 1979), pp. 310–343. A good study on recent trends in U.S.-Uruguayan relations with a useful statistical appendix.

Verdisco, Aimee E. "Between Accountability and 'Reivindicación': Development and Intranational Differentiation in Uruguay." Ph.D. diss., State University of New York at Buffalo, 1996.

Weinstein, Martin. *Uruguay: The Politics of Failure.* Westport, Conn.: Greenwood Press, 1975. A comprehensive analysis of Uruguayan politics; especially good for the study of the 1900–1960s period.

Paraguay

Abente, Diego. *Stronismo, Post-Stronismo, and the Prospects for Democratization in Paraguay.* Working Paper No. 119, Kellogg Institute, University of Notre Dame, 1989.

Bouvier, Virginia M. *Decline of the Dictator: Paraguay at a Crossroads* (Washington, D.C.: WOLA, 1988).

Cardozo, Efraim. *Breve historia del Paraguay.* Buenos Aires: EUDEBA, 1965. A good and short introduction to Paraguayan history.

Grow, Michael. *The Good Neighbor Policy and Authoritarianism in Paraguay.* Lawrence: Regents Press of Kansas, 1981. A very well documented study of the 1939–1949 period.

Hicks, Frederick. "Interpersonal Relationships and Caudillismo in Paraguay." *Journal of Inter-American Studies and World Affairs* 13 (January 1971), pp. 89–111. A very interesting, although somewhat outdated, study of Paraguayan politics.

Lewis, Paul H. *The Politics of Exile: Paraguay's Febrerista Party.* Chapel Hill: University of North Carolina Press, 1968. An in-depth study of the Febrerista Party.

_____. *Paraguay Under Stroessner.* Chapel Hill: University of North Carolina Press, 1980.

Pastore, Carlos. *La Lucha por la tierra en el Paraguay.* Montevideo: Editorial Antequera, 1972. A very good social history of Paraguay with special emphasis on an analysis of the agrarian process.

Warren, Harris G. *Paraguay and the Triple Alliance: The Post-War Decade 1869–1878.* Austin: Institute of Latin American Studies, University of Texas Press, 1978. The best analysis of the first postwar decade.

PART TWELVE

BRAZIL

29

BRAZIL: FROM INDEPENDENCE TO 1964

MICHAEL L. CONNIFF

Brazil's independence in 1822 was unusual among the anticolonial movements in the Western Hemisphere, and it launched the new country on a trajectory different from the rest of Latin America. Throughout much of the nineteenth century, Brazil enjoyed a stable and prosperous monarchy envied in neighboring countries. Much of the stability, however, was due to the avoidance of major decisions affecting the society and economy, decisions that by the 1880s became urgent and indeed overwhelmed the government's capacity to act. The monarchy was swept away in 1889 and replaced by a transitional military regime, whose leaders created a republican system that lasted for forty years. This era, known as the First Republic, saw Brazil gradually modernize along the lines of Western Europe and North America.

Brazil established closer relations with the rest of the American republics, especially the United States, during these years. The sui generis political system, however, broke down in 1930 during a presidential succession crisis. The man who emerged victorious from the crisis (known as the Revolution of 1930) was Getúlio Vargas, Brazil's leading political figure of the twentieth century. Until his suicide twenty-four years later, Vargas dominated national politics in various roles, both in power and out. Afterward, other politicians, following directions charted during the Vargas era, attempted to preserve democratic and constitutional government in the face of growing military interest in power and increasingly difficult international and economic circumstances. In 1964, the army, joined by some civilian forces, ended the country's brief "experiment in democracy" and inaugurated what became one of the most resilient military governments in Latin American history.

THE FIRST AND SECOND EMPIRES

Brazilian independence came at the hands of Prince Pedro of Alcantara, who governed the prosperous colony on behalf of his father, King João VI of Portugal. João and the entire Portuguese court had resided in Brazil's capital city, Rio de Janeiro, from 1808 until 1821 in order to elude Napoleon's hostile armies and then to manage the burgeoning economy of their giant tropical possession. By long tradition, the British had played a role in protecting the Portuguese Empire, in exchange for which England was granted free access to Brazilian resources and trade. João had more to fear than foreign threats to his colony, however: Independence wars were raging across the continent, and similar movements had erupted in Brazil as well. Thus, when João returned to Portugal, he instructed his son Pedro, who remained as prince regent, to assume the leadership should independence become inevitable. Thereby a dynastic, if not a colonial, relationship would continue between Portugal and Brazil.

Pedro—brash, impetuous, ambitious, and advised by persons sympathetic to independence—was all too ready to take command of the colony. On September 7, 1822, in response to insults from the Portuguese Parliament (temporarily in the ascendancy), Pedro declared Brazil independent and soon received the crown of the newly created empire. With the help of the British, he quelled several pro-Portuguese rebellions and received recognition from the United States, England, Portugal, and finally, the Vatican. True to the spirit of the Enlightenment, which inspired many of his supporters, Pedro gave the country a quasi-parliamentary government in the Constitution of 1824. He retained and exercised an overriding authority, however, the so-called moderating power.

Pedro's reign, known as the First Empire (1822–1831), proved turbulent and ill starred. The great prosperity of the preceding decades broke in the mid-1820s as a hemisphere-wide depression set in. Even coffee, rapidly becoming Brazil's leading export, experienced a slump. Pedro's authoritarian style, deemed necessary during the independence period, now irritated Brazilians, as did a scandalous extramarital affair. The decline in his popularity was also due to prolonged meddling in the Portuguese succession struggles (João VI died in 1826) and to a costly and unsuccessful war against Argentina over the Banda Oriental (to become Uruguay in 1828). In 1831, confronted with financial insolvency, street demonstrations, and a hostile Brazilian elite, Pedro abdicated.

The end of the First Empire contributed to a prolonged period of internal conflict, because the emperor's son (also named Pedro) was only five years old and could not ascend to the throne until he was eighteen. Brazilian political leaders quickly formed a regency triumvirate to rule in the prince's name. They lacked the legitimacy a true monarch would have enjoyed, however, and the country drifted toward dissolution. Nearly every region experienced an uprising of some sort, and two—the Cabanagem in Amazonas (1835–1840) and the Farroupilha in Rio Grande do Sul (1835–1845)— were outright civil wars. Ineffectual central rule permitted considerable authority to shift into the hands of officers, typically *coronéis* ("colonels"), of the newly created National Guard. Most *coronéis* were in fact prominent planters or cattlemen who used their commissions to legitimate armed control over their rural dominions.

Pedro II, it is generally agreed, symbolically and personally brought peace to the country in the 1840s and made it a true nation in the 1850s. In 1840, he was approached by leading politicians who proposed that Parliament declare him of age immediately in order to stem the provincial warfare and aimlessness of government. Young Pedro agreed, and the following year he was duly crowned Pedro II, ushering in the Second Empire (1841–1889).

In the 1840s, two principal parties became consolidated, the Liberals and the Conservatives, and Pedro II relied on each in alternation to staff high executive posts in the government. Within several years, a workable, albeit authoritarian, version of the British parliamentary system was in operation, allowing Pedro to exercise the moderating power while more experienced men ran the affairs of state on a daily basis. From 1853 to 1868, in fact, Pedro managed a bipartisan government of some sophistication during the conciliation era. Powers that had been ceded to the provinces during the 1830s were reconcentrated in the imperial court, and in several major cases (notably the Queiros Law of 1850, which ended the African slave trade), Pedro displayed considerable statesmanship.

The Brazilian economy recovered its dynamism during the 1840s, aided by the growth of coffee exports from the Paraiba Valley northwest of Rio de Janeiro. Since the time of independence, landowners in the region had secured their hold on huge tracts, which were planted in coffee. By mid-century, Brazil had become the world's leading supplier of coffee, and the new planter elite dominated imperial government. The general prosperity kept government solvent, spurred infrastructure development and ancillary industries, and financed a major war in the south against the Paraguayan dictator Francisco Solano López (War of the Triple Alliance, 1864–1870). Yet the Paraiba Valley coffee boom was relatively short-lived because planting methods caused great erosion and relied heavily on slave labor, which was becoming scarce.

Labor shortages were chronic throughout Brazilian history, due in part to poor treatment of Amerindians, blacks, and racially mixed persons over the centuries. After the end of the African slave trade, planters faced an apparently insoluble dilemma: The slave population was growing older and less productive, and no new laborers could be attracted as long as slavery existed. Since the 1820s, the government had attempted to attract European immigrants, but with few exceptions, these attempts had not relieved the general shortage of plantation labor.

The decline of the Second Empire began during the War of the Triple Alliance and gathered momentum in the following decades. Pedro's obstinacy in eliminating Solano López prolonged the war, nearly destroying Paraguay and severely taxing the Brazilians. The war became unpopular, and Pedro's esteem fell correspondingly. Inflation, indebtedness, financial crises, food shortages, and disruption of the labor supply were among the more serious consequences of the war. Politically, the costs were also high. The bipartisan conciliation arrangement failed, and Pedro was obliged to exercise far more than moderating powers. Moreover, army officers, having fought loyally for five years under trying circumstances, resented demobilization and inattention from the court after 1870.

Some officers began openly to criticize the government and to advocate republicanism, to which the government responded with an order requiring prior clearance from the minister of war for any political statements. The ranking general, Marshal Deodoro de Fonseca, objected to these restrictions and launched a campaign to defend officers' prerogatives and to further the cause of republicanism, which he personally embraced. A critical juncture in this campaign was the formation of the Military Club in 1887 to protest orders that the army pursue slaves who ran away from their owners. Indeed, the causes of republicanism and of the abolition of slavery had become closely intertwined by this time.

The antislavery movement of the 1880s ranks as a major *tomada de conciencia,* or moral crusade, in Brazilian history. Based in the cities and drawing upon new professional groups, the movement enlisted thousands of supporters from all walks of life and carried on an unprecedented propaganda effort. The issue split the two parties and caused great administrative instability. Emancipation advocates penetrated the coffee zones and encouraged slaves to revolt or run away, which many did. By 1887, the level of tension and violence was so high that many planters manumitted slaves voluntarily, so the end was clearly in sight. Pedro, however, was in Europe for treatment of his diabetes, and the final emancipation decree, known as the Golden Law, was promulgated by Princess Regent Isabel on May 13, 1888, amid great rejoicing.

The euphoria that accompanied emancipation lasted for several months but did not save the monarchy. Isabel was recognized as talented, but by now, too many people believed that a basic change of government was necessary. Meanwhile, the planters, dominant throughout the two empires, no longer defended the monarchy. In these circumstances, the army became the critical arbiter, and Deodoro became the reluctant agent of Pedro's overthrow on November 15, 1889.

THE OLD REPUBLIC

The beginnings of civilian-military rivalry in Brazilian government are rooted in the five-year transition period during which Deodoro (1889–1891) and army Marshal Floriano Peixoto (1891–1894) ruled the country more or less dictatorially. To be sure, Deodoro declared Brazil a federal republic, but once in power, he and his successor found it difficult to step down, for political as well as circumstantial reasons. For one thing, the country had very few persons experienced in representative government and quite a few who desired restoration of the monarchy. Civil uprisings of various sorts punctuated the 1890s and made strong rule necessary. For another, the country was plunged into a depression following a crisis in the London capital market, the economic effects of which were extremely harmful for Brazil.

The United States quickly recognized Deodoro's government and initiated trade overtures designed to end the long-standing advantages enjoyed by the British. The same depression that assailed Brazil impeded freer imports into the United States, but in 1896, President Cleveland made a permanent friend of the baron of Rio Branco by favoring the latter's case over the Argentineans' in arbitration of the Missiones Territory. When Rio Branco became foreign minister in 1901, he replaced

Brazil's traditional orientation toward London with one favoring Washington, in what came to be known as the unwritten alliance.

Ruy Barbosa, a firebrand republican appointed minister of government in 1890, held a constitutional convention and orchestrated the adoption of a charter like that of the United States. The Constitution of 1891 provided for a federal republic, a broad bill of rights, a president elected for a nonrenewable four-year term, a bicameral legislature, a separate judiciary, and important powers vested in the states. Among the last were supervision of all elections, collection of export taxes (important for the coffee states), maintenance of militias, financial autonomy, and state-enacted constitutions. Although for several years the constitution was unenforced, due to army control, depression, and civil wars, it did last until 1930 and gave shape to the country's modern administration.

A republican leader from São Paulo, Prudente de Moraes, skillfully maneuvered himself into the presidency in 1894 and ended Brazil's first period of military rule. During his four years of turbulent administration, he did little to institute formal democracy but he did lay solid claim to the presidency on behalf of his state, whose exports of coffee were all that stood between Brazil and financial ruin. São Paulo gradually pulled ahead of the rest of the states, driven by coffee exports but also drawing on the dynamic leadership of its elite families. Immigrants now flowed into São Paulo to work on plantations and eventually to settle in cities and towns throughout the temperate south. The rail system, installed during the last quarter of the nineteenth century by British companies, made possible an integrated regional economy in which the transition from export agriculture to manufacturing was not only easy but natural. For these reasons, São Paulo emerged as the leading state in the federation during the Old Republic and exercised great influence over the national administration in Rio.

During and after the administration of Manuel Ferrax de Campos Sales (1898–1902), politics settled into predictable patterns, albeit not those the constitution prescribed. The main reason for the renewed stability was the return of coffee prosperity and, with it, respite from the difficult economic problems of the 1890s. Campos Sales rescheduled the debt held by Brazil's international creditors, the English branch of the Rothschilds, and arranged with the governors of leading states to have a free hand in meeting conditions imposed by the bankers: return to a convertible hard currency and balanced budgets. In exchange for federal autonomy in financial policies, Campos Sales conceded substantial prerogatives to the governors of the leading states, in what came to be known as "the politics of the governors."

During the first three decades of this century (and in some respects longer), Brazil's governments operated according to two unwritten codes, "the politics of the governors," covering relations between presidents and governors of leading states, and *coronelismo*, which regulated relations between most governors and regional bosses (called *coronéis* because, at first, many were colonels in the National Guard). The politics of the governors gave to the heads of major states the right to choose presidential successors and to rule their states with no federal interference. In practice, this meant that the governors of São Paulo (the economic power) and Minas Gerais (the most populous and best-organized state) aspired to and often won the presidency in rigged, coordinated elections. Their candidates usually ran unopposed, and in the 1920s, a gentlemen's agreement (called *café com leite* ["coffee with cream"]) stipulated that the presidency alternate between the two states.

Rio Grande do Sul, a quasi-garrison state with a disciplined single-party regime, also played an important role in the politics of the governors, although it never captured the presidency. By judiciously opposing the São Paulo–Minas alliance, Rio Grande could represent the interests of the smaller states in the Northeast, much like a broker. This occasionally gave Rio Grande the chance to veto official candidates and to play a spoiler role in federal politics.

Military power definitely enhanced the states' influence during the Old Republic, so that during crises a kind of military federalism prevailed. Police forces maintained by the larger states were veritable armies, capable of offering a good fight to the national armed forces should the occasion arise. State police also made it possible for governors to rule their own territories more effectively.

Each governor had to manage local politics in order to guarantee his influence in national affairs. Most did so through the Republican parties, formal networks of politicians who kept their subordinates in line and carried out their governors' commands. On the informal level, however, governors made deals with regional bosses, the famous *coronéis,* by which the latter supplied votes (usually fraudulent) and military backing on request. The governors in turn provided the *coronéis* with jobs, public works moneys, important positions in the state assemblies and executives, armed support when needed, and almost total freedom in local affairs. The *coronéis,* then, were potentates in their regions; most were already powerful by virtue of owning ranches, plantations, or businesses.

Coronelismo existed in most states (all had to elect congressmen and governors), but the politics of the governors was limited to a few. The rest of the states had to adjust their actions in accordance with what the big three did. The possibilities for alliances were enormous, and many strange combinations emerged during presidential contests. In all, it was an effective, quasi-federal oligarchical system for rotating the presidency among the most powerful states.

The army's part in republican politics made it the functional equivalent of a "big state." In a sense, the army inherited the moderating power of the emperor, and even after Floriano stepped down in favor of a civilian, the army kept watch as guarantor of the republican system it had spawned.

Military intervention brought side effects not contemplated by commanders. In the 1920s, hundreds of younger officers and cadets joined the revolutionary movements of *tenentes,* so named because many were lieutenants. They objected to using the army to control the smaller northeastern states (from which many came). They protested rural poverty, illiteracy, violence against labor, imperialism, and undemocratic government. The *tenente* movements were insufficient in themselves to overthrow the government, but they bolstered reformist sentiments in the urban middle classes. The *tenentes* also expanded the army's political mission from guarantor of democracy to socioeconomic reformer. The most famous *tenente* exploits were their capture of São Paulo city for nearly a month in 1924 and their subsequent "long march" of 15,000 mi (24,135 km) through the backlands to publicize rural poverty and backwardness.

Just as the *tenente* movements broke down the army's internal unity, dissident political groups in the major states also gummed up the politics of the governors and *coronelismo*. As cities grew and industrialization proceeded, the political system seemed outmoded and archaic. Too many groups, especially in the cities, found themselves virtually disfranchised in national elections. In addition, the so-called social questions—poverty, illiteracy, poor health, and alienation among the lower classes—demanded the attention of presidents and governors whose priorities lay elsewhere. Thus the 1920s, although quite prosperous, saw a new kind of political unrest: middle-class reformism and demands for more representative government. This was the scenario for the Revolution of 1930.

The politics of the governors worked well when Minas Gerais and São Paulo could agree on a presidential candidate; if they couldn't, Rio Grande gained considerable leverage by breaking the impasse. In 1928, incumbent Paulista president Washington Luis broke the *café com leite* pattern and chose a Paulista candidate for the 1930 election. The governor of Minas, Antonio Carlos de Andrada, convinced he was being cheated out of the presidency, made a deal to support Getúlio Vargas of Rio Grande, with the implicit understanding that four years hence *he* would be the official candidate. Vargas accepted and created the Liberal Alliance coalition to conduct his campaign. The Revolution of 1930, then, began as a succession crisis and contested presidential election. What made this election different was the heavy voter recruitment conducted by both sides, especially among middle- and working-class voters in the cities. Vargas posed as a reformer, despite the fact that he was a conventional politician with a record of working within the system. He was, above all, an extremely versatile mediator, and he nearly won the election with his daring campaign: He polled over 48 percent of the record turnout of 1.9 million.

THE 1930 REVOLUTION AND THE SECOND REPUBLIC

Vargas and the older politicians were prepared to live with defeat, but a number of younger men in Rio Grande and Minas Gerais decided to overthrow the government, on the grounds that Vargas had been fraudulently denied the presidency. The onset of the depression heightened their resolve to take the government by force.

These younger leaders recruited a number of *tenente* officers to staff the revolt, and they convinced Vargas and Antonio Carlos de Andrada to go along with the plot. Two outstanding figures emerged at this point: Oswaldo Aranha, coordinator of the revolution, and Colonel Pedro Aurélio Góes Monteiro, chief of staff of its armed forces. Already counting on the state police of Rio Grande and Minas, they won over enough army officers in the south to make their revolt militarily feasible. After several false starts in mid-1930, they launched their revolt on October 3. Troops from Minas secured that state and awaited the drive north by the main body of revolutionaries from Rio Grande. As the final showdown neared in late October, the army high command in Rio de Janeiro decided to intervene to prevent massive bloodshed. It deposed the incumbent president and negotiated an agreement whereby Vargas would become provisional president. He was sworn in on November 3.

The Revolution of 1930 brought about many changes in the political system of the country and is held to have initiated a Second Republic. Moreover, the concurrent depression altered the economy deeply, a process that interacted with politics. Finally, large-scale migration to cities commenced at this time, so that by the end of the first Vargas presidency, Brazil would be ripe for mass politics. Most of these changes occurred in unplanned fashion, however, because the Revolution of 1930 had no clear blueprint or mandate for such sweeping changes.

Vargas's principal challenge after taking office was to stabilize the country and secure his hold on power. For nearly a year, he experimented unsuccessfully with various coalitions until he decided to create a dictatorship while relying heavily on *tenente* leaders who had fought with him in 1930. This course alienated civilian politicians and provoked a civil war in São Paulo in mid-1932. Always conciliatory, Vargas agreed to restore civilian representative government once his control was secure, and in 1933 he oversaw elections for a constitutional convention. Many of the reforms attributed to Vargas and the Revolution of 1930 were actually portions of the *tenente* program adopted during the dictatorial interlude of 1931–1932.

The constitution promulgated in 1934 ended the provisional government and confirmed Vargas in the presidency for four years. The Liberal-progressive regime of the mid-1930s was not at all to Vargas's liking, so he began to rely on the federal police, the army, and conservative political groups to help contain what he believed were threatening leftist movements. Thus, politics became increasingly polarized. Symptomatic were extremist clashes and uprisings. Yet perhaps more important in the long run was the emergence of a populist movement in Rio de Janeiro, led by former *tenente* Pedro Ernesto Baptista.

Pedro Ernesto, a wealthy surgeon who had aided the *tenentes* in the late 1920s, had become their leader during the period of dictatorship, at which time he was appointed mayor of Rio. He became Brazil's first genuine populist leader by forming a multiclass reform movement in the country's largest city. Vargas quashed the populist experiment in mid-1936. Nevertheless, Pedro Ernesto proved that urban voters could be recruited for coalition politics in large numbers, a lesson to be demonstrated amply following World War II.

By 1936, Vargas had decided to stay in power as long as possible, so he gradually assembled a plan to abort the presidential elections scheduled for 1938 and impose another dictatorship, this time inspired by European fascism. Briefly, Vargas's associates helped create a climate of political crisis that justified suspension of democratic procedures. The army was especially interested in such a policy, for most high-ranking generals regarded normal political byplay as a temptation for Communist agents to subvert Brazil. On November 10, less than two months before the election date, Vargas and the army carried out a *continuismo* coup, which gave him a new term and near-dictatorial powers under a fascist constitution. The new regime, called the Estado Novo (New State) after Salazar's in Portugal, lasted until late 1945; it has also been termed the Third Republic.

Vargas's New State was milder than most European fascist regimes, though it was harsher than anything Brazilians had experienced for several generations. Until 1942, Vargas assumed a posture of strict neutrality in the war and allowed fascist sympathizers to operate freely. The police and army seemed to be the warmest supporters of the Axis.

In early 1942, however, Vargas broke relations with the Axis and began supporting the United States. Brazil sent 25,000 men to participate in the Italian campaign of 1944, the Brazilian Expeditionary Force (FEB). This qualified Brazil to receive lend-lease military and other aid from the United States and established a cooperative relationship between the two military forces that lasted into the 1970s. In 1949, the Pentagon aided Brazil in establishing the Superior War College (ESG), which developed a full-scale plan for Brazilian development and national security.

In internal politics after 1942, Vargas tried to assuage critics and to appear a man of the people. Indeed, an elaborate publicity campaign proclaimed Vargas to be "the protector of the working class" because of the favorable decrees he had signed during his administration. These benefits had multiplied during the New State, albeit in exchange for putting the union movement under the control of the Ministry of Labor.

In 1945, Vargas tried to make a risky transition from dictator to democrat and failed. The mood of the country would no longer tolerate censorship, police spying, political prisoners, and totalitarian powers invested in the executive. Even the army, fighting for democracy in Europe, favored a return to constitutional representative government. Vargas, a wise politician with friends throughout the country, recognized the public mood and announced that elections would be held in December. He created two parties, one made up of traditional politicians from leading states, called the Social Democratic Party (PSD), and another called the Brazilian Labor Party (PTB). The latter was based exclusively in the Ministry of Labor and sought to tap the support of workers in Rio, São Paulo, and Rio Grande do Sul. The PSD nominated General Eurico Dutra for the presidency, apparently with Vargas's blessing.

Opposition to Vargas grew during the year. He tried to change his image, removing some of the worst autocrats and courting leftist support, and it seemed the country would return to democracy. However, the opposition (which coalesced into the Brazilian Democratic Union, UDN) continued to attack him energetically. Indeed, such was Vargas's influence that politicians took stances for or against him rather than for programs or ideologies. This overwhelming presence convinced many, including Dutra, that Vargas would again execute a *continuismo* coup to stay in power, as he had in 1937.

The army high command, led by Dutra and Góes Monteiro, ushered Vargas out of office in late October and held the elections on schedule. Dutra won, but he was hardly a popular choice. Short, pudgy, reclusive, Dutra won only because of support from parties Vargas had created. Elections in 1946 and 1947 showed that the Communists enjoyed the support of about 10 percent of the voters and that populists like Adhemar de Barros in São Paulo could attract great multiclass support in urban areas.

Dutra presided over what amounted to a caretaker government. His undertakings included a new constitution in 1946, a return to free market economics, establishment of the Superior War College, and a ban on the Communists in 1947. Dutra followed U.S. wishes in foreign policy and was rewarded with credits under the Point Four Program and from the World Bank. Yet he provided little leadership and even lost control of his own party, the PSD. By 1950, the voters were ready for a change, and Vargas offered them one.

Vargas had begun rebuilding his career soon after his overthrow in 1945. He was elected to Congress from several states, cultivated the image of "father of the poor," and campaigned on his labor record. (Government inattention to falling real wages in the postwar years inadvertently helped him.) He proclaimed the need for greater economic independence and industrial expansion, together with wage increases to broaden the internal market. His new program is sometimes referred to as "developmentalist nationalism." As the 1950 election approached, Vargas pulled ahead and even made a deal to receive the São Paulo votes of Adhemar de Barros.

Vargas won 49 percent of the votes in the hotly contested three-man race, a relative landslide. Brazil enjoyed a year and a half of prosperity due to high commodity prices, and Vargas made good his promise to raise real wages. He also asked Congress to nationalize the petroleum and electric power industries. In support of the draft laws, Vargas pointed out that these sectors were crucial for industrial development, but because they were foreign owned, national planners could not influence management decisions. Apparently Vargas had, during the preceding fifteen years, completely changed his ideas about the role of the state.

Vargas's new economic nationalism and prolabor policies were increasingly formulated by younger, aggressive men around the aging president. João Goulart, PTB leader from Rio Grande and minister of labor from 1953 to 1954, was prominent among these new forces pushing Vargas to the left. Vargas, in fact, was losing control over the government, unable in his late sixties to manage the bureaucracy that he had done so much to inflate.

Economic and political crises mounted in 1954, and Vargas grew more desperate. The end of the Korean War brought reduced prices for the country's exports. On Labor Day, Vargas decreed a 100 percent wage increase, but other sectors—including military officers whose pay was in arrears—protested and nearly brought the government down. Corruption had become endemic in the higher echelons of the regime, though Vargas himself was honest. Finally, one of his bodyguards, apparently acting alone, made an attempt on the life of Carlos Lacerda, UDN leader and

Vargas's most outspoken foe. Vargas said, "I feel like I am standing in a sea of mud." His days were clearly numbered.

In August 1954, an air force uprising brought the army back into politics—and gave Vargas his second ouster in less than ten years. At this point, however, the president decided on a different course. Rather than face an ignominious retirement and continued vilification by his enemies, Vargas took his own life. His dramatic suicide note spoke of covert forces that jeopardized the very sovereignty of the nation. Only he had defended the people against subjugation by international companies like the great oil monopolies, and now that he was gone, the people would need to redouble their vigilance. The suicide note wrought a political miracle, resurrecting Vargas's reputation and casting him as a martyr for the nation.

Vargas's fame as a populist comes largely from the early 1950s, yet paradoxically, he accomplished little during his second term in office. The national petroleum monopoly, Petrobras, stands as a sole monument. By comparison, his first term (1930–1945) virtually remade the Brazilian state and ushered in major socioeconomic changes. The early Vargas years will remain controversial, but they were unquestionably the most dynamic in this century.

Vice-President Café Filho took over the executive branch in 1954, but he was little more than a weak stand-in assailed by powerful pressures. To his credit, he managed honest elections in 1955, in which Juscelino Kubitschek of the Minas PSD won a narrow plurality. Army units almost blocked the succession, objecting to the vice-president-elect, João Goulart, but a countercoup restored constitutional rule. Kubitschek took office in early 1956.

The new administration promised "fifty years of progress in five" and indeed accomplished a great deal. Kubitschek followed the economics of the "structuralists," who argued that daring and unorthodox measures were required to break through obstacles to progress. Brazil gave lucrative concessions to U.S. and European firms to start up the now-booming automobile industry. It built hydroelectric dams and highways in the rural areas. It set up regional development agencies such as the famous SUDENE for the depressed Northeast. And finally, Brasilia, the twenty-first-century capital, was built at the geographical center of the country, more as a symbol of economic independence than a contributor to it. Much of this rapid expansion, however, was financed through enormous budget deficits, which, after a lag, caused high inflation. Moreover, many of the new industries enjoyed subsidies and tax credits that shielded them from competition and protected inefficiency. Unquestionably, Kubitschek, for better or worse, followed Vargas's lead in pursuing an end to dependence on imported manufactures and capital.

Politically, Kubitschek managed quite well by balancing wage increases with bigger profits for business. Lucrative construction contracts kept political cronies happy and party coffers full. Meanwhile, Goulart, chastened by the abortive military coup against him, kept a low profile and tried to live down his reputation as a labor radical. In a sense, Kubitschek managed to "export" dissidence by drawing on international resources to prime the pump and keep everyone happy. When the borrowing became excessive, the International Monetary Fund cut him off, leading to Brazil's angry withdrawal from the agency. Kubitschek then made a memorable proposal to the United States for a vast developmental effort to be called Operation Pan-America. Several years later, the idea germinated and became the Alliance for Progress.

Elections held in 1960 saw voters bolt the old parties and images to support a newcomer, Janio Quadros, for the presidency. Having enjoyed a meteoric rise from schoolteacher to governor of São Paulo in the 1950s, Quadros had a fresh quality untainted by the old parties and alliances. His campaign symbol was a broom, with which he promised to sweep the rascals out of office. He eschewed party affiliation and accepted the UDN nomination only because it was traditionally the party of the "outs." Quadros was eccentric, a loner, appealing but aloof, a savior who appeared out of nowhere.

Two other factors helped Quadros's victory in 1960. Center-of-the-road politics had begun to fade away, leaving the field increasingly to radicals of the left and right, who attacked one another indecorously to win voters in the big cities. During the 1950s, a subtle but important change had occurred. Urban voters no longer reacted en masse to whatever was served up on the political platter; rather, they had become more discriminating and interest oriented. According to one analyst, class politics replaced mass politics in the big cities, raising the level of competitiveness and complexity. In this perspective, Quadros was the last of the consensual populists who could appeal to the masses and middle class without a program. Unfortunately for those who placed their trust in him, Quadros's presidential career lasted a scant seven months.

Quadros's victory, backed by the disorganized UDN, seemed to give him unusual freedom of action, but his inexperience made it hard to work with Congress. He instituted budget retrenchment to check inflation yet kept the economy moving with Alliance for Progress and IMF funds. He promised a bold new foreign policy in keeping with a changed world situation. Brazil would pursue its interests in the international arena regardless of old sympathies (e.g., with the United States). He envisioned Brazil leading the Third World nations, especially those of Africa, with which Brazil shared historic ties. Finally, Quadros dispatched Vice-President Goulart (reelected in 1960) on a goodwill and trade mission to Russia and Communist China.

Quadros lacked patience and staying power, however, and he soon wilted in the hothouse political environment of Brasilia. Frustrated with slow congressional deliberations over many of his programs, he decided in August 1961 to force the issue by resigning. Congress would not (he assumed) allow him to leave, for Goulart was in China and the new administration had barely been set up. A more cooperative Congress would beg him to stay. Yet Quadros mishandled the ploy and made it impossible for Congress to call him back even had the will existed, which was doubtful. Quadros's departure was accepted, and congressional and military leaders debated whether to allow Goulart to assume the presidency. A compromise agreement stipulated that Goulart could become president if Congress amended the constitution to create a parliamentary system with limited executive powers.

With hindsight, it is clear that the Quadros resignation and Goulart succession were critical events in the chain that led to the military coup of 1964. Quadros symbolized the failure of consensus and moderate politics. Goulart—notwithstanding years of "good behavior"—was still considered a dangerous radical and the alter ego of Vargas. The interaction between Goulart, Congress, the army, and the United States was extremely complex, and ultimately disastrous for the Goulart presidency and for Brazilian democracy.

CONCLUSION

Looking back over nearly a century and a half of Brazilian history since independence, we can discern several major themes or continuities. The political elite, whether Pedro II's nobility or Vargas's cronies, distrusted representative government because the masses were too backward and uneducated. The elite gradually remedied the situation with schools, hospitals, and literacy campaigns, but never quickly enough. The masses were expected to—and did—follow unquestioningly. Even the architects of the great populist expansion of the 1930–1964 period assumed that the masses were not fully capable of participatory democracy. Second, the coercive powers of the army were always posed to prevent civil disturbances, whether slave uprisings or Communist revolts. By this century, the army had assumed the role of "moderating power" from the 1824 Constitution, whereby it could save the country should the politicians lose their way. The army has continually intervened in politics since the 1880s. Third, Brazil moved rapidly through several economic phases— from sugar and coffee production in the nineteenth century to light manufacturing in the early twentieth to heavy or basic industry by mid-century. This progression concentrated more people and resources in the major coastal cities. Finally, constitutions have been only imperfect guides to the operation of politics, which, instead, was based upon old traditions as well as shifting balances of power. All these trends were evident in the events leading to the 1964 coup.

SUGGESTED READINGS

Burns, E. Bradford. *A History of Brazil*. New York: Columbia University Press, 1970. A fine, well-written synthesis from colonial to modern times.

Conniff, Michael L. *Urban Politics in Brazil*. Pittsburgh: University of Pittsburgh Press, 1981.

Conrad, Robert. *The Destruction of Brazilian Slavery, 1850–1888*. Berkeley: University of California Press, 1972. Portrays the events leading to emancipation, the burning issue of the day that helped bring down the monarchy.

Dean, Warren. *The Industrialization of São Paulo, 1880–1945*. Austin: University of Texas Press, 1969. An essential account of the rise of São Paulo to economic preeminence by shifting from coffee to manufacturing.

Dulles, John W.F. *Vargas of Brazil*. Austin: University of Texas Press, 1967. Still one of the best political biographies covering this century.

Flynn, Peter. *Brazil: A Political Analysis*. Boulder, Colo.: Westview Press, 1978. An excellent survey from independence on, emphasizing trends that culminated in the 1964 coup.

Graham, Richard. *Britain and the Onset of Modernization in Brazil*. New York: Cambridge University Press, 1968. A broad and sympathetic portrayal of development under Pedro II, especially as influenced by the British.

Haring, Clarence H. *Empire in Brazil*. Cambridge: Harvard University Press, 1958. Traditional account of politics during the First and Second Empires.

Levine, Robert M. *The Vargas Regime*. New York: Columbia University Press, 1970. Monographic study of the period 1934–1938, during which Vargas moved from democrat to dictator.

Love, Joseph L. *Rio Grande do Sul and Brazilian Regionalism*. Stanford: Stanford University Press, 1970. One of the first detailed studies of state-level politics during a time when a few major states dominated the nation.

McCann, Frank D., Jr. *The Brazilian-American Alliance*. Princeton: Princeton University Press, 1973. Diplomatic and military focus that highlights the Washington-Rio axis during World War II.

Poppino, Rollie. *Brazil: The Land and the People*. New York: Oxford University Press, 1973. Fine survey from colonial times to the present, with emphasis on socioeconomic themes.

Skidmore, Thomas E. *Politics in Brazil*. New York: Oxford University Press, 1967. Standard work on the later Vargas years and the period that culminated in the 1964 coup.

Stein, Stanley J. *Vassouras*. Cambridge: Harvard University Press, 1957. Classic study of coffee in the Paraiba Valley before São Paulo dominated the industry.

Stepan, Alfred. *The Military in Politics*. Princeton: Princeton University Press, 1970. Major study of the military after World War II tracing the military's involvement in politics up to and after the 1964 coup.

Wirth, John D. *The Politics of Brazilian Development*. Stanford: Stanford University Press, 1970. Fine study of Vargas's policymaking style based on three case studies spanning his first and second terms.

30

BRAZIL: MILITOCRACY AND FRUSTRATED DEMOCRATIZATION

BRADY TYSON,
RENÉ A. DREIFUSS,
AND JAN K. BLACK

Brazil has often been portrayed and characterized as a nation existing on two levels—the "two Brazils"—where an incredibly rich, developed, educated, and very small minority managed to dominate the poor majority, many living on a subsistence level, passive, semieducated, unorganized, leaderless.[1] Two Brazils sharply cut into various dichotomies: rural and urban social and cultural environments, industrial and agrarian economies, coast and hinterland, plains and rain forests. The growing gap between the rich and the poor—less than 10 percent of the population currently own 50 percent of the national wealth—and conflicting demands for material modernization and social change that weak formal political institutions were unable to mediate led to an impasse in the early 1960s. The consequent demand for "order" against the "chaos" deriving from incipient social mobilization paved the way for the civilian-military coup of 1964.

During the later years of the military regime, in the 1970s and early 1980s, the notion of two Brazils was synthesized by economist Edmar Bacha into an expression, "Belindia," to explain this emerging newly industrialized country: one part considered to be like Belgium—European, consumer oriented, developed, modern, growing through those years from 10 to 20 million people—and the other like India, an underdeveloped nation with a great mass living in miserable conditions, increasing its numbers from 60 million to about 110 million people in the same period.[2] "Belindia" summarized the dilemmas that Brazil confronted. But alongside the uneasy coexistence of the two Brazils, in the military period and over the next decade, there emerged a burgeoning new middle sector, comprising perhaps 20 to 30 million (of about 160 million total population). The sector now struggles to maintain its economic and social foothold in a complex modern society, facing a stern stabilization program imposed by the current government, after years of persistent inflation and even hyperinflation.

In Brazil today, it is easy to see the bustling, prosperous upper and middle sectors of society in their great modern cities with large shopping centers and luxurious, extensive residential areas and to imagine that this top 25 percent of the population is a symbol of hope for the "other Brazil," hope that with time the whole nation will be pulled upward toward a minimal standard of living. But in fact the skewing of income distribution in Brazil is among the world's worst. Brazil is the fifth largest country by population, tenth in gross national product, but fifty-second in terms of per capita gross national product. In educational national achievement, Brazil ranks seventy-fourth—lower than Madagascar, Ghana, Indonesia, Zimbabwe, Tunisia, Zaire, and Egypt.[3]

THE COUP OF 1964 AND THE NATIONAL SECURITY STATE

The "Revolution" of 1964, when the military seized power in a coup after a destabilization campaign devised by civilians, marked an abrupt change of direction in Brazilian political life. Top officers of the armed forces, profoundly disturbed by the often tumultuous political life as civilian leaders struggled to cope with the growth of population, the uneven impact of modernization on the nation, and the rising tide of expectations and discontent, toppled constitutional president João Goulart in 1964. Leaders of political, academic, labor, and other sectors identified with basic reforms (including members of the Congress and former presidents) were summarily stripped of their offices; several thousand prominent persons had to flee, and hundreds were arrested as the military assumed total control of the state apparatus.

Plans for the Modernization of Brazil

But the "Revolution" of 1964 was not a traditional Latin American military coup, designed to restore an old, tottering elite system. From the beginning, some of the military conspirators had an ideological framework of reference, combining notions of economic and administrative modernization and political containment, synthesized in the motto "Development and National Security," which had been developed in the Escola Superior de Guerra (Advanced War School). The ESG, as it was known, had been for years a meeting ground of civilians and military, allowing for a specific and guided cross-fertilization, and directed by a cadre including General Humberto de Alencar Castelo Branco (head of the General Staff of the army at the time of the coup), who became the first president-general. The new regime also had a set of very specific economic and state-reform projects, devised by the study and doctrine groups of the Instituto de Pesquisas e Estudos Sociais (Institute of Research and

Social Studies, or IPES). The institute had bases in the major cities of Brazil, where hundreds of entrepreneurs, economists, engineers, academics, media personnel, and military officers met on a daily basis during the years that preceded the coup, in a joint effort to destabilize Goulart's national-reformist government and organize the Brazilian elites. After the coup, IPES became a major government recruiting ground, providing some of the most important cabinet ministers and cadres of the new state administration, as well as the economic rationale and master plan.[4]

The new president-general, Castelo Branco, announced that he intended to return power to the civilians within eighteen months, assuming that the problems defined by the military as arising from "corruption and communism" could be tackled by taking out of political life the leaders of agitation and that other civilian leaders would readily accept the rationale of the national project developed by the ESG-IPES officers, entrepreneurs, economists, and engineers—the so-called technobureaucrats—over the previous years. But the military soon discovered there were three problems they had not anticipated.

First, not even conservative civilian political leaders and normally apathetic citizens would be easily persuaded to accept the leadership of the military. Criticism and resistance, initially from the student milieu, the media, intellectuals, and trade unionists, continued and increased in spite of repression and censorship. Repression and torture began the day of the coup, though they were sporadic initially. But what at first seemed to be the development—by vigilante groups, members of the three services, and civil and military police—of separate repressive teams that practiced torture in their disparate efforts to quell dissent soon became part and parcel of a nationwide repressive system under the unified command of top military officers. Castelo Branco had believed it would be possible to live with a relatively sanitized Congress, purged of its most assertive critics. The short-lived successor government of President-General Arturo Costa e Silva, already under pressure from radical positions springing from within the armed forces as well as from the entrepreneurial milieu, increased political repression. There was some congressional reaction, coupled with growing discontent over governmental economic policies among urban middle classes and the noisy resistance of high school and university students. Going against the rising tide of discontent, the High Command dictated a comprehensive "Institutional Act Number 5" (a decree known as "A1-5," promulgated in December 1968) that closed the Congress, extended the cancellation of civil rights to many other political leaders, and centralized power in the presidency-general.

Second, the challenges of modernizing, integrating, and disciplining the economy and society were much more complex than the ESG military and the IPES entrepreneurs had imagined, and they became aware that any serious national project of modernization would take more time and face more resistance from conservative business (who opposed entrepreneurial modernization on the IPES format), from traditional military officers (siding with hard-liners in their anti-Communist campaign, their rejection of civilian government, and their lust for jobs in the public administration), and from politicians who feared the consequences of the institutional and economic reforms implemented by the government. This broad spectrum of interests coalesced to underpin Castelo Branco's successor, Costa e Silva, a troop commander who had no contact with the ESG officers but whose bid for the presidency gained the support of the middle-rank officers. Although expressing himself through a discourse that sounded more nationalistic than his predecessor's, Costa e Silva allowed for the continuation of the economic internationalization coupled with a reinforcement of state agencies, while making space in the forefront of economic events for diverse industrial, agrarian, and commercial interests who were displaced by the former government.

Third, Castelo Branco had signed a basic law on agrarian reform, still considered a model for such programs. Everyone knew that it was necessary to stem the flow of poor and untrained peasants to the cities and make them more productive, content, and secure in the heartland. However, as the government soon discovered, the implementation of such a land reform would have led them to direct confrontation with the pugnacious landowners—agrarian production was still a main component of the GNP and exports from this sector were fundamental—who had a stronghold in Congress within the traditional parties, as well as important alliances with the state governments, judiciary, police, press, and private militia. As a result, very little was done and the problem festered.

Castelo Branco's government was able to carry out an important administrative reform that favored industrial modernization and set the basis for a major overhaul of the financial system, enhancing concentration of economic power and wealth. But as did his successor, he failed to obtain popular support for governmental policies, to maintain a dialogue with civilian politicians, to appease middle-class discontent, to deal with trade union and student unrest, and to develop bureaucratic leadership and efficiency. These problems, along with new demands for deepening state and economic reform, voiced by modernizing business interests—which would hit hardest the urban workers and important middle-class segments—finally pushed the military into a two-pronged maneuver. Through the first one, they sought to intensify industrialization and internationalization of the economy—seeking capital and know-how—and to reinforce the state apparatus, thus building toward great-power status.

On the other hand, the military had to tackle the social and political corollary of the economic proposal they endorsed: basically a model of high concentration and primitive accumulation through overexploitation. Thus, the second thrust involved mounting a ruthless apparatus of repression, which would override political resistance stemming from dislodged interests and popular opinion and an effective propaganda machine. The latter subjected the public to doctored TV and radio programs, propaganda films, and favorable cover stories in weekly magazines. On top of it all, appealing to jingoism ("Love it or leave it" was the motto), the regime established effective censorship of news and investigative journalism. The military would steer the helm of government for the next fifteen years, occupying not only the streets but the state apparatus, while entrepreneurs, economists, and engineers mapped the course.

The Economic "Miracle" and the High Tide of Repression

In August 1969, General Emilio Garrastázu Médici became president on the incapacity of Costa e Silva, victim of a stroke, after his vice-president, Pedro Aleixo, a civilian politician, was barred from taking office. Médici had been director of the National Information Service (SNI), which combined functions of police and political intelligence with operational capacity. General Médici anchored his government to a triad: military control and repression were left in the hands of army minister General Orlando Geisel, leadership of the economy was the task of finance minister Antonio Delfim Neto, and developing infrastructure projects with political and marketing impact was coordinated by transport minister Corone Mario Andreazza. During Médici's five-year term, state violence was increased to levels hitherto unknown in modern Brazil, while the repressive apparatuses of the three services and those that were specifically created in those years, such as the Doi-Codi units, became powers on their own, although inscribed within the newly created National Information Service. Only with the next president, General Ernesto Geisel, did the repression abate.

A heated debate continues even today as to whether the economic "miracle" (1968–1973, averaging 11 percent per year growth in that period) was caused by policies of the Médici government or whether it was just part of a regular cycle in which a significant accumulation of investment power had reached a ready market. Regardless, the military presided over an economic boom: "Growth euphoria" stimulated national planners, bankers both in Brazil and in the creditor nations, industrialists, and commercial leaders in Brazil.[5] Economic growth marched ahead while the foreign debt ballooned, and the rich became even richer, more satisfied, and less sensitive: The poorest 50 percent suffered a drastic drop in their share of the GNP, which went down from 26 percent in 1960 to 11 percent in 1976, while the richest 5 percent increased their hold from 27 percent to 39 percent over the same period of time. Even though a certain amount of the wealth did dribble down, the poor essentially had to choke down the "miracle" : An average industrial laborer had to work eighty-eight hours to buy a minimum food basket in 1965; ten years later, the total hours needed increased to 163, without changes in the quality or quantity of the contents. As Médici's government exerted its power, trade unions succumbed to repression and management pressure, and an unlimited, unorganized mass of cheap labor was offered on the market; there was no other balancing political sector to restrain the distributional skewing of the "miracle."

The External Debt and the End of the "Miracle"

From 1967 until 1982, Brazil, like many other Third World countries, contracted large foreign debts in the expectation that the country's production could grow rapidly and thus overcome the development gap. By 1990 Brazil had a foreign debt of more than $120 billion, and, what was more serious, economic growth had plummeted since the end of the "miracle" in 1973. Many of the loans were contracted to build major works—highways, bridges, dams, great hydroelectric plants—that were intended to stimulate the economy. The military government and its civilian economic advisers believed that industrial development would trickle down to the poor, but they failed to understand that postindustrial technology did not generate nearly enough new jobs. They were still stuck with the vision of industrial—not postindustrial—technology and its consequences.

TRANSITION TO "DEMOCRACY"

The "economic miracle" gave a free ride for several years to the military leadership, even though it did not address the deep social and structural imbalances and injustices. By 1974, however, the worldwide oil crisis had profoundly rocked the vulnerable Brazilian economy, and some military factions had had enough of growing opposition in the middle class, restlessness among industrial workers, and general loss of respect for the armed forces. Médici's successor, General Ernesto Geisel, launched a deliberate process of relaxing political constraints and stretching political freedom, although he was severely challenged by the extreme right-wing military and its civilian backers. This challenge culminated in the torture and killing of journalist Wladimir Herzog and industrial worker Manoel Filho. Geisel responded with the immediate dismissal of the army commander of the Second Military Region, based in São Paulo, where both men were held prisoners for interrogation. Geisel's strategy (masterminded by General Golbery do Couto e Silva, creator of the SNI and a key actor in both ESG and IPES) of *distensão* (relaxing tension) would lead to a "slow, gradual, secure" political opening. Although strained by a stop-and-go process aimed at hitting opposition right and left, it proved successful. The "April package" was introduced in 1977 to secure political control in Congress by granting overrepresentation to the north and northeastern states, conservative strongholds. Some of the more progressive politicians were stripped of their political rights. Meanwhile, however, in a bold move, army minister Silvio Frota, who spearheaded the alignment opposing political opening, was pushed into handing in his resignation. Thus Geisel paved the way for vertical control of the army, split from the intelligence and repression network.

In 1979 the last of the military presidents, João Batista Figueiredo, assumed the presidency and continued the deliberate process of return to the rule of law. In that year an amnesty bill was signed that served both to shield members of the armed forces from charges of "excesses" (torture and other similar acts) and to relieve some of the repressed resentment on the part of the opposition. Also that year the artificial two-party system, imposed in 1965, was scrapped, allowing more space for political groups in a multiparty system. Despite resistance and renewed violence from the extreme right and amid the largest civic mobilization ever witnessed in Brazil (with more than 10 million people demanding civilian government), this tortuous process eventually led to free but indirect elections in 1984. Only five years later, Brazilians would exert their right to vote and elect, freely and directly, their first president since 1960. Then, Janio Quadros had been elected by almost 6 million votes in a country of 60 million people. Thirty years later, voters alone were more than 80 million, and two-thirds of the population had been born after the coup of 1964.

Labor Strikes and the "New Union Movement"

In 1974 the metalworkers' (essentially, the automobile workers') union, protesting the steady decline of labor's earning power, began to pressure the government. The metalworkers' union had always had a privileged position among unions, its members enjoying higher skills, higher wages, and thus more power, and it had a history of struggle for more equitable contracts. In that period of ferment and conflict, in the union's stronghold, the triangle of the three southeastern industrial cities known as "ABC," Luís ("Lula") Inacio da Silva, a rank-and-file toolmaker, emerged as a leader. In 1978 the first illegal strikes began, giving birth to "new unionism"[6] and to the Labor Party (PT), led by Lula.

The Emergence of the Progressive Church

Soon after the coup of April 1, 1964, the military and the police embarked on a campaign to "sanitize" Brazilian society, and torture was sometimes used even against progressive clergy and nuns. The bishops were stung by the indifference to their pleas to the military, who had become involved in torture and other forms of repression of priests, nuns, and lay leaders involved in the Basic Reform Movement during the Goulart period. For a time, the most significant actions of opposition were led by bishops who protested against torture and deaths under torture. But bishops and their allies, concerned about the plight of the dispossessed majority of the nation, began to develop some plans for the future that would "empower" the poor. Soon, encouraged by the "opening" initiated by Pope John XXIII, the bishops began to take seriously their precarious situation, and the result was the "progressive church" or "the Church of the People."

The Roman Catholic Church had been, until 1965 or 1966, an ally of the establishment in Brazil, but the Catholic Action Movement, brought to the nation by young Brazilian priests who had been studying in France and Belgium, introduced a new style and mentality that had become a major factor in the Basic Reform Movement during the presidency of João Goulart. Soon scattered by opposition from the Church hierarchy, allied with the military at the time of the "Revolution" of 1964, many radical young Catholics sowed the seeds of a broader, grassroots movement through the human rights movements in the early phase of the dictatorship and then in the flowering of the Basic Ecclesiastical Communities (CEBs).[7] For a time, the CEBs tried to be a political force, but under pressure from conservative forces they retreated to local, human rights issues.

Parties and Elections

The party system that prevailed during the second republic (1945 to 1965) was a legacy of the Vargas era. The military dictatorship, after purging the Congress and the parties along with other institutions, abolished all existing parties in 1965; in their place, it established a controlled two-party system, comprising a government party, the National Renovating Alliance (Alianza Renovadora Nacional, or ARENA), and a "loyal opposition," the Brazilian Democratic Movement (Movimento Democrático Brasileiro, or MDB). This system was to provide a façade of continuity of democratic institutions, but the Brazilian polity, not easily taken in, labeled them the parties of "yes" and "yes, sir."

Party and electoral rules were changed regularly between 1964 and 1985 to ensure the continued dominance of promilitary legislators. When it appeared, from 1979 onward, that the MDB was beginning to take itself seriously and to gather momentum as an opposition movement, the two-party system was demolished in favor of a multiparty one. A reorganized ARENA became the Democratic Social Party (Partido Democratico Social) and the MDB became the PMDB, the Party of the Brazilian Democratic Movement (Partido de Movimento Democrático Brasileiro).

A Façade Attains Reality

Little by little the façade that earlier served to legitimize the dictatorship attained reality. The elections of November 1982 produced stunning victories for the opposition, and in 1984, for the first time in more than twenty years, the electoral college chose a civilian president, Tancredo Neves of the opposition party PMDB. Undergoing surgery, however, Neves missed his scheduled inauguration in March 1985; he died on April 21. Vice-President José Sarney, who then assumed the presidency, had been a late defector from the military government's Democratic Social Party (PDS).

The elections of 1986, featuring some 45,000 candidates representing thirty parties, resulted in a sweeping victory for the ruling PMDB; it took all but one of the then twenty-three governorships and won absolute majorities in both houses of Congress. It did so building in part upon the popularity of the Cruzado Plan, a stabilization gimmick that froze prices and allowed for a minor salary and wage adjustment. Between them, the PMDB and its coalition partner, the Liberal Front Party (PFL), a spin-off of the conservative PSD, won 90 percent of the contested offices. Such a sweep, however, did not suggest that Brazil was en route to the kind of monopolistic one-party system so common in the Third World. Personalism and regionalism continued to reign supreme. One found little trace of party loyalty or discipline; thus the PMDB victory, impressive as it was, suggested neither a high level of consensus within the polity nor predictability in the policymaking process. Then PMDB senator Fernando Henrique Cardoso, of the state of São Paulo, compared the party to a bus in which all of the passengers wanted to go in different directions.

Indeed, many who had supported the PMDB on the strength of its economic policies were stunned when, only days after the election, President Sarney lifted price controls. Workers accused the government of betrayal. Rioting broke out in Brasília and strikes began to unsettle the industrial heartland, contributing to impressive victories for Leonel Brizola's Democratic Workers' Party (PDT) and Lula's PT in major metropolitan areas in the municipal elections of 1988.

The Congress elected in 1986 served also as a constituent assembly for the purpose of drawing up a new constitution. That constitution, promulgated in 1988, was expected to resolve issues of economic decisionmaking and to guarantee redistribution of land and income and effective protection of rights. The new document, unfortunately, failed to live up to those expectations. Rather, it is full of contradiction, reflecting social conflict rather than resolving it. Even the very fundamental choice between the preexisting presidential system and a proposed parliamentary one was put on hold for a 1993 plebiscite, which opted for retaining the presidential system. The new constitution did, however, extend the vote to all citizens over sixteen, including illiterates; and it dictated the restoration of direct elections for president and vice-president, elections that Sarney managed to postpone until 1989.[8] The presidential election, to a five-year term with reelection precluded, allows for a runoff if no candidate receives an absolute majority in the first round.

Receding Hopes for Popular National Sovereignty

The new constitution devoted considerable attention to the elaboration of civil and human rights, and, indeed, since the withdrawal of the military the rights of the affluent have generally been respected. Not so, however, those of the more numerous and always vulnerable poor.

Land reform legislation has produced very little redistribution, in part because peasant leaders who have sought to present claims have so often paid with their lives. The Brazilian Pastoral Commission for Land documented more than 1,200 murders of activist peasants, union leaders, priests, and lawyers in connection with land disputes in the 1980s. Human rights organizations attribute such casualties to death squads in the hire of landlords who operate with the support or at least tolerance of local authorities. Similar death squads, apparently serving business interests, operate with seeming impunity in urban areas and are believed responsible for the murder of several thousand street children each year.

Brazil's prospects of gaining a measure of sovereignty and of making "democracy" something more than a charade should be much greater than those of most Latin American countries. Its political and intellectual leadership is highly sophisticated and creative. More important, it has a network of grassroots organizations and political parties that despite its weaknesses is more vibrant than that of most countries in the Third World and some in the First.

Brazil has almost 160 million people, half of the territory and population of South America, and commands the world's ninth largest economy, with a GNP estimated at almost $700 billion and a per capita income of $4,375. Over the course of the 1980s, the country expanded and diversified its economic and political relationships. Its exports quadrupled, reaching $46 billion by the 1990s. It became a major exporter of intermediate-technology products, weapons included. It even became one of the world's top producers of petroleum. What is more, Brazil engaged itself in the formation of Mercosur, a common market and free-trade agreement initiative, formed together with Argentina, Uruguay, and Paraguay, through the Treaty of Asunción, signed in March 1991. The combined population of the four founding countries is estimated at 200 million people. Their average per capita income of $5,000 represents 30 percent more than that of the totality of Latin America. Together with associate countries—Chile and Bolivia—the Mercosur constitutes itself into a regional space with more than 220 million people and a GNP greater than $1,050 trillion. Brazil and Argentina together represent more than 50 percent of the GNP of Latin America and 97 percent of the GNP of the Mercosur, whose growth has been 3.5 percent yearly since 1990.[9]

By the end of the 1980s, however, Brazilian independence had been tempered by debt and hyperinflation. Consequently, it suffered also from increasing denationalization of decisionmaking on the most essential elements of economic policy, as creditors, multilateral financial institutions, aid donors, and investors gained ever greater leverage.

THE 1990S: DEMOCRACY WITHOUT JUSTICE, GROWTH WITHOUT EQUITY

For most Brazilians, the elections of 1989 represented the first opportunity to cast a direct vote for a presidential candidate. This electorate, 85.6 percent of which turned out for the runoff, numbered more than 82 million, compared to an electorate of 15.5 million at the time of the last direct presidential election in 1960. The electorate in 1989 was young, about half under thirty, and almost three-fourths urban, whereas that of 1960 had been predominantly rural. Young, urban voters might be expected, on balance, to favor the more liberal candidate; but they are also more heavily exposed to television, and the conservative former governor of Alagoãs, Fernando Collor de Mello, young and attractive and serving up a populist appeal, had mastered the medium. With seemingly limitless funds, he rose from obscurity to surprise the oddsmakers and edge out the early favorites, Lula and Brizola.

The December runoff pitted Collor's personalist vehicle, the Party for National Reconstruction (Partido de Reconstrução Nacional, or PRN), in concert with the PFL, PDS, and PTB, against Lula's PT in a coalition, known as the Brazilian Popular Front, with the PSB, the Green Party (Partido Verde, or PV), and the Communist Party of Brazil (Partido Comunista do Brasil, or PC do B). Lula also enjoyed the crucial support of Brizola's PDT. The PMDB, occupying the extreme center, proved characteristically ambivalent about the runoff, but its breakaway faction, the Party of Brazilian Social Democracy (Partido da Social Democrácia Brasileira, or PSDB), also known as the Tucanos, supported Lula.

Collor's Triennium from Obscurity to Impeachment

Collor's 4-million-vote margin of victory represented slightly fewer votes than those that were blank or for other reasons discarded. Along with more traditional election-day *jeitos,* the conservative coalition on that day made good use of public opinion polls, pinpointing the constituencies of the two candidates to rearrange the public transportation system in key districts, shifting buses, most of which are privately owned, from major urban concentrations, for example, to more rural and provincial areas.

The gubernatorial and legislative elections of October 1990 featured some 70,000 candidates vying for more than 1,500 offices. Almost two-thirds of the winners in congressional races were newcomers. Otherwise, the elections followed a familiar pattern: While results in the predominately rural congressional races favored parties of the center and right, giving Collor the potential of a working majority, governorships and mayoralties in the most populous and most industrialized areas went to candidates of the center to left.

Collor, after some two years of economic decline and allegations of corruption, had lost much of the public support that had propelled him to the presidency. Attempting to court the relatively progressive PSDB, he was nevertheless becoming increasingly dependent on the far more conservative PFL. By mid-1992, he had found it necessary to replace his entire cabinet with the exception of those members representing the military.

With both inflation and unemployment climbing, Collor found that his lack of political definition and the low profile of his own party, which had served him well initially, allowing him to shift alliances as he changed policy course, had become liabilities. They underlined his isolation when polls suggested that his fortunes were sinking. The coup de grâce for this beleaguered government came with revelations of Collor's complicity in an elaborate bribery and influence-peddling scheme. Demonstrations involving millions of Brazilians, particularly students, reinforced the resolve of legislators who launched an impeachment campaign.[10]

On September 29, 1992, the Federal Chamber of Deputies voted 441 to 38 in favor of impeachment. Vice-President Itamar Franco of the PMDB became acting president while Collor awaited trial by the Senate; following Collor's conviction, Franco became president to serve out the remaining two years of Collor's term.

An Interim of Shared Leadership

The government of Itamar Franco, a provincial politician, inherited most of the problems that bedeviled its predecessor. The corruption scandals that had previously centered around the presidency now moved into the Congress, felling members in virtually wholesale fashion. The shadow of kickback schemes and other financial shenanigans that so sullied the body politic did not touch Itamar Franco personally; a man of modest tastes, he seemed indifferent to the perks and temptations of office. But he fell victim to the sort of sex scandal to which Brazil's *teleno-*

velas had so addicted the TV-viewing public. A very public romp with a less-than-fully-clad showgirl at the 1994 Rio Carnival, allegedly set up by the media, made him a figure of ridicule.

Itamar's low-key and weakly undergirded government seemed at first ill prepared to deal with any of the country's deepening problems, least of all the juggernaut of five-digit inflation. The parliamentary style of governing, leaving considerable latitude to cabinet members, was perhaps the only one available to a regime whose political support was broad but shallow. But such an approach, deriving initially from weakness, was ultimately judged a strength, as initiatives fell more and more to the very able former senator from São Paulo, Fernando Henrique Cardoso. Cardoso served first as foreign minister, but it was as finance minister, after mid-1993, that he began to make his mark.

In June 1994, Cardoso launched his Plano Real, introducing and bulwarking a new currency. There was nothing new about new currencies in Brazil at this juncture, but this one, pegged loosely to the dollar, was underwritten by a mountain of hard-currency reserves. It was no doubt protected as well by the anxieties of foreign would-be investors about the popularity of Lula and the PT and their hesitance to undermine the most promising alternative to a labor-based government.

When the real was introduced, prices for most goods quadrupled almost overnight; but in the months that followed, prices held more or less steady as the real fluctuated within a narrow band, even increasing somewhat in value at times vis-à-vis the dollar. Thus the initial price shock to consumers accustomed to living on the rack was ameliorated over time by the hope that they were indeed witnessing the miracle of price stabilization.

While Cardoso's political skills should not be underrated, the effectiveness of the Plano Real, proved the most decisive factor in the elections of 1994. It convinced the middle classes that Cardoso was the only one who could defeat inflation and thus convinced the upper classes that he was the only one who could defeat Lula. It should also be noted that there were opinion leaders who were more comfortable with Lula's platform and his constituency but who feared that Brazil under a labor-left government would be devastated by capital flight and credit freezes.

Four public opinion polls published in May 1994, just before the unveiling of the Plano Real, showed Lula leading in the presidential contest, with the support of 36 percent to 42 percent of the electorate. Cardoso was running a distant second, with a following of 15 percent to 23 percent. Five months later, in the poll that mattered, Cardoso won in the first round with about 54 percent of the vote to 22 percent for Lula. Cardoso's victory was broadly based geographically. He defeated Lula in all of the twenty-seven states except Rio Grande do Sul and the Federal District. The coalition backing Cardoso (PSDB, PTB, and PFL) won only 210 of the 514 seats in the Chamber of Deputies, but an accord reached in December with the PMBD, holding 107 seats, gave Cardoso what he called "unorganized majority support" going into his inauguration on January 1, 1995. The National Congress saw considerable turnover in the 1994 election; 70 percent of its members were new.

Cardoso's Catch-22

Cardoso's career in electoral politics was his second. He had first gained international prominence as a social scientist, one of the originators of dependency theory, which held that links to external political and economic interests stood as an obstacle to national sovereignty and social justice. His election to the presidency might be seen, then, as less a political victory than an intellectual one. He found that he could achieve "power" only by running against himself—that is, as the candidate of major domestic and foreign financial interests—thus validating his now orphaned theories.

At his inauguration, Cardoso pledged that social justice was to be his top priority, and some who spoke for the nonaffluent dared to believe. They found grounds for optimism in the fact that as a candidate he had already sold out his friends in order to appeal to his enemies. They reasoned that as president he could only sell out his enemies. That, however, appears to have been wishful thinking.

Cardoso's legislative agenda has catered to his neoliberal allies who dominate the Congress. Price stabilization and economic growth appeared to call for the acceleration of privatization, the proceeds of which were to cover the federal government's deficit. Dozens of state-owned enterprises were put up for sale, including the Companhia Vale do Rio Doce, the world's largest iron mine. Although the sacrosanct Petrobras would remain in public hands, it would be forced to compete with foreign investors, as the state's monopoly in the oil sector was to be ended.

State monopolies in telecommunications and shipping were to be ended as well, and national companies were to be stripped of any advantages they held over foreign ones. Tax reforms were to enhance revenue collection and to cut indebted states adrift. Another reform, in the works during 1996, would permit presidential reelection.

A 1995 report by the United Nation's Economic Commission for Latin America and the Caribbean (UNECLAC) heaped praise on Cardoso's stabilization program, highlighting dramatic reduction in inflation, economic growth, shrinkage of unemployment, and rising real wages and gross capital formation. Such achievements were not to be taken lightly, and indeed opposition forces appeared to have given Cardoso a lengthy honeymoon. But by midyear frustration was mounting, even among some groups, such as progressive bishops and NGOs, that had been supportive initially.

A new development initiative, Comunidade Solidária, under the guidance of Ruth Cardoso, the president's wife and a highly respected anthropologist, aroused some hopes, as did a new program to deal with human rights abuses and a commitment to compensate some families victimized by the military regime. But Cardoso's land reform proposal was generally viewed by progressive groups as woefully inadequate, and his initial veto of a minimum wage increase was greatly resented. A salary freeze of more than twenty-two months imposed upon public functionaries, including medical staff, university lecturers, and federal administrators, took its social and political toll. Salaried workers were also perturbed by proposals to shrink social security benefits, privatize parts of the program, and terminate job security in the public sector. Environmentalists and defenders of the rights of indigenous peoples were stunned by the issuance of a presidential decree on January 9, 1996, allowing loggers, miners, farmers, and business owners to contest in court the boundaries of areas set aside as nature and indigenous reserves.

To those who have fought long and hard for the resurrection of democracy, Brazil's party and electoral systems still represent unfinished business and in many ways a project derailed. The kind of democracy that is compatible with the new version of free enterprise may be the best that money can buy. With campaign contributions routinely in the millions of dollars, corruption becomes institutionalized and virtually all politicians are to some degree vulnerable, though Brazil has avoided some of the worst abuses of the process seen in the United States by requiring that television stations offer free time for live appearances by major candidates.

The combination of intraparty and interparty contests in a single "open list" for congressional offices reinforces the tendency to personalism and party fragmentation and leaves an electorate that is largely semiliterate with an overly challenging task.[11] Party stability is further challenged by the ease with which elected officials change from one to another. It was reported in October 1995 that forty-three members of the National Congress had switched parties in the previous eight months.

The strengths of Brazilian democracy are manifest in the fact that both of the major contenders in the last presidential election—Fernando Henrique Cardoso, the extraordinarily sophisticated and insightful social scientist, and Lula, the skillful community organizer and eloquent spokesman of popular interests—are a cut above the best in the political stables of most countries of North or South. The weaknesses of the system are set in relief by the enormity of the challenge they face. These two remarkable men have in general continued to treat each other with respect and to keep open the crucial channels of communication. But it is not clear that the best of their efforts would suffice to bring about an upward shift in burden sharing and to bridge the country's ever-growing gap between rich and poor.

NOTES

1. For an extensive discussion of the "basic dualism of Brazilian society," see Helio Jaguaribe, *Alternativas do Brasil* (Rio de Janeiro: José Olympia Editora, 1989), chapter 2.

2. Edmar Bacha and Herbert S. Klein, eds., *A Transição Incompleta: Brasil desde 1945*, volume 1, *População/Emprego/Agricultura/Urbanização*, and volume 2, *Desigualdade Social/Educação/Saude Previdenci* (Rio de Janeiro: Paz e Terra, 1986).

3. Jaguaribe, *Alternativas do Brasil*, p. 27.

4. For in-depth coverage of the coup and its aftermath, see René A. Dreifuss, *1964: A Conquista do Estado: Ação Política, Poder e Golpe do Estado* (Petrópolis: Editora Vozes, 1981).

5. See Edmar Bacha and Malan in Alfred Stepan, ed., *Democratizing Brazil: Problems of Transition and Consolidation* (New York: Oxford University Press, 1989), p. 123. The "miracle" was fueled by the "peace" between labor and management imposed by the army: Strikes were declared illegal and the army broke any attempts to strike.

6. "New unionism" is a movement that intends to be free of the old's inherited "corporatist" system, instituted by Getulio Vargas. The "old unionism," or corporatist system, makes the union movement almost a branch of the government, regulated by the minister of labor.

7. The Basic Ecclesiastical Communities began in 1965–1966 as a way to give more vitality to the Catholic Church among the poor, given the need for supportive communities, the scarcity of priests, and the lack of social programs. The CEBs blossomed by 1985 or 1986, with 100,000 to 110,000 basic communities. Because of opposition from the conservative Church leaders and the Vatican, the movement has not grown much since then.

8. For a detailed account of the wheeling and dealing that characterized the deliberations of the constitutional assembly and the role of Sarney during that period, see René A. Dreifuss, *O Jogo da Direita* (Petrópolis: Editora Vozes, 1989).

9. *El País* (Montevideo), February 11, 1996.

10. Ben Ross Schneider, "Brazil Under Collor: Anatomy of a Crisis," *World Policy Journal* 8 (Spring 1991), pp. 321–347.

11. "As lições da eleição," *Cadernos do Terceiro Mundo,* November 1994, p. 8.

SUGGESTED READINGS

In English

Bernard, Rui, and Huberto Kirchheim (coordinators). *The Roots of Poverty and Hunger in Brazil.* Translated by Jaime Wright. New York: Random House, 1986.

Black, Jan Knippers. *United States Penetration of Brazil* (Philadelphia: University of Pennsylvania Press, 1977).

_____. *Sentinels of Empire: The United States and Latin American Militarism* (Boston: Allen and Unwin, 1986).

Chacel, Julian M., Pamela S. Falk, and David V. Fleischer, eds. *Brazil's Economic and Political Future.* Boulder, Colo.: Westview Press, 1988.

Dassin, Joan, ed. *Torture in Brazil: A Report by the Archdiocese of São Paulo.* Translated by Jaime Wright. New York: Random House, 1986.

Harrison, Lawrence E. "Brazil: Scapegoating Debt." *Washington Post,* February 9, 1989.

Helder Camara, Archbishop. *Spiral of Violence.* Translated by Della Couling. Denville, N.J.: Dimension Books, 1971.

Kucinski, Bernardo. *Brazil: State and Struggle.* London: Latin American Bureau, 1982.

Mainwaring, Scott. *The Catholic Church and Politics in Brazil, 1916–1985.* Stanford, Calif.: Stanford University Press, 1986.

O'Donnell, Guillermo. "Challenges to Democratization in Brazil: The Threat of a Slow Death." *World Policy Journal,* Spring 1988, pp. 281–300.

Skidmore, Thomas. *The Politics of Military Rule in Brazil, 1964–85.* New York: Oxford University Press, 1988.

Stepan, Alfred, *Rethinking Military Politics: Brazil and the Southern Cone.* Princeton, N.J.: Princeton University Press, 1988.

_____, ed. *Democratizing Brazil: Problems of Transition and Consolidation.* New York: Oxford University Press, 1989.

Wirth, John D., Edson de Oliveira Nunes, and Thomas E. Gobenschild. *State and Society in Brazil: Continuity and Change.* Boulder, Colo.: Westview Press, 1987.

In Portuguese

Almeida, María Hermínia T. de., and Bernardo Sorj, eds. *Sociedade e Política no Brasil Pos–64.* São Paulo: Editora Brasiliense, 1984.

Bacha, Edmar, and Herbert S. Klein, eds. *A Transição Incompleta: Brasil desde 1945.* Volume 1: *População/Emprego/Agricultura/Urbanização.* Volume 2: *Desigualdade Social/Educação/ Saude Previdenci.* Rio de Janeiro: Paz e Terra, 1986.

Bresser Pereira, Luiz. *Pactos Políticos: Do Populismo a redemocratização.* São Paulo: Editora Brasiliense, 1985.

_____, ed. *Dívida Externa: Crise e Soluções.* São Paulo: Editora Brasiliense, 1989.

Chaui, Marilena. *Conformismo e Resistencia: Aspectos da Cultura Popular no Brasil.* São Paulo: Editora Brasiliense, 1986.

D'Alva Gil Kinzo, Maria. "O Quadro partidário e a Constituinte." *Revista Brasileira de Ciência Política* 1, 1 (March 1989), pp. 91–124.

DaMatta, Roberto. *O Que Fax O brasil, Brasil?* Rocco, 1986.

Dreifuss, René A. *1964: A Conquista do Estado: Acão Política, Poder e Golpe do Estado* (Petrópolis: Editora Vozes, 1981).

_____. *O Jogo da Direita* (Petrópolis: Editora Vozes, 1989).

Faoro, Raymundo. *Os Donos do Poder: Formação do Patronato Político Brasiliero.* Editora Globo, 1958.

Jaguaribe, Helio. *Alternativas do Brasil.* Rio de Janeiro: José Olympio Editora, 1989.

Machado, Ivan G. Pinheiro, ed. *Nova Republica: Um Balanco.* L&PM Editores, 1986.

Rattner, Henrique, ed. *Brasil 1990: Caminhos alternativos do Desenvolvimento.* São Paulo: Editora Brasiliense, 1979.

31

CONCLUSION: AN INTEGRATED NEIGHBORHOOD

JAN KNIPPERS BLACK

GETTING TO KNOW THE NEIGHBORS

One of the complaints commonly voiced by Latin Americanists as the century draws to a close is that the U.S. government is paying too little attention to Latin America. Central Americans on the receiving end of U.S. bombs and bullets in the 1980s might counter that official U.S. attention is, at best, a mixed blessing.

The relative inattention of the late 1990s was owing in part to the shift from muddled Cold War concerns to more straightforward commercial ones, and thus a shift in watchdogs from military and intelligence operatives to international financial institutions. It reflected also a general perception on the part of pundits and policymakers that this recently raucous part of the world had "matured." In fact much of what Anglo-Americans are inclined to see as change in Latin America actually represents change in our perceptions of Latin America, as well as in our perceptions of our own society.

Latin America is more familiar to us now. That is due only in part to the enormously increased volume of academic studies inspired by the birth of a multidisciplinary field. It is also due to increased travel and investment by U.S. citizens and to expanded U.S. public and private programs of exchange, propaganda, proselytizing, relief, and development. The perspectives of diplomats and others, whose writings provided our images in decades past, derived almost exclusively from contacts with the political and economic elites. But thousands of Peace Corps volunteers and other Americans coming of age since the 1960s have come to know Latin America's peasants and workers and marginalized would-be workers as real people—friends.

Can it be that Latin America's poor, stereotyped in the not-so-distant past as ignorant and passive, have only recently become clever, energetic, and enterprising? Or is it that we are only beginning to learn of the courage required to overcome official intimidation and of the ingenuity required to survive on the edge? Is it possible that Latin America's middle classes, traditionally hedonistic and lackadaisical, have only recently been energized? Or can it be that we have only recently realized that the professional who seems never to be in his office actually juggles three offices: his bureaucratic post, his chair at the university, and his private practice?

A student of mine once commented that "Brazilian women don't work; they have maids." No doubt there are still women throughout the Americas who are pampered and cloistered. But now that we know the maids as well as the mistresses, we know that the issue "to work or not to work" is even phonier for most Latin American women than for their Anglo-American counterparts. In fact, we have now seen that the greater the economic or political threat to survival, the more central will be the role of women in combating that threat. Women have long been the economic and organizational mainstays of the poorest urban shantytowns. More recently, the large-scale involvement of women in danger-fraught human rights networks and in revolutionary movements has been particularly striking. To declare that Latin Americans, for reasons of work roles or sex roles, intellect or temperament, are unequal to the task of their own development on their own terms is to declare our ignorance of them.

While Latin America has been overrun in the past half century with U.S. slogans, products, and advisers, there has also been movement in the other direction. Latin American scholars have set the tone for studies by U.S. academic specialists in Latin American affairs. Some of the best U.S. novelists have experimented with literary styles pioneered by Latin American novelists. Latin American graphic arts, music, and cinematography have gained in popularity with U.S. audiences. U.S. churches have been influenced by the Liberation Theology that swept first, like a firestorm, through Latin America's religious communities. Some of Latin America's "best and brightest," driven from their own countries by dictatorial regimes supported by the U.S. government, have settled in the United States and have deepened our own national debates about domestic and foreign policy.

Of course, Anglo-America and Latin America share the shame of past and present mistreatment of native American and Afro-American populations. Furthermore, much of what is now the United States shares with much of Latin America the heritage of Spanish conquest and settlement and 300 years of Spanish colonialism. Indian and Spanish cultures, never quite suppressed in the southwestern United States, are now being revitalized by the annual influx of Mexican and Central American workers, estimated to be in the millions, seeking employment that eludes them at home. Miami, of course, has been Cubanized, and the northeastern part of the United States has absorbed great numbers of Caribbeans. As these workers, refugees, and immigrants, documented or otherwise, move from state to state and city to city in search of work, no part of the United States is wholly immune from the process of Latinoization.

There were some 30 million Hispanics in the United States in 1996. It is estimated that by the year 2010, they will surpass blacks in numbers to become the largest ethnic minority in the United States. Although some people lament the trend, I lament only its causes. There is no reason to doubt that Latin Americans will enrich our culture and our national life as have past waves of immigrants.

Finally, we are getting to know Latin Americans as a consequence of our government's incessant meddling in their affairs. Despite the wonders of technology and the imaginative means of intimidating whistleblowers, government secrets have become ever harder to keep. The media sooner or later catches up with our boys in camouflage. Their exploits in the 1980s, along with the images of peasants fighting and dying and of leaders pleading, in flawless English, for arms or for reason, were brought into our homes nightly in living color.

A question raised urgently and often in the United States in the 1980s was, Will Central America become another Vietnam? There are many arguments as to why it did not, but the most important may be that the Central Americans are our neighbors. The Vietnamese were to North Americans a most exotic people. While we opposed U.S. involvement in that distant war for a myriad of reasons, we were not prepared to understand the problems and aspirations of the people of Indochina. Latin Americans, by contrast, are now a familiar people.

AMERICA IS ONE

U.S. presidents always begin their Columbus Day speeches before the assembled dignitaries of the Organization of American States with the assertion that America is one. Such assertion is followed by rhetorical fluff about individualism, democracy, godliness, private enterprise, and the security threat. But there is a growing unacknowledged reality to the oneness of America. Latin America is increasingly sharing not only the blessings of U.S.-style modernization but its demons as well. And many of the problems that have long plagued Latin America are more and more apparent and bedeviling in the United States itself. The clearest trend in the Americas is a trend toward convergence—if not of interests, at least of problems.

Latin America, now predominantly urban, boasts or frets of several of the world's largest cities. To Latin America, as to the United States, urbanization has brought both advantages and disadvantages. It has led to new, more effective forms of political organization and has facilitated the extension of services—electricity, running water, health care, public schools—to a greater proportion of the population. It has extended the reach of the communications media, enhancing their ability to disseminate information, misinformation, and disinformation. In Latin America, as in the United States, urbanization has weakened the constraints, but also the socialization and the security, that flowed from extended family systems. To Latin America, more recently than to the United States, it has also meant traffic congestion, pollution, and anonymous, impersonal street crime.

Latin American economies have long suffered from fluctuations in world prices for a limited number of minerals or agricultural products and from deterioration in the terms of trade for such primary products. Before World War II, agriculture contributed twice as much to regional gross product as manufacturing did. Although most Latin American countries are still highly dependent upon the export of one or two primary products, manufacturing's share of gross regional product, by the late 1960s, was well above that of agriculture. In the 1970s, Brazil began to earn more from the export of manufactures than from that of primary products. By the 1990s, more than half of Latin America's exports were at least processed. At the same time, however, the importation of capital goods and, in the case of most countries, of energy to fuel the industrialization process led to soaring debts and other problems.

While Latin America has been industrializing, the United States has been moving in the other direction. Spurred by incentives, offered by both U.S. and foreign governments, and lured by cheap labor, U.S.-based corporations have shifted capital—and jobs—to the Third World, including Latin America. Thus, the United States, for several decades the virtually unchallenged provider of manufactured goods to Latin America, has itself become increasingly dependent upon foreign investment, the importation of manufactured goods, and the export of primary products, particularly wheat.

In most Latin American countries, as in the United States, the idea of stimulating the economy from the bottom up—of expansion of the domestic market and production to meet effective mass demand—has been abandoned in favor of production for export and/or for the relatively affluent. Modernization, in Latin America as in the United States, has meant increasingly capital-intensive—as opposed to labor-intensive—industry, resulting in chronic unemployment. In the absence of stunningly innovative policy, the unemployment problem in both Americas promises to get worse.

Since the Iberian conquest of the New World, the concentration of landownership has been among Latin America's most obstinate problems. Conquistadores and others favored by the Iberian monarchs carved out for themselves enormous estates complete with the previous native American claimants or imported African slaves to do the work. But the land grabs of the colonial period pale by comparison to those inspired since the mid-nineteenth century by the growth of export markets for primary products. Effective and enduring land reform has been rare in the twentieth century, and in some countries the ongoing process of seizure of peasant lands leaves an ever-increasing proportion of the rural population dependent upon seasonal work for the large landholders. As semi-feudal estates are transformed into agribusinesses and machines replace workers, displaced peasants will be left with neither land nor wages.

In the 1970s, many Latin American governments, recognizing that their agricultural sectors had been neglected or milked while import-substitution industrialization was being promoted, turned their attention to the modernization of agricultural production and offered new incentives for the exportation of agricultural products. One consequence was that lands that had been used to produce staples for domestic consumption were converted into production for export. Export earnings, not usually redistributed in any form to the general population, have risen, but increasingly, basic foodstuffs must be imported, resulting in higher prices for the consumer.

As is often pointed out in comparisons of Anglo-America and Latin America, Anglo-America was early blessed with a land tenure pattern of small holdings, or family farms. However, while the U.S. government, in the 1960s, spoke of the need for land reform in Latin America, the process of concentration of landholdings, favoring agribusiness conglomerates, assumed a dizzying pace in the United States. By the 1990s, the family farm was clearly an endangered species.

Denationalization, the process whereby the ownership or control of resources passes from national to foreign hands, has long been a major problem for Latin America. For the first century or so of independence, it was primarily the land and mineral resources that attracted foreign investors, with the diplomatic—and sometimes military—backing of their governments. Transportation, public utilities, and other infrastructural projects also were often undertaken and controlled by foreigners. By the mid-twentieth century, foreign firms and multinational corporations had begun to capture, or recapture, domestic markets for durable consumer goods and to buy out or squeeze out local industries. More recently, foreign firms have competed successfully for control of distribution and services as well.

For most of the century in Meso-America and for several decades in South America, the denationalizers have been predominantly U.S.-based corporations. Since the 1970s, however, firms based in Western Europe and Japan have been gaining rapidly in the competition for Latin American markets and for the fruits of Latin American land and labor. The same European and Japanese companies, along with those of Middle Eastern oil potentates and East Asian "tigers," have also been increasing their shares of U.S. consumer markets, at the expense of U.S.-based companies, and their shares of ownership of U.S. farmland and urban real estate, banks, and industries.

A kindred and more insidious problem in the United States, which has received less attention even though it is far more serious, is that of "delocalization." The same multinational banks, conglomerates, and chains that have displaced Latin American businesses and rendered Latin American economies dependent have also bought out or squeezed out local businesses in Tennessee and Michigan and New Mexico. Such companies, which pay campaign debts in Washington and taxes in the Bahamas, have no national or local allegiances. When they see greater profits to be made in São Paulo or Seoul, they leave Nashville or Albuquerque jobless with no regrets; they were never a part of the community.

Several Latin American countries made headway in the 1960s and 1970s toward gaining control over their resources and their economics. Expropriation of mineral resources was particularly common, and was so popular that even the most *en-*

treguista right-wing military dictators rarely dared to try to reverse it. The assumption that subsoil resources are national domain was inherited by most of the Latin American countries from the Spanish crown. Mexico, in 1917, declared its petroleum and other subsoil resources social property, to be owned and exploited by and for the people as a whole; it made the claim an economic reality in 1938. Most other Latin American countries subsequently established public corporations to manage the production, importation, or distribution of petroleum and other energy products. Meanwhile, in the United States, an ever-smaller number of companies make ever-larger profits, while consumers undergo a price-gouging energy crisis every fifteen to twenty years.

Attempts by Latin American nationalists to regain control of their economies have often been undertaken at great cost. Such attempts generally have the effect of adding the great weight of the multinational corporate community and the U.S. government to the ever-present schemes against popular governments. And foreign creditors and multilateral financial institutions weighed in heavily in the 1980s and 1990s with pressure for privatization and debt-for-equity swaps. Nevertheless, the extension of national control over the economy is central to the agenda of popular movements in Latin America. Political leaders have been forced in the 1990s, by the globalized control of credit conditionality, to backtrack on the issue. But the issue will surely be revisited, perhaps as regional rather than national challenges to global economic interests. In the United States, the ideas of public control over national or local resources and, in general, of placing public interest over private profit are still in the category of heresy.

For Latin America, the 1980s was a decade of turmoil. Civilian rule was restored in Argentina only after the military regime instigated and suffered humiliating defeat in a war with Great Britain over the Falklands/Malvinas Islands. Military regimes held on in Chile and Paraguay until the end of the decade. In Central America, following upon the success of the Nicaraguan Revolution in 1979, insurgency and counterinsurgency raged throughout the 1980s in El Salvador and Guatemala; and efforts of the Reagan administration to reestablish U.S. hegemony in the region swept Honduras, Costa Rica, and even Panama into the turmoil. Such conflict exacerbated debt exposure and other economic disasters, resulting in what came to be known throughout Latin America as the "Lost Decade." After having grown since mid-century at rates averaging 4 to 6 percent annually, Latin American economies in the 1980s experienced a negative per capita growth rate of – 8 percent, along with inflation levels ranging to four or five digits and high levels of unemployment and underemployment.[1] It was estimated in 1990 that three-quarters of the population was suffering from some degree or manifestation of malnutrition.

Economic growth was resumed in the 1990s in several countries, especially Mexico, Chile, Argentina, and finally Brazil, spurred largely by massive privatization of public assets and services. But the new wealth did not trickle down, and the gap between rich and poor continues to grow. Likewise in the United States since the 1970s, the gap has been growing—generally the outcome not of policy failures but of policy decisions.

Meanwhile, the debt trap that is bankrupting so many Latin Americans is thereby destroying markets for U.S. manufacturers and wiping out jobs for U.S. workers. In fact, it is sadly ironic that even as the United States struggles against the encroachment of Japan, the European Union, and the newly industrializing countries on traditional markets, it continues, through unqualified support for the global creditor cartel, to destroy economies in the one area where it had the greatest trade advantages and to leave those countries with few profitable exports save the two least welcome, officially, in the United States: drugs and people.

Moreover, Latin American debts, like Third World debts in general, are increasingly owed to private banks. To many of the same banks, the United States now owes much of its national debt of some $5 trillion. The U.S. debt tripled in the 1980s, and, though the annual deficit dropped in the 1990s, both the debt itself and its proportional claim on the budget are expected to increase over the next decade. To an even greater extent than is true of most Latin American countries, the rising U.S. debt may be attributed to unproductive military spending.

Indices of health, education, services, and infrastructure suggest that the quality-of-life gap between the United States and Latin America has been narrowing steadily in the period since World War II. Even discounting the limitations of statistics and of index-making, this indicates very promising long-term progress for Latin America. In the shorter term, however—since the 1970s, for example—it also suggests slowed progress or even retrogression on the part of the United States. The U.S. National Commission on Excellence in Education reported in 1983 that functionally illiterate U.S. citizens numbered some 23 million, more than the entire population of most Latin American countries. The American Association of State Colleges and Universities reported a $500-per-student decline between 1980 and 1995 in state appropriations for public universities and colleges, largely a result of the increased state costs for prisons and health care. At the beginning of the 1990s, Americans were spending more per capita on health care than any other people in the world; yet 37 million lacked any kind of medical insurance. Immunization programs for children had been among the casualties of budget cuts in the 1980s, and cases of measles had multiplied tenfold in ten years. After a decade in which the number of pregnant women receiving no prenatal care climbed by 50 percent, the United States ranked twenty-second in the world in infant mortality prevention, placing it squarely in a Third World category. Life expectancy for white Anglo-Saxons continued to rise, but for minorities it had begun to drop.

More than 5 million Americans who needed housing assistance in 1990 were not getting it, up from 3.5 million in the mid-1970s. The census bureau reported in 1989 that one-fifth of American children (under age eighteen) and more than one-third of American Blacks were living in poverty. Among the policy decisions reflected in these trends were changes in tax laws since the late 1970s that, according to the Congressional Budget Office, had left 90 percent of Americans paying more while the richest 10 percent paid up to a third less. Meanwhile, the richest 5 percent of the population enjoyed a real increase in their income of 46 percent. The income of the richest 400 Americans alone grew by $50 billion in the 1980s. In 1989, the wealthiest 10 percent of households owned three-quarters of all investment assets.

While the gap between Latin America and the United States has been narrowing, the gap between the United States and the more prosperous and egalitarian states of Western Europe has been widening. As Latin America, in aggregate, becomes more nearly a part of the "developed" world, the United States becomes more nearly a part of America. Whether or not Latin America is perceived to have been developing in the late twentieth century depends upon which countries, which years, and which indices one chooses to emphasize. What is more readily apparent, however, is that the United States has been underdeveloping.

Even if Latin America and Anglo-America increasingly share the blessings and the curses of modernization—along with such problems as competition from stronger economies, excessive dependence on the export of primary products, concentration of landownership, the undermining of local businesses by multinational corporations, staggering debts, chronic unemployment, and a growing gap between rich and poor—is it not obvious that the two Americas are centuries apart in matters of government and politics? Perhaps. But there, too, similarities and convergences can be found.

In the 1960s and 1970s, much of Latin America experienced the rise of a new and very modern kind of military dictatorship—institutional, technocratic, self-confident, and ruthless. In demobilizing civilian political organizations and imposing their new order, these military establishments were assisted by paramilitary, intelligence, and police networks with expertise in surveillance, torture, and assassination. This development is not unrelated to the economic problems mentioned above. Those who are left on the margins by modernization, who are needed neither as workers nor as consumers, and who are written off by the economic planners cannot simply be ignored. They are the ill-fed, ill-clothed, ill-housed masses who are presumed to constitute a threat to the established order. The greater their numbers and the greater their sophistication and potential for political organization, the more elaborate will be the apparatus of repression required to contain them. But there are limits to the efficacy of rule by brute force, and the wielders of economic power—domestic and foreign—rediscovered the fact that a civilian government that is uninterested in acting upon or unable to act upon a popular mandate, and unwilling or unable to control military and paramilitary forces, is often a better hedge against social change than a repressive military government.

The 1980s witnessed the withdrawal of the generals from Latin America's presidential palaces and a process of "redemocratization." But the withdrawal has been only partial—not to a safe enough distance to allow democracy a free rein. And the new democracies, to a large extent, represent the victory of form over substance. Redemocratization has been accompanied by increasing indebtedness and surrender of economic sovereignty, the discrediting of reformist leaders and programs, and a return to economic elitism buffered by parties and parliaments and the ritual of elections. Civilian leaders have sometimes appeared to be virtual prisoners in their own presidential palaces, and violence, particularly against the poor, continues unabated.

Politics in Latin America has often been associated, in the minds of Anglo-Americans, with violence and petty corruption. But political assassination has also become common in the United States, and in the aftermath of Watergate, the Iran-Contra affair, and so many other recent scandals in the heart of the U.S. government, Anglo-Americans should at least be learning humility. Meanwhile, Latin American politicians—democrats and demagogues alike—are drawing upon U.S. expertise in a more sophisticated, institutionalized form of corruption. Consultants, pollsters, and fund-raisers, credited with political miracles in the United States, are being hired by Latin American candidates to pass on the art of taking money from the rich and votes from the poor on the pretext of protecting each from the other. Media campaigns and media advisers may be expected to replace political organizations and machines, and campaign contributions, legal and more substantial, may replace under-the-table bribes. Where elections in Latin America retain any representational meaning at all, we are likely to see the increasing capitalization and frivolization of the process.

It should not go unnoticed in the United States that it was the most highly developed politically of the Latin American states that suffered the cruelest fate during the era of militocracy. Many of the same anti-egalitarian economic policies that were imposed on Brazil in the 1960s and the Southern Cone countries in the 1970s by counterrevolutionary military regimes have since been adopted in the United States without a rupture in democratic processes. Perhaps the majority in the United States has been saved—by the myth of a classless society, the alienation of almost half of the eligible electorate, and the lack of effective political organization—from a fate worse than economic deprivation.

But not all U.S. citizens are spared the kind of official violence that is commonly employed in Latin America and elsewhere to contain a growing sector of marginalized, would-be workers. Such containment in the politically decentralized United States is carried out by increasingly autonomous local police forces. Police brutality, particularly against minority groups, is common from coast to coast. Amnesty International has called attention to such brutality on the part of the New York City police, and Human Rights Watch has cited the abuse of female prisoners in several state institutions. The U.S. federal prison population doubled in the 1980s to some 700,000 and in the mid-1990s exceeded 1 million, the highest per capita prison population of any industrialized Western country. One in every four African-American men in their twenties was in jail or on parole or probation.

Except for such brief skirmishes as those in response to the inner-city riots following the assassination of Dr. Martin Luther King and to Vietnam War protests, the United States has been spared the spectacle of troops on the streets. But it has not been spared the general trend toward militarism. The enhanced power of the U.S. military establishment during the Cold War was expressed primarily in the increasing militarization of the U.S. foreign policymaking apparatus and in the military's ever-increasing peacetime share of the national budget.

The role expansion of military establishments in the two Americas proceeded in tandem. The incorporation of Central America and the Caribbean into the U.S. sphere of influence in the early twentieth century, through military intervention and, in some cases, direct military occupation, left a more modern form of militarism firmly entrenched. In the 1950s and 1960s, the U.S. military, on the premise of the need for a global strategy in the face of a permanent global war, undertook the organizational and technological modernization of the South American military establishments as well. An aspect of the Cold War worldview, inculcated or reinforced through U.S. training, was the idea that the political arena is the battleground of the Cold War, and, as such, too important to be left to the politicians. It is not surprising, then, that the U.S. intelligence technicians and techniques employed to ferret out "subversives" in Latin America came to be unleashed on U.S. citizens as well. The people of the United States have reaped at home what they allowed the U.S. government to sow abroad. As the late U.S. senator Hubert H. Humphrey commented in 1973:

> With Watergate we have seen officials of our government commit criminal acts that strongly resemble the practices and methods directed against foreign governments and other peoples. Counterespionage, coverups, infiltration, wiretapping, political surveillance, all done in the name of national security in faraway places, have come home to haunt us. The spirit and the purpose of domestic policy is said to condition our foreign policy. The reverse is also true.[2]

Like Watergate, the more effectively suppressed Iran-Contra scandal of the 1980s proved once again that a democracy cannot maintain an empire without detriment to the essentials of its democratic character.

The end of the 1980s also marked the end of the Cold War. Soviet leader Mikhail Gorbachev had simply opted out. But as the Christmas season 1989 U.S. invasion of Panama demonstrated with great clarity, the end of the Cold War did not mean the end of U.S. intervention. The Cold War was never the reason for such intervention; it was only the rationale, and a new rationale, in the form of the "War on Drugs," has already been adopted.

PUTTING TO REST A TROUBLED CENTURY

A little more than half a century ago, in times not so different from the early 1990s, when in the United States the lines outside soup kitchens were lengthening and the ranks of the homeless swelling, and when the United States was in disrepute beyond its own borders for such practices as gunboat diplomacy, a newly elected Democratic president, Franklin Delano Roosevelt, pledged nonintervention and ushered in a period of Good Neighborliness toward Latin America. Under cover of the Cold War, and more recently of the Drug War, subsequent U.S. presidents have failed to honor that pledge. But the gunboat diplomacy of the late twentieth century has proved as subversive to the spirit of American democracy as did that of the century's youth, and a renewed pledge of nonintervention is overdue.

Such a pledge must be understood to cover not only interventions undertaken for straightforwardly strategic or political motives previously covered by the now defunct Cold War. It must subsume also any and all substitute rationales for the ongoing pursuit of indefensible objectives. Given the recent history of military abuse of civil liberties and human rights in Latin America and given our professed intent to support fledgling democracies, there can be no excuse for continuing to extend aid in any form to Latin American armed forces or for promoting arms sales—and thus arms races.

Little wonder that Latin America's democratic leaders, threatened at the least with trade disruption and credit freezes and all too often with military conspiracy or even U.S. military intervention if they moved to reward their own constituencies with a measure of economic democracy, have been skeptical of U.S. protestations of common economic interests. The fact is, however, that the ordinary people of the United States and of Latin America, as opposed to the high-rollers who place their bets in a global game, occupy the same hemisphere. Now more than ever, as economic communities are roped off in Europe and Asia, Americans of North and South are destined to share either prosperity or destitution.

The economic time of troubles felt throughout the hemisphere in the 1980s has generally abated, at least in terms of the figures and purposes that matter most to economists, investors, and creditors. But policy continues to favor capital over labor, global enterprise over national and local business, financial sleight of hand over production and consumption for internal mass markets, and exploitation and depletion over conservation and regeneration. The same policies that have stripped Latin America of internally generated capital, obliterated social services, suppressed local markets, and kept labor cheap have served to draw U.S. capital—and jobs—abroad.

Having contributed, through unqualified support for a set of policies now known as "structural adjustment," to the impoverishment of the only area where the U.S. had a traditional trade advantage, the U.S. government proceeded to place already shortchanged U.S. workers in the position of competing for jobs with even more desperate Latin American workers. It cannot be said that this system has failed—every system works for somebody—but it has failed the people of the Americas, all of the Americas, and for the sake of us all it must be reversed.

The bureaucracies and mindsets generated by the Cold War and by an exploitative boom-and-bust approach to development are inappropriate for the challenges of the twenty-first century. The Clinton-Gore administration pledged to promote economic democracy in the United States. That end would be furthered by promoting economic democracy in Latin America as well. For better or worse, given NAFTA and other integrative initiatives, the economies of Anglo- and Ibero-America will be increasingly intertwined and the well-being of their peoples interdependent.

Though wiser policy might have delayed it, the passing of Pax Americana is not a matter of choice. In the commercially driven new world order, the world's mightiest military machine is a devalued currency—just so much Confederate money. For half a century, the Cold War provided cover for the pursuit of private and bureaucratic interests in Latin America and for the use of Latin America in posturing and saber-rattling for domestic political advantage. The stripping away of that cover should make it possible and even necessary, at last, to base policy on the legitimate interests of Americans and on a profound understanding of Latin American reality.

NOTES

1. *The IDB* (Washington, D.C.), Vol. 16, No. 9–10, September–October 1989, pp. 6–9.
2. Hubert H. Humphrey, "The Threat to the Presidency," *Washington Post,* May 6, 1973.

ABOUT THE BOOK
AND EDITOR

This textbook, extensively revised and updated in this new third edition, introduces the student to what is most basic and most interesting about Latin America. The authors—each widely recognized in his or her own discipline, as well as among Latin Americanists—analyze both the enduring features of the area and the pace and direction of change. The book conveys the unifying aspects of Latin American culture and society, together with the distinct characteristics of major subregions and countries.

Highlights of the third edition include discussions of the resolution of conflict in Central America, the tenuous trend toward redemocratization in South America, and the traumatic impact of drugs and debt throughout the hemisphere. Contributors also carefully examine developments in the 1990s such as emphasis on the export sector, a trend toward privatization, general retrenchment with regard to social welfare programs, spurts of economic growth, steady growth in income gaps, and the recognition that distinctive ecological zones are threatened. The expanding influence of Latin American intellectual, literary, and artistic contributions is also given special attention.

Jan Knippers Black is a professor in the Graduate School of International Policy Studies at the Monterey Institute of International Studies in California and a senior associate member at Saint Antony's College, Oxford. Previously, she has served as research professor of public administration at the University of New Mexico and as senior research scientist and chair of the Latin American Research Team in the Foreign Area Studies Division of American University.

ABOUT THE CONTRIBUTORS

Diego Abente Brun is vice-president of the Senate of the Republic of Paraguay and vice-president of his party, Encuentro Nacional. He was elected to the Senate after about a decade as assistant and associate professor of political science at Miami University, Ohio. He is the author of several articles on the politics of Paraguay, Uruguay, and Venezuela that have appeared in scholarly journals, including *Comparative Politics, Latin American Research Review, Journal of Latin American Studies, Journal of Interamerican Studies,* and *The Americas.* He is currently working on a book on the politics of Paraguay.

Peter Bakewell is professor of history at Emory University in Atlanta. He has previously taught at Cambridge University and at the University of New Mexico, where he also served as associate editor of the *Hispanic American Historical Review.* Among his many publications are definitive studies of colonial-era silver mining in Mexico and Bolivia. His most recent book is *A History of Latin America: Empires and Sequels, 1450–1930* (1997).

Jan Knippers Black is a professor at the Monterey Institute of International Studies and senior associate member at Saint Antony's College, Oxford. Previously she was research professor of public administration at the University of New Mexico and senior research scientist and chair of the Latin American Research Team in the Foreign Area Studies Division of American University. A former Peace Corps volunteer in Chile, she holds a Ph.D. in international studies from American University in Washington, D.C. Her publications include *United States Penetration of Brazil* (1977); *Sentinels of Empire: The United States and Latin American Militarism* (1986); *The Dominican Republic: Politics and Development in an Unsovereign State* (1986); *Development in Theory and Practice: Bridging the Gap* (1991); and *Recycled Rhetoric and Disposable People* (forthcoming). She has also edited and coauthored several books and published more than 100 chapters and articles in reference books and anthologies, journals, magazines, and newspapers.

E. Bradford Burns was professor of history at the University of California, Los Angeles. After receiving his Ph.D. from Columbia University, he spent thirty years studying Latin America, particularly Brazil. He traveled extensively in the area and occasionally lived there. The author of numerous essays on Latin America, he also wrote and edited twelve books about the area. His first, *The Unwritten Alliance: Rio Branco and Brazilian-American Relations,* won the Bolton Prize (1967). Professor Burns had three popular texts, *A History of Brazil* (2d ed., 1980), *Latin America: A Concise Interpretive History* (5th ed., 1990), and *Latin America: Conflict and Creation* (1993). His recent books included *At War in Nicaragua* (1987). He died on December 19, 1995.

Peter Calvert is professor of comparative and international politics at the University of Southampton, England. He was educated at Campbell College, Belfast; Queens' College, Cambridge; and the University of Michigan, Ann Arbor. He took his doctorate at Cambridge. In 1964 he was appointed lecturer in politics at Southampton and in 1984 was appointed to a personal chair there. He specializes in the politics and international relations of the Western Hemisphere, with a particular interest in environmental issues; he was a delegate to the Earth Summit in 1992. Among his recent publications are *Latin America in the Twentieth Century* (2d ed., 1993, with Susan Calvert), *An Introduction to Comparative Politics* (1993), *The International Politics of Latin America* (1994), and *Politics and Society in the Third World* (1996, with Susan Calvert).

Michael L. Conniff directs Latin American and Caribbean Programs and teaches history at the University of South Florida in Tampa. He has published books on Brazil—*Urban Politics in Brazil* (1982)—and Panama—*Black Labor on a White Canal* (1985) and *Panama and the United States* (1992). He has edited several books, including *Latin American Populism in Comparative Perspective* (1982), *Modern Brazil* (1991, with Frank McCann), and *Africans in the Americas* (1994, with T. J. Davis). He has two works forthcoming in 1998: *A History of Modern Latin America* (with Larry Clayton) and *Populism in Latin America*. Until recently, he served as executive secretary of the Conference on Latin American History.

René Armand Dreifuss, a naturalized Brazilian, obtained degrees from the University of Haifa and the University of Leeds before receiving his Ph.D. in political science from the University of Glasgow in 1980. Formerly professor of political science at the Universidade Federal de Minas Gerais and visiting researcher at the Universidade Federal de Rio de Janeiro, he is a professor in the Social Sciences Department of the Universidade Federal Fluminense. Founder and director of the Nucleus of Strategic Studies at UFF, he is also an associate of the Nucleus of Strategic Studies of the Universidade de Campinas and of the Fundação-Escola de Servicio Publico (FESP) in Rio de Janeiro. His many publications include *1964: A Conquista do Estado* (1981), a best-seller; *A Internacional Capitalista* (1986); *O Jogo da Direita* (1989); and *A Época das Perplexidades* (1996).

José Z. García is professor of political science and director of the Latin American Institute at New Mexico State University in Las Cruces. He has lived in Ecuador and Peru and has done extensive research on military factionalism in Peru. More recently, he has been researching the military in Central America; he is currently working on a book on the Salvadoran military. Professor García is experienced in practical politics as well; he served for several years as chair of the Democratic Party of New Mexico's Doña Ana County.

William P. Glade is professor of economics at the University of Texas at Austin and director of the Mexican Center at the university's Institute of Latin American Studies. He is also senior scholar in the Woodrow Wilson International Center for Scholars, Smithsonian Institution, Washington, D.C., where he earlier served as senior research associate and acting secretary of the Latin American Program. From 1989 to 1992, he was associate director in charge of educational and cultural affairs at the United States Information Agency. Recent publications include articles on systemic transformation in Latin America and the former centrally planned economies and two edited volumes—*The Privatization of Public Enterprises in Latin America* (1991) and *Bigger Economies, Smaller Governments: Privatization in Latin America* (1996)—and, with Charles Reilly, *Inquiry at the Grassroots: An Inter-American Foundation Fellowship Reader* (1993).

Alfonso Gonzalez is professor of geography at the University of Calgary in Alberta. Since receiving his Ph.D. from the University of Texas, Austin, he has been on the faculty at San Diego State College, Northeast Louisiana State College, Southern Illinois University, and the University of South Florida, where he served as chair of the Department of Geography. Professor Gonzalez specializes in Latin American geography, with particular attention to population, settlement, and socioeconomic development. He has performed field and archival research in several areas of Hispanic America, especially the coastal region of southwestern Mexico, and has presented and published numerous papers.

Mary Grizzard is the author of three books and many articles and chapters on Latin American cultural history, with an emphasis on the role of politics in cultural expression. She was a tenured professor in Latin American art history at the University of New Mexico until becoming a senior fellow in arms control at the Arms Control and Disarmament Agency in Washington, D.C. Since 1995 she has directed projects for the Immigration and Naturalization Service and has served as a foreign affairs specialist in the Department of the Army, Pentagon. She continues to teach art history at the American University in Washington, D.C., and to write on Latin American cultural history. She holds a Ph.D. from the University of Michigan.

Fred R. Harris, a former member of the U.S. Senate (D-Oklahoma, 1964–1972), is a professor of political science at the University of New Mexico, teaching U.S. politics and U.S.-Mexico relations. He has been a Fulbright Scholar in Mexico, a visiting professor at the Universidad Nacional Autónoma de México, a Distinguished Fulbright Lecturer in Uruguay, and has taught and lectured extensively in Mexico and Latin America. He is the author of twelve books, including an introductory university text, *America's Government* (1990, with Gary Wasserman), now in its fourth edition, and *Estudios sobre Estados Unidos y su Relación Bilateral con México* (1986, with David Cooper).

Tamara Holzapfel is professor emerita of Spanish and former chair of the Department of Modern and Classical Languages at the University of New Mexico. Her numerous publications on Spanish American literature have appeared in *Hispania, Revista Iberoamericana, Latin American Theatre Review, Modern Drama,* and other scholarly journals. She has collaborated as book editor and has contributed chapters to anthologies of literary criticism. She is past associate editor of the *Latin American Research Review* and continues to serve on the editorial boards of the *Latin American Theatre Review* and *Studies in Twentieth Century Literature*.

Eldon Kenworthy is professor of politics at Whitman College in Washington State and a partner in a small reforestation project in Costa Rica. His book *America/Américas: Myth in the Making of U.S. Policy Toward Latin America* (1995) also deals with cultural projections, albeit in a foreign policy context. Kenworthy holds a Ph.D. in political science from Yale University.

Anthony P. Maingot is professor of sociology and editor of *Hemisphere* at Florida International University in Miami. He has previously taught at Yale University and at the University of the West Indies in Trinidad and served as acting dean of International Affairs at Florida International. A citizen of Trinidad, Professor Maingot studied at the University of Puerto Rico and the University of California, Los Angeles, before receiving his Ph.D. from the University of Florida. He was a member of the Constitutional Reform Commission of Trinidad and Tobago from 1971 to 1974 and president of the Caribbean Studies Association from 1982 to 1983.

John D. Martz has written or edited eighteen books plus numerous articles, many of which deal with the Andean republics. His most recent books are *United States Policy in Latin America: Decade of Crisis and Challenge* (1995) and *The Politics of Clientelism in Colombia: Democracy and the State* (1996). Since 1988 he has served as editor of *Studies in Comparative International Development.* He was editor of *Latin American Research Review* from 1975 to 1980. He is presently distinguished professor of political science at Pennsylvania State University.

Richard Millett is professor of history and chair of the Latin American Studies Committee at Southern Illinois University, Edwardsville. Professor Millett, who earned his Ph.D. at the University of New Mexico, is author of *Guardians of the Dynasty* (1977) and coeditor of *The*

Restless Caribbean: Changing Patterns of International Relations (1979). A regular visitor to Central America, he has made frequent appearances on national television interview programs and before congressional committees to testify on the crisis in that area.

Martin C. Needler is dean of the School of International Studies at the University of the Pacific and a trustee of Saint Antony's College, Oxford. He has previously held teaching positions at Dartmouth College, the University of Michigan, and the University of New Mexico and postdoctoral fellowships or research positions at UCLA, Harvard, and the University of Southampton. He has published thirteen books, principally on Latin American politics and U.S. foreign policy, including *Political Development in Latin America* (1968), *Politics and Society in Mexico* (1971), *The Problem of Democracy in Latin America* (1987), and *Mexican Politics: The Containment of Conflict* (3d ed., 1995). His *Identity, Interest, and Ideology: An Introduction to Politics* came out in 1996. Professor Needler holds a Ph.D. in political science from Harvard.

Jorge Nef is professor of political studies and international development at the University of Guelph. He graduated from the University of Chile and has studied at Vanderbilt University, the Facultad Latinoamericana de Ciencias Sociales, and the University of California. A past president of the Canadian Association of Latin American and Caribbean Studies (CALACS) and editor of the *Canadian Journal of Latin American and Caribbean Studies,* he is a fellow of the Centre for Research on Latin America and the Caribbean (CERLAC) and the Centre for Refugee Studies (CRS), both at York University. In addition to his recent *Human Security and Mutual Vulnerability* (1995), he has authored numerous books and monographs as well as many articles. He has been a consultant for national and international agencies in international development and a participant in the Expert Groups of the South Commission in Geneva (1989). In 1995 he traveled to Chile with "Team Canada" during the prime minister's visit and was an expert witness for the Senate's Committee on Foreign Affairs. His most recent research has focused on issues of governability, conflict resolution, and human security in the context of global and inter-American relations.

James Petras is professor of sociology at the State University of New York at Binghamton. His publications span a broad range of topics on Latin American and global developments, and a number of them are translated into other languages. They include *U.S. Hegemony Under Siege: Class, Politics and Development in Latin America* (1990); *Democracy and Poverty in Chile* (1994); and *La Continuación de la Historia* (1996).

James Lee Ray is professor of political science at Vanderbilt. He previously served on the faculties of Florida State University in Tallahassee and the University of New Mexico, where he was chair of the Department of Political Science from 1982 to 1984. Professor Ray is author of *Global Politics* (forthcoming) and has published articles in a number of journals, including *International Interactions, International Organizations, International Studies Quarterly,* and *Journal of Conflict Resolution.* He contributed chapters to *Prisoners of War?* (1990) and *The Long Postwar Peace* (1990).

Steve C. Ropp is professor of political science at the University of Wyoming. He holds a Ph.D. in political science from the University of California, Riverside. Professor Ropp is the author and coeditor of a number of books and articles on Panamanian and Central American politics. His current research focus is on human rights norms and domestic practice in the region.

Karl H. Schwerin is professor of anthropology at the University of New Mexico. Since receiving his Ph.D. from the University of California, Los Angeles, he has conducted fieldwork in several Latin American countries, with particular emphasis on economic and subsistence patterns, adaptive strategies, and processes of culture change. Professor Schwerin has served as president of the American Society for Ethnohistory and the University of New Mexico chapter of the scientific research society Sigma Xi. From 1987 to 1993, he chaired the Department of Anthropology at the University of New Mexico. He has published four books and numerous papers on a broad range of topics relating to Latin America and tropical societies worldwide. At present he is investigating the bases for ethnic identity formation in Latin America and continuing a long-term study on the ethnographic researches of the French explorer Alcide d'Orbigny.

Wayne S. Smith, a visiting professor of Latin American Studies at the Johns Hopkins University in Baltimore and a senior fellow at the Center for International Policy in Washington, D.C., was a U.S. Foreign Service officer for over twenty-five years. When he left the service in 1982 because of profound disagreements with the Reagan administration's policies, he was chief of mission at the U.S. Interests Section in Havana and was recognized as the Department of State's leading expert on Cuba. Smith holds three master's degrees, and his Ph.D. is from George Washington University in Washington, D.C. His published works include *The Closest of Enemies: A Personal and Diplomatic Account of U.S.-Cuban Relations Since 1957* (1987) and *Toward Resolution: The Falklands/Malvinas Dispute* (1991), which he edited.

Fred Gillette Sturm is professor of philosophy at the University of New Mexico. He holds a Ph.D. from Columbia University and has done funded research at the Institute for Brazilian Studies of Vanderbilt University, the Universidade de São Paulo, the Centro de Estudios Filosóficos of the Universidad Nacional Autónoma de México, and the Universidade de Coimbra. He is past president of the Society for Iberian and Latin American Thought (SILAT), an honorary member of the Instituto Brasileiro de Filosofia, a fellow of the Centro de Estudos de Pensamento Luso-Brasileiro, and an "effective member in perpetuity" of the Academia Brasileira de Filosofia.

Brady Tyson is professor emeritus of international relations at the American University's School of International Service and the initiator of that school's International Development Semester program. During the Carter administration, he served as a special assistant to Andrew Young, U.S. ambassador to the United Nations. Professor Tyson, whose Ph.D. is from American University, has studied and taught in Brazil, visits that country regularly, and has published numerous articles about its political processes.

Nelson P. Valdés is professor of sociology at the University of New Mexico. Born in Cuba, he came to the United States in 1961. Since 1977 he has traveled to Cuba on more than a dozen occasions. Professor Valdés holds a Ph.D. in history from the University of New Mexico and has published five books and numerous articles on Cuba. He is presently working on a manuscript dealing with the ideological roots of the Cuban revolutionary movement. He founded and served as director from 1986 to 1996 of the Latin America Data Base, a computerized database producing two electronic newsletters: the *Central America Update* and the *Latin American Debt Chronicle.* Professor Valdés is a board member of the Center for Cuban Studies (New York) and the Instituto de Estudios Cubanos (Miami). He is also the Latin American analyst for the Pacific News Service.

Arturo Valenzuela is Professor of Government and Director of the Center for Latin American Studies at Georgetown University. He served as Deputy Assistant Secretary of State for Inter-American Affairs in the first Clinton administration. He is a member of the Council on Foreign Relations, Board Member of the National Democratic Institute for International Affairs, and former Board Member of America's Watch. He serves on the editorial boards of *The Journal of Democracy, The Third World Quarterly,* and *Current History.* The author or coauthor of six books on Chilean politics, he is the co-editor and coauthor with Juan Linz of *The Failure of Presidential Democracy* (1995). Professor Valenzuela previously taught at Duke University and has been a Visiting Scholar at Oxford University, the University of Sussex, the University of Florence, the University of Chile, and the Catholic University of Chile.

J. Samuel Valenzuela is professor and former chair of the Department of Sociology at the University of Notre Dame. He was formerly on the faculties at Yale and Harvard Universities and has been senior associate member at Saint Antony's College, Oxford University. He is the author of *Democratización vía Reforma: La Expansión del Sufragio en Chile,* coauthor of *Religion, Class, and Gender: Constructing Electoral Institutions and Party Politics in Chile,* and coeditor of *Military Rule in Chile: Dictatorship and Oppositions* and of *Chile: Politics and Society.* He has also written numerous articles on the intersection between labor and politics and on democratization and electoral politics.

Henry Veltmeyer, professor of sociology and international development studies at Saint Mary's University, Halifax, Nova Scotia, is currently a visiting professor in political science at the Autonomous University of Zacatecas in Mexico. He has written and contributed to the publication of a wide range of articles and books on the dynamics of global development and Canadian political economy as well as the sociology of Latin American development. His publications include *Rethinking Development: Caribbean Perspectives, Canadian Corporate Power,* and, with James Petras, *Neoliberalism and Class Conflict in Latin America.*

Thomas W. Walker is professor of political science and director of Latin American studies at Ohio University. He holds a Ph.D. in political science from the University of New Mexico. He has been doing research in Central America for three decades and has served on international electoral observation teams in Nicaragua in 1984, 1990, and 1996. Walker is the author, editor/coauthor, or coeditor of nine books on the politics of Central America, including *Understanding Central America* (2d ed., 1993), *Nicaragua: The Land of Sandino* (3d ed., 1991), and *Nicaragua Without Illusions: Regime Transition and Structural Adjustment in the 1990s* (1997).

Larman C. Wilson, professor emeritus of international relations and former associate dean at the School of International Service, the American University, specializes in international law and organization and inter-American relations. He has been a fellow of the Academy of International Law in The Hague and of the OAS's Inter-American Juridical Committee in Brazil. He has done research in the Dominican Republic, Mexico, and Spain. His publications include articles, book chapters, and monographs on inter-American relations; he is coauthor of two books, including (with Pope Atkins) *The Dominican Republic and the United States: From Colonialism to Transnationalism* (forthcoming).

INDEX